Electronic Media

(formerly *Telecommunications*)

Eleventh Edition

Electronic Media

An Introduction

Lynne Schafer Gross

California State University, Fullerton

The McGraw·Hill Companies

McGraw Hill · Connect Learn Succeed™

ELECTRONIC MEDIA: AN INTRODUCTION, ELEVENTH EDITION

Published by McGraw-Hill, a business unit of The McGraw-Hill Companies, Inc., 1221 Avenue of the Americas, New York, NY 10020. Copyright © 2013 by The McGraw-Hill Companies, Inc. All rights reserved. Printed in the United States of America. Previous editions © 2010, 2006, and 2003. No part of this publication may be reproduced or distributed in any form or by any means, or stored in a database or retrieval system, without the prior written consent of The McGraw-Hill Companies, Inc., including, but not limited to, in any network or other electronic storage or transmission, or broadcast for distance learning.

Some ancillaries, including electronic and print components, may not be available to customers outside the United States.

This book is printed on acid-free paper.

2 3 4 5 6 7 8 9 0 DOC/DOC 10 9 8 7 6 5 4

ISBN   978-0-07-3526164
MHID   0-07-3526169

Vice President & Editor-in-Chief: *Michael Ryan*
Executive Director of Development: *Lisa Pinto*
Publisher: *David Patterson*
Develoment Editor: *Penina Braffman*
Marketing Specialist: *Alex Schultz*
Project Manager: *Jessica Portz*
Cover Designer: *Studio Montage, St. Louis, MO*
Cover Image: *Ingram Publishing/SuperStock RF (top), Digital Vision, Getty Images RF (middle),* © *The McGraw-Hill Companies, Inc./John Flournoy, photographer (bottom)*
Buyer: *Sandy Ludovissy*
Media Project Manager: *Sridevi Palani*
Compositor: *MPS Limited*
Typeface: *10/12 Times New Roman*
Printer: *RR Donnelley - Crawfordsville*

All credits appearing on page or at the end of the book are considered to be an extension of the copyright page.

Library of Congress Cataloging-in-Publication Data
Gross, Lynne S.
    Electronic media : an introduction / Lynne Schafer Gross.—11th ed.
        p. cm.
    Summary: "Electronic Media: An Introduction provides students the essentials for interacting with electronic media whether they plan to become media producers or shrewd media consumers. The text discusses the most current media forms and the functions of those forms as they relate to advertising, promotional, regulatory, ethical and global issues. Students will explore types of media careers and learn how to obtain those jobs by developing networking and interviewing skills and by preparing strong application materials"—Provided by publisher.
    Includes bibliographical references and index.
    ISBN 978-0-07-352616-4 (pbk.)
1. Telecommunication. 2. Broadcasting. I. Title.
TK5105.G759 2013
384—dc23

                                                                                    2012024001

www.mhhe.com

ABOUT THE AUTHOR

Lynne S. Gross has taught radio-television-film production and theory courses at California State University, Fullerton (where she was Vice Chair of the Communications Department), Pepperdine University, Loyola Marymount University, UCLA, USC, and Long Beach City College. She is the author of 12 books and numerous journal and magazine articles.

She was recently Associate Producer for the instructional video series *Journeys Below the Line* and before that was Program Director for Valley Cable TV. She has served as Producer for several hundred television programs, including the series *From Chant to Chance* for public television, *Effective Living* for KABC, and *Surveying the Universe* for KHJ-TV.

Her consulting work includes projects for Children's Broadcasting Corporation, RKO, KCET, CBS, the Olympics, Visa, and the Iowa State Board of Regents. It has also taken her to Malaysia, Swaziland, Estonia, Russia, Australia, New Zealand, and Guyana, where she has taught radio and television production and consulted on movie planning and postproduction equipment.

She is active in many professional organizations, serving as a Governor of the Academy of Television Arts and Sciences and President of the Broadcast Education Association. Awards she has received include the Rosebud Award for Outstanding Media Arts Professor in the California State University System, the Frank Stanton Fellow for Distinguished Contribution to Electronic Media Education from the International Radio and Television Society, and the Distinguished Education Service Award from the BEA.

PREFACE

Purpose

The electronic media constitute one of the most potent forces in the world today. They influence society as a whole, and they influence every one of us as an individual. As each year passes, the media grow in scope. The early pioneers of radio would never recognize today's vast array of electronic media—broadcast television, cable TV, satellite radio and television, the internet, DVRs, video games, smartphones, pods, pads. Neither would they recognize the structure that has evolved in such areas as regulation, advertising, and audience measurement. They would marvel that their early concepts of equipment have led to such developments as audio boards, cameras, graphics generators, nonlinear editors, fiber optics, and satellites. If they could see the quantity and variety of programming available today, they might not recognize that it all began with amateurs listening for radio signals on their primitive crystal sets.

All indications are that the electronic media will continue to change at a rapid pace. As they do, they will further affect society. All people, whether individuals working in the communications field or individual members of society, have a right to become involved with media and have an obligation to understand why people need to interact with the media. Some knowledge of the background and structure of the industry is an essential basis for this understanding. A major goal of this book is to provide just that kind of knowledge so that both practitioners in the field and members of the general public can make intelligent decisions about the role of media in society.

Revisions in This Edition

Because the media landscape changes so quickly, each edition of this book (which was first published in 1983 and originally had the title of *Telecommunications*) has undergone major revision. This edition is no exception. There are changes on almost every page, but what follows are a few of the major changes made in each chapter.

Chapter 1—An Overview of Electronic Media—A new section entitled Chronological Highlights and Interactions serves as an overview to the book and includes thumbnail photos to pique student curiosity. New artwork freshens the chapter, and the statistics, especially those dealing with ownership and use of media, have been updated.

Chapter 2—The Internet, Portable Platforms, and Video Games—Except for some early historical information, this chapter is almost a total rewrite. It needed to take into account items that did not exist or barely existed when the last edition was printed, such as Facebook, Twitter, smartphones, iPad, and clouds. The changes in audio and video on the internet necessitated a major rework of those topics.

Chapter 3—Cable, Satellite, and Telco TV—At the suggestion of reviewers, this chapter and Chapter 4 were reorganized into media forms rather than the previous edition's early and modern organization. Television provided by phone companies has been given more space and several new sections have been added, one dealing with how these three media forms interact with each other.

Chapter 4—Broadcast Television—In order to keep this textbook a reasonable size (and it is actually a little shorter than the previous edition), some of the older material needed to be condensed or removed. Such was the case with color TV, LPTV, UHF, and HDTV. There also are new sections dealing with network changes, government interactions, and broadcasting's relationship to newer technologies.

Chapter 5—Radio and Audio—Consumer audio (phonograph, CDs, MP3, apps) was added to this chapter along with material about internet radio. This chapter, too, underwent some pruning, and, at the suggestion of reviewers, some of the Golden Era of Radio material was condensed but highlighted in a "Zoom-In" box.

Chapter 6—Movies and Home Video—There are four new sections in this chapter dealing with home video, (VHS, DVR, clouds, etc.), something that has had a major impact on movies. Some of the earlier movie material was compressed, and a new "Zoom In" box on sequels with new photos should further liven the chapter.

Chapter 7—Careers in Electronic Media—This chapter was new last edition and was extremely well received. It didn't need as much revision as some of the other chapters, but it has revised material about online job applications and added material suggested by reviewers, such as working outside the comfort zone, being emotionally smart in the workplace, and needing to show productivity.

Chapter 8—Programming—The slant of this chapter changed because of all that has happened regarding programming on the internet. Also, many of the examples were updated (Oprah's syndicated show is gone; *Glee* is here). A new "Zoom In" box delves into the scheduling mess related to Jay Leno and Conan O'Brien, and nine new photos highlight programming changes.

Chapter 9—Sales and Advertising—So much has changed in advertising that this chapter was almost totally reorganized and massively rewritten. More than half the exhibits have changed and the sections and subsections are very different from the last edition. The emphasis is now on process rather than individual advertising forms, and more space is devoted to gaining audience attention.

Chapter 10—Promotion and Audience Feedback—Promotion was expanded because, with so many options available, it has become very important.

Audience research methods have changed, too, because of cross-platform viewing. New biometric and neuroscience methods, such as eye tracking, have been added, and Twitter and Facebook receive mentions for their role in audience behavior.

Chapter 11—Laws and Regulations—A new section dealing with privacy, especially as it relates to social media and smartphones, highlights the changes in this chapter. Some of the material added includes WikiLeaks, the Casey Anthony case, and copyright as related to social media. Equal time, ownership, and obscenity have been thinned out, and the fairness doctrine is now an R.I.P. "Zoom In" box.

Chapter 12—Ethics and Effects—Information on the interrelationship of laws and ethics now has its own section that includes new information about hacking. The News Corp. phone tapping scandal and several other current examples of ethical failings have been added. Some of the older research studies and facts have been removed and replaced with new ones.

Chapter 13—Technical Underpinnings—This chapter is a major rewrite from the opening quote about a young child trying to turn on the TV by swiping to the closing paragraph that mentions the possibilities of computers that can talk and autosteroeoscopic (without glasses) 3-D TV. New sections discuss the technology behind smartphones and wi-fi, and information on all technologies is updated.

Chapter 14—The International Scene—There is a whole new section on globalization that details the ways production companies throughout the world are interacting. The sections on indigenous programming and the digital age were totally rewritten, and, as with some other chapters, elements of the historical information were removed or condensed.

Features of the Book

Exhibits

The book contains over 275 photos, drawings, and charts to enhance the reader's understanding of concepts and ideas. More than 60 of these visual exhibits are new to this edition.

Issues and the Future Boxes

All the chapters should lead the reader to assess the strengths and weaknesses of the particular subject being discussed. Toward this end, each chapter contains an "Issues and the Future" box. This feature should help prepare readers for fast-changing events that they will read about in newspapers and magazines and on the internet.

Zoom In Boxes

Each chapter includes several "Zoom In" boxes. Many of these boxes are designed to increase critical thinking. They discuss current and controversial issues,

often of an ethical nature, and end with a series of questions designed to stimu-
late the reader's thinking. Other boxes relate historical information to help readers understand the genesis of today's media events. For this edition, 11 of the
"Zoom In" boxes are new, five are greatly revised, and 14 from the old edition
have been removed, mainly because they were dated.

Review Guides

Marginal notes appear in each chapter. These notes highlight the main subjects
being discussed in the adjacent paragraphs. Taken together, these notes serve as
review points for the reader. Throughout the text, important words are boldfaced.
These terms are all defined in the glossary and should serve as another aid to
learning.

Suggested Websites

Each chapter lists several pertinent websites that readers may wish to visit to
supplement their knowledge. Websites are also mentioned in chapter notes and
within the text itself.

Further Study

Extensive notes at the end of each chapter provide many sources for further study
of particular subjects.

Beginnings and Endings

Each chapter begins with a pertinent quote and a short introduction. At the end of
each chapter, a summary outlines major points in a manner slightly different from
that given within the chapter. For example, if the chapter is ordered chronologi-
cally, the summary may be organized in a topical manner. This should help the
reader form a gestalt of the material presented.

Flexible Chapter Sequence

The chapters may be read in any sequence. Some of the terms that are defined
early in the book, however, may be unfamiliar to people who read later chapters first. The glossary can help overcome this problem. It includes important
technical terms that the reader may want to review from time to time, as well
as terms that are not necessary to an understanding of the text but may be of
interest to the reader.

Supplementary Materials

This edition of the text, like the former, includes a valuable website at www
.mhhe.com/gross11e. Among other items, the site contains useful practice quizzes
for the student and an instructor's manual and testbank.

Acknowledgments

This book represents the combined efforts of many people, including the following reviewers who offered excellent suggestions:

David A Nelson, University of Central Oklahoma

Terry Bales, Santa Ana College

John Hart, California State University, Fullerton

Bruce Drushel, Miami University

In addition I would like to thank the book team at McGraw Hill, especially Nicole Bridge for her suggestions and guidance and for her technical assistance with formatting the text and exhibits.

LYNNE SCHAFER GROSS

BRIEF CONTENTS

CONTENTS

ELECTRONIC MEDIA FORMS

A wide variety of electronic media exists for the dissemination of entertainment and information. The media both complement and compete with one another, experiencing the slings and security of the free enterprise system. Some people wonder how many forms of media the market can bear; others marvel at how many it does bear. As these media develop, change is inevitable, brought about by both external and internal forces. Although all the electronic media forms are relatively young, they are already rich in history and adaptation. The first chapter of this section gives an overview of the various media; the succeeding chapters handle such media forms as the internet, portable platforms, video games, cable TV, satellite TV, broadcast TV, home video, radio, and movies.

Chapter 1

AN OVERVIEW OF ELECTRONIC MEDIA

You would be hard-pressed in modern American society to find someone who does not interact with electronic media on a daily basis—someone who does not surf the internet, watch TV, listen to the radio, download music to an iPod, go to a movie, play a video game, send an email, talk on a smartphone. In fact, many people in this age of multitaskinginteract with several media at the same time. They watch a movie downloaded from the internet while playing a video game and texting a friend.

> What they [college students] like most about their mobile devices is that they can reach other people. What they like least is that other people can reach them.
>
> **Naomi Baron, American University Professor who conducted a study on mobile devices**

In addition, everyone has opinions that relate to media. Our opinions decide whether a movie or a TV series is a hit or a dud. We vote for our favorite *American Idol* singer. We argue about the media's coverage of political candidates. We talk about the tactics used in commercials and the sex and violence seen on TV and heard in radio song lyrics. We worry about the predators on the internet and whether or not our cell phones will cause cancer.

The media are constantly changing. Not very long ago there was no internet, no iPad, no Twitter. Within the past few decades, a number of technologies that were highly touted have gone by the wayside—subscription TV, VCRs, teletext. The way people used electronic media and how they perceived the media were quite different 10 years ago from what they are today.

1.1 A Rationale for Study

Even though everyone has a basic knowledge of the field of electronic media, there are many reasons to study it. Anyone who is aiming toward a career in this area will profit from an intimate knowledge of the history and organization of the industry. Those armed with knowledge have a greater chance for career survival than those who are naive about the inner workings and interrelationships of networks, stations, cable TV facilities, the internet, movie studios, advertisers, unions, telephone companies, the government, and a host of other organizations that affect the actions of the industry. As the various forms of communications expand, they create new and exciting jobs. Knowledge of the past will help people predict the direction of their future jobs. Knowing about media can also help practitioners set their own personal values so that they can help mold the industry into a form that they feel is effective in a positive way.

career options

At a broader level, individuals owe it to themselves to understand the messages and communication tools of our society because they are so crucial in shaping our lives. Rare is the individual who has not been emotionally touched or repulsed by a scene in a movie. Rare, too, is the individual who has never formed, reinforced, or changed an opinion on the basis of information heard on radio or seen on TV or the internet. Knowledge of the communications industry and its related areas can lead to a greater understanding of how these forces can influence and affect both individual lives and the structure of society as a whole. It can also teach each individual the most effective methods for interacting with media.

understanding

In addition, the electronic media are fascinating and worthy of study in their own right. Those in the field are associated with glamour and excitement (and power and greed), both on-screen and off (see Exhibit 1.1). Although the day-to-day workings of the industry can be as mundane as they are in any other field, the fact that it is a popular art that includes the rich and famous makes this industry of special interest. The ramifications of the power that the electronic media exert over society are most deserving of study.

fascination

1.2 Chronological Highlights and Interactions

Although all electronic media forms can be discussed as entities unto themselves (as they are in the following chapters of this section), in reality, they are intertwined. What happens with television can affect radio; successful programming on cable TV can hurt broadcast TV ratings; a Facebook page can be supplemented with audio and video; the internet and smartphones can change distribution patterns for radio, television, telephones, movies, and more. What follows is a brief chronological recounting of some of the major media interactions and highlights over the past 100 years. It illustrates a slow, consistent path for media during the early years of the 20th century, followed by a more frenetic introduction of media forms toward the end of the century and into the 21st century. The facts and photos will become more meaningful as you read the remainder of the book, but this will give you a quick overview of the significance of media, especially in relation to each other.

1.2a 1920s

An early radio station

A case can be made that radio was the only true electronic media in the 1920s. Movies existed, but film was a chemical medium that was edited and projected mechanically. With the addition of sound in 1927, movies did utilize electrons, but sound was much more primitive than what we experience today. The telephone also existed in the 1920s and needed electrons to carry its signals, but, although it was first proposed as a device to carry music and other sounds to mass audiences, it became an interpersonal one-to-one instrument that was not considered part of the mass media family. There had been experiments related to television as far back as the 1880s, but it was not present in any viable form. Radio had been around for several decades, but its primary use was as a safety device for ships at sea, especially after the 1912 sinking of the *Titanic*. In the early 1920s some visionaries saw the possibility of using radio for entertainment purposes, something that eventually came to be known as **broadcasting**. Radio got off to a rocky start financially but eventually attracted advertising money that could be used to pay for programming and networks.

1.2b 1930s

The 1930s constitute part of what has been frequently referred to as the "Golden Era of Radio." As an entertainment medium, it was viewed primarily as a competitor to vaudeville and movies. And, indeed, it did lower the attendance for both, especially when popular programs such as *Amos 'n' Andy* and the *Jack Benny Show* were on the air. The price of this entertainment programming (free) was welcomed by those who lived through the Great Depression. The major programming **formats** (drama, comedy, children's programs, news, sports) were developed by the major radio networks (NBC, CBS, ABC) involved with radio during the 1930s. Radio also had a major interaction with newspapers because radio announcers started reporting the latest news before the evening newspaper editions had hit the streets. At first the newspapers were able to stifle radio because they were more powerful, but before the 1930s ended, radio had become an important source for news.

Jack Benny and Mary Livingston

1.2c 1940s

Radio was also the dominant electronic medium during the 1940s—an extremely long run for one media form by today's standards. Part of this was due to the fact that experimentation related to television came to a halt during World War II. So did experimentation for a new type of radio called frequency modulation (FM), which would eventually become more popular than AM (amplitude modulation) radio, the original radio form. Postwar radio was extremely profitable, allowing radio companies to invest heavily in television. By the end of the decade that new medium was rising in popularity and the Federal Communications Commission (FCC) instituted a **freeze** on TV station authorizations in order to organize the TV frequencies.

Edward R. Murrow

1.2d 1950s

Television replaced radio as the dominant electronic medium during the 1950s. It was broadcast live in black and white on tiny screens, but "radio with pictures" caught the fancy of the nation. Because television took the formats and the stars previously associated with radio programming, many predicted that radio would disappear. But it did not. It reinvented itself with music programming that featured disc jockeys. It essentially lost its network structure and became local-station oriented. Movies, which had survived and even thrived alongside radio, were now considered to be in great jeopardy because people could watch pictures in their own homes. The movie industry countered with large screens and special techniques, such as **3-D**, that could not be replicated in the home. A tiny business known as **Community Antenna Television (CATV)** also emerged during the 1950s to retransmit local television signals by wire into areas where they could not be received, usually because of hills or obstructions. A little section of the Defense Department, called ARPA, began research on what eventually became the internet.

Lucille Ball

1.2e 1960s

Kennedy funeral

Broadcast television, with the addition of color and videotaped programming, dominated the 1960s. The programming reflected the unrest of the time and gradually integrated African Americans into entertainment and news roles. Radio still garnered loyal audience members who liked the music fidelity of the newer FM stations. Movie companies embraced television and used the stations and networks as an income source by allowing them to broadcast movies from the past. Although these movies were still chemically based, they were being distributed electronically. First-run movies for theaters recovered from the blow TV had given them in the 1950s by switching to independently produced films that were cheaper and more intimate in content than the blockbuster films from the movie studios of the 1950s. CATV, which by now was known as cable TV, was becoming a thorn in the side of broadcast TV. The cable systems were starting to send wired signals from distant TV stations (a practice known as **distant signal importation**) to the homes that subscribed to their service. The local stations felt threatened by this and appealed to the Federal Communications Commission, which in the 1960s established regulations that primarily favored the broadcasters. The Defense Department continued its research, aided by professors at various universities, and by 1969 had developed a little network of computers called **ARPANET**.

1.2f 1970s

All in the Family

The first email was sent over ARPANET during the 1970s, but it did not lead to any quick adoption of what eventually became the internet. The decade still belonged to broadcast television, with some of the programming being edgier now that the medium was maturing. **Syndicators** distributed network reruns, movies, and other fare to fill time on **independent** stations. They also sold programs that stations **affiliated** with the three networks (NBC, CBS, and ABC) could air during hours when the networks did not provide programming. Public broadcasting that had been structured in the late 1960s became popular, especially with its children's programming. HBO started in a limited way but signaled the cable rush that would come in the next decade. The first videocassette recorder (VCR) for home recording was introduced and VHS and Betamax began a format rivalry. And the first major video game, *Pong*, was invented during the 1970s.

1.2g 1980s

Cable TV wrestling

Media began to multiply in the 1980s. Cable TV became a dominant force with cities being wired at a rapid rate and new cable networks springing up in rabbit-like fashion. Cable TV's structure differed from broadcast in that the cable systems passed through many networks, rather than affiliating with one, as broadcast stations did. Also, many cable networks were geared to attract a specific audience (a concept known as **narrowcasting**) rather than the general audience targeted by the broadcast networks. Satellite TV got off to a shaky start then faltered, except for people who bought very large satellite dishes, like those used by the cable TV systems. Videodisc player manufacturers tried to unseat the popularity of videocassette recorders, but were unsuccessful. The movie industry felt threatened by videocassettes, just as it had by radio and television, so it brought a copyright lawsuit against the recorders. The movie business lost but then found videocassettes to be a friend because people rented and bought movies on tape in droves, further supplementing the movie industry's coffers. A new network, Fox, started on broadcast television and the Hispanic television audience gained prominence. Radio somewhat limped through the 1980s, although several networks emerged to sell programming to the locally oriented stations.

1.2h 1990s

Radio, movies, broadcast TV, cable TV, satellite TV, cell phones, videocassettes, videodiscs, video games, the internet, and more—they all coexisted during the 1990s. A major problem became the size of the advertising pie. Although a few media forms rely on direct sales to consumers, most obtain the bulk of their money from advertisers. Having so many channels and so many systems greatly fractured the size of the audience for any one program or service. Advertisers who once split their budgets between radio and TV now had many more options but less knowledge about how effective their overall campaigns were. The internet was the "new kid on the block" that grew quickly in popularity. At the beginning of the decade it consisted only of text and rudimentary graphics, but soon it was providing news, stock market quotes, sports, and other information traditionally provided by radio and TV, as well as newspapers and magazines.

Satellite dish

1.2i 2000s

"Digital" was the watchword of the 2000s. All broadcast TV stations switched from **analog** to **digital** transmission, a requirement of the Federal Communications Commission. Some radio stations and networks switched to digital also, although they were not mandated to do so by the FCC. DVDs (the first "D" stands for "digital") became popular, overcoming the stalled progress of the old analog videodiscs. DVRs, such as TiVo, caused analog VHS video recorders to head toward extinction. The Telecommunications Act of 1996 encouraged businesses to enter each other's fields. For example, cable TV companies began offering phone services and phone companies started providing digital TV over fiber optics. Digital technologies allowed the internet to grow in capacity and speed so that both video and audio could be streamed and downloaded online and social media could thrive. Although internet companies hit a financial speed bump at the beginning of the decade, advertisers became cognizant of new forms of advertising devised by enterprising young entrepreneurs and started switching ad dollars from more traditional media to the internet. On top of all that, it was the decade that introduced the iPod, iTunes, Xbox, YouTube, Hulu, Facebook, and other digital innovations.

Google search

1.2j 2010s

The 2010s continued a frenetic introduction of new digital devices and procedures. Apple introduced the iPad, which changed the way many people work. Smartphones became the norm for people on the go. Twitter became a major method of communication with people connecting frequently in 140 characters

Steve Jobs

or less text messages. Movies, which were slower to convert to a total digital process than other media, made the final step when a majority of movie theaters converted from analog film projection to digital projection. This conversion also allowed theaters to project 3-D. People began working from computer software stored on clouds (company servers) and even placed their music, video, and text files on the clouds. Traditional and newer distribution forms abounded, but the element that continued to matter the most was content—captivating stories and meaningful information.

1.3 Ownership of Media Devices

Statistics and studies tell us a great deal about the relationship of people and society to the electronic media. Americans own a large number of electronic communication devices (see Exhibit 1.2). Some of these exhibit consistent ownership while others have risen and declined.[1]

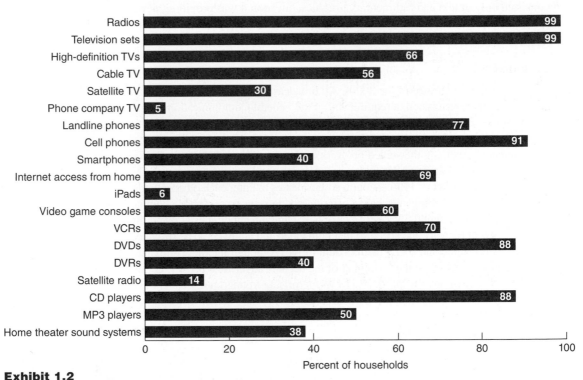

Percentage of American Households with Various Electronic Media Devices and Services

Device	Percent
Radios	99
Television sets	99
High-definition TVs	66
Cable TV	56
Satellite TV	30
Phone company TV	5
Landline phones	77
Cell phones	91
Smartphones	40
Internet access from home	69
iPads	6
Video game consoles	60
VCRs	70
DVDs	88
DVRs	40
Satellite radio	14
CD players	88
MP3 players	50
Home theater sound systems	38

Percent of households

Exhibit 1.2

Americans own many devices that help them keep entertained, informed, and connected. How many of these do you own?

For decades, surveys have shown that just about every household has at least one radio and one TV set. In fact, the average household owns 6 radios and 2.6 TV sets, and two-thirds of homes have 3 or more sets. The mandatory advent of **digital television** in 2009 led many people to buy new sets that could take advantage of the improved high-definition quality. Within a short period of time, two-thirds of homes had digital sets and that number is still growing. **radios and TVs**

Originally homes received both radio and television through the airwaves for free, with the costs being covered by advertising. But when cable TV started, it operated under a different business plan that charged consumers to receive a variety of channels. Today 91 percent of people receive their television through some sort of subscription service. At one point cable companies had wired over 70 percent of homes, but as competition rose in the form of **satellite TV** and TV services provided by phone companies such as Verizon and AT&T, cable's slice of the pie shrank. Today it only covers 56 percent of homes with its competition covering 35 percent. **types of TV**

Ownership in the telephone realm has undergone great change. Not too long ago, almost 100 percent of the population had **landline** phones. Then along came **cell phones** which, at first, were just other phones in addition to the landline phone. Now 25 percent of people have a cell phone but no landline, while only 17 percent have a landline and no cell phone. **Smartphones**, which enable access to the internet and other services, are part of the cell phone number, constituting a little less than half the cell phones, but that number is increasing. The percent given in the chart is for households, but in most cases multiple people in one household own cell phones, meaning that there are more cell phones than people in the United States. **phones**

Internet access from home, which didn't even register on any charts until the 1990s, continues to grow at a rapid rate. Most of those who do not have the internet at home can access it at work or at internet cafes or libraries. Apple's iPad, introduced in 2010, quickly racked up sales. That number seems destined to rise quickly, especially given that 17 percent of households that have iPads have two or more. **internet**

When Wii was introduced in 2006, **video game** console ownership zoomed up from 44 percent to 60 percent. Although many of the Wii consoles now sit unused, it is estimated that over 80 percent of people play video games. Console ownership has remained steady at about 60 percent. **games**

Devices to record video signals in the home have been popular since the late 1970s. At one point, over 90 percent of homes had **videocassette recorders (VCRs)**. That number is now down to 70 percent, having been overtaken by digital devices. No doubt some of those 70 percent are stored away in a closet. The number of homes with **DVD players** has also shrunk from a high of 94 percent to 88 percent. Ownership of **digital video recorders (DVRs)**, such as TiVo, continues to rise. **recorders**

In the audio realm, **satellite radio** is subscribed to by 14 percent of the population, a number that might grow as automobile manufacturers install more systems in cars. **Compact disc (CD)** players are in 88 percent of homes, but some may have been abandoned as their owners listen to most of their music on **MP3** **audio** players, many of which are iPods. Home theater sound systems have remained stagnant for quite a few years, perhaps because the housing market is deflated.

America is a land of gadgets. A typical American 8 to 18 years old lives in a house with three TV sets, three radios, three MP3 players, and two video game consoles. The possession of electronic media devices is not equal throughout society, however. As expected, the rich own many more gadgets than the poor. For example, 9 percent of households with an income over $75,000 have iPads while only 3 percent of households with an income under $75,000 have them. Similar numbers for high-speed internet are 93 percent and 85 percent. Likewise, education affects ownership; 89 percent of people with college degrees have internet accessibility in their homes while only 57 percent with only high school diplomas do.

1.4 Use of Electronic Media

hours spent

Of course, people don't just own these electronic media devices; they use them. Studies show that people spend an average of 3.1 hours a day online, 3 hours listening to radio, and 4.7 hours watching TV. The fact that people multitask means that this does not add up to 10.8 hours a day. The best guesstimate is that people, on average, spend a little over seven hours a day with radio, TV, video games, and the internet, but that does not include the amount of time people talk on the phone, text, listen to recorded music, or go to the movies. Regardless of what the exact number is, people spend a great deal of time with media, making their devices a very significant part of life.

The number of hours that the TV set is on in the average household has remained fairly stable in recent decades (see Exhibit 1.3), although there has been a definite trend away from viewing broadcast television (NBC, CBS, ABC, Fox, etc.) to watching cable TV (MTV, USA, Lifetime, ESPN, etc.).

internet and TV

"Watching TV" is becoming a complicated concept because people can watch traditional TV programs on the internet and can also watch programming fare that is being created specifically for the internet. Younger people are more

Exhibit 1.3

The number of hours a TV set is on grew rapidly during TV's first few decades, then leveled out.

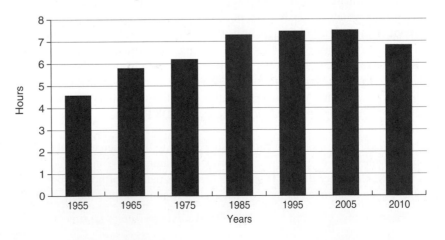

Average Hours a TV Set Is On in Households

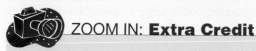 ZOOM IN: **Extra Credit**

For those of you who like statistics, here are a few additional miscellaneous facts about the electronic media.

1. Two-thirds of people regularly watch TV while eating dinner.
2. People who own Apple computers are more likely to have other electronic gadgets than are people who own PCs. For example, 63 percent of people with a Mac computer are likely to own an iPod versus 35 percent of other computer owners.
3. About 62 percent of radio listening is done away from home.
4. Of mobile phone owners, 8 percent stream audio and 7 percent stream video.
5. YouTube receives 48 hours of new uploaded footage every hour.
6. Two-thirds of adults sleep with their cell phones next to their bed.
7. Among those who text, 84 percent say they send and receive texts "just to say 'Hello.'"
8. Forty-nine percent of Americans say they watch too much TV.

Can you explain these statistics?

likely to stream TV programs on the internet than their elders. Among Millennials, 44 percent watch TV online while only 28 percent of Gen Xers and 21 percent of Baby Boomers do.

Young people are also more likely to attend movies, doing so about 11 times a year versus 4 times for their parents. They also play more video games and text more often. Of the 83 percent of teens who text, the average one sends or receives about 3,000 text messages a month while only initiating or answering 200 phone calls a month. Phone calls have been steady over the years while texting took a rapid jump in the late 2000s. For example, Twitter grew 500 percent between 2008 and 2009. In general, people like the electronic media. Only 6 percent of people would even consider giving up television or the internet.

young

Statistics abound regarding how people use media. Some are self-evident; others are puzzling. Some remain fairly stable over the years while others fluctuate or even disappear. The "Zoom In" box gives some interesting examples you may wish to contemplate. You might also want to consider how and why you use the various devices that you own.

1.5 The Functions of Media

Several decades ago, theoreticians claimed that the main functions of media were to entertain, inform, and persuade. As electronic media expanded and became more important to the social fabric, so did their functions. Today one way to look at the functions is to consider that the electronic media are involved with (1) presenting entertainment, (2) disseminating news and information, (3) aiding commerce, (4) transmitting culture and customs, (5) acting as a watchdog, (6) providing relaxation and companionship, and (7) connecting people to each other. These purposes are not mutually exclusive. It is entirely possible that one

list of functions

Exhibit 1.4

Jon Stewart of *The Daily Show* sometimes bemoans the amount of work that goes into the program because it must summarize the news—and make it funny. Do you believe this show is both entertaining and informative? Can you think of ways that it fulfills the other functions of media?

major function

passivity

criticisms

importance

television program, for example, could serve all these functions (see Exhibit 1.4).[2]

1.5a Presenting Entertainment

Entertainment occupies the lion's share of time or space for many forms of electronic media. Movies, for example, are almost totally entertainment based (see Exhibit 1.5), as are video games. Approximately three-fourths of the programming on TV qualifies as entertainment; for radio stations with a music format, the percentage is even higher. The internet started out primarily delivering information, but as its capacity to deliver audio and video improved, people began using the internet for entertainment purposes. Portable devices, such as an iPod filled with music, also provide entertainment.

Electronic media companies provide so much entertainment because that is what people seem to want. Ratings for dramas are almost always higher than ratings for documentaries. Individuals, however, certainly have the ability to choose not only how much entertainment they want, but also what type of entertainment they desire. Sports fans can always find something on some medium devoted to sports, and even a group as narrow as *CSI* aficionados can get their fill by using broadcast TV, cable TV, DVDs, internet downloads, and other media forms.

For many years entertainment was a passive activity; people watching TV were often referred to as "couch potatoes" because they just sat on their couches and watched what someone else produced. Today watching passively is still a major mode for entertainment, but there are more opportunities for active participation in entertainment. Many programs encourage viewers to interact with the show's websites. Sites such as YouTube and Facebook encourage people to program their own creative ideas. Some movies allow viewers to select the ending, and the user has great control over how video games progress.

The media do not always fulfill their entertainment function to the satisfaction of everyone. Politicians, citizens groups, parents, and others complain about the amount of sex and violence in TV programs, video games, movies, and music lyrics. Although the electronic media do provide excellent entertainment, some of it is trite or just plain bad. When some idea catches on for one network, others quickly imitate it, and the imitations are usually not as good as the original. Some believe that this is particularly true of the reality genre. Started because it was inexpensive, it has now spawned across many networks. However, entertainment will no doubt continue to be the dominant function of electronic media. People like to be entertained, and the electronic media are well equipped to provide entertainment.[3]

1.5b Disseminating News and Information

Although entertainment may rank as the top function of electronic media in terms of quantity and accessibility, there are many times when the importance of news or information transcends anything of an entertainment nature. When there is a terrorist attack, a fire, a tornado, or some other imminent danger, people turn to the

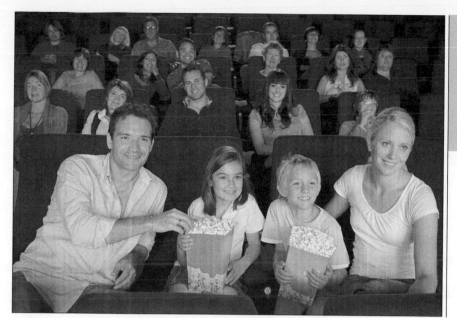

Exhibit 1.5
Although documentaries are shown in movie theaters, the dominant purpose of movies is to entertain people, such as this family.

media. This certainly happened on September 11, 2001, when terrorists crashed airplanes into the World Trade Center; internet sites were overloaded and people were glued to their TV sets. Radio is particularly valuable in emergency circumstances because most people have battery-operated radios that continue to work when other media do not. This happened when Hurricane Katrina (see Exhibit 1.6) hit New Orleans in 2005; other media forms failed, but radio stations stayed on the air. The telephone also becomes important, especially now that emergency agencies can use reverse 911 to call many people to give them information. During the 2007 Virginia Tech shootings, students kept in touch with each other and exchanged information through cell phones and internet blogs.

routine information

It does not take an emergency for the information function to be valuable, however. If you want to know whether to carry an umbrella or what route you should take to work, the media can instruct you. They can also provide the latest economic information (unemployment statistics, stock market results), as well as information about the media (what's playing at the local theater, what's on TV tonight). During political campaigns, most people learn about the candidates through the media. Both radio and television are valuable for providing useful general information, but the internet and mobile media are proving even more valuable because the information you need is always available. You don't have to wait for your radio or TV station to broadcast the weather; you can access your favorite weather site and obtain the information instantaneously.

news

Most people like to stay up-to-date on the news of the day, and the electronic media provide ways of doing that. For many years, the broadcast network evening news was the main source of news for many people. Those newscasts still lead in number of viewers, but the numbers have eroded greatly from the 1980s as audience members have turned to cable TV 24-hour-a-day news services, all-news radio, the internet, and other sources.

Exhibit 1.6
When Hurricane Katrina flooded New Orleans, radio stations were able to stay on the air even though other forms of communication failed.

noncrucial information

In addition to information that you need, the media also provide information that is interesting but not crucial. Although you can get through life without knowing about the mating patterns of the cockroach, a well-presented chronicle on the subject can convey provocative, and sometimes useful, information. Many TV channels provide informational programming ranging from cooking shows to science experiments to history reenactments, and the amount of information available on the internet is growing exponentially.

personalized news

People who use the internet or mobile devices for news can take an active role by personalizing their internet pages with news stories from around the world that contain specific words or phrases—Egypt, SAT scores, bipolar disorder. Some services automatically text you on a smartphone any time there is a new story with the words or phrases you have indicated.

criticisms

There are many complaints about news and information, ranging from "it's boring" to "it's sensationalized." Because news departments of media entities need to make money, they sometimes resort to titillating stories that will attract audience members rather than hard news. Reporters don't always get it right. In the effort to be fast, they sometimes broadcast incorrect information. Often news is capsulated, with very little content for any one story. Most people think the news is biased—against whatever their point of view is. On the other hand, there are so many news venues now that individuals can find some source that agrees with their political leanings and thus can avoid being exposed to the views of others—a danger in a democracy.

Documentaries become controversial when they present a point of view while programs that are purely informational, such as nature shows, do not attract a large audience. Although there is a great deal of information on the internet, anyone can place it there, so its accuracy is suspect.[4]

1.5c Aiding Commerce

Like it or not, advertising is a major part of the electronic media business. In the past, advertising was considered part of the persuasion function of the media because commercials were geared primarily to persuade consumers to buy products. Advertisers still hope purchases will be the outcome of most commercials, but commercials have changed, and the media now aid commerce in other ways.

persuasion

Research has shown that humor is effective in helping people remember commercials and the products they advertise. Also, visual effects have improved greatly from what they were in the early days of electronic media. As a result, some commercials are not as hard sell as they used to be; they may contain only a short reference to the product while emphasizing humor and effects.

humor and effects

Another trend is to match consumers with products that interest them. In some cable TV service areas, not everyone sees the same ads; they are tailored to the demographics of a particular area, and switching equipment at the cable headquarters sends different ads to different homes. Google has made important inroads into matching consumers and advertisers. When you type in the name of a product, the screen displays places where you can buy that product. Companies have paid to have their links included, but generally these links are helpful to the person doing the search, and they are unobtrusive. In general, many of the ads you see on internet pages are specifically directed to you and deal with topics you have been searching or material you have written in emails.

tailoring

Exhibit 1.7

This woman is watching a cable TV home shopping channel that helps aid commerce.

shopping

Media, the internet in particular, enable commerce between individuals through sites such as eBay and craigslist that help people sell possessions they no longer want or find people to provide services they desire. The internet has also changed shopping patterns. Many people order products through the internet without setting foot in a store; the products are delivered to their homes via one of the truck delivery services. Some products, such as music and movies, are delivered over the internet and do not involve any form of conventional transportation.

In many ways, advertisers need to work harder to gain the attention of potential customers. People with DVRs easily skip through commercials, and the clutter of commercials on radio and TV means that any one commercial can get lost in the crowd. Advertisers have responded, in part, by placing their products within TV programs, movies, and video games, a practice known as **product placement.** They also create entire programs about single products (**infomercials**) or multiple products (**home shopping** channels) (see Exhibit 1.7).

gaining attention

criticisms

Hardly anyone will admit to liking commercials—except, perhaps, the ones that accompany the Super Bowl. Commercials are particularly controversial when aimed at young children who are not sophisticated enough to sort out the deceptive hype. Some people take offense at the personal products that certain networks and stations air, such as feminine hygiene and condoms. Companies are constantly rethinking their marketing strategies, hoping that new ideas will be more acceptable and more productive. Any changes they make are likely to involve the electronic media in a major way.[5]

1.5d Transmitting Culture and Customs

unintentional

The electronic media transmit culture and customs without even trying. A TV program about lifestyles of the rich and famous may not show the customs most Americans are used to, but it does show a slice of Americana. American sitcom mothers are usually portrayed as loving, cheerful, and devoted to their children—cultural values held high for mothers. A home show such as *Martha Stewart Living* conveys a message about what constitutes the good life. A documentary about Ethiopia details that country, but if that documentary is made by a French company, it may have a slant that reflects France as much as Ethiopia. A dramatic movie about ancient China will reveal the history and customs of that time, but will no doubt also reveal traits of modern times. People talking on cell phones convey their attitudes and values. The music that pours from an iPod is part of culture (see Exhibit 1.8).

Exhibit 1.8

Music, being played here on an iPod, is an important part of culture.

intentional

criticisms

Sometimes the transmitting of culture and customs is intentional. Spanish-language networks, Vietnamese-language stations, German internet sites, and similar entities have as part of their mission transmitting the values of the culture related to their languages. Religious programming is intent on disseminating the beliefs of a particular religion. Public service campaigns often try to enforce or change customs—fasten your seat belt; don't text and drive. People who interpret the news, such as conservative radio talk show hosts, liberal TV commentators, bloggers, or even individuals on Facebook, are trying to transmit their ideas of what society should be like.

By transmitting culture and customs, people involved with the media also create **stereotypes** and give false impressions. Sitcoms, in order to garner a laugh, often exaggerate negative traits of a particular group of people. A movie that casts a particular minority as villains can be accused of creating a false stereotype. If programming from one culture is shown in another culture, this can result in culture clash. Governments have tried (largely unsuccessfully) to prevent programming from reaching their citizens because it shows customs that are not accepted in that country. Leaders in poor countries worry that if their citizens see lifestyles and customs of wealthier countries, they will become discontent and dissatisfied with their leaders.[6]

1.5e Acting as a Watchdog

In the United States, one of the functions of the media is to watch over aspects of society, particularly the government. Media have a responsibility to report defects, not ignore them. Most of this watchdog function falls to journalists. They keep a close eye on the actions of politicians and report indiscretions—large or small. Sometimes this reporting creates an adversarial relationship between the government and the press. This is not the case in many other countries; in other societies, the press is a public relations arm of the government and primarily keeps people informed about the good things the government is doing for them.

politicians

During election campaigns, the American press reports on the candidates and the election process, informing people so that they can make more intelligent voting decisions (see Exhibit 1.9). As part of their watchdog function, journalists also interpret. For example, after the president gives a speech, they tell us what the most important points were. They try to explain why the price of gasoline is rising or why unemployment is on the increase.

election campaigns

Sometimes various media entities just present material and let members of the public draw their own conclusions. C-SPAN, for example, cablecasts the proceedings of various government bodies, including the House of Representatives. People can watch, without commentary from journalists, and make their own observations. On the internet are political sites of every flavor that people can examine to form (or reinforce) their points of view.

conclusions

The government is not the only body that the media watch over. They keep an eye on business, reporting misuse of funds and executive improprieties. The media also report on failures and successes in education, recreation, religion, and other aspects of society.

others

Exhibit 1.9

The media cover all aspects of election campaigns.

criticisms

The people being watched do not look favorably upon the watchdog function of the media. They feel they are being treated unfairly by overzealous journalists looking to blow any minor indiscretion into a major story. Some people who might make good public servants will not enter politics because they do not want

companion

to put themselves and their families through the brash scrutiny of the press.[7]

1.5f Providing Relaxation and Companionship

Electronic media can fulfill the function of providing relaxation and companionship just by being there. For example, TV can be an excellent companion for older people who live alone. A simple turn of a radio switch can bring relaxing music. Some people find relaxation in sorting through their email, playing video games, or texting (see Exhibit 1.10).

vicarious experience

Part of the reason that media can be relaxing is that they provide vicarious experiences. After a hard day at work, many people want to forget their own problems and become wrapped up in the lives of fictional characters whose problems far surpass theirs. Vicarious experiences can also serve as a release from boredom, or they can simply help pass the time. They can serve as an emotional release. Horror movies allow people to scream in a theater, and tear-jerkers allow them to cry without other people looking at them strangely.

criticisms

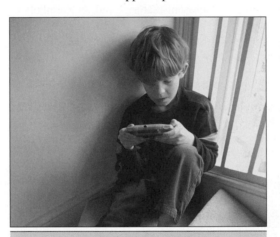

To some, relaxation is a synonym for laziness, and they do not buy into the value of media as an agent of relaxation. And, indeed, some people become so narcotized by media that they spend hours in front of a TV set or computer screen when they would

Exhibit 1.10
Playing video games can be a source of relaxation.

be better off going out and socializing or exercising.

Although media can provide relaxation and companionship, they can also waste a lot of time. Television, in particular, is criticized for being a "boob tube" and delivering content that requires no thinking or action on the part of the viewer. It is blamed for obesity because people tend to eat while watching, and they watch passively rather than engaging in any physical activity that might shed a few pounds. Video games receive similar criticism, but at least they involve hand-eye coordination, and some of them require bodily movement.[8]

1.5g Connecting People to Each Other

Electronic media have always provided material that enables people to have something in common. When a movie comes out, people talk about it—and

producers hope the word-of-mouth buzz will sell more tickets. In the heyday of
radio drama, large numbers of people listened to the same program at the same
time and then talked about it with their friends and co-workers the next day.
For many years, network TV served the same "water cooler" function. Today
viewing and listening are more fragmented, so people are less likely to have conversations in which everyone has seen or heard the same material, but even if a
few people haven't seen a particular show, they have probably heard about it—
through the media.

conversations

In addition to providing content that connects people who have all experienced it, many media forms provide for direct contact between people. Email
over the internet is one example; people who would never have bothered to write
a letter to someone will dash off an email or a text message. The current generation of high school and college students is often referred to as the "connected
generation," in part because of their high use of smartphones and other communication devices (see Exhibit 1.11).

But they aren't the only ones who use media to connect. Their parents find old
high school and college classmates through social media sites. Talent agents use the
internet to scout for promising actors and musicians. Bloggers connect with people
they have never met. People who play multiple-player video games or have social
media sites on the net make new friends they never would have met otherwise. Internet dating services bring people together, and the most common form of dating is
going to the movies. Chat groups act as support for people with various diseases, people who have been victims of abuse, or people who simply share common interests.

direct contact

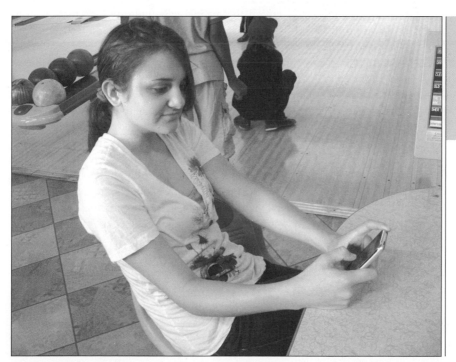

Exhibit 1.11
Text messaging
has become an
important form of
communication,
especially for young
people.

criticisms

Media may help people to connect, but they also help them to disconnect—the boy who is too immersed in a video game to talk to his parents, the teenager who drowns out the world with an iPod, the father who won't answer his daughter's question because he is watching a TV sports event. Also, the ease of connecting makes it easier for people to express hate through emails or phone messages and to prey upon unsuspecting people such as children and the elderly. All the multitasking that is needed to stay connected can interfere with the ability to concentrate. There are those who believe that the degree to which people interact with media is causing a new type of attention deficit disorder (ADD).[9]

1.6 The Democratization of Media

gatekeepers

One major change in electronic media in recent times is that people in general are now much more in control of the media. This is a major **paradigm shift** from earlier times when **gatekeepers** controlled most the public's use of media. Gatekeepers included network executives who chose the series to be aired and decided what time they could be watched; news producers who selected which stories would make it to the evening newscast; radio music directors who selected the music their station would play; and movie studio executives who gave the green light to film projects and then decided when and where they would open. Today those people still exist, but they have much less power than in the past, in part because people with DVRs record programs and watch them when they want to. In a way we are all programmers who can decide, from many options, what we want to see or hear when we want it.

supplying news

There are so many news outlets that people can choose which they want to frequent. In addition, people with camcorders or cell phone cameras often supply material for the newscast if they happened to be where major news breaks (see "Zoom In" box). Individuals select their own music, filling their MP3 players with what they like, not necessarily what a radio station music director might select. People have many more options for watching movies than just going to a theater, and they can create their own little movies and exhibit them on the web.

user-generated content

User-generated content has greatly democratized electronic media. Much of what happens in the world does not get reported or programmed by the major media companies. That leaves plenty of room for individuals to report on events of importance to them. Parents can distribute an announcement about the birth of their baby over the internet. People can post facts, anecdotes, photos, videos, and just about anything else on social media sites. Music lovers can create and operate their own radio stations. Any number of people have had success marketing their materials through the internet.

other aspects

Cable TV facilities have **public access** channels, and although they are somewhat "yesterday," they are another outlet through which people can produce video material and gain an audience. Callers to radio talk shows play a more important role than they used to, often setting the agenda for the show. Individuals provide apps that improve the performance of smartphones and other devices. All these examples and many more have changed the nature and basic structure of the media, making them more accessible and democratic.[10]

ZOOM IN: **We're All Reporters**

A large number of people carry news recording equipment with them all the time. The first time this became obvious was in July 2005 when bombs ripped through London's subway system and victims trapped below ground used the cameras built into their cell phones to record the events and email the images to British TV networks. Because of the dangerous conditions, members of the press were not allowed near the places where the explosions had occurred, so the original reports were based on these citizens' footage.

The London incident was far from the first (or last) time that non-journalists would contribute to the news. Much of what was seen of the devastation of the December 2004 tsunami in South Asia was taken by tourists with camcorders who were vacationing in Thailand. As far back as 1991, George Holliday used his camcorder to record the arrest and beating of Rodney King by the Los Angeles police—a tape that was played repeatedly by news organizations and used in the trials of the police officers involved. The 2010–2011 earthquakes in Chili, New Zealand, and Japan were reported first by people who were in the vicinity with recording devices.

At another level, there are non-journalists who purposely gather news and then try to sell the footage to news organizations. Others put together news stories for their blogs or websites. Some

local stations and networks encourage amateurs to submit footage. Local TV stations, especially, do not have staff to cover all that happens in the community and welcome outside contributions.

This "citizen journalism" has its problems. One is determining the authenticity of the footage. Unscrupulous people seeking to dupe a news organization may send anonymous footage that is fictional. Another problem is that overzealous amateur reporters who have not been trained in journalistic procedures may get in the way of fire or rescue crews or put themselves in harm's way. The quality of the footage is often poor—shaky, with too many zooms.

To cope with these problems, some media outlets do not air footage sent anonymously and also make contributors sign documents attesting to the authenticity of the material. Some stations offer courses to train people who wish to contribute news footage. This is win-win because the independent "reporters" make contact with the stations and can then sell their wares more easily, and the stations receive better footage from people who they know have had some training.

If you were a news director of a TV station, under what circumstances would you air amateur footage? Can you think of a time when you might have been able to capture footage that could be used by a news organization?

A scene from the 1991 tape a citizen made of the Los Angeles police arresting Rodney King.

1.7 Convergence, Proliferation, and Resilience

Convergence, proliferation, and resilience are in some ways contradictory and in other ways complementary. **Convergence** refers to bringing together various media forms and facilities. **Proliferation** refers to distributing media content to a wide variety of venues through an ever-increasing number of distribution platforms. **Resilience** refers to the ability of various forms of electronic media to adapt and continue to exist. Interestingly, although different forms are brought together, they are also more widespread, and they seem to be able to withstand a changing landscape.

convergence

One aspect of convergence involves the blending of separate media to create new types of information and entertainment suppliers. Studios stream movies over the internet; DVDs play on a TV set or a computer screen; radio stations podcast programs. Another type of convergence involves media businesses that supply similar things. Cable companies and phone companies provide high-speed internet access; satellite TV shows much of the same programming as cable TV. As companies try to grapple with what the future will bring, they cover their bets by merging and investing in various forms. In so doing, they often converge parts of their business. If, for example, a company has radio, broadcast TV, cable TV, and internet interests, it may use the same news reporters to gather news for all the entities, even though the presentation of the news is different for each one.

proliferation

Because companies cover their bets, they are also eager to adopt new distribution methods that will further the impact of their products and increase their financial bottom lines. The result is that media products are everywhere. Not only are they accessible in your home, but they appear on your grocery cart, in the restaurant where you eat, at the gas station, and in doctors' waiting rooms—a phenomenon known as **location-based** video.

Portable equipment is responsible for many lifestyle changes. Children can now watch movies or play video games in the backseat of a car while traveling, eliminating some of the "Are we there yet?" phenomenon. Salespeople can call from the road to set up new appointments. If you enjoy any form of media-oriented work or leisure, you are probably contributing to the bottom line of one of the big conglomerates such as Time Warner, Viacom/CBS, Sony, News Corp./Fox, Comcast/NBCU, or Disney.

resilience

The media business is very fast-paced, with media forms changing at a rapid clip. However, despite all the new media, for the most part the older media remain. Movie theaters have been declared dead any number of times, but they still exist (see Exhibit 1-12). They have changed emphasis over the years from grand palaces in the cities to multiplexes in suburban malls, but they have not disappeared.

When TV stole radio's comedy and drama programming in the 1950s, many pundits said radio would disappear, but it didn't. The audience for broadcast TV keeps shrinking, but it, too, is looking for ways to adapt. The internet and mobile media are riding high now, but invariably something will come along to challenge that dominance.[11]

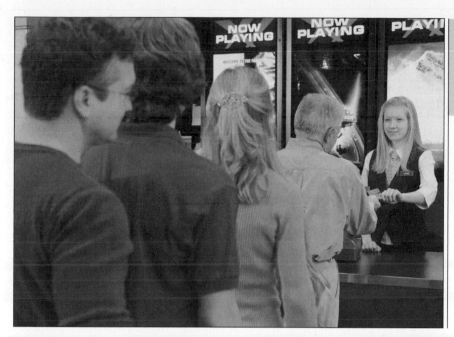

Exhibit 1.12
Movie theaters have been written off many times, but they are still going strong.

1.8 Issues and the Future

The field of electronic media has innumerable issues, many of which will be dealt with in the remaining chapters of this book. They include issues that are internal to the media such as which network will attract the most viewers. The issues also relate to outside forces that the media cannot control, such as decisions made by the FCC or the courts. Within a field that is so technologically oriented, new equipment breakthroughs can raise issues, such as the degree to which photos should be digitally manipulated.

    One generalization that can be made about the future is that the significance of electronic media will probably increase. People are becoming more dependent on these media and will probably use them to a greater extent than at any time in the past. Based on recent history, the number of electronic gadgets and the number of channels of distribution will also continue to increase, whether they are needed or not. New uses for media seem to occur daily, some of them a solution in search of a problem. Perhaps media will be used to replace air travel for business-to-business communication. Perhaps they will be used to help solve health care problems.

    TV set penetration may decline as people decide to use their computer to receive programming. It is also possible that the smartphone may become the second TV set for people and households will no longer have three or

internal and external

significance

more sets. The proliferation of TV in doctors' offices, grocery stores, and the like may prove pointless if people are so absorbed with their portable devices that they are no longer captive to location-based video.

criticisms

The criticisms related to media—sex and violence, lack of originality, sensationalism, inaccuracy, bias, stereotyping, overzealousness—probably won't change. They represent human characteristics that have been around for ages.

advertising

Media functions may change and increase. The one that seems destined for the most change is that of aiding commerce. The old advertising models are not working well and, given that advertising provides the main financial support for the various media, those in the advertising business need to find ways to increase effectiveness.

Individuals have the tools to further democratize the media. Each new recording device seems to be smaller and easier to use. Whether individuals will continue to have the time and inclination to produce programming and website material remains to be seen.

cycles

Convergence and proliferation tend to come and go in cycles. Companies merge and buy out other companies until they become large and unwieldy; then they start breaking themselves down into smaller pieces. As you read the remainder of this book, you may notice that media forms have always converged to some extent and that program material has proliferated over the years. The difference today is in degree; everything is faster and more intense, making for exciting challenges for anyone making a career in the media business.

1.9 Summary

The electronic media are well used and well known. Those who wish to work in media jobs should learn the intricacies of the field, and those who use the media should understand their effects.

Radio was the dominant electronic media form for several decades. When TV became popular in the 1950s, radio had to reinvent itself. In the 1980s cable TV began providing competition to broadcast TV and cable was then followed by satellite and telco TV. The internet became popular in the 1990s, and the 2000s saw the introduction of many more digitally based media. The 2010s continue to increase both the number and speed of new electronic media forms.

People own many communication devices, but their importance and penetration shift as they compete with each other. People use these devices many hours a day, with young people's usage patterns being somewhat different from those of older people.

The functions of the electronic media include presenting entertainment, disseminating news and information, aiding commerce, transmitting culture and customs, acting as a watchdog, providing relaxation and companionship, and connecting people to each other. In all areas, there are criticisms of how the media handle their functions.

Recent times have seen a democratization of the electronic media as individuals take control of what they watch and when they watch it. Individuals also contribute to the news and create user-generated content. Convergence is bringing various media forms together as companies work to hedge their bets. Proliferation of media has increased over the years. Through it all the media forms remain resilient.

Suggested Websites

www.broadcastingcable.com (the website for a magazine that contains a great deal of information about electronic media)

www.c-span.org (C-SPAN, a watchdog organization that cablecasts government activities)

www.pewtrusts.org/our_work_category.aspx?id=230 (a site for statistics about electronic media)

www.stateofthemedia.com (the latest in facts and observations about the media)

www.youtube.com (YouTube, a site for watching and sharing videos)

Notes

1. In gathering statistics about electronic media, it is difficult to find apples and apples. Some figures are based on households and some on individuals; some give percentages, and some give raw numbers; some figures are for all media and some just for selected electronic media; it is hard to find all of the ones for a specific year, although finding them for 2010 was somewhat easy because many statistics were gathered as part of the census. Independent sources are certainly the best to use, as companies and advertisers who list statistics often give them a biased slant. Certainly it is possible to use statistics to prove just about anything you want—see Darrel Huff's perennial tongue-in-cheek favorite *How to Lie with Statistics* (New York: Norton, 1954). Nevertheless, statistics do lend interest and credence to the significance of electronic media, and even though they may not be totally accurate, they do show past behavior and future trends. To put the statistical material together for sections 1.3 and 1.4, the author accessed a wide variety of sources during the summer of 2011, the most significant of which were the following: www.census.gov; www.broadcastingcable.com; www.variety.com; www.hollywoodreporter.com; www.latimes.com; www.wallstreetjournal.com; www.stateofthemedia.com; www.nielsenmedia.com; and www.pewtrusts.org.
2. The entertain, inform, and persuade functions are well delineated in Chapter 4, "The Purposes of the Media," in Edd Applegate, *Print and Broadcast Journalism: A Critical Examination* (Westport, CT: Praeger, 1996). The functions given here are the author's.
3. "TV Season by the Numbers," *Variety*, June 20–26, 2011, 17; "Network Fear: The Net as a Copilot," *Los Angeles Times*, March 27, 2007, E-1; and "CBS: Scheduling for Strength," *Broadcasting & Cable*, May 23, 2011, 12.
4. "Crisis Coverage Showed TV Reporting at Its Best," *Hollywood Reporter*, September 13, 2001, 3; "Flood Victims Turn to Facebook," *Broadcasting & Cable*, June 27, 2011, 12; "This Just In: How Is Your House Faring?" www.nytimes.com/2011/06/27/us/27airwaves.html (accessed June 27, 2011); and "The Impact of Virginia Tech on the News," *Broadcasting & Cable*, April 23, 2007, 14.
5. "Strike Up the Brand," *Hollywood Reporter*, April 4–6, 2008, S-10; "The Golden Age of TV Shopping," *Wall Street Journal,* November 11, 2010, D-1; "Marketers Targeting Generation of Millennials," *Broadcasting & Cable*, April 11, 2011, 28.

6. "Getting Your Faith on Demand," *Broadcasting & Cable*, February 14, 2011, 13; and "Latino TV Gets Serious," *Newsweek*, March 20, 2007, 48.

7. "CNN Rolls Out Election Express," *TV Technology*, October 17, 2007, 6; and Joseph Graf and Sean Aday, "Selective Attention to Online Political Information," *Journal of Broadcasting & Electronic Media*, March 2008, 86–100.

8. "Pass the Remote—and the Bifocals," *Emmy*, September/October 2008, 12; and "Study: Young Kids Immersed in TV," *Broadcasting & Cable*, November 3, 2003, 22.

9. "Y U Luv Texts, H8 Calls," *Wall Street Journal*, October 14, 2010, D-1; and "Staying Connected," *Newsweek*, December 1, 2003, E14.

10. "Why Everybody Is a Reporter," *Broadcasting & Cable*, August 22, 2005, 14; "Cell Phones Change the View of Disaster," *Los Angeles Times*, July 8, 2005, 1; and "The Changing Face of Broadcast Journalism, *TV Technology*, July 6, 2011, 4.

11. "Place Your Bets," *Broadcasting & Cable*, February 14, 2011, 24; "Jumping on the Band Wagon," *Emmy*, September/October 2006, 82–85; "Television Everywhere," *Broadcasting & Cable*, July 24, 2006, 14–15; and "Whither Television Broadcasting?" *TV Technology*, May 1, 2009, 25.

Chapter 2

THE INTERNET, PORTABLE PLATFORMS, AND VIDEO GAMES

Here are some things that were not available at the beginning of the 21st century: iPod, iTunes, iPhone, iPad, Xbox, hotspots, YouTube, Hulu, Skype, Facebook, and Twitter. The technological innovation that has occurred since 2000 has been a blur. Each month seems to bring faster computer speeds and greater storage capacities that expand capabilities of the internet, portable platforms, and video games. Traditional media such as radio, television, and movies were separate for many years, but these new inventions now incorporate material from all of them—as well as from newspapers, magazines, the record business, the telephone industry, and many other media entities.

If you understand it, it's obsolete.
Mosaic Computer, Inc.

The interactive capabilities of the internet, portable platforms, and video games have taken media in a new direction. Previous media forms were basically one way—the producers of content distributed to the public, most of whom simply listened to or watched the material passively. Now anyone can be a producer, distributing to those who click on their site or download their information. When people interact with internet-based media, whether for shopping, texting, emailing, blogging, or any of many other activities, they are in an active stage that involves thinking and doing. The internet did not start out that way, however. It had humble beginnings and then took hold in ways no one had originally envisioned.

2.1 Origins of the Internet

computers

The internet's roots can be traced to two phenomena in the middle of the 20th century. First was the development of computers. Electromechanical calculating machines existed more than 100 years ago, but the first practical **vacuum tube** computer was developed by the U.S. Army during World War II to calculate ballistic artillery trajectories quickly. The general public learned of computers for the first time in 1952 when UNIVAC (see Exhibit 2.1), a computer manufactured by Remington-Rand, was used for election coverage. With only 5 percent of the vote counted, it predicted that Dwight Eisenhower would defeat Adlai Stevenson for president.

cold war

The second phenomenon leading to the internet was the cold war. In 1957, the Soviet Union launched the first communications satellite, *Sputnik*. Realizing the potential of space-based communication for defense, in 1958 President Dwight Eisenhower formed the Advanced Research Projects Agency, commonly called ARPA, and it became part of the Defense Department. Its mission was to manage and direct scientific research in the pursuit of a stronger military.[1]

In 1962, Joseph C. R. Licklider, a professor at the Massachusetts Institute of Technology (MIT), was selected to direct ARPA's behavioral science office. "Lick" put together a team of young researchers to develop his vision of using computers to enhance intelligence. One of these scientists, Bob Taylor, became frustrated that the three computer connections he had in his office at the Pentagon in 1966 (University of California at Berkeley, Strategic Air Command in Santa Barbara, and Lincoln Labs at MIT) could not talk with one another because each had a different computer language and operating protocol. He realized that research and communication

Exhibit 2.1

Dr. J. Presper Eckert (center) describes the functions of the UNIVAC 1 computer he helped develop in the 1950s to newsman Walter Cronkite.

could be greatly enhanced if scientists at one location could interact with computers at other locations.
He hired a team to make this happen.

The scientists reasoned that if each computer
had to learn the language of the other computers,
that would require too much computing power—
computers in the 1960s didn't have anywhere near
the calculating ability of today's laptops, in spite
of their room-filling size. They decided that each
computer would have a smaller computer, called
an **Interface Message Processor (IMP),** which
would translate data, leaving the larger computer
free to do its calculations. In January 1969, the
bid to build an IMP went to a small Massachusetts
engineering firm, Bolt, Baranek, and Newman
(BBN) (see Exhibit 2.2), which met a deadline of
just nine months and delivered the first IMP to the
University of California, Los Angeles (UCLA).
On September 2, Leonard Kleinrock led a team
that hooked up a mainframe computer to the IMP and soon had the big and little
machines sharing messages (see Exhibit 2.3). Thus was born ARPA's computer
network, **ARPANET,** the forerunner of today's internet.

Exhibit 2.2
The BBN team that developed the first IMP in 1969.

IMPs

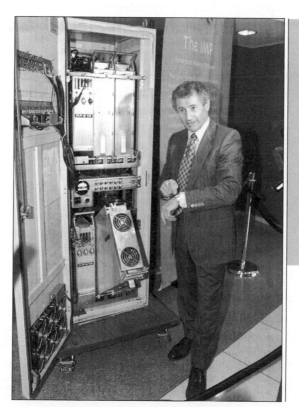

Exhibit 2.3
Len Kleinrock is
pointing out that his
modern-day watch
has more computing
power than the first
IMP installed at UCLA
in 1969. Kleinrock
has said that in the
early days he thought
the internet would
be useful, but what
he never envisioned
was that someday his
97-year-old mother
would be using it.

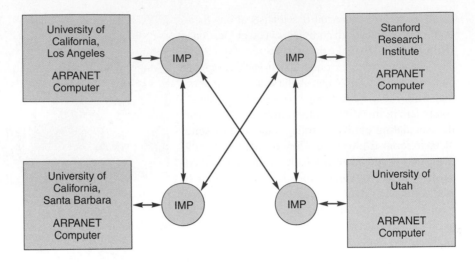

Exhibit 2.4

Diagram of the Interface Message Processors connected to the first four ARPANET computers in December 1969.

ARPANET

At first this network grew slowly. By December 1969, four universities were hooked up (see Exhibit 2.4). In 1984, there were approximately 500 computers on the ARPANET when the National Science Foundation took it over. Since it was no longer part of the Defense Department, people stopped using the name ARPANET and began referring to this interconnected network of computers as the "internet." Through the rest of the 1980s, the number of linked computers grew astronomically. By 1991, more than 300,000 computers were connected, and the internet was no longer the domain of research universities. It had permeated corporations and was beginning to enter homes.[2]

Exhibit 2.5

Vinton Cerf, often referred to as the "Father of the Internet."

2.2 Standardizing the Internet Design

The idea of networking computers did not belong to ARPA alone. Other computer networks sprang up, such as USENET and TELNET. Each network had its own way of transferring messages and files among its computers. For all the networks to be interconnected into one big network, it was clear that one standard scheme, or protocol, had to be created and adopted for file sharing. The task of creating this single standard went to Vinton Cerf (see Exhibit 2.5), a graduate student in 1969 at UCLA—where the ARPANET launched—who became a professor at Stanford in 1972. He decided there needed to be a computer between each network that functioned in the way IMPs functioned between computers—concerning themselves only with a common language for information sharing rather than with the complex codes of each network.

Cerf called this new scheme **Transmission Control Protocol/ Internet Protocol (TCP/IP),** and it is the internet protocol used today. The idea was to enclose each information packet in a **datagram,** something like an envelope that contains a letter. The letter itself is not important for delivery, but the envelope is. The datagrams would contain standardized information for delivery so that the packets were sent to the appropriate computers. Those computers would then decode the packets (open the envelopes) to access the content. TCP/IP was used by programmers for other networks (e.g., TELNET), so their networks could interface with the ARPA-NET. Though there was no directive that all computer networks be interconnected, this seemed to be happening because researchers saw the usefulness of this standard protocol.[3]

TCP/IP

Because the idea of interconnecting computers for defense was born during the cold war, it was important that the network be able to survive a nuclear attack. Paul Baran, a researcher at the RAND Corporation, was charged with designing this network in the 1960s. Baran sketched three different types of networks (see Exhibit 2.6). A *centralized* network has all the information flow to and from a central unit, such as the Pentagon, making it too vulnerable because, if the central unit goes down, the entire network goes down. A *decentralized* network has a number of different units through which information flows, which makes it less vulnerable, but if any one unit goes down, the part of the network connected to that unit goes down. A **distributed network** has no central unit, making it the least vulnerable because it has multiple paths for information flow. Like a fishing net, each piece is connected to more than one other piece, so if one piece breaks, the information can be routed around that break and moved to its destination. This was the network pattern chosen for the internet.

distributed network

This distributed network consists of many **nodes**—the dots on the sketch in Exhibit 2.6. A node functions like a post office. When it receives information, it routes it to the next node, which in turn routes it to the next, and so on, until the information gets where it's going. If any path or node is broken, the information is returned to the previous node, which then reroutes it through a different path or node. Of course, all this happens at the speed of electrons.

How does a node know where to route information? Leonard Kleinrock of UCLA had the answer: **packet switching.** On the sender's computer, a message (text, graphic, photo, audio, video) is broken up into little packets of digital ones and zeros. The computer assigns a datagram (header) to each packet, noting its

packet switching

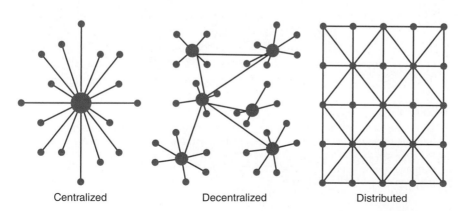

Centralized   Decentralized   Distributed

Exhibit 2.6

A drawing representing Paul Baran's 1960s sketch of three types of computer networks.

origin, destination, date, time, contents, and where it belongs in the overall message. The computer launches the packets into the distributed network. The packets are switched along different paths (e.g., copper wire, coaxial cable, fiber optic, satellite). They arrive at the receiver's computer and are reassembled as the original message. If you have ever watched a web page load on a slow computer, you have seen how the page "chunks in" piece by piece. Each piece is a packet, arriving at the computer and loading into its respective place. This packet switching on a distributed network became the backbone design of the internet.[4]

2.3 The Beginning of Email

Tomlinson

The pioneer credited with the invention of **electronic mail (email)** is Ray Tomlinson. While working on the ARPANET for BBN in 1971, he thought it would be a good idea if the scientists could share messages across computers in addition to sharing research data files. On his own time—writing email was not part of anyone's job description—he tweaked an electronic messaging program that allowed users to send messages to others' mailboxes on the same computer system. Combining that program with an experimental file transfer program, he was able to send an electronic message to himself between two networked computers sitting in the same room (see Exhibit 2.7).

Exhibit 2.7

The first email computers in 1971. Ray Tomlinson sent himself a test message from the computer in the back to the one in the front. Although the computers were side by side, this first network email was delivered via the ARPANET, to which both computers were connected. Note: The computers are on the tables by the racks; the machine on the left is a Teletype.

ZOOM IN: **Email Myths**

No one was more surprised about interest in email than Ray Tomlinson, its creator. To this engineer who graduated from Rensselaer and MIT, creating email was no big deal and certainly nothing that he took any pains to record. In fact, one of his colleagues told him not to tell his boss what he had done because that wasn't part of his job. He was supposed to just work on a file transfer system.

On his website, Tomlinson points out some myths that have arisen about the invention of email. One is that he invented the "at" sign. Actually @ had been around for a long time, but he may have saved it from extinction because it was used so rarely that some were considering removing it from the keyboard.

He also did not press shift-2 to type @. On the keyboard he used, @ was just to the right of "P" where the left bracket and brace are on modern English keyboards.

Although some accounts have said that the first email message was "QWERTYUIOP,"

Tomlinson points out that what he said is that it was something *like* QWERTYUIOP. It could have been "TESTING 1 2 3 4" or something equally insignificant, but he does think it was uppercase.

Ray Tomlinson, the creator of email.

That first email message is lost to history. Tomlinson doesn't remember it, but guesses it could have been something as simple as the top row of capital keys—QWERTYUIOP (see "Zoom In" box). Nonetheless, the use of electronic mail caught on like wildfire, making it the first "killer application" of the new ARPANET. By the next year, 1972, nearly every network user was regularly sending and receiving electronic messages. In addition to exchanging research information, these scientists engaged in heated debates about the Vietnam War (an early chatroom) and developed an early computer-based video game they called Space War.[5]

2.4 The World Wide Web

Another important aspect of the internet is the **world wide web (www),** also known simply as "the web." It consists of a vast array of content provided by corporations, nonprofit associations, universities, government agencies, and individuals from all over the planet. The pioneer credited with inventing the web is Tim Berners-Lee (see Exhibit 2.8), a British physicist working at the European Center for Nuclear Research in Geneva, Switzerland. Berners-Lee wanted to accelerate automatic information sharing among scientists at different institutions around the world. He reasoned that research could be swapped almost

Berners-Lee

Exhibit 2.8

Tim Berners-Lee, often called the "Father of the World Wide Web."

hyperlinks

URLs

instantaneously using the internet. To make this happen, he combined three ideas. One was the *TCP/IP* protocol created by Vint Cerf, discussed previously. Another was *hyptertext,* a term first used in the 1960s related to the concept of connecting virtual documents in computers. Third was the *Domain Name System (DNS),* created in the 1980s to translate web and email addresses into standard numbers that computers can read to route information packets through the internet.

Putting all this together, Berners-Lee introduced, in 1990, a network computer language called HyperText Markup Language (HTML). It made instant information sharing possible by creating **hyperlinks**—words and images that appear highlighted in one document and that allow users to click and be taken instantly to other documents. He envisioned this automatic, instantaneous, global sharing of information as a spider's web spun around the world, so he called his creation the world wide web.

Berners-Lee also wrote the protocol that made possible the transfer of hypertext documents: HyperText Transfer Protocol (HTTP). To be available on the web, each document must be assigned a unique **uniform resource locator (URL),** also called a web address. Thus was born the string of code letters that make up the addresses you see when you use the web (e.g., http://www.mcgraw-hill .com/index.html).[6]

2.5 Privatizing the Internet

privatization

Until the 1990s, the internet was used primarily by government offices and universities. Started by the U.S. Defense Department, it had evolved into a worldwide amorphous entity. It had political support, most notably from Senator (and later Vice President) Al Gore, who had sponsored legislation in the 1980s and early 1990s that funded and expanded the **information superhighway**—a useful metaphor for the grid of cables, fiber optics, and wireless transmitters that allow information to flow among networked computers. As the internet grew, it no longer needed government funding and intervention; it could operate on its own. In 1992, Congress passed legislation that privatized the net, allowing individuals and corporations to profit from it commercially.

This resulted in a free ownership structure. Most electronic media are owned by companies, such as media giants Time Warner, Disney, and Sony, as well as smaller private companies. These businesses create and distribute content using channels, such as radio and television networks, that they also sometimes own.

no owners

Unlike these traditional media, however, no one owns the internet. Anyone can be an information provider. You don't need a license, government approval, or a lot of money.[7]

The privatization of the net greatly increased its use among individuals and corporations. By the end of 1993, 3.2 million computers were connected, representing about 10 million users. By the end of 1994, about 10,000 web **servers** were online, of which some 2,000 were commercial.[8]

2.6 Refining the Internet

In the internet's early days, the people using it were fairly technically minded and could wade through complex codes and operational procedures to exchange information. However, once it became private and ordinary people started using it, much attention was devoted to making the internet user-friendly. Three refinements of the 1990s were browsers, internet service providers, and search engines.

History credits Marc Andreessen (see Exhibit 2.9), a graduate student at the University of Illinois, as the inventor of the first truly viable **browser** for personal computers, Mosaic. Developed in 1993, Mosaic guided users to the information they sought. Mosaic had an easy-to-use interface, incorporating both text and graphics, as well as powerful search capabilities, especially for its day.

Mosaic browser

In 1994, Andreessen joined forces with Silicon Graphics founder Jim Clark to develop and market his browser. They renamed the company Netscape Communications and boasted the lion's share of the browser market: as high as 80 percent in 1995. But when Bill Gates's Microsoft launched its computer operating system Windows 95 in August of that year, it included a free browser called Internet Explorer. Although Explorer initially was considered inferior to Netscape, after a few years and a few generations of improvements it was able to surpass Netscape in market share, and it still holds the lead today. Netscape still exists with a browser called Firefox, which has a small percentage of usage, and other browsers, such as Safari, have been developed.[9]

Netscape

ISPs

To use a web browser, one must connect to the internet. Various **internet service providers (ISPs)** offer this connection. The first ISP, called The World, came to market in 1990. The two major browsers, Microsoft Internet Explorer and Netscape-Firefox, operate as ISPs. Other popular ISPs have included Yahoo, America Online (AOL), Earthlink, and Verizon. ISPs sometimes provide subscribers with specially prepared information and services in addition to internet access. For example, some can open up at log-in with news tailored to the client's interests. At first, ISPs charged for internet access by the minute, but now most are free, supported by advertising.

Prior to actual ISPs, there were text information providers. The main one was CompuServe, started in 1979 as a service that consumers could access from rather modest computers to view large amounts of information (news, sports scores, stock market quotes, weather, etc.) stored within a large CompuServe computer. Early CompuServe and its contemporary services were expensive and complicated, and the standards, operational procedures, and codes necessary to obtain the information

Exhibit 2.9

Marc Andreessen, creator of Mosaic, the first commercial browser.

Exhibit 2.10
Google founders
Sergey Brin and
Larry Page.

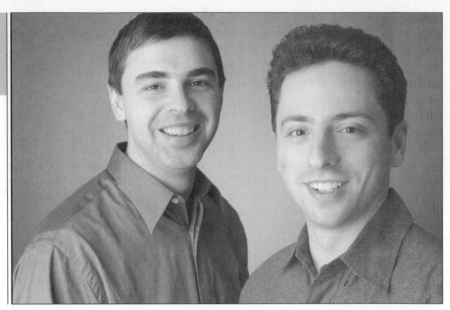

CompuServe

search engines

Google

made the whole concept inaccessible to most people. In 1997, AOL purchased CompuServe, folding some of its services into AOL's ISP.[10]

Compared with early CompuServe, searching and retrieving information from the web today is relatively simple. The development of ISPs and browsers naturally led to **search engines**—giant indexes of information. Attempts at search engines date back to the early 1990s when students at several universities set up systems that indexed names of files. A number of improvements followed, such as being able to search for words, photos, and music.

In 1998 Sergey Brin and Larry Page (see Exhibit 2.10), students at Stanford University, founded Google, the most popular of today's search engines. Not only does Google claim to index the most web pages and register the most hits, but it has led to a new verb: To "google" means to search for something on the web. Google and some of the other search engines use a **raw website return** scheme in which the user enters keywords into a box and the engine scours the web for pages that contain those keywords. Google has since branched out to offer many other technological services other than its search engine.[11]

2.7 Ups and Downs of Internet Companies

As the internet companies of the 1990s grew, merged, and bought each other out, many of them provided browsers, internet service, search engines, email, websites, and a host of other services that were springing up on the internet. They were joined by commercial companies, which, because the internet had been privatized, saw it as a means of making money and coined the term **e-commerce** (electronic commerce).

e-commerce

In 1995, amazon.com, founded by Jeff Bezos (see Exhibit 2.11), sold its first book and quickly became the net's biggest retailer. Many cyberstores followed, some existing only on the net and others as offshoots of brick-and-mortar businesses. Pierre Omidyar founded AuctionWeb in 1995 and changed the name to eBay in 1997; the first item sold was a broken laser pointer for $14.83. Omidyar actually called the buyer to make sure he realized the pointer was broken and the buyer said, "I collect broken laser pointers." Realtors, toy stores, stock brokers, airlines, herbal medicine companies, and many others established an internet presence. Many of these did not make money initially, but they felt there was great potential.[12]

The "product" that made money consistently almost from the beginning was sex—taking in about $1 billion a year. Approximately one-third of all internet usage is visits to porn sites, most of which display a little free material before charging. About 70 percent of visits to these sites are during the 9 A.M. to 5 P.M. workday. Other web-based activities that came to the fore during the 1990s were **instant messaging (IM)** for live chatting, **bulletin boards** for posting messages, web logs (**blogs**) for chronicling life's events, **chatrooms** for private conversations, and **distance learning** for college coursework.[13]

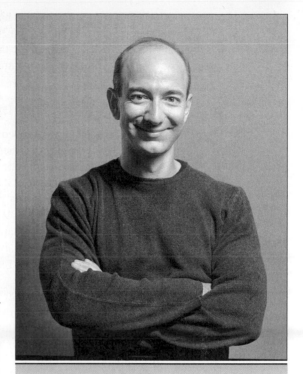

Exhibit 2.11
Amazon.com founder Jeff Bezos.

other services

Because of the rapid development and enormous public acceptance of the internet during the 1990s, the companies involved with it caught the fancy of the stock market. They could sell stock at phenomenal prices, even though they weren't earning any profits. For example, when the auction site eBay went on the stock market in 1998, its stock soared 163 percent the first day of trading, and Pierre Omidyar became an instant billionaire. That same year, Yahoo's stock multiplied sevenfold. This financial euphoria came to a temporary end in the early 2000s, however, when investors started evaluating the dot-com companies more realistically. Many of their stocks plummeted. People who thought they had created a "golden goose" found themselves in hard times. However, a number of young people became very rich during the short period that the stocks were riding high.[14]

Within a few years, the boom-then-bust wave smoothed out, and public internet corporations could sell stock at reasonable prices. For example, in 2004 Google announced its first public stock offering, and because it was the most used search engine in the world, speculation was that the stock would sell very high, perhaps as much as $160 per share. By the time the sale finally happened in August of that year, reality had set in, and Google shares sold for $85, a respectable

stock ups and downs

price, though not as high as had initially been expected. Internet stocks, and most other stocks, dipped again in 2009 because of the recession. When Facebook went public in 2012, the price of the stock actually went down after the initial public offering, causing quite a controversy.[15]

2.8 Audio on the Internet

Internet technology improved rapidly during the 1990s. The decade started with crudely typed words but rather quickly moved into attractive layouts that featured graphics. Toward the middle of the decade a few people began experimenting with audio on the net. At first the audio "hiccuped" as the computer **buffered** the information: The processors and **modems** of the day weren't fast enough to accommodate the data. But as technology and storage improved, both smooth playback and sound quality became acceptable. RealAudio (later called RealPlayer), released in 1995 by Progressive Networks, provided software for **encoding** audio so it could be **compressed** (see Chapter 13) as well as software that consumers could use to **decompress** the audio and hear it through their computer speakers. Shortly thereafter, other companies, such as Microsoft (Windows Media) and Apple (QuickTime) provided similar software. Internet radio stations (see Chapter 5) sprung up that allowed people to hear the station live through **streaming audio** and also allowed them to **download** files to computers to listen **on-demand** at a later time.[16]

software

When it became easy to store audio on a computer, another phenomenon surfaced: music **file sharing.** People in chatrooms began sending each other cuts from CDs to reduce the cost of purchasing music. Shawn Fanning (see Exhibit 2.12), a 19-year-old college dropout, developed software in 1999 that made this exchange easier, and in 2000 he launched Napster. Anyone could download the software for free and send a request to Napster for a particular song. During its peak month, February 2001, Napster reported 2.8 billion songs downloaded. The encoding system used for this exchange, **MP3,** had been introduced in 1998 for the audio part of digital video editing. Once people downloaded music onto their computers, they could play it through their speakers, burn it to a CD, or transfer it to newly developed MP3 players. A website, MP3.com, was developed as a place where new artists could release music for people to sample at no cost.

Napster

Exhibit 2.12
Shawn Fanning, creator of Napster.

Teenagers and college students became enamored with Napster and MP3. For a while, "MP3" was the second-most-searched term on the internet, after "sex." Because Napster attracted such immediate attention and heavy use, Fanning was able to obtain financial backing from Silicon Valley companies. But the recording companies did not take well to Napster. Citing copyright violations, the Recording Industry Association of America

(RIAA) sued, followed soon by the heavy metal group Metallica and others. In 2001, the courts ordered Napster to shut down, and it filed for bankruptcy.[17]

Several companies, including Grokster and Kazaa, tried to pick up where Napster left off with free file sharing by using a different computer configuration, but the courts eventually ruled that they, too, were violating copyright, and they either closed down or switched to legal pay services. In addition, starting in 2003, the RIAA initiated a historic series of lawsuits. On behalf of the major recording labels it represented, the RIAA brought litigation against 261 people, many of them quite young, who had shared music files illegally. The cases got so much publicity that they had a chilling effect that led many people to stop downloading music for free.[18]

lawsuits

Also, the record industry, noting a downturn in music sales, changed its tactics from total opposition to downloading to working with legal downloading services, such as Apple's iTunes, to allow music to be purchased over the internet at reasonable rates. They started to realize that the internet was an ideal distribution system for music that could eventually lessen their costs because it did not need brick-and-mortar buildings or an elaborate distribution network of wholesalers. Certainly it is still possible to obtain music illegally for free using the internet, but the extent to which that happens has greatly declined since Napster's heyday. Record companies now seem willing to take less money per song than they used to, and music fans seem willing to pay at this lower rate, especially if being sued is the alternative. There has definitely been a decrease in the acrimony that once existed.

changed tactics

Another element of audio on the internet involves **Voice over Internet Protocol (VoIP)**—a telephone system that doesn't operate through traditional telephone company facilities. Rather, VoIP converts voice to digital at the handset and then sends the information over the internet as packets of data, using the packet technology developed by Vinton Cerf and Leonard Kleinrock. A caller connects a microphone, internet phone, or regular landline phone to a computer, and software does the rest. Two companies that provide VOIP are Skype (see "Zoom In" box) and Vonage. For Vonage, callers pay a monthly fee for unlimited calling around the world, using their regular phones. Cable systems and ISPs have licensed the technology to offer their customers internet phone service. Skype charges for calls to regular landline phones and cell phones but also has a free service wherein Skype users can call each other if both are talking through microphones connected to their computers.[19]

VoIP

2.9 Video on the Net

Video on the internet developed later than audio, primarily because the files are larger and require more advanced technology. **Streaming video** was mostly experimental in the early 1990s. For the information to get through the internet **pipes**—the physical cables, fiber optics, microwaves, and satellites that make up the internet's delivery grid—and onto the computer monitor, only some of the video information was sent. It did not have as many frames or as high resolution as regular video, so the picture was jerky and fuzzy. The picture also had to be small, and the overall material had to be short; otherwise, it would take hours to download. But as high-speed internet connections, usually referred to

technical limitations

ZOOM IN: Skype's Multinational History

The inventors of Skype are Scandinavians who did much of their initial computer engineering work with engineers in Estonia. One of the primary inventors, Niklas Zennstrom, is a native of Sweden, and the other, Janus Friis, is from Denmark. Skype was not their first venture. They developed the music sharing site Kazaa in 2000 and several years later sold it to an Australian company.

Then, in 2003, they brought out Skype and it quickly became quite successful. They sold it to eBay in 2005 for $2.6 billion, using some of the money to pay $100 million to record labels because Kazaa was engaging in illegal music downloading when they developed it.

eBay found that Skype didn't fit the synergies of its other holdings and decided to sell it. But there were legal problems because Zennstrom and Friis still owned key technologies on which Skype had been built. In addition, a European satellite company filed a trademark suit over the name "Skype." Eventually, in 2009, part of the company was sold to a group of investors. By this time Skype had added many features such as video, conference calls, and instant messaging, and it had competition from others, including Google Talk. In 2011 Microsoft bought Skype for $8.5 billion—quite a jump from its 2003 beginnings.

Scandinavian countries of Sweden and Denmark, and nearby Estonia.

as **broadband,** became available and other technologies improved, video on the internet became more viable.[20]

Some of the first material to stream was promotional in nature. TV program websites featured short clips from shows, and movie sites featured **trailers.** Stations and networks **webcast** news stories because they are short, and several sites gathered short independent and student films and made websites specifically for these projects. Sports organizations, such as the National Basketball Association, showed highlights of games. Interviews and music videos also fit into the "short but sweet" category.

early content

As the years passed, some producers became a little more adventuresome and used the interactive aspects of the internet for their programming. In 1999, Warner showed a cartoon, *The God and the Devil Show,* in which God and Satan interviewed people. Viewers could then send the people to either heaven or hell. Viewers could also be the "judge" for *People's Court,* or play *Wheel of Fortune* or *Jeopardy!* on Sony's site. Starting in the late 1990s, some video suppliers offered full programs on the net, primarily on a one-time-only basis. For example, Comedy Central webcast an episode of *South Park*. In 2004, NBC provided coverage of the Summer Olympics on the net, showing events not seen during its evening tape-delayed televised broadcasts. Production companies also began producing short comedies and dramas named **webisodes** to be shown only on the internet; some of these webisode ideas were picked up by broadcast and cable networks and made into series.[21]

The video sharing site YouTube was founded in 2005 by Chad Hurley and Steve Chen (see Exhibit 2.13), who met while they were employees of Pay-Pal. Apparently while at a San Francisco party, they hatched the idea for a site that would collect and organize short videos from a wide variety of sources and make them available to the public at large. The service started in April 2005 and grew quickly. Just one month after it started, it was hosting 30,000 viewers a day. By November 2005 it was showing more than 2 million videos per day and by July of 2006 that number had reached 100 million. In the fall of 2006, only a year and a half after YouTube was founded, Google bought it for $1.65 billion.[22]

Exhibit 2.13
Steve Chen and Chad Hurley, founders of YouTube.

The site includes how-to videos, comedy sketches, trailers for movies, and many other types of fare, but many of its most popular videos are from amateur videographers who shoot with consumer cameras and load (and sometimes edit) the material on their computers. From there, they upload to YouTube's vast storage network. YouTube also allows organizations and individuals to set up their own channels within its structure; the Motion Picture Academy and the Public Broadcasting Service are among those who have channels. Many of the videos have enabled their creators to have their 15 minutes (or more) of fame. In the summer of 2006, episodes of what appeared to be a video diary of "Lonelygirl" appeared on YouTube. Hundreds of thousands of people viewed them, thinking they were real. Eventually the creators confessed that this was a fictionalized account. Singers have been signed to recording contracts based on their YouTube performances, and people have been hired to write for Comedy Central. Politicians also use YouTube to upload both serious and light-moment videos of themselves, hoping to enhance their image with the YouTube crowd.[23]

As the capabilities of the internet expand, YouTube and many other companies are webcasting longer forms of video, such as movies and TV shows. NBC and Fox (see Chapter 4) founded Hulu as a free service in 2007 primarily to webcast shows they had already aired. Eventually they teamed up with other program sources and became mostly a pay service. Several entire cable TV channels (see Chapter 3) moved from cable to the internet. Movie studios (see Chapter 6) have joined together several times to found services to webcast movies for a fee, but Netflix, which originally distributed movies on DVD, has been most successful at gaining a paying audience for its products.[24]

Internet video is a moving target, dispersing in a multitude of directions and peopled with participants who come up with new ideas at an accelerated rate. But, as with all technologies, there are always new forms around the corner to challenge the existing leaders and push possibilities even further.[25]

2.10 Social Networking

Early 1990s chatrooms and bulletin boards were forms of **social networking** in that they helped people connect with others and share interests. A little later, dating sites hooked together those looking for partners, and classmates.com let people connect with people they had known in high school and college. In 2002 a

Friendster

site called Friendster was set up by computer programmer Jonathan Abrams as a safe place to meet new people by looking at user profiles. The site had 3 million users in the first three months using the pattern of people joining and then asking their friends to join. It grew to over 100 million, but it suffered from technical and management difficulties and began losing members. Today Friendster is owned by a Malaysian company and is primarily a gaming site.[26]

MySpace

Some of Friendster's members went to MySpace, which had actually been started in 1999 but became better known in 2003. Its roots are a little muddy because it received financial and logistical support from another company called eUniverse, and most of the early users were eUniverse employees, but Tom Anderson and Chris DeWolfe are given credit for much of the innovation and success of the site, which built up to 115 million users worldwide. It had more features than Friendster with its members posting bios, photos, blogs, videos, and other things that fit their fancy. It attracted some 3 million bands, as well as numerous comedians, filmmakers, and wannabees who wanted to be seen. In 2005, Rupert Murdoch's News Corporation (parent of Fox Broadcasting) bought it for $580 million and a year later made a deal with Google wherein Google provided search functions and advertising. News Corp., being a large company, did not seem to be able to act quickly in response to technological changes and also never solidified a unified vision for the site. Starting in the fall of 2008, it bled about a million users a month and in 2011 News Corp. sold it for a mere $35 million to Tim Vanderhook, the CEO of a small company, who brought in singer Justin Timberlake to help change the site's focus back to one for independent artists.[27]

Facebook

The downfall of MySpace was caused, at least in part, by the growth of Facebook. It was started in 2004 by Mark Zuckerberg while he was a student at Harvard and grew rapidly starting about 2007. At first Facebook was solely for college and high school students, but Zuckerberg opened it to everyone and, like MySpace, encouraged all types of member postings. However, as a small company, Facebook is nimble and able to adapt quickly. It seamlessly integrated various forms of communication such as instant messages, text messages, email, photo and video postings, and live video chats. It includes many specific features such as the ability to write on someone's "wall" or indicate that you "like" someone's post, personal profiles, status updates, common interest user groups, and social gaming. In 2010, the movie *Social Network,* based on Facebook and starring Jesse Eisenberg (see Exhibit 2.14) as Mark Zuckerberg, was one of the contenders for best picture. Facebook has not been without its controversies. Zuckerberg originally hacked into Harvard's computer network to copy private dorm ID images, an act that caused Harvard to shut down his initial site and charge him with breach of security and other offenses, charges that were ultimately dropped. Several of his fellow students accused him of using their ideas. Facebook has been faced with complaints about privacy and security. However, it has accumulated 750 million users and is the third largest web company after Goggle and Amazon.[28]

Exhibit 2.14
Actor Jesse Eisenberg who portrayed Mark Zuckerberg in *Social Network.*

Twitter is a different type of social network in that its main features involve writing short messages and following people or things of interest. It was founded in 2006 as an experimental side project to a podcasting company called Odeo. The three main people involved with its establishment were Jack Dorsey, who was interested in dispatch systems, and Evan Williams and Biz Stone who worked on blogging software. The executive suites of Twitter have been a revolving door filled with drama. Dorsey was the first CEO; then Williams took over and Dorsey became chairman of the board and also started another company. Williams then left but stayed on the board and Dick Costolo, formerly with Google, became CEO. Stone involved himself as an advisor on philanthropy but also consulted with other companies. In short, none of the founders work full time at the company. Nevertheless, it has grown phenomenally from about 1.5 million messages (**tweets**) a year in 2007 to 65 million tweets a day in 2010. Because of technical restrictions, Twitter's tweets can be no longer than 140 characters. They can be sent in a wired or wireless fashion on Twitter's website or through the use of various other devices. Although individuals can **text message** each other and set up profiles, one of the main aspects of Twitter revolves around the principle of followers. When someone chooses to follow another Twitter user, that user's tweets are sent to the person—and to all the other followers. Many celebrities use Twitter to send messages to their fans— anything from what they had for breakfast to music recommendations to political opinions.[29]

Twitter

Although Facebook is currently the largest social network, and Twitter is close behind, there are others, such as Google+, trying to be a replacement. There are also smaller social networks for more focused groups such as churchgoers, dog lovers, or surfers. Social networking has become a major force in society, including for the media business. The film industry uses social networks to promote its movies, and rock bands use them to create a buzz. Reality TV consumption also correlates well with heavy use of social media.[30]

2.11 The Rise of Portable Platforms

reasons

Portable platforms arose from a need people felt to carry digital material from one place to another. Someone who typed a document on a desktop computer wanted to be able to work on that document in an airplane. People on the go wanted to be able to access the internet to look at their email or find a weather report when they were in a hotel room or a coffee shop. Kids wanted to play video games or watch a favorite DVD while riding in the back seat of a car.

developments

As computer storage and speed grew, laptop computers became feasible. These could be carried in a briefcase and used in the same manner as a desktop. They could also be configured to receive the internet first through phone wires and later at wireless **hotspots**—areas served by **wi-fi** transmitters that could pick up the internet. Small video game consoles and DVD players allowed entertainment to travel anywhere. Cell phones and smartphones opened up new vistas of portability as did pods and pads.

People now want entertainment and information when they want it and where they want it. They also want it on whatever portable device they happen to have with them at the time. They want control, convenience, choice, and connection. And, for the most part they are able to obtain it.[31]

2.12 Cell Phones

The **cellular phone** was one of the earliest successful portable platforms. Portable wireless phones actually existed as far back as the 1920s, but they were cumbersome and expensive and did not catch on with the general public. AT&T's Bell Labs developed the concept for what eventually became the cell phone in 1947. But the Federal Communications Commission (FCC) had no inclination back then to assign spectrum for wireless telephones, so AT&T kept the idea on the shelf for decades.

history

In 1981, the FCC authorized spectrum space for cell phones. The first commercial cell phone call is credited to Bob Barnett, an executive at the phone company Ameritech. In 1983, from his car in Chicago, he phoned Alexander Graham Bell's grandson in Berlin. The quality wasn't great, but the commercial viability of cell phones was apparent. Cell phones caught on fairly quickly; by 1993, some 20 million had been sold, and people throughout the world were using them.[32]

operation

Cell phones operate through low-powered transmitters and receivers, each serving a small geographic area called a cell. When a person talking on a cell phone in a car leaves a particular cell, the call is transferred seamlessly to a transmitter in the next cell. Because the transmitters are so low frequency, many people can be talking on the same frequency in the same cell without causing interference. It is estimated that at any one time there are over 10 million drivers using cell phones in cars in the United States. This has led to safety concerns as tests have shown that talking on a cell phone can be as dangerous as drinking and driving. Many states have outlawed certain types of cell phone use, such as use in cars by drivers under 18. Some states only allow automobile cell phone calls that utilize **Bluetooth** or similar products that transmit phone calls through the car's built-in microphone/speaker system. The original cell phones were used only to make phone calls. It wasn't until the mid 2000s that cell phones morphed into smartphones.[33]

2.13 Smartphones

Smartphones emerged by combining features of phones with those of **personal digital assistants (PDAs),** such as Apple Newton and Palm Pilot, which were available in the 1990s. The first of the PDAs were primarily a substitute for the paper calendar or date book—a way for people to keep track of what they needed to do each day. As time progressed, they also stored contact information about friends and business associates and added calculators, alarm clocks, email, and internet access.

PDA origin

The first phone/PDA combination was the IBM Simon released in 1993, but it did not catch on nationwide. More successful were the Erickson and Nokia smartphones that used the Symbian open operating system and a Microsoft product that used Windows. These were all marketed in the early 2000s, using the term "smartphone."

early smartphones

In 2002 Research in Motion released the first BlackBerry. Because it was optimized for wireless email, it became more popular than earlier phones. In 2007 Apple came out with its first iPhone, which was controlled through a touchscreen and had the best web browser of the time. Apple allowed third parties to design **applications (apps)** for its phone and in 2008 opened an app store that became very successful. People have submitted, for free or for sale, about 500,000 applications for such things as fitness aids, travel tips, low battery warnings, foreign language translation, videos, and games. In 2008 Google released Android and its market share increased quickly. Like other smartphones, Google's includes the original PDA features plus GPS navigation, web browsing, media playing, and many other functions, either native to the phone or available as apps.[34]

BlackBerry, iPhone, Android

Smartphones (and cell phones) operate through telephone companies such as AT&T, Verizon, and T-Mobile. Sometimes a phone manufacturer (such as Apple) will contract with one specific phone company (such as AT&T), meaning that anyone who buys an iPhone must use AT&T as its service provider. This has not resonated well with consumers so the practice is diminishing.[35]

service providers

Text messaging is a feature of smartphones that has become very popular. The 140-character messages possible through Twitter can be sent over the phone as well as over the internet. Someone can send and receive texts anywhere that there is cell phone reception without having access to the internet. Also, a number of producers have created **mobisodes,** program material produced specifically for the small screen video and headset audio of the smartphone platform. Smartphones have changed how people communicate and how they obtain information. Their impact has been significant in a very short period of time.[36]

texting

2.14 Pods and Pads

genesis

Apple is the main company that has popularized **pods** and **pads** with its iPod and iPad. The idea for a new form of MP3 player that was hard-drive based and tied to a music delivery system where users could obtain music legally came from Tony Fadell, who pitched it to several companies before approaching Apple. Apple's executives, including CEO Steve Jobs, were enthusiastic about the idea and hired Fadell in early 2001 to head a team to develop it. The project was kept very secret, and when Jobs announced it in October of 2001, people were surprised that Apple would offer a music player, especially one that didn't operate at all like its computers.[37]

iTunes

But the iPod became very popular, especially after the iTunes Music Store opened on the internet in 2003. Jobs had worked hard with music publishers and record companies to convince them that it was in their interest to allow Apple to sell music singles (instead of albums) for the low price of 99 cents each. To appease the music industry, Apple applied a form of copyright protection called **digital rights management (DRM)** onto the music that consumers downloaded from iTunes. It limited the number of times that someone could copy the music from one computer to another, first to three and later to five. This iTunes concept did help reduce illegal copying.[38]

features

There are other pods, but Apple dominates and has come up with many updates of its product, which now sports a screen, allows for apps, and is referred to as iPod Touch. Apple added radio and television programs to iTunes and the term **podcasting** was invented to refer to the act of sending material to a pod, whether it came from iTunes or elsewhere. Apple now has a service wherein people can save and access their whole music collections from an Apple server.

iPad

The iPad is also a product of Apple that was introduced in 2010 (see Exhibit 2.15). For a company that was almost defunct in 1997, the iPod, iPhone, and iPad have served it well. The iPad, although not a phone, has many of the features

Exhibit 2.15
Steve Jobs introducing the iPad in 2010.

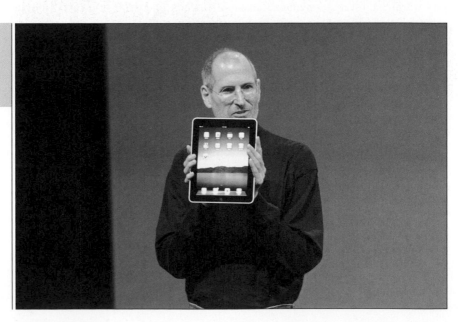

of a smartphone—games, photos, email, internet access, apps, etc. Because it is about the size of a piece of paper (although thicker), it is also a device for reading books, magazines, and newspapers.

Amazon.com was the first company to come out with an **e-book** reader, the Kindle, in 2007. With the capacity to hold about 200 books, it sold out in a little over five hours. Kindle was designed strictly for reading books, so it does not support color. Rather, its black and white screen is ideal for reading in all types of lighting conditions. The books can, of course, be purchased from amazon.com and downloaded wirelessly. Other companies, such as Sony and Barnes & Noble, have come out with readers, but the main competition for book reading seems to be between Kindle and iPad.[39]

Kindle

The iPad, because it has many other functions, may also replace other portable platforms, such as the laptop. It is already being used extensively within the entertainment business. Producers read scripts on it, directors post crew instructions such as call sheets with it, and hairstylists use it to take photos to keep track of how actors' hair looked in certain scenes. It has apps to help cinematographers with lighting settings and apps for making notes and highlighting material. Instead of jotting down ideas on napkins, people draw them on a digital tablet.[40]

industry features

2.15 The Early Days of Video Games

Video games are now ubiquitous, but that has not always been the case. The first popular video games were in amusement arcades, usually near pinball machines. The "Father of Video Games" was Nolan Bushnell, an egotistical but likable entrepreneur who founded Atari in northern California in 1972. He and his main engineer, Al Alcorn, invented *Pong,* an electronic version of table tennis, which they placed in arcades. It became so popular that the main technical problem was that the coin boxes filled up with quarters too quickly. Atari's next successful step was a home version of *Pong,* which sold out almost instantly during the Christmas 1975 season. It was encased in a separate unit that plugged into a TV set, allowing the operator to interact with the set by manipulating the unit's joystick.

Pong

Atari was not the first console video game that connected to a TV set. In 1972 Magnavox had come out with a product called Odyssey, developed by Ralph Baer, that had two controllers and an overlay that stuck to the face of the TV tube. One overlay was a tennis court for a tennis game, and another was a hockey court. Magnavox sued Atari for violating Baer's patent, but they settled amicably. Atari paid Magnavox a small amount, and Magnavox became the first licensee for Atari's products, so everyone won. Atari had the better technology in that *Pong* had sound and the ball speeded up as the player improved.

Magnavox

Bushnell came up with the idea of putting the chip for the game into a cartridge that would slip into the console unit. That way people could buy individual games without having to buy a whole console for each game. But he didn't have enough money to develop this concept, so he sold Atari to Warner Communications. Bushnell's company had a very laid-back culture that pleased his creative workers (see "Zoom In" box), and Warner was a much more straight-laced, formal company, so the cultures clashed. In addition, the first product that Warner

Bushnell sells

ZOOM IN: **Inside Atari**

Nolan Bushnell hired young people for Atari, many of whom were unkempt and undisciplined. He recruited them from some of the seedier parts of northern California during the era when the "flower children" were in full bloom. Bushnell didn't pay much attention to when they got to work, what they wore, whether or not they engaged in personal hygiene, or what they imbibed. But he did care about results in terms of creating video games. So he set deadlines for them to accomplish certain tasks, and if they met the deadlines, he threw them a party—something that proved to be an excellent incentive. Atari, rightfully, became known as a party company.

One of the scruffiest employees he hired was a young man named Steve. Steve had a friend, also named Steve, who was never officially an employee of Atari but who hung out at the company with his buddy Steve and kibitzed with other employees. After a while the two Steves decided to form their own company, and they asked Bushnell if he wanted to invest. He declined. In case you haven't already guessed, the first Steve was Steve Jobs and the other was Steve Wozniak, the founders of Apple Computer.

But don't weep for Bushnell because he missed a great financial opportunity. After he got kicked out of his own company, he went on to make his fortune by founding the Chuck E. Cheese chain.

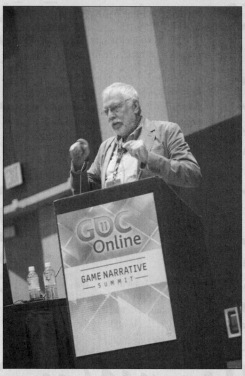

Nolan Bushnell, who still makes presentations and consults for the game industry.

and Atari worked on together failed (in part because they didn't get it out in time for Christmas), so in 1978 Warner fired Bushnell from his own company. Over the next several years Atari's products sold well, and for several years in the early 1980s Atari accounted for more than half of Warner's earnings. But Warner never treated the game inventors well, and most of them left.[41]

Pac-Man

Meanwhile Atari acquired some competitors, including the American company Midway, which in 1980 brought out a Japanese-developed game it had licensed called *Pac-Man.* (The name in Japan had been the Japanese equivalent of Puck-Man, but the Midway executives were afraid people would change the first letter of Puck-man, so they changed the name to *Pac-Man.*) *Pac-Man* was a round character (in the true 8-bit color of the time) with a big mouth that ate everything in his path. He became a national personality that was licensed for products such as toys and food. He even had his own song and TV show.

Nintendo

Another competitor was Nintendo, a Japanese playing card company that had been formed in 1889, but which decided in 1980 that it wanted to cash in on the U.S. video game market. It came out with a game called *Donkey Kong* (again the title was the result of a translation problem). It had a "story" to motivate the action: A gorilla runs away from a carpenter and steals the carpenter's girlfriend, so the carpenter chases the gorilla through a factory to rescue the girl. The carpenter's name was Mario, and he, like Pac-Man, caught the fancy of the public. Nintendo gave Mario a family and developed many more games around him that are still among the more popular game franchises today.[42]

2.16 Games Falter and Rebound

Back at Atari, things weren't going so well. Having lost its best creative people, Warner, in a 1982 move of desperation, licensed the game console rights for *Pac-Man*. They put it on their Atari 2600 console, but it never worked right. It was hard to control, the characters didn't move well, and it was just plain ugly. Warner had a lot of unsold inventory. Then, in what turned out to be an even bigger mistake, they brought in Steven Spielberg to help them make a game based on his popular 1982 movie, *E.T.: The Extra-Terrestrial*. They couldn't get this game to work either, and legend has it that they bulldozed a hole in the desert to bury all the unused inventory. In 1984 Warner sold Atari at a loss.[43]

disasters

The *Pac-Man* and *E.T.* fiascos affected the whole industry, and for several years hardly anyone was playing video games either in arcades or in their homes. In 1986, Nintendo launched a new console, NES, that had better graphics and sound and brought video games to a new level. Accenting its Mario games, Nintendo revived the video game industry. Sega, another Japanese company, came out with a console in 1986, and for a number of years the video game business belonged to the Japanese.[44]

In the mid to late 1980s, computer manufacturers became interested in games, especially Steve Jobs and Steve Wozniak who founded Apple Computer and who had games in their blood (see previous "Zoom In" box). They made sure the computers they developed had the technological capabilities to handle gaming. One of Apple's employees, Trip Hawkins, left Apple and founded Electronic Arts (EA), a company that created software for games, originally games for computers although later it developed games for consoles also. EA (see Exhibit 2.16) made its mark with sports games and attractive packaging that featured sports stars who endorsed the games. EA had problems with its first football-based game, however. Technology only allowed there to be seven players on each team. Football players nixed the seven-player concept and would not endorse it. Eventually, when technology improved, EA developed a very successful interactive football game, *Madden*.[45]

EA

Husband and wife team Ken and Roberta Williams also developed games in the 1980s. She wrote stories as the basis for games such as *Mystery House* and *King's Quest*. The latter was the first **third-person perspective** game, in which the player could move the characters through the game. Ken developed the technology for the graphics needed for Roberta's stories and in doing so advanced

third-person perspective

Exhibit 2.16

As evidence that video games are big business, Electronic Arts built this large complex in Los Angeles to take advantage of the talent in the film and TV industry located there.

video game possibilities. In the early 1990s, Robyn and Rand Miller released *Myst* for the Macintosh computer. It was a totally absorbing story with advanced graphics that people immersed themselves in for hours, or even days. Another popular game was *Sim City,* in which players could build simulations of people and run their lives, something that its creator, Will Wright, likened to having a dollhouse. The games of the 1970s and 1980s had been "script driven"—the same monster would appear behind the same tree every time the game was played. But now games changed depending on how the player interacted with them.[46]

In the early 1990s, the **first-person shooter** games arrived, led by *Doom.* For these games, the player's eyes were the monitor and players could see their hands and the gun in front of them. When *Doom* came out, its creators, IDS Software, tried to upload it to a server so that people could download it. But so many people were waiting for it and writing notes asking when it was coming that IDS

first-person shooter

couldn't get it uploaded and had to tell everyone to stay off the site for a while. The first-person shooter games were quite violent and bloody and caught the attention of parents' groups and the government. Congress held hearings, and the games were blamed for a number of social problems, including the 1999 Columbine massacre. The result was that the gaming industry developed a ratings code (such as M for "Mature" and AO for "Adults only") to give consumers information on which to base their purchases.[47]

video and sound

Video games' visual and sound effects also improved greatly during the 1990s. *Sherlock Holmes, Consulting Detective,* was the first computer game to incorporate **full-motion video.** It was released on CD-ROM, as were many games during that decade. Once full-motion video was possible, producers began using recognized actors to star in the games or to serve as body models for animated characters. Sound effects dazzled with futuristic audio as well as wind, rain, and other aural elements to make the players feel as though they were really in their virtual worlds.[48]

2.17 Game Console Wars

Nintendo-Sega

In the 1990s, Nintendo was riding high as the leader of video consoles. It had used a 1984 Russian-based puzzle game called *Tetris* to launch its new console, Game Boy. (Incidentally, the Russian inventor of the game did not get money for his invention; the Communist Party took it over and sold it around the world.) Sega Master System still existed and occasionally gave Nintendo a run for its money, especially when it came out with a very fast-paced game, *Sonic.* Consoles were no longer tied to TV sets; they were stand-alone units.

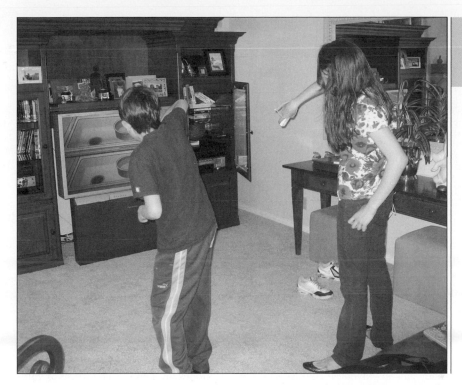

Exhibit 2.17
Brother and sister compete playing Wii.

Sony-Microsoft

In 1995 Sony entered the game business with PlayStation. Its technology was so far ahead of Sega's that Sega dropped out of the video game business. In 2001, Microsoft joined in with Xbox. Skeptics weren't sure that Microsoft, which previously had dealt only with software, could develop a hardware game console, but the product proved to be very successful and Microsoft was able to launch a successful game franchise with *Halo,* an alien invasion video game. In the mid-2000s, Nintendo upped the ante with Wii (see Exhibit 2.17), a video game concept that involves not just the thumbs but the entire body. In 2008, video game company Take-Two Interactive brought out *Grand Theft Auto IV* for PlayStation and Xbox, and it sold a record $500 million in the first week. Video game console companies Nintendo, Sony, and Microsoft are still avid competitors.[49]

2.18 Games for the Internet and Beyond

many players

Meanwhile the internet was growing, and gamers started using it as a distribution means for their games. This brought about an entirely new game-playing experience. For example, the internet game *Majestic* infiltrated people's lives by sending them cryptic emails, menacing phone calls, threatening faxes, and other "real-life" information related to the game. In addition, people around the world who didn't know each other could play games with each other. One of the first games, *Quake,* enabled six people to play each other. These people formed clans and had meetings in Texas where *Quake* players could actually meet the clan people they had been playing with. As the internet technology improved, games could accommodate millions of people. *World of Warcraft (WoW),* for example, had more than 11.5 million people playing it worldwide. They paid a fee and could then customize much of their play.[50]

social networks   Social networks have provided an excellent outlet for video games. Zynga Inc. has done well with *Farmville* and *Cityville* on Facebook. It does not charge people to play the games but rather sells virtual products that can help people move through the game more efficiently. Although many people play without buying these goods, enough do purchase them that Zynga makes a profit.[51]

audience base   Video games, which originally targeted young males, have broadened their audience base. There are educational games for young children, games that appeal primarily to women, and games such as Bingo and chess that attract an older demographic. The military uses game technology to train enlistees, many of whom have excellent hand-eye coordination from growing up with games. In arcades, players can don gloves with motion sensors that make a projected virtual world react to their movements. Gamers can enjoy lifelike simulations of flying, turning upside down, and fighting with monsters. Some games are created so players can get into the programming and modify them and others are designed to be shown in 3-D. Games are based on movies and movies are based on games. Same for TV shows. Some game consoles also allow for TV programs and movies to be seen through the console. As each new platform arises, games join in. They can be played on laptops, iPods, smartphones, and iPads. The world of gaming has certainly changed from the days of *Pong.* [52]

2.19 Issues and the Future

Many of the current and future issues related to the internet, portable platforms, and video games revolve around how they will affect more traditional media and how they will affect each other. As the trend shifts from using broadcasting and cable TV for entertainment and information to using the internet, major changes are likely to take place. For one, there is a need for a bigger slice of wireless frequencies to accommodate portable devices. At present, a plan is afoot to take these frequencies from local broadcast stations. Needless to say, this plan is opposed by the stations.[53]

frequencies needed

net neutrality   There is an internal debate going on between those who have content on the internet and those who provide access to the net. It involves a concept called **net neutrality.** Search engines and owners of websites are in favor of net neutrality because they want everything on the internet to have an equal chance of being seen by users. The service providers, such as cable TV and phone companies, oppose net neutrality. They want to manage the traffic on their networks to prevent sluggish operation. Sometimes that means blocking certain sites or messages that are hogging too much bandwidth. Proponents of net neutrality say that blocking material threatens freedom of speech. This is an issue that has potential to be to be "resolved" and then brought up over and over through court decision and layers of regulations.[54]

Many companies hedge their bets and become involved with multiple distribution forms. How much should a company invest in a new business that might hurt an old one? Some feel that MySpace, for example, went downhill because News Corp. was paying too much attention to its older businesses and not enough to developing social networking. However, new media forms often bring forth new players. YouTube enabled anyone with a digital camera to produce material, some of which was watched more intently than product of the more traditional media. But now the more traditional media are moving to take over YouTube and social networking by placing their material there. Gone will be dancing cats and aspiring comics in favor of network dramas and comedies. Will this take away from the pioneering flavor of the internet?

traditional versus new

Texting is now a major part of income for telephone companies. However, there are signs that the texting fad may be fading. Phone companies are looking at this with a nervous eye. Texting seems to be replacing email because it is so much more "with the moment." Most texting is undertaken on portable platforms, and the small screen experience leaves things to be desired. If the larger pads add phone functions, will they replace smartphones?[55]

There are elements within one form of media experience that can affect particular aspects of the form. For example, will there be a need for video game consoles with games so available on social networks, smartphones, and pads? Games as apps may be cheaper and more convenient than games tied to a particular console. If some company perfects 3-D games, will that wipe out other aspects of the game industry?[56]

inter effects

The internet, portable platforms, and video games are also ripe for many sociological issues. People can access much more information more quickly than in the past. Is it information overload? Is the quick access saving time or merely eating up time? Some people experience FOMO (fear of missing out) if they don't check their smartphones constantly. Is this stressful? Or is fiddling with a smartphone just a way of avoiding eye contact or a conversation with a "real" person? Some people play video games for hours on end with an intensity resembling addiction. Many people access Facebook or other internet sites when they are at work. Is this fair to their employers?

social effects

These new media forms may change life as we know it. Email may bring the end of the post office. Online banking may eliminate the need for checks. Newspapers, books, and other paper products may no longer be available in their hard copy forms. Perhaps e-books will bring about a resurgence in reading because they are easier to carry around than traditional books. Some predict the end of the English language as we know it because of all the abbreviations that have arisen to accommodate the 140-character tweets.[57]

Social networks and smartphones can help friends get together on short notice because they can communicate where they are and what they are doing. However, they can also congregate too many people. People who have followings on Twitter can bring most of their followers to a particular place,

major changes

reliance

sometimes causing riots or protests that get out of control because of the mass of people involved.[58]

Almost anyone who has ever lost an internet connection for a day or a smartphone for an hour or an important cell phone call while behind a building knows we have all become very reliant on these new technologies. This overreliance leaves us very vulnerable to cyber attacks or even technological hiccups.

The positives of the internet, portable platforms, and video games seem to far outweigh the negatives because these devices continue to grow and change as technological improvements allow for greater electronic speed and capacity. With each technological advance, creative minds find new ways to use the technology, which then drives the technology even further.

2.20 Summary

The early visionaries associated with ARPA, such as Licklider, Kleinrock, Cerf, and Baran, worked on methods to interlink computers and send information through them by developing IMPs, TCP/IP, a distributed network, and packet switching. Once the internet was formed, the emphasis was on using technology in practical ways. Tomlinson created email and Berners-Lee constructed the world wide web. About the same time, Bushnell was using technology to create the *Pong* video game. When there was a need to make the internet user-friendly, others, such as Andreessen, Brin, and Page, developed browsers, ISPs, and search engines. Technology has also been important in making the internet portable through cell phones, smartphones, pods, and pads. It was instrumental in providing video games to arcades, consoles, and the internet.

In addition to being technological marvels, the internet, portable platforms, and games are also important economic, political, and social phenomena. The privatization of the internet that led to growth of e-commerce through such sites as amazon.com and eBay changed how many products are marketed. Music, in particular, has changed its business model as a result of Napster, iTunes, and pods. YouTube enabled everyone to become a producer. Video games are available on a multitude of platforms, including pads, and have included third-person perspective, first-person shooter and many other types of games. Chatrooms, VoIP, and social networking sites such as MySpace and Facebook have altered how people interact. Cell phones and smartphones have led to instant communication, aided by Twitter's tweets. Older media have had to adapt to changes brought about by these new technologies and, although society has embraced the internet, portable platforms, and video games, they are not without their problems.

Suggested Websites

http://openmap.bbn.com/~tomlinso/ray/home.html (Ray Tomlinson's site that describes the beginning of email) www.amazon.com (one of the first e-commerce sites)

www.skype.com (a VoIP site)

www.twltter.com (Twitter's home page)

www.zynga.com (a video game production company site)

Notes

1. "A Brief History of the Net," *Fortune,* October 9, 2000, 34–35.
2. "The Birth of the Internet," *Newsweek,* August 8, 1994, 56–57.
3. "Internet Pioneers: Vint Cerf," http://www.ibiblio.org/pioneers/cerf.html (accessed May 1, 2008).
4. *The Internet: Behind the Web,* Video, History Channel, 2000.
5. "The Evolution of the Internet," *Telecommunications,* June 1997, 39–46.
6. "How the WWW Is Put Together," *Byte,* August 1995, 138; and Barbara K. Kaye and Norman J.Medoff, *The World Wide Web* (Mountain View, CA: Mayfield, 1999).
7. Rijiv C. Shah and Jay P. Kesan, "The Privatization of the Internet's Backbone Network," *Journal of Broadcasting & Electronic Media,* December 2007, 93–109.
8. "The Birth of the Internet," 56–57; and "A Brief History of the Net," 34–35.
9. "The Killer Browser," *Newsweek,* April 21, 2003, E-6–E-11.
10. "A Trip to Cyberspace," *Los Angeles Times Advertising Supplement,* Summer 1995, 8.
11. "The World According to Google," *Newsweek,* December 16, 2002, 47–49.
12. "Once Upon a Time," *Newsweek,* February 21, 2005, E10.
13. "Selling Sex on the Web," *Newsweek,* June 12, 2000, 76J.
14. "Tale of Two Onliners: Stripped vs. Steady," *Hollywood Reporter,* October 19–21, 2001, 1.
15. "Facebook's $100 Billion Question," *Wall Street Journal,* February 3, 2012, B1.
16. "That Dammed Streaming," *Broadcasting & Cable,* May 14, 2001, 42.
17. "The Noisy War Over Napster," *Newsweek,* June 5, 2000, 46–52.
18. "Grokster Case Fit to Be Tried," *Hollywood Reporter,* June 28–July 4, 2005, 1.
19. "Hi! The Net Is Calling," *Newsweek,* January 31, 2005, E4–E5; and "Microsoft Agrees to Buy Skype," *Los Angeles Times,* May 11, 2011, B-1.
20. "The Not Ready for Prime Time Medium," *Broadcasting and Cable,* May 25, 1998, 22–28; and "TV Goes Online—in a Flash," *Broadcasting and Cable,* November 18, 2006, 14.
21. "New Venue for Video on the Internet," *TV Technology,* July 27, 1998, 16.
22. "Google-YouTube May Be Good Fit," *Hollywood Reporter,* October 9, 2006, 7.
23. "AMPAS Sets Up Channel on YouTube," *Hollywood Reporter,* February 22–24, 2008, 8; "'Lonely' at the Top," *Hollywood Reporter,* June 20, 2007, S-2; and "The Call of the Web," *Emmy*, March/April, 2008, 26–27.
24. "TV Channels Move to Web, Think Outside the Cable Box," *Wall Street Journal,* August 10, 2007, B-1; "Serving Up Movie Downloads," *TV Technology,* September 5, 2007, 30; and "Test Tube," *Variety,* June 20–26, 2011, 1.
25. "Cisco Expects Video to Lead Consumer Internet Traffic," *TV Technology,* June 22, 2011, 6.
26. "How to Kill a Great Idea," http://www.inc.com/magazine/20070601/features-how-to-kill-a-great-idea.html (accessed August 12, 2011).
27. "MySpace Fetches $35 Million in a Fall as Swift as Its Rise," *Los Angeles Times,* July 1, 2011, A-1.
28. "Facebook Pokes Its Rivals," *Wall Street Journal,* November 16, 2010, C-12; and "The New Wisdom of the Web," *Newsweek,* April 3, 2006, 47.
29. "Twitter Quitters," *Newsweek,* July 18, 2011, 22; and "Twitter Tries to Dig Up a Profit," *Los Angeles Times,* January 30, 2011, B-1.
30. Michael A. Stefanone, Derek Lackaff, and Devan Rosen, "The Relationship between Traditional Mass Media and 'Social Media': Reality Television as a Model for Social Network Site Behavior," *Journal of Broadcasting and Electronic Media,* September 2010, 508–525.
31. "Life in the Fast Lane," *Emmy,* Issue No. 7, 2011, 17.

32. "AT&T's $12 Billion Cellular Dream," *Fortune,* December 12, 1994, 100–12.
33. "Cellphone Gridlock," *Fortune,* March 22, 2010, 38.
34. "BlackBerry Down," *Newsweek,* July 11, 2011, 30; "The Rise of Apps, iPad and Android," *Wall Street Journal,* December 28, 2010, B6.
35. "Buh-Bye, Wireless Guys," *Newsweek,* February 15, 2010, 24.
36. "Married to the Mobisode," *Hollywood Reporter,* April 4–10, 2006, 19–20.
37. "Apple's Jobs Unveils Song Service,'" *Los Angeles Times,* April 29, 2003, C-1.
38. "The Power of iPod," *Newsweek,* October 23, 2006, 72–74.
39. "Amazon Kindles E-reader War," *Variety,* September 28–October 4, 2009, 13; and "Tablets & E-book Readers," *Consumer Reports,* September 2011, 43–47.
40. "The iPad Cometh," *Emmy,* Issue No. 3, 2011, 236–239; and "Laptop Killer?' Pretty Close," *Wall Street Journal,* April 1, 2010, D1.
41. "Atari and the Video Game Explosion," *Fortune,* July 27, 1981, 40–46; and "After Years of Chaos and Loss, Atari Tries Rebooting," *Los Angeles Times,* August 3, 2010.
42. *Video Game Invasion: The History of a Global Obsession,* DVD, Game Show Network, 2004.
43. "Warner Sells Atari to Tramile: Will Report a Loss of $425 Million," *Los Angeles Times,* July 4, 1984, D-1.
44. *Video Game Invasion.*
45. "EA Raises the Ante for Rival," *Los Angeles Times,* February 25, 2008, C-1; and "Electronic Arts' Digital Makeover," *Fortune,* December 12, 2011, 60.
46. "Online Games Get Real," *Newsweek,* February 5, 2001, 62–63.
47. "The Players," *Wall Street Journal,* March 22, 1999, R14.
48. "Games in the Video Age," *AV Video,* April 1996, 75–76.
49. "The 'Halo" Effect," *Variety,* September 6–12, 2010, 1; "Consolations for a Console," *Newsweek,* February 12, 2001, 7; "Wii's Unintended Consequences," *Newsweek*, June 2, 2008, E16; and "Just How Grand Is $500 Mil?" *Hollywood Reporter,* May 8, 2008, 1.
50. "Family Values," *Newsweek,* November 25, 2002, 47–53.
51. "Zynga Expands Its Online Games Empire," *Los Angeles Times,* June 1, 2011, B-1.
52. "How to Be a Player," *Variety,* May 24–30, 2010, 1; and "Games for the Rest of Us," *Los Angeles Times,* July 21, 2009, C-1.
53. "FCC Aim to Boost Web Still Remote," *Wall Street Journal,* March 17, 2010, A4.
54. "Net Neutrality Back in Spotlight," *Broadcasting & Cable,* November 12, 2007, 19–23.
55. "Carriers Sweat as Texting Cools Off," *Wall Street Journal,* June 9, 2011, B1.
56. "TV's Future All Boxed In?" *Variety,* November 8–14, 2010, 1.
57. "The End of Paper?" *Fortune,* March 16, 2009, 66–72; and "Why Email No Longer Rules," *Wall Street Journal,* October 12, 2009, R1.
58. "Police Struggle to Tame Twitter," *Los Angeles Times,* August 16, 2011, 1.

Chapter 3

CABLE, SATELLITE, AND TELCO TV

Today cable TV, satellite TV, and telco TV compete with each other. They all offer multitudes of channels of TV programs and they also compete in the areas of phone and internet service. Their histories are very different, however. Cable TV started in the 1940s, but it mainly retransmitted broadcast signals, such as those from ABC, NBC, and CBS. It struggled for several decades before it became a major player in the field of electronic media. Satellite TV didn't take hold until the

New media have meant new values. Since the dawn of history, each new medium has tended to undermine an old monopoly, shift the definitions of goodness and greatness, and alter the climate of men's lives.

Erik Barnouw, A Tower in Babel, 1966

1990s, although it sputtered during the 1980s while cable was enjoying glorious high-growth days. Telephone companies have been around since the 1870s, but for over 100 years they provided only landline telephone service. It wasn't until the 2000s that they began competing with cable and satellite by offering packages that included TV, internet, and phone.

3.1 The Beginnings of Cable TV

In the 1940s when television broadcasts first began, there were not very many TV stations and some people lived in areas, such as valleys, that could not receive the over-the-air signals from these stations. The only way that they were able to see TV was to put up an antenna where the signal could be received and run that signal through a wire to where they wanted it (see "Zoom In" box). As a result, neighbors in remote and mountainous areas built rudimentary cable TV systems in order to provide television reception for themselves (see Exhibit 3.1).[1]

beginnings   Within a short time, small "mom-and-pop" companies took over the stringing of cable as a moneymaking venture, charging the people who wanted to

 ZOOM IN: **Where Did Cable TV Begin?**

There are several stories about how cable TV actually began. One is that a man who sold TV sets in a little appliance shop in a hilly area of Pennsylvania started cable TV in 1948. He noticed that he was selling sets only to people who lived on one side of town. After investigating, he discovered that the people on the other side of town could not obtain adequate reception, so he placed an antenna at the top of a hill, intercepted TV signals, and ran the signals through a cable down the hill to the side of town with poor reception. When people on that side of town

bought a TV set from him, he would hook their home to the cable.

Another story is that a "ham" radio operator in Oregon was experimenting with TV signals because of his interest in the field and because his wife wanted "pictures with her radio." He placed an antenna on an eight-story building and ran cables from there to his apartment across the street. Neighbors became excited about the idea, so he wired their homes, too. The initial cable subscribers helped pay for the cost of the equipment, and he charged newcomers $100 for a hookup.

Pennsylvania, with its many hills and mountains, had a need for the retransmission of early cable TV.

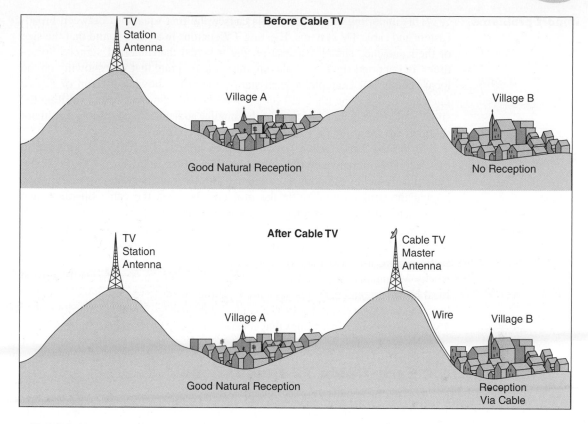

Exhibit 3.1

This diagram shows the structure of very early cable TV when its purpose was to bring TV signals to areas that could not receive them.

receive television an initial installation fee and monthly fees compatible with modest profits. If there were no local signals available, these companies carried the three network signals by importing them from stations in nearby communities, a practice that became known as **distant signal importation.** With 65,000 subscribers and an annual revenue of $10 million in 1953, cable TV was only a minor operation. Most broadcasters were unconcerned about this business that was growing on the fringes of their signal contour.[2]

During the 1950s and 1960s, cable TV became more sophisticated. Wires placed on telephone poles replaced the house-to-house wire loops augmented here and there by a tree. In addition to importing signals into areas where there was no television, cable companies began importing distant signals into areas where there were a limited number of stations. For example, if a small town had one TV station, the cable system would import the signals from two TV stations in a large city several hundred miles away.

import problems

This importing of distant signals caused the first squabbles between broadcasters and cable TV systems. Existing TV stations in an area found that the size of their audience shrank because people watched the imported signals. Sometimes an imported signal was playing the same program that was showing on the local station. For example, a local station might be showing a rerun of *I Love Lucy* and find that the imported station was showing the same rerun, splitting the show's audience in half. Because of the smaller audience, local stations could not sell their ads for as high a price as before the importation.

In the late 1950s, some stations in areas affected by cable TV appealed to the Federal Communications Commission (FCC) for help. The FCC, however, maintained a policy of nonintervention in cable TV matters during the early years, hoping the courts would settle the problems between the cable operators and broadcasters. But the situation only became more confused as court cases piled up.

court cases

One court case, referred to as the *Carter Mountain* case, however, did set a precedent. In 1963 a court ruled that the FCC could refuse to authorize additional facilities to Carter Mountain Transmitting Corporation, a cable company in the Rocky Mountains, because the cable company might damage the well-being of local broadcast stations. This gave the FCC the power to restrict cable to protect broadcasters. As a result, the FCC abandoned its hands-off policy regarding cable TV and began initiating rulings that generally favored broadcasters.[3]

3.2 Early Cable TV Regulations

In 1963, the FCC issued a notice that covered two main areas: (1) All cable systems would be required to carry the signal of any TV station within approximately 60 miles of its system; and (2) no duplication of program material from distant signals would be permitted 15 days before or 15 days after a similar local broadcast. The rule of local carriage, which became known as **must-carry,** caused little

must-carry

or no problem at the time because cable owners were glad to carry the signals of local stations. However, must-carry would raise many issues in the future—issues that still plague the broadcast-cable relationship.

The 30-day provision did cause bitter protest from cable operators because it limited their rights with regard to what they could show on their distant imported stations. This rule, known as **syndicated exclusivity,** meant that if a local station was going to show an *I Love Lucy* rerun on June 15, a cable TV operator would have to black out that rerun on a distant imported station for the whole month of June. The cable TV industry marshaled its forces and succeeded in having the 30-day provision reduced to only one day. This, of course, angered the broadcasters. The debate and actions related to syndicated exclusivity lasted many years.

syndicated exclusivity

Another report issued by the FCC in 1966 put more restrictions on cable service. This order came when about 600 cable systems were starting construction and 1,200 had applications pending. All these systems were required to prove to the FCC that their existence would not harm any existing or proposed broadcast station. By not increasing its staff to handle this load, the FCC was, in essence, freezing the growth of cable. This made broadcast station owners very happy. But the effect of this ruling on cable operators was not what the FCC had envisioned.

Cable companies that were unable to expand were sold to large corporations that could withstand the unprofitability of the freeze period. **Multiple-system operators (MSOs)**—companies that owned a number of different cable systems in different locations—became quite prevalent by the 1970s.[4]

    Another regulatory issue that caused consternation between broadcasters and cable operators during the 1970s was the payment of **copyright** fees. When cable systems transmitted broadcast signals, they did not pay any fees to those who owned the copyright to the material. In some instances, networks or stations created the material, so they owned the copyright. In other cases, the networks or stations purchased program material from film companies or independent producers and paid copyright fees. The stations, networks, film companies, and independent producers believed the cable companies should pay copyright fees for the retransmission of material because these retransmission rights were not included in the broadcast TV package. Cable operators thought they were exempt from paying fees for retransmission rights because they were merely extending coverage. In 1976, a new copyright law was passed, and one of its provisions was that cable TV systems were required to pay **compulsory license** fees to a newly created government body called the Copyright Royalty Tribunal. This body would then distribute the money to copyright owners. The amount of this compulsory license fee was 0.7 percent of the cable operator's revenue from basic subscriptions, and the copyright law gave the tribunal authority to adjust the rate for inflation. Although both cable operators and copyright holders seemed happy with this plan at the time, it would prove contentious in the future.[5]

MSOs

copyright

3.3 Early Cable TV Programming

Despite its legal problems, the cable TV business did make a few forays into programming, mostly during the 1960s and 1970s. When cable TV first began, it was simply a **common carrier;** that is, cable companies picked up signals and brought them into homes for an installation charge and regular monthly fees and did not provide any programming themselves. The very early systems had only three channels for the three broadcast networks. As television and its resulting technology grew, cable systems provided as many as 12 channels of programming. Different cable systems placed varying programming on these 12 channels, but this usually consisted of all the local stations and, if there weren't many local stations, then the cable system would bring in stations from nearby communities.

    Gradually, however, some cable facilities began to undertake their own programming. The most common "programming" involved unsophisticated weather information. Cable TV operators would place a thermometer, barometer, and other calculating devices on a disc and have a TV camera take a picture as the disc slowly rotated. This would then be shown on a vacant channel, so people in the area could check local weather conditions. Some systems had news of sorts. This might involve a camera focused on bulletins coming in over a wire-service machine or on 3-by-5-inch cards with local news items typed on them (see Exhibit 3.2). It was a simple, inexpensive, one-camera type of local

common carrier status

simple programming

Exhibit 3.2

A simple cable TV system whereby local announcements are placed on the TV screen one after the other as the drum rotates.

origination. Some cable systems had more complex local programming, usually in the form of local news programs, high school sports events, city council meetings, and talk shows on issues important to the community.[6]

In October 1969, the FCC issued a rule that required all cable TV systems with 3,500 or more subscribers to begin local programming. This was a burden on many cable systems that did not have the funds to build studios, buy equipment, and hire crews. As a compromise, the FCC changed the order so that systems that did not want to produce programming themselves could simply make equipment and channel time available to members of the community who wished to produce programs.

This brought about a different type of local programming known as

public access

public access. Individuals or groups used the equipment provided by the cable operator to produce programs without the operator's input or sanction, and those programs were then cablecast over one of the system's channels. This differed from **local origination,** which was what programming planned and produced by the cable system came to be called. In most areas, public access was not a huge success, and the equipment provided by the cable company remained largely unused for lack of interest. In other areas, particularly where cable systems showed an active interest in local programming, some exciting and innovative projects were undertaken. Sometimes, unfortunately, the people using public access time were would-be stars who used cable for vanity purposes or people from fringe groups who promoted various causes or even lewd modes of behavior. Such individuals and groups gave public access an unsavory reputation.[7]

movies

Another form of local programming instituted by some cable systems was the showing of movies. A cable company would use one of its channels to show movies that only subscribers who paid an extra fee could receive. These movies were leased from film companies and shown without any commercial interruptions. Regulations prevented cable systems from showing the well-known films that broadcasters wanted to show during prime time, but because the small cable systems had only a limited number of subscribers willing to pay for the movies, they could not afford to lease blockbuster movies anyway. The channels for movies were not a huge success, but they did bring extra income to some cable systems.

Throughout the 1960s and 1970s, promises were made, broken, and remade concerning the potential services and programs that would be available through cable, such as home security systems and home shopping services. For the most part, however, early cable was a medium to bring broadcast signals to areas with poor reception.

3.4 HBO's Influence

The stage was set in 1975 for a dramatic change in cable programming when Home Box Office (HBO) began distributing movies and special events via satellite. Home Box Office was actually formed in 1972 by Time, Inc., as a movie/special pay service for Time's cable system in New York. The company decided to expand this service to other cable systems and to set up a traditional **microwave** link to a cable system in Wilkes-Barre, Pennsylvania. During the next several years, HBO expanded its microwave system to include about 14 cable companies, but this was not a successful venture, and it was not profitable for Time.

Exhibit 3.3
A live in-concert taping by HBO of singer Diana Ross before a regular nightclub audience at Caesar's Palace in Las Vegas. This was one of HBO's early programs.

In 1975 Time decided to show the Ali-Frazier heavyweight championship fight from Manila by satellite transmission on two of its cable systems. The experiment was very successful, and HBO decided to distribute all of its programming by satellite (see Exhibit 3.3). As soon as HBO sent its signals to a satellite (which was then a relatively new technology), they could be received throughout the country by any cable system that was willing and able to buy a receiving dish.

HBO then began marketing its service to cable systems nationwide, which was no easy chore. The original receiving dishes were 10 meters in diameter and cost almost $150,000, a stiff price for cable systems, many of which were just managing to break even. But satellite technology moved quickly enough that by 1977 dishes in the range of 3 meters sold for less than $10,000. Another problem that HBO encountered involved the rules that had been established by broadcasters that prevented cable from bidding on programming, such as movies and sports events, that conventional broadcasters wanted to show. HBO and several cable TV system owners took these rules to court, and in 1977 the courts set aside the rules, allowing HBO to develop as it wanted. Another problem HBO had when it first started marketing its service was its financial relationship with cable systems. At first, it offered the cable system owners 10 percent of the amount they collected by charging subscribers extra for HBO programming. Approximately 40 percent of the fee was to go to HBO and 50 percent to the program producers. When cable owners complained about their percentage, HBO raised it so that the systems retained about 60 percent of the money and HBO and the program producers split the other 40 percent.

satellite placement

marketing

With receiving dishes manageable in both cost and size, with appealing programming, and with financial remuneration at a high level, cable systems began subscribing to HBO in droves. Likewise, HBO became very popular with individual cable subscribers who were willing to pay extra to receive commercial-free movies. By October 1977, Time announced that HBO turned its first profit.

Soon after HBO started distributing programming via satellite, Ted Turner, who owned a low-rated UHF TV station, WTBS, in Atlanta, Georgia, decided to

superstation

put his station's signal on the same satellite as HBO. This meant that cable operators that bought a receiving dish for HBO could also place Turner's station on one of their channels. This created what was referred to as a **superstation** because it could be seen nationwide. Cable operators paid a dime a month per subscriber for the superstation signal, but they did not charge the subscriber as they did for the HBO pay service. The economic rationale was that the extra program service would entice more subscribers. The charge to the cable companies did not cover the superstation's costs, but the station could charge a higher rate for its advertisements once the superstation had a bigger audience. With two successful program services on the satellite, the floodgates opened and cable TV took on a new complexion.[8]

3.5 The Beginnings of Satellite TV

FCC ruling

Satellite TV would eventually become a competitor for cable TV, but it got off to a slow start. When satellites were first launched in 1962, the technology was very complicated—well beyond what typical homeowners could handle. But the technology developed and reception dishes became more user-friendly, so in 1979 the FCC issued a ruling that no one needed a license to have a **TV receive-only (TVRO)** satellite dish. In other words, individual households were allowed to own satellite dishes that received (but did not send) programming.

beginnings

One outcome of this 1979 ruling was that Satellite Television Corporation (STC) informed the FCC it wanted to develop a new programming service that would go directly from satellites to homes. The satellites would have higher power than the ones being used by cable TV systems to receive cable TV networks, so the consumer dishes could be smaller and cheaper than the dishes the cable systems needed. The FCC agreed with the basic idea and invited all interested parties to apply for licenses for this service, which was then called **direct broadcast satellite (DBS).** In 1982, the FCC approved eight DBS applications and expected that the services would be operational by 1985.[9]

failures

The FCC mandated that the companies prepare "due diligence" reports in 1984 to make sure the services were on track. With great fanfare, market researchers proclaimed that 50 percent of people would subscribe to DBS, but the companies ran into many technical and financial problems as they dealt with the realities of launching high-power satellites. Several of the original DBS applicants flunked their "due diligence" tests, and others didn't even bother to fill out the forms. In a surprising 1984 move, STC, the company that had pioneered the DBS concept, announced it was pulling out of the business after having invested five years and $140 million gearing up. Prospects for DBS dimmed and no services were on the air by 1985.[10]

backyard satellite

Another result of the 1979 FCC ruling that no one needed a license to own a TVRO was that individuals, particularly those in rural areas where TV reception was poor, bought the large dishes used by cable TV systems and set them up in their backyards. This became known as **backyard satellite** reception. The dishes cost about $3,000, but the people who bought them could then receive all the cable programming for free. This caused a minor stir among cable TV program suppliers, but the number of backyard dishes was so small that the cable providers did not aggressively pursue the issue.[11]

3.6 Cable TV's Gold Rush

What cable TV did pursue was its own phenomenal subscriber growth, sparked mainly by the development of its satellite-delivered programming services. The number of homes subscribing to cable TV more than doubled between 1980 and 1985 (see Exhibit 3.4), and the amount of money cable companies brought in skyrocketed. In 1979, pay revenues grew 85 percent over 1978 figures. The industry predicted that this peak would subside to about 50 percent growth, but in 1980 pay revenues grew another 95.5 percent. Between 1975 and 1980, cable TV profits grew 641 percent. With figures such as these, it is no surprise that cable experienced a veritable gold rush.[12]

statistics

One way this gold rush manifested itself was in franchising. In most areas, the local city council became the agency that issued cable **franchises** and stipulated how the cable system was to conduct business. Local governments assumed this responsibility in part because the national government would not intervene in cable TV matters during its early years and in part because cable TV companies had to tear up city streets to lay cable, and that took the approval of the city government. Competing applicants for a cable franchise would present their plans for operation, including such items as the method of hookup (for example, telephone poles or underground cable), the fees to be charged to the customer for installation and for regular monthly service, and the percentage of profit that the company was willing to give the city for the privilege of holding the franchise. Based on this information, the council awarded the franchise to the company it believed was most qualified. During the early years of cable, this was a sleepy process; usually only one or two companies applied for a franchise in a given area. Areas with good reception did not even bother with franchising because no companies applied.

franchising

Year	Number of Systems	Number of Subscribers	Percent of Homes	Pay Cable Subscribers	Number of Cable Networks
1955	400	150,000	.5	—	—
1960	640	650,000	1.4	—	—
1965	1,325	1,275,000	2.5	—	—
1970	2,490	4,500,000	7.6	—	—
1975	3,506	9,800,000	12.0	469,000	—
1980	4,225	16,000,000	20.0	9,144,000	28
1985	6,844	32,000,000	43.0	30,596,000	56
1990	9,575	54,280,000	58.9	40,100,000	79
1995	11,218	58,834,440	62.5	43,730,000	128
2000	10,845	66,054,000	71.3	49,200,000	224

Exhibit 3.4
Growth of cable TV.

However, with the cable TV boom, cities that could not have given away cable franchises in earlier years because of their clear reception of over-the-air broadcast TV signals suddenly became prime targets for cable and its added programming services. Most city governments were not accustomed to dealing with such matters. Gradually, through the use of consultants, city councils established lists of minimal requirements that they wanted from the cable companies. Cable companies, in their fervor to obtain franchises, usually went well beyond what the cities required. They, too, hired consultants, who contacted city leaders to learn the political structure and needs of the city and to decide how the company should write its franchise proposal to ensure the best possible chance of winning the contract. Only one company could receive a franchise for a particular area; therefore, cries of corruption sometimes accompanied the procedures.[13]

PEG

The development of local programming became an important part of the franchising process. Cities usually requested that cable companies set aside a certain number of channels for access by community groups. These were often referred to as **PEG** (public, education, government) access channels. To program these PEG channels, cable companies promised to provide equipment and sometimes personnel.

Cable companies began promising cheaper rates, shorter time to lay cable, more channels, more equipment, and generally more everything as franchising competition became intense. Sometimes the winning cable company was unable to meet all the requirements stipulated in the bid, especially concerning the speed with which the system was to be built. The laying of cable, however, did move forward at a rapid rate.

larger MSOs

As the cable companies promised more, they realized they might not recover their investment for about a decade. This hastened a process that was already prevalent within the cable industry—the takeover of small mom-and pop cable operations by large multiple-system operators and then the consolidation of these MSOs with other large companies. Major companies emerged in the cable industry, partly because they wanted to be part of the gold rush and partly because only large companies had the resources to withstand the expenses of the franchising process and the other start-up costs of laying cable, marketing, and programming.[14]

other participants

Other groups also began to stake their claims in cable's gold rush. Advertisers who saw cable reaching close to 30 percent of the nation's households in the early 1980s began placing ads on cable's programming channels, both local and national. Members of the various unions and guilds that operate in the broadcasting industry were not involved in cable programming when it first began because the cable companies did not recognize the unions. After several long, bitter strikes during the early 1980s, however, the unions won the right to be recognized and to receive residuals from cable TV. Thus, the same people who worked in broadcast programming began working in cable programming.[15]

Perhaps the biggest winners in the cable gold rush were the equipment manufacturers that supplied the materials needed to build the cable systems. Suppliers of the converters that enable a regular TV set to receive the multitude of cable channels, the satellite dishes, and the cable itself found their order desks piled high. Space on a satellite became a precious commodity as more companies wanted to launch national programming services.[16]

Although large companies, advertisers, unions, and equipment manufacturers all flocked to cable during the late 1970s and early 1980s, the most noticeable cable growth was in the area of programming.

pay cable

3.7 Growth of Cable TV Programming Services

Shortly after Time became successful with its HBO service, Viacom launched a competing **pay cable** service, Showtime (see Exhibit 3.5). Other pay cable services started in rapid succession: The Movie Channel, a 24-hour-a-day service from Warner-Amex; Spotlight, a Times-Mirror movie service; Bravo (see Exhibit 3.6) and The Entertainment Channel, both cultural programming services; The Disney Channel, a family-oriented pay service featuring Disney products; and Playboy, "adult" programming that included R-rated movies, skits, and specials.[17]

Other new satellite-delivered programming services were launched as what became known as **basic cable.** Some of these were supported by advertising, some were supported by the institutions that programmed them, and some were supported by small amounts of money that cable systems paid to the programmers. Most **narrowcast,** meaning they had a specific niche audience in mind. Among them were:

Exhibit 3.5

Jason Robards starring in Eugene O'Neill's *Hughie,* one of Showtime's cablecasts of a Broadway production.

> ESPN, all-sports programming started by Getty Oil
>
> Black Entertainment Television, programming about and for African Americans
>
> CBN, Christian-oriented family programming
>
> Nickelodeon, a noncommercial children's service
>
> CNN, 24 hours a day of news started by Ted Turner
>
> USA, a network with a variety of programming (see Exhibit 3.7)
>
> C-SPAN, public service-oriented programming, including live coverage of the House of Representatives
>
> ARTS, an ABC-owned cultural service

Exhibit 3.6

A scene from *The Greek Passion* performed by the Indiana University Opera Company and taped by Bravo. This was the first opera to be taped for cable television.

Exhibit 3.7
An early wrestling match on USA.

basic cable

CBS Cable, an advertising-supported cultural service owned by CBS

MTV, the creator of music videos

Satellite News Channel, a Westinghouse-ABC joint venture of 24-hour news, established to compete with CNN

Daytime, a service geared toward women

Cable Health Network, programming about physical and mental health

The number of superstations also grew and were considered part of basic cable. Ted Turner's WTBS was first, but soon after, WGN in Chicago and WWOR in New York also went on satellite.[18]

local programming

Local programming took on an entirely new dimension. The older cable systems that only had 12-channel capacity usually allocated one channel to local programming. The newer systems that took advantage of improved technology to provide 20, then 54, then more than 100 channels usually promised an entire complement of local channels. At least one of these channels was reserved for local origination—programming that the cable system itself initiated. A number of others were some combination of public access. Some systems had **leased access** channels for businesses or individuals interested in buying time on a cable channel to present their messages. Not all the local programming planned by cable systems and local groups materialized, but the quality of access programming improved greatly from the early days when it consisted mainly of vanity TV.[19]

interactive services

Interactive cable was highly touted. Promises were made that cable would perk the coffee, help the kids with homework, do the shopping, protect the home, and teach the handicapped. In some areas of the country, a fair amount of interactive cable was undertaken. The pioneer and most publicized system was Qube, which Warner-Amex operated in Columbus, Ohio, starting in 1977. The basic element of Qube was a small box with response buttons that enabled Qube subscribers to send an electronic signal to a bank of computers at the cable company that could then analyze the responses. An announcer's voice or a written message on the screen asked audience members to make a decision about some question, such as who was most likely to be a presidential candidate, what play a quarterback should call, or whether a city should proceed with a development plan. Audience members made their selection by pressing the appropriate button in multiple-choice fashion. A computer analyzed the responses and printed the percentage of each response on the participant's screen.[20]

Home security was another interactive area that cable entered. Various burglar, fire, and medical alarm devices connected to the cable system. A computer in a central monitoring station sent a signal to each participating household about every 10 seconds to see if everything was in order. A signal was sent back to the cable company monitoring station, which then notified the police if any of the doors, windows, smoke detectors, or other devices hooked to the system were not as they should be. These interactive services were largely unprofitable, but cable TV seemed like such a gold mine that companies were willing to experiment.[21]

home security

In retrospect, all of this was too much too fast, and by the mid-1980s the bloom was off the rose. A number of cable programming services merged or went out of business, advertisers became more cautious, and MSOs sold some of their systems. All of this was a necessary correction to the hype that existed in the cable world, and once it was over, cable remained a viable business.[22]

retrenchment

3.8 Cable TV Regulations Revisited

As cable grew, the animosities between broadcasters and cablers increased. Must-carry, which originally caused little anxiety for either broadcasters or cablecasters, became controversial. When there were few cable networks, cable companies were happy to carry all local TV stations. But as cable programming sources grew, cable system owners wanted must-carries outlawed so that they could use their channels to carry the more profitable satellite services rather than local stations. They claimed that because they had to carry little-watched religious, educational, and ethnic broadcast stations, they did not have channel space for public access, C-SPAN, and other cable programming services. Local broadcast stations wanted to be carried on the systems and even thought cable systems should pay them because they were of great value to cable. During the 1980s, must-carries were outlawed and reinstated a number of times, depending on which forces lobbied the hardest or won the court cases.

must-carry

In 1992, a new law provided that broadcasters could choose either must-carry or **retransmission consent.** If they chose must-carry, they were guaranteed a spot on the cable system. If they chose retransmission consent, they could ask the cable system to pay them for the privilege of carrying their signal. If the cable system paid, the broadcasters would be richer, but the cable system had the option of not carrying the station if it opted for retransmission consent. This led to a certain amount of acrimony in which popular stations pulled their signals from cable systems that refused to pay. However, in many instances, the broadcasters

retransmission consent

and cable systems found a way to compromise. Instead of asking for money for retransmission of their signals, the stations asked for channel space on the cable system, so they could program additional material. For example, ABC and Hearst, which owned ESPN, agreed to let cable systems carry all ABC and Hearst-owned stations in return for a channel on which they could place a new service, ESPN2.[23]

copyright

Copyright issues resurfaced in 1983 when the Copyright Royalty Tribunal, acting under its right to adjust fees, ordered cable systems to pay 3.75 percent of their gross receipts (a hefty increase) for their imported distant signals. In 1993, Congress abolished the Copyright Royalty Tribunal, replacing it with ad hoc arbitration panels chosen by the Librarian of Congress. These arbitration panels have leaned toward even higher rates, but most cable systems, now that they have so many cable networks, have stopped distant signal importation.[24]

In 1984, Congress passed the Cable Communications Policy Act, delineating the role of cable systems and local governments. The main positive change for cable operators was that cities with at least three broadcast stations could no longer regulate the rates that cable systems charged their customers for basic service. Instead, these charges were determined by the marketplace. However, the

de- and reregulation

cable industry did not behave nobly under **deregulation.** Because cable had monopolistic power—there was generally only one cable system in any particular area—many cable systems raised basic cable rates as much as 50 percent over seven years. Cable was also laissez-faire about customer relations, making customers wait on the phone for long periods. This led to **reregulation,** culminating in a 1992 law giving the FCC authority to determine reasonable rates for basic services and to set service standards. The FCC rolled back rates and mandated that cable operators provide a 24-hour-a-day toll-free number and a convenient customer service location. Congress also ordered cable networks to sell their programming to anyone who wanted it, not just cable systems. This was done to help and encourage other types of technologies, so they could compete with cable.[25]

3.9 Satellite TV Revived

One of these competing technologies was satellite TV, which was essentially resurrected from the dead during the 1990s. After STC backed out of the direct broadcast satellite business in 1984, interest in the field remained dormant for quite a few years. In the early 1990s Rupert Murdoch of Fox, whose company News Corp. was involved in satellite businesses in other parts of the world, became interested in U.S. satellite-to-home opportunities and formed an alliance with NBC, Cablevision Systems, and Hughes Communications for a system to be called Sky Cable. The Sky Cable alliance dissolved quickly, the victim of clashing ideas and egos. Hughes, however, plodded along with the idea and eventually joined forces with USSB, a company owned by Stanley Hubbard that was one of the few original DBS applicants still interested in developing the service. In 1993, Hughes successfully launched a high-power satellite, and in 1994 Hughes and USSB jointly offered a 150-channel digital satellite service that became known

DirecTV

as DirecTV. The widespread consumer acceptance of DirecTV surprised even the most avid satellite TV supporters. Within six months, more than 500,000 households had paid $700 each for the receiver dish and the decoder box that would enable their television sets to display programming coming directly from high-powered satellites.[26]

Why did Hughes/USSB succeed when all the 1980s ventures had failed? A number of factors were involved. Hughes, a satellite-building company, was able to perfect a high-power satellite that could deliver to homes. Also, with the help of RCA and Sony, it developed small, reliable 18-inch dishes that could be mounted on the sides of houses (see Exhibit 3.8). Digital technology had improved greatly during the decade, and by offering digital signals, DirecTV could feature high-quality picture and sound. Digital improvements also allowed DirecTV to offer more than 100 channels, including ones for major sports events and top-rated movies. The law Congress passed in 1992 ordering cable networks to sell their programming to anyone who wanted it, cleared the path for USSB and Hughes to obtain well-known popular programming such as that on ESPN, MTV, and C-SPAN. Perhaps most important of all, people were angry with their cable companies for raising rates, being slow to fix technical glitches, and not answering their phones. They were willing to spend $700 to quit their cable services and try something new.

Exhibit 3.8
DirecTV's 18-inch reception dish developed by Sony and RCA.

reasons for success

The success of DirecTV was also a factor in killing off most of the backyard satellite reception. The companies with programming on satellites had become more upset that the backyard dish owners were receiving the programming for free. Many services began **scrambling** their signals. This brought forth a surge in illegal decoders, but as scrambling improved and antipiracy laws loomed, these decoders became problematic. Many people who had the large dishes opted for the smaller dishes that DirecTV offered. They were more cost-effective and convenient and did not carry the stigma of illegality.[27]

backyard satellite

While DirecTV was becoming successful, Rupert Murdoch still lingered in the wings. In 1995, he formed an alliance with MCI to establish a satellite TV service. This proved to be too expensive for Murdoch, so he looked for an additional partner and found one in Charlie Ergen, who owned another would-be DBS company, EchoStar. Again egos and finances destroyed the relationship, and eventually Ergen established his own service, Dish Network, which has competed quite effectively with DirecTV. Murdoch did eventually get his satellite TV system in 2003, when he purchased DirecTV for $6.6 billion. He didn't keep it long, however, selling it in 2006 to cable TV entrepreneur John Malone.[28]

Dish

One drawback of satellite TV services of the 1990s was that they lacked permission to deliver local stations to their subscribers. Although they tried a number of times to obtain this permission through Congress, the more powerful cable TV business lobbied successfully to keep them at bay. However, in 1999, Congress passed a bill allowing satellite services to retransmit local stations into their local

local programming

areas, often referred to as **local-into-local.** Being able to deliver these stations has given satellite TV a valuable asset.[29]

interactive

Another drawback for satellite TV was the difficulty of providing interactive services, such as internet and telephone because satellite broadcasting is only one-way—consumers cannot broadcast back from their satellite dishes. To solve this problem, DirecTV and Dish formed alliances with companies providing interactive services and then sold TV, internet, and phone as a package.[30]

3.10 Programming Changes

The multitude of cable TV programming networks launched during the 1980s experienced many changes (see "Zoom In" box). Exhibit 3.9 shows what happened to the networks listed in section 3.7. Some of the basic cable channels, in addition to changing ownership, had to change their stripes to keep current. For example, MTV started out programming only music videos. As time went on, this programming drew less attention, so MTV changed to a schedule that included some non-music programs aimed at the same audience that appreciated music videos (see Exhibit 3.10).[31]

 ZOOM IN: **Two Coups**

Two highly touted cable network failures warmed the hearts of cable practitioners because the networks had been started by broadcasters who exhibited a high-and-mighty attitude. One was the CBS-owned cultural service, CBS Cable. With its deep pockets, CBS planned to produce commercially viable original cultural television that was a cut above what any cable companies could afford. It also used those deep pockets to mount a very aggressive marketing campaign. When most cable networks were trying to convince cable systems to carry them by holding receptions with celery and carrot sticks, CBS Cable was offering shrimp and lobster. But neither the cable systems nor the advertisers bought into CBS's plans. The system owners resented what they saw as a broadcaster's attempted encroachment into the cable business, and very few signed up to cablecast the network. Advertisers followed suit. CBS hung on for several years, then stopped programming in 1983 after losing $50 million.

Another well-publicized 1983 coup occurred when Ted Turner's Cable News Network slew the broadcast giants ABC and Westinghouse. Turner, a well-respected maverick in the cable TV business, had gone out on a limb in 1980 to form a 24-hour TV news service—something

that was very expensive and innovative. His concept was starting to catch on when, in 1982, ABC and Westinghouse decided to combine their considerable news resources and create their own 24-hour channel, Satellite News Channel. Turner, working from an inferior but more flexible position, outmaneuvered the broadcasting executives and managed to buy them out in October 1983. This meant less competition for CNN, which was then able to proceed on less tenuous financial footing because it did not have to compete for advertisers with Satellite News Channel.

Ted Turner, seen here with then-wife Jane Fonda.

Showtime—merged with The Movie Channel

The Movie Channel—merged with Showtime

Spotlight—went out of business

Bravo—converted from pay to basic

Entertainment Channel—gave its programming to ARTS, which became A&E

Disney—converted from pay to basic

Playboy—changed how hard-core its programming was based on viewer response

ESPN—changed ownership from Getty to ABC

Black Entertainment Television—was purchased by Viacom

CBN—changed from religious programming to family-oriented programs

Nickelodeon—accepted commercials and changed ownership from Warner to Viacom

CNN—changed ownership when Warner bought Ted Turner's networks

USA—brought in a consortium of owners

C-SPAN—added Senate coverage in addition to House of Representatives

ARTS—took programming of the Entertainment Channel and became A&E

CBS Cable—went out of business

MTV—changed from music videos to include other types of programming

Satellite News Channel—was bought out by CNN

Daytime—merged with Cable Health Network to form Lifetime

Cable Health Network—merged with Daytime to form Lifetime

Exhibit 3.9
Here is what happened to the cable networks mentioned earlier in section 3.7.

Exhibit 3.10
During the 1992 presidential campaign, MTV encouraged its young viewers to become participants in the political process. To this end, MTV invited Democratic candidate Bill Clinton to participate in a program in which he answered questions from 18- to 24-year-olds.

Exhibit 3.11

These four foulmouthed third graders became a big hit on the Comedy Central animated show *South Park.*

new networks

Not many new cable networks were launched in the 1990s, but those that were include Court TV (now called truTV), Comedy Central (see Exhibit 3.11), the History Channel, and TV Land. Many of the more recent channels have come from well-established companies that operate other channels. These companies have the infrastructure to develop and sell channels that will have only small numbers of interested viewers. For example, a do-it-yourself channel that programs primarily information about remodeling homes was started by the same company that owns Home and Garden Television and the Food Channel. Noggin, an educational channel, comes from Viacom, which also has Nickelodeon. Sometimes new channels are just vehicles for repackaged programs from another channel. For example, Discovery has reorganized the material it has cablecast over the years into channels dealing with such subjects as science and health.[32]

on-demand

As technologies have improved, new programming concepts related to program accessibility have taken hold in the cable and satellite arena. The first was **pay-per-view (PPV).** It authorizes viewers, who pay an extra one-time-only sum, to see special events such as boxing matches and first-run movies. Interactive equipment allows the viewer to push a button on a remote-control-like device that enables the special programming to be delivered to a particular channel on the TV set. Those who do not subscribe to the PPV program see a blank screen on that channel. **Near-video-on-demand (NVOD)** takes PPV one step further. One movie is shown on several channels, each of which starts it at a different time— usually 15 minutes apart. The viewer who wants to see the movie but misses the 8:00 P. M. starting time on Channel 57 can catch it on Channel 58 starting at 8:15. NVOD is similar to PPV in that the movie is sent to all paying subscribers at the same time; it is just sent more often. Even further up the technological chain is **video-on-demand (VOD).** Individual viewers can watch programs precisely when they want to. VOD uses a large **server** at a cable system that contains an enormous amount of information—movies, TV programs, video games, and so on. When a consumer asks for a particular movie (or anything else), it can be **downloaded** on one of the cable system channels into a digital box on top of the customer's TV set. The movie will also remain in the cable server so other customers can request and receive it. The consumer can then play the movie, stop it, rewind, and fast forward at will. PPV, NVOD, and VOD have been popular with some subscribers, but they have not been as successful or profitable as the operators' would wish.[33]

Activity on the local public access and local origination channels has slowed greatly from its hyped period of the early 1980s. Cable systems that had promised truckloads of production equipment to local organizations tried their best to delay these costly obligations. Local programming departments that had included five or six employees dwindled. The only local programming for some systems consisted of messages typed on the screen about local news and events. They had, in essence, reverted to a sophisticated version of the early 3-by-5-inch cards. Some systems joined to form regional cable networks that programmed primarily sports. Local programming has not disappeared, but it does not fill the multitude of channels promised in many of the original franchise agreements.[34]

local programming

Interactive services took a nosedive. Warner-Amex killed its highly touted Qube system by 1984, mainly because it was not profitable. In the 1990s, Time Warner experimented with interactive technology by installing a system in Florida called Full Service Network (FSN). Because of Warner's involvement, some jokingly referred to FSN as "Qube Squared." After two years of operation (1995–1997), Time Warner pulled the plug on FSN, attributing the closure to high costs and technical problems. Interactive services have been taken over by the internet, which handles them much more effectively. Cable systems, by offering internet service as part of their packages, are fulfilling their interactive functions somewhat vicariously.[35]

interactive

3.11 Telephone Company Entry

Telephones, of course, are not a new technology. History credits Alexander Graham Bell (see Exhibit 3.12) with the invention of the telephone in 1876. Bell and two of his friends started the Bell Telephone Company to lease phones and charge for short-distance phone calls. For long-distance calls, they formed a subsidiary, American Telephone and Telegraph Company (AT&T), which eventually became the parent organization, owning both long-distance and local phone companies. AT&T operated as a monopoly, regulated by the government. The telephone business grew into a major national and international industry, but it remained primarily a voice service connecting one individual with another. Improvements were made in switching systems and phone installation, but because AT&T was a monopoly making a guaranteed profit, it had little incentive to add new services for the customer.[36]

early phone companies

Exhibit 3.12
Alexander Graham
Bell demonstrating
an early telephone.

breakup of AT&T

During the 1970s, the Justice Department took a hard look at AT&T's monopoly. Several companies wanted to sell telephones competitively to consumers, and some businesses, such as MCI and Sprint, wanted to compete in long-distance service. Addressing these issues, the Justice Department in 1980 issued a consent decree that broke up AT&T. "Ma Bell" had to divest itself of its 22 local phone companies. These were spun off into seven new "baby Bells," called **regional Bell operating companies (RBOCs),** which served seven sections of the country. The consent decree also allowed independent companies to compete in long-distance service, giving customers a choice, and it permitted independent companies to manufacture telephones for customers to buy.[37]

new services

With strong competition, the phone companies began offering a new array of services. Some features, such as the hold button and answering machines, had been part of phone technology previously, but the **postdivestiture** period of the 1980s brought many new options. These included redial, speed dial, call waiting, conference calling, and caller ID. Cordless phones evolved, fax machines came to the fore, and automated voice systems replaced company telephone operators.[38]

Over the years, the RBOCs merged, with several of them coming together in 2000 to form a new company, Verizon. In 2005, one of the RBOCs, SBC, bought the AT&T name and went into business as AT&T. Although there still are other

AT&T and Verizon

national, regional, and local phone companies, the two that dominate the telecommunications business are AT&T and Verizon.[39]

video services

In the 2000s, both these companies decided to provide phone, internet, and television service to compete with the cable and satellite businesses. Verizon launched its TV service FiOs in 2005 and has succeeded in capturing a respectable share of customers. AT&T launched Uverse in selected parts of the country in 2008.[40]

3.12 Regulations Continued

Some of the regulatory issues that affected cable TV in its earlier years continued to plague it into the 21st century. Must-carry/retransmission has been a particularly thorny issue. Because many of the broadcast stations opted for being paid for retransmission of their signals rather than settling for free must-carry, there have been numerous instances when cable systems and broadcasters have reached a stalemate. Their contracts come up for renewal every several years and often TV stations want more money for their signals. Cable systems, of course, do not want to pay more, so the stations threaten to withhold the programming. The stations have a particularly strong hand if a big event such as the Super Bowl is coming up and the cable system's customers will be very upset if they cannot see the game. There have been enough high-profile standoffs that the FCC approved a proposal for "good faith" negotiations, wherein the station signals stay on the cable systems while negotiations are underway. The retransmission rules also now apply to satellite TV and telco TV, and in 2011 DirecTV and several stations owned by Northwest Broadcasting did have a stand-off at Super Bowl time that was resolved close to game time with a temporary agreement.[41]

retransmission

Another issue involves **net neutrality** (see Chapter 2). The companies that provide access to the internet, such as cable TV systems and phone companies, want to be able to manage the access so that their connections operate smoothly. But that may mean slowing down access to some websites so that others can operate. Major search engines and websites, such as Google, Amazon, and Yahoo, fear they will be the ones slowed down so that sites owned by the phone or cable companies can be given preferential treatment. They want rules that require providers to be "neutral" and allow all sites equal opportunity to be accessed on the net. The FCC has sided with the companies favoring net neutrality, but some courts have ruled in favor of cable or phone companies. The issue is far from resolved.[42]

net neutrality

Another government action that affected cable, satellite, and telco companies was the **Telecommunications Act of 1996.** The main legislation that governed the broadcasting industries for many years was the **Communications Act of 1934.** Although written largely for radio (see Chapter 5), it served broadcasting well for decades, mainly because the American system of government allows laws to be interpreted by the courts and regulatory bodies such as the FCC. These interpretations lead to precedents that can accommodate changing times. In addition, the act was amended to take into account alterations such as those related to using television for electioneering (see Chapter 11). But by the 1990s it was definitely showing its age because of the advent of many new technologies such as cable and satellite TV.

Congress passed a sweeping new law, the Telecommunications Act of 1996. It did not replace the Communications Act of 1934, but it dealt with newer technologies and ramifications that related to older technologies. The act's provisions directly related to cable were mainly deregulatory, once again allowing cable systems to set their own rates for basic services. This time, however, cable systems faced growing competition from satellite TV and were intent on keeping

Telecom Act

their customers happy, so most of them made only modest rate increases. Perhaps the most significant provisions of the Telecommunications Act, stemming from the lawmakers' desire to foster competition within the telecommunications industry, were those that encouraged the intermingling of the broadcast, cable, satellite, online, and telephone businesses. It took a while for this to take hold, in part because of the technical and financial complexities, but today consumers have many options for receiving television programming, internet access, and telephone service.[43]

3.13 Competitions Galore

internal and internet competitions

The phone, satellite, and cable companies compete among themselves. Cable TV companies were the first to offer television services so have the largest share of the subscription pie, but telco TV, because it is the newest, has the latest technology. The telephone companies, because they were first with phone service, still dominate in that area but cable TV has done well by providing phone service that travels over the internet. Both these services offer programming over wires, either cable or **fiber optics.** Satellite TV, because it comes through the airwaves, does not require an infrastructure of wires so can be put in place more quickly. All three carry basically the same TV programming and offer internet and phone services, but they compete with pricing and with the types of program packages they offer to customers.

Exhibit 3.13

James Gandolfini accepts a best actor Emmy for his portrayal of Tony Soprano in HBO's *The Sopranos*. This series was the first cable network offering to top the commercial broadcast networks for the Emmy for best drama.

Emmys

They also compete with the internet (see Chapter 2) and with broadcast TV (see Chapter 4). Internet-based companies stream some of the same programming offered by cable, satellite, and telco TV but, at least for the present, do so for lower cost. In general, the internet model allows consumers to purchase one program without subscribing to entire networks. In covering their bets, cable, satellite, and telco companies also utilize the internet, purposely positioning their programming there in order to create another revenue stream. In the broadcast TV area, cable and its cousins obviously compete with broadcasters regarding retransmission fees, but they also attempt to build co-operative entities. In 2011 Comcast, a major cable TV company, merged with broadcast network NBC with the goal of enhancing broadband opportunities for both companies.[44]

Another area of competition involves competitions themselves. For example, for many years Emmys went only to broadcast TV programs. But HBO began creating its own high-quality programming in the 1990s, and, in the 2000s, HBO's *The Sopranos* (see Exhibit 3.13), an ongoing dramatic series about a New Jersey mafia family, won numerous Emmys including for best drama. AMC, a cable channel that once featured old movies, also won Emmys for its critically acclaimed *Mad Men*. Some of the satellite TV services are considering creating their own original programming so may be the next new entity in line for an Emmy.[45]

3.14 Issues and the Future

The big challenge for cable TV involves the fact that it is losing subscribers. Part of this may be economic; people just don't have the money to spend on a non-necessity such as TV programming. Younger people are abandoning cable or not even bothering to subscribe to it in the first place; it's just not the "place to be."[46]

loss of subscribers

Some of the erosion involves people switching to satellite and telco TV, but more of it seems to be related to the internet. Some Congressional representatives have suggested that cable offer **à la carte** services. In other words, consumers would be able to order and pay for only the channels they want to watch instead of having to buy the packages of channels that the cable systems (and satellite and telco companies) offer. Of course, these companies are opposed to this because they would sell less. The internet model, however, allows for viewing individual programs, something that seems more in line with consumer desires.[47]

à la carte

The internet can more easily offer programming to people when they want it, where they want it, and on whatever device they desire. It has more flexibility than the older PPV, NVOD, and VOD models of cable and its cousins. There are also some who feel cable companies have created way too many cable channels and that they are hurting themselves by having these networks compete with each other. Perhaps it is time to thin the ranks of cable networks and concentrate on those that are most popular. Again, the internet, because it does not have a channel structure, is able to accommodate networks and some, such as those that have not been able to find space on cable system set-ups, have been placed on the internet.[48]

channel overload

The trend within the cable industry has been toward consolidation. Small MSOs joke about being listed among the top 25 cable system owners, not because they have grown but because of all the mergers and buyouts among the large MSOs. As companies merge and buy each other out, the total number of companies involved in cable, satellite, and telco TV shrinks, but the companies get larger. Many of the cable companies that own distribution systems also own networks, so they have an incentive to run their own networks on their systems. This may not always serve the viewers' best interests, especially if the systems are trying to curtail access by networks owned by another company. For example, a Time Warner cable system might be more likely to give consumers incentives to subscribe to HBO, which it owns, than to Showtime, which is owned by Viacom, even though some of those consumers would prefer Showtime.[49]

MSO size

There are some issues that may plague cable, satellite, and telco for a while. Net neutrality is one of them. However, it may be solved by technology. As engineers continue to increase the speed, size, and flexibility of servers and internet nodes, there may be less need to restrict certain websites or search engines.

net neutrality

Cable, satellite, and telco companies will not disappear, but they may have a less significant role in the electronic media structure than they have in the past or they may change to embrace the internet more firmly.

3.15 Summary

Cable TV, satellite TV, and telco TV have different histories, but they have all been affected by legal and programming issues. Cable started out in the 1940s as mom-and-pop common carrier services in areas with poor reception. By the 1980s, when cable had a great growth spurt, MSOs dominated. Satellite started in the 1980s when people were allowed to have TVROs. But the technology was complicated and it wasn't until the 1990s that satellite TV took hold. Phone service was affected by the 1980 breakup of AT&T and the creation of RBOCs. Two of these offshoots started offering TV, internet, and phone service in the 2000s.

Legal rulings regarding distant signal importation and its related syndicated exclusivity affected cable in its early days. The must-carry rules, which at first caused no problems, have continued to be an issue for cable, satellite, and telco operations. Retransmission consent, a supposed solution to must-carry problems, has created its own difficulties. Copyright fees and compulsory licenses have also complicated life for cable TV entities. The franchising process has included local legal ramifications that cable must consider. Deregulation was favorable for cable companies but their irresponsible actions brought reregulation. Satellite TV was affected by the FCC TVRO license ruling and then subsequently by failure to pass FCC-mandated due diligence tests. Congress's 1992 law requiring cable TV to sell its programming to other entities helped satellite TV survive as did Congress's local-into-local bill. The Telecommunications Act of 1996 affected cable, satellite, and telco companies because it encouraged them to enter each other's businesses. Net neutrality is now a thorn in all their sides.

Cable TV's first programming was very simple, such as a camera on a thermometer. When the government ruled that cable companies must at least provide equipment to community members, public access programming was born. Systems also programmed local origination and movies. The latter was emphasized by HBO, which was the first successful cable network. It was followed by superstations and many pay cable and basic networks. Most of these narrowcast and underwent many changes. Franchising brought about PEG access and leased access. For a while interactive cable, especially QUBE, was a rage, and systems experimented with home security. PPV, NVOD, and VOD were common with cable, satellite, and telco TV but not as successful as those companies would have liked. In recent times, cable TV has produced high-quality programming that wins Emmys.

Suggested Websites

www.directv.com (home page for satellite service DirecTV)

www.dishnetwork.com (home page for satellite service Dish)

www.hbo.com (cable network Home Box Office's main site)

www.mtv.com (home page for cable network MTV)

http://www22.verizon.com/Residential/aboutFiOS/Overview.htm (information about Verizon's FiOs offerings)

Notes

1. David L. Jaffe, "CATV: History and Law," *Educational Broadcasting,* July/August 1974, 15–16; and Thomas F. Baldwin and D. Stevens McVoy, *Cable Communication* (Englewood Cliffs, NJ: Prentice-Hall, 1983), 8–10.
2. Jaffe, "CATV," 34.
3. "Cable: The First Forty Years," *Broadcasting*, November 21, 1988, 40.
4. Jaffe, "CATV," 35.
5. "Righting Copyright," *Time,* November 1, 1976, 92; and Margaret B. Carlson, "Where MGM, the NCAA, and Jerry Falwell Fight for Cash," *Fortune,* January 23, 1984, 171.
6. Ron Merrell, "Origination Compounds Interest with Quality Control," *Video Systems,* November/December 1975, 15–18; and Sloan Commission on Cable Communications, *On the Cable: The Television of Abundance* (New York: McGraw-Hill, 1972).
7. Richard C. Kletter, *Cable Television: Making Public Access Effective* (Santa Monica, CA: Rand Corporation, 1973); and Charles Tate, *Cable Television in the Cities: Community Control, Public Access, and Minority Ownership* (Washington, DC: The Urban Institute, 1972).
8. *HBO Landmarks* (New York: Home Box Office, n.d.), 1; and Patrick Parsons, "The Evolution of the Cable-Satellite Distribution System," *Journal of Broadcasting & Electronic Media,* March 2003, 1–17.
9. "Lofty Bid for First DBS System," *Broadcasting,* December 22, 1980, 23.
10. "Another Nail in the DBS Coffin: Comsat Bows Out," *Broadcasting,* December 3, 1984, 36.
11. "Backyard Satellite Dishes Spread but Stir Fight with Pay-TV Firms," *Wall Street Journal,* April 2, 1982, 25.
12. Census Bureau, *Statistical Abstracts of the United States, 2000* (Washington, DC: Department of Commerce, 2000), 567–74; *Cable Television Developments* (Washington, DC: National Cable Television Association, 1995), 1–7; and "Cable Revenues Gain Faster Than Profits, Survey Finds," *Broadcasting,* November 30, 1981, 52.
13. "Cities Issue Guidelines for Cable Franchising," *Broadcasting,* March 9, 1981, 148; and "Dirty Tricks," *Panorama,* May 1981, 57–59.
14. "Entertainment Analysts Find Cable Mom-Pop Days Are Gone; Big Bucks Rule the Day," *Broadcasting,* June 15, 1981, 46.
15. "Cable Television Is Attracting More Ads; Sharply Focused Programs Are One Lure," *Wall Street Journal,* March 31, 1981, 46; and "Scribes Back at Typewriters," *Daily Variety,* July 16, 1981, 1.
16. "All You Ever Wanted to Know About Buying an Earth Station," *TVC,* May 15, 1979, 16–19.
17. "Viacom Becomes Second Satellite Pay Cable Network," *Broadcasting,* October 31, 1977, 64; and "Disney Previews Pay-TV Channel," *Daily Variety,* April 13, 1983, 1.
18. "Basic-Cable Programming: New Land of Opportunity," *Emmy,* Summer 1980, 26–30; and Peter W. Bernstein, "The Race to Feed Cable TV's Maw," *Fortune,* May 4, 1981, 308–18.
19. Don Kowet, "They'll Play Bach Backwards, Run for Queen of Holland," *TV Guide,* May 31, 1980, 15–18; and Ann M. Morrison, "Part-Time Stars of Cable TV," *Fortune,* November 30, 1981, 181–84.
20. "The Two-Way Tube," *Newsweek,* July 3, 1978, 64.
21. "Home Security Is a Cable TV, Industry Bets," *Wall Street Journal,* September 15, 1981, 25.
22. "Cable's Lost Promise," *Newsweek,* October 15, 1984, 103–5.
23. Michael G. Vita and John P. Wiegand, "Must-Carry Regulations for Cable Television Systems: An Economic Policy Analysis," *Journal of Broadcasting & Electronic Media,* Winter 1994, 1–19; "Court: Must-Carry Is Constitutional," *Electronic Media,* December 18, 1995, 6; and "Looking Back at Retransmission," *Electronic Media,* March 4, 2002, 1.
24. "Congress Abolishes Copyright Royalty Tribunal," *Broadcasting & Cable,* November 29, 1993, 18; and "Cable Price Hike," *Broadcasting & Cable,* October 23, 2000, 29.
25. "Free at Last: Cable Gets Its Bill," *Broadcasting,* October 15, 1984, 38; "Cable Rates Up 50% Since Deregulation," *Daily Variety,* September 5, 1991, 1; and "FCC Reins in Cable TV Rates," *Christian Science Monitor,* February 24, 1994, 3.

26. "Hubbard Broadcasting: Into DBS from Day One," *Broadcasting & Cable,* December 6, 1993, 30–68; and "Hughes Sees Payoff from DBS Gamble," *Aviation Week & Space Technology,* May 1, 1995, 58–59.

27. "All But Unanimous: VideoCipher-Plus," *Broadcasting & Cable,* February 17, 1992, 12.

28. "Rupe Finally Bags His Bird," *Daily Variety,* April 10, 2003, 1; and "Can John Malone Remake His Cable Empire in the Sky?" *Broadcasting & Cable,* January 1, 2007, 18–19.

29. "DirecTV Makes Local Deals," *Broadcasting & Cable,* December 13, 1999, 16.

30. "DirecTV Adds Internet and Phone Network," http://www.broadcastingcable.com/index.asp?layout=articlePrint&articleID=CA6468980 (accessed March 27, 2008).

31. "Sorting Through the Fallout of Cable Programming," *Broadcasting,* October 17, 1983, 29.

32. "Cable's Court Is in Session," *Broadcasting & Cable,* July 8, 1991, 49; and "CTV: Punch Line-ups Unveiled for Comedy Service," *Broadcasting & Cable,* March 4, 1991, 54.

33. "Pay-Per-View Seems a Sure Thing Despite Marketing, Technical Obstacles," *Wall Street Journal,* February 6, 1989, A9A; "Near Video on Demand Has Arrived," *Daily Variety,* May 13, 1994, 1; and "The VOD Roll-Out," *IC,* May 2000, 18–24.

34. "Public Access, Spotty Success," *Los Angeles Times,* July 16, 1999, B-2.

35. "Time Warner to Unplug FSN," *Electronic Media,* May 5, 1997, 8.

36. J. Brooks, *Telephone: The First Hundred Years* (New York: Harper and Row, 1975).

37. "Ma Bell's Big Breakup," *Newsweek,* January 18, 1982, 58–59.

38. "The Exploding Fax Universe," *Computer Telephony,* March 1995, 123; "Cutting the Cord," *Wall Street Journal,* November 9, 1990, R-1; and "Small Scale Telephony," *Byte,* May 1995, 125.

39. "Ma Bell Finally Gets Cable," *Hollywood Reporter,* June 25, 1998, 1.

40. "FiOs Joins the Millionaires Club," *Hollywood Reporter,* January 29, 2008, 10.

41. "Super Bowl Looms with Northwest Broadcasting, DirecTV Yards Apart," http://www.broadcastingcable.com/article/print/462987 (accessed January 27, 2011).

42. "Court Chokes Net Neutrality," *Hollywood Reporter,* April 7, 2010, 65.

43. "New Law of the Land," *Broadcasting & Cable,* February 5, 1996, 8.

44. "U.S. Oks Comcast's Bid for NBC," *Los Angeles Times,* January 19, 2011, B-1.

45. "Why the Sopranos Sing," *Newsweek,* April 2, 2001, 48–55.

46. "Pay TV's Affordability Crisis," *Hollywood Reporter,* July 29, 2011, 30.

47. "Media Chiefs Confront Cable TV Challenges," *Los Angeles Times,* June 15, 2011, B-3.

48. "Time to Screen Out Unloved Channels," *Wall Street Journal,* June 27–28, 2009, B10; and "TV Channels Move to Web, Think Outside the Cable Box," *Wall Street Journal,* August 10, 2007, B1.

49. "Top MSOs Own 90% of Subs," *Broadcasting & Cable,* May 24, 1999, 34.

Chapter 4

BROADCAST TELEVISION

At one time broadcast television was the only game in town. Stations sent their black and white signals through the airwaves to antennas that were on rooftops of people's homes. From there the signal went by wire to the family TV set, where programming was displayed on tiny TV screens. The signals did not travel very far, usually not beyond the boundaries of the city where they originated. Most cities had three or fewer stations and, if you missed a program when it aired, there was no way to watch it at a later time. Nevertheless, it was a wonder to the people of the 1950s and it quickly became an important part of the American fabric. Within a short period of time television became a blur of technological change and programming turnover.

Television had a negative impact on both radio (see Chapter 5) and movies (see Chapter 6), but broadcast television in turn encountered the

Many people are disappointed because television has not been put to general use already. They have been reading about it for so long that they are beginning to doubt that it will ever be of much importance. But those who are working with television are confident that someday television will be widely used to entertain people and to inform them.

"What Will Be the Future of Television?"
The Junior Review, February 13, 1939

Exhibit 4.1

Early mechanical scanning equipment. Through a peephole, a technician observes the image recreated through the rotating disc. The scanning disc at the other end of the shaft intervenes between an illuminated transparency and the photoelectric cell. This cell is in the box that is visible just beyond the driving shaft.

Alexanderson

Farnsworth

Exhibit 4.2

Philo T. Farnsworth in his laboratory about 1934.

competitive challenges of cable TV, satellite TV, telco TV (see Chapter 3), and the internet (see Chapter 2). Some believe that the broadcasting structure of a few networks and many stations is past its prime. Yet broadcast TV still commands the largest audiences, albeit quite a bit eroded from its heyday. Today only a small percentage of people receive their broadcast TV through the airwaves. Each station's signal is now placed on cable, satellite, or telco systems where it appears as one channel of programming among many. But, in part because it was first, broadcast television has an intriguing history.

4.1 Early Experiments

The first experiments with television used **mechanical scanning** (see Exhibit 4.1), invented in Germany in 1884. This process depended on a wheel that contained tiny holes positioned spirally. A small picture was placed behind the wheel, and each hole scanned one line of the picture as the wheel turned. Even though this device could scan only very small pictures, attempts were made to develop it further. For example, a General Electric employee, Ernst F. W. Alexanderson, began experimental programming during the 1920s using a revolving scanning wheel and a 3-by-4-inch image. One of his "programs," a science fiction thriller of a missile attack on New York, scanned an aerial photograph of New York that moved closer and closer and then disappeared to the sound of an explosion.[1]

Other people developed **electronic scanning,** the system that was later adopted. One developer was Philo T. Farnsworth (see Exhibit 4.2), who in 1922 astounded his Idaho high school teacher with diagrams for an electronic TV system. He applied for a patent and found himself battling the giant of electronic TV development, RCA. In 1930 Farnsworth, at the age of 24, won his patent and later received royalties from RCA.[2]

The RCA development was headed by Vladimir K. Zworykin, who patented an electronic pickup tube called the **iconoscope.** Beginning in the early 1930s, he and other engineers (including Alexanderson) systematically attacked such problems as increased lines of scanning, brightness, and image size. They started with a system that scanned 60 lines using a model of Felix the Cat (see Exhibit 4.3). Gradually they improved this scanning to 441 lines.[3]

In 1939, David Sarnoff, then president of RCA and a strong advocate of TV, decided to display television at the New York World's Fair (see Exhibit 4.4). President Franklin D. Roosevelt appeared on camera and was seen on black-and-white sets with 5-inch

Exhibit 4.3

Felix the Cat as he appeared on the experimental 60-line, black-and-white TV sets in the late 1920s. This picture was transmitted from New York City all the way to Kansas.

Exhibit 4.4

David Sarnoff dedicating the RCA pavilion at the 1939 New York World's Fair. This dedication marked the first time a news event was covered by television.

tubes. RCA (which owned NBC) by this time had an experimental TV program schedule broadcasting only in New York that consisted of one program a day from its studio, one from a mobile unit traveling the streets of New York, and several assorted films. The studio productions included plays, puppets, and household tips. The mobile unit consisted of two huge buses, one jammed with equipment to be set up in the field and one containing a transmitter. It covered such events as baseball games, airport interviews with dignitaries, and the premiere of *Gone with the Wind.* The films were usually cartoons, travelogues, or government documentaries.[4]

RCA's contributions

CBS, which existed as a radio network in the 1930s, began experimentation with color television, utilizing a mechanical color wheel of red, blue, and green that transferred color to the images. This color system was not compatible with the system RCA was using. In other words, the sets being manufactured could not receive either color or black-and-white pictures from the CBS mechanical system, and proposed CBS receivers would not be able to pick up existing RCA black-and-white pictures. In 1940, a group led mainly by RCA personnel tried to persuade the Federal Communications Commission (FCC) to allow the operation of the 441-line system. The FCC, however, was not certain this system had adequate technical quality, so it established an industrywide committee of engineers, the National Television System Committee (NTSC), to recommend standards. This committee rejected the 441-line system and in 1941 recommended a 525-line system that became the standard in the United States for many years.

color TV

Originally there were to be 13 **very high frequency (VHF)** channels, but channel 1 was eliminated to allow spectrum space for FM radio, so for many years channels 2 through 13 were available for over-the-air broadcast. Twenty-three stations went on the air in 1941 and 1942, 10,000 sets were sold, and commercials were sought. The first commercial was bought by Bulova and consisted of a shot of a Bulova clock with an announcer intoning the time. All of this

growth

stopped, however, in 1942 because of World War II. During the war, only six stations remained on the air, and most sets became inoperable because spare parts were not being manufactured for civilian use.[5]

4.2 The Emergence of Broadcast Television

color feud

Television activities did not resume immediately after the war. The delay was partly due to a shortage of materials and partly to the expense of building and operating a station. In addition, CBS and RCA were still feuding about color. CBS stated that its mechanical color system was so well developed that TV station allocations should not continue until the FCC resolved the color question. RCA promised black-and-white sets on the market by mid-1946 and a color system shortly thereafter that was electronic and compatible with its black-and-white sets. In 1947, the FCC declared that CBS's color system would be a hardship on set owners because they would have to buy new sets. It therefore stated that television should continue as a 525-line black-and-white system. Television emerged as a mass medium in 1948. The number of stations, sets, and audiences all grew more than 4,000 percent within one year. Advertisers became aware of the medium, and networks began more systematic programming.[6]

networks

Television networks had existed before 1948 as offshoots of radio networks. As early as 1945, TV networks were organized by NBC, CBS, and ABC. A fourth network, DuMont, existed for a short while. The network programming was broadcast through local stations. In the late-1940s, when most cities had only one or two TV stations, NBC and CBS usually recruited them as **affiliates,** making it difficult for ABC and DuMont to compete. ABC survived because it merged in 1953 with United Paramount Theaters and thus gained an increase in operating funds. DuMont, however, went out of business in 1955.[7]

4.3 The Freeze

stations

Television grew so uncontrollably that in the fall of 1948 the FCC imposed a **freeze** on television station authorizations because stations were beginning to interfere with one another. The proposed six-month freeze lasted until July 1, 1952. During this period, 108 stations were on the air, and no more were authorized to begin operation. What occurred between 1948 and 1952 could be termed an explosive lull. Many cities, including Austin, Texas; Denver, Colorado; and Portland, Oregon, had no television stations. Others had only one or two. New York and Los Angeles were the only cities to boast seven. Although TV networking still could not be considered truly national, the number of sets, audience size, advertising, and programming continued to grow. By 1952, 15 million homes had sets, the largest of which had 20-inch tubes and sold for about $350.

allocation tables

When the FCC ended the freeze in 1952, it established a station allocation table that assigned specific channels to specific areas of the country. Between 1948 and 1952, the FCC realized that the 12 VHF channels being used would not be sufficient to meet demand. The FCC engineers added 70 channels in the **ultra-high frequency**

(**UHF**) band, for a total of 82 channels. In addition, the FCC reserved 242 stations (80 VHF and 162 UHF) for noncommercial educational television.[8]

4.4 Early TV Programming

During the 1948–49 season, 30 percent of sponsored evening programs on broadcast TV were sports related. Wrestlers, both men and women, competed to outdo one another in costumes, hairdos, and mannerisms. The large number of TV sets in bars spurred the sports emphasis. During the 1949–50 season, however, sports comprised less than 5 percent of evening programming, and children's programming was tops, indicating that TV had moved to the home.

In TV cities, movie attendance, radio listening, sports event attendance, and restaurant dining were all down—especially on Tuesday night, which was Milton Berle night. People with TV sets stayed home and often invited their friends (or allowed their friends to invite themselves) to watch this ex-vaudevillian's show, which started in 1948 and included outrageous costumes, slapstick comedy, and a host of guest stars (see Exhibit 4.5). "Uncle Miltie" on his *Texaco Star Theater* became a national phenomenon and was the reason many people bought their first television set.[9]

The programming forms used by early TV were very similar to those used during the heyday of radio—comedy, drama, soap operas, public affairs, and children's programs (see Chapter 5). Some of them were reconstructed radio shows with radio stars such as Jack Benny and ventriloquist Edgar Bergen (who didn't last long because people could see his lips move).

In 1951, *I Love Lucy* (see Exhibit 4.6) began as a maverick of the TV world because it was filmed earlier, whereas other shows were aired live. There was a stigma against film at the time, partly because it added to the cost and partly because the TV networks inherited the live tradition from radio and assumed that all shows should be produced live. The film aspect was particularly useful and dramatic when Lucille Ball became pregnant, and the story line dealt with Lucy's pregnancy. The episode involving the birth of Lucy's baby was filmed ahead of time, and Lucille's real baby was born the same day the filmed episode aired—to an audience that comprised 68.8 percent of the American public. Eventually, the filming more than paid for itself because the program became the first international hit. Copies of the film were dubbed into numerous languages and sold overseas.[10]

Television newscasts of the 1950s developed slowly. Networks found it easy to obtain news and voices, but pictures were another matter. At first they contracted with the companies that supplied the newsreels then shown in movie theaters. This did not exactly fit television's bill because much of it was shot for in-depth stories, not news of the day. Networks hired their own film crews, but limited budgets and bulky film equipment meant that camera operators could attend only planned events, such as press conferences and ribbon-cuttings. The 15-minute newscasts tended to be reports on events that had been filmed earlier.[11]

Interview-type public affairs shows were a further development. *Meet the Press* (which is still on the air) began its long run of probing interviews with

Exhibit 4.5
Milton Berle in one of his outlandish costumes. His *Texaco Star Theater* was TV's first big hit.

sports, Uncle Miltie, and Lucy

news

public affairs

Exhibit 4.6

Lucy tries to make a hit playing the saxophone. The *I Love Lucy* series, starring Lucille Ball, captured America's heart and can still be seen in reruns.

prominent people. *See It Now* started in 1951 as a news documentary series featuring Edward R. Murrow. A historic feature of the first program was showing for the first time both the Atlantic and Pacific oceans live on TV. At this point, television could be proud of its achievements. Sets had increased in size and quality, TV programming had increased in hours and variety, the public was fascinated with the new medium, and advertisers were providing increasingly strong financial backing.[12]

4.5 Blacklisting

To this fledgling industry came some of the country's best-known talent. They came from radio, Broadway, and film—all of which were experiencing downturns as television was burgeoning. Unfortunately, some of these people became caught in the anti-Communist **blacklisting** mania of the 1950s led by Senator Joseph R. McCarthy. A 215-page publication called *Red Channels: The Report of Communist Influence in Radio and Television* gave information about 151 people, many of whom were among the top names in show business, which suggested they had Communist ties. Some of these charges, such as associating people with "left-ist" organizations to which they had never belonged, were proved to be

Red Channels

false. Other allegations were true, but were "leftist" only by definitions of the perpetrators of *Red Channels*. These included such "wrongdoings" as signing a cablegram of congratulations to the Moscow Art Theater on its 50th birthday.

Although many network and advertising executives did not believe these people were Communists or in any way un-American, they were unwilling to hire them, in part because of the controversy involved and in part because sponsors received phone calls that threatened to boycott their products if programs employed these people. Some well-established writers, for the better part of a decade, found that all the scripts they wrote were "not quite right," and certain actors were told they were "not exactly the type for the part." Many of these people did not even know they were on one of the "lists" because these were circulated clandestinely among executives.

In time, the blacklist situation eased. Ironically, broadcasting was influential in exposing the excesses of the Communist witch hunt, which had spread beyond the entertainment industry. Edward R. Murrow prepared several programs on Senator McCarthy, who had alarmed the country by saying that he had a list of hundreds of Communists in the State Department. The Murrow telecasts helped expose this claim as false. In 1954, television covered hearings in which

McCarthy's downfall

McCarthy took on the army. As the nation watched, McCarthy and his aides harassed and bullied witnesses. Public resentment built against McCarthy, and the Senate voted 67 to 22 to censure him.[13]

4.6 The Live Era

Programming of the 1950s was predominantly live. *I Love Lucy* continued to be filmed, and several other programs jumped on the film bandwagon as foreign countries began developing broadcasting systems. Americans could envision

ZOOM IN: **The Challenges of Live Programming**

Live programming, especially dramas, created problems for writers, actors, and technicians. Costume changes needed to be essentially non-existent. The number of story locales was governed by the number of sets that could fit into the studio. These sets were arranged in a circle on the periphery of the studio so the cameras could have easy access to each new scene. Timing was sometimes an immense problem. In radio, scripts could be quite accurately timed by the number of pages, but television programs contained much action, the time of which often fluctuated widely in rehearsals. One writing solution was to plan a search scene near the end of the play. The actor could find what he or she was looking for right away if the program was running long or could search the room for as long as necessary if the program appeared to be moving too quickly.

Because the programs were live, they were usually performed twice—once for the Eastern and Central Time zones and a second time for the Mountain and Pacific Time zones. During the interval between the two broadcasts, the cast and crew would go out to eat and drink. The second performances were usually a little more "lively" than the first ones.

A scene from *Marty*, a 1953 drama starring Rod Steiger and Nancy Marchand that was originally aired live and later made into a movie.

the reuse of their products in other countries and, hence, the possibility of recouping film costs. Reruns in the United States were as yet not thought of, although some programs were kinescoped, so they could be shown at various times. These **kinescopes** were low-quality, grainy film representations of the video picture. Most of the popular network series of the day, however, originated in New York and were telecast as they were being shot (see "Zoom In" box). Local stations produced some of their own programming, such as children's shows, that were also live.

kinescopes

The programming of the early 1950s is often referred to as the "golden age of television." This is mainly because of the live dramas produced during this period. One of the most outstanding plays was Rod Serling's *Requiem for a Heavyweight* (see Exhibit 4.7), the psychological study of a broken-down fighter. Another was Paddy Chayefsky's *Marty,* the heartwarming study of a short, stocky small-town butcher who develops a sensitive romantic relationship with a homely schoolteacher.[14]

"golden age"

Weaver

Exhibit 4.7

Requiem for a Heavyweight, starring Jack Palance as the fighter and Keenan Wynn as his manager.

Exhibit 4.8

Dave Garroway with chimps J. Fred Muggs (left) and Phoebe B. Beebe. Muggs was discovered in classic show-business style by one of *Today's* producers, who spotted him in an elevator.

In addition to conventional drama, innovative formats surfaced, many of them the brainchild of Sylvester L. "Pat" Weaver, president of NBC from 1953 to 1955. One of his ideas was the spectacular, a show that was not part of the regular schedule. One outstanding spectacular was *Peter Pan,* which was viewed by some 165 million Americans. Weaver was also involved in developing the *Today* and *Tonight* shows. *Today* was first hosted by Dave Garroway (see Exhibit 4.8), who had a chimpanzee as a sidekick. *Tonight* originally starred Steve Allen and from 1962 to 1992 was hosted by Johnny Carson. Weaver believed that programs should be controlled by the network rather than by advertising agencies. Most radio shows and early TV program content had been produced by **advertising agencies** (see Chapter 5). Weaver developed a **magazine concept** whereby advertisers bought insertions in programs, whose content was supervised and produced by the networks.[15]

While commercial television was prospering, educational television programming was struggling. Although the FCC had reserved channels, activating the stations was difficult because of the huge sums of money needed. The stations were not allowed to engage in advertising, and the organizations interested in establishing stations—universities, school districts, nonprofit community organizations—were not known for deep pockets.

Fortunately, the Ford Foundation stepped in and provided money for facilities and programming. Two innovative programming concepts it funded were the Chicago TV College and the Midwest Program on Airborne Television Instruction (MPATI). The Chicago project (see Exhibit 4.9) was a fully accredited set of televised courses that enabled students to earn two-year college degrees through a combination of at-home viewing and on-campus class attendance. MPATI used an airplane that circled two states to broadcast programs to schoolchildren. The Ford Foundation also helped establish a **bicycle network** system for distributing programming, the National Educational Television and Radio Center, which operated out of Ann Arbor, Michigan. This helped stations acquire programming, but because tapes were mailed to stations in a round-robin fashion, nothing timely could be exchanged. Despite this outside help, educational programming of the 1950s and 1960s was, in a word, dull. It was produced on a shoestring budget and consisted primarily of talking heads discussing issues and information.[16]

Exhibit 4.9
Professor Harvey M.
Karlen conducting a
lesson on national
government for
Chicago TV College.

Ford Foundation

4.7 Color TV Approval

Color TV underwent a number of changes and did not become widespread for several decades. CBS continued to advocate its mechanical system while RCA favored an electronic one. In 1950, in a reversal of its 1947 decision, the FCC accepted the CBS system, believing it provided higher quality color pictures. RCA, however, continued to fight the CBS system by refusing to program in color and by gaining allies among other set manufacturing companies and TV stations. CBS ran into difficulty manufacturing its color sets, and a general state of confusion concerning color reigned in the TV industry.

CBS system accepted

To help solve the problem, the National Television System Committee, the same committee of engineers that had decided on the 525-line system, volunteered to study the situation. Because this committee included more members who favored the RCA system than the CBS system, very few people were surprised when it recommended the compatible system. To its credit, however, the RCA system had improved, in part in response to suggestions from the NTSC. The FCC took the NTSC recommendation and in 1953 sanctioned RCA's electronic compatible system. At the time, even CBS supported the adoption.

RCA system accepted

For a long time, however, RCA-NBC was the only company actively promoting color. NBC constructed new color facilities and began programming in color, but both CBS and ABC dragged their heels, and most local stations did not have the capital needed to convert to color equipment. Consumers were reluctant to purchase color TV sets because they cost twice as much as black-and-white sets, and the limited color programming did not merit this investment. But as more color sets were sold, the prices fell, and programming in color increased, causing even more sets to be sold. Not until the late 1960s were all networks and most stations producing color programs.[17]

slow growth

4.8 Prerecorded Programming

The days of live broadcast programming, other than news and special events, began to disappear in the mid-1950s for several reasons. One was the introduction of videotape in 1956. The expense of the equipment prevented it from taking hold quickly, but once its foot was in the door, videotape revolutionized TV production. Programs could now be performed at convenient times for later airings. As the equipment became more sophisticated, a taping could be stopped for costume and scene changes. As the equipment became even more sophisticated, mistakes could be corrected through editing.

videotape

film

Exhibit 4.10

Gunsmoke, the longest-running western. It started on CBS in 1955 and lasted until 1975. Shown here are two of the principals, Dennis Weaver and James Arness.

The live era, however, began to yield to film even before tape took hold. Film companies were originally antagonistic toward TV because it stole much of the audience that attended movie theaters. Some film production companies would not allow their stars to appear on TV and would not even allow TV sets to appear as props in movies. The 1953 merger of United Paramount Theaters and ABC opened the door for Hollywood film companies and the New York TV establishment to begin a dialogue. The first result of this dialogue was a one-hour weekly series, *Disneyland,* produced for ABC by the Walt Disney Studios. This was a big hit, and soon several other major film companies were producing film series for TV. Among the early filmed TV series, westerns predominated. By 1959, 32 western series were on prime-time TV. The one with the greatest longevity was *Gunsmoke* (see Exhibit 4.10), which revolved around Dodge City's Matt Dillon, Chester Goode, Doc, and Miss Kitty.

The TV boom continued in the late 1950s— more TV sets, more viewers, more stations, more advertising dollars. To this rising euphoria came a dark hour.[18]

4.9 The Quiz Scandals

Quiz programs on which contestants won minimal amounts of money or company-donated merchandise existed on both radio and television. In 1955, however, a new idea emerged in the form of *The $64,000 Question* (see Exhibit 4.11). If contestants triumphed over challengers for a number of weeks, they could win huge cash prizes. Sales of Revlon products, the company that produced and sponsored *The $64,000 Question,* zoomed to such heights that some were sold out nationwide. The sales success and high audience ratings spawned many imitators. Contestants locked in soundproof booths pondered, perspired, and caught the fancy of the nation.

The $64,000 Question

Then, in 1958, a contestant from *Twenty-One* described situations that indicated the program was rigged. The networks and advertising agencies denied the charges, as did Charles Van Doren, a Columbia professor who was the most

Van Doren

Exhibit 4.11

Master of ceremonies of *The $64,000 Question* was Hal March (right). Gino Prato, an Italian-born New York shoemaker, mops his brow while listening to a four-part question about opera.

famous of the *Twenty-One* winners. A House of Representatives subcommittee conducted hearings, and in 1959 Van Doren testified. He read a long statement describing how he had been persuaded in the name of entertainment to accept help with answers in order to defeat a current champion who was becoming unpopular. Van Doren was also coached on methods of building suspense, and when he did win, he became a national hero and a leader of intellectual life. He asked to be released from the show and finally was allowed to lose after months on the program. He initially lied, he said, so that he would not betray the people who had faith in him.

In retrospect the **quiz scandals'** negative effect on TV was short-lived. The medium was simply too pervasive a force to be permanently afflicted by such an incident. Congress did amend the Communications Act to make it unlawful to give help to a contestant, but for the most part the networks rectified the errors by canceling the quiz shows and reinstating a higher percentage of public-service programs. **effects**

Networks also took charge of their programming to a much greater extent. All three networks decreed that from then on most program content would be decided, controlled, and scheduled by networks, which would then sell time to advertisers. This was a further extension of Weaver's "magazine concept." Beginning in 1960, most program suppliers contracted with the networks rather than with advertising agencies. This made life more profitable for the TV networks, too, because they established profit participation plans with the suppliers.[19]

4.10 Reflections of Upheaval

Broadcast television journalism gathered force and prestige during the 1960s—the decade of civil rights revolts, the election of John F. Kennedy, assassinations, the Vietnam War, and student unrest. The networks encouraged documentaries and, in 1963, increased their nightly news from 15 to 30 minutes, thereby assigning increased importance to their news departments. Anchoring on camera **news**

Exhibit 4.12

A Huntley-Brinkley newscast. Chet Huntley broadcast from New York, while David Brinkley, seen on the television screen, broadcast from Washington, DC.

documentaries

civil rights

debates

for NBC were Chet Huntley and David Brinkley (see Exhibit 4.12), and CBS had Walter Cronkite, the person who became known as the most trusted man in America.

The quiz scandals helped precipitate a rise in documentaries. To atone for their sins, networks increased their investigative fare. Documentaries were now easier to produce because technical advances allowed film and sound to be synchronized without an umbilical cord between two pieces of equipment, and wireless microphones enabled speakers to wander freely without having to stay within range of a mike cord. News-gathering flexibility became even greater when portable video cameras were developed at the end of the 1960s.

Many documentaries reported on racial problems. *Crisis: Behind a Presidential Commitment* chronicled the events surrounding Governor George Wallace's attempted barring of the schoolhouse door to prevent blacks from attending the University of Alabama; *The Children Are Watching* dealt with the feelings of a six-year-old black child attending the first integrated school in New Orleans. Television reacted to the civil rights movement in another way—it began hiring African Americans. Scriptwriters began including stories about blacks, and Diahann Carroll (see Exhibit 4.13) in *Julia* became the first black TV heroine.

Television was credited, through the debates between John F. Kennedy and Richard M. Nixon, with having a primary influence on the 1960 presidential election results. Kennedy and Nixon met for the first debate at the studios of Chicago's CBS station. Kennedy, tanned from campaigning in California, refused the offer of makeup. Nixon, although he was recovering from a brief illness, did likewise. Some of Nixon's aides, concerned about how he looked on TV, applied Lazy-Shave, to create a clean-shaven look. Some people believe that Kennedy's apparent victory in the first debate had little to do with what he said. People who heard the program on radio felt Nixon held his own, but those watching TV could see a confident, attentive Kennedy and a haggard, weary-looking Nixon whose perspiration streaked the Lazy-Shave. Three more debates were held, and Nixon's makeup and demeanor were well handled, but the small margin of the Kennedy victory is often attributed to the undecided vote that swung to Kennedy during the first debate.[20]

Exhibit 4.13

Diahann Carroll (left) was the first African American heroine in a TV series.

Three years later, television devoted itself to the coverage of the assassination of John F. Kennedy (see Exhibit 4.14). From Friday, November 22, to Monday, November 25, 1963, there were times when 90 percent of the American people were watching television. One New York critic wrote, "This was not viewing. This was total involvement." From shortly after the shots were fired in Dallas until President Kennedy was laid to rest in Arlington Cemetery, television kept the vigil, including the first "live murder" ever seen on TV as Jack Ruby shot alleged assassin Lee Harvey Oswald. Many praised television for its controlled, almost flawless coverage. Some thought TV would have made it impossible for Lee Harvey Oswald to receive a fair trial and that it was the presence of the media that enabled the Oswald shooting to occur.[21]

Exhibit 4.14

The Kennedy funeral. This off-monitor shot shows JFK's son saluting the flag covering his father's caisson.

Television brought war to the American dinner table for the first time in history. The networks established correspondents in Saigon as the troop buildup began in Vietnam during the mid-1960s. Reports of the war appeared almost nightly on the evening news programs. In 1968, amid rising controversy over the war, Walter Cronkite decided to travel to Vietnam and returned believing that the United States would have to accept a stalemate in that country (see Exhibit 4.15).

Kennedy assassination

Vietnam

demonstrations

Much of the controversy surrounding the war originated on the country's campuses, where students became increasingly dissident. This, too, was covered by the media, as was the 1968 Democratic convention in Chicago, where youths outside the convention hall protested the nomination of Hubert Humphrey. The media became embroiled in the controversy. On the one hand, they were accused of inciting the riot conditions because the demonstrators seemed to be trying to attract media coverage. On the other hand, many people inside the convention hall learned of the protest by seeing it on a TV monitor and might not otherwise have known of this show of discontent.[22]

Exhibit 4.15

Walter Cronkite visiting Vietnam.

4.11 A Vast Wasteland?

In 1961, Newton Minow, Kennedy's appointee as chairman of the Federal Communications Commission, spoke before the annual convention of the National Association of Broadcasters. During his speech, Minow, who had

ZOOM IN: **Still a Wasteland?**

Here are some other excerpts from Newton Minow's 1961 speech. How do you think they apply (or don't apply) to television today?

When television is good, nothing—not the theater, not the magazines or newspapers— nothing is better. But when television is bad, nothing is worse.

You will see a procession of game shows, violence, sadism, murder, western badmen, western good men, private eyes, gangsters, more violence and cartoons. And, endlessly, commercials— many screaming, cajoling, and offending.

It is not enough to cater to the nation's whims— you must also serve the nation's needs. If some of you persist in a relentless search for the highest rating and the lowest common denominator, you may well lose your audience.

I am unalterably opposed to government censorship. There will be no suppression of programming that does not meet with bureaucratic tastes.

We need imagination in programming, not sterility; creativity, not imitation; experi-mentation, not conformity; excellence, not mediocrity.

The power of instantaneous sight and sound is without precedent in mankind's history. This is an awesome power. It has limitless capabilities for good—and for evil. And it carries with it awesome responsibilities—responsibilities which you and I cannot escape.

Newton Minow.

seemed favorable toward broadcasting, startled his audience with the following words:

> I invite you to sit down in front of your television set when your station goes on the air and stay there without a book, magazine, newspaper, profit-and-loss sheet, or rating book to distract you—and keep your eyes glued to that set until the station signs off. I can assure you that you will observe a vast wasteland.

Minow's speech   The term **vast wasteland** caught on as a metaphor for television programming (see "Zoom In" box). The executives were not happy with Minow's phrase.[23]

During the early 1960s, the dominant fare on TV was violence. The original versions of such programs as *The Untouchables, Route 66,* and *The Roaring 20s* all featured murders, jailbreaks, robberies, kidnappings, and blackmail. Saturday morning children's programming was also replete with violent cartoons. A surge against

violence   violence, aided by Minow's challenge, spurred a shift to shows about doctors, such as *Dr. Kildare,* and more comedies, such as *The Dick Van Dyke Show, Gilligan's Island, The Beverly Hillbillies,* and *Hogan's Heroes* (see Exhibit 4.16).

During the 1960s, old Hollywood movies established themselves on TV (see Chapter 6). In 1961, NBC's *Saturday Night at the Movies* began a prime-time movie trend that, by 1968, saw movies every night of the week. This rapidly depleted Hollywood's supply of old films, and some of the low-quality films that made it onto the airwaves enhanced the vast wasteland theory. In 1966, NBC made a deal with Universal to provide movies that were specially made for television and would not appear in theaters first. This concept caught on, and by 1969, all three networks had **made-fors** on a regular basis.

Also during the 1960s, the number of local stations that were on the air grew. Most cities had more than three stations, and because there were only three networks, some of the stations, referred to as **independents,** did not have a network to feed them programming. Although some of these stations produced their own programming, most of them bought the bulk of it from **syndicators**—companies that had started businesses to provide programming for these stations. Syndicated programs were sent to stations on tape, and they could air them whenever they wanted. By this time the U.S. television industry had discovered the value of the rerun, so much of what the syndication companies provided was reruns of programs that had been on one of the networks. They also provided packages of older movies, often giving them a theme—such as horror movies or Cary Grant movies. This type of programming fare gave Minow further fuel for his "vast wasteland" comment.[24]

Exhibit 4.16

Hogan's Heroes, a comedy set in a World War II prisoner-of-war camp, was on CBS from 1965 to 1971.

movies

local station fare

4.12 The Public Broadcasting Act of 1967

Meanwhile, educational broadcasting was undergoing its own transformation. The Ford Foundation, feeling that it was shouldering too much of the support for educational television, cut back on funding. A number of organizations and councils appeared and disappeared, trying to solve the financial problems, but the result was a lack of focus and political infighting.

The Carnegie Foundation finally came to the rescue by setting up the Carnegie Commission on Educational Television. This group of highly respected citizens spent two years studying the technical, organizational, financial, and programming aspects of educational television and in 1967 published its report. The commission changed the term *educational television* to *public television* to overcome the pedantic image the stations had acquired. It also recommended that "a well-financed and well-directed system, substantially larger and far more

Carnegie Commission

pervasive and effective than that which now exists in the United States, be brought into being if the full needs of the American public are to be served."[25]

Most of the Carnegie Commission's many recommendations were incorporated into the Public Broadcasting Act of 1967. There were two major changes between the Carnegie recommendation and congressional passage of the act, however. First was the addition of radio. The Carnegie Commission addressed itself only to TV, but the radio interests that led to National Public Radio were included by Congress (see Chapter 5). Second, the Carnegie group recommended that **public broadcasting** be given permanent funding, perhaps through a tax on TV sets, but Congress opted for one year's funding of $9 million with additional funding to be voted on later.

Public Broadcasting Act

The Public Broadcasting Act of 1967 provided for the establishment and funding of the Corporation for Public Broadcasting (CPB) to supply national leadership for public broadcasting and to make sure that it would have maximum protection from outside interference. Government money was given to CPB, which in turn gave money to stations and networks. In this way public broadcasters were protected from government influence. The CPB's 15-member board (later changed to 9) was appointed by the president with the consent of the Senate. The main duties of the board were to help new stations get on the air, to obtain grants from federal and private sources, to provide grants to stations for programming, and to establish an interconnection system for public broadcasting stations.

CPB

The CPB was specifically forbidden from owning or operating the interconnection system. The corporation, therefore, created the Public Broadcasting Service (PBS), an agency to schedule, promote, and distribute programming over a wired network (the use of wires disappeared in 1978 when PBS became the first network to distribute programming totally by satellite). PBS had a governing board consisting of station executives. This service was not to produce programs, but rather to obtain them from such sources as public TV stations, independent producers, and foreign countries. Hence a three-tier operation was established: (1) The stations produced the programs; (2) PBS scheduled and distributed the programs; and (3) CPB provided funds and guidance for the activities.

PBS

programs

Exhibit 4.17
Fred Rogers (right) with Mr. McFeely, one of the many characters who visited regularly on *Mister Rogers' Neighborhood.*

The advent of the Corporation for Public Broadcasting and its accompanying funding allowed public television to embark on innovative programming of high quality. The first series to arouse interest was the successful children's series *Sesame Street,* first produced in 1969 by a newly created and newly funded organization, the Children's Television Workshop (CTW). This series helped strengthen PBS as a network because it was in demand throughout the country.

Other early PBS series that met with sustained popularity were *Mister Rogers' Neighborhood* (see Exhibit 4.17), a children's program produced in

Pittsburgh; *The French Chef,* Julia Child's cooking show produced in Boston; *Black Journal,* a public affairs series dealing with news and issues of importance to African Americans produced in New York; and *Masterpiece Theatre*, a series produced in Boston that presented many acclaimed British dramas.[26]

4.13 Government Actions of the 1970s

The organization for public broadcasting set up by the Public Broadcasting Act of 1967 looked good on paper, but it had problems in operation. A major controversy surfaced during the Nixon administration when the CPB, which had been formed to insulate public broadcasting from government, became somewhat of an arm of the government. The conflict centered on programs that were critical of the government, primarily nationally aired documentaries. The administration carried its ire into the budgeting area, and Richard Nixon vetoed a bill that would have given public broadcasting $64 million for 1972–73. With this action, the chairperson and president of CPB resigned, and Nixon appointed new people to the posts who were more in line with his way of thinking. With CPB now more in tune with the administration, a schism developed between CPB and PBS over who should control the programming decisions for public broadcasting. PBS wanted to continue the documentaries while CPB pressed for an emphasis on cultural programming that would be less political in nature. The controversy continued but gradually abated as Watergate consumed the administration and Nixon was forced to resign.[27]

Nixon

In 1970, the FCC adopted a rule barring networks from acquiring a financial interest in independently produced programs and from engaging in domestic syndication of these programs or of their own network-produced programs. This rule, called **financial interest–domestic syndication (fin-syn),** was adopted because the FCC thought the networks, which at the time had about 90 percent of the prime-time audience, were too powerful in the programming business. The rule stated that networks could produce only 3.5 hours of the 22 prime-time hours available each week.

fin-syn

The bulk of the shows during the next several decades were produced by independent production companies (see Exhibit 4.18). Some of the most popular were the following:

The Mary Tyler Moore Show (on CBS from 1970 to 1977). The independent production company was MTM run by Grant Tinker, Mary's husband at the time. It was the first show to feature an unmarried career woman. Its three **spin-offs**—*Rhoda, Phyllis,* and *Lou Grant*—were based on characters in the show and were also produced by MTM.

All in the Family (on CBS from 1971 to 1979). The production company was Tandem, headed by

Exhibit 4.18
The cast of *All in the Family* on the set of their Queens home.

Norman Lear and "Bud" Yorkin. It was the first situation comedy to deal with previously taboo subjects such as politics, ethnicity, and sex, mainly through its bigoted lead character, Archie Bunker. Among other shows produced by Tandem were *Maude* and *Sanford and Son*.

Happy Days (on ABC from 1974 to 1984). The company was Miller-Milkin-Boyette, the last names of the three principals. The series was created by Garry Marshall and dealt with 1950s teenagers, including Ron Howard as the lead and Henry Winkler as "The Fonz," a high school dropout. It spawned other hits such as *Laverne and Shirley* and *Mork and Mindy*.

Dallas (on ABC from 1978 to 1991). The production company, Lorimar, was started by Irwin Molasky, Merv Adelson, and Lee Rich. The series dealt with the sordid lives of rich people in Dallas. In the final episode of the 1980 season, the scheming oil baron, J. R. Ewing, was shot. The summer was abuzz with speculation about "Who shot J. R.?"

The Cosby Show (on CBS from 1984–1992). The principals of the production company, Carsey-Werner, were Marcy Carsey and Tom Werner. The show starred Bill Cosby and was a sitcom about his fictional family, which in some ways resembled his real family of four girls and one boy. Other Carsey-Werner shows included *A Different World* and *Roseanne*.[28]

After these programs aired on the networks, the rights reverted to the production companies, which gained the profits from syndication. Fin-syn lasted until 1995, when the networks were able to prove their power was no longer dominant, given all the other programming sources that had arisen. The abolishment of fin-syn enabled the networks to produce more of their own product and to profit from it financially. Obviously, the independent Hollywood production companies that had supplied the programming were not happy with this situation and eventually most of them disappeared.[29]

PTAR

In 1971, the FCC established the **prime-time access rule (PTAR).** The purpose was to break the networks' monopoly on programming between 7:00 and 11:00 P.M. so that some of this time could be programmed by stations to meet community needs. The rule stated that networks would be allowed to program only three hours a night on stations in the top 50 markets, leaving the other hour to their local affiliates. During this hour, there were to be no old network programs or old movies; all programs had to be new. However, the rule was modified so that prime-time access became 7:30 to 8:00 P.M., Monday through Saturday. Although prime-time access was established to allow stations to broadcast local programming of high quality, this did not happen to any significant degree. The stations filled the time with the cheapest thing they could find—game shows and remakes of old formats, although some developed local **magazine shows.** As the years progressed, various entities involved argued about the efficacy of the rule, and in 1995 the FCC abolished it.[30]

family hour

Family hour began in 1975 as an attempt to curtail sex and violence before 9:00 P.M., when children are most likely to be watching. The family-hour concept originated with the code of the National Association of Broadcasters (NAB), an industry organization. Some believed the code came about as a result of subtle pressure from the FCC and, hence, represented an abhorrent attempt by the commission to regulate program content. The family-hour idea was widely opposed by writers, producers, and directors, who took the concept to court. Eventually courts decided that the FCC had overstepped its powers and that the family-hour restrictions should be removed from the NAB code.[31]

4.14 Network Changes

The 1980s were not financially good times for over-the-air commercial television. Stations and networks were faced with competition from cable TV, which splintered the audience and the advertising dollar. Profits were down almost universally, and some stations even went bankrupt. This downturn in broadcasting, combined with a national phenomenon of company takeovers, led to major changes in the management and ownership of all three networks.

ABC The first network affected was ABC, which was purchased in 1985 for $3.5 billion by Capital Cities Communications, a company one-third the size of ABC. Although the takeover was termed "friendly," it was the first time in history that a major network had been purchased, and it was referred to as "the minnow swallowing the whale." CapCities kept ABC for 10 years and then sold it to Disney for $18.5 billion, a tidy profit for a minnow.[32]

NBC Less than a year after Capital Cities bought ABC, a second major network, NBC, was purchased as part of an overall takeover of its parent company, RCA. The purchaser was General Electric, a company that had been involved in the formation of NBC radio and then eased out of ownership by RCA (see Chapter 5). This, again, was called a "friendly takeover." In 2004, NBC spread its wings further and merged with Universal, garnering the network a strong production facility.[33]

CBS Things were not so "friendly" in the CBS executive suites. In 1985, Ted Turner attempted an unfriendly coup that CBS thwarted only by buying back much of its own stock, an act that greatly damaged CBS's financial footing. In 1986, CBS founder, William Paley, who had retired, came back to CBS and formed an alliance with Lawrence Tisch, who also was nibbling at the edges of CBS in what some thought was a takeover bid. Tisch was appointed chief operating officer, so his "takeover" did not involve any formal exchange of stock. In 1995, Tisch arranged to sell CBS to Westinghouse for $5.4 billion, placing another pioneer radio company back in the network business (see Chapter 5). In 1997, Westinghouse changed its name to CBS and then, in 1999, merged with Viacom, a major TV distribution company.[34]

Fox and other networks A new network, Fox, appeared on the scene in 1987. Rupert Murdoch, an Australian media baron who had recently obtained U.S. citizenship, purchased 20th Century Fox and six TV stations owned by Metromedia. He then built a network using his six stations and other independent stations throughout the country. Fox increased the number of programs offered to its affiliates slowly, but a number of its shows, such as *The Simpsons* (see Exhibit 4.19), quickly became hits, and during the 1990s Fox established itself as a major network.[35]

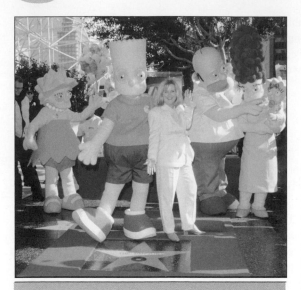

Exhibit 4.19

The Simpsons. This cartoon family of self-proclaimed losers gained great popularity in its prime-time spot on the Fox network and earned themselves a star on the Hollywood Walk of Fame. The real person in the center is Nancy Cartwright, the voice of Bart Simpson.

Fox's success encouraged the 1995 launch of two other networks, United Paramount Network (UPN) and the WB Network. The ownership of these networks underwent some convoluted changes. Paramount merged with Viacom, which then merged with CBS, meaning that Viacom/CBS owned two networks, CBS and UPN. A 1940s rule stipulated that a company could own only one network, but in 2001 the FCC relaxed that restriction allowing both UPN and CBS to be owned by one company. Warner underwent ownership changes in 2000 when America Online bought it in a highly hyped deal that created AOL Time Warner. This deal did not live up to expectations; Warner finally exerted dominance over the internet company and in 2003 separated from AOL. In the final analysis, neither UPN nor WB garnered a large audience, so in 2006 Warner and CBS merged the two networks into CW, "C" for CBS and "W" for Warner.[36]

4.15 More Government Interaction

deregulation

The 1980s, under the presidency of Ronald Reagan, were years of **deregulation,** wherein the government reduced rules and regulations for many types of businesses. Broadcasting was no exception. For example, in 1984, the number of years that a broadcast station could hold a license before having to renew it with the government was lengthened from three years to five, and the number of TV stations one entity could own was increased from 7 to 12, provided the 12 stations were not in markets that collectively contained more than 25 percent of the nation's TV homes.[37]

Telecommunications Act

The **Telecommunications Act of 1996** further loosened restrictions on broadcasters. It lengthened the five-year license renewal period to eight years, eliminated the 12-station numerical cap, and raised the coverage area from 25 percent to 35 percent. But the amount of sex and violence on television bothered members of Congress, so they included regulatory provisions related to that subject. The main one was that TV sets had to be equipped with a **V-chip,** a device that consumers could use to block programs with violence, sex, or other undesirable material. The television industry was required to develop a ratings system to earmark these programs and then encode the programs electronically so the chip could identify them and block them from coming into households where they were not wanted. (see Exhibit 4.20).[38]

retransmission

Another law that had an important effect on broadcast TV was one that allowed broadcasters to choose whether they wanted **must-carry** or **retransmission consent**. Must-carry had been a major issue between broadcasters and

TV Program Ratings

TV-Y—for all children

TV-Y7—directed toward older children
    TV-Y7-V—mild violence
    TV-Y7-L—mild coarse language
    TV-Y7-FV—fantasy violence

TV-G—for general audience

TV-PG—parental guidance suggested
    TV-PG-V—moderate violence
    TV-PG-L—mild coarse language
    TV-PG-S—mild sexual situations
    TV-PG-D—mild suggestive dialogue

TV-14—probably unsuitable for children under 14
    TV-14-V—strong violence
    TV-14-L—moderate coarse language
    TV-14-S—moderate sexual situations
    TV-14-D—moderate suggestive dialogue

TV-MA—mature audiences only
    TV-MA-V—extreme violence
    TV-MA-L—strong coarse language
    TV-MA-S—strong sexual situations

Exhibit 4.20
The television program rating system.

cablecasters for years (see Chapter 3). But this 1992 law allowed broadcast stations to choose whether they wanted to ensure they were carried on local cable systems for free (must carry) or wanted to have the right to ask cable systems to pay for the privilege of carrying their signal (retransmission consent). If they chose the latter, the cable systems had the right to refuse to pay, and then the station would not receive money and also would not be carried on the cable system. After a rather unstable period, most stations chose retransmission consent and most cable systems were willing to pay the stations, which were a valuable asset on their systems. The stations became used to this extra money stream and, in fact, the networks they were affiliated with started to ask for some of the money because they supplied much of the programming.[39]

4.16 Programming Changes

There have been content and structure changes related to modern broadcast TV programming. One major change is the addition of a new genre—**reality TV.** The genre came to the fore in the 1990s, featuring actual events or reenactments of events, some of which were bizarre. Networks and stations liked these programs because they garnered fairly large audiences and were inexpensive to produce. The reality genre experienced a big jump in popularity in the summer of 2000 when CBS broadcast *Survivor,* the trials and tribulations of specially selected ordinary citizens as they overcame challenges of living in the South Seas and competed for a $1 million prize by voting each other off the island (see Exhibit 4.21).

reality TV

Exhibit 4.21

The original *Survivor* took many twists and turns before Richard Hatch was voted the winner of the $1 million prize. Here the Tagi tribe, which included Hatch, arrives on the island.

The series was such a success that many clones and variations appeared in the following years, including more *Survivor* series and NBC's *The Apprentice,* starring Donald Trump, who made "You're fired" a well-known phrase as contestants aspiring to a job with his firm were eliminated. High-stakes game shows, which had been sparse in prime time since the scandals of the 1950s, also made a comeback, particularly with the 1999 ABC hit *Who Wants to Be a Millionaire?* hosted originally by Regis Philbin (see Exhibit 4.22). Fox's singing competition show, *American Idol,* which started in 2002, became a ratings leader week after week and year after year, and NBC's *The Voice* showed that a gentler style of singing competition show could become popular.[40]

Music became popular in the drama genre, too, with Fox's *Glee,* about a group of misfits in a high school glee club, becoming a

other shows   major hit starting in 2009. Other older **genre** programs captured the audience's fancy, including comedies such as *Cheers, Seinfeld, Friends,* and *The Office* (see Exhibit 4.23) and dramas such as *Law and Order, 24, CSI, ER,* and *LOST.* Production qualities for these shows improved greatly from the early days and many episodes of dramas were prepared with the care and expense usually reserved for theatrical movies.[41]

4.17 Growth of Hispanic Television

As the demographics of the nation changed to include more Spanish-speaking people, Spanish-language programming increased. The two largest program distributors are Univision and Telemundo.

Univision traces its roots back to 1955 and the establishment of the first U.S. Spanish-language TV station, KCOR, in San Antonio, Texas. The station was a money-loser and in 1961 was sold to people who had ties to what became Mexico's main TV force, Televisa. The new owners improved the station's fortunes, mainly by airing Televisa's programming. In 1963, the group signed on KMEX-TV in Los Angeles and called itself Spanish International Network (SIN). For more than 20 years SIN was shown on Spanish-language broadcast TV stations and as a cable TV network.

In 1986, the owners sold the network to a partnership of Televisa and Hallmark Cards. This group changed the name to Univision and started producing some programs specifically for Hispanic Americans, such as *TV Mujer,* a magazine show aimed at Latinas living in

Exhibit 4.22

Host Regis Philbin on the set of *Who Wants to Be a Millionaire?*

the United States. In 2007, Univision was sold to a group of equity investors, most of whom were not of Hispanic descent. The relationship between Televisa and Univision deteriorated over the years, with Televisa threatening to stop supplying Univision with its popular **telenovelas.** Televisa felt it was not being properly compensated and, in 2009, after a nasty court battle, won a handsome financial payment from Univision. The agreement assured that Televisa would continue to supply Univision with telenovelas.[42]

Univision and Telemundo

Telemundo was launched as TV station, WKAQ, in Puerto Rico in 1954. During the 1970s and 1980s, the station produced many popular Puerto Rican telenovelas. In 1987, a Spanish-language Los Angeles station purchased WKAQ and several other stations and set up the Telemundo Group. The group went through a number of management changes and programming failures—including trying to let the Hollywood community produce its telenovelas. In 2001, NBC purchased Telemundo and has successfully achieved its aim of narrowing the ratings gap between Telemundo and Univision. Telemundo has always produced most of its own programming, and NBC has supported this policy financially and philosophically.[43]

Although Univision still leads in the ratings, both networks are successfully ensconced in cable TV and Spanish-language broadcasting. This success has encouraged others to enter the Spanish-language TV business.[44]

Exhibit 4.23

Steve Carell, star of *The Office*, a sitcom about everyday life at a paper company, accepting a Golden Globe award.

4.18 Digital TV and HDTV

In 2009, the United States switched from **analog** TV to **digital television (DTV).** Digital TV had been a long time coming and brought about a certain amount of confusion. Part of the problem lay in misunderstanding of the terms digital TV and **high-definition television (HDTV).** The two are intertwined but not the same. Digital TV uses technology similar to computers, with signals coded as either off (0) or on (1). High-definition TV has more lines on the TV screen—about 1,000 as compared to the 525 lines of the traditional **standard-definition (SD)** analog TV—and also has a wider screen (see Chapter 13). HDTV can be analog or digital, and digital TV can be standard or high definition, but the 2009 change was mostly related to digital HDTV.

DTV and HDTV

HDTV was originally developed by the Japanese in the 1970s as an analog system. At one point during the 1980s, it was almost adopted in the United States and other parts of the world, but the plan fell apart. In 1990, the American company General Instrument proposed an all-digital high-definition system that had the technical advantages inherent in digital technology, such as clearer sound

history

and no loss of quality when tapes are copied. In 1993, a consortium of companies called the Grand Alliance joined to further develop this digital system, which in 1997 was adopted by the FCC to be the American system. In 1998, the FCC gave broadcast stations new frequencies for digital HDTV transmission—channels that were to be developed while the stations continued to broadcast on their old analog channels. All stations were supposed to have their digital channels up and running by May 2002, but because of technical problems and because it costs up to $4 million to convert to digital, many stations fell behind schedule. After several postponements of the conversion to digital, it finally took place in 2009.[45]

must-carry

Consumers with analog sets have had to buy new sets, buy conversion boxes for their old sets, or be attached to cable TV systems that convert digital signals to analog. One of the controversies that has arisen related to the conversion is the old issue of must-carry. The frequencies given to broadcast stations for their digital signal were originally intended to carry just one HDTV digital channel. But as technology improved, stations found they could use the frequencies to broadcast one or two additional standard definition signals, called **secondary channels.** A number of stations are doing just that, with programming they provide themselves or purchase from other sources, such as continuous local weather, Spanish-language programming, and movies. The stations want the cable systems to carry all of their channels, but the FCC has ruled, at least for the present, that the cable systems must carry only the **primary channel** that is high definition. The FCC has also ruled that cable systems need to carry both digital and analog versions of primary channels for three years. Cable systems are lobbying to carry only the digital versions.[46]

auctions

The FCC has taken back the analog frequencies that the TV stations originally had and **auctioned** them off. Most of them have gone to cell phone companies, particularly AT&T and Verizon, with some going to satellite TV companies. Eventually these companies may use them to enhance wireless services.[47]

The adoption of high-definition TV, combined with large screens and **surround sound** systems, leads to a better television viewing experience. It may also lead to structural changes within the industry as different production and distribution companies vie for their piece of the pie. But change is nothing new for this dynamic industry.

4.19 Broadcasting and Newer Technologies

ratings decline

The new distribution technologies that have sprung forth since the 1970s have had a great effect on broadcast television. The first was cable TV, which rose rapidly in the 1980s (see Chapter 3). People were predicting that broadcasting would falter and cable would dominate. To some extent this happened, but it happened slowly—an evolution, not a revolution. Programming on ABC, CBS, and NBC, which once could commandeer ratings in the high 20s now struggles to get as high as 10 (see Exhibit 4.24). However, the broadcast ratings are still higher than those of most cable network programs, and broadcasting is still considered the way to reach a mass audience.[48]

The Prime-Time Share of Audience for Broadcast Television

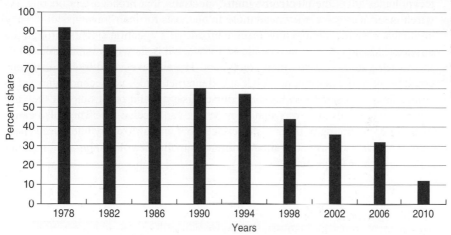

Exhibit 4.24

The share of audience for broadcast TV has dipped continuously since the advent of cable TV networks and other new technologies.

Hulu

Broadcasters have not remained oblivious to the power and potential of the internet (see Chapter 2). They have used it as another platform for their programming, mainly by allowing people to access old programs through their computers, often for free. The networks set up **streaming video** and **downloading** capabilities on their websites and also utilized their sites to obtain interest and participation from their audience members. People could vote for their favorite singers, suggest plot ideas, and in other ways be a part of the network interactive process. In 2007 NBC and Fox joined together to form Hulu and were later joined by ABC. Hulu became the place to go to view NBC, Fox, and ABC TV programs (and some other fare) for free. However, in 2011 the three networks rethought the "for free" idea and required payment for newer and more popular programs.[49]

portable standard

Portable platforms are on the minds of broadcasters also. TV stations have approved a technical standard for delivering local broadcast signals to smartphones, pads, small digital TV sets, laptops, in-car entertainment systems, and the like. Stations are experimenting with sending their regular programming plus additional material such as weather reports and traffic updates. Broadcasters also use these portable devices in conjunction with their programs. Twitter activity greatly increases when tied to a TV show, something that benefits both the broadcasters and Twitter and leads to more of a shared experience for audience members. Both Twitter and Facebook are often "second screens" that are in operation while people watch network programs.[50]

NBC-U Comcast merger

In 2011, what was NBC-Universal merged with Comcast. Now Comcast, as the largest cable TV and internet provider, has control over a major broadcast network and studio. Part of the stated reason for the merger was to increase opportunities for multiplatform interaction. The government imposed restrictions on the merger so that Comcast could not overwhelm competing companies. For example, it must allow others to show NBC programming. But the merger does provide an opportunity to change business models of media practitioners and the user experience of media consumers.[51]

frequency
jeopardy

The biggest threat to broadcasters related to new technologies is that these technologies covet the **electromagnetic spectrum** that broadcasters occupy. As wireless services grow, they need more frequencies for their transmissions. They argue that very few people now receive broadcast TV station signals through the airwaves. Most people watch broadcast TV when it is shown by their cable, satellite, or telco services or on their computers. The airwaves used by local stations could be used for smartphones, high-speed internet, pads, and technologies yet to come. Broadcast station owners, of course, disagree and point out that they are the only potentially free way that poor people can receive TV. They also claim that they are planning to offer more services that will utilize any underused spectrum. They have, however, warmed somewhat to the idea of being paid for giving up some of their frequencies.[52]

4.20 **Issues** and the Future

marginalization

The main issue facing broadcast television is whether or not it will be marginalized. As other technologies gain in audience and acceptance, the old broadcasting model has to struggle to remain relevant. For example, local broadcasting stations seem to add little to the media structure. The only locally based programming produced by many stations is local news, but cable systems could take over that task. Most stations simply pipe through programming sent by networks or show old movies and TV shows. There is no technical reason why CBS or any other network could not simply put its programming on a cable channel, in the same manner as USA or Discovery, and bypass the local stations. The historical loyalty between broadcast networks and the stations that carry their programs is what prevents this. But that relationship has its rocky moments.[53]

financial fate

Financially, owning a TV station used to be referred to as a "license to print money." But, now that there are many platforms where advertisers can place their money, this saying no longer holds. Because of rising costs and lower advertising income, broadcasters have become dependent on retransmission fees from cable systems, but the stability of those is uncertain. The networks have been fortunate that reality programming has become popular because it is cheaper to produce than most other types of programming. If audiences grow tired of this programming, networks and stations may encounter more of a financial crunch caused by the cost of additional dramas and sitcoms.[54]

fin-syn effects

Now that fin-syn no longer exists, networks are producing much of their own programming. Independent producers are few and far between. This translates into fewer points of view in programming and a loss of some creative voices.

public
broadcasting

Public broadcasting, even more than its commercial brethren, seems to have become irrelevant. Many cable networks show documentaries and art-oriented programs, which originally were the domain of PBS. The cable networks have more money to produce these shows because they can advertise. As government funding flounders, public television finds it hard to produce material that will catch the fancy of audience members.

The merger of NBC-U and Comcast has the potential for taking broadcasting in innovative directions. But many companies that are that large have stumbled under their own weight. They are not nimble enough to react quickly as the tastes of the fickle public change.

merger

If broadcasters fail to handle their businesses in innovative ways, they may find their fortunes waning. Some station owners, especially those near retirement age, may see selling their station frequencies as a way to save the value of their assets. If that snowball starts to roll, the broadcasting structure, as it exists, may disappear.

frequencies

On a brighter note, none of this will happen quickly. Broadcasting has remained strong longer than any of the media forms with which it competes. Other forms have fallen by the wayside while networks and stations have survived in viable fashion. Broadcasting's viability will depend on the resourcefulness of the young people who lead it into the future.

future

4.21 Summary

Broadcast TV, as the original form of television, has a rich history that includes developments in technology, government interactions, and programming.

Experimentation with mechanical and electronic scanning dates back to the 1880s and involves work by Farnsworth and Zworykin. Once the picture was adequately developed in the 1940s, color became a major issue. CBS favored a mechanical wheel while RCA proposed an electronic system compatible with black and white screens. The RCA system eventually won FCC approval, but it wasn't until the 1960s that color TV was widespread. Videotape recorders were invented in the 1950s and changed production techniques. Portable equipment made it easier to cover news stories. The switch from analog to digital TV and HDTV improved quality in 2009. Broadcast TV has been influenced by the newer technologies such as cable TV and the internet.

Many laws from Congress and rulings from the FCC have affected broadcast TV. The FCC made the decision to go with the 525-line system used for many years and also imposed the freeze from 1948 to 1952 that led to a reorganization of frequencies. Senator Joseph McCarthy was the main force behind blacklisting and it was the Senate that censored him. FCC Chairman Newton Minow's chastisement of broadcasters for their "vast wasteland" led to programming changes. Congress passed the Public Broadcasting Act of 1967 that established the public TV structure. Regulations established and retracted fin-syn, PTAR, and family hour. The deregulation of the 1980s lengthened the terms of licenses and, in general, favored station owners. The Telecommunications Act of 1996 brought about the v-chip and program ratings. The retransmission policies have brought a second stream of money to broadcasters.

Television programming has come a long way from the buses full of equipment that experimentally covered events in New York in the 1930s. The earliest of regular programming was sports because most sets were in bars. When TV entered the home in the late 1940s, children's programming was popular. Most watched of all was Milton Berle. Soon thereafter, *I Love Lucy* started as a show that was filmed, unlike most other shows of the period, which were live. These live dramas of the 1950s were highly acclaimed as were some of the contributions of Pat Weaver, such as spectaculars and the *Today* show. Once many programs were filmed, westerns became very popular. News was a minor programming form in the 1950s because of the difficulty of managing equipment to cover events. The quiz scandals temporarily tainted TV. In the 1960s, broadcasters programmed many documentaries and also covered the turmoil of the decade including the Vietnam War, the riots outside the convention hall in Chicago, the Kennedy-Nixon debates, and Kennedy's funeral. Most of the shows of the 1970s were produced by independent production companies, and some were more edgy than in the past. During the 1980s, network ownerships changed and Fox was added as a network. In the 1990s Hispanic TV grew and reality TV became a popular genre. Today many of the popular shows have excellent production techniques.

Suggested Websites

www.philotfarnsworth.com (the official family site for TV inventor Philo T. Farnsworth)

www.davidsarnoff.org (the David Sarnoff library, which contains articles about his life and about TV and radio in general)

www.chicagotelevision.com/dumont.htm (a site devoted to the history of the DuMont Network)

www.americanrhetoric.com/speeches/newtonminow.htm (complete text and audio of Newton Minow's speech)

www.museum.tv (site for the Museum of Broadcast Communications, which contains a wealth of information about the history of TV)

Notes

1. These early mechanical systems are described in A. A. Dinsdale, *First Principles of Television* (New York: Wiley, 1932) and in the first volume of the authoritative three-volume history of broadcasting by Erik Barnouw published in New York by Oxford University Press. The titles and dates are *A Tower in Babel: A History of Broadcasting in the United States to 1933* (1966); *The Golden Web: A History of Broadcasting in the United States 1933–1953* (1968); and *The Image Empire: A History of Broadcasting in the United States from 1953* (1970).
2. For more on Farnsworth, see Donald G. Godfrey, *Philo T. Farnsworth: The Father of Television* (Salt Lake City: University of Utah Press, 2001).
3. Barnouw, *A Tower in Babel,* 66, 154, 210. For Zworykin's own view of the electronics of TV, see Vladimir Zworykin, *The Electronics of Image Transmission in Color and Monochrome* (New York: Wiley, 1954).

4. Barnouw, *The Golden Web*, 126.
5. Ibid., 126–30.
6. Ibid., 242–44.
7. "The Death of the DuMont Network," *Emmy*, August 1990, 96–103.
8. Robert K. Avery and Robert Pepper; "An Institutional History of Public Broadcasting," *Journal of Communication*, Summer 1980, 126–38; and Barnouw, *The Golden Web*, 295.
9. Barnouw, *The Golden Web*, 285–90.
10. "For the Love of Lucy," *Emmy*, July/August 2006, 60–63.
11. Mike Conway, "A Guest in Our Living Room: The Television Newscaster before the Rise of the Dominant Anchor," *Journal of Broadcasting & Electronic Media*, September 2007, 457–78.
12. Matthew C. Ehrlich, "Radio Prototype: Edward R. Murrow and Fred Friendly's *Hear It Now*," *Journal of Broadcasting & Electronic Media*, September 2007, 438–56.
13. *Red Channels: The Report on Communists in Radio and Television* (New York: Counterattack, 1950); and "Hollywood Blacklist," *Emmy*, Summer 1981, 30–32.
14. Barnouw, *The Image Empire*, 22–23.
15. "Pat Weaver: Visionary or Dilettante?" *Emmy*, Fall 1979, 32–34.
16. Clifford G. Erickson and Hyman M. Chausow, *Chicago's TV College: Final Report of a Three-Year Experiment* (Chicago: Chicago City Junior College, 1960); and Mary Howard Smith, *Midwest Program on Airborne Television Instruction: Using Television in the Classroom* (New York: McGraw-Hill, 1960).
17. Daniel E. Garvey, "Introducing Color Television: The Audience and Programming Problems," *Journal of Broadcasting*, Fall 1980, 515–26; and "Color-TV Gaining Momentum," *Hollywood Reporter*, October 2, 1963, 1.
18. "The Videotape Recorder Turns 50," *TV Technology*, April 12, 2006, 26–27; and "The End of the Trail," *Emmy*, September–October 1984, 50–54.
19. "Dress Rehearsals Complete with Answers?" *U.S. News*, October 19, 1959, 60–62; and Susan L. Brinson, "Epilogue to the Quiz Show Scandal: A Case Study of the FCC and Corporate Favoritism," *Journal of Broadcasting & Electronic Media*, June 2003, 276–88.
20. "Debates in Retrospect," *New Republic*, November 21, 1960, 18–19.
21. "Covering the Tragedy: President Kennedy's Assassination," *Time*, November 29, 1963, 84; and "Did Press Pressure Kill Oswald?" *U.S. News*, April 6, 1964, 78–79.
22. Michael J. Arlen, *Living Room War* (New York: Viking Press, 1969); and "Looking Back at 'The Living Room War,'" *RTNDA Communicator*, March 1987, 12–13.
23. "The Wasteland Revisited," *Broadcasting & Cable*, May 16, 2011, 30.
24. Some of the works that deal with TV programming include: Irving Settl, *A Pictorial History of Television* (New York: Frederick Ungar, 1983); Alex McNeil, *Total Television: A Comprehensive Guide to Programming from 1948 to the Present* (New York: Viking Penguin, 1991); "The Twenty Top Shows of the Decade," *TV Guide*, December 9, 1989, 20–27; and "The Unforgettables," *Emmy*, July/August 2006, 60–63.
25. The Public Broadcasting Act of 1967, Public Law 90-129, 90th Congress (November 7, 1967).
26. Robert M. Pepper, *The Formation of the Public Broadcasting Service* (New York: Arno Press, 1979); "Jolly Good," *Emmy*, Issue No. 2, 2011, 26–27; and "In the Beginning, Before PBS," *TV Technology*, April 11, 2007, 46–47.
27. "Twenty Tumultuous Years of CPB," *Broadcasting*, May 11, 1987, 60–75.
28. "The 80 Greatest Moments on TV," *Hollywood Reporter*, December 22, 2010, 94–97; and "Still Digging the Big D," *Emmy*, Issue No. 7, 2011, 20–21.
29. "Fin-Syn," *Broadcasting and Cable*, January 24, 2000, 30.
30. "FCC Gives Prime-Time Access Rule the Ax," *Los Angeles Times*, July 27, 1995, D-1.
31. "'Family Hour' OK but Not by Coercion," *Daily Variety*, November 5, 1976, 1.
32. "Capcities/ABC," *Broadcasting*, March 25, 1985, 31; and "Disney to Buy Cap Cities/ABC for $19 Billion, Vault to No. 1," *Los Angeles Times*, August 1, 1995, A-1.
33. "General Electric Will Buy RCA for $6.28 Billion," *Los Angeles Times*, December 12, 1985, A-1; and "Feds Bless NBC-U Wedding Plan," *Daily Variety*, April 21, 2004, 4.
34. "CBS Gleam in Ted Turner's Eye," *Broadcasting*, March 4, 1985, 35; "Tisch Does What CBS Feared in Turner," *Wall Street Journal*, November 20, 1987, 6; and "Group W-CBS Deal OK'd," *Electronic Media*, November 27, 1995, 2.

35. "The Fox Files," *Hollywood Reporter,* April 15, 2002, S1–S2; and "Ground Breakers," *Emmy,* Issue No. 6, 2009, 30–37.

36. "You Got Bailed: TW, AOL Split," *Hollywood Reporter,* May 29–31, 2009, 1.

37. "FCC Strikes the Flag on TV Ownership Rules," *Broadcasting,* August 13, 1984, 35.

38. "New Law of the Land," *Broadcasting & Cable,* February 5, 1996, 8; and "Finally, Ratings Agreement," *Electronic Media,* July 14, 1997, 1.

39. "Looking Back at Retransmission," *Electronic Media,* March 4, 2002, 1

40. "Taking 'Survivor' Lessons," *Broadcasting & Cable,* August 21, 2000, 12; and "What's So Real About Reality TV?" *Emmy,* October 2000, 47–49.

41. "For Hugs and Hard Work, It's Gotta Be Glee," *Emmy,* Issue No. 2, 2011, 22.

42. "Univision Sale Facing Vote Today," *Hollywood Reporter,* September 27, 2006, 6; and "Televisa, Univision Settle," *Los Angeles Times,* January 23, 2009, C-1.

43. "NBC to Acquire Telemundo Network for $1.98 Billion," *Los Angeles Times,* October 12, 2001, C-1; and "Best of Both Worlds," *Emmy,* Issue No. 5, 2011, 78–81.

44. "Hispanic TV Takes Off in the U.S.," *Wall Street Journal,* September 7, 2000, B-1.

45. "HDTV: From 1925 to 1994," *TV Technology,* August 4, 2004, 42; "FCC Starts Digital Clock," *Daily Variety,* April 4, 1997, 1; and "Staggering Toward DTV," *Broadcasting & Cable,* February 16, 2009, 4; and "Life After Analog TV," *Broadcasting & Cable,* June 15, 2009, 3.

46. "Local Stations Multiply," *Broadcasting & Cable,* March 10, 2008, 16–17.

47. "AT&T, Verizon in Airwaves Grab; A Win for Google?" *Wall Street Journal,* March 21, 2008, B-1.

48. "A Collective Sigh of Grief for Networks," *Hollywood Reporter,* May 22, 2009, 8.

49. "Hulu's Site's Owners Call off Sale," *Los Angeles Times,* October 14, 2011, B-1; and "The Call of the Web," *Emmy,* March/April, 2008, 26–27.

50. "Mobile DTV Standard Approved," *TV Technology,* November 4, 2009, 8; and "Taking the Passivity Out of Watching TV," *TV Technology,* March 18, 2011, 10.

51. "NBComcast," *Hollywood Reporter,* November 13, 2009, 24–25; and "With Comcast-NBCU Closed, Staffers Brace or Change," *Broadcasting & Cable,* January 31, 2011, 4.

52. "Television's Spectral Gold Mine," *Wall Street Journal,* October 10–11, 2009, B12; and "FCC to Push Ahead on Broadband Agenda," *Wall Street Journal,* April 9, 2010.

53. "This Way, Not That," *Emmy,* Issue No. 1, 2010, 11.

54. "Going for Broke," *Emmy,* Issue No. 2, 2010, 40–43.

Chapter 5

RADIO AND AUDIO

Radio knows how to reinvent itself. At present it consists largely of music, talk, and news. This, however, has not always been the case. During the 1930s and 1940s, radio was the main source of national entertainment programming. Most of the models of entertainment and information that are common to the media today were formed by radio during those years. When television took away radio's audience in the 1950s, some believed radio would die, but today it is a viable medium that enters homes, automobiles, and many other places people inhabit.

> It is inconceivable that we should allow so great a possibility for public service as broadcasting to be drowned in advertising chatter.
>
> **Herbert Hoover, while serving as Secretary of Commerce**

It, like other older media, has been affected by the internet and portable platforms. The accessibility of music through other audio channels has been a particular challenge to radio stations—a challenge that is still continuing. Although radio must continually reassess its role in society, it has a rich history to aid it.

5.1 Early Inventions

The beginnings of radio are veiled in dispute. People living in various countries devised essentially the same inventions. Ironically, this was partly because no communication system was available for people to learn what others were inventing. This led to numerous claims, counterclaims, and patent suits.

Maxwell and Hertz

Many people believe that radio originated in 1873 when James Clerk Maxwell, a British physics professor, published his theory of electromagnetism, which predicted the existence of **radio waves**. During the 1880s, a German physics professor, Heinrich Hertz, undertook experiments to prove Maxwell's theory. Hertz actually generated the radio energy that Maxwell had theorized at one end of his laboratory and transmitted it to the other end.[1]

Marconi

Guglielmo Marconi (see Exhibit 5.1) expanded upon radio principles. Marconi, the son of a wealthy Italian father and an Irish mother, was scientifically inclined from an early age. Fortunately, he had the leisure and wealth to pursue his interests. Soon after he heard of Hertz's ideas, he began working fanatically, finally reaching a point where he could transmit the dots and dashes of Morse code using radio waves. Marconi wrote to the Italian government in an attempt to interest it in his project but to no avail. His determined mother decided he should take his invention to England. There, in 1897, he received a patent and the financial backing to set up the Marconi Wireless Telegraph Company, Ltd. Under the auspices of this company, Marconi continued to improve on **wireless** technology and began to supply equipment to ships. In 1899, he formed a subsidiary company in the United States.[2]

Fleming and DeForest

People became intrigued with the idea of transmitting voices. In 1904, John Fleming of Britain took a significant step in this direction when he developed the **vacuum tube,** which led the way to voice transmission. Three years later, American inventor Lee De Forest (see Exhibit 5.2) patented the **audion tube,** which was an improvement on Fleming's tube in that it was capable of amplifying sound

Exhibit 5.1

Guglielmo Marconi shown here with wireless apparatus (about 1902).

to a much greater degree than was previously possible. De Forest, like Marconi, was fascinated with electronics at an early age and later secured financial backing to form his own company. However, he experienced management and financial problems that frequently rendered him penniless and led him to sell his patent rights. De Forest strongly advocated voice transmission for entertainment purposes. In 1910, he broadcast the singing of Enrico Caruso from the New York Metropolitan Opera House. Several years later, he started a radio station of sorts in the Columbia Gramophone Building, playing Columbia records (he later referred to himself as the first disc jockey) in hopes of increasing their sales.[3]

5.2 The Sinking of the *Titanic*

During its early stages, radio grew with very few government controls. The first congressional law to mention radio was passed in 1910; it required all ships holding more than 50 passengers to carry radios for safety purposes.

The rules concerning this safety requirement were not very effective, as was proven with the 1912 sinking of the *Titanic*. As the "unsinkable" *Titanic* sped through the night on its maiden voyage, radio operators on other ships warned it of icebergs in the area. The *Titanic*'s radio operator, concerned with transmitting messages for the many famous passengers, passed the warnings on to the captain, who disregarded them. The wireless operator transmitted SOS signals when the *Titanic* struck the fatal iceberg about midnight on April 14, but none of the nearby ships that could have helped save some of the 1,500 passengers and crew who died heard the distress calls because their wireless operators had signed off for the night.

The operators on land who had been receiving the passengers' messages also heard the distress calls, so for the first time in history people knew of a distant tragedy as it was happening. One wireless operator decoding the messages in New York was reputed to be David Sarnoff (see Exhibit 5.3), who later became

Titanic calls

Exhibit 5.3

David Sarnoff working at his radio station position atop the Wanamaker store in New York where he heard the *Titanic*'s distress call.

an important broadcasting person. He and others relayed information about the rescue efforts to anxious friends and relatives and to newspapers. This brought wireless communication to the attention of the general public for the first time.

Soon after the sinking of the *Titanic,* Congress passed the Radio Act of 1912; it emphasized safety and required everyone who transmitted on radio waves to obtain a license from the secretary of commerce. The secretary could not refuse **licenses** a license but could assign particular wavelengths to particular transmitters. Thus, ship transmissions were kept separate from amateur transmissions, which, in turn, were separate from government transmissions. All this was done without any thought of broadcasting as we know it today.[4]

5.3 World War I

patent problems   In 1917, during World War I, the U.S. government took over all radio operation. Prior to this, Marconi's company, still the leader in wireless, had aroused the concern of American Telephone and Telegraph (AT&T) by suggesting the possibility of starting a wireless phone business. AT&T, in an effort to maintain its supremacy in the telephone business, had acquired some wireless patents, primarily those of Lee De Forest. The stalemate that grew out of the refusal of Marconi's company, AT&T, and several smaller companies to allow one another to interchange patents had stifled the technical growth of radio. Because of the war, these disputes were set aside so the government could develop the transmitters and receivers needed.

World War I also ushered two other large companies into the radio field: General Electric (GE) and Westinghouse, both established manufacturers of light **GE and** bulbs. GE and Westinghouse assumed responsibility for manufacturing vacuum **Westinghouse** tubes because both light bulbs and radio tubes require a vacuum. General Electric had also participated in the development of the **alternator,** used to improve long-distance wireless.

The patent problem returned after the war, and GE began negotiating with **navy intervention** Marconi's company to sell the rights to its alternator. The navy, which had controlled radio during the war, feared this sale would enable the Marconi company to achieve a monopoly on radio communication. The navy did not want radio controlled by a foreign company, so it convinced GE to renege on the Marconi deal. This cancellation left GE sitting with an expensive patent from which it could not profit because GE did not control other patents necessary for its utilization, but the patent placed GE in an excellent negotiating position.[5]

5.4 The Founding of RCA

What ensued was a series of discussions among Marconi, AT&T, GE, and Westinghouse that culminated in the formation of Radio Corporation of America (RCA) in 1919. The Marconi American subsidiary, realizing that it would not receive navy contracts as long as it was controlled by the British, transferred its assets to RCA. AT&T, GE, and Westinghouse bought blocks of RCA stock and agreed to make patents available to one another, thus averting the patent problem and allowing radio to grow. This was undertaken with ship-to-shore transmission in mind, not entertainment broadcasting.[6]

company involvement

One person who saw entertainment possibilities was David Sarnoff, a Russian immigrant who at age 15 had become an employee of Marconi and at age 21 received distress messages from the *Titanic*. Apparently, at the age of 24, he wrote a memo to Marconi management suggesting entertainment radio that read in part as follows:[7]

> I have in mind a plan of development which would make radio a "household utility" in the same sense as the piano or phonograph. The idea is to bring music into the home by wireless. . . . The receiver can be designed in the form of a simple "Radio Music Box" and arranged for several different wavelengths, which should be changeable with the throwing of a single switch or pressing of a single button. . . . The same principle can be extended to numerous other fields as, for example, receiving lectures at home which can be made perfectly audible; also, events of national importance can be simultaneously announced and received. Baseball scores can be transmitted in the air by the use of one set installed at the Polo Grounds. . . . This proposition would be especially interesting to farmers and others in outlying districts removed from cities. By purchase of a "Radio Music Box," they could enjoy concerts, lectures, music recitals, etc. . . .

Sarnoff's memo

This idea was not acted upon, and Sarnoff, who joined RCA when RCA bought out Marconi, had to wait for a more propitious time.

5.5 Early Radio Stations

Meanwhile, many amateur radio enthusiasts began undertaking experiments. One was Frank Conrad, an employee of Westinghouse in Pittsburgh (see Exhibit 5.4). From his garage he programmed music and talk during his spare time. A local department store began selling wireless reception sets and placed an ad for these in a local newspaper, mentioning that the sets could receive Conrad's broadcasts. One of Conrad's superiors at Westinghouse saw the ad and envisioned a market. Until this time, both radio transmission and reception had been for the technical-minded who could assemble their own sets. It was obvious that sets could be pre-assembled for everyone who wished to listen to what was being transmitted.

Conrad

Exhibit 5.4
Frank Conrad, who worked with experimental equipment and supervised the construction of KDKA.

Exhibit 5.4

Frank Conrad, who worked with experimental equipment and supervised the construction of KDKA.

Conrad was asked to build a stronger transmitter at the Westinghouse plant, one capable of broadcasting on a regular schedule so that people who purchased receivers would be assured listening fare. In 1920, Westinghouse applied to the Department of Commerce for a special type of license to begin a broadcasting service. The station was given the call letters KDKA (see Exhibit 5.5) and was authorized to use a frequency away from amateur interference. Because Westinghouse was the first to acquire this type of license, KDKA is generally considered

Exhibit 5.5

A tent atop a Westinghouse building in Pittsburgh served as KDKA's first studio. It caused some of early radio's unusual moments, such as the whistle of a passing freight train heard nightly at 8:30 and a tenor's aria abruptly concluded when an insect flew into his mouth.

the first radio station, but other stations that were experimenting at the same time also lay claim to the title of "first." KDKA launched its programming schedule with the Harding-Cox election returns, interspersed with music, and then continued with regular broadcasting hours. Public reaction could be measured by the long lines at department stores where radio receivers were sold.[8]

KDKA's success spurred others to enter broadcasting, including David Sarnoff, who now received more acceptance for the ideas in his memo. He convinced RCA management to invest $2,000 to cover the Jack Dempsey–Georges Carpentier fight on July 2, 1921, through a temporary transmitter set up in New Jersey. Fortunately, Dempsey knocked Carpentier out in the fourth round, for soon after, the overheated transmitter became a molten mass. This fight, however, helped to popularize radio, and both radio stations and sets multiplied rapidly. By 1923, radio licenses had been issued to more than 600 stations, and receiving sets were in nearly 1 million homes.[9]

The stations were owned and operated primarily by those who wanted to sell sets (Westinghouse, GE, RCA) and by retail department stores, as well as radio repair shops and universities that wanted to offer college credit courses that people could listen to in their homes. Unfortunately, all stations were on the same frequency—360 meters (approximately 830 on the AM dial). Stations in the same reception area worked out voluntary arrangements to share the frequency by broadcasting at different times of day. However, as more stations went on the air, interference became common. This was particularly hard on students trying to hear their lessons for college credit courses, and many universities had to cease this form of instruction.

Programming was no problem for these early radio stations. People were mainly interested in the novelty of picking up any signal on their battery-operated crystal headphone receivers. Programs consisted primarily of phonograph record music, call letter announcements, and performances by endless free talent who wandered in the door eager to display their virtuosity on this new medium (see "Zoom In" box).[10]

One programming form of the era was dubbed **potted palm music**—the kind played at teatime by hotel orchestras usually flanked by potted palms (see Exhibit 5.6). Sometimes a vocalist was featured, and sometimes a pianist or small instrumental group played. Sopranos outnumbered all other "potted palm" performers. Often the performers who "appeared" on radio wore tuxedos or evening gowns.

Drama was also attempted, even though engineers at first insisted that men and women needed to use separate microphones placed some distance from each other. Performers found it difficult to play love scenes this way. Finally engineers "discovered" that men and women could share a microphone.

From time to time radio excelled in the public-affairs area, broadcasting political conventions and presidential speeches. Religious broadcasts were also part of early radio. Evangelist Aimee Semple McPherson operated a station in Los Angeles that frequently wandered off frequency. When the secretary of commerce threatened to shut down her station, she wired back, "Please order your minions of Satan to leave my station alone. You cannot expect the Almighty to abide by your wavelength nonsense."[11]

KDKA

boxing broadcast

interference

music

drama

information

ZOOM IN: **The Joys of Early Radio Programming**

Sometimes the use of amateurs on early radio created awkward situations. For example, a woman who was a strong advocate of birth control asked to speak on radio. The people at the station were nervous about what she might say, but when she assured them that she only wanted to recite some nursery rhymes, they allowed her into the studio. She then broadcast, "There was an old woman who lived in a shoe/She had so many children because she didn't know what to do." She was not invited back.

A Chicago man wanted to discuss Americanism over a Chicago station and even submitted a script ahead of time. He appeared at the station with a group of bodyguards, who assured no buttons were pushed to take him off the air. It turned out that he was a potentate of the Ku Klux Klan, and, digressing from the script, he extolled the virtues of white supremacy.

A young man in New Jersey wanted to let his mother know how he sounded over the air, so he dropped in at WOR, which had just opened a studio near the music department of a store. The singer the studio was expecting had not arrived, so this young man was put on the air before he even had time to notify his mother. He sang to piano accompaniment for more than an hour as a messenger rushed sheet music from the music counter to the studio.

A carbon microphone of the type used by many early performers.

Exhibit 5.6

Los Angeles's first station, KFI, began broadcasting in 1922. Although the audience heard only the audio, special attention was given to the studio's decor, including the potted palms.

5.6 The Rise of Advertising

As the novelty of radio wore off, people were less eager to perform, and some means had to be found for financing programming. Many ideas were proposed, including donations from citizens, tax levies on radio sets, and payment from radio set manufacturers. Commercials evolved largely by accident.

AT&T was involved mainly in the telephone business and, although it was a partner with RCA, was reluctant to see radio grow because such growth might diminish the demand for wired services. One of its broadcasting entries was closely akin to phone philosophy. It established station WEAF in New York as what it termed a **toll station:** AT&T would provide no programming, but anyone who wished to broadcast a message could pay a "toll" to AT&T and then air the message publicly, in much the same way as private messages were communicated by dropping money into pay telephones. In fact, the original studio was about the size of a phone booth. The idea did not take hold. AT&T realized that before people would pay to be heard, they wanted to be sure that someone was listening. As a result, WEAF began broadcasting entertainment material, drawing mainly on amateur talent found among its employees. Still there were no long lines of people willing to pay to have messages broadcast.

WEAF toll experiment

Finally, on August 22, 1922, WEAF aired its first income-producing program: a 10-minute message from the Queensboro Corporation, a Long Island real estate company, which paid $50 for the time. The commercial was just a simple courtesy announcement because AT&T ruled out direct advertising as being in poor taste. Many people of the era said that advertising on radio would never sell products and every dollar that WEAF obtained was a painful struggle.

Queensboro ad

Eventually, AT&T convinced the Department of Commerce that WEAF should have a different frequency. The argument was that other broadcasters were using stations for their own purposes, while WEAF was for everyone and therefore should have special standing and not be made to broadcast on 360 meters. As a result, WEAF and a few other stations were assigned to the 400-meter wavelength. This meant less interference and more broadcast time. The phone booth was abandoned, a new studio was erected, and showmanship took hold.[12]

WEAF frequency change

5.7 The Formation of Networks

AT&T began using phone lines for remote broadcasts because it was still predominantly in the phone business. It aired descriptions of football games over its long-distance lines and established toll stations in other cities that it interconnected by phone lines—in effect, establishing a network. During this time, AT&T did not allow other radio stations to use phone lines and also claimed sole rights to sell radio toll time. At first, other stations were not bothered because they were not considering selling ads. In fact, there was an anti-advertising sentiment in the early 1920s. For example, people thought that toothpaste should never be advertised because it was an intimate product. As the AT&T toll network emerged and began to prosper, however, other stations became discontented with second-class status. The fires were further fanned by a Federal Trade Commission inquiry that accused AT&T, RCA, GE, and Westinghouse of creating a monopoly in the radio business.

NBC

A series of closed hearings held by the major radio companies resulted in the 1926 formation of the National Broadcasting Company (NBC)—owned by RCA, GE, and Westinghouse. AT&T agreed to withdraw from radio programming in exchange for a long-term contract assuring that NBC would lease AT&T wires. This agreement earned the phone company millions of dollars per year. NBC also purchased WEAF from AT&T, thus embracing the concepts of both toll broadcasting and networking.

In November 1926, the NBC Red Network, which consisted of WEAF and a 23-station national hookup, was launched in a spectacular debut that aired a symphony orchestra from New York, a singer from Chicago, a comedian from Kansas City, and dance bands from various cities throughout the nation. A year later, NBC's Blue Network was officially launched, consisting of different stations and different programming.

In 1932, GE and Westinghouse withdrew from RCA, largely because of the U.S. attorney general's order that the group should be dispersed and partly because David Sarnoff, now president of RCA, believed his company should be its own entity. Another series of closed-door meetings resulted in a divorce settlement. RCA became the sole owner of NBC, and GE and Westinghouse received RCA bonds and some real estate. In retrospect, it appears that RCA walked off with the lion's share of value. But all this happened during the Depression, and GE and Westinghouse were not eager to keep what they thought might be an expensive broadcasting liability.[13]

CBS

ABC

Both RCA and NBC have an interesting parentage. NBC was originally owned by RCA, GE, and Westinghouse, which ousted AT&T in forming NBC. RCA was formed by GE, Westinghouse, and AT&T, which ousted Marconi during RCA's formation. The exact details of all these corporate maneuvers will probably never be known.

Exhibit 5.7
William S. Paley originally worked with his father, who owned a cigar company. The younger Paley took a six-month leave to get CBS going, but he never returned to the cigar business.

What eventually became the Columbia Broadcasting System (CBS) was founded in 1927 by a man who wanted to supply radio talent to stations. His plans did not work out, and his failing company was bought by the family of William S. Paley (see Exhibit 5.7). Paley became president and built a radio network that was similar in organization to NBC in that it consisted of a chain of stations. The network became successful, and during the 1930s and 1940s, Paley lured much of the top radio talent from NBC to CBS.[14]

The American Broadcasting Company (ABC) came into existence because of Federal Communications Commission (FCC) actions in the early 1940s. By 1940, the networks had established a power base that the FCC thought could be detrimental, so it attempted to limit their power by issuing rules that prohibited any company from owning more than one national radio network. Thus in 1943, NBC had to sell its Blue Network to a group of investors who, in 1945, changed the network's name to the American Broadcasting Company.[15]

A fourth radio network, Mutual Broadcasting Company, was formed in 1934 when four stations decided to work jointly to obtain advertising. Unlike the other networks, Mutual owned no stations. Instead, it sold ads and bought programs and then paid the stations in its network to carry the programs and the network ads. It also allowed stations to sell their own ads. Mutual, too, was involved with FCC regulations. NBC and CBS affiliate contracts stipulated that the local stations could not carry programs from a different network. In 1938, Mutual gained exclusive rights to broadcast the World Series, but the NBC and CBS contracts would not allow their affiliated stations to carry these games, even in cities where there were no Mutual stations. The people wanted the games, the stations wanted to carry them, and advertisers wanted to pay for the coverage. Nevertheless, many Americans did not hear the 1938 World Series. The FCC determined that this type of program thwarting was not in the public interest and issued a ruling that no station could have an arrangement with a network that hindered that station from broadcasting programs of another network.[16]

Mutual

5.8 Chaos and Government Action

The problem of broadcast frequency overcrowding continued to grow during the 1920s. Secretary of Commerce Herbert Hoover was besieged with requests that the broadcast frequencies be expanded and that stations be allowed to leave the 360-meter frequency band on which most of them were broadcasting. Hoover made attempts to improve the situation by altering station power and broadcast times, and he called four national radio conferences to discuss problems and solutions, but he was unable to deal with the problem in any systematic manner because he could not persuade Congress to give him the power to do so.

Hoover and radio

One ramification of the frequency situation was that commercial stations overpowered educational radio stations. In the early 1920s, educational and commercial stations often alternated hours on a shared frequency. If the commercial station decided it wanted a larger share of the time, it would petition the government and usually win because it could afford an expensive, time-consuming hearing in Washington while the educators could not. In addition, Hoover urged people who wished to enter broadcasting to buy an existing station rather than add one to the already overcrowded airwaves. As a result, many educational facilities were propositioned by commercial ventures and sold out.[17]

educational stations

By 1925, the interference problem was so widespread that Hoover threw up his hands and told radio station operators to regulate themselves as best they could. During 1926–27, 200 stations were created, most of them using any frequency or power they wished and changing at whim. With so much chaos, Congress finally acted and passed the **Radio Act of 1927.** The act proclaimed that radio waves belonged to the people and could be used by individuals only if they had a license and were broadcasting in the "public convenience, interest, or necessity." All previous licenses were revoked, and applicants were allowed 60 days to apply for new licenses from the newly created Federal Radio Commission (FRC). The commission then granted 620 licenses in what is now the **amplitude modulation (AM)** band.[18]

Radio Act of 1927

Several years later Congress passed the **Communications Act of 1934,** which created the Federal Communications Commission. This act was passed primarily because Congress decided that all regulation of communications

Communications Act of 1934

Exhibit 5.8

A home radio receiver with a loudspeaker speaker from about 1924.

should rest with one body. The FCC was given power over not just radio but also telephone and other forms of wired and wireless communications. As the act was being formulated, educators lobbied for 15 percent of the frequencies to be reserved for educational radio; however, they were unsuccessful in their bid.[19]

5.9 The Golden Era of Radio

With the chaotic frequency situation under control, radio was now ready to enter the era of truly significant programming development—a heyday that lasted some 20 years. Improvements in radio equipment helped. **Earphones** that only one person could use had already been replaced by **loudspeakers** so that the whole family could listen simultaneously (see Exhibit 5.8). Station equipment improved to include microphones with greater fidelity (see Exhibit 5.9). Portable equipment was introduced, even though it was cumbersome because of the size of early batteries (see Exhibit 5.10)

equipment improvements

Radio became the primary entertainment medium during the Depression. In 1930, 12 million homes were equipped with radio receivers; by 1940, this number had jumped to 30 million. During the same period, advertising revenue rose from $40 million to $155 million. In 1930, NBC Red, NBC Blue, and CBS offered approximately 60 combined hours of sponsored programs a week. By 1940, the four networks (Mutual had been added) carried 156 hours.[20]

Exhibit 5.9

An early station setup that included a multi-tubed audio board, a microphone, and receivers.

Exhibit 5.10

Early backpack equipment for remote radio broadcasting.

Exhibit 5.11
Amos 'n' Andy as it appeared when broadcasting from NBC's Hollywood Radio City. Freeman Fisher Gosden is on the left side of the table with Madaline Lee; Charles J. Correll is on the right. Sitting in the left foreground is the announcer, Bill Hay.

Amos 'n' Andy

The first program to generate nationwide enthusiasm was *Amos 'n' Andy* (see Exhibit 5.11). It was created by Freeman Fisher Gosden and Charles J. Correll, who met while working in vaudeville. Gosden and Correll, who were white, worked up a blackface act and tried it on WGN radio in Chicago as *Sam 'n' Henry*. When WGN did not renew their contract, they took the show to WMAQ in Chicago and changed the name to *Amos 'n' Andy* because WGN owned the title *Sam 'n' Henry*.

Correll and Gosden wrote all the material themselves and played most of the characters by changing the pitch and tone of their voices. Gosden always played Amos, a simple, hardworking fellow, and Correll played Andy, a clever, conniving, and somewhat lazy individual who usually took credit for Amos's ideas. According to the scripts, Amos and Andy had come from Atlanta to Chicago to seek their fortune, but all they had amassed was a broken-down automobile, known as the Fresh-Air Taxicab Company of America. Much of the show's humor revolved around a fraternity-type organization called the Mystic Knights of the Sea headed by a character called Kingfish, who was played by Gosden. The show's success caught the attention of the NBC Blue Network, which hired the two in 1929. Their program, which aired from 7:00 to 7:15 P.M. Eastern time, became such a nationwide hit that it affected dinner hours, plant closing times, and even the speaking schedule of the president of the United States.[21]

Benny

Many other comedians followed in the wake of the success of Correll and Gosden (see "Zoom In" box). One of the most listened to was Jack Benny. He and his wife and co-star Mary Livingston (see Exhibit 5.12) were sponsored for many years by Jell-O and Lucky Strike cigarettes. The show featured such surefire laugh provokers as an ancient Maxwell automobile that coughed and sputtered (aided by a talented sound effects man), Benny's perennial age of 39 years, a constant "feud" with fellow comedian Fred Allen, and Benny's horrible violin playing.

ZOOM IN: **A Sample of Old-Time Radio Comedians**

The simplicity of the comedy of the 1930s and 1940s may seem a little corny, but it captivated the audiences of the time. George Burns and Gracie Allen, who were husband and wife, started in vaudeville and worked together in radio, TV, and film. Many of the jokes of their radio program were plays on words based on Gracie's supposed empty-headedness. At one point she started searching for her "lost brother" by suddenly appearing on other shows to inquire about him. In 1940, she and George started a campaign of "Gracie Allen for President" and she actually received some write-in votes at election time.

Chester Lauck as Lum (left) and Norris Goff as Abner

where they grew up. In 1936, Waters changes its name to Pine Ridge in honor of the Lum and Abner show.

Edgar Bergen was a ventriloquist with a dummy named Charlie McCarthy. Bergen wasn't a particularly skilled ventriloquist, but that didn't matter on radio where no one could see his lips move. He had an excellent sense of comedic timing and developed the character of Charlie well. Charlie was a precocious child who was particularly fond of women and had supposed love affairs with about all the 1930s and 1940s beauties and even the 1950s movie star Marilyn Monroe. He also had a running feud with W. C. Fields, a regular on the show. The feud led to one-liner barbs such as: W. C.: "Step out of the sun, Charlie. You may come unglued." Charlie: "Mind if I stand in the shade of your nose."

Gracie Allen and George Burns

Childhood friends Chester Lauck and Norris Goff developed two hillbilly characters, Lum and Abner, who owned the Jot 'Em Down grocery store in the fictional town of Pine Ridge, Arkansas. The two were constantly coming up with money-making ideas, only to be thwarted by their main nemesis, Squire Skimp, who was a city slicker. However, Lum and Abner usually redeemed themselves in the end. Lauck and Goff often based their script ideas on events in Waters, Arkansas,

Left to right: W. C. Fields, Dorothy Lamour, Charlie McCarthy, and Edgar Bergen

Music, especially classical music, was also frequently aired. NBC established its own orchestra led by Arturo Toscanini (see Exhibit 5.13). *Your Hit Parade,* which featured the top-selling songs of the week, was introduced in 1935, and people who later became well-known singers, such as Kate Smith and Bing Crosby, took to the air. The big bands of the 1940s could also be heard over the airwaves (see Exhibit 5.14).

Some programs featured the general public. Among many talent shows, the most famous was *The Original Amateur Hour,* which, like today's *American Idol,* spawned stars—including Frank Sinatra. Quiz shows, such as *Professor Quiz,* rewarded people for responding with little-known facts. Stunt shows, such as *Truth or Consequences,* which required people to undertake silly assignments if they answered questions incorrectly, attracted large and faithful audiences.

Exhibit 5.12

Jack Benny and Mary Livingston performing in 1933.

Many programs were developed for children, including *Let's Pretend,* a multi-segment program that emphasized creative fantasy; *The Lone Ranger,* a western; *Quiz Kids,* a panel of precocious children who answered questions; and *Little Orphan Annie,* a drama about a child's trials and tribulations. During the day, many stations broadcast continuing dramas. These programs, called soap operas because soap manufacturers were frequent sponsors, always ended with an unresolved situation to entice listeners to "tune in tomorrow." Most did.

In the area of drama, the networks first tried to rebroadcast the sound of Broadway plays but discovered that this was akin to sitting in a theater blindfolded. So the networks hired writers to script original dramas for radio.

music

amateur participation

daytime shows

Exhibit 5.13

Arturo Toscanini, seen here conducting the NBC orchestra, was coaxed out of retirement in Italy by David Sarnoff, head of NBC and classical music lover. A special studio was built for the orchestra; because of its unique construction, it was referred to as the world's only floating studio.

drama

These dramas usually used many sound effects and were sponsored by one company that often incorporated its name into the program, such as *Lux Radio Theater* or *Collier's Hour.* In 1938, Orson Welles produced *The War of the Worlds,* a fantasy about a Martian invasion in New Jersey. Upon hearing the broadcast, an estimated 1.2 million people succumbed to hysteria. They panicked in the streets, fled to the country, and seized arms to prepare to fight—despite the fact that the *Mercury Theater* program included interruptions to inform the listeners that the presentation was only a drama.

The Depression spurred the growth of commercials. During the 1920s, advertisements were brief and tasteful and price was not mentioned. As radio stations and all facets of the American economy began digging for money, the commercial standards dissolved. Some advertisers believed commercials should irritate, and broadcasters, anxious for the buck, acquiesced. The commercials became long, loud, and cutthroat.

commercials

Most radio programs were produced not by the networks but by **advertising agencies.** These agencies found that personal help programs could effectively promote products. Listeners would send letters to radio human relations "experts" detailing traumas and transgressions and asking for help. Product box tops accompanying a letter qualified it for an answer; or the suggested solution might involve the sponsor's drug product or the contentment derived from puffing on the sponsor's brand of cigarette. By 1932, more airtime was spent on commercials than on news, education, and religion combined. The commercials brought in profits for networks and stations and for the advertising agencies that were intimately involved in most details of programming, including selecting program ideas, overseeing scripts, and selling and producing advertisements for the shows.

stunts

There were also many events that could be termed stunt broadcasts, such as those from widely separated points, gliders, and underwater locations. One music program featured a singer in New York accompanied by an orchestra in Buenos

Aires. These stunt broadcasts paved the way for the broadcasting of legitimate public events from distant points. In 1931, 19 locations around the world participated in a program dedicated to Marconi. People heard the farewell address of King Edward VIII when he abdicated the British throne and the trial of the man who kidnapped aviator Charles Lindbergh's baby.

Radio also figured in politics of the day. President Franklin Delano Roosevelt effectively used radio for his **fireside chats** (see Exhibit 5.15) to reassure the nation during the Depression. Louisiana's firebrand Governor Huey Long was often heard on the airwaves, and Father Charles E. Coughlin, a Detroit priest, tried to build a political movement through radio.[22]

Exhibit 5.15
President Franklin Delano Roosevelt delivering a "fireside chat."

5.10 The Press-Radio War

News was destined to become one of radio's strongest services, but not without a struggle. At first, announcers merely read newspaper headlines over the air, but gradually networks began purchasing news from **wire services.** In 1932, the Associated Press sold presidential election bulletins to the networks, and programs were interrupted with news flashes. Newspapers objected to this on the grounds that news on radio would diminish the sale of papers. From 1933 to 1935, a **press-radio war** ensued.

A meeting of newspaper publishers, network executives, and wire service representatives, held at the Biltmore Hotel in New York in 1933, established the **Biltmore Agreement.** It stipulated that networks could air two five-minute newscasts a day, one in the morning after 9:30 A.M. and one in the evening after 9:00 P.M. so they would not compete with the primary hours of newspaper sales. No "hot-off-the-wire" news was to be broadcast, and newscasts were not to have advertising support because this might detract from newspaper advertising. Newspaper publishers ensured that these provisions appeared in the Biltmore Agreement because they were the most numerous, most powerful, and wealthiest of the meeting participants.

Biltmore Agreement

But the ink on this agreement was barely dry when its intent began to be subverted. The newspaper publishers had agreed to allow radio stations and networks to have **commentators.** Radio took advantage of this provision, and often these commentators became thinly disguised news reporters. NBC and CBS began their own news-gathering activities. At NBC, one person gathered news simply by making telephone calls. Sometimes he scooped newspaper reporters because almost anyone would answer a call from NBC. In addition, he could reward news sources with highly prized tickets to NBC's top shows.

work-arounds

events

The public became increasingly aware of news as world tensions grew prior to World War II. Advertisers became interested in sponsoring news radio programs because of the growing potential listener market. At one point, two services agreed to make their news available to advertisers, which would then broadcast it over radio, but they would not make it available to radio stations directly. This arrangement led to a breakdown of broadcast news blackouts, and radio began to develop as an important news disseminator. Americans heard actual sounds of Germany's march into Austria and the voices of Adolf Hitler and Benito Mussolini.[23]

5.11 World War II

war efforts

The government did not take over broadcasting during the 1940–45 World War II period as it had during World War I. It did, however, solicit radio's cooperation for bond purchase appeals, conservation campaigns, and civil defense instructions. Among the most famous of these solicitations were singer Kate Smith's marathon broadcasts for war bonds, which sold more than $100 million worth. Many of the plays and soap operas produced during this period dealt with the war effort, and some even tried to address segregation, which was an issue because of racial separation in the armed forces.

news function

The news function greatly increased as up-to-date material was broadcast at least every hour. At one point CBS newsman H. V. Kaltenborn didn't leave the studio for 18 days and went on air 85 times to analyze news from Europe. One of the best-known voices heard from overseas was that of Edward R. Murrow (see Exhibit 5.16), whose broadcasts from London detailed what was happening to the English during the war.[24]

prosperity

Radio stations enjoyed great economic prosperity during the war. About 950 stations were on the air when the war began. No more were licensed, so these 950 received all the advertisements. A newsprint shortage reduced ad space in newspapers, and some of that advertising money was channeled into broadcasting. As a result, radio station revenue increased from $155 million in 1940 to $310 million in 1945.[25]

Exhibit 5.16
Correspondent Edward R. Murrow broadcasting on CBS.

5.12 The Early Development of Audio Recording

One result of the war was the perfection of **audiotape recorders.** Prior to the 1940s, the main audio recording technique employed **phonograph** discs. The phonograph was patented by Thomas Edison in 1877. Although for most of its life, this invention used a disc that was commonly called a **record**, the first phonographs used a cylinder wrapped in tinfoil to capture the sound. A major drawback of this cylinder was that it could not be duplicated. In 1887, a metal disc was introduced that could record sounds and then be duplicated by using a mold. Hundreds of discs could be made from this mold, making the mass production of records possible. Phonographs that played records that were 10-inches in diameter and revolved at 78 revolutions per minute (rpm) were popular in American homes during the early 1900s as a means for playing music (see Exhibit 5.17). In the 1940s the 78 rpm was largely replaced by smaller records that could spin at 45 rpm and then long-playing (LP) vinyl records that were 12 inches in diameter, spun at 33 rpm, and could hold about 25 minutes on two sides.[26]

The only magnetic recording known in America before World War II was **wire recording.** To edit or splice the recording, someone had to tie a knot in the wire and fuse it with heat—a very cumbersome technique. During the war, American troops entering German radio stations found them operating without any people. The broadcasting was handled by a machine that used plastic tape of higher fidelity than Americans had ever heard from wire. This plastic tape could be cut with scissors and spliced with adhesive. The recorders were confiscated, sent to America, and improved, and they eventually changed programming procedures because material could be recorded for later playback. The first tape recorders were bulky and required that tape be threaded from one reel to another (see Exhibit 5.18). Although they were used mostly in radio studios, some wealthy music aficionados purchased them for their homes. The widespread use of consumer-grade tape recorders would not occur for several decades when smaller tape recorders were developed.[27]

Exhibit 5.17
An early phonograph. This one had to be hand-cranked in order to play the music.

phonographs and tape recorders

5.13 The Rise of the DJ

TV takeover

Postwar radio prospered. Advertisers were standing in line, and the main programming problem was finding a way to squeeze in the commercials. To the networks, especially NBC, this boon provided the necessary capital to support the then-unprofitable television development. Radio fed the mouth that bit it. On the local level, this prosperity created a demand for new radio station licenses as both entrepreneurs and large companies scrambled to cash in on the boom. The 950 wartime stations expanded in rabbitlike fashion to more than 2,000 by 1950. Advertising revenues increased from $310 million in 1945 to $454 million in 1950. The bubble burst, however, as advertisers deserted radio to try TV. This left radio networks as hollow shells. The 2,000 local stations found that the advertising dollars remaining in radio did not stretch to keep them all in the black. In 1961, almost 40 percent of radio stations lost money.[28]

After the war, radio networks returned to prewar programming—comedy, drama, soap operas, children's programs, news. However, a new phenomenon appeared on the scene—the disc jockey (DJ). Several conditions precipitated this emergence. A court decision in 1940 ruled that if broadcasters purchased a record, they could then play it. Previously, records had been stamped "not licensed

records and radio

Exhibit 5.18

A reel-to-reel tape recorder used in radio stations and some homes.

for radio broadcast." This was due, in part, to the musicians' union, which insisted that all broadcast music utilize musicians rather than phonograph records. During the mid-1940s, the musicians' union was appeased with a musicians' welfare fund to which record companies contributed. This opened the door to records on radio and led to a symbiotic relationship between radio and the record business.

The beginnings of this relationship can be traced to several people, most notably Alan Freed, Gordon McLendon, and Todd Storz. During the early 1950s, Freed, a Cleveland DJ, began playing a new form of music he called rock and roll (see "Zoom In" box and Exhibit 5.19). The music caught the fancy of teenagers and gave radio a new primary audience and a new role in society—a mouthpiece for youth. McLendon and Storz were both station owners who began programming Top 40 music. According to radio lore, Storz was in a bar one night trying to drown his sorrows over the sinking income of his radio stations when he noticed that the same tunes seemed to be played over and over on the jukebox. After almost everyone left, a waitress went over to the jukebox. Rather than playing something that had not been heard all evening, she inserted her nickel and played the same song that had been selected most often. Storz decided to try playing the same songs over and over on his radio stations. Top 40

Top 40

radio was born. McLendon programmed the same Top 40 format and promoted it heavily.[29]

At the same time that recorded music was being introduced on radio, radios were becoming more portable and Americans were becoming more mobile. The public (especially the young) appreciated the DJ shows, which could be enjoyed while they engaged in other activities, such as studying or talking with friends. Another important reason for the rise of the DJ was that station man-

advantages

agement appreciated the lower overhead, fewer headaches, and higher profits associated with DJ programming. A DJ did not need a writer, a bevy of actors, a sound effects person, an audience, or even a studio. All that was needed were records, and these were readily available from companies that would eagerly court DJs (who were the ones who selected the music they would play on the air) in the hope that they would plug certain tunes, thus assuring sales of the records.[30]

payola

This courtship slightly tarnished the DJs' image during the late 1950s when it was discovered that a number of DJs were engaged in **payola,** accepting money or gifts in exchange for favoring certain records. To remedy the situation,

ZOOM IN: **The Father of Rock and Roll**

Alan Freed, who referred to himself as the Father of Rock and Roll, wasn't the first to air the type of rhythm and blues music that became rock, and he wasn't the first to use the term "rock and roll," but he put the two together. In the 1950s, rhythm and blues was considered African American music that whites shouldn't listen to, and "rock and roll" was a term used in relation to the sex act. By popularizing rhythm and blues with white audiences, Freed has been credited with breaking down racial barriers among young people of the 1950s decade.

Freed, who was born in 1921, became interested in radio while in college. After World War II, he landed jobs in small radio stations and then, in 1950, went to Cleveland, where he was an afternoon movie show host for a TV station and also played rock and roll late at night on WJW, which was otherwise a classical music station. He called himself Moondog, after an instrumental that he liked. He organized a rock and roll concert at a large Cleveland stadium that had to be shut down because of near-riot overcrowding. That brought him fame, and WJW gave him more air time.

His reputation traveled to New York and in 1954 WINS hired him to turn that station into a rock and roll station. He continued to arrange concerts to showcase rock and roll musicians, some of which became rowdy. In 1958 he was indicted for inciting a riot at a Boston concert, and although charges were eventually dropped, WINS did not renew his contract, and he moved to WABC, New York. In 1959 he got caught up in a payola scandal, and when he wouldn't sign a form saying he had never accepted payola, WABC fired him. In 1960 he pleaded guilty to several counts of commercial bribery. Although the penalty he received was mild, the bad publicity ruined his career. He died in 1965 at the age of 43 of cirrhosis of the liver brought on by alcohol. When the Rock and Roll Hall of Fame opened in 1986, he was one of the first inductees.

Alan Freed.

Congress amended the Communications Act so that if station employees received money from individuals other than their employers for airing records, they had to disclose that before broadcast time under penalty of fine or imprisonment. This helped control the practice of payola, but every now and then it still rears its head.[31]

decline of networks

The stations' need for the networks declined as the stations courted DJs and top talent left radio for TV. The increasing number of stations also meant that more stations existed in each city, so more of them were programming independently of networks. The overall result was a slow but steady erosion of network entertainment programming.

a.

BIRTHPLACE OF
ROCK 'N' ROLL

When radio station WJW disc jockey Alan Freed (1921-1965) used
the term "rock and roll" to describe the uptempo black rhythm
and blues records he played beginning in 1951, he named a new
genre of popular music that appealed to audiences on both sides
of 1950s American racial boundaries – and dominated American
culture for the rest of the 20th century. The popularity of
Freed's nightly "Moon Dog House Rock and Roll Party" radio
show encouraged him to organize the Moondog Coronation Ball–
the first rock concert. Held at the Cleveland Arena on March 21,
1952, the oversold show was beset by a riot during the
first set. Freed, a charter inductee into the Rock and Roll Hall
of Fame, moved to WINS in New York City in 1954 and continued
to promote rock music through radio, television, movies,
and live performances.

THE OHIO BICENTENNIAL COMMISSION
THE ROCK AND ROLL HALL OF FAME
THE OHIO HISTORICAL SOCIETY
2003   46-18

b.

Exhibit 5.19

Because rock and roll was first broadcast by Alan Freed
in Cleveland, the Rock 'n' Roll Museum (a) was built in
that city. Its plaque (b) tells of the early beginnings of the
format.

Armstrong

FM's slow start

5.14 FM Radio Development

During the early 1930s, David Sarnoff mentioned to Edwin H. Armstrong that someone should invent a black box to eliminate static. Armstrong did not invent just a black box, but a whole new system—**frequency modulation (FM).** He wanted RCA to back its development and promotion, but Sarnoff had committed RCA funds to television and was not interested in underwriting a new radio structure despite its obviously superior fidelity.

Armstrong continued his interest in FM, built an experimental 50,000-watt FM station in New Jersey, and solicited the support of GE for his project. During the late 1930s and early 1940s, an FM bandwagon was rolling, and some 150 applications for FM stations were submitted to the FCC. The FCC altered channel 1 on the TV band and awarded spectrum space to FM. It also ruled that TV sound should be frequency modulated. Armstrong's triumphant boom seemed just around the corner, but World War II intervened, and commercial FM had to wait.

After the war, the FCC reviewed spectrum space and decided to move FM to another part of the broadcast spectrum, ostensibly because it thought sunspots might interfere with FM. Armstrong protested this move because it rendered all prewar FM sets worthless and saddled the FM business with heavy conversion costs. Armstrong was further infuriated because, although FM sound was to be used for TV, RCA had never paid him royalties for the sets it manufactured. In 1948, he sued RCA. The suit proceeded for more than a year, and the harassment and illness it caused Armstrong led him to leap from the window of his 13th-floor apartment to his death.[32]

FM continued to develop slowly. With television on the horizon, there was little interest in a new radio system. Many of the major AM stations acquired FM licenses as insurance in case FM replaced AM, as its proponents were predicting. AM stations simply duplicated their AM programming on FM, which did not increase the public's incentive to purchase FM sets. In fact, for a while an industry joke ran, "What do the letters 'FM' in FM radio stand for?" The answer was "Find me."

One brighter spot for FM was on the education front. In 1945, educators convinced the FCC to reserve the 20 FM channels between 88.1 and 91.9 exclusively for noncommercial radio. Most of these stations were used by universities, although some were owned by nonprofit community groups, and others were operated by religious organizations. In 1949, the National Association of Educational Broadcasters (NAEB) formed a **bicycle network** to provide programming for educational stations. The programs were duplicated at a central location and then sent by mail from one station to another on a scheduled round-robin basis.[33]

noncommercial radio

As general interest in high-fidelity music grew, FM's interference-free signal became an asset to commercial stations. In 1961, the FCC authorized stereo sound transmission for FM, which led to increased awareness of the medium. At first, classical music dominated the FM airwaves. When hi-fi equipment became inexpensive enough to be purchased by teenagers, rock music became prominent FM fare. This led to an increased number of listeners, followed by an increased number of advertisers. A further aid to FM's success was a 1965 FCC ruling that in cities of more than 100,000 population, AM and FM stations with the same ownership had to have separate programming at least 50 percent of the time. This helped FM gain a foothold because it now developed its own distinctive programming. During the 1970s, FM developed so successfully that it began taking audiences away from AM. In 1972, AM had 75 percent of the audience, and FM had 25 percent. By the mid-1980s, those percentages had reversed, and AM stations were the ones losing money.[34]

FM success

The switch to FM was mostly caused by the superior sound quality of the medium, including the capability for **stereo** sound. AM proponents tried to combat this by developing an AM stereo system, but AM stereo was not as good as FM stereo and did not give AM a competitive boost.[35]

AM stereo

5.15 The Restructuring of Public Radio

The educational stations at the lower end of the FM dial received some sprucing up with the passage of the Public Broadcasting Act in 1967. This act was adopted mainly to benefit educational television, but radio was also included. The term "educational" was dropped and "public radio" was used instead. The act resulted in funding for a network, National Public Radio (NPR), which began operating from Washington, DC, in 1970. It replaced the bicycle network of the NAEB and today delivers programming by satellite. NPR's mission was to upgrade the quality of public radio programming with news, music, talk shows, documentaries, and programming from other countries. One of the most popular early programs was the in-depth evening news program *All Things Considered,* which is still on the air (see Exhibit 5.20).

NPR

Over the years, some structural elements of NPR were not popular with many of the stations, most notably the fact that most of the programming was produced in Washington, DC Local stations thought their programs deserved wider dissemination. A group of public stations in 1982 formed American Public Radio,

Exhibit 5.20

Anchor Robert Siegel at National Public Radio's headquarters in Washington, DC, during a broadcast of *All Things Considered*.

PRI and APM

which in 1994 changed its name to Public Radio International (PRI). PRI is an independent, nonprofit network that does not receive direct federal funding. Station members pay fees that support the national office in Minnesota and the satellite distribution system. In 2004, Minnesota-based American Public Media (APM) decided to distribute programs it owned and produced itself rather than through PRI, so there are now three distributors of public radio programming—NPR, PRI, and APM.

local programming

The public broadcasting networks do not fill all the airtime on the 750-plus public radio stations that affiliate with them. Local programming includes music—classical, jazz, swing, and other forms not generally heard on commercial radio. Some stations also produce their own public-affairs programs, dramas, and children's programs.[36]

5.16 College Radio

network affiliated

A number of colleges and universities own NPR-, APM- and/or PRI-affiliated stations that program primarily network material and operate much like public radio stations owned by community groups in that they have a paid staff and no involvement from the student body. Other colleges affiliate with the networks but allow for some student involvement, such as airing programs produced by students in radio production classes or offering student internships.

student run

However, what the term "college radio" usually conjures up is an independently operated radio station owned by the college but operated by students as both a learning experience and a form of expression (see Exhibit 5.21). In addition to the college stations, more than 300 high school stations operate in this manner. Many of these high school stations offer computer-programmed music during school hours and live DJ programming after school. These student stations, like other noncommercial stations, are located at the lower end of the FM band. They originally arose because of a 1948 FCC ruling authorizing low-powered, 10-watt educational stations that generally reached only a 2- to 5-mile radius and were inexpensive to operate. These **10-watter** college and high school radio stations grew rapidly, and most have since increased their power. The student-run stations are important to musicians because they are the main outlet for alternative music and are often the first to air new groups and new sounds.

In addition to FM stations, some colleges and high schools have closed-circuit stations that operate only on campus, programming primarily to the cafeteria or the dorms. Others operate low-power AM or FM stations that are designated to provide traffic and weather information. Student groups supplement this programming material with announcements about campus events. Many colleges have placed their FM stations on the internet, and a number have established internet-only student stations.[37]

other types if stations

5.17 The Changing Structure of Commercial Radio

On the commercial front, the business structure of radio underwent a number of significant changes in the latter part of the 20th century. Radio networks, which hit a low in the 1960s, began to reemerge, but in a different form. They no longer brought common programming to the nation but instead developed numerous satellite services with different features and formats, each intended for a particular niche of stations. Some stations used only bits and pieces from the network, some used the network music along with local personalities, and others used a preponderance of network material—often obtaining it from several different networks. Obviously the old rules against one company owning more than one network were dropped.[38]

reemergence of networks

Network ownership also changed. A new radio network, Westwood One, purchased Mutual in 1985 and NBC radio networks in 1987. Westwood One then entered into an arrangement whereby it was managed by Infinity Broadcasting, which later became part of CBS. In 1995, Disney bought ABC, including its radio properties, and then in 2006 Disney sold the radio interests to Citadel. CBS radio underwent several ownership changes as its parent organization merged with various companies, but today CBS radio remains a major part of the overall CBS structure. More than 500 companies now distribute radio programming, primarily by satellite. Some call themselves *networks,* and others call themselves *syndicators* or *program producers.*[39]

deregulation

Another big change in the structure of the radio business involved **deregulation,** particularly that encompassed in the **Telecommunications Act of 1996** that greatly relaxed station licensing procedures and ownership restrictions. License renewal, which used to be a very complicated procedure occurring every three years, became a simplified process that occurs only every eight years. In previous decades, a particular company could own no more than seven AM and seven FM stations and could have no more than one of each in any listening area. Now there are no national ownership limits, and local ownership limits have been changed so that, in some markets, one company can own eight stations. This deregulation resulted in companies with large financial resources, such as Clear Channel, buying and operating many radio stations.[40]

programming changes

As the structure of radio changed, so did the programming. The large stations owners, partly to avoid risk and partly to lower costs, began consolidating their programming staffs. They centralized the music selection, coming up with playlists indicating what music should be played on each station. These playlists were no longer generated by local disc jockeys but were the result of audience research and management input. The parent companies also instituted **voice tracking**, which was largely a substitute for local DJs. With voice tracking, announcers for a few stations do "intros" and "outros" to music for a large number of the company's stations. These intros sound local because the announcers incorporate material about the local community, but they are being piped in from a distant city. Voice tracking saves companies a great deal of money because the disc jockeys don't sit around while the music plays. In fact, they don't even hear the music; they just record voice for several hours.[41]

ethnic and talk radio

Another change in radio was the growth of ethnic radio. Black-oriented stations and foreign language stations existed for many years. But by the mid-1990s, more than 400 stations were operating with an ethnic format. In Los Angeles, for example, Spanish-language stations often rated number one during rating periods. Talk radio has become important to the social fabric of America. Talk-show hosts help set and challenge public policy, and listeners freely express their opinions and viewpoints. Shock jocks stir controversy with their sexual and scatological language and their often outlandish antics on and off the radio.[42]

5.18 Consumer Audio Options

Audio tapes and discs also underwent changes in the latter part of the 20th century. In the 1980s, the 33 rpm LP vinyl record was replaced by the **compact disc (CD)**. CDs used digital technology rather than the older analog technology, thus allowing for higher fidelity sound. Consumers took to the inexpensive CD players, both portable and console models, and soon CDs that could hold 74 minutes of stereo music were outselling records. CD shipments went from 23 million in 1985 to 287 million in 1990 while, during the same period, LP shipments tumbled from 167 million to 11 million.[43]

CDs

Audiocassette recorders became popular in the 1970s. The tape was housed in a small case, so it did not need to be threaded from one reel to another as had been the case with the older recorders. In 1980, the low-cost portable stereo Sony Walkman was introduced in the United States and gained great popularity. It was made for people on the go who wanted to listen to music while jogging or engaging in other activities. It reigned supreme until replaced by hard drive **MP3** players such as the iPod (see Chapter 2). Radio stations joined into the iPod frenzy by **podcasting.** Consumers could listen to stations' entire feeds or just to particular programs. There are also many **apps** that allow people to hear terrestrial, satellite, or internet radio on their **smartphones.**[44]

newer technologies

5.19 Satellite and HD Radio

Satellite radio and HD radio use digital technology. **Satellite radio** is a subscription service that involves broadcasting directly from a satellite to receivers in cars or homes. It needs a different radio receiver than the ones used for terrestrial radio stations. One of its advantages is that signals can be picked up anywhere in the country; someone could drive from California to Maine and hear the same program service the entire way. Satellite radio started in 2001 when XM Satellite Radio began broadcasting, followed by Sirius Satellite Radio. Both companies had received permission to develop their services in 1997 when they paid the FCC more than $80 million for the frequencies. Each service developed more than 100 channels with programming from established networks and programming specially developed by their companies, much of it free of advertising. Sirius captured "shock jock" Howard Stern, who switched from conventional radio in 2006, in part because the FCC was cracking down on indecency, and government agencies have no authority over satellite radio programming content. The quality and convenience of satellite radio garnered close to 15 million subscribers between the two companies, but that was not enough to turn a profit, so Sirius and XM merged in 2008 and have since branched out to offer their channels on the internet as well as from satellites.[45]

Sirius and XM

Conventional broadcasters developed their own form of digital radio, which they refer to as **HD radio**. HD radio was not mandated by the FCC as was digital television, so some stations added digital services and some did not. Technology squeezes the digital signal into the same frequencies that the station uses for AM

digital services

or FM broadcasting and also allows for better reception, higher fidelity, and the possibility to add services such as a second channel or traffic information on demand. People must buy a special radio in order to hear HD radio, but then the programming is free. About 1,300 radio stations have added an HD service, but it has not been highly adopted by consumers. AM and FM broadcasting will continue in their present form regardless of the fate of HD radio.[46]

5.20 Internet Radio

early activities

It is difficult to pinpoint when radio programs first became a part of the internet, but it could have been on April Fools' Day in 1993 when the now defunct Internet Multicasting Service started a talk radio program called "Geek of the Week." It is known that the University of Kansas was a pioneer in internet radio, placing its student station, KJHK-FM, on the net in December 1994. The first commercial station to use the internet, KLIF-AM in Dallas, didn't do so until September 1995. That year internet radio stations proliferated rapidly. Hobbyists, music fans, college students, and just about anyone who wanted to could create an internet-only radio station. No one needed a license and the equipment required was minimal and inexpensive.[47]

streaming and on-demand

Many over-the-air radio stations engage in **streaming audio** by putting their live feed onto the internet in addition to broadcasting it. This means that people all over the world, not just those in its terrestrial signal area, can hear the station. Because computers can store information, both internet-only and over-the-air stations found they could place program material on the internet that consumers could download and listen to at their convenience in an **on-demand** basis. They have built files of past play-by-play sports coverage, yesterday's DJ shows, updated news clips, public-affairs programs, and so on.[48]

growth

The radio stations, whether over-the-air or internet-only, have built elaborate websites to go with their audio. They encourage listeners to email requests for music or questions for talk shows. In some instances, they include such elements as live shots of their disc jockeys playing music, photos of the artists whose music is being played, or written statistics to accompany a ball game. Of course, it is possible for the consumer simply to listen to internet radio while doing something else at the computer—word processing, spreadsheets, games. As internet radio grew, it began to attract advertisers. The ads could be part of the program material or they could be part of the webpage— for example, **banner ad** links for listeners to click through to the advertiser's website.[49]

Today there are thousands of internet stations. Many of them pay a modest monthly fee to services such as loudcity.net (see Exhibit 5.22) that netcast, organize, and promote internet radio stations, helping listeners find the particular stations that interest them. Internet radio is a viable option for audio listening and an easy, inexpensive way for those who want to create radio to have an outlet and a way to express their individual tastes and opinions about music and other subjects.

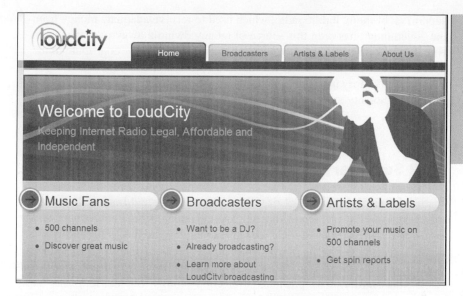

Exhibit 5.22
A screenshot of loudcity.net, which organizes and distributes internet radio stations.

5.21 Issues and the Future

The various forms of radio both complement and compete with each other. There was great fear among broadcasters when satellite radio started that Sirius and XM would drain listeners and advertisers from them. But the two forms seem to co-exist and many people who install satellite radio also listen to terrestrial radio. Internet radio is now considered a threat by traditional broadcasters, but their ability to be part of internet radio, means they can use it to their advantage. The amount stations collect in advertising revenue for their internet service goes to the same company bottom line as what they collect for terrestrial broadcasting.

competition

Much of radio content is music and there are many ways for people to obtain this music—without commercials. They can download it from the internet, buy CDs, or obtain it for their portable platforms. Many consumers only want to hear the songs that they really like. Radio does not lend itself to such narrow music listening, so radio has lost listeners to the new technologies that allow for individualizing music selections. The news functions of radio have also been challenged by the internet and portable platforms. Consumers do not need to wait for "traffic on the fives" or weather reports each hour when they have such information available instantly and constantly on laptops or smartphones.

music and news

Many bemoan the deregulation that resulted in the consolidation of radio in the hands of large companies. They point to a sameness of radio programming and the increasing difficulty that new music groups have in getting airplay because the big companies want to play it safe with what has worked in the past. They sense stagnation in radio programming.

consolidation

Radio broadcasting, which used to be profitable, now has trouble making money. There are so many stations that the advertising money available cannot

money

support all of them. Public radio, which used to receive adequate money from the government, has seen this source of money dwindle away over the years. However, public radio has a loyal following and listeners do contribute to the operation of their local stations which then, in turn, support the networks.

Radio's history is full of cataclysmic changes, but it has a history of adapting to meet society's needs. Its resilience in reinventing itself during the 1960s could serve as a model as it marches forward in the 21st century.

5.22 Summary

Radio has survived periods of experimentation, glory, and trauma. Early inventors, such as Maxwell, Hertz, Marconi, and De Forest, would not recognize radio in its present form. Many people who knew radio during the 1930s and 1940s do not truly recognize it today. Radio has endured and along the way has chalked up an impressive list of great moments: picking up the *Titanic*'s distress calls, broadcasting the Harding-Cox presidential election returns, broadcasting the World War II newscasts of Edward R. Murrow, surviving the television takeover, and adjusting to new technologies.

Government interaction with radio illustrates the medium's growth as a broadcasting entity. Early laws dealt with radio primarily as a safety medium. The fact that government took control of radio during World War I but not during World War II indicates that radio had grown from a private communication medium to a very public one that most Americans relied on for information. The need for the government to step in to solve the problem of overcrowded airwaves during the late 1920s proved the popularity and prestige of radio. The ensuing Communications Act of 1934 and the various FCC regulations helped solidify the government's role in broadcasting. When Congress passed the Public Broadcasting Act of 1967, it set the groundwork for the reorganization of public radio. Government was involved in the development of FM and the initiation of satellite radio and HD radio. It also deals with issues in radio such as payola. The lessening of ownership regulations stipulated in the Telecommunications Act of 1996 and the changes in programming it brought about are further evidence that radio has survived.

Companies from the private-enterprise sector have also played significant roles in the history of radio, starting with the Marconi company and progressing through the founding of RCA by AT&T, GE, and Westinghouse. These early companies contributed a great deal in terms of technology, programming, and finance. The networks and stations, each in their own peculiar way, set the scene for both healthy competition and elements of unhealthy intrigue. Intrigue also characterized the rivalry between newspapers and radio in the pre–World War II days, and free enterprise in its purest sense altered the format of radio when television stole its listeners. The formation of new networks such as Westwood One and the revitalization of networks and syndicators are further proof that radio has survived.

Radio programming is indebted to early pioneers who filled the airwaves with boxing matches and "potted palm" music, and to *Amos 'n' Andy,* Jack Benny, and others who are remembered for creating the golden era of radio.

Today countless DJs, talk-show hosts, and newscasters on terrestrial, satellite, and internet radio let us know that radio has survived.

Suggested Websites

www.clearchannel.com (site of Clear Channel, the company that owns the most radio stations)

www.Live365.com (a service that organizes and promotes internet radio stations)

www.paleycenter.org (the Paley Center for Media that has facilities in New York and Los Angeles with exhibits related to the history of radio and examples of old time radio shows)

www.siriusXM.com (satellite radio service SiriusXM)

www.westwoodone.com (site for Westwood One radio networks)

Notes

1. Orrin E. Dunlap, Jr., *Radio's 100 Men of Science* (New York: Harper and Brothers, 1944), 65–68, 113–17.
2. Degna Marconi, *My Father Marconi* (New York: McGraw-Hill, 1962).
3. Lee De Forest, *Father of Radio: The Autobiography of Lee De Forest* (Chicago: Wilcox and Follett, 1950).
4. Erik Barnouw, *A Tower in Babel: A History of Broadcasting in the United States to 1933* (New York: Oxford University Press, 1966), 77.
5. Robert W. Morrow, "Nationalizing American Radio: Anti-Monopoly, Nationalism, and the First Alexander Bill, 1915–1917." *Journal of Radio and Audio Media*, May 2011, 17–32.
6. Barnouw, *A Tower in Babel*, 57–61.
7. There is some question as to whether this memo was actually written in 1915. Some sources say 1916; others say the ideas may not have come until 1920. Sarnoff himself said many times that he wrote the memo in 1915. The dispute over the memo is chronicled in Louise M. Benjamin, "In Search of the 'Radio Music Box' Memo," *Journal of Broadcasting & Electronic Media*, Summer 1993, 325–35; and Louise Benjamin, "In Search of the Sarnoff 'Radio Music Box' Memo: Nally's Reply," *Journal of Radio Studies,* June 2002, 95–106.
8. Yochi J. Dreazen, "Pittsburgh's KDKA Tells Story of How Radio Has Survived," *Wall Street Journal*, May 15, 2001, A-1.
9. Robert E. Summers and Harrison B. Summers, *Broadcasting and the Public* (Belmont, CA: Wadsworth, 1966), 34.
10. Barnouw, *A Tower in Babel*, 85, 86, 100.
11. Ibid., 180.
12. William P. Banning, *Commercial Broadcasting Pioneer: WEAF Experiment, 1922–1926* (Cambridge, MA: Harvard University Press, 1946), 150–55.
13. "The First 60 Years of NBC," *Broadcasting*, June 9, 1986, 49–64.
14. "Farewell to the Man in the CBS Eye," *Broadcasting*, November 5, 1990, 35–39.
15. "The Silver Has Turned to Gold," *Broadcasting*, February 13, 1978, 34–46.
16. "How Sweet It Was," *Broadcasting & Cable*, April 19, 1999, 74–76.
17. J. Wayne Rinks, "Higher Education in Radio 1922–1934," *Journal of Radio Studies*, December 2002, 303–16.
18. Louise Benjamin, "Working It Out Together: Radio Policy from Hoover to the Radio Act of 1927," *Journal of Broadcasting & Electronic Media*, Spring 1998, 221–36.

19. *Public Law No.* 416, June 19, 1934, 73rd Congress (Washington, DC: Government Printing Office, 1934), sect. 303.

20. Summers and Summers, *Broadcasting and the Public*, 45–50.

21. Andrews and Ahrgus Julliard, *Holy Mackerel: The Amos 'n' Andy Story* (New York: Dutton, 1986).

22. For more information on radio programming, see Michele Hilmes, *Radio Voices: American Broadcasting 1922–1952* (Minneapolis: University of Minnesota Press, 1997); and Vincent Terrace, *Radio's Golden Years: The Encyclopedia of Radio Programs 1930–1960* (San Diego: A.S. Barnes, 1981).

23. "Genesis of Radio News: The Press-Radio War," *Broadcasting*, January 5, 1976, 95.

24. Paul White, *News on the Air* (New York: Harcourt, Brace, 1947).

25. Summers and Summers, *Broadcasting and the Public*, 46.

26. "How We Got there," *Hollywood Reporter*, December 28, 1999, 10–14.

27. Eric Barnouw, *The Golden Web: A History of Broadcasting in the United States 1933–1953* (New York: Oxford University Press, 1968), 46.

28. *Broadcasting Yearbook*, 1975 (Washington, DC: Broadcasting Publications, 1975), C-289 and Ward L. Quaal and James A. Brown, *Broadcast Management* (New York: Hastings House, 1976), 292.

29. Michael C. Keith, *Radio Programming* (Boston: Focal Press, 1987), 3.

30. Arnold Passman, *The DJs* (New York: Macmillan, 1971).

31. "Gov't Gets 1st Payola Conviction," *Daily Variety*, May 23, 1989, 1; and "FCC Launches Payola Probes of 4 Radio Giants," *Los Angeles Times*, April 20, 2006, 1.

32. "Armstrong's Legacy," *TV Technology*, October 17, 2001, 14–15; and Christopher H. Sterling and Michael C. Keith, *Sounds of Change: A History of FM Broadcasting in America* (Chapel Hill, NC: University of North Carolina Press, 2008).

33. Donald N. Wood and Donald G. Wylie, *Educational Telecommunications* (Belmont, CA: Wadsworth, 1997).

34. "AM Radio Plays Hard to Be Heard Again As Audience Dwindles," *Insight*, July 4, 1988, 44.

35. Bruce Klopfenstein and David Sedman, "Technical Standards and the Marketplace: The Case of AM Stereo," *Journal of Broadcasting & Electronic Media*, Spring 1990, 171–94.

36. "New Name, Focus for American Public Radio," *Daily Variety*, December 20, 1993, 52 and Sara Magee, "All Things Cultured: An Analysis of Popular Culture Coverage on National Public Radio's *All Things Considered,*" *Journal of Radio and Audio Media*, May 2011, 47–64.

37. Jim McCluskey, "An Examination of New and Existing FCC Policies and Procedures Affecting Student/Noncommercial Radio Stations," *Feedback*, Fall 1998, 32–36; and "These DJs Are Well-Schooled," *Los Angeles Times*, May 22, 2004, E-19.

38. "New Radio Networks Spring Up," *New York Times*, January 11, 1980, III-6.

39. "Westwood One to Buy NBC Radio Networks for $50 Mil," *Daily Variety*, July 21, 1987, 1; and "Citadel Jumps to Top of Radio Dial," *Hollywood Reporter*, February 7–13, 2006, 12.

40. Wenmouth Williams, "The Impact of Ownership Rules and the Telecommunications Act of 1996 on a Small Radio Market," *Journal of Radio Studies*, Summer 1998, 8–18.

41. "'96 Act Killed Radio's Star," *Hollywood Reporter*, December 14, 2006, 6; and "DJ is Not Going Away Quietly," *Los Angeles Times*, November 5, 2011, D-1.

42. "Radio Rides Hispanic Population Boom," *Broadcasting & Cable*, October 6, 1997, 46; and Stephen Earl Bennett, "Americans Exposure to Political Talk Radio and Their Knowledge of Public Affairs," *Journal of Broadcasting & Electronic Media*, March 2002, 72–86.

43. Bureau of Census, *Statistical Abstracts of the United States, 2000* (Washington, DC: Department of Commerce, 2000), 573.

44. "Why Podcasts Are Comedy's Second Coming," *Hollywood Reporter*, October 7, 2011, 24; and "Setting the Course for Radio's Sea Change," *Los Angeles Times*, October 11, 2011, B-1.

45. "Voices from the Heavens," *Los Angeles Times*, November 1, 2001, T-1; "Stern Has Sirius Intentions," *Hollywood Reporter*, October 7, 2004, 1; and "FCC Staff Back XM-Sirius Merger," *Wall Street Journal*, June 16, 2008, B1.

46. "New Wave of Radio Choices," *Los Angeles Times*, May 27, 2007, C-3.

47. Barbara K. Kaye and Norman J. Medoff, *The World Wide Web* (Mountain View, CA: Mayfield). 78–80.

48. Cheryl L. Evans and J. Steven Smethers, "Streaming into the Future: A Delphi Study of Broadcasters' Attitudes Toward Cyber Radio Stations," *Journal of Radio Studies*, Summer 2001, 5–28.

49. Web Radio Adds Video to Audio," *Broadcasting & Cable*, August 9, 1999, 32.

Chapter 6

MOVIES AND HOME VIDEO

Originally, movies were not part of electronic media. They were shot on film, a chemical medium, and edited with mechanical machines that incorporated razor blades and adhesive tape. They were shown in dark theaters using mechanical projectors that lit up beaded cloth-like screens. They were totally separate from radio, and when broadcast television came along, movies and TV had an adversarial relationship (see Chapter 4). However, in the 1950s old movies became broadcast TV fare and, when cable TV channels started, some of them used movies as their primary content (see Chapter 3).

In the 1980s, consumer home video was developed in the form of videocassette recorders. People used the recorders mainly to watch

Things you would never know if it weren't for the movies:

Once applied, lipstick will never come off, even when swimming under water.

All grocery bags contain at least one stick of French bread.

When staying in a haunted house, women should investigate any strange noises in their most revealing underwear.

It is always possible to park directly outside the building you are visiting.

A man will show no pain while taking the most ferocious beating but will wince when a woman tries to clean his wounds.

When a car is being driven down a dark road at night, the light under the dashboard will always be lit.

Anonymous Internet Humor

movies. As home video transformed through discs, hard drives, and clouds, movies remained major content. Most movies are still produced primarily to show in movie theaters, but some are made specifically for television or for home video. Regardless of the distribution method, they are employing more and more electronics. Many are now shot using high definition cameras, edited with computer programs, and projected with digital equipment. This chapter will cover theatrical movie history and will discuss the role of home video and its increasing importance in the electronic media field.

6.1 Early Developments

stroboscopic toys

The motion picture business grew out of photography and **stroboscopic** toys. One of the toys of the early 1800s was a flat disc with the picture of a parrot on one side and the picture of a cage on the other. When someone spun the toy, the parrot appeared to be in the cage. This demonstrated a phenomenon called **persistence of vision** in which the human eye retains images for short periods. That is why film, which is actually a series of projected still images, appears as moving pictures.[1]

Stanford bet

In 1877, Leland Stanford, the governor of California, had a $25,000 bet with a friend that when a horse gallops, all four of its feet are off the ground at the same time. He hired Eadweard Muybridge, who was experimenting with continuous motion photography, to prove his theory. Muybridge rigged 24 cameras that were triggered in synchronized fashion by string stretched across a racetrack. The photos showed that Stanford was right (see Exhibit 6.1), and he won the bet—although the experiment cost him $40,000.[2]

The major developments in early film in the United States were undertaken in the 1880s by George Eastman and Thomas Edison, with his assistant W. K. L. Dickson. Eastman had undertaken experiments with rolls of celluloid film that he intended for still cameras, but the flexible film lent itself well to what eventually became movies. Edison was looking for a way to have pictures accompany his audio invention, the phonograph, and was persuaded by Dickson to use Eastman's celluloid film. So, in a way, the first movie concept was a music video.

Edison, Dickson, and Eastman

Dickson went on to invent an electrically powered camera and a battery-powered viewer. Edison thought that images should be projected to one person at a time rather than to a large audience because the image would be clearer and because he believed he could earn more money this way. So the viewer that Dickson invented was a peephole machine called a **Kinetoscope** (see Exhibit 6.2). In the 1890s, Kinetoscope parlors appeared around the country; for a few pennies, people could watch a movie that was about 20 seconds long.[3]

Dickson and Edison had abandoned sound for their movies by this time, but Edison still thought his phonograph was a much more important invention than anything related to movies. They built a small studio to shoot movies. Its exterior

Exhibit 6.1
Some of the photos taken by Eadweard Muybridge to enable Leland Stanford to prove that a horse has all four feet off the ground while galloping.

was tar paper to keep out unwanted light, and it soon became known as the Black Maria (see Exhibit 6.3). The roof opened to let in sunlight, and the whole building rotated so it could catch the light as the day progressed. The camera in the room could move, but Dickson never changed its position when shooting any one film.

Projection and portability were developed by others, primarily the Lumière brothers (Auguste and Louis) of France. They created one of the first functional projectors, and in 1895, the first movie theater open to the paying public showed movies in the basement of a Paris café. The Lumières also utilized a smaller hand-cranked camera that they took outside to film everyday events.[4]

Lumière brothers

Exhibit 6.2
A Kinetoscope. People viewed through the peephole on the top.

6.2 The First Movies

The first known Edison-Dickson movie is *Fred Ott's Sneeze* (1894), a short scene of one of Edison's mechanics sneezing. Other movies consisted of jugglers, animal acts, and dancers who paraded through the Black Maria. The Lumière movies showed factory laborers leaving work, a baby eating, and a train pulling into a station. The train had people in the theater ducking as it came toward them on the screen. One Lumière film was a precursor to slapstick comedy. In it a boy is standing on a hose. A man picks up the hose, the boy steps off the hose, and the man's face is pelted with water. Projection caught

Exhibit 6.3

The Black Maria was covered with tar paper and rotated to follow the sun.

Méliès and Porter

Exhibit 6.4

A scene from Edwin S. Porter's *The Great Train Robbery*.

Biograph and Vitagraph

on in the United States, too, and an 1895 Edison-Dickson film called *The Kiss* caused quite a stir. As the name implies, it showed two people kissing, something that wasn't publicly accepted in that era.[5]

The very early movies were shot with no camera movement and no editing. Gradually more production values crept in. Frenchman George Méliès, who was a magician, experimented with special effects such as split screens, double exposures, and stop motion. In 1902, he employed special effects in the name of "science fiction" for his best-known movie, *A Trip to the Moon*. Edwin S. Porter, who worked as a director for Edison, extended the art in films such as *Life of an American Fireman* (1903) and *The Great Train Robbery* (1903) (see Exhibit 6.4). Among his techniques were cutting back and forth from one scene to another and panning the camera. He also used some medium close-ups, such as a shot of an outlaw pointing a gun at the audience that made viewers jump in their seats.[6]

6.3 Studio Beginnings

Two other companies joined the moviemaking ranks—Biograph and Vitagraph. Biograph was formed by W. K. L. Dickson, who left Edison and became his rival. Because Edison (as Dickson's former employer) held the patents on Dickson's inventions, Dickson had to invent the motion picture camera twice. Biograph, Vitagraph, and Edison competed fiercely. For example, in 1899 Biograph set up a large number of lights to film a boxing match at Coney Island. When the Biograph people discovered a Vitagraph camera filming the fight several rows back, they sent detectives to confiscate Vitagraph's equipment. A fight ensued that many people thought was better than the fight in the ring. Eventually Vitagraph succeeded in recording the fight and took the film back to its lab. The next morning the Vitagraph people found that the film had been stolen during the night by folks from Edison.[7]

In 1909, because of all the bad blood and lawsuits among the film companies, nine New York companies, led by Edison, decided to form the Motion Picture Patents Company (often referred to as the Trust or the MPPC). The nine companies were to share patent rights and also keep all other companies from entering the film production business. To accomplish this, they agreed not to sell films to distributors who bought from anyone else, and they also arranged with George Eastman's company, Kodak, to sell film only to these nine companies.[8]

Distributors had become important because movie theaters were springing up around the country. Most of these were storefronts with a few chairs and a screen, but some were plush and accompanied the silent films, now often a half-hour long, with piano music performed live as the movie was rolling. The theaters originally charged customers a nickel to view a film, so they became known as **nickelodeons.** Most of the early film viewers were working-class people, but the wealthy joined in when the theaters became fancier.[9]

The MPPC didn't keep its lock on film forever. Filmmakers who didn't knuckle under to the Trust became independent producers and distributors, and some of them moved to faraway California to escape the eye of the New York–based companies. They could also purchase film cheaply, some of it manufactured in Mexico. William Fox started what became 20th Century Fox, and Carl Laemmle formed the company that became Universal.[10]

6.4 Griffith and His Contemporaries

David Wark (D. W.) Griffith, a would-be actor, became a talented director who worked briefly for Edison and then switched to Biograph. He experimented with many aspects of filmmaking, such as lighting subjects from below, moving the camera in long tracking shots, and creating flashbacks. He also used close-ups and medium shots, which most previous directors had avoided, thinking that people wouldn't pay to see only part of an actor. Many of his movies contained last-minute rescue scenes, which allowed him to employ **parallel editing** in which he cut back and forth between the victim and the rescuer. Griffith regularly cast the same talented actors—Lionel Barrymore, Lillian Gish, Mary Pickford—and he worked with a creative cameraman, "Billy" Bitzero. (See Exhibit 6.5.)

techniques

The Birth of a Nation

Eventually Griffith left Biograph because his movies became too long and expensive for Biograph's tastes. In the silent film era, the director could talk to the actors as they were acting, and the owners of Biograph became upset when Griffith wanted to spend time and money on rehearsals. Griffith went to an independent company, Mutual, where he made a deal that allowed him to make one movie a year of his choice in addition to the movies Mutual assigned him.

In 1915, Griffith, a Southerner by birth, released *The Birth of a Nation,* which cost $115,000. It was a historical film about the Civil War in which the heroes were Ku Klux Klan members. The movie advanced filmmaking in that it had huge sets, battle scenes, many rehearsals, and dynamic editing. The racist subject matter, however, caused riots throughout the country. Although the movie was banned in a number of cities, it made a great deal of money and could be considered the first blockbuster. Griffith's next film, *Intolerance* (1916), cost $2 million but was not successful. It intercut four stories and four last-minute rescues that occurred in different centuries, something that was too difficult for

Exhibit 6.5
D. W. Griffith directing a silent movie.

ZOOM IN: **Accusations and Applause**

Charlie Chaplin was one of the actors who became caught up in the blacklisting of the 1950s (see Chapter 4). The accusations that he was a Communist stemmed in part from the fact that he was a foreigner, having been born in England in 1889, where he became a popular child actor before coming to the United States to pursue his career in 1910. The FBI claimed that Chaplin was sympathetic to leftist beliefs and put together a document of more than 1,900 pages against him. Accusations included that he had given a reception for a prominent labor leader and that he was often the guest of a millionaire whose son became a Communist. When Chaplin was questioned about being a Communist, he had no concrete answer except that he didn't want to create any revolution; he just wanted to create a few more films. He was quoted as saying, "I am a citizen of the world," and he participated in War Bond drives for the allies. The FBI finally admitted in 1948 that, despite its 1,900-page document, it had no evidence that Chaplin was a Communist.

All the accusations, however, affected Chaplin and his career. He stopped impromptu performances and often stayed away from the studio, lonely and depressed. In 1952, with McCarthyism in bloom, Chaplin took a trip back to his native England. The FBI, under J. Edgar Hoover, planned to bar his reentry through U.S. customs, despite its lack of evidence. Rather than face the situation, Chaplin made his home in Switzerland with his wife Oona (daughter of playwright Eugene O'Neill) and their eventual eight children.

In 1972, the Academy of Motion Picture Arts and Sciences gave Chaplin an honorary award for "the incalculable effect he has had in making motion pictures the art form of this century." At the Academy Awards ceremony, he received an unprecedented five-minute standing ovation. To view Chaplin receiving his award, go to www.youtube.com/watch?v=J3Pl-qvA1X8.

Charlie Chaplin.

audiences to follow. After that, Griffith's Victorian sensibilities seemed to be out of touch with the Roaring Twenties, and his movies did not generate large audiences.[11]

During this period, Mack Sennett and Charlie Chaplin experimented with comedy. Although they worked together for a while, they did not get along because they had different views of comedy. Sennett preferred sight gags such as people bumping into things or falling into swimming pools. Frequently he spoofed Griffith's last-minute rescues. Chaplin preferred more character-driven comedy, albeit with a few sight gags. He developed and acted the character of the Little Tramp, an immigrant worker who was at the fringe of society but who aspired to be with the rich and powerful. The character allowed Chaplin, who mainly improvised rather than working from a completed script, to show both the good and bad aspects of wealth as well as his gifted abilities with comedic pantomime. Chaplin knew both wealth and poverty, having been at one point in a home for destitute children and at another point the first actor to sign a million-dollar contract (see "Zoom In" box).[12]

Chaplin and Sennett

6.5 Hollywood during the Roaring Twenties

The scene was set for Hollywood to dominate film production in the 1920s. American filmmaking had gained importance during the late teens because World War I made film production overseas difficult and the New York film production power base deteriorated. In 1917, the courts outlawed the MPPC, but it was already losing its dominant film production role to the independents in California, which preferred to produce long films to be shown in comfortable theaters rather than short films for nickelodeons. The indies also allowed the stars more personal recognition, whereas the Trust rarely gave screen credits. The stars appreciated this new approach, so the "Biograph Girl" left Biograph and went to an independent where she could be known by her real name, Florence Lawrence. "Little Mary" became Mary Pickford.

Pickford and Fairbanks

As the stars assumed their own personas, the public became interested in their personal lives. The era of the Roaring Twenties was not the height of morality, and Hollywood exaggerated the characteristics of the time. Although many movies had moralistic, sentimental plots, others hinted at lust and promoted materialism. The press highlighted stories of drugs, alcohol abuse, and divorce among Hollywood luminaries. In 1920, Mary Pickford, who was then "America's Sweetheart," went to Las Vegas and divorced her husband, Owen Moore. Three weeks later she married Douglas Fairbanks (also divorced), who played gallant, pure, exuberant roles. This marriage shocked (and captivated) the nation (see Exhibit 6.6). The public interest proved that movies had left the novelty phase and become an important social force.[13]

Exhibit 6.6

Mary Pickford and Douglas Fairbanks on the deck of a ship during their honeymoon.

Hays Office

In 1922, partly in reaction to stories of sex and sin in Hollywood, the industry formed the Motion Picture Producers and Distributors of America (MPPDA). It was headed by Will Hays, a Presbyterian elder and ex–postmaster general, who took on the charge of cleaning up Hollywood movies and Hollywood's image. Hays headed the agency for 23 years, so it was often referred to as the Hays Office. His efforts were only partially successful during the 1920s, but in 1930, pressured by religious leaders and the threat of government censorship, the movie business adopted the Motion Picture Production Code to which producers voluntarily submitted movies. It contained many provisions, but mainly it stated there were to be no sexual acts or innuendos in movies and bad characters were to be punished.[14]

Movie companies proliferated during the 1920s. Adolph Zukor's Paramount Pictures became very powerful. Zukor acquired a number of motion picture production companies and set up a distribution arm for the films his combined company produced. He established the practice of **block booking,** in which a movie theater had to buy lesser-quality Paramount films to be able to show the more popular features. This angered theater owners, but Zukor had the might to enforce it. Eventually he purchased theater chains so that it was easy for Paramount to produce, distribute, and exhibit all its movies. In a similar fashion, Marcus Loew established Metro-Goldwyn-Mayer by buying several film production companies, and he also owned the Loews theaters. This **vertical integration** of companies that produced films, distributed them, and then exhibited them in theaters grew during the 1920s. One variation on the theme was United Artists, formed in 1919 by three of the most important actors (Douglas Fairbanks, Mary Pickford, and Charlie Chaplin) and the most important director (D. W. Griffith). Each principal in the company produced his or her own films, and United Artists distributed them.[15]

vertical integration

genres

Because most movie producers were in California, they took advantage of the landscape and the sun and started making westerns; John Ford became a particularly well-known director of this genre. Comedy continued, too, with Harold Lloyd, Buster Keaton, and Laurel and Hardy as headliners. A few documentaries were produced in the 1920s, most notably Robert Flaherty's *Nanook of the North* (1922), a feature-length story of an Eskimo family.[16]

theaters

The theaters themselves became larger and plusher, with ushers and ornate decorations that catered to rich and poor alike. Two of the most elaborate were Radio City Music Hall in New York and Grauman's Theater in Los Angeles, both of which hired orchestras to play music to accompany the silent films. Other theaters employed piano or organ players, and some even had people backstage who spoke words of dialogue. But that would soon change.

6.6 Sound

As mentioned previously, Edison's early idea was that movies would have sound—or, more accurately, that sound would have pictures. Others, including Lee De Forest, experimented with sound. In fact, it was De Forest's **audion tube** used for radio (see Chapter 5) that allowed sound to be amplified for movies.

Before synchronized talk occurred, some films had synchronized music to fit the action. Some newsreels shown in theaters of the time had synchronized sound; for example, Fox Movietone showed George Bernard Shaw talking.

But Warner Bros.' *The Jazz Singer* (see Exhibit 6.7), which opened on October 6, 1927, was the first full-length movie to use sound in such a way that it was part of the narrative story. Part of the movie was silent and part was sound. The sound parts were very static visually—for example, a static shot of Al Jolson in blackface singing "Mammy" in a theater. But Jolson exuded warmth and style when he talked and sang and audiences loved it.

Much of the film community pooh-poohed sound, considering it to be a passing fad, but the public demanded it. By 1929, most movies were sound. The conversion to sound was difficult technically. Cameras had to be placed in an isolation booth so that their noise would not be recorded. Microphones were hidden on sets, and actors couldn't move far away from them or the sound would fade. Eventually, someone thought of putting a microphone on a pole above the actors and having a technician move it as the actors moved. Also, cases built for cameras silenced them. As technology improved, production values returned. Theaters had to convert from silent to sound, but with audience members flocking to sound movies, it behooved theaters to convert quickly.

Exhibit 6.7

The story of *The Jazz Singer* was such that Jolson was singing "Mammy" as a stage actor, but within the movie, he was singing for his mother and his girlfriend.

Life was difficult for many of the actors and actresses who were silent stars. Some could not make the conversion to sound because of their voice quality. Talking movie scripts were less visual and less slapstick. New stars such as Clark Gable, Katharine Hepburn, Humphrey Bogart, Claudette Colbert, John Wayne, and Bette Davis captured the nuances needed for sound and replaced the older stars.[17]

The Jazz Singer

conversion to sound

6.7 The "Golden Years" of Moviemaking

The 1930s and 1940s (roughly from the beginning of sound to the beginning of television) were powerful years in the moviemaking business and are sometimes referred to as the "Golden Years." Part of this time is also often called the **studio years.** Major Hollywood studios (MGM, Paramount, 20th Century Fox, Warner, RKO, Universal, Columbia) mass-produced movies in almost assembly-line fashion. Directors were assigned scripts, sets, actors, and crew. Actors were under contract to individual studios, and the studios prepared materials that would utilize their talents and make them more valuable to the bottom

studio power

Exhibit 6.8
Mae West.

the Code

box office health

musicals

line. Crew members had very specific jobs that they undertook from one movie to another. Lighting was created to make the stars look good, not to aid the drama of the movie. But despite all these restrictions, craftsmanship emerged, and many of the movies of this period are still considered classics.[18]

Another element that had an effect on moviemaking was the MPPDA (Hays Office) Code. As mentioned previously, a voluntary code had been established in 1930. It might not have been enforced except that in 1933 the Catholic Legion of Decency threatened to have Catholics boycott movies. Although banned by the voluntary code, sexual innuendos still appeared, but now they were verbal as well as visual. Mae West (see Exhibit 6.8), in particular, used her throaty voice and undulating hips to sing songs with titles such as "I Like a Guy Who Takes His Time" and to make comments such as "Are you packing a rod or are you just glad to see me?"

The Catholic leadership was strong enough to influence many of the MPPDA provisions, such as one that stipulated that a producer who released a movie without getting approval through the MPPDA would be fined $25,000. To obtain approval, the movie had to pass the code's moral restrictions. Sexual language, promiscuity, and "unnatural" sex were not permitted, but even hints of sex between married couples were frowned upon. Long-wedded Nick and Nora Charles of *The Thin Man* (1934) each had a separate twin bed. Many words were prohibited in scripts—not only *damn* and *hell,* but also words such as *guts* and *louse,* which were considered lacking in gentility. Anything illegal could not be shown as pleasant or profitable, so gangsters no longer lived fancy lives before meeting their comeuppance. Mae West's career plummeted.[19]

This led to movies that were basically escapist fare and showed life in a good light, even though it was the Great Depression. Audiences enjoyed movies as an inexpensive form of entertainment that carried them away from their day-to-day troubles. Theaters started showing double features during the 1930s because this sounded like a better deal to moviegoers. Usually at least one of the features was a **B picture** (a movie that was relatively inexpensive to produce because it didn't have big-name stars or expensive sets), but people still flocked to see them. The box office was healthy during most of the Depression and was particularly healthy right after World War II. In 1946, an average of more than 90 million tickets a week were sold, the highest of any year in film history. Today's figure is about 26 million.[20]

Films of various genres were popular during the 1930s and 1940s. Now that song and dance could be synchronized, musicals became a well-known genre. MGM specialized in them, and its director/choreographer, Busby Berkeley, cranked them out (see Exhibit 6.9). Many were "backstage" stories of life in the theater business. They were thin on plot but contained dazzling musical numbers with complicated choreography and varied camera angles. There were musicals for children (often starring Shirley Temple), musicals on ice, and musicals under water, among others.

Westerns and comedies continued to be popular with the Marx Brothers, among others, performing crazy, unpredictable antics. Frank Capra directed movies about life in America such as *Mr. Smith Goes to Washington* (1939) and *It's a Wonderful Life* (1946), which glorified simple people struggling against those with power and money. Gangster films, albeit with gangsters who fit the provisions of the code, became popular during these years. Disney produced animated family movies, first short films such as *The Three Little Pigs* (1933) and then full-length features, the first of which was *Snow White and the Seven Dwarfs* (1937). Patriotic war movies were produced during World War II. Some of these were documentaries directed by major feature-film directors, such as John Ford's *The Battle of Midway* (1942) and Frank Capra's *Why We Fight* series (1942). Also during the war, "film noir" became a popular genre, with its dark, conflicted heroes and heroines. One of the classic films of this genre was *Casablanca*.[21]

Exhibit 6.9

An elaborate musical number from Busby Berkeley's *Golddiggers of 1933*.

Hitchcock

Welles

Two of the most influential directors of the Golden Years were Alfred Hitchcock and Orson Welles. Hitchcock was one of a number of directors who started in England and moved to the United States. His movies—with such well-known actors as Jimmy Stewart, Cary Grant, Ingrid Bergman, and Grace Kelly—include alarming crimes that occur in public places and humor in the face of impending doom. Tiny details reveal clues and normal and abnormal behaviors are separated by a very thin line. He was a master at using editing to increase the sense of horror without actually showing gory events, such as in the shower scene from *Psycho* (see Exhibit 6.10).[22]

Orson Welles did not produce a large body of work as Hitchcock did. His most famous film is *Citizen Kane,* released in 1941, which is based on the life of William Randolph Hearst. The Hearst family was less than pleased with his portrayal of the lead character, and the movie did not have a Hollywood "happily-ever-after" ending. It didn't do very well at the box office, but it did extend the art of filmmaking. The movie used **deep focus** shots to show alienation and **low angle** shots to accentuate abuse of power. With his background in radio drama (see Chapter 5), he also advanced sound with echoes, well-placed sound effects, and spatial cues. The film has garnered critical acclaim and was named the greatest film in movie history by the American Film Institute (see Exhibit 6.11).[23]

Exhibit 6.10

In the shower scene in *Psycho,* Hitchcock cut together 72 short shots without actually showing the brutal slaying, but the blood trickling down the drain at the end lets the audience know exactly what has happened.

AFI's List of the Greatest Movies of All Time

1. *Citizen Kane* (1941)
2. *Casablanca* (1942)
3. *The Godfather* (1972)
4. *Gone with the Wind* (1939)
5. *Lawrence of Arabia* (1962)
6. *The Wizard of Oz* (1939)
7. *The Graduate* (1967)
8. *On the Waterfront* (1954)
9. *Schindler's List* (1993)
10. *Singin' in the Rain* (1952)

Exhibit 6.11

The American Film Institute nominated 400 movies to be on a list of the all-time best movies and then asked 1,500 members of the film community to select the 100 best. The criteria were historical significance, critical recognition and awards, and popularity. This list shows the ones that made the top 10.

early color

stable color

Exhibit 6.12

The 1939 film *Gone with the Wind*, starring Vivien Leigh and Clark Gable, was shot in color and was fourth on the AFI all-time best movie list.

star costs

6.8 Color

Some of the early films had been delicately hand colored frame by frame, and some were tinted to convey a particular mood, such as red for passion and blue for night. In 1917, Technicolor was founded and established a monopoly over experiments regarding color. By the 1920s, it had developed a two-color process that involved blue-green and red-orange. This was adequate for clothing and sets, but it made people look a strange orange color.

In 1933, Technicolor introduced a three-color process that used three lenses and three separate rolls of film (one sensitive to cyan, another to magenta, and the third to yellow) that were joined when the film was processed. Shooting with this color process was tedious and expensive, so it was reserved for very special films such as the 1939 classics *The Wizard of Oz* and *Gone with the Wind* (see Exhibit 6.12). Later the three rolls of film were joined during shooting, but the color faded quickly. It wasn't until the late 1960s, when a stable color system was developed, that shooting in color became the norm rather than the exception.[24]

6.9 Hard Times

When World War II ended in 1945, the movie business was booming. As previously mentioned, 1946 was the all-time high year for ticket sales. By 1953, the weekly attendance rate had dropped 75 percent from what it had been immediately after the war. The movie industry was in a slump that lasted until about 1963. Several factors caused this downturn.[25]

The creative people within the movie industry didn't help. Stars and directors, in particular, knew their value to the studio and began demanding higher pay. This increased the costs of moviemaking beyond what the studios could bear, and eventually they began letting the stars' contracts expire. This led to a major change in the studio system because talented people were now free to work for anyone, not just the studio that employed them.

In addition, the movie industry suffered a legal setback in 1948. For years the major studios engaged in vertical integration, producing movies, distributing them, and exhibiting them in theaters that they owned. This helped the studios to become very profitable because they could guarantee that their movies would play, even if they were less than wonderful. In 1938, the Justice Department began looking into this practice, using a test case of *United States v. Paramount.* In 1948, after 10 years of litigation, the Supreme Court agreed with the Justice Department and outlawed vertical integration. The studios had to give up production, distribution, or exhibition. Most chose exhibition and sold their theaters. This changed the economic model of the studio system and contributed to its collapse. Now the movie theater owners decided what films would be shown. This increased the risk in producing movies because they were no longer guaranteed a box office. B pictures disappeared and eventually so did the double feature.[26]

In the midst of coping with the changes brought about by *United States v. Paramount,* the movie industry lost some of its best talent because of the **blacklisting** of the McCarthy era (see Chapter 4). In 1947, the House Un-American Activities Committee called 47 screenwriters, actors, and directors to Washington to answer accusations about leftist leanings. Ten of the witnesses, referred to as the **Hollywood 10,** refused to answer what, in retrospect, were inane, insulting questions and were jailed for contempt. For the most part, their careers were ruined because the studio executives, fearful that the investigations would extend to them, did not hire those who had been tainted by the accusations.[27]

Another culprit was television. People could stay in their homes and be entertained—for free. As the postwar population moved from the cities to the suburbs, they preferred this stay-at-home mode to driving into the central city where the movie theaters were located. At first the movie industry reacted very defensively to television. It wouldn't allow TV sets to be shown in films, and studios tried to prevent the actors and actresses they had under contract from appearing on TV. Eventually they learned "if you can't fight them, join them," and the studios found ways to make money from video enterprises. But that was a long time coming.[28]

The movie industry's initial response to the curse of television was technological. It incorporated large screens and special effects that were beyond the capability of the home and the television set (see "Zoom In" box). Scary **three-dimensional (3-D)** movies, such as *Creature from the Black Lagoon* (1954), graced a few screens, but the novelty soon wore off. Filming in 3-D used two cameras placed slightly apart. To show the film, two projectors threw images on the screen, and the red and blue glasses people wore combined the two images to make them look like one three-dimensional shot.

Cinerama was popular for a bit longer, but it, too, was not successful at getting people to leave their couches to enjoy a theater experience. Cinerama consisted of three interlocking projectors and a wraparound screen that made the movie extend to viewers' peripheral vision (see Exhibit 6.13). This was accompanied by six-track stereo sound. The first Cinerama movie, *This Is Cinerama,* was shown in 1952; Stanley Kubrick's *2001* was the last in 1968, but Cinerama was essentially dead before that.

Another 1950s idea was **CinemaScope.** A special **anamorphic** lens squeezed a wide picture onto a frame of film; then an anamorphic lens on the

vertical integration outlawed

blacklisting

television

3-D

Cinerama

ZOOM IN: **Grandmaster of Gimmicks**

Many gimmicks were used to bring people into theaters during the 1950s and early 1960s, but some of the best came from producer-director William Castle. Born in New York in 1914, Castle, as a teen, worked (often by lying his way in) in just about every aspect of Broadway theater—lighting, makeup, set building, directing, writing, acting—before coming to Hollywood. He made use of his theatrical experience to add fun to the moviegoing experience. He was the ultimate showman and a great pitchman. Most of his movies were B picture thrillers with spooky premises and hyped advertising, but moviegoers were happy to suspend belief and fall for his spiels. Here are some of his movies and their gimmicks.

- *House on Haunted Hill* (1959): During points in the movie, inflatable plastic skeletons attached to a guy wire flew over the audience.

- *The Tingler* (1959): Some of the seats in the movie theater were wired with a motor that gave the seat occupant a tingling sensation. The premise of the movie was that the tingler was a creature that attached to the spines of people who were really scared. One of the movie characters was trying to catch the tingler, and at an appropriate point in the movie, the seat motors activated. The people in the selected seats reacted, of course, often jumping out of their chairs screaming. The other moviegoers were left to wonder what was going on or to laugh at their friends who were being "attacked."

- *Mr. Sardonicus* (1961): Before entering the theater, people were given glow-in-the-dark pieces of paper that indicated thumbs up or thumbs down. During the movie, there was a Punishment Poll in which people held up their papers to indicate whether they thought the villain should be punished. It really didn't matter how the audience voted; it was always thumbs down because there was only one ending for the movie.

- *Zotz* (1962): Castle distributed magic Zotz coins—which did absolutely nothing.

- *Macabre* (1958): The advertising read, "If it frightens you to death, you'll be buried free of charge." There was also a "Fright Break" during the movie so, if you were really scared, you could go sit in the "Cowards Corner." Yeah, sure!

CinemaScope   projector unsqueezed it and showed it on a curved screen. This was cheaper than 3-D or Cinerama because it did not involve multiple cameras and projectors, but theaters wishing to show CinemaScope movies had to invest in anamorphic lenses, curved screens, and stereo sound. Eventually the wide-screen concept caught on, but mainly for showing 70 mm film instead of 35 mm.[29]

Exhibit 6.13
How Cinerama worked. Each projector threw a different image onto part of the screen, and the over all image melded together. The speakers allowed for six-track stereo sound.

6.10 The Road Back

Although the number of movie tickets sold per week has never surpassed the 1946 high, the movie business started to improve gradually during the 1960s. A significant factor was a change in the basic structure of the industry that finally led to profitability. The combination of low movie attendance, abolishment of vertical integration, and high costs of production led to a downgrading of power for the major studios. They could no longer afford to keep high-maintenance actors and directors on contract, and they could not ensure that the movies they produced would actually be shown in theaters. As the studio system crumbled, **independent** production companies rose, slowly but steadily, to fill the vacuum.

These independent companies did not keep talent under contract. They pulled together actors and crew to make a movie and then disbanded. They had very little

**independent
producers**

Exhibit 6.14

Woody Allen is representative of the independent directors. He openly disdained the studio system and worked out of New York rather than Hollywood. Most of his movies involve an outsider neurotic character that he uses to explore social structures such as sexuality, conformity, and religious stereotypes. Here, Allen is shown in his 1973 film *Sleeper*.

overhead and a great deal of flexibility. They did have problems, however. For one, they had to raise money to make the movie. In the past, banks had lent money to the big studios, knowing they would stay in business. Banks were more leery of small companies that were likely to evaporate. With less money, independents steered clear of the extravaganzas that the major studios produced, such as *Quo Vadis,* a 1951 film from MGM that used 5,500 extras, and *Cleopatra,* a Fox film that cost $44 million in 1963. Instead, they concentrated on movies that were stronger on plot and sensibilities but that used only a few characters and unpretentious sets and costumes.

The independents also gave the artists more power. No longer were directors and actors given unalterable scripts. They were encouraged to stamp the movies with their artistic style. Some of the independents were directors who created their own material. They were well aware of European filmmaking (see Chapter 14) and its **auteur** (French for "author") theory of directors as prime creative forces who were encouraged to instill personal reflections and statements within their films (see Exhibit 6.14).[30]

The films made by independents helped bring about a movie renaissance because they caught on with audiences, albeit different audiences than attended in the 1930s and 1940s. Movies became more geared toward the young, who were eager to leave the house and have a place to go that was not under the watchful eye of elders. The subject matter that appealed to these younger audiences revolved around sex and violence. In previous decades, the code would have prevented this subject matter, but in 1951, the Supreme Court had ruled that movies were considered part of the press and, as such, were protected by the First Amendment. Before this (based on a 1915 decision), movies had been considered art and were not protected by the First Amendment.

youth

code

The code didn't disappear, but it was revised several times to allow for changing mores. The Motion Picture Producers and Distributors of America had been renamed the Motion Picture Association of America (MPAA), and Jack Valenti headed it for many years. In 1968, the MPAA established the backbone of the present rating system—G for general audience; PG for parental guidance; R for restricted (those under 17 need to attend with an adult); and X, no one under 17 allowed. Later, in 1984, PG-13 was added for slightly racier PG films, and in 1990, the MPAA created NC-17 that meant no one under 17 was allowed—this because X had been appropriated by producers of pornography.[31]

Films of the 1950s included quite a few westerns and musicals, but they were stronger on story than their predecessors. Both these genres have had to struggle,

ZOOM IN: **Why Marilyn?**

Wander through the tourist shops in Hollywood today and you will see a large number of souvenirs related to Marilyn Monroe. There are Marilyn paperweights, Marilyn T-shirts, Marilyn refrigerator magnets, Marilyn license plates, and so on. Books, websites, and documentaries about Marilyn abound. The skirt-blowing photo from *The Seven Year Itch* has become legendary. Why does the public still have such a fascination with Marilyn? It has been more than half a century since she was in movies. She only starred in a handful of films, and often she was late coming to the set and couldn't remember her lines. True, aspects of her personal life were movielike:

- Illegitimate birth as Norma Jeane Mortenson on June 1, 1926.
- Childhood with foster care, an orphanage, various friends and relatives, and occasionally her mentally unstable mother.
- "Discovered" while working in a parachute factory when a photographer took an army picture of her to show women working to support the war effort.

- Marriages to Joe DiMaggio and Arthur Miller and "close associations" with Jack and Bobby Kennedy.
- Drugs.
- Untimely, mystery-shrouded death (suicide? overdose? foul play?) on August 5, 1962.

Why has this 1950s icon survived in such a high-profile manner through several generations? Why not Katharine Hepburn, who was a far superior actress? Why not Betty Grable, who had better legs? Why not Zsa Zsa Gabor, who had more husbands? Why Marilyn?

Souvenirs related to Marilyn Monroe.

and, with a few exceptions, have not reached the status of their glory days in the 1950s. *The Sound of Music,* released in 1965, did become a big hit. Many producers at the time thought the musical had made a comeback and came out with expensive copycat musicals, but they all failed at the box office. The 1950s also included the rise of Marilyn Monroe's career (see "Zoom In" box) and the comedies of Dean Martin and Jerry Lewis and Bob Hope and Bing Crosby. Another popular genre was the rebel youth film. Some examples are *On the Waterfront* (1954) with Marlon Brando and *Rebel Without a Cause* (1955), starring James Dean.[32]

genres

By the 1960s, the films had much more social commentary and psychology, including antiheroes and attacks on American social mores. For example, Stanley Kramer's 1967 *Guess Who's Coming to Dinner?* dealt with racial tension, and Stanley Kubrick's 1964 *Dr. Strangelove or How I Learned to Stop Worrying and Love the Bomb* was a dark comedy that attacked America's war interests.

changing content

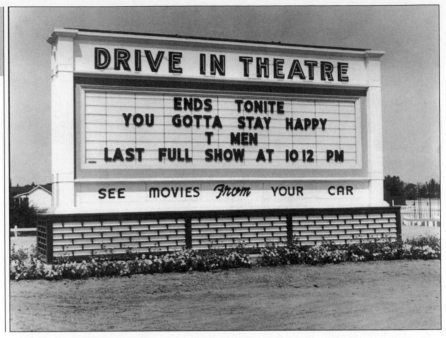

**other positive
factors**

Reasons other than the rise of the independents also enabled the movie in-dustry to get back on its financial feet. The nemesis, television, actually became a benefactor. Television stations and networks began programming old movies (see Chapter 4). The fees they paid were an unexpected welcome addition to the stu-dios' coffers. The theaters also moved closer to where the people were. First were the drive-ins (see Exhibit 6.15) that fit with Americans' love for their cars. Then came movie complexes in suburban shopping areas. These were not the large, lush palaces of the older city theaters but multiplexes of small theaters that could show a variety of movies. Of course, the price of movie tickets rose and rose, so, although attendance has never surpassed the 1946 level, revenues far exceed the levels of previous years.

6.11 Mythmakers Lucas and Spielberg

Lucas

The movie business was doing well enough by the 1970s that the inexpensive production elements of the 1960s could be set aside and movies could again em-ploy expensive production techniques. Special effects became popular, especially with the 1977 release of George Lucas's *Star Wars* (see Exhibit 6.16). Lucas's incorporation of flying spaceships and **Dolby** noise reduction ushered in a new form of movie experience.

He and Steven Spielberg led moviemaking away from the dark, negative films of the 1960s into films that were more like the older Hollywood escapist fare. They embraced elements of myths, such as strong heroes, quest-like journeys, and happy endings; and they made movies with entertainment value as a primary

Exhibit 6.16

Because of the clear delineation of "good guys" and "bad guys," some people referred to the *Star Wars* movies as westerns set in outer space. The characters Storm Trooper (left) and Darth Vader are examples of this delineation.

Exhibit 6.17

Harrison Ford as Indiana Jones in *Raiders of the Lost Ark* constantly overcame obstacles.

purpose. Spielberg's *Indiana Jones* films, starring Harrison Ford, personify the hero who overcomes unbelievable obstacles (see Exhibit 6.17).

Lucas stopped directing after his 1983 *Return of the Jedi* and did not return to that aspect of his career until 1999, when he released the first of three **prequels** to *Star Wars*. During his hiatus from directing, he concentrated on the development of special effects through his Industrial Light + Magic company, located in northern California. This company and several others have taken digital special effects to new levels that make the original *Star Wars* pale by comparison.

Spielberg remains prolific, usually directing several films a year. He has made some of the highest grossing films, including *Jaws* (1975), *E.T.: The Extra-Terrestrial* (1982), *Jurassic Park* (1993), and *Super 8* (2011). Some of his films lean toward social messages, such as his 1993 Oscar-winning *Schindler's List,* which deals with the Holocaust, and *Munich* (2005), which deals with the aftermath of the murder of 11 Israeli athletes at the 1972 Olympics. In 1994, Spielberg, along with Jeffrey Katzenberg and David Geffen, established a movie studio, DreamWorks SKG.[33]

Spielberg

6.12 Analog Home Video

"Home video" did not become a common term until the 1980s, but there were ways before that for people to record events of importance to them—birthday parties, vacations. The most common was **Super 8** film, introduced by Kodak in 1965. Because the size of the film was much smaller than the 35 mm used for

Super 8

Exhibit 6.18
An early VHS
videocassette
recorder.

professional movies, and because the equipment needed was fairly inexpensive, consumers could make their own short movies.[34]

videocassette recorders

Then in 1975 Sony introduced the **Betamax,** the first **videocassette recorder (VCR)** specifically designated for home use. It was followed the next year by the **video home system (VHS)** put out by Matsushita (see Exhibit 6.18). Both these recorders used 1/2-inch tape, but they were not compatible. In other words, a tape recorded on a Betamax would not play back on a VHS machine. Obviously, both formats were **analog** because **digital** technologies were not prevalent yet. A format war ensued between the two and eventually VHS became the most popular standard. The concept of the VCR gradually replaced Super 8 because of its flexibility and ease of operation.

Although people did buy video cameras and use the videocassette recorders to tape vacations and such, some of them also hooked the recorders to their TV sets in order to record feature films that were broadcast over the airwaves. The videocassette manufacturers took advantage of this consumer interest to refine their products so they could record for several hours unattended. The companies also added timers that would record programs while the owner was away. **Video stores,** such as Blockbuster, sprung up where people could buy or rent tapes of movies to play at home.[35]

lawsuit

At first the movie industry fought the onslaught of VCRs, fearing that people would record, rent, or buy movies instead of going to the theater. In a landmark lawsuit started in 1976, Universal and Disney brought suit against Sony, claiming that any device that could copy their movies violated copyright laws and should not be manufactured. The case dragged through the courts for years, but in 1984 the Supreme Court ruled that home VCRs do not, in or of themselves, violate copyright laws. This decision was fortunate for Sony and for consumers because by 1984 more than 13 million recorders had been sold.[36]

In the end, home video did not destroy Hollywood—it saved Hollywood. People bought and rented movies on tape in droves. The home video market created another revenue stream. By the early 1990s, movie studios were earning more from video sales and rentals than from theatrical box office sales.[37]

Analog **videodiscs** became available slightly after tapes. In 1978, MCA and a number of other companies brought to market the **laser disc,** which used a laser beam that read information embedded in a plastic disc. RCA followed in 1981, introducing a **capacitance disc** (see Exhibit 6.19); it had a diamond stylus that moved over grooves similar to those of a phonograph record. Although attempts were made to develop videodisc machines that would record, none of these attempts were effective. Discs became somewhat popular for playing back movies, but analog videodiscs never became a dominant consumer medium, in part because of their inability to record.[38]

Exhibit 6.19
RCA's stylus videodisc player.

analog discs

6.13 Digital Discs

The **digital videodisc** (**DVD**), however, which was introduced in 1997, became a big hit with consumers. It had technical quality far superior to that of analog tape and because of this high quality, the movie studios repeated their earlier fear of videocassettes and refused to place material on discs. In addition to worrying that people would stay home instead of going to theaters, the Hollywood moguls worried about copyright because the discs could be so easily copied. Disc manufacturers came up with better copyright protection and a few movie executives supported DVDs, believing that people would buy them. This did, indeed, happen and DVD sales helped bolster the income studios received from home video. Between 1997 and 2001, 20 million households bought DVD players. By 2002, some movies were selling more DVD copies than VHS copies, a trend that accelerated to the point that video stores now carry few, if any, VHS tapes.[39]

movie studio
reaction

At one point, there were two competing DVD formats—one supported by Sony and Philips and the other supported by Toshiba and Time Warner. Remembering the Betamax-VHS battle, the two sides met to try to establish one format. IBM helped forge a compromise because it could see the possibilities for using DVDs for computer storage. Companies then developed DVDs that could record as well as play back and that added to the appeal and practicality of the DVD. As a result, "DVD," which had started out standing for "digital videodisc," was redubbed "**digital versatile disc.**" The machines that could record were used not only for movies but also for music, games, text, and other data.[40]

formats

Movie studios started enhancing the extra material that they had originally put on some of the older analog discs. In addition to interviews with directors and other background information, they now created such features as games related to the movie, multiple endings, original directors' cuts, and documentaries on the "making of." Other companies offered self-help DVDs, and TV producers put entire seasons of their series on DVD, creating an added source of income.[41]

enhancements

high-definition discs

As high-definition was becoming a television reality, disc equipment manufacturers also began preparing for high-definition DVDs. At first it appeared there would once again be a format war between Toshiba, which had developed a format called **HD DVD,** and Sony, whose development was called **Blu-ray.** But by 2008 the major studios had endorsed Blu-ray, mainly because it had six times the capacity of the rival format, and Toshiba stopped development of HD DVD. Blu-ray, however, was not destined to have as successful a run as the original digital DVDs. Time marches on and discs, although they are still plentiful, are becoming an "old technology."[42]

Exhibit 6.20

A first generation digital video recorder.

profit problems

features

6.14 Enter TiVo

TiVo is a brand name, but it has become the generic word to describe **digital video recorders (DVRs).** Several companies introduced DVRs in 1999, but it was TiVo, with its clever graphics and user-friendly interface, that caught on (see Exhibit 6.20). TiVo, however, could not figure a way to make money. The problem was that the technology was easy to duplicate, and cable and satellite companies started including their own DVR products in their service packages. TiVo tried licensing its product to others, only to find that the companies canceled the licenses and went with their own product. In a legal action that lasted from 2008 to 2011, TiVo won a patent lawsuit mainly against the satellite service Dish and received $500 million.[43]

DVRs use high-capacity microchips to store many hours of video on solid-state hard drives. They convert the signal coming into the TV set from a wire or antenna into digital form, and then compress and store the information until someone plays it back, at which time the signal is decompressed. DVRs also enhance viewing. They allow users to pause and fast-forward through commercials. They display an accurate schedule of everything that is going to be on TV and suggest what a person might want to record based on what has been recorded the past. Movies can be accessed by particular actors or particular genre. Over the years, features have been added to DVRs to make them computer-friendly. This is largely because of a trend for people to watch movies (and other video fare) on their computer screens.[44]

6.15 The Internet and the "Cloud"

movie studio sites

As with radio and television, movies and home video have been greatly affected by newer technologies (see Chapters 3, 4, and 5). The movie companies themselves saw the mess that the music industry found itself in because of music file sharing (see Chapter 2), and decided not to repeat that in their business. Before the internet developed fully enough to allow people to exchange the large files required by movies, the various studios were making plans to distribute their movies themselves in a manner that would be acceptable to consumers and would keep people from being tempted to distribute illegally. Usually several studios went together to establish a website where consumers could download old (or semi-new) movies for a low rental fee. None of these ventures were overwhelmingly successful, and some of the studios wound up selling the sites to commercial companies.

Netflix

The internet downloading that, to date, was most successful came from Netflix. In 2002, Netflix began a mail-based DVD rental system that successfully stole some of the business from video stores. People paid a monthly fee and could keep the movies as long as they wanted without a late fee. They just had to return movies before they could order more. In 2010, Netflix decided to offer the movies either through mail or over the internet, and the internet downloading became very popular. Netflix then made a few mistakes with its pricing, so the jury is still out on the long-term success of their internet venture.[45]

variations

Currently, many sites provide movie downloads, each with a different business plan. Some only have very old movies; some want long-term commitments from customers; some are willing to pay studios large sums and others (such as Apple) want to leverage their success to get lower fees; some offer downloads to portable platforms and social media as well as regular computer streaming.[46]

clouds

The latest home video recorder is not in the home and is not a traditional recorder. It is referred to as "the **cloud**." The cloud is actually one or more very large **servers** owned by a company (Google, Apple). The idea is that people put all their computer material on this server and then are able to access it from anywhere with any computer. They keep not only movies on this cloud but also music, documents, and even computer programs. Very little is resident on a laptop or desktop computer. Everything comes transparently from a remote location that is out there on a cloud.[47]

6.16 Moviemaking Today

studio structure

Today most movie studios have adopted an organizational model that is a combination of the independent era and the studio era. The major studios (Disney, Fox, NBC-U Comcast, Paramount, Sony/MGM, and Time Warner) do not have stars or others under contract. They hire people film by film, using the independent model. However, they give independent film companies space in their facilities, help underwrite their films, and then act as distributors for the films in which they have an interest. Sometimes several film companies join to finance a film, as in the collaboration of Paramount and Fox on James Cameron's 1997 blockbuster *Titanic*. Banks sometimes underwrite consortiums of companies to produce a variety of films, knowing that some will be hits and others duds.[48]

Another trend in movie-making involves a revival of 3-D (see Exhibit 6.21). In 2009 Fox released James Cameron's 3-D science fiction film *Avatar*. It became the highest grossing film of all time, in part due to the skill of Cameron

Exhibit 6.21
3-D is back.

3-D

and his associates in executing newly developed three-dimensional techniques. As a result, many other movies were produced in 3-D and older movies were converted to 3-D. None have been as successful as *Avatar,* some because they were rushed through production, some because the 3-D was not well executed, and some because they did not have a good story.[49]

Digital technology has greatly democratized the art of moviemaking. When movies were shot on film, individuals could not afford the expense. But high-quality digital cameras and inexpensive computer video editing programs have made moviemaking much more affordable. Independent producers and students can now work with some of the same equipment that "the big guys" use. The re-

independents

sult is that the pool of talented moviemakers has grown. The independent producers can show their movies at festivals such as Sundance, they can put them on the internet, and they can distribute them on DVDs.[50]

digital cinema

Digital has also come to movie theaters in the form of **digital cinema.** Until recently, movies were projected using film, even though they might have been shot and edited digitally. Technology was developed to project them digitally, thus saving the studios money because copies of movies on digital media are cheaper than copies on film. The problem was that the theaters had to invest a great deal of money into the equipment for projecting the digital movies and they did not stand to gain financially from the conversion. Eventually the studios agreed to pick up the tab for much of the theater conversion and that is enabling theaters to change from film to digital projection.[51]

content

From a content point of view, movies continue to evolve. Today's technology enables many special-effects–laden movies. In fact, some would say that movies are so special effects driven that story is given little attention—but then lack of story is not a new criticism for the movie industry. Animation has particularly profited from improved technologies that have been showcased in such movies as *Cars* and *Wall-E.* Some **sequels,** such as those for *Shrek* and *Pirates of the Caribbean,* have done better than the originals, a phenomenon that was not true in the past (see "Zoom In" Box).[52]

ZOOM IN: **Ahh, Sequels**

It has been said that no Hollywood executive ever got fired for approving the production of a sequel. If a movie has done well at the box office, the chances are that another movie based on the same concept will do well, too. A sample of the diverse offerings that have been well mined for sequels includes:

X-Men
Happy Feet
Paranormal Activity
Pirates of the Caribbean
Francis, the Talking Mule
Shrek
Spider Man

For which of these do you think the sequels were better than the original movies?

Here are some ideas that have been suggested (tongue in cheek) for sequels.

Groundhog Day Revisited
Friday the 14th
127 Hours 2: The Other Arm

Dude, Where's My Minivan?
The Karate Adult
The Three Facelifts of Eve
Titanic II
Rocky: Teeth in a Glass

6.17 **Issues** and the Future

piracy

Piracy has always been a big concern of the movie industry. Sometimes movies appear on the black market in foreign countries before they are even released. The FBI and movie trade organizations have been very helpful in curbing piracy at home and abroad, but the problem still persists. Illegal distribution of films has been a continuing issue in the movie business, but at least pirated copies in the past were often of low quality because they were distributed in analog form, such as on VHS tape. Digital material can be reproduced without loss of quality, so if a movie is intercepted somewhere in the digital production-distribution-exhibition chain, high-quality illegal copies can be made and sold. However, digital technologies are here in forms other than digital motion picture theater presentation so there are more entities behind elimination of piracy than ever before. The cloud, for example, presents problems of security and reliability in addition to problems of piracy. We have all become very dependent on the internet and yet it occasionally crashes. If most material is resting on a distant server and needs the internet to deliver it and the internet fails, society as a whole will be faced with major short-term and long-term problems.[53]

distribution patterns

Another major issue involves the distribution pattern of movies. At present, most major movies are first shown in theaters and, after they have completed their run, are made available for other distribution methods such as pay per view, broadcast TV, DVDs, and internet downloading. The period of time between when a movie is released for theaters and when it is released for another distribution means is called a **window.** Theaters want a long window because that way they can accumulate the most money by being the only place people can see a new movie. Studios, however, like the idea of being able to promote a movie all at once for the various distribution methods, and they can charge more for their movies on pay-per-view services if they offer them within days of the theatrical release than if they wait a few weeks or months. Studios also sometimes garner more money from home video than they do from theatrical release, so they are anxious to shorten the window. This is a constant battle and one that has yet to be satisfactorily resolved.[54]

3-D longevity

Will 3-D have legs? It had been the "new rage" several times throughout history. As already mentioned, 3-D movies were produced in the early 1950s as one way to counter television. In the early 1970s several soft porn movies were produced with a system called Stereovision. A resurgence of interest for 3-D films took place from 1980 to 1983 that was mostly horror film oriented. In the late 1980s, the large screen IMAX format started being used frequently for 3-D. James Cameron produced several 3-D movies before *Avatar*, but they were not widely distributed. In general, excitement about 3-D has waned each time the novelty wore off. Time will tell whether or not the post *Avatar* interest will be more long-lasting.[55]

Theaters still excel over all the home video possibilities in terms of the experience of seeing and hearing a movie in a dark, acoustically-designed room. But in an era when a movie made for the theater might be shown via NBC, USA cable, DirecTV, FiOs, DVD, Telemundo (translated into Spanish), a network in Germany, iTunes, Netflix, YouTube, and many a DVR, producers must be very savvy and take into account who the audience members are likely to be and where they may be watching the movie.

6.18 Summary

Movies and home video have undergone many changes through the years, in terms of both technology and elements related to content. Technologically, the first moving pictures were stroboscopic toys that utilized persistence of vision. Thomas Edison and his assistant, W. K. L. Dickson, invented the film camera and the Kinetoscope for viewing films; they made movies in a studio called the Black Maria with film supplied by George Eastman. The Lumière brothers of France made the first projector, and eventually nickelodeons and elaborate theaters appeared to show the movies. There were so many companies with competing interests that in 1909 the Motion Picture Patents Company was created, with New York companies Edison, Biograph, and Vitagraph as the main participants.

Equipment continued to improve, and film companies moved to California where they could take advantage of the sunny weather and get away from the New York stranglehold on production and film stock. Sound was developed and became very popular after the 1927 showing of *The Jazz Singer.* Several different forms of color were developed in the 1920s and 1930s, but color did not become stable until the late 1960s.

During the 1950s, the movie industry tried technological wizardry to stem the erosion of the audience to television. Cinerama, CinemaScope, and 3-D were tried, but to little avail. People have been more receptive to the technology of later decades that has centered on special effects.

Home video became prevalent in the 1980s, although Super 8 film had been used before that. Analog VHS tape recorders had a long run of popularity while analog discs were far less popular. DVDs and DVRs, became available in the late 1990s, and high-def DVDs have since been developed. They are still used, although recently people have been starting to store their material on clouds.

Electronic editing and digital video cameras have become part of the movie production process, and digital electronics are now prevalent in distribution and exhibition. These digital resources are part of what has enabled a revival of 3-D.

In terms of content, the stroboscopic "movies" were simply moving images, such as a parrot in a cage. Edison and Dickson's movies were mostly vaudeville acts, while the Lumières took the camera outside and filmed everyday events. Early filmmaker George Méliès experimented with special effects, and Edwin S. Porter cut back and forth between scenes. D. W. Griffith developed the narrative film and produced the controversial *The Birth of a Nation* in 1915. Charlie

Chaplin developed comedy with his Little Tramp character. During the silent film era of the 1920s, movie stars came to the fore, and fans became interested in their lives. Movie content was somewhat risqué, and Will Hays was brought in to head the MPPDA and clean up movies. Zukor established block booking so all the Paramount films would be shown in theaters.

When film studios were set up in California, they began filming westerns because the land and climate lent itself to this genre. Once sound was introduced, the studios were able to produce musicals and fare that was more dramatic than in the past. The MPPDA Code's moral restrictions influenced movie content, but people flocked to the movies in record numbers. Two important directors of the studio era were Alfred Hitchcock, who used editing to increase tension, and Orson Welles, who used camera angles and focus to accentuate emotion.

When the movie industry hit bad times because of television and the outlawing of vertical integration, movie content changed. Independent producers came to the fore; they made cheaper films by hiring people for only one film at a time, thereby reducing overhead. Their films, released mainly in the 1960s, were more artistic and personal and contained the stamp of the auteur. A court ruling put movies under the First Amendment, so they were able to contain more sex and violence. Movies of the 1970s reverted back to more positive themes and happy endings. Lucas and Spielberg led the way with *Star Wars* and the *Indiana Jones* films.

Home video equipment was used primarily to view movies, and it also gave Hollywood another source of income. It enabled people to watch movies in many different places and at times that they desired. Sometimes they could even select the ending for a movie. Today, in selecting their content, moviemakers must take into account all the various platforms on which movies are viewed.

Suggested Websites

www.oscars.org (the Academy of Motion Picture Arts and Sciences, the organization that gives out Oscars)

www.afi.com (the American Film Institute, the organization that devised the list of the greatest movies of all time)

www.imdb.com (the Internet Movie Database, which gives facts about almost all movies)

www.mpaa.org (the Motion Picture Association of America, which lobbies for the movie industry and oversees the ratings system)

www.TiVo.com (the site for the DVR, TiVo)

Notes

1. Joseph McBride, ed., *Persistence of Vision* (Madison: University of Wisconsin Press, 1968).
2. Kevin MacDonnell, *Eadweard Muybridge* (Boston: Little, Brown, 1972).
3. "Vintage Instruments," *American Cinematographer,* January 2003, 70–77.
4. Georges Sadoul, *Louis Lumière* (Paris: Seghers, 1964).

5. Benjamin B. Hampton, *A History of the American Film Industry from Its Beginnings to 1931* (New York: Dover, 1970).

6. John Frazer, *Artificially Arranged Scenes: The Films of Georges Méliès* (Boston: Twayne, 1980); and Charles Musser, *Before the Nickelodeon: Edwin S. Porter and the Edison Manufacturing Company* (Berkeley: University of California Press, 1991).

7. Anthony Slide, *The Big V: A History of the Vitagraph Company* (Metuchen, NJ: Scarecrow, 1996).

8. Robert Anderson, "The Motion Picture Patents Company: A Reevaluation," in Tino Balio, *The American Film Industry* (Madison: University of Wisconsin Press, 1985).

9. The "odeon" part of "nickelodeon" stood for admission to a theater, from the Greek word *odeon*.

10. "The First Moguls," *Hollywood Reporter,* May 26, 2005, S1–S8.

11. Tom Gunning, *D. W. Griffith and the Origins of American Narrative Film: The Early Years at Biograph* (Chicago: University of Illinois Press, 1991).

12. Charles Chaplin, *My Autobiography* (New York: Simon and Schuster, 1964); Mack Sennett, *King of Comedy* (New York: Doubleday, 1954); and David Robinson, *Chaplin: His Life and Art* (New York: McGraw-Hill, 1985).

13. Booton Herndon, *Mary Pickford and Douglas Fairbanks* (New York: Norton, 1977).

14. Leonard J. Leff and Jerold L. Simmons, *The Dame in the Kimono: Hollywood, Censorship, and the Production Code from the 1920s to the 1960s* (New York: Grove Weidenfeld, 1990).

15. Tino Balio, *United Artists: The Company Built by the Stars* (Madison: University of Wisconsin Press, 1976); and "Mind of the Mogul," *Hollywood Reporter,* July 2000, 44.

16. Tag Gallagher, *John Ford* (Berkeley: University of California Press, 1985); Daniel Moews, *Keaton* (Berkeley: University of California Press, 1977); Adam Reilly, *Harold Lloyd* (New York: Collier, 1977); Charles Barr, *Laurel and Hardy* (Berkeley: University of California Press, 1968); and Erik Barnouw, *Documentary: A History of the Non-Fiction Film* (New York: Oxford University Press, 1992).

17. Evan W. Cameron, ed., *Sound and the Cinema: The Coming of Sound to the American Film* (Pleasantville, NY: Redgrave, 1980).

18. "The Screens Most Glamorous," *Hollywood Reporter,* December 22, 2010, 34–38.

19. Paul W. Facey, *The Legion of Decency: A Sociological Analysis of the Emergence and Development of a Pressure Group* (New York: Arno, 1974).

20. "The Numbers," http://www.the-numbers.com/market/ (accessed October 21, 2011).

21. Jane Feuer, *The Hollywood Musical* (Bloomington: Indiana University Press, 1993); and "Of Mice, Moguls, and Cartoon Stars," *Los Angeles Times,* March 21, 2004, E-26.

22. Donald Spoto, *The Art of Alfred Hitchcock* (New York: Anchor, 1992)

23. Charles Higham, *The Films of Orson Welles* (Berkeley: University of California Press, 1970); and http://www.afi.com/100years/movies.aspx (accessed October 22, 2011).

24. Rod Ryan, *A History of Motion Picture Color Technology* (New York: Focal Press, 1978); and "The Color-Space Conundrum," *American Cinematographer,* January 2005, 88–110.

25. Jack C. Ellis, *A History of Film* (Englewood Cliffs, NJ: Prentice Hall, 1990), 252.

26. Michael Coant, *Antitrust in the Motion Picture Industry* (Berkeley: University of California Press, 1960).

27. Larry Ceplair and Steven Englund, *The Inquisition of Hollywood: Politics in the Film Community* (New York: Doubleday, 1980).

28. Ken Auletta, *Three Blind Mice: How the TV Networks Lost Their Way* (New York: Random House, 1991), 76.

29. Dan Symmes, *Amazing 3-D* (Boston: Little, Brown, 1982); David W. Samuelson, "Golden Years," *American Cinematographer,* September 2003, 70–77; and Dennis P. Kelley, "When Movies Played Downtown: The Exhibition System of the San Francisco Theater Row, 1945–1970," *Journal of Film and Video,* Summer/Fall 2002, 71–89.

30. John Baxter, *Hollywood in Sixties* (Cranbury, NJ: A. S. Barnes, 1972).

31. "Valenti Passes the Torch," *Daily Variety,* July 2, 2004, 1.

32. "My Week with Marilyn," *Hollywood Reporter,* October 21, 2011, 62–63.

33. Thomas G. Smith, *Industrial Light and Magic* (New York: Del Rey, 1986); Donald R. Mott and Cheryl McAllister Saunders, *Steven Spielberg* (Boston: Twayne, 1986); "Paramount Confirms Studio Deal," *Los Angeles Times,* December 12, 2005, C-1; and "The Man Who Found Spielberg," *Hollywood Reporter,* December 22, 2010, 55–56.

34. David Cheshire, *The Book of Movie Photography* (New York: Alfred A. Knopf, 1984), 34–37.

35. "High Tech: The New Videocassettes," *Emmy,* Summer 1980, 40–44.

36. "3rd Quarter VCR U. S. Population Pegged at 13 Mil," *Daily Variety,* October 25, 1984, 1.

37. "Home Front," *Emmy,* June 1995, 44–46.

38. "Take the Videodisc—Please," *TV Guide,* December 26, 1981, 12–14.

39. "Thou Shall Buy DVD," *Fortune,* November 8, 1999, 201–8.

40. "Agreement Reached on New Format for Video," *Los Angeles Times,* September 16, 1995, D-1.

41. "Fox Gives Viewers a Taste of TV-DVD Starter Sets," *Hollywood Reporter,* March 17, 2005, 55.

42. "Par Completes Blu-Ray's Sweep," *Hollywood Reporter,* February 21, 2008, 19; and New Movie Purchases on DVD, Blu-ray Fall 19%," *Los Angeles Times,* May 3, 2011, B-3.

43. "Dish, EchoStar Settle TiVo Suit," *Los Angeles Times,* May 3, 2011, B-3.

44. "TiVo Digital Recorder," *Los Angeles Times,* October 11, 2001, T-3.

45. "How the Assault on Netflix Will Shake Out," *Hollywood Reporter,* March 25, 2011, 37–39.

46. "Facebook's New Offer for Friends: Movies," *Los Angeles Times,* March 9, 2011, B-1.

47. "Cloudburst," *Los Angeles Times,* July 23, 2011, D-1.

48. "Money Crunch," *Hollywood Reporter,* August 2001, 121.

49. "Conquering New Worlds," *American Cinematographer,* January 2010, 32–47; and "Global B. O. Hails 'Avatar' Its All-Time King," *Variety,* February 1–7, 2010, 8.

50. "What the New Sundance Deals Look Like," *Hollywood Reporter,* January 26, 2011, 40.

51. "D-Cinema Closer to Close-Up," *Hollywood Reporter,* August 15, 2006, 6; and "Fresh Kodak Concerns Surface," *Wall Street Journal,* July 28, 2010, B5.

52. "Summer Movie Sequels," *Funny Times,* August 2011, 8; and "Sequel Madness," *Newsweek,* May 23, 2011, 71–77.

53. "Pirate Party Fires Volley," *Variety,* June 14–20, 2010, A-4.

54. "Shattered Windows," *Variety,* August 23–29, 2010, 1.

55. "3-D Reaches a Tipping Point," *Variety,* June 15–21, 2009, A-2.

ELECTRONIC MEDIA FUNCTIONS

The various forms of electronic media must operate within the confines of certain guidelines. They should handle their finances responsibly; they must supply a product that someone wants to utilize; they need to find someone to pay for their product; it behooves them to know their audience size and composition; they must abide by certain rules and regulations and by dictates of conscience; they must make sure the product reaches its destination. The nuances of the various functions vary from one form of electronic media to another. The first chapter in this section deals with the careers that support the functions; the following chapters deal with functions such as programming, sales, advertising, promotion, audience research, legal actions, ethical behavior, technical processes, and international influence.

Chapter 7

CAREERS IN ELECTRONIC MEDIA

The information age is here, making jobs in electronic media important in terms of social significance and impact. The field is expanding as new processes and distribution means come to the fore. Whereas electronic media used to involve only radio and television, they now cover a vast array of areas including video game production, DVD sales, website creation, satellite radio promotion, internet advertising, movie research, cell phone technical development, and satellite TV legislation. It is a good time to be interested in a career in electronic media. Books, articles, and websites that deal with the best jobs for the future usually list entertainment and information among the top.[1]

> **We are looking to hire people with passion and conceptual thinking.**
>
> **Bruce Rosenblum, executive vice president, Warner Brothers Media Research and Insights.**

However, there are many people seeking electronic media jobs. Gaining employment in this field has never been easy because more people would like to be employed than there are jobs. It is difficult to gather reliable statistics about the number of people employed in electronic media. Directors cross over from commercials to broadcast fare to cable programs to movies; people who work for advertising agencies spend some time on radio, TV, and the internet and some on print; some American media experts work mainly in other countries. Likewise, it is difficult to determine just how many people aspire to jobs in the field. More than 550 colleges have programs related to the field, but some of their graduates will enter newspapers, the theater, or fields totally unrelated to their major. Conversely, students from other majors will enter electronic media.

If you aspire to enter the field, the amount of competition you face is relevant but not overly important. What really matters is how well you prepare yourself to enter the field and how capably and flexibly you perform your duties once you have a job.

7.1 Desirable Traits for Electronic Media Practitioners

Electronic media–related jobs are not for everyone. Those who crave routine, want security, or like working by themselves had best look elsewhere. Because the field is so competitive, people who do not *really* want to work in the business usually fall by the wayside. A number of traits are particularly important for media people. You don't need to have all of them for every job, but if you don't have most of them, this business probably isn't for you (see Exhibit 7.1).[2]

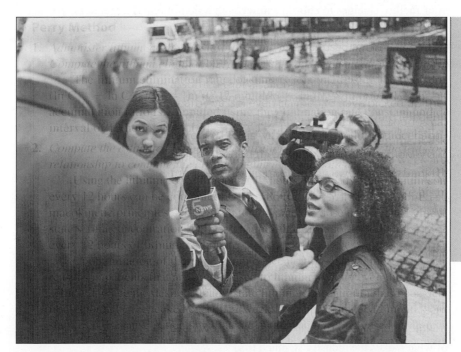

Exhibit 7.1
News reporting is a good example of a job that requires the traits discussed here. Can you think of reasons why these reporters would need interpersonal skills, flexibility, versatility, dependability, positive attitude, energy, productivity, resilience, ability to "have a life," and skill to do the job?

interpersonal skills

Interpersonal skills. Most media projects involve teamwork, so you must be able to get along well with others. There may be 200 people on a movie or TV set, all needing to interact with each other to accomplish a special effect. In an office environment, the programming executives must work closely with the sales and promotion departments to ensure a successful program launch. Reporters interact with newsmakers and members of the public. The engineers who designed the internet had to work with each other both in person and over long distances. One director selects his crew by interviewing the most talented people he can find for each position and then selecting the ones he would most like to go camping with—not a bad idea, because some of the lifestyle related to electronic media is not too far removed from camping.

flexibility

Flexibility. Because the media world changes so rapidly, you, too, must be willing to change. If you are in any job that involves equipment, you must be able to learn new operating methods and new computer programs several times a year. You can't count on your employer to train you; usually you need to learn on your own. Networks often need to make changes when the ratings are low; if you fight the changes, you can find yourself in the unemployment line. When a promising new program distribution form, such as the iPad comes along, you should be nimble and position yourself to take advantage of its capabilities. Another element of flexibility is geographic flexibility. You may need to spend six months on a movie location in Malaysia. You may need to "commute" between New York and Los Angeles.

versatility

Versatility. Closely related to flexibility is versatility. It behooves you to be able to do more than one thing. If you are an excellent studio camera operator, but your facility changes to **robotic cameras** that do not require operators, you need to find something else to do. If you know how to operate all the equipment, if you know how to maintain equipment, if you understand budgeting, you are more likely to remain employed.

dependability

Dependability. Because the media industry is so people driven, those in it depend on each other. After you work with someone for a while, you develop a mutual trust, and that trust is a large part of what makes the media business function. Punctuality is a very important part of dependability. Many functions of the media are run by the clock—the news starts at 5:00, not 5:07.

positive attitude

Positive attitude. People don't like to be around someone with a sour disposition, someone who is constantly complaining. Many things are wrong with the media business, but if you dwell on them, there is little chance that you will help to correct them. A good sense of humor helps you have a positive attitude. It also helps to exude an attitude that shows you are trying to do what is best for the organization you are working for and are not thinking only of yourself.

energy

Energy. Hours are long and activity is high. There aren't many jobs in the media world where you sit at a desk all day. Often you must use initiative to undertake some task that needs attention but that other people are too busy to do. In most jobs, you will gain energy from your fellow workers. The camaraderie that develops when working on a movie, an internet site, or a radio sales project is part of what makes the industry so much fun.

Productivity. You will find much of your energy needs to be put into productivity. As media consolidate and costs rise, people are asked to take on more roles. You need to be able to multitask so that you can work on several projects at once and complete them efficiently. You need to be emotionally smart so that you do not waste time on tasks that will not be productive. Keep in mind the saying: "God, give me the serenity to accept the things I cannot change, the courage to change the things I can, and the wisdom to know the difference." **productivity**

Resilience. Just about everyone has down periods during a career. You may make a mistake that gets you fired, but often a lack of employment is not your fault. When the economy is in trouble, executives may renege on innovative ideas you propose. When the actors go on strike, many people are out of work. When sitcoms are out of favor, writers lose their jobs. You can't let unfortunate circumstances keep you down. You must realize that security is not part of the media business, dust yourself off, and try again. **resilience**

Ability to "have a life." The media business can devour you. It is difficult to keep relationships when you are traveling constantly and working long hours. You need to take care in selecting your significant others, and you need to communicate well with them so that they understand the needs of your job and are accepting of those needs. The nature of the business can make it difficult to give proper attention to spouses and children; on the plus side, it's a fascinating business, and close relatives can share it with you if you are open to devising ways that they can become involved. Try to engage in some activities other than work, such as a hobby or charity work, so you don't put all your emotional energy into your job. In addition, save some money so you are not in a dire financial situation if you lose your job. **ability to have a life**

Skills to do your job. You do need to be able to accomplish what you are asked to do. A cinematographer must have an eye for picture composition and know the capabilities of the camera. A programmer must understand ratings. A reporter must know the legalities related to journalism and have excellent writing skills. But most people can master the skills needed for a career in electronic media; it's not nuclear physics or brain surgery. What is important is the ability to use your skills in a constructive manner that enhances the other traits that you need as a media practitioner. **skills**

7.2 College Preparation

If you feel you have the traits needed for a career in electronic media, an excellent way to begin your preparation is to enroll in one of the colleges or universities that offer courses in the field. If you are in high school, you might want to consider first attending one of the many community colleges that have excellent hands-on media programs. If you are looking for a four-year college, you want to consider personal factors such as location, cost, and extracurricular opportunities, but you can find colleges with media programs by surfing the internet or by consulting books that describe the offerings.[3] **colleges**

Often the coursework you are looking for is in a radio-TV-film department, but courses and majors are also found in many other departments— **majors**

Exhibit 7.2
Weathercasters need to have knowledge of meteorology.

communications, theater arts, English, journalism. In reality, a college education is not essential for most entry-level jobs, but people who do the hiring for entities such as radio stations, TV networks, movie productions, cable systems, and internet start-ups are interested in hiring people with promotion potential and generally believe that a college education makes people well rounded and builds good work habits. Some executives do not even bother to look at résumés of people who do not have college degrees.[4]

Although courses that specifically cover electronic media are advisable, you should also have a broad knowledge in other fields (see Exhibit 7.2). If you want to enter the news field, you will be almost useless if you are a good camera operator but know nothing about national or international affairs. Political science, history, and writing courses are a must for reporters. Likewise, accountants and salespeople should take business courses; engineers should know electronics and computer science; people wanting to work in international aspects of media should study foreign languages; and directors should be knowledgeable about drama, music, and psychology.

You should learn as much as you can about budgeting and finance because you will be working in an environment where costs are tight, and

courses

other knowledge

people who can draw up accurate budgets are valued. You need computer skills because almost everyone employed in electronic media works with computers. They are used to design sets, edit videos, bill clients, schedule programs, write news stories, and accomplish a host of other tasks. And, although it may sound redundant, people aspiring to communications jobs should know how to communicate. Take courses to improve your writing and speaking skills because one of the main complaints of employers is that employees cannot express written or spoken thoughts clearly.[5]

7.3 Outside Activities

work experience

Engaging in media activities beyond the classroom enables you to come closer to "real world" work experiences that will help you obtain a job. If your university has a radio station or TV facility, become involved (see Exhibit 7.3). Try to exhibit the same interpersonal skills, flexibility, dependability, and other personal qualities that you will need for a job. If you can find a part-time job in the media business, do so. It will build your work ethic and add a valuable line to your résumé. If you cannot find a job within media, take whatever job you can. People with no work experience have a hard time getting a job, so any job will show that you know how to work. Sometimes when you have a job that is not related to media, you can volunteer to take on an extra task that is communications oriented. Perhaps you can design a flyer or produce a video that the organization can use to promote itself.

Another way to make yourself salable on the job market is to win awards. Students who win prizes for productions, scripts, or articles are often highly sought after because they have proven their ability to rise above the competition. Quite a few organizations have contests or festivals especially for students, and others accept student entries to compete with entries from established professionals (see Exhibit 7.4).[6]

Exhibit 7.3
Working at a student radio station is a good activity to undertake while in college.

You should also read industry trade journals. Some, such as *Broadcasting & Cable, Variety,* and the *Hollywood Reporter,* cover many aspects of the entertainment business. Others, such as *Radio Ink, TV Technology,* and *Game Informer* are more specialized by industry or occupation. Most **trades** have not only hard copies but also daily web reports and breaking news announcements that can be delivered to smartphones, pads, or whatever platforms you request (see Exhibit 7.5).

awards

trades

One note of caution regarding outside activities: Be careful what you post on the internet. Remember that employers surf the net, too, and that "clever" video of you acting foolish at a party or spoofing an employer might just lose you the chance for a desirable job.

Contests

Academy of Motion Picture Arts and Sciences Student Academy Awards
(www.oscars.org/awards/saa/index.html)

Academy of Television Arts and Sciences College Television Awards
(www.emmysfoundation.org/college-television-awards)

Broadcast Education Association Festival of Media Arts (www.beafestival.org)

The Christophers Video Contest for College Students (www.christophers.org)

David L. Wolper documentary Student Achievement Award
(www.documentary.org/content/enter-ida-awards-competition-online-now)

National Religious Broadcasters Student Achievement Awards (www.nrb.org)

UFVA Student Film and Video Festival (www.ufva.org)

Exhibit 7.4
Winning a contest provides a good entry for a résumé.

Trades
Billboard (www.billboard.biz)
Broadcasting & Cable (www.broadcastingcable.com)
Emmy (www.emmys.tv/emmy-magazine)
Game Informer (www.gameinformer.com)
Hollywood Reporter (www.hollywoodreporter.com)
Journal of Broadcasting & Electronic Media (www.tandf.co.uk/journals/HBEM)
Journal of Film and Video (www.press.uillinois.edu/journals/jfv.html)
Mix (www.mixonline.com)
Radio Ink (www.radioink.com)
TV Technology (www.tvtechnology.com)
Variety (www.variety.com)

7.4 Internships

types

Many college electronic media programs include **internships** either as a requirement or an option. You can also obtain an internship on your own, but doing so is
difficult. Many companies do not have insurance that covers interns who are not
enrolled for college credit and, therefore, are reluctant to offer private internships.
Also, if you undertake your internship through your college, you usually have an
advisor who can help you make the most of your experience.

application

Your school will probably have a list of places that regularly accept interns,
and you can either choose from that list or find another place. Often you will
need to go through an interview process very similar to that for a job. Companies
do not want interns who might be disruptive or not fit into the company culture.
Although paying internships are available in some industries, you probably will
not receive money for your electronic media internship.

duties

Most internships involve a combination of work and observation. You
may be allowed to sit in on a sales meeting, watch a movie being produced,
do research for a news story, or proofread budget figures. You should not be
confined to the copying machines, although a limited amount of photocopy-
ing, phone answering, and coffee procuring might be part of the internship. If
you find that your internship experience is not valuable, talk to your college
advisor.

jobs

However, most internships are very worthwhile. They give you a taste
of the business and a chance to prove yourself. Even if the main thing you
learn is what you *don't* want to do, that is a valuable experience that you cannot duplicate in the classroom. Often it is a good idea to accept an internship
in an area that is outside your comfort zone because it builds confidence in
your ability to work in the media business as a whole. Sometimes internships
lead to jobs, so it is best to start them shortly before you plan to graduate.

You are more likely to receive a job offer in good economic times or from a large company with turnover. But to do so, you must gain the trust of the people you intern with, and you must show that you possess the traits (interpersonal skills, flexibility, dependability, etc.) mentioned previously.[7]

Generally you complete your internship near your college so that you can take courses at the same time. However, there are also prestigious full-time internships in other locations that you might want to apply for. One of them is the summer internship program of the Academy of Television Arts & Sciences, a program that has been listed in the top 10 of all internship programs in the country (see Exhibit 7.6). You receive a stipend and have the opportunity to work at a top Hollywood organization full-time for six to eight weeks.

Exhibit 7.6

These students—who hailed from Southern Methodist University, University of California at Berkeley, State University of New York at Genesco, University of Miami, Western Michigan University, Occidental College, and Skidmore College—completed summer internships hosted by the TV Academy.

special internships

7.5 Networking

There is a saying in the media business that "It's not what you know but who you know." Actually, in order to succeed, you need both "what you know" and "who you know." But the importance of meeting people and keeping in touch with them cannot be overemphasized. Start with your college classmates. At least one of them may be in a position to hire you at some point. Collect contact information (email, Facebook, Skype, Twitter, phone, etc.) for everyone you are interested in working with; occasionally update them on your activities and make sure you have their current contact information. Do the same for several of your instructors. Throughout your career, you will need letters of recommendation; by keeping your professors updated, you will be providing them with information they can include in a recommendation.

who you know

When you participate in an internship or work in a part-time media job, meet as many people as you can and add them to your contact list. Use your college assignments as a way to tour facilities and interview people in the business that you can contact later. Busy executives are more likely to take time to talk with a student doing research than they are to talk to someone who seems interested only in obtaining a job. It is also wise to join organizations to meet people in the field (see Exhibit 7.7). Many of these organizations have special reduced rates for students. Even though you are just a student member, you can attend meetings and join committees and in that way extend your network.[8]

meeting people

Exhibit 7.7

Joining organiza-
tions helps you
network.

Organizations

Academy of Motion Picture Arts and Sciences (www.oscars.org)

Academy of Television Arts & Sciences (www.emmys.tv)

Alliance for Women in Media (www.allwomeninmedia.org)

Broadcast Education Association (www.beaweb.org)

College Broadcasters, Inc. (www.askcbi.org)

International Radio & Television Society Foundation, Inc. (www.irtsfoundation.org)

Media Communications Association (www.mca-i.org)

National Academy of Television Arts & Sciences (www.emmyonline.org)

National Association of Broadcasters (www.nab.org)

National Association of Television Program Executives (www.natpe.org)

National Cable & Telecommunications Association (www.ncta.com)

National Religious Broadcasters (www.nrb.org)

Radio Television Digital News Association (www.rtdna.org)

Society of Motion Picture and Television Engineers (www.smpte.org)

University Film and Video Association (www.ufva.org)

USTelecom: The Broadband Association (www.ustelecom.org)

7.6 Job Applications

database

Many job application forms are on the internet and are specific to each job. Some require that you fill in specific information related to each job; others ask for general information and then request that you attach your **résumé**. In either case, you are well advised to have a "database" of information about yourself available. This is simply an organized list of what you have done in your life; from it, you can select the items that best fit any particular job. For example, if you are applying for a sales job, you will want to include your people-oriented skills and experience. If the job is more technical, you will want to emphasize analytical elements of your background. Your database can include the same material that you put on a résumé; it just contains more than the résumé. If you are filling out a company-created application form, you can select the items from your database that answer the specific questions.

If you are asked to submit a résumé (see Exhibit 7.8), you should begin with the strongest material. If you have had several internships, you might want those near the top of the résumé; if you have won two TV production contests, lead with those. You also need to consider what items will be most important to the person who might hire you. With computer technology, it is easy to tailor your résumé to suit the needs of each job.

résumés

One-page résumés are best for beginning jobs. Polished-looking desktop-published résumés are so easy to compose that they are the accepted norm. As you design your résumé, keep in mind that the recipient will probably look at it for only 20 seconds. Use bold, italics, and font changes to facilitate reading rather than hinder it. Have a uniform style throughout the résumé—don't use all caps

MARION RICHARDSON
1234 18th Street, Apt. 7; Anytown, AZ 12345
Cell Phone: 1-234-555-1234   Email Address: MRichardson@site.com

Job-Related Experience

Intern, KKKK-TV, Anytown. Sorted national newswire copy for the evening newscasts and suggested and researched local subjects for coverage. Helped write copy for several newscasts. Also worked in sales, assisting the sales manager by organizing leads.

Website Coordinator, Hatch Restaurant, Anytown. Wrote up changes for the restaurant webmaster so that the website remained up-to-date.

Producer/Director, "A Helping Hand." Produced the project in my advanced TV production class about the director of a Disabled Student Center.

Producer, Public Service Announcement for Children's Ways. Produced the project in my beginning TV production class and presented it to Children's Ways, which had it broadcast on Channel 7 of the Anytown Cable TV system.

Education

Bachelor of Arts degree, Communications Department, Anytown University, 2010
Associate of Arts degree, Anytown Community College, 2008

Awards

Dean's Honor Role with 3.8 grade point average, Anytown University
Honorable Mention Award of $100 from The Christophers Video Contest for Students for "A Helping Hand."
Best Producer Award for Children's Way PSA, Anytown University Awards Night

School Activities

Secretary of Publicity for the Associated Student Body, Anytown University
Treasurer of Television Society, Anytown University
Member of the Women's Basketball Team, Anytown Community College
Feature Editor of the school newspaper, Anytown High School

Employment

Hostess, The Hatch Restaurant, Anytown, 2008–2010
Sales Clerk, Evans Department Store, Anytown, 2006–2008
Youth Counselor, Park and Recreation Department, Anytown, 2004–2006

Exhibit 7.8
A résumé can take many forms; this is one example.

for one heading and caps and small letters for another. Spelling and punctuation errors should be nonexistent. A résumé is a sales tool; it should sell, among other things, your ability to communicate (see "Zoom In" box).[9]

Some jobs require that you submit a compilation (often called a **demo reel** or a **portfolio**) of your work. Such a compilation (be it a DVD, material on your Facebook page, or a folder) should lead with your best work. If you put together an audio or video demo reel and the first 30 seconds doesn't grab a busy executive, he or she will probably look no further. Likewise, if the first several pages of a portfolio are not exciting and relevant to the job, the rest will go unseen.[10]

reel or portfolio

Sometimes job applications require a separate written piece, often called a **cover letter**, that highlights elements of your résumé (and demo reel) that you feel are particularly applicable to the job at hand (see Exhibit 7.9) You can also use the cover letter to include information about why you are interested in the job and the organization.

cover letter

ZOOM IN: **What Not to Put on Your Résumé**

Following are some items that have supposedly appeared on résumés or job applications.

- Received a plague for Salesperson of the Year.
- Reason for leaving last job: maturity leave.
- Am a perfectionist and rarely if if ever forget details.
- Personal interests: Donating blood. Fourteen gallons so far.

- As indicted, I have over five years experience in computer programming.
- Instrumental in ruining entire operation of a research department.
- Finished eighth in my class of ten.

Why is it important to proofread your résumé? What other advice could you give to the "authors" of these statements?

Exhibit 7.9

A sample cover letter.

Date

Person's Name
Person's Title
Company
Street Address
City, State and ZIP Code

Dear Person's Name:

I am about to graduate as a radio-TV major from Thunderbolt University and am interested in employment as a country-western disc jockey.

As you can see from my enclosed résumé, I was disc jockey for a country-western program five hours a week on our campus FM and Internet radio station. The show gained a large loyal audience while I was on the air. I believe this success can be attributed mainly to my sincere interest in and knowledge of country-western music. I have been collecting records since I was twelve and have followed the careers of the artists carefully.

I am also an effective salesman and received a Salesperson of the Month award for selling video games and consoles. I will be happy to combine sales work with my disc jockey activities.

If you are interested in hiring a hardworking, effective disc jockey, I will be happy to send you an audition tape.

Sincerely yours,

Your Signature

Your Name
Your Street Address
Your City, State and ZIP code
Your Phone Number
Your Email Address

7.7 Finding the First Job

You may be one of the lucky ones to receive a job offer at the end of an internship. More likely you will need to spend time and energy looking for a job. The best method for obtaining a job is to use "who you know." Contact the people in your network and let them know you are job hunting. Even if most of them don't have any specific job openings, they can lead you to other people who may be able to employ you.

Another method is to answer ads for jobs that interest you. The internet has many sites that list electronic media job availabilities (see Exhibit 7.10). You can also send cover letters and résumés to stations, networks, cable systems, and other organizations. Again, the internet can help you find addresses and website URLs. However, when you send a general application to a company, your chances of getting a reply are low. Obviously, if they do not have any positions available, they cannot hire you. If you find a company you think you would particularly like to work for, research it thoroughly and steer your cover letter to an area where you think you could be of most value.[11]

If your university has a campus career center, visit it, because the people there have contacts that might lead to job possibilities. In some cities, there are agencies that place people in temporary jobs within entertainment-oriented companies. This is a fertile avenue because if you prove your worth in a temporary job, you may be offered a permanent position. You can also use the services of an employment agency or place a "situations wanted" ad in a newspaper or on an internet site. Neither of these approaches is likely to yield much success, however. Electronic media companies do not have trouble finding potential employees, so they rarely need to look beyond the résumés they receive.

Many jobs, particularly in the production area, are **freelance.** You do not have a permanent job; for example, you work as a crew member on a movie, knowing that when the movie finishes shooting you will be out of a job and need to find

contacts

sending material

agencies

freelancing

Sites for Finding Jobs

Entertainment Careers (www.entertainmentcareers.com)

EntertainmentJobs.com (www.entertainmentjobs.com)

4 Entertainment Jobs (www.4entertainmentjobs.com)

JournalismJobs.com (www.journalismjobs.com)

MediaLine (www.medialine.com)

Media Match (www.media-match.com)

Media Post (www.mediapost.com)

Monster.com (www.monster.com)

Showbizjobs (www.showbizjobs.com)

TV Jobs: Broadcast Employment Services (www.tvjobs.com)

TV and Radio Jobs (www.TVandRadioJobs.com)

Exhibit 7.10
Some of these websites may help you find a job.

another one. Taking a low-level (low-pay) freelance job right after college graduation is a good way to get to know other freelancers who may then recommend you for other jobs. "Paying your dues" is an accepted practice in the media field.

moving from within

You don't need to hold out for your "dream job"; just get your foot in the door. Entry-level jobs, such as a production assistant for a movie or TV show, a call screener for a radio talk show, or an administration assistant for an internet start-up, may not seem to utilize your talents, but that is the level at which most people start. Once you are on the inside, your options become broader. Many organizations hire from within, so you can move about within the company. Also, once you are working in the industry, you can greatly expand your "who you know" network and open up new opportunities for yourself.

Finding a job can be difficult, especially in poor economic times. Some people feel that finding a job is harder work than doing the job. Talk to as many people as you can who have jobs in the field and ask how they got their first job. You will hear many different stories, but some of them may be applicable to you. Also there are many books you can read that give advice for obtaining a satisfying media job.[12]

7.8 Interviewing

video phone

Most jobs require an interview. Sometimes this interview is conducted over the internet using Skype or another video phone service. If you are required to have an internet interview and you have never done one before, practice with a friend or relative. Little mannerisms that might not be noticed when someone is interviewing you in a large room can be very noticeable on a close-up of a video screen. Maintain eye contact with the camera so that the person interviewing you feels you are looking directly at him or her. Mainly relax and be yourself. Treat the interview just as you would if you were sitting across a desk from someone.

preparation

Whether the interview is virtual or person-to-person, you should prepare carefully. If you are interviewing with a station or network, watch or listen to their programming. Examine the company website thoroughly so that you can talk intelligently about your potential role in the company and so that you know some background about the people who might be interviewing you. If you can talk about the overall media business in a knowledgeable manner, you will also receive high points. Here is where keeping up on news by reading the trades helps.

attire

Plan what you are going to wear. The type of clothes will depend on the type of job and type of company. A suit would not be appropriate if you are interviewing for a grip position but could be appropriate for a sales job. People in small independently owned companies usually dress more casually than people in large conglomerates. Looking at how people dress in the photos on a company website can give you ideas on what to wear.

time

On the day of the interview, give yourself plenty of time. If you are talking over the internet, assume that there will be some technical difficulties. If you are driving to the interview site, assume you will encounter traffic and parking difficulties. If you are early, you can always walk around the block—a much better alternative than rushing in late. If you wait in a reception area, observe your surroundings. Often companies have awards or examples of their work hanging on the walls that you can refer to during the interview.

    If you meet your interviewer in person, shake hands firmly, but if you are nervous, sit down as soon as possible so your knees don't shake. Either in person or over the net, let the interviewer begin the discussion. Small talk will often precede discussion of the actual job, and something you read in the trades or the reception area may come in handy. Throughout the interview, be positive, enthusiastic, and confident. Express your interest in the specific job and in media in general; if you are interviewing for a job in television, don't say, "I never watch TV." It is appropriate to ask questions about the job, but answer more questions than you ask. Don't be concerned about matters such as vacations and fringe benefits until you are sure someone wants to hire you. Emphasize your strong points that are most closely akin to the job you are applying for, but also maintain flexibility. Occasionally people start an interview for one job but end with a different one. Let the interviewer terminate the interview, but try to orchestrate the end so the interviewer feels that not hiring you will be a loss. One way to do this is to return briefly to some subject discussed earlier that seemed to particularly pique the interviewer's interest.

    A few days after the interview, send a follow-up note (email, text, letter). This will bring you to the mind of the interviewer again and serve as a timely refresher in case he or she has been interviewing other candidates. Make the note short, summarizing points about yourself that you think the person liked the best.[13]

procedure

follow-up

7.9 Diversity

The media business used to be criticized for being a bastion of white males, but in recent decades the percentage of women and minorities has been climbing. The area that has seen the most progress for some minorities is acting. First blacks and then Latinos experienced significant increases in movie and television roles. Asians are less prominent, and Native Americans are practically invisible. Gays have made visible gains in their portrayals, but the disabled complain because production companies often hire able-bodied people, even when the role is that of a disabled person. Most older actors, particularly women, are offered fewer parts than when they were younger.

    Behind the scenes, both women and minorities can now move into positions such as producers, script supervisors, station managers, and salespeople. Writing, directing, and cinematography are three areas in which women and minorities still lag. Discrimination against older writers is particularly severe. There are more women in top executive jobs than there used to be, but both women and minorities are scarce among union members.[14.]

    Diversity is a subject discussed frequently by media practitioners and politicians, and there are organizations that work to further career possibilities and networking opportunities for women and minorities (see Exhibit 7.11). Most of the flagrant favoritism toward white males that existed in the early decades of radio and television is gone, but overall the field has made less progress in diversifying itself than some other occupations.[15]

acting

behind-the-scenes

organizations

Exhibit 7.11
These media organi-
zations help promote
diversity.

Diversity Organizations

Asian American Journalists Association (www.aaja.org)

National Association of Black Journalists (www.nabj.org)

National Association of Hispanic Journalists (www.nahj.org)

Native American Journalists Association (www.naja.com)

National Association for Multi-Ethnicity in Communications (www.namic.com)

Native American Public Telecommunications (www.nativetelecom.org)

National Black Programming Consortium (www.nbpc.tv)

National Hispanic Media Coalition (www.nhmc.org)

National Lesbian & Gay Journalists Association (www.nlgjany.org)

7.10 Unions and Agents

job requirements

Some jobs require membership in a **union** or **guild.** (Unions and guilds have different historic antecedents, but in today's society they are very similar.) These organizations negotiate with networks, stations, production companies, and others to make sure their members receive proper pay and working conditions. Getting into a union can be a catch-22; you must have a job to join a union, but you must join the union to get a job. Breaking into that vicious circle is often difficult.

Unions allow nonunion workers to be hired when all the union members are employed—something that is most likely to happen when many movies and TV pilots are being produced. The people in your network can most easily hire you at that time and shepherd you through the union membership process. Most of the crew-oriented entertainment production unions (e.g., those for cinematographers, makeup artists, set designers, script supervisors, etc.) are under the jurisdiction of the International Alliance of Theatrical Stage Employees (IATSE).

guilds

The main labor organizations for actors have been the Screen Actors Guild (SAG) and the American Federation of Television and Radio Artists (AFTRA). In 2012 these two organizatins merged. Established directors belong to the Directors Guild of America (DGA), producers belong to the Producers Guild of America (PGA), and writers have the Writers Guild of America (WGA).[16]

nonunion

Of course, there are many electronic media jobs, such as those in management and sales, which do not require union or guild membership. Even within production and news, where the unions are most visible, you can work without being a union member. Radio and TV stations in small markets, some cable TV networks, independent movie production companies, internet organizations, video game producers—most of these are not unionized. Many recent college graduates work freelance on independent movies, albeit for much less money than union members who are working on major Hollywood movies. In order to avoid requirements related to unions, some of the large unionized companies locate their productions in "right to work" states; these are states, mainly in the

South and Midwest, which have laws that require unionized workplaces to allow employees to work whether or not they are union members.

Actors, musicians, writers, directors, and other creative people often need **agents**. Their function is to find work for their clients in return for a percentage— usually 10 to 15 percent. Many production companies will not deal directly with actors and others; they deal only through agents. Newcomers have little chance of being noticed without an agent. Getting an agent when you have little experience can be difficult. It is much easier for an agent to find work for someone with an established name than someone in the "Who's she?" category. The best way to attract an agent is to have completed a sizable body of work (community playhouse, actors' workshops, scripts) to show that you are really serious about working in the business.[17]

agents

7.11 Compensation

On the average, electronic media jobs are not especially high-paying. True, superstars and some top executives make millions, but they are few and far between. Others earn a decent but not sensational living. There is no standard pattern on fringe benefits, but many employers provide medical insurance and vacations for full-time, but not freelance, employees. People who belong to unions can often obtain benefits from them.

pay

What undoubtedly attracts most people to electronic media is the glamour, excitement, and power of the profession (see Exhibit 7.12). All of these are present (albeit to a lesser degree than most people think), and they do make for a richer, more rewarding life than many people experience in other day-to-day occupations.

other benefits

Exhibit 7.12
Co-producer Michele Tasoff talks with Barack Obama during a break in the taping of *The Tonight Show.*

7.12 Types of Job Possibilities

variations

You don't need to decide the particulars regarding the type of electronic media job you want. Once you obtain a position, you can move around. In fact sometimes the industry does the moving for you. It changes so rapidly that you are unlikely to keep the same job doing the same thing for your entire career. Also, your job may vary depending on the organization you work for. At a small independently owned radio station, the person hired to oversee programming might also work an on-air shift, sell ads, produce commercials, and even sweep the floor. At a large network, the programming department may have many people, with specific employees in charge of comedy, drama, daytime programs, and children's programming. The type of media is another factor. The sales department at a commercial TV station is primarily concerned with selling to advertisers. Within a satellite TV system, the selling is aimed toward subscribers.

Some students may know exactly what they want do—"I've wanted to direct movies since I was five years old." Even so, they need to know how the industry operates, and they need to explore the paths they can take to reach their goals. Other students may be open to any option but want to narrow the field of possibilities.

narrowing the field

One method for determining what direction(s) you might focus your career is to make a matrix (see Exhibit 7.13). Down the side, you can list major media forms. Across the top, you can list job possibilities; to get started, you can list the categories discussed in the remainder of this chapter. However, as you read this chapter and the rest of the book, you will discover specific jobs that are excellent entry-level positions, and you can add them to your list. Once you finish your

Exhibit 7.13 Building a matrix like this may help you decide what jobs you want—and don't want.

	Production	News	Programming	Engineering	Sales	Administration
Job Matrix						
Internet						
Portable Platforms						
Cable TV						
Satellite TV						
Telco TV						
Commercial TV						
Public TV						
Commercial Radio						
Public Radio						
Movies						
Home Video						
Corporate TV						

matrix, you can combine various media and jobs and ask yourself what interests you most. Would you consider a sales job in radio? Would you like to be an administrator of an internet start-up? Do you want to be a news reporter for a cable TV channel? If you find there are areas that don't interest you, eliminate them.

7.12a Production

Production jobs are the ones people think of most readily when considering job possibilities in electronic media. Everyone has heard of **actors, directors, producers,** and **writers,** and many people are attracted to the media because they want to fill one of those roles. These four positions are generally referred to as **above-the-line** jobs and, as you might expect, they are the most difficult jobs to obtain. The good news is that there are many other creative jobs, usually referred to as **below-the-line** positions, which are excellent careers in themselves but can also lead to other jobs. (The terms "above-the-line" and "below-the-line" come from production budgets, in which costs associated with actors, directors, producers, and writers are summarized at the top. Then a line is drawn and below that line are the costs associated with craft and technical jobs.)[18]

All you need to do is take a look at the closing credits for a movie or TV show to see that there are often hundreds of people involved in the production process. Some jobs, such as camera operator and editor, are fairly well understood, but other jobs, such as the ones listed in Exhibit 7.14 are lesser known but fulfilling. How specific jobs are executed depends, to some degree, on the type of production. Game shows are produced in a **studio** with multiple cameras sending signals to a nearby **control room** where the director and other crew members sit to select the pictures and sound that will be recorded. Documentaries are shot at whatever location is appropriate, usually with only one camera. Sports events come live from sports venues and involve roving cameras and a truck that acts as a control room. It is possible that during your career you will operate a camera for all three types of productions, but the techniques needed for each will be different.

Areas other than television and movies also include creative production jobs. Radio disc jockeys create their banter and interact with the music they play. Webmasters handle the design and creation of websites. Video game creators constantly push the envelope as advancing technologies allow them to be more creative.

You might want to consider working in **corporate video,** a fertile area that job applicants often ignore. Many organizations, such as businesses, governments, churches, hospitals, and educational institutions, make use of video, the internet, DVDs, and other media to enhance their operations (see Exhibit 7.15). Finding a job in this area, either freelance or full-time, is somewhat easier than finding one in conventional media, and many people are able to move back and forth between corporate video and other fields.

Somewhat related to corporate video is **event video.** Even as a college student, you can earn decent pay recording and editing weddings, birthday parties, retirement parties, and the like. For production practice, you can produce material for social networking sites, but at present there isn't an obvious way to earn money in that field.

above-the-line

below-the-line

type of production

other areas

corporate video

event video

Selected Below-the-Line Production Jobs

boom operator: holds the microphone on a long pole above the talent during
production.

color timer: makes sure the colors in the frames of the final product are consistent
and in line with what the director wants.

Foley artist: creates noises such as walking on gravel or clinking of glasses to
accompany a movie.

gaffer: heads the lighting crew as they position the lights.

lead person: supervises the set dressers—the people who buy and arrange pillows,
magazines, and other elements that give a proper ambience to the set.

location scout: finds appropriate places to shoot a production that are in line with
what the script needs.

matte artist: creates computerized backgrounds that are part of visual effects.

production designer: oversees the "look" of a production, making sure the set,
props, costumes, makeup, etc. work together and are consistent with the needs
of the story.

property master: finds or constructs props and makes sure they are properly placed
on the set.

pyrotechnician: oversees the setting of fires that are part of special effects.

rigging grip: sets up lights that are near the ceiling of a studio.

script supervisor: works closely with the director making sure all the scenes are
shot and making notes about what actors are wearing and doing so that there are
no continuity problems in the finished product.

sound designer: oversees how sounds such as music, sound effects, and dialogue
will be incorporated into the movie and coordinate with the picture needs.

stand-by painter: touches up paint that gets damaged during rehearsal or
production.

technical director: operates the switcher to select shots during a studio shoot.

In short, there are many opportunities related to production. You need to understand the basics of equipment and aesthetics, something that is usually taught at the college level in production courses. Reading about production helps, but undertaking projects for fun or profit is what will sharpen your skills and prepare you for when that "dream job" comes along.[19]

7.12b News

structure

News can be considered one type of production. It involves cameras, microphones, sets, and many elements common to other programs. However, most of the people in the news field are trained in broadcast journalism because news has special laws and reporting techniques. Generally a **news producer** oversees each newscast, organizing it and deciding what to include. There are no actors; rather there are **news reporters** and **anchor people** (see Exhibit 7.16). There may be writers, but they mostly rewrite material that has come from other sources rather than creating their own material. In addition, there are **assignment editors** who

From One Generation to Another

"One generation will commend your works to another; they will tell of your mighty acts." Psalm 145:4

VIDEO

Here are links to five videos about Zion and about the new stewardship campaign. Enjoy!

	Click this link to play video	*Description*	*Length*
	Pastor.avi	An introduction to the stewardship campaign from Senior Pastor Mark Rossington	4:52
	Schools.avi	A video about Zion's schools	3:22
	History.avi	A video about Zion's history	6:38
	Oswald.avi	A skit in which Oswald learns about stewardship from his sidekick Eddie	5:46
	Helicopter.avi	A birds-eye fly-over of Zion's campus	1:29

Exhibit 7.15

An opening page of a church's CD-ROM, which uses photos, text, and hyperlinks to video clips.

keep track of stories that need to be covered and send reporters to cover these stories. News people can work for stations and networks, or they can work for other companies that supply news, such as **news agencies** or companies with helicopters that broadcast traffic information to a number of stations. Reporters generally have no idea what they are going to do when they report to work. Their duties evolve as the events of the day evolve. Some news operations work toward specific deadlines, such as the 5:00 P.M. news. Others, such as 24-hour news services, have constant deadlines.

There are differences in news procedures for different media forms. Radio is obviously different from television in that radio doesn't have pictures, and there- **variations**
fore reporters and anchors need to provide mind's eye pictures for the listeners.

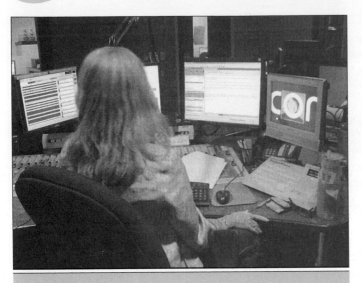

Exhibit 7.16

Radio news anchor Tammy Trujillo undertakes various tasks. Obviously, she reads the news from a script, such as the one seen on the computer screen to her right. She also does her own engineering, operating an audio board and audio playback devices. She follows the list of items to be broadcast on the screen to the left and signs off that each element has aired. She also looks for new stories. She can use the monitor to the far right to check video feeds from television stations or news agencies and a monitor directly in front of her to access databases and the internet.

For radio, reporters and anchors operate their own equipment. Most television reporters have camera operators with them, although some stations require reporters to operate their own cameras by placing them on tripods and standing in front of them for introductions and interviews. Anchors in a TV studio may operate the **teleprompter** on which their script is written, but there are crew members to operate most of the studio and control room equipment. Many people supply news on the internet, some of whom are **bloggers** with no training in journalism, but generally they are not paid. The people who select and organize the news for websites of news organizations are employees of those organizations.

The news business can be gritty in that you often wind up at fires, floods, or shootings, and you are expected to ask hard questions of people who do not want to be questioned. But you are at the forefront of current events, and you meet fascinating people from all walks of life.[20]

7.12c Programming

different systems

Programming jobs encompass deciding what should be distributed to the public and when. Some programmers have very little choice; they simply pass through what the network or networks send them. A programmer for a local cable TV system, for example, has almost no say as to what is shown on ESPN, MTV, or any other cable network, but often that person has a say as to which cable networks the system will carry. In other situations, particularly at the broadcast and cable networks, the programming department has a great deal of power because it is in charge of the company's primary product.

The heads of programming—usually called program directors, program managers, or vice presidents of programming—do not make major programming decisions by themselves. The sales department has input in terms of what programs will be the easiest to sell to advertisers. Top management often has a major say regarding programming; in fact, if program acquisition is fairly uncomplicated, a general manager may handle it and there will be no program manager.

hot seat

But programmers who are on the hot seat at major networks have a hectic, and often short-lived, existence. There is no routine way to produce hits. The public is fickle and what works one month may not work the next. The program head who is perceived to have lost touch is quickly replaced. But the programming department can be an exciting, powerful place, and programmers work with very creative people as they find, develop, and schedule programs. This process will be discussed in Chapter 8.

The word *programming* has several other meanings. Within the computer world, programming refers to writing the code that controls computer functions. Programming a video game, for example, does not refer to scheduling but rather to creating it in such a way that it will respond to the actions of the players. Consumers also program their TiVos or other recording devices to record a program at a particular time and store it for later viewing. In this case, consumers are taking away some of the power of network programmers. Programming also has a different connotation on the internet. Anyone can be a programmer and place material on a website, although it takes a lot of effort to program successfully (see "Zoom In" box).[21]

other programming

7.12d Engineering

The people who develop, operate, maintain, and install equipment and systems needed for producing and distributing material for various electronic media are often referred to as engineers. Sometimes they work within a company department called engineering or technical services. The current trend, however, is to hire many of these people, especially those who operate and maintain equipment, on a freelance rather than a permanent basis.

jobs

Engineers are very important when an electronic media entity is starting. In fact, it is technical people who usually design and test new technologies such as the internet, cell phones, satellites, or high-definition TV. Equipment companies, such as Sony and Panasonic, hire engineers to develop new products and improve old ones. Distribution systems must operate technically before programming can be sent out to listeners, viewers, or surfers (see Chapter 13).

start-up

In electronic media companies that have engineering departments, the head of the department is called the chief engineer. Among this person's duties are scheduling the people and equipment, tending to the transmitter or satellite dishes, overseeing maintenance, and making recommendations to top management regarding new equipment purchases. In the cable TV and telco businesses, the chief engineer oversees the installation of the wires in the community.[22]

head person

7.12e Sales

Sales jobs are easier to attain and usually more lucrative than production jobs. There are many jobs attached to the sales function because sales represents the lifeblood of most media forms. Without income a business cannot exist, and people involved with sales are the main ones who bring in the money.

In many companies, sales and marketing are in the same department. Usually sales involves direct selling, and marketing involves everything else—hosting lunches for potential advertising clients, preparing materials to include in telephone bills to get people to sign up for more services, and working with the programming department to develop shows that appeal to potential customers.

marketing

ZOOM IN: One Unique Way to Program for the Internet

Felicia Day was an actress who had played some quirky supporting roles but felt she wasn't really going to make it in the established media business. So she capitalized on one of her other interests, video games, and wrote a script about people who played video games online, giving herself the lead as a geekish girl who was addicted to the games.

This was in 2007 and the idea of playing video games online wasn't big yet, so nothing came of the script. But a friend who became her co-producer, Kim Evey, suggested producing the script for the internet, given that online gamers spend their time there. That was the start of *The Guild*. To shoot the episode Felicia and Kim borrowed cameras, asked crew members to work for free, filmed in people's homes, commandeered set dressings from objects headed for recycling, and managed to produce the show for a couple hundred dollars of their own money.

The Guild started to gain an audience, so the duo wanted to continue producing, but the self-funding was on the brink of collapse. Utilizing guts and creative thinking, they placed a Pay-Pal button on the site and asked their viewers to donate. Amazingly, well over 500 people from all over the world donated and the series was able to continue a 10-episode season. "Somebody gave us $500 once, and I emailed him to find out if he had misplaced the decimal, but he hadn't," Day remarked. With the help of PayPal contributions, she was able to pay cast and crew and started pitching her idea to producers. Although some were interested, they weren't willing to pay much for the rights.

Felicia and Kim then came up with the idea of self-producing a DVD. They sold several thousand copies, all of them packaged in Felicia's kitchen. The proceeds enabled them to keep producing another season. Since that time they have utilized every free method of publicity that comes along—Twitter, Facebook, interviews on public radio—to create a buzz about the show. Microsoft and Sprint have offered financial support and new viewing platforms, such as Xbox and smartphones. Although the budget for *The Guild* is nowhere near that of network TV series, Felicia and Kim regularly meet payroll and have carved out a fun career for themselves and numerous others.

What elements of Felicia's story illustrate the desirable traits discussed at the beginning of this chapter?

Felicia Day.

A combined sales and marketing department is usually headed by a vice president of marketing. The head of sales, usually called a sales manager or sales director, is under the vice president. This person hires, trains, and evaluates salespeople; sets sales policies; controls sales expenses; and communicates with other departments within the company.

The main element sold in many media companies is advertising time. As a result, audience research is often part of the sales department because **ratings** are important to selling time. Ratings are gathered by outside companies, such as Nielsen and Arbitron (see Chapter 10), but people at a station or network need to know how to read the reports and interpret them so that the sales force can use the figures that most enhance the particular situation. People who are interested in audience research are highly valued in the industry and can easily find work.

research

Traffic is another area connected to sales—one that provides excellent entry-level positions. The department's responsibility includes listing all the programs and commercials to be aired each day in a **log** (see Exhibit 7.17). Traffic is usually part of the sales department because the most important job involved with

traffic

Time Scheduled	Programs/ Announcements	Length	Source	Type	Actual Time	Remarks
8:00:00	News of the hour	5 min.	Net	N		
	Cancer Fund	30 sec.	LS	PS		
	Mason Ford	30 sec.	Rec	C		
8:05:00	Steve Stevens Show	23 min.	LS	E		
	Pop-a-Hop	30 sec.	Rec	C		
	Arbus Tires	30 sec.	Rec/LS	C		
	C-C Cola	15 sec.	Rec	C		
	Articycle	30 sec.	LS	C		
8:28:00	Station Break	2 min.	LS	SI		
	Crisis Helpline	30 sec.	LS	PS		
	Richers	30 sec.	Rec	C		
8:30:30	News and Weather	2 min.	LS	N		
	Sid's Market	30 sec.	LS	C		
8:32:00	Steve Stevens Show	13 min.	LS	E		
	Fuel 'n' Lube	30 sec.	Rec	C		
	Coming Events	1 min.	LS	PS		
8:34:00	Sports Special	30 min.	LR	S		

Source Abbreviations: LS-Local Studio; LR-Local Remote; Net-Network; Rec-Recorded
Type Abbreviations: PS-Public Service Announcement; C-Commercial; PR-Station Promo; SI-Station Identification; E-Entertainment; N-News; S-Sports; R-Religious; PA-Public Affairs

Exhibit 7.17
This is what a radio station log might look like.

the log is scheduling the various commercials. After sales are made, someone, with the aid of a computer, must make sure each advertiser's schedule of ads is actually aired under the conditions stipulated in the sales contract.

Many media entities sell hookups or subscriptions directly to consumers. For example, cable TV systems, satellite companies, and telephone companies sell their services to individuals. Although this is sales, companies sometimes place this function in a department called **customer service.** This is a softer term intended to make the customers believe they are being serviced rather than sold goods. Customer service also handles complaints and questions, so this is an easy place for someone to get a foot in the door.

customer service

distributors

Some electronic media products are sold through distributors and retailers, just as clothing and food are. DVDs and console-oriented video games are examples. Movies are sold through a slightly different distribution process that involves agreements between the production studios and the movie theaters.

promotion

Another area closely related to sales is **promotion,** which involves getting out the word about a program, station, network, movie, internet site, video game, portable device, and so on. Promotion is much more important today than it used to be. When three broadcast networks dominated, they could do most of their promotion during late August right before they started their new seasons. Now programs change frequently, and people have so many listening and viewing choices that all media forms must constantly remind people to partake of their product. The sales department works closely with promotion because salespeople cannot sell ads for programs that do not have an audience. Chapter 9 deals in more detail with information pertinent to sales and advertising, and Chapter 10 deals with promotion and audience research.[23]

7.12f Administration

Electronic media companies are businesses, many of them with shareholders or owners who expect a financial return. Therefore, media companies have administrative positions that are similar to those of other businesses. For example, most companies have people who handle finances. Often headed by a **chief financial officer (CFO),** finance departments are involved in many of the decisions that affect all aspects of the company. They are charged with keeping companies on the straight and narrow and warning top executives if profits or stock prices appear to be in danger of falling. **Controllers** oversee profit and loss and expenditures, and **treasurers** handle cash, making sure the company has enough money on hand to pay its bills and also investing the company's money so that it will earn interest. Accountants establish and oversee computerized ledgers and print out various reports that keep track of the financial health of the company (see Exhibit 7.18). The finance department pays the bills and collects the money owed to the company. If someone (such as an advertiser) does not pay a bill, it is the finance department's job to see that the money is collected.

finance

Financing within the movie industry has a rather unsavory reputation. The business is so risky that it is hard to obtain financing, and, once obtained, the

Balance Sheet As of _____ (Date)		
Assets	**This Year**	**Last Year**
Current Assets		
Cash	_____	_____
Current investments	_____	_____
Receivables, less allowance for doubtful accounts	_____	_____
Program rights	_____	_____
Prepaid expenses	_____	_____
Total current assets	_____	_____
Property, plant & equipment at cost	_____	_____
Less: Accrued depreciation	_____	_____
Net property, plant & equipment	_____	_____
Deferred charges and other assets	_____	_____
Programming rights, noncurrent	_____	_____
Intangibles	_____	_____
Total assets	$_____	$_____
Liabilities & Stockholders Equity		
Current Liabilities		
Accounts and notes payable	_____	_____
Accrued expenses	_____	_____
Income taxes payable	_____	_____
Total current liabilities	$_____	$_____
Deferred revenue	_____	_____
Long-term debt	_____	_____
Other liabilities	_____	_____
Stockholders Equity		
Capital stock	_____	_____
Additional paid-in capital	_____	_____
Retained earnings	_____	_____
Treasury stock	_____	_____
Total stockholders equity	$_____	$_____
Total liabilities & stockholders equity	$_____	$_____

Exhibit 7.18

A typical balance sheet, one of the many forms the finance department prepares on a regular basis.

nature of moviemaking allows room for "creative bookkeeping." Actors, writers, directors, and others often negotiate to receive a percentage of the profit from the movie, and many times they believe they are cheated because the point at which the movie makes a profit is obscured in statistics.

Some companies, especially large ones, have **human resources** departments. Headed by a director or manager, these departments handle procedures related to hiring and firing. They place ads to fill openings within the company,

**human
resources**

screen résumés, and recommend a number of candidates to the person who is trying to fill the vacancy. If an employee is to be fired, the human resources department makes sure proper procedures are followed, such as giving the person several notices of poor performance before the actual firing. Human resources is also responsible for handling the company benefits package and for making sure the company abides by equal employment guidelines. If there are unions within the company, human resources is often in charge of overseeing union–management negotiations. In smaller companies that don't hire people very often, human resource duties may be handled by a staff member who has other duties.

CEOs

All companies have a "boss"—a "buck stops here" person. The title given this person varies from one situation to another. At radio and TV stations and cable systems, the person is usually called a station manager or general manager. At networks and internet companies, the person is referred to as a president. Often the term **chief executive officer (CEO)** designates the person at the top of the organization. There are several ways to become a CEO. One is to form your own company, sometimes in conjunction with several other people. Many internet start-ups have been formed that way with the founders becoming instant CEOs—and in some cases instant millionaires. Another way is to inherit a company, as is the case with the current CEOs of the cable TV company Comcast, the radio company Clear Channel, and the conglomerate News Corp. that Rupert Murdoch inherited from his father. Another method of becoming a CEO is to rise through the ranks, as the current CEOs of Time Warner, Disney, Viacom, and Sony have done. You do not need to spend your entire career with one company to become a CEO. Sometimes companies bring in top people from other companies (see "Zoom In" box).[24]

The duties of those in top management vary, but generally they provide the leadership and direction for the unit they oversee. They set goals for the company, trying to keep in mind both long-term and short-term success. They stand at the front of the firing line if a crisis occurs. They are the ones who must decide what to do if the competition is trying to hire away a well-liked anchor, if sales are lower than predicted, if the stock prices take a dangerous dip. Top management also deals with the outside world. Executives join professional and community organizations, and they try to anticipate the competition's next move. One of the most important jobs of top managers is to hire and motivate good people. They have to create and oversee a team of department heads who work together for the overall good of the company, and they must mediate if departments collide. They find means, other than pay increases, to keep employees involved and productive when times are bad.

The electronic media business is awash with lawyers. Most companies have them on staff or on call because there are so many laws and regulations that affect media (see Chapter 11). Many producers, programmers, finance executives, and CEOs have law degrees because so much of what they do is of a legal nature. Having an entertainment law degree makes a person more employable in many types of media occupations.[25]

ZOOM IN: **Two Paths to Glory**

There is more than one route to the top. Jeff Bezos (see Exhibit 2.11) did it by forming his own company, and Howard Stringer did it by working his way up in two major companies.

Jeff Bezos, founder of amazon.com, was born in 1964 in Albuquerque, New Mexico, and showed mechanical aptitude at a young age. After graduating from Princeton, he worked on Wall Street helping create computer networks. He had a promising future there, but he also knew that internet usage was growing and, after some methodical research, decided that book distribution would be a good internet business. In 1994 he moved to Seattle, where he could have access to a book wholesaler, and started amazon.com, named after the Amazon River with its numberless branches.

The company grew quickly and inspired other online retailers but hit a rough spot when Barnes and Noble launched a rival website. Bezos remained optimistic even when amazon.com's stock dropped from $100 to $6 a share. Armed with his ability to handle numbers and statistics, he continued to grow the company and offered many more products. He became involved in other projects, such as Kindle, the portable reading device used to download books from amazon.com, and a human spaceflight project. He has been ranked 35 on a list of the world's wealthiest people.

Howard Stringer, chairman and chief executive officer of Sony, was born in Cardiff, Wales, in 1942 and obtained a B.A. and M.A. in modern history at Oxford University. He is actually Sir Howard Stringer, having received the title of Knight Bachelor from Queen Elizabeth in 1999. He moved to the United States in 1965 and had a 30-year career at CBS, where he earned nine individual Emmys as a writer, director, and producer. He held numerous positions at CBS News, including executive producer of the *CBS Reports* documentary unit and executive producer of *CBS Evening News*.

From 1988 to 1995, he was president of CBS. Among his accomplishments were con-

Howard Stringer.

vincing David Letterman to bring his show from NBC to CBS and presiding over CBS's rise from last to first place in 1993. In 1995 he left CBS to become CEO of a new company, TELE-TV, founded by three phone companies to deliver home entertainment and information services. In 1997 Sony hired him as president of Sony Corporation of America. His appointment to the position of chairman and CEO of Sony Corporation in 2005 surprised many because he is the first foreign-born CEO of a major Japanese electronics company.

If you have aspirations to head a large company, which path do you think you would prefer? Which people do you think have the greatest chance of holding their jobs the longest? Which do you feel can have more of an impact on society?

7.13 Issues and the Future

Finding jobs in electronic media has never been easy. Hard work is the norm. One consolation is that when times are bad, it is no harder to find media jobs than it is jobs in other areas. In fact, sometimes the electronic media are better than other fields because movies, TV, and the internet provide relatively cheap entertainment that is appreciated by people stressed out from a bad economy.

finding employment

technology

New technologies often render some electronic media jobs obsolete—but they also create new jobs. Jobs for telecine operators (people who transfer film to a digital video medium) may be declining because fewer productions are shot on film. At the same time a new category of job called multiple platform marketers (people who figure out how to use social media, portable devices, satellite radio, and such to build awareness for products and services) is created because of the all the new distribution technologies.

project orientation

Many media companies are now project oriented rather than function oriented. A group of people is hired to do one public relations campaign, one program, or one sales push. At the end of the project, they are let go and other groups are hired for other projects. This form of organization presents both opportunities and challenges for those looking for work.

programming

The functions needed to operate media businesses will remain intact, but the one that is most likely to change is programming. Now that people have so many options for viewing programs when they want to view them, the programming department needs to put more effort into leading people to particular programs on all avenues of distribution. This will have an impact on sales because commercials may not always follow along with the programs. There are many opportunities for people new to the business to come up with business models that can produce profits in a constantly changing technological world.

industry process

Regardless of what job you have, you will always need to understand the broad processes that operate in electronic media. A set designer who has two job offers needs background information about the industry in order to decide which job might have the greatest longevity. A salesperson who is considering applying for a managerial position needs to know the latest trends in order to decide whether such a move is likely to be financially rewarding. The following chapters of this book deal with the major aspects of the business by discussing programming processes, sales and advertising, promotion and ratings, laws and regulations, ethics, the technical underpinnings of the media, and the important role that the world at large plays in the electronic media scene.

7.14 Summary

Whether you are interested in electronic media jobs in production, news, programming, engineering, sales, or administration, you need to first consider whether you have most of the traits needed for the field. While in college, you should take not only electronic media courses but others such as political science (for news) and accounting (for administration). A part-time job or internship while you are in college will help build your network. As you begin looking for a job, make yourself a database so that you can fill out applications and prepare polished résumés. Search for jobs in a multitude of ways—contacts, the internet, career centers. Also be aware of diversity issues and the possible need to join a union.

Don't expect high pay, especially in the most competitive and artistic areas such as production and news. In these areas, below-the-line positions are easier to obtain than above-the-line, but there are many new and interesting positions in production and news that people don't always consider. Programming is undergoing many changes, making it an exciting spot for people with innovative ideas. You have a chance of doing better financially in engineering, sales, and administration positions. Engineering requires technical ability and is at the forefront of invention. Sales and related areas are important to a company's financial health and also include exciting, little-known jobs. Administration can be rewarding, especially if you become a successful CEO, but lawyers and finance people also have productive professional lives.

Suggested Websites

www.internshipprograms.com (a site where you can search for internships of any type in any part of the country)

www.rileyguide.com/interview.html (advice for interviewing)

www.aftra.com/aftra/aftra.htm (the site for the American Federation of Television and Radio Artists, a union for actors and on-air news people)

www.dga.org (the Directors Guild of America site)

www.watchtheguild.com (the website for Felicia Day's series *The Guild*)

Notes

1. J. Michael Farr and Laurance Shatkin, *Best Jobs for the 21st Century* (Indianapolis, IN: Jist Works, 2003); "Digital Makes the Grade with Grads," *Variety,* February 21–27, 2011, 1; and U.S. Department of Labor, "Occupational Outlook Handbook," http://stats.bls.gov/oco/ (accessed November 1, 2011).

2. "Get a Life," *Emmy,* November/December 2007, 32–33; "Getting the Ol' Crew Together," *P3,* February 2008, 12; and "The Price of Job Security," *Variety,* June 13–19, 2011, 13.

3. Academy of Television Arts & Sciences, *Television, Film, and Digital Media Programs* (New York: The Princeton Review, 2006); and "Choosing Communications as a Major," www.ask. com/questions-about/Choosing-Communications-as-a-Major (accessed November 1, 2011).

4. Ann C. Hollifield, Gerald M. Kosick, and Lee B. Becker, "Organizational vs. Professional Culture in the Newsroom: Television News Directors' and Newspaper Editors' Hiring Decisions," *Journal of Broadcasting & Electronic Media,* Winter 2001, 92–117.

5. Daniel B. Wackman, *Media Executives' Opinions about Media Management Education* (Minneapolis, MN: Media Management and Economics Resource Center, n.d.); and "Reading, Writing . . . Helming," *Variety,* August 15–21, 2011, 4.

6. For information on contests and festivals, go to http://www.studentfilmmakers.com/ or http://www.withoutabox.com.

7. "Interns Learn a Lot, But It's Rarely What They Were Expecting," *Wall Street Journal,* May 11, 2005, B-1; "The Great American Internship Swindle," *Newsweek,* November 28, 2011, 22; Mark Oldman, *Vault Guide to Top Internships* (New York: Vault Career Library, 2008); and Garth

Gardner and Bonny Ford, *Gardner's Guide to Internships in New Media 2004* (Washington, DC: Garth Gardner Co., 2004).

8. For a list of additional organizations, go to http://www.1800miti.com/associations/92-broad .html.

9. "Your Most Important Product," *Emmy,* February 2001, 34.

10. "A Real Good Reel," *Emmy,* February 2001, 35.

11. Christina Edwards, *Gardner's Guide to Finding New Media Jobs Online* (Washington, DC: Garth Garner Co, 2004); and "Jobs Back in Biz Picture," *Variety,* February 21–27, 2011, 1.

12. Examples of books that offer advice about getting a job in the electronic media field include: Steve Heller and David Womack, *Becoming a Digital Designer: A Guide to Careers in Web, Video, Broadcast, Game, and Animation Design* (Hoboken, NJ: Wiley, 2008); Fran Harris, *Crashing Hollywood* (Studio City, CA: Michael Wiese Productions, 2003); and Chris Schneider, *Starting Your Career in Broadcasting* (New York: Allworth, 2007).

13. Joyce Lain Kennedy, *Job Interviews for Dummies* (Hoboken, NJ: Wiley, 2008).

14. "Fewer Women Working in Primetime TV," *Hollywood Reporter,* August 24, 2011, 6; and C. Ann Hollifield and Clay W. Kimbro, "Understanding Media Diversity: Structural and Organizational Factors Influencing Minority Employment in Local Commercial Television," *Journal of Broadcasting and Electronic Media,* June 2010, 228–47.

15. "The Picture Isn't Perfect, But It Is Better," *Broadcasting & Cable,* February 7, 2005, 22; and "Some Screenwriters Are More Equal Than Others," *Wall Street Journal,* October 25, 2005, D-8.

16. For more information see www.iatse-intl.org/home.html; and "S.F. Unit Asks SAG to End Drive against AFTRA Pact," *Hollywood Reporter,* June 24, 2008.

17. Lists of agents can be obtained from some of the guilds, such as the Screen Actors Guild, 5757 Wilshire Blvd., Los Angeles, CA 90036, or the Writers Guild of America, 7000 W. Third St., Los Angeles, CA 90048.

18. The video series *Journeys Below the Line* (for which the author is the Associate Producer) gives an overview of craft and technical jobs in television. It can be obtained from First Light Media Publishing, www.firstlightvideo.com. Background instructional information can be found at www.journeysbelowtheline.com.

19. Books that deal with media production include: Stanley R. Alten, *Audio Basics* (Belmont, CA: Wadsworth, 2011); Herbert Zettl, *Television Production Handbook* (Belmont, CA: Wadsworth, 2011); Lynne Gross and Larry Ward, *Digital Moviemaking* (Boston: Cengage, 2009); and Norman Medoff and Edward J. Fink, *Portable Video* (Boston: Focal Press, 2012).

20. Books that deal with news include: C. A. Tuggle, Forrest Carr, and Suzanne Huffman, *Broadcast News Handbook* (New York: McGraw-Hill, 2006); and Frank Barnas and Ted White, *Broadcast News Writing, Reporting and Producing* (Boston: Focal Press, 2010).

21. "How a Girl Geek Made It Big on Her Own," *Hollywood Reporter,* July 20–14, 2011, 12–13; and Philippe Perebinossoff, Brian Gross, and Lynne Gross, *Programming for TV, Radio & the Internet* (Boston: Focal Press, 2005).

22. For more on engineering, see Graham A. Jones, *A Broadcast Engineering Tutorial for Non-engineers* (Boston: Focal Press, 2005); and Jerry Whittaker, *Standard Handbook of Broadcast Engineering* (New York: McGraw-Hill, 2005).

23. Books that deal with the sales area include: Charles Warner and Joseph Buchman, *Media Selling: Broadcast, Cable, Print, and Interactive* (Ames: Iowa State Press, 2009); Paul Weyland, *Successful Local Broadcast Sales* (New York: American Management Association, 2007); and Susan Tyler Eastman, Douglas A. Ferguson, and Robert Klein, *Media Promotion & Marketing for Broadcasting, Cable & the Internet* (Boston: Focal Press, 2006).

24. Material for the box on Bezos and Stringer was obtained from various sources, including www .sony.com/SCA/bios/stringer.shtml and www.woopidoo.com/biography/jeff-bezos/index.htm.

25. Books dealing with aspects of administration include: Walter McDowell and Alan Batten, *Understanding Broadcast and Cable Finance* (Boston: Focal Press, 2008); Alan B. Albarran, *Management of Electronic Media* (Belmont, CA: Wadsworth, 2009); Wayne Overbeck, *Major Principles in Media Law* (Boston: Cengage, 2011); and Peter Pringle and Michael F. Starr, *Electronic Media Management* (Boston: Focal Press, 2011).

Chapter 8

PROGRAMMING

Programming involves deciding what should be distributed to the public and when. In a limited way, you are a programmer when you decide what to put on your Facebook page. Facebook can be accessed by anyone at any time, so usually "when" is not important, but perhaps you want to give a tribute to a friend, so you decide to post a photo of the two of you on your friend's birthday. Actual programming, of course, is a more complicated process, but it should come as no surprise that the internet has influenced the whole programming process. In fact, every time there is a successful new distribution technology, it disrupts the concepts of programming.

> Anyone pitching a show right now that's not thinking about how it's going to live across multiple platforms doesn't have their eye on the audience. You have to fish where the fish are.
>
> **Kevin Reilly, Fox entertainment president**

In the early days, when there were just three television networks, most of their strategizing revolved around competing with each other. As cable and satellite brought more channels, programmers needed to think about how to brand their services to attract specific audiences. With the coming of the internet, social media, and portable platforms, programmers have had to design new ways to combine older programming practices with various facets of interactivity.

Many other factors affect programming. One of the most challenging is societal changes. The neatly packaged nuclear family sitcoms of the 1950s don't work in today's society. Audience fatigue is another factor. When MTV was founded in 1981, its programming revolved totally around music videos. The young people of the 1990s grew tired of that, and MTV had to retool to include dramas, sitcoms, and other forms of programming. In the 2000s, the MTV audience was flocking to the internet, so MTV developed more than 300 websites.[1]

8.1 Sources of Programs

Programming is not an easy job. Many people want to produce radio programs, movies, and television programs, so there are many sources to choose from. After a programmer has decided what to select, the projects must be nurtured to develop in a manner that will attract an audience, and they must be scheduled so that the audience can find them. Many programmers do not last long in their jobs. The public can be fickle and if programmers are not successful at selecting and scheduling the right programs at the right time, they are usually replaced.

8.1a Self-Produced

examples

Much of programming is produced by the organization that distributes it. A local radio station hires a disc jockey for its evening drive time music/talk program. A local TV station produces several news programs a day. A cable system shows live coverage of the city council meeting on its **local origination** channel. CBS produces some of its soap operas at its network facilities in Los Angeles. NBC produces its morning show, *Today,* from its New York studios. ABC employees decide what to put on the network's website. ESPN sends sports crews to cover the events it cablecasts. DirecTV has experimented with original programming. Vuguru, the web service launched by ex-Disney CEO Michael Eisner, produces its own short comedies and **mockumentaries**. A hospital's video department makes a tape about pediatric care to show in waiting rooms.[2]

An advantage of self-producing programs is control; programmers can decide what they want and determine how programs are produced. However, there are so many hours that need to be filled with programming that most networks, stations, and other distribution forms find they must obtain programming from other sources.

8.1b Related and Nonrelated Media

Program departments often get material from each other, especially if they are related. When *Queer Eye for the Straight Guy* (see Exhibit 8.1) became a hit on the NBC-owned cable channel Bravo, NBC put it on its main network. Disney has placed some of the ABC network sitcoms on its ABC Family cable channel in an effort to give that channel a boost. In some cities where one company owns several TV stations, the stations share news crews and reports.[3]

In radio, related stations obtain similar program material if companies that own a group of stations decide on the music for all their stations. Also, if a station owner undertakes **voice tracking** (see Chapter 5), then the various stations have the same announcer, even though the announcer may talk about local news and weather.[4]

Local TV stations **affiliate** with particular networks and obtain much of their programming from them. So although the CBS soap opera might be an original production of the CBS network, it is a program that the CBS-affiliated TV stations throughout the country obtain from the network to help fill their broadcast day. In a similar manner,

Exhibit 8.1

Queer Eye for the Straight Guy started in 2003 on Bravo, one of the smaller cable networks in which NBC has an interest. It became a bigger hit than the programmers had predicted, so NBC placed it on its broadcast network and also continued its showings on Bravo.

public TV stations obtain programs through PBS, and Spanish-language stations tap into material from Telemundo. Occasionally, especially with public radio and TV, the stations supply programs to the networks. Cable, satellite, and telco TV systems affiliate with many networks (MTV, USA, ESPN, HBO, etc.) because they provide many channels to the consumer. In a similar vein, SiriusXM satellite radio has channels from different radio networks, including NPR and Spanish-language CNN.[5]

related sources

Even when programmers are not related through company ties or affiliation agreements, they often receive programming from each other. HBO and Fox have produced for ABC. NBC has gotten some of its programming from PBS. *Medium* was produced by CBS Studios but aired on NBC; when NBC canceled it, CBS picked it up and continued its run. If one programmer is producing a show another programmer wants, they sit down and negotiate, and eventually "our lawyer talks to your lawyer."[6]

nonrelated sources

The internet has become a source of programming for networks because it is a good place to test out concepts. Inexpensively produced programs are acceptable on that venue and if something gains traction or buzz, one of the broadcast or cable networks is likely to express an interest in airing it (see "Zoom In" box).[7]

8.1c Majors and Independents

Another source that programmers tap for material is **major** production companies—the ones that also produce theatrical movies. Again, this often involves "synergy." CBS and Showtime may order series from Paramount because all are part of the Viacom family. NBC is connected to Universal, from which it obtains, among other things, the many episodes of *Law & Order* that it airs

ZOOM IN: **Up from the Internet**

Here are four examples of projects that started on the internet and moved to other media:

- *Sanctuary* was made by a Canadian cast and crew who became enamored with the idea of combination television sets and computer screens and decided to do the first high-definition online series that people could watch on their widescreen TVs. The production, which was backed by a private Canadian investor, was expensive, in part because its science fiction concept involved people who operate a sanctuary for extraordinarily powerful creatures. The original episodes webcast in 2007 were well received, but the finances were not available to continue. Several of the people involved with *Sanctuary* had connections with the Sci Fi network and were able to convince that cable network to pick up the show for a very modest price, made possible because the producer, director, and lead actress worked for free. The series was successful and renewed under better financial conditions, then continued on the air for a number of seasons.

- Steven Tsapelas, Angel Acevedo, and Brian Amyot put 11 episodes of *We Need Girlfriends* on YouTube. The series, which is about recent college grads trying to understand the New York dating scene after being dumped by their girlfriends, drew as many as 700,000 views per episode. It also drew the attention of *Sex and the City* creator Darren Star, who negotiated a script commitment from CBS.

- Michael Reiss put *Queer Duck* on a little-known website, icebox.com, in 1999. It was a cartoon series about a gay duck who lived with his boyfriend, Openly Gator. A friend designed and animated the show from his home computer. Showtime decided it wanted the series to run along with its drama series, *Queer as Folk,* and invested 10 months in legal wrangling to get the series from icebox. After it aired on Showtime in 2002, Michael and others turned the idea into a movie that was distributed by Paramount in 2006. And what is Michael Reiss's day job? He writes for *The Simpsons.*

- Even big name stars start projects on the internet. Lisa Kudrow of *Friends* fame made a series of web episodes starring herself as a self-proclaimed webcam psychotherapist who lacks expertise in her field and is in need of counseling herself. Showtime liked the idea and picked up the series to cablecast as *Web Therapy.*

Lisa Kudrow.

Exhibit 8.2

Law & Order illustrates a variety of programming arrangements. The program started in 1990 as an offering from Dick Wolf Productions, a small independent production company. The production company moved onto the Universal Studio lot and utilized the facilities and distribution function of that major studio. Universal sold *Law & Order* to a variety of cable networks such as USA, A&E, and TNT, but its biggest customer was NBC, which regularly programmed the original series and its three spin-offs on that network. In 2004, NBC bought Universal, so it now owns the series, but Dick Wolf retains creative input.

(see Exhibit 8.2). ABC has Disney and Fox has 20th Century Fox. But it's not all "in the family." For example, *Law & Order* has been seen on many broadcast and cable outlets owned by various companies. Warner Brothers regularly has shows on most, if not all, the broadcast networks.[8]

The major production companies also sell the movies they produce to pro- **majors**
grammers. A particular movie might be seen on network TV, local stations, several cable and satellite networks, the internet, and DVDs. Often the majors set up **windows** for their movies. A window is the time between when a film is shown in the theater and when it is shown elsewhere. Usually pay services and home video can negotiate a shorter window than commercial networks; in other words, a movie might be available for **pay-per-view** within a month after theatrical distribution but not available to be shown on network TV for a year. In recent years, majors have been eager to get movies into the lucrative pay market and have shortened or eliminated that window.[9]

In addition to the major production companies, there are smaller **independent** production companies that supply programming. When **financial interest-domestic syndication** was in effect (see Chapter 4), these companies were very important and provided the commercial broadcast networks with most of their prime-time programming. But now that fin-syn has been abolished and networks can "roll their own," small companies are hurting. When they do get the ear of a commercial network, they usually have to make financial concessions and give the network part ownership in the programs they produce.

independents

Sometimes independents attach themselves to a major production company in an **umbrella deal.** The major gives them office space and some financing and, in return, gets the right to distribute whatever they produce. Some cable TV networks still welcome productions from independent production companies, but they generally do not pay as well as the commercial networks. Independent producers are also active in providing **webisodes** for the internet and **mobisodes** for portable platforms. They produce movies and informational programs for video stores and computer downloading, and they hire themselves out for corporate videos.[10]

8.1d Syndicators

Other players in the programming business, called **syndicators,** supply programs to a variety of programming outlets. They are in the business of acquiring programs from others or producing programs themselves and then selling those programs to local radio and TV stations, cable networks, or anyone else who wants to buy them. Unlike many TV networks, which require all affiliated stations to run the programming they supply at the same time, syndicators give their customers total discretion as to when they air the program. So *Jeopardy!,* a show that is syndicated by King World Productions, conceivably could air on Channel 8 in Dallas at 3:00 P.M., Channel 9 in Philadelphia at 7:30 P.M., and the cable Game Show Channel at 10:30 A.M.

types of programming

Syndicators acquire programming in a variety of ways. One way is to buy programs that have already been on major networks. These programs, referred to as **off-net,** have the advantage of a track record. The syndicators can tell stations how the programs have fared in the past, and the programs may have a built-in audience of people who want to see their old favorites again. Now that people can obtain network shows on DVDs or download them from the internet, however, the value of off-net has declined. Syndicators also handle old movies, usually obtaining packages of several movies from various movie studios. The movies, too, have a track record, but by the time they get to stations and cable, they may have been shown so many places that most interested people have seen them. Syndicators also sell material that has not been seen before because it is made specifically for syndication and is referred to as **first-run syndication.** Examples are *Wheel of Fortune, Judge Judy,* and *The Ellen DeGeneres Show.*[11]

radio

Syndication is also common in radio, but in radio it is hard to tell a syndicator from a network because generally radio networks do not require affiliates to air their programs at the same time; both networks and syndicators provide short bits of material that customers are free to use as they wish (see Exhibit 8.3).

Provider	Services
American Blues Network	Rhythm and blues music in a 24 live hour format
Business Talkradio	Business news, financial advice, and lifestyle programming
CBS Radio Networks	News, sports, information features, and music
Hispanic Communications Network	Spanish-language news and features
Metro Weather Service	Tailored weather forecasts
Monitor Radio	News and commentary from the Christian Science Monitor
Motor Racing Network	Live auto racing coverage and news and talk about auto racing
North American Network	Talk shows about health, consumer protection, and other subjects
Progressive Radio Network	Programs on physical and psychological health, particularly as it relates to substance dependence
Radio Spirits	Old-time radio shows
Sports Byline USA	Sports talk shows
Westwood One Radio Networks	News, entertainment, business, music, concerts, and sports

Exhibit 8.3
A partial list of radio networks and syndicators.

Most stations want to sound local, so they do not emphasize that they are playing network or syndicated programming. Some stations affiliate with more than one network and buy from more than one syndicator.

8.1e Others

In summary, the most common ways for programming departments to obtain material are to produce it themselves; obtain it from some other programming department (related or not); or get it from a network, major production company, independent production company, or syndicator. But there are many other sources. Foreign language stations and various cable channels obtain programming from other countries. Radio stations deal extensively with music companies. Sports franchises negotiate with broadcasters to have their games televised. Religious programs are produced by churches. Video game producers obtain rights from movies to make them the basis of a game, and vice versa. Advertisers are getting back into the business of supplying programming. Members of the public contribute to programming on cable access and the internet. Just about anything is possible. That's why the programming department is a creative, exciting place.[12]

miscellaneous sources

8.2 Development

Many TV programs, TV series, and movies that are being developed from scratch (and some that are acquired from other sources) go through a **development** process that takes them from idea to distribution. Even if you are only "programming" your social network page, you probably spend some time thinking about what you are going to include and how you are going to edit any video clips you may have.

ideas
In the network world, development is a complicated process. Ideas don't just spring off the page and become programs. They must be nurtured, tested, and fine-tuned before they are ready for public consumption. The development process starts when someone comes up with an idea. The person may be a network executive who hears a radio news story on the way to work and decides it would make a good TV movie or watches a short clip on YouTube and decides it could be made into a series. He or she calls creative people (independent producers, people within the network, the creator of the YouTube clip) and asks them to flesh out the idea. Or an independent producer may hear that news story or see that clip and set up a meeting to **pitch** the idea to several network executives (see Exhibit 8.4).[13]

pilots

variations
If the network executives like the fleshed out idea, they may eventually commission (pay for) a full script. If the idea is for a series, as opposed to a single program, the executives may request a **pilot**—one program as it might appear in a series. Pilots are viewed by network executives and tested on potential viewers (see Chapter 10). If the program idea gets past the pilot stage, the network authorizes production.

Exhibit 8.4

The TV movie *In the Line of Duty: Ambush at Waco*, starring Tim Daly as the Branch Davidian leader David Koresh, is an example of a program that was based on a news event, in this case the February 28, 1993, storming of the compound at Waco, Texas. NBC contacted producer Ken Kaufman on March 1 and asked him to produce a program on Waco for the *In the Line of Duty* series he was supplying to the network. It aired on May 23.

Of course, it's not as simple as all that. In fact, development is frequently referred to as "development hell." Often there are rights to be procured, especially if the idea is based on something already published, such as a book, or on something that has already been distributed, such as a YouTube clip or a programming concept that was successful in another country. The executives may want the location or the age of the lead actor changed to take into account a **demographic** they want to attract.

Network or movie studio heads may come close to accepting a new idea, then decide it is safer to put their resources into making a **sequel** to a popular movie or a **spin-off** involving characters from a popular TV series. A children's program idea that the creators thought was just right for the Disney Channel may be passed on by Disney but eventually accepted by Nickelodeon. There are bound to be negotiations concerning the budget, and the stars' agents will get involved. And, of course, getting a meeting in the first place to discuss the idea is a daunting task for a newcomer.

Then there is the weeding-out process. Broadcast network executives may hear hundreds of pitches, pay for 100 scripts, decide to ask for pilots for 20 shows, then only produce 5. They may not even ask for a pilot because pilots are expensive and often lead nowhere, so some executives make their decisions based on scripts.[14]

8.3 The News Process

News is handled very differently from other programs and series. Because it is based on whatever is happening in the world, there is no pitch-pilot development process. There are people who decide which stories to put on the air and how much emphasis to give each, but these decisions are made more quickly than the decisions involved with selecting dramas, reality shows, and other forms of programming.

8.3a News Gathering

Gathering news is a complex process. The major providers—CNN, Fox News, NBC, CBS, ABC, local TV stations, all-news radio stations—have their own reporters who go to local, national, and international places where the news is happening to gather the facts. Sometimes these reporters find their own stories because they know the locale—if they notice new stop signs at an intersection, they investigate to see why they were put there. Other times they are given stories to cover by an **assignment editor,** a person located at the news headquarters who keeps a list of stories that are likely to become important—the city council will be considering parking problems at 1:00; this is the anniversary of a fire, so there should be a follow-up story to cover what has been done to prevent this type of fire in the future. Other times they are assigned stories by the head of the news organization—for example, they may be assigned to cover a conflict in the Middle East or a flood in Thailand (see Exhibit 8.5).

reporters

stringers

Most news organizations also use stories from **stringers**—people who are not on the payroll but who are paid for stories or footage they supply that is actually used. These people are particularly valuable for breaking news stories occurring in areas where the news organization does not usually have a reporter.

Large organizations that program news on a variety of platforms use the same reporters and same information for various outlets. For example, NBC, CNBC, and MSNBC share resources, not only for their broadcast and cable outlets, but also for their internet sites. Broadcast networks make footage available to their affiliates. This works in reverse, too. Affiliated stations supply footage to networks, particularly when a major story occurs in their city. Cable News Network makes news

Exhibit 8.5

In 2003 when the war with Iraq started, specific reporters were "embedded" with the troops. They went with them in the military equipment and used digital equipment to beam pictures and sound that were telecast live in the United States.

major providers

available to others besides CNN, including local broadcast stations. Since its beginnings in the 1980s, CNN has been particularly aggressive in selling (or sometimes giving) its news to foreign countries. As a result, CNN receives credit on news clips seen on many countries' local newscasts.

news agencies

Another source of news, particularly for organizations that don't have their own elaborate news-gathering structure, is **news agencies.** Sometimes these groups are referred to as **wire services,** a term that predates electronic news when organizations gathered news for newspapers and sent the information over wires to machines in newspaper offices that printed out the stories. Today, most news agencies sell not only written copy but also **sound bites** and video footage, which they transmit via satellite. The oldest American-based news agency is the Associated Press. A variety of other news services also supply news, such as Reuters, Accu-Weather, and Agence France-Presse. Some of them provide wide coverage of international news; some provide specialized news, such as weather or sports; and some are local. News agencies have a bevy of reporters stationed at strategic points who gather news the same way other reporters do.

the public

The general public serves as another source of news. People call stations or networks with tips on news stories. Now that many people have **camcorders** or cell phone cameras, ordinary citizens sometimes supply news organizations with footage just because they happen to have their camera with them when a major event occurs and they can easily send the video over the internet to a network or station. In addition to video and audio files, individuals also put news on the internet, in the form of **blogs** or social media entries. Some news organizations look at blogs for leads to stories while others are skeptical of their accuracy.

news releases

Many organizations prepare written **news releases** or **video news releases (VNRs)** that they send to networks and stations, hoping that the material will be included in the news. For example, Congress has a special room where senators and representatives can tape VNRs to send to stations in the districts or states they represent. Sometimes news releases do give news organizations story ideas, but often they are simply self-promotion.

equipment

In addition, news organizations often have satellite equipment to monitor weather conditions. By using **scanners**—devices that monitor police and fire radio communications—they sometimes arrive at the scene of a crime before the police. Some news organizations have their own helicopters, so they can gather news and traffic information from the air.[15]

8.3b News Compilation

While reporters gather worldwide, national, and local news, other people perform different duties that lead to newscasts. The number of people needed depends on the emphasis given to news. A small radio station may have a news staff of one person who decides what stories to broadcast, rewrites news agency copy, makes a few phone calls to confirm facts or gather material for stories, writes the script for a three-minute news update once an hour, and also reads the news over the air.

people needed

At a large news organization, a **news director** has overall responsibility for the news operation, hiring and firing people, and setting the general guidelines for the approach. Each individual newscast is overseen by a **news producer,** who organizes the program and decides what will be included. If a newscast is to include special types of information, such as consumer affairs or entertainment news, **segment producers** may oversee those particular items. Assignment editors, as already mentioned, keep track of the stories that need to be covered and send reporters to cover these stories. Writers rewrite news agency copy and stories sent in by reporters and prepare the introductions and conclusions for the total newscast.

At most radio stations, the process of selecting the stories that air is ongoing **radio** because news is broadcast many times throughout the day. Radio networks generally feed stories to stations as they occur and also provide several news programs throughout the day. Thus, the news producer of a station affiliated with an ABC radio network might decide that the 8:00 A.M. news should consist of five minutes of ABC news as broadcast by the network; a story on a fire in Delhi that came in from Associated Press but was not covered by ABC; an update on the condition of a hospitalized city official that the producer obtained by phoning the hospital; a report on a liquor store robbery gathered by one of the station's reporters; a report of a murder received from the local news agency; and the weather as received from the weather bureau. The stories of the Delhi fire and liquor store robbery may be included in the 9:00 A.M. news, slightly rewritten and accompanied by two stories excerpted from the 8:00 ABC news broadcast, a report phoned in live by a station reporter covering a school board meeting, an update on the hospitalized official, and the weather. All-news radio stations that broadcast news continuously throughout the day have many crews, a variety of news sources, and a large staff of people working at the station; this costs money, making an all-news format expensive.

Most broadcast television news has a more defined countdown because the **television** major effort is devoted to the evening news. There are exceptions, of course, including late night and early morning newscasts incorporated into both network and station schedules. CNN, Fox News Channel, MSNBC, and other 24-hour news cable services have procedures closely akin to all-news radio stations. News producers at most local TV stations and the major broadcast networks spend the day assessing the multitude of news items received to decide which will be included on the evening news and in what order. This is no easy task given that a half-hour newscast (22 minutes without commercials) is equivalent to only three columns in a newspaper. Decision making about what stories to air goes on until close to airtime, when the "final" stories are collected and timed. The anchors get into position, the director and crew prepare for the broadcast, the material to be included in the newscast is put in order, the teleprompter copy is readied, the computer graphics are polished, and the newscast begins. Last-minute changes can still occur, for the news is sometimes changed even as it is being aired if something noteworthy happens while the newscast is in progress.

Presentation of news is another important area. News for radio is sometimes **presentation** read by disc jockeys or reporters. Stations, however, vary both content and presentation of news broadcasts in relation to their audience. A rock station has a faster-paced presentation than an oldies station. All-news radio stations generally

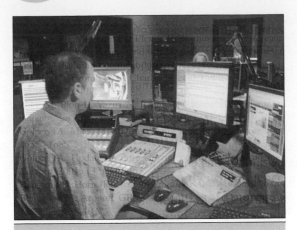

Exhibit 8.6

The setup for two news anchors at an all-news radio station.

websites

have anchor teams to present the news (see Exhibit 8.6). Because TV news can be a moneymaker for local stations, they are particularly eager to lead the ratings; therefore, local stations attempt to find newscasters who appeal to viewers. The networks hope to establish trustworthy, congenial newscasters who maintain a loyal audience.

News organizations also update their websites constantly. The people in charge of the website rework the news that is gathered for broadcast or cablecast so that it fits with the style and content of the website. They can include the same video clips used in a newscast, or they can reedit the material. They can also include material that does not make it to the newscast because the web does not have time limitations. Some sites allow people to tailor the news they receive by requesting that news about certain topics be sent to their portable devices as soon as it is available.[16]

8.4 Formats

formats and features

Within radio, the main element that is developed by stations is the **format**—the particular type of material that they program. Some formats used by commercial radio stations include adult contemporary, classic rock, top 40, country, alternative, all-news, and talk. Within the context of the format, stations may develop special features, such as local sports, farm reports, and traffic reports. Radio networks and syndicators also develop original programming, such as business reports, live concerts, and health information. Public radio stations usually develop and program classical or offbeat music and public affairs shows that seek out cultural and thought-provoking elements of the community.[17]

decision factors

Many factors affect what format and features a particular station chooses. One consideration is the programming already available in the station's listening area. For example, a jazz format may be chosen because no other station in town offers that type of music. If the local area has few jazz music fans, however, this format will not draw an adequate audience. Therefore, the composition of the listening audience is another important factor. A rural audience will probably be more interested in farm reports than will a city audience. The interests of the community and the interests of the station management can also affect programming. If the town has a popular football team, the station might broadcast football games. If the station manager is particularly interested in boating, he or she might promote boating reports.

Getting material ready to be distributed, whether through the pitch and pilot process, by gathering news, or by establishing a format and features, can be an arduous process. Even when it's finished, the work is not over. Scheduling can be crucial to success or failure.

8.5 Scheduling

Concern with scheduling is most intense on television networks, but other media deal with scheduling also. In radio, the main scheduling element that programmers use is a **clock,** which shows all the segments that appear within an hour's worth of programming (see Exhibit 8.7). Generally, each time segment within an hour resembles that same time at other hours. For example, if news comes on at 9:15, it will also come on at 10:15, 11:15, and so on. In this way, the listener knows what to expect of a station at each segmented time of the hour. Most stations change their clocks to some degree during different **dayparts.** For example, a station may give more frequent traffic reports from 6:00 A.M. to 9:00 A.M. when people are commuting than from 9:00 A.M. to 4:00 P.M. For a station with a music format, the program manager (either local or corporate) must also consider what music to play, how often to play it, and when to stop airing it because its popularity has worn out.[18]

radio

The movie business is not as schedule intensive as radio or TV, but it does have a scheduling cycle. Many movies, especially high-budget ones, are released in the summer or during holiday periods when people have leisure time to spend at theaters. Video games are often scheduled to come out near Christmas to maximize sales. The internet, because it is always available, has less to do with scheduling than some media, but websites need to be kept up-to-date, lest surfers lose interest and do not return.[19]

other media

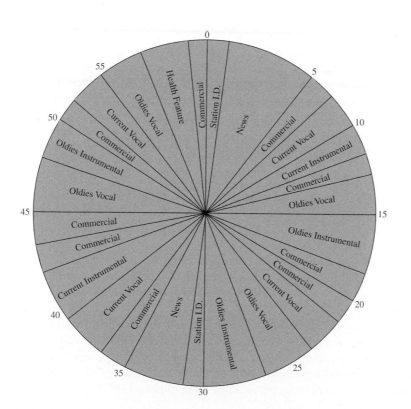

Exhibit 8.7
A typical radio station clock.

8.5a Scheduling Factors

Programmers in the television business spend a great deal of time deciding how and when to schedule each program. Nowadays, of course, people can totally rearrange the carefully crafted schedule by using their **digital video recorders,** viewing DVDs, or downloading material from the internet. But scheduling considerations are still important for television programmers because many people use TV to relax. They just want to turn on the power button, surf with their remote control until they find something they like, and then stay put. For that reason, when a program is scheduled can be important to its longevity. If it is against a major hit, it probably will not do well. If it is scheduled at a time when the audience members who would be most interested are not available because they are at work or sleeping, it is unlikely to gain a following.

For the broadcast networks, prime time is the scheduling period that receives the most attention because that is when most people watch TV. The major scheduling meetings for prime time occur in the spring to set the schedule for the fall season. However, with high program turnover and the recent tendency to start new series during the summer and other parts of the year, prime-time scheduling is considered at other times of the year, too. To determine a schedule, the executives consider not only where to put new programs but also which old programs to cancel or move to a new time. In making these decisions, they consider ratings of present programs, fads, production costs, overall program mix the network hopes to attain, ideas that have worked well or poorly in the past, the kind of audience to which a program will appeal, and types of programs that the other networks may be scheduling.[20]

Cable networks with programs that do well in prime time, such as HBO, engage in serious thinking similar to broadcast networks when they consider where to place their programs. Other cable networks engage in **narrowcasting,** in which they are only trying to attract a particular demographic—sports enthusiasts, children, music aficionados. They usually schedule the best of what they have to offer during prime time. But some channels don't put their best foot forward during that time period. For example, 9:00 P.M. is not a good time to attract children.[21]

TV stations affiliated with a network only have to worry about scheduling during the periods when the network does not feed them material, usually late morning, late afternoon, and the middle of the night. The most crucial programming they deal with is their locally produced news, which they try to schedule under the best circumstances. Other than that, they often schedule syndicated material and repeats of programs.

A new scheduling factor for networks and stations involves when and how to schedule their programs for home video and the internet. Because Hulu, Netflix, and other downloading and DVD services have become so popular, TV show producers have found that they can recoup extra money by packaging their programs for these new distribution means. But, like movies, showing TV shows on other platforms has the potential to reduce the viewership for the networks' prime distribution system. Programmers are still experimenting with how to release their shows. Some make them available on the internet the day after they air; others wait until the end of the season to release the shows on DVD.[22]

8.5b Scheduling Strategies

A number of scheduling strategies have arisen over the years. For example, networks often attempt **block programming**—the scheduling of one type of program, such as situation comedies, for an entire evening. This is undertaken in an attempt to ensure **audience flow**—the ability to hold an audience from one program to another. Cable networks that narrowcast essentially have block programming for their entire schedule, but sometimes they break down their already narrow programming so that, for example, they target World War II history buffs for an entire evening. Public broadcasting has also tried block programming, with some evenings devoted to fiction and some to nonfiction.

If networks are introducing a new series, they may program it between two successful existing series with the idea that people will stay tuned through the whole block. This is usually referred to as **hammocking.** Another concept, called **tentpoling,** involves scheduling new or weak series before and after a very successful program. **Stripping** is a scheduling strategy that is used mostly by TV stations and cable networks. They show programs from the same series at the same time Monday through Friday, usually during daytime hours. That way audience members can find the show easily (see Exhibit 8.8).

methods

Scheduling is a controversial process. Producers always want their shows scheduled at the best time and resist having to pull some other program along (unless, of course, they have produced that program as well). They are quick to blame poor performance on poor scheduling. Of course, there are times when everything seems right—a show comes from a reputable source, it goes through thorough development, and it is scheduled at an ideal time—and still it fails. Other times a show doesn't seem to work but network executives believe in it and reschedule it until it finally clicks. Programmers have not come up with a fail-safe method for guaranteeing a hit. In the end, it is usually the public that determines what lives on and what gets canceled.[23]

8.6 Drama

Programmers are well advised to know the **genres** of programs that have worked in the past and the upsides and downsides of each form. Drama, for example, is a basic, enduring, high-profile form of entertainment that has been part of electronic media since its beginning. Dramatic stories were part of early movies, and early radio had many dramatic series. Today drama is rarely heard on radio. Movies, of course, are still heavy on drama, and many of them are part of television, either as movies made for TV or as movies originally made for the theater that are then shown on various forms of television.

qualities

Drama comes in many forms, one of which is soap operas. Each program is serialized in such a way that it entices the viewer to "tune in tomorrow"; the plot lines trail on for weeks, and adversity is the common thread. A variation on the soap opera, the **telenovela,** has been imported from Latin America. It has continuing stories, but no one telenovela goes on forever; it usually only lasts for several months. Soaps had enduring popularity during the daytime for many decades, but quite a few have been canceled lately so they seem to be losing their luster.

soaps

Exhibit 8.8

Programming scheduling strategies.

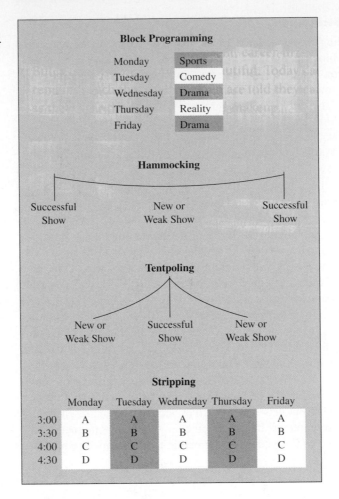

Block Programming

Monday	Sports
Tuesday	Comedy
Wednesday	Drama
Thursday	Reality
Friday	Drama

Hammocking

| Successful Show | New or Weak Show | Successful Show |

Tentpoling

| New or Weak Show | Successful Show | New or Weak Show |

Stripping

	Monday	Tuesday	Wednesday	Thursday	Friday
3:00	A	A	A	A	A
3:30	B	B	B	B	B
4:00	C	C	C	C	C
4:30	D	D	D	D	D

miniseries and docudramas

Dramas sometimes come in the form of **miniseries** that last for several episodes but do not go on indefinitely. One of the most successful miniseries was the 1977 *Roots*, Alex Haley's saga of his slave ancestors, which aired eight straight nights to the largest TV audience up to that time. *Roots* was also one of the first series to be called a **docudrama**—a program that presents material that has a factual base but includes fictionalized events. Both the miniseries and docudrama forms still exist, but they are not aired as often or as successfully as they were during the late 1970s and early 1980s.[24]

prime-time forms

Prime-time TV dramas have taken many forms over the years. Dramas of the 1950s, usually referred to as **anthology dramas,** were series (*Playhouse 90, Philco Television Playhouse*), but the drama presented each week was an individual story that did not have the same characters as other dramas within the series. Although these plays were popular with the public, they became less acceptable to advertisers, who were trying to sell instant solutions to problems through a pill, toothpaste, or coffee. The sometimes depressing, drawn-out relationships and

Exhibit 8.9

The cast of *LOST*, a drama about a group of people stranded on an island after their plane crashes. Story lines covered multiple episodes; in fact, some of them were not even resolved when the series ended after its six season run from 2004 to 2010.

problems of the dramas were inconsistent with advertiser philosophy, which led to their demise by the 1960s.

Anthology dramas were replaced by **episodic dramas,** which had set characters and problems that could be solved within 60 minutes. With series such as *Gunsmoke, Route 66,* and *Marcus Welby, M.D.,* plot dominated character, and adventure, excitement, tension, and resolution became key factors. The nature of episodic dramas has changed over the years. For example, in the 1980s dramas with more complexity, such as *Hill Street Blues* and *ER,* debuted. Audiences had to watch carefully to follow the plot. HBO pushed the envelope in the late 1990s with *The Sopranos,* a highly acclaimed series about the inside workings of a New Jersey mob family. In the 2000s, a number of dramas, such as *24* and *LOST* (see Exhibit 8.9) had serial elements in that story lines covered multiple episodes. These dramas were also highly produced, with production values that often rivaled those of movies. AMC, a cable network known for old movies, not original drama, changed its image in 2008 with the debut of *Mad Men,* an acclaimed drama about 1960s advertising executives.[25]

A downside of dramas is that they are expensive to produce. As media fragment and audiences for any one show become smaller, it is harder to justify the costs. Also, dramas, by nature, contain suspense and conflict, elements that often lead to violence. This violence is highly criticized by politicians and citizen groups, sometimes necessitating changes on the part of program producers (see Chapter 12).

criticisms

8.7 Comedy

forms

Comedy, like drama, has historically been a mainstay of media. Situation comedies, first on radio and then on TV, aim to make people laugh—not an easy task. It takes strong-penned writers and talented performers to crank out humorous lines. Although sitcoms are the primary form of TV comedy, other forms do exist. *Saturday Night Live* has had a long run with skits that spoof many facets of society. Stand-up comics appear, particularly on cable channels.

Many of the early situation comedies made an attempt to be believable, but the necessity to crank out programs accelerated a trend toward paper-thin characters and canned laughter. One mainstay became the idiotic father ruling over his patient and understanding wife and children. A breakthrough in comedy series occurred in the 1970s with the debut of *All in the Family,* whose bigoted lead, Archie Bunker, harbored a long list of prejudices. This series, unlike any previous comedy series, dealt with contemporary social and political problems (see Chapter 4). The 1990s had a fair amount of caustic comedy. The Fox network had two hit shows in this category: *Married . . . with Children* dealt irreverently with marriage, and *The Simpsons* glorified the underachiever. Comedy Central's *South Park* showed irreverence toward just about everything. These sitcoms and others were criticized for their negative approach and for their constant references to sex, but they received audience loyalty and spawned many other hard-edged comedies.

sitcoms

For a period of time in the early 2000s, sitcoms appeared to be an endangered species (see Exhibit 8.10). *Frasier* and *Friends* went off the air voluntarily, and networks seemed to be abandoning comedy for reality shows. By 2010 comedies seemed back in favor with such popular offerings as *Modern Family* and *The Big Bang Theory.*[26]

8.8 Reality

early

Reality TV came to the fore as its own genre in the 1990s. Prior to that there had been programs featuring real people engaged in real activities, with some, such as *Candid Camera,* dating back to the 1950s. But they did not achieve the popularity that they gained in the 1990s and 2000s, and they did not carry the label of "reality TV." One of the initial appeals of modern reality programming to networks was the low cost. The first shows featured primarily heroic and unusual feats by ordinary citizens. There were no actors to pay, no sets to build, and the technical requirements were minimal. Originally the genre was looked down upon as cheap programming whose appeal would be short-lived.

Survivor

Then, in the summer of 2000, reality went in a new direction when Mark Burnett (see Exhibit 8.11) produced *Survivor* for CBS. The program involved a number of ordinary citizens placed on an island, where they undertook unusual tasks and voted each other off the island. The winner of this *Survivor* series received $1 million, a small price to pay for the return that CBS received. An estimated 72 million people watched the final episode, giving CBS the highest ratings it had had in years. Since that time, reality has become a popular genre, with many of the programs eliminating people until only one is left.

Exhibit 8.10

Is this show a comedy? In 2005, *Desperate Housewives* put itself up for awards in the comedy category. This raised the eyebrows of those who wondered how a show that dealt with suicide, drug addiction, murder, and blackmail could be considered a comedy rather than a drama. The producer, Marc Cherry, admitted that part of the reason was that the drama pool for awards was very strong while the comedy pool was weak because networks were not programming very many sitcoms. The strategy paid off as seen in this photo of cast and producer receiving the Golden Globe for Best Musical or Comedy TV Series.

criticisms

The term "reality TV" has been extended to some other forms or programming that were originally considered game shows or music shows—for example, ABC's *Who Wants to Be a Millionaire?* and Fox's *American Idol*. The shows have been criticized for being inane and for endangering people as the grossness and difficulty of the tasks they must perform escalate. But they are still relatively inexpensive, and, although they don't garner as large audiences as they used to, they have had a longer life than their detractors predicted.[27]

8.9 Games

Game shows have long been popular on electronic media. Their formula involves ordinary people using skill or luck to win prizes—and exude

Exhibit 8.11

Mark Burnett (left) shown here with Survivor host Jeff Probst, is often considered the king of reality TV. After the original *Survivor*, he went on to produce many spin-offs of the show and many other reality shows.

Exhibit 8.12

Longtime host Pat Sajak and card turner Vanna White of *Wheel of Fortune*.

excitement. Audience members, both in the studio and at home, empathize and agonize along with the contestants.

Early radio's quiz shows were not as hyped as today's TV game shows. Some of them were quite intellectual, such as *Quiz Kids,* which presented difficult questions to precocious children. Television took over the quiz program idea early in its history. Most of the initial TV shows had modest prizes for the winning contestants, but during the mid-1950s, the stakes began to increase with such programs as *The $64,000 Question.* The 1958 **quiz scandals** (see Chapter 4) gave a temporary blow to game shows. No chance-oriented shows dared touch the airwaves for a while, but gradually, low-stakes programs referred to as game shows emerged during daytime hours. The prize for *The Dating Game,* for example, was an expense-paid date for the contestant and the person he or she selected. The most watched, longest-running syndicated game show is *Wheel of Fortune* (see Exhibit 8.12), which started in 1975.[28]

Games of another sort, **video games** (see Chapter 2), consume a great deal of recreational time. They are praised for developing eye-hand coordination but criticized for being violent and a waste of time.

8.10 Music

radio

Music is the mainstay of radio, but it is difficult to keep track of the various music formats because music is constantly evolving. Music that might be referred to as "new wave" doesn't stay "new" for long. When a particular type of music, such as rock, becomes popular, it tends to be subdivided into categories (hard rock, classic rock, album-oriented rock) so that stations can have a unique sound.

older forms

Historically, music had a more minor role in TV than in radio. Dick Clark's *American Bandstand,* a glorified disc jockey program on which teenagers danced to the current hits, had the greatest longevity of any music show, starting in 1952 and being shown in some form for about 40 years. Public broadcasting and some cable channels frequently air concerts from venues around the country. In 1981, MTV started programming music videos and soon they were appearing everywhere—on commercial networks, local stations, cable networks, and at dance clubs. They have lost some of their popularity but remain a good way to showcase bands.

Amateur shows featuring singers and musicians go back to the early 1950s. But they received a revival in 2002 under the banner of reality shows when *American Idol* started. Its concept of searching for a superstar by narrowing down contestants caught on and other similar programs appeared, both for singers and dancers. In 2009, Fox programmed a musical series, *Glee,* about high school

Exhibit 8.13

Some of the cast of *Glee*.

glee club misfits who battle with their own problems and those of competing on the glee club circuit. The plot lines had social significance and the music was interwoven and performed by a talented cast (see Exhibit 8.13).[29]

Modern music such as rap is criticized for its sexual and violent lyrics, especially those that demean women. As with some other forms of programming, there are periodic inquiries from government and citizen organizations about the negative effects this music has on youth.

newer forms

8.11 News

As previously mentioned, news is currently available in a large number of forms at any time of the day or night. Such has not always been the case. Radio had to fight the newspaper industry in order to provide any news (see Chapter 5), and for many years both radio and TV reported news only at specific times of day. Journalists were referred to as **gatekeepers** because they decided what people needed to know. Some radio and TV news departments still operate that way, but most also have websites that people can access at any time. In addition, there are stations and networks that program news 24 hours a day.

gatekeepers

There are also many more sources for news, so it is easy to find news content and style that are agreeable, whether you are conservative or liberal, young or middle-aged, rich or poor. News junkies can get their fill, while those only interested in major headlines that affect their lives are also easily accommodated. In times of disaster, almost everyone depends on the electronic media as the main source of help and information—directing victims to shelters, communicating vital health and safety information, and calming jangled nerves (see Chapter 1).

variety

politics

The electronic media are particularly important when it comes to delivering political information, such as candidate debates, campaigning, coverage of the Democratic and Republican conventions (see Exhibit 8.14), and election night coverage. Election night coverage was particularly dicey in 2000, when the networks declared the results of the presidential election vote count in Florida and then had to change their story several times as the nation waited for weeks to find out whether Al Gore or George W. Bush would become president. The rush to judgment by the news media was highly criticized.[30]

There are numerous other criticisms of news, many centered on what news the electronic media present and how they present it. Television, particularly, is obsessed with visual stories and sometimes downplays an important story simply because no exciting pictures accompany it. Sometimes stories are so highly visual that the

Exhibit 8.14
Numerous reporters cover the Democratic and Republican nominating conventions.

criticisms

facts become obscured. The weather, for example, can contain so many computer graphics, satellite feeds, and digital effects that viewers are left wondering whether it will rain.

Both radio and TV provide encapsulated news. Five-minute radio updates, revolving 20-minute newscasts of all-news stations, and 30-minute evening news broadcasts cannot cover the day's news in depth, explaining and analyzing it. Yet the news that is chosen is often trivial. Greater coverage is given to a politician eating a taco than to his or her views on crime. If a station or network achieves a scoop, it dwells on that story even though the story is relatively unimportant. In the rush to get a story first, a news organization may get a story wrong.

Tasteless coverage of victims is also a problem. Some reporters succeed in interviewing people who have just seen a close relative killed or have lost all their possessions in a disastrous flood. Overall, the emphasis is on sensationalism, with murder, rape, and prostitution given more airtime than weighty national and international economic and political issues. The phrase "If it bleeds, it leads" has been used to describe the phenomenon of gaining audience attention with sensational stories. In their sensationalizing, news media are often accused of judging guilt before a suspect has had a chance to receive a court trial. "Trial by the press" is a frequently used ploy of lawyers who think their clients cannot get a fair trial because of adverse radio and TV publicity.

Another criticism is that news is biased. Some claim it is a product of the "liberal Eastern establishment," while others bemoan the conservative slant of Fox news and talk radio. Politicians and businesspeople, who are often targets of news darts, are particularly prone to cry bias. But it is the duty of journalists to act as society's watchdog and report improprieties of public servants and others whose activities have a major effect on the well-being of the citizenry.[31]

8.12 Sports

types

The most highly publicized sports programs are those that show America's major sports—football, basketball, baseball—on the broadcast and cable networks. Archery, badminton, tractor pulling, and every other conceivable type of sport, however, can be found somewhere on radio, TV, or the net. Throughout the country, local radio, TV, and cable systems have their own sports programs, often in conjunction with a local college or university. A growing number of radio stations have an all-sports format that includes play-by-play and call-in talk shows. Regional cable TV sports networks that show local teams on a number of cable systems are particularly popular. Team and league websites stream sports events, or at least highlights, over the internet.

history

Throughout their short history, sports and electronic media have had an unusual symbiotic relationship. The Dempsey-Carpentier boxing match gave early radio its first big boost (see Chapter 5); early TV had its wrestling matches (see Chapter 4); ESPN was one of the first successful cable networks (see Chapter 3).

rights

As sports proved its value to broadcasting, the **rights fees** television paid to air the games skyrocketed. For example, the rights to the National Football

League season grew from $4.65 million in 1962 to $50 million in 1970 to $500 million in 1998 to $4 billion in 2010. During the 1990s, the networks sometimes lost money on sports events; they had to give money back to advertisers because they could not deliver the audience size they promised. This still happens occasionally, but for the most part the rights fee issue has been solved by compromise. The sports teams slowed the acceleration rate of their rights fee increases, advertisers spent a little more money, and fans remained loyal, especially for major events such as the Super Bowl and the Olympics (see Exhibit 8.15).[32]

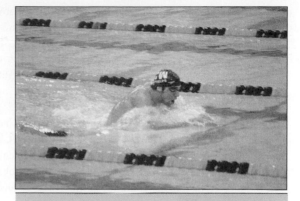

Exhibit 8.15
Michael Phelps's successful quest for eight gold medals at the 2008 summer Olympics kept viewers tuned in.

Another controversial aspect of sports and broadcasting involves **blackouts.** When TV first started broadcasting sports events, attendance at games plummeted (for example, a 32 percent plunge for baseball between 1948 and 1953). Sports owners realized they were cutting their own throats when they televised all their games. As a result, Congress enacted a law in 1973 that allows major sports games to be blacked out (not aired) up to 90 miles from the origination point unless the game is sold out 72 hours in advance. The biggest critics of this policy are the fans who are occasionally deprived of seeing the game on TV.

blackouts

There are occasional outcries from the sports world against TV equipment that is so sophisticated it out-umpires umpires and out-referees referees. But the sophistication of modern TV equipment often enhances the viewing with slow motion, split screens, cameras placed within racing vehicles, microphones picking up sounds on the field, and virtual graphics that show such elements as the strike zone or the nationality of the swimmer in each lane of the Olympic pool.

equipment

Whatever the problems are with the sports–electronic media relationship, it is not likely that either party will initiate divorce proceedings. The fans would not approve.[33]

8.13 Talk Shows

Early radio had talk shows, but not of the kind it has today because the telephone technology that allows viewers to call in was not available. The talk shows were simply in-studio interviews with people in the news. Today's radio talk shows on both commercial and public radio still have many in-studio elements, but they also involve audience members. Some are devoted almost entirely to members of the public who call to express opinions on specific or general subjects. Others feature experts on various subjects who then answer listeners' questions. Talk radio has gained increasing importance in the political world, serving as a sounding board for ideas and disagreements.

radio

public service

The earliest TV talk show was *Meet the Press,* which started in 1947 and can still be seen Sunday mornings on NBC. It and other programs like it feature interviews with people of political and social stature who discuss important issues of the day. Programs with this public-service orientation exist on commercial networks, local stations, public TV, and cable systems. Sometimes they are criticized for being boring, but most of them now have quality production values.

different times

A lighter form of talk show appeared in the 1950s with the advent of *Today* and *The Tonight Show* (see Chapter 4). *Today,* a morning show, covered a broad swath of both news and feature material. It contained interviews, newscasts, weather, and interactions by the host(s). *Today* and its morning competitors still adhere to the same general formula despite many changes in on-air and off-air staff.

The Tonight Show, with the exception of the opening monologue, was primarily an interview show, but unlike the more serious talk shows, many of its interviewees were entertainment celebrities. It and its many late-night clones capitalize on the average person's desire to know what makes celebrities tick and also highlight the hosts who often include unusual make-believe characters or crazy skits as part of the shows (see "Zoom In" box).[34]

The daytime talk shows with hosts such as Geraldo Rivera and Oprah Winfrey came to the fore in the 1970s. Oprah reigned as the queen of talk for 25 years and when she ended the show in 2011 in order to concentrate on her cable network, many hosts were hoping to fill her spot (see Exhibit 8.16). The afternoon talk shows tend to feature celebrities or a group of unknown people with unusual stories to tell. Some of these shows became controversial because of the increasingly bizarre subjects discussed (sex changes, satanic worship, daughters who date their mothers' boyfriends). After a show that resulted in the death of one of the participants, the shows tamed down, although some of them are still criticized for exploiting people.[35]

The cost of talk shows depends primarily on the quality and demands of the guests and host. Some talk shows are almost free; they are beset with requests from aspiring authors and the like who wish to appear on the program for publicity purposes. Other shows pay top price to obtain "hot properties" of the show business and political worlds.

Exhibit 8.16

Anderson Cooper was one of the newer daytime talk show hosts hoping to take the place of Oprah Winfrey.

8.14 Documentaries and Information

definition

The definition of a documentary has changed over the years. Film theorists who studied and produced documentaries before the days of television believed that documentaries had to deal with controversial subjects and present a point of view. Television's early documentaries, such as those presented by Edward R. Murrow

ZOOM IN: **The Jay-Conan Brouhaha**

If ever there was a programming scheduling mess, it was in 2009 when NBC made changes regarding *The Tonight Show*. The seeds dated back to 2004 when NBC announced that Conan O'Brien would succeed Jay Leno as host in 2009. At the time NBC's nighttime schedule was:

10:00–11:00 P.M.—a drama
11:00–11:35 P.M.—a break so that local affiliated stations could air their news
11:35 PM–12:35 A.M.—*The Tonight Show* hosted by Jay Leno
12:35 1:35 A.M. *Late Night* hosted by Conan O'Brien

NBC made the announcement in 2004 because it wanted to give Conan a guaranteed future so he would not be tempted to defect to another network. So far, so good. When 2009 came, Conan was eager to take over *Tonight* but Jay wasn't really ready to retire. Fearful of losing Jay to another network, NBC offered him the 10:00–11:00 timeslot for *The Jay Leno Show*. This had an extra advantage to NBC in that talk shows are much cheaper than the dramas that usually occupied that time period. In June of 2009 Conan started hosting *Tonight* and in September 2009 Jay started his show. So far, so good.

However, talk shows do not commandeer the ratings that dramas do so, although Jay's show had acceptable ratings by talk show standards, it did not do well against the other networks' 10:00–11:00 programming. The main complainers were the NBC network affiliates because they no longer had a large lead-in audience to their 11:00 newscasts. In most cities the NBC affiliates started losing audience (hence, advertising money) to the other stations in their area. The ratings for Conan's *Tonight* show were also lower than what Jay's ratings had been—something that Conan's producers attributed to the domino effect of Jay's low ratings leading to low news ratings leading to low ratings for *Tonight*. To top it off, Jay wasn't happy with his 10:00 spot. So far, not so good.

NBC executives decided they had to do something. The media were all over the story and Conan's fans and Jay's fans were tweeting to support "their guy." The executives decided to go back to drama programming at 10:00 and give Jay a half-hour show from 11:35–12:05 and then broadcast *Tonight*, hosted by Conan, from 12:05 to 1:05. They told Conan that his alternative was to leave the network. He chose that alternative because he didn't want to be following Leno for the rest of his life. His last *Tonight* show was January 21, 2010.

Needless to say, there was a tremendous amount of legal maneuvering involving non-compete stipulations, who got paid what, and who owned the characters Conan had created. NBC stipulated that Conan could not appear on another network before September 2010, so he went on a "Legally Prohibited from Being Funny on Television" national tour. Although Fox had been courting him, that fell apart, and in September of 2010 he started an 11:00–midnight show on cable channel TBS. Jay Leno went back to hosting *Tonight* in his old 11:35–12:35 spot—and life went on.

Good, or not so good? Can you think of any way that this awkward situation could have been avoided? Did the NBC executives make the right decisions? Did Conan make the right choice? Was Jay at fault for any of this?

Jay Leno.

Conan O'Brien.

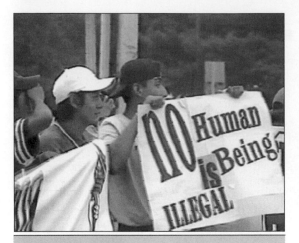

Exhibit 8.17

This documentary, *Farmingville*, which was aired on *P.O.V.*, covered a neighborhood on Long Island, New York, that was torn by conflict over immigrant workers.

on *See It Now* (see Chapter 4), were in that mold. They presented bold, strong programs on controversial subjects.

Hard-hitting documentaries were still present during the 1960s, but their controversial subject matter caused the networks many headaches in terms of lawsuits and the need to prove that they were handling all sides fairly. As a result, the networks turned to softer documentaries such as *The Louvre* and *The White House Tour with Jacqueline Kennedy*. During the 1970s, **minidocs** became prevalent. Often produced by local TV stations, they consisted of several minutes about a particular subject. Stations sometimes aired information about one subject over a week, covering a different aspect of it for three to five minutes during each day's newscast. Then they would edit all the minidocs into one unified documentary to air as a program by itself.

In 1978, CBS started *60 Minutes* as a magazine program that consisted of a number of mini-

changes

docs of 5 to 20 minutes each. Purists do not consider *60 Minutes,* or its imitators, to be documentaries because they do not go into enough depth, and some of the subjects are more featurelike than documentary. The success of *60 Minutes,* however, is significant in terms of its influence on society. A number of times, it has effected change by exposing a fraudulent practice or unsavory scheme, and as a result, it, too, has been embroiled in controversy.

Public television has two long-running prime-time documentary series, *Frontline* and *P.O.V.* (*Point of View*), both of which started in the 1980s. *Frontline* is produced by people employed by public TV stations, but *P.O.V.* consists of documentaries produced by independent videomakers who are not part of the established media structure (see Exhibit 8.17).

examples

Cable TV's Discovery Channel, formed in the 1980s, opened the door for more documentary production. Most of its programming is fairly noncontroversial, dealing with wildlife, science, and other aspects of nature. Similarly, the National Geographic nature specials, the *Biography* series on A&E, and much of the programming on History and The Learning Channel (TLC) qualifies as documentaries by today's standards.

information

There are many other types of programs and internet sites that provide general information, covering such subjects as health, cooking, home decorating, and farming. C-SPAN covers the House of Representatives and the Senate and many important conferences and meetings. Some of the best instructional programming is produced in the corporate realm, where programs intended to train employees or showcase products and services are well produced and effective.[36]

8.15 Religion

Religious programming has been part of electronic media since their beginnings. Radio evangelists were common, and from the beginning religious organizations made frequent use of TV. The structure varies depending on the philosophy and finances of the particular religions. Some religious groups own TV stations or cable channels that program religious material of one denomination 24 hours a day; in other situations several denominations share a facility with each paying for its share of the time. Individual churches buy time on networks while still others are given time by media facilities for their Sunday morning services. Some radio stations have religious music formats that sound similar in style to Top 40; others include a great deal of talk. Some facilities produce locally based programs; others air mostly programming that comes through a network (see Exhibit 8.18).

radio and TV

Religious organizations also make frequent use of newer media. They webcast funerals so that people in distant places can feel they are participating; they use video-on-demand to target people with particular spiritual needs; they create websites for collecting money; they set up Facebook pages and create apps to extend the brand awareness of particular religions; they utilize Skype conversations for people who cannot attend church; they program material for DVDs and use satellite technologies and franchise marketing techniques to grow flocks throughout the world. Some people feel that religious experiences cannot be authentically replicated online, but many of the new technology experiments that churches have undertaken have been successful—spiritually and financially.[37]

newer technologies

Exhibit 8.18

For many years evangelist minister Dr. Robert H. Schuller broadcast *Hour of Power* from this Crystal Cathedral in Garden Grove, California. The program was shown on many broadcast TV stations and on the cable networks Lifetime, TBN, Discovery, and Church Channel. However, financial problems engulfed the church and it went bankrupt.

8.16 Children's Programming

radio and movies

Children watch and listen to much of the media fare that is targeted toward adults, but through the years, companies have produced a great deal of material specifically aimed at children. The two media forms that first provided for children were movies and radio. Today, radio airs very little for children, other than Radio Disney, a network that features music and contests for kids. Kids' movies, on the other hand, are still very popular, with many parents as well as their offspring.

early television

Television networks started children's programming early with an emphasis on puppets, such as Howdy Doody. The longest-running kids' show on commercial network TV (1955 to 1982) was *Captain Kangaroo,* starring Bob Keeshan. Children's programming was important on early local TV stations, too. Most programs consisted of a host or hostess whose main job was to introduce cartoons and sell commercial products. During the 1960s, networks overwhelmingly adopted the likes of *Felix the Cat* and *Tom and Jerry*—and therein began a controversy.

For many years, these cartoons dominated Saturday morning TV, making for one of the most profitable areas of network programming. The cartoons were relatively inexpensive to produce, and advertisers had learned that children can be very persuasive in convincing their parents to buy certain cereals, candies, and toys. The result was profits in the neighborhood of $16 million per network just from Saturday morning TV.

The situation changed gradually. Parents who managed to awaken for a cup of coffee by 7:00 A.M. on Saturday noticed the boom-bang violent, noneducational content of the shows, along with the obviously cheap mouth–open/mouth-closed animation techniques. A group of Boston parents became upset enough

ACT

to form an organization called Action for Children's Television (ACT), which began demanding changes in children's programs and commercials. Researchers realized that children under five were watching 23.5 hours of TV a week and that by the time they graduated from high school, they would have spent 15,000 hours in front of the tube. The Children's Television Workshop developed *Sesame Street,* and its successful airing on public TV proved that education and entertainment could mix.

government actions

All this led to a long, hard look at children's TV. In 1969, the U.S. Surgeon General appointed an Advisory Committee that selected 12 researchers to investigate the effects of television violence on children. After these 12 had worked for two and a half years, the committee concluded that a modest relationship exists between viewing violence on TV and aggressive tendencies.

Led and cajoled by ACT, a number of organizations demanded reforms in children's TV. They noted that there were some fine children's programs on TV—*The Wonderful World of Disney* and *Mister Rogers' Neighborhood*—but they were after changes in the cartoons, slapstick comedy, and deceptive commercials. In 1974, the FCC issued guidelines for children's television that stated, among other things, that stations would be expected to present a reasonable number of children's programs to educate and inform, not simply entertain. The FCC also stated that broadcasters should use imaginative and exciting ways to further a child's understanding of areas such as history, science, literature, and art.

Exhibit 8.19
SpongeBob SquarePants, one of Nickelodeon's popular programs, was created by former marine science teacher, Steve Hillenburg. He also drew the talking sponge, dopey starfish, and cranky squid who encounter adventures with charming naiveté.

By the mid-1970s, most stations and networks acquiesced, at least in part, to the reform demands. Programs that attempted to teach both information and social values hit the airwaves. These were more expensive (and less watched) than cartoons, so the amount networks and stations spent on children's programs increased. ABC developed after-school specials that dealt dramatically with socially significant problems faced by children, such as divorce and the death of a friend. In cable TV, Nickelodeon was established in 1979 to show solely nonviolent children's programming.

social values

With the 1980s, the tide turned, and the FCC, in the spirit of deregulation, dismissed the idea of maintaining or adopting standards for children's programming. The 1974 guidelines were ignored. The networks, eyeing their sinking children's TV profits with fear, canceled many of the expensive education-oriented programs and returned to the world of cartoons. In the mid-1990s, Fox began programming the *Mighty Morphin Power Rangers,* which some called the most violent children's cartoon ever—and it became a huge hit. In 1990, Congress passed a law that dealt mostly with restricting commercials within children's TV programs (see Chapter 9).

deregulation

Today, there is less furor about children's programs, in part because the networks have faded into the background. They still offer children's programming, but some have turned their Saturday morning programming over to other companies that rent the network time to broadcast programming they produce or acquire. In addition, there are a multitude of sources for video material for children, both socially redeeming educational material and "brain-numbing" cartoons. Nickelodeon has become the top purveyor of popular children's programs (see Exhibit 8.19), and PBS still has many offerings in this area. In addition the Disney Channel, Cartoon Network, The Hub, and other cable networks program for children.

In addition, many DVDs are available for children—some are videos of TV programs that have aired or movies that have been shown in theaters, but others include entertainment or information made specifically for DVDs. Similarly there are children's games and learning materials available for pods, pads, and smartphones.[38]

other media

8.17 Issues and the Future

genre changes

structural changes

newer media

fatigue

criticisms

Programming is always in a state of flux, in part because public tastes change quickly and in part because it is high profile. There are always major issues that are in the process of changing. For example, soap operas that at one time seemed destined to last forever now look more like a genre on the verge of extinction. For many decades, going back to radio, they have been a stalwart part of afternoon programming. They were able be deal with subject matter, such as rape and incest, that was taboo on primetime TV. But as talk shows became racier and reality TV pushed the envelope, the fictional characters of soaps seemed less intriguing than the real people who vividly exposed their real problems. Of course, now reality TV seems to be waning also so some new (or old) genre may replace it.

In a similar vein, independent producers ruled the airwaves during the 1970s and 1980s, but now the networks produce much of their own programming, marginalizing the independents. Radio, which was originally a nationally based medium became a local medium and now seems headed back toward a national sound of sameness as big companies program their radio stations in a similar, safe manner. Is there really a need for local TV stations when all they do (other than news) is pipe through network programming and show the same syndicated fare that is on cable or satellite TV? Will syndicators be needed now that off-network material is available on DVDs or through internet downloads?

The biggest unknown related to programming is what eventual role the internet and portable devices will play in distributing entertainment and information. These technologies have yet to be fully developed in terms of their program potential, and their future course will affect the fortunes of the older media.

As media forms proliferate, so do programming choices. Although this would appear to be a good thing for the consumer, it can lead to choice fatigue. You can spend all evening with the remote control just clicking through the channel options. It is easy to settle into programs that fit your comfort zone and do not challenge you with opposing viewpoints. This is particularly true of news and documentaries.

Criticisms leveled at programs are not likely to go away. Sex and violence will continue to draw fire, but program producers are not likely to give them up because they are elements that sell programs. News will be criticized, especially when journalists must make quick decisions on important topics or when they exhibit viewpoints that are not popular with certain members of the populace. Because children are so impressionable, there may be new watchdog organizations demanding improvements in children's TV. Those involved with both entertainment and information programming will make mistakes—they are human beings. But both the media and the people who produce for them will become stagnant if they do not try new ideas, many of which are likely to fail, but some of which will showcase the talents of numerous individuals, including programmers.

8.18 Summary

Different types of programs wend their way through the programming process in various ways. The three forms most likely to be programmed during network prime time are dramas, which have historically been a mainstay of TV, in anthology, episodic, miniseries and docudrama form; sitcoms, which have had their ups and downs; and reality TV, the newest genre, which incorporates games and talent shows. All three forms are sometimes produced by the network and sometimes obtained from majors and indies. They go through a development process that often includes pitches and pilots, and they are carefully scheduled in prime time, often incorporating block programming, hammocking, and tentpoling. Networks deliver these programs to their affiliated stations or cable systems.

Game shows and afternoon talk shows often come from syndicators, who also market off-net and made-for syndication programs. They are likely to be stripped.

Music is predominant on radio, where it is part of a format and where it is usually scheduled with a clock and dayparts in mind. Music videos have also been popular on television, where they started out being narrowcast on MTV. Specific music shows, such as *American Bandstand, American Idol,* and *Glee* have achieved great popularity.

News is programmed quite differently than other forms of programming because of its immediacy. It comes from reporters, stringers, news agencies, the general public, VNRs, helicopters, and many other sources. News producers, assignment editors, website designers, anchors, and others are involved in getting it to the public through radio, scheduled commercial and public TV news broadcasts, 24-hour cable news networks, and constant-access internet sites.

Sports events are usually produced by the entity that airs them and involve paying rights fees to the sports franchise and dealing with blackouts. Sports and media have a long-term symbiotic relationship, and some networks and stations are devoted totally to sports.

Public-affairs talk shows are usually produced by whatever organization distributes them; on broadcast networks they often air in the early morning. Daytime and nighttime talk shows have lighter content often involving celebrities. They are syndicated or self-produced.

Documentaries often come from independent producers and are narrowcast on cable TV channels. Religious organizations produce their own material and utilize radio, television, and many newer technological approaches to get across their messages.

Children's programming is a controversial area that is to some extent governed by laws and influenced by citizens' groups. Several cable networks are devoted to children's programs, and public broadcasting has played a role in this area. Commercial networks produced children's programs in the early years, but now some networks have farmed out this programming to other companies.

All forms of programming have come under criticism, some of which is generated by the need to try new ideas.

Suggested Websites

www.ap.org (Associated Press, a news agency)

www.cnn.com (news channel Cable News Network)

www.espn.go.com (sports channel ESPN)

www.mtv.com (music channel MTV)

www.natpe.org (National Association of Television Program Executives, an industry organization that deals with programming)

Notes

1. "I Want My (Web) MTV," *Newsweek,* April 14, 2008, E8–E9.
2. "Why Cable Originals Are Crucial," *Broadcasting & Cable,* October 13, 2003, 42; "ESPN Turns 25," *TV Technology,* September 8, 2004, 14; "Direct Action," *Emmy,* Issue No. 4, 2011, 12; and "Digital Studios Take Cues from Hollywood," *Los Angeles Times,* July 12, 2011, B-1.
3. "A Season of Seeing Double," *Broadcasting & Cable,* September 30, 2002, 7; and "Why Local News Is in a Fix," *Broadcasting & Cable,* August 7, 2006, 10.
4. "A Giant Radio Chain Is Perfecting the Art of Seeming Local," *Wall Street Journal,* February 25, 2002, 1.
5. "Can These Marriages Be Saved?" *Broadcasting & Cable,* January 14, 2002, 6; and "Online Education, *Broadcasting & Cable,* April 17, 2006, 9.
6. "To Each His Own," *Hollywood Reporter,* May 22–24, 2009, 1; and "Public Partnering," *Broadcasting & Cable,* January 21, 2002, 32.
7. "Star Commits to 'Girlfriends' from YouTube," *Hollywood Reporter,* November 2–4, 2007, 2; "The Web's First Fall Season," *Wall Street Journal,* September 9, 2000, B-1; "With the Swift Death of 'Quarterlife,' *Sanctuary* is True Web to TV Pioneer," *Hollywood Reporter,* November 18, 2008, 6; and "Deconstructing Lisa Kudrow," *Emmy,* Issue No. 4, 3011, 68–71.
8. "Law and Disorder," *Wall Street Journal,* July 12–13, 2008, 1; and "Hollywood's TV Factory," *Wall Street Journal,* September 2, 2011, D1.
9. "DVD Growth Spurs Spending Spurt on Home Video Marketing," *DVD Exclusive,* August 2004, 24; and "Shattered Windows," *Variety,* August 23–29, 2010, 1.
10. William M. Kunz, "Prime-Time Television Program Ownership in a Post-Fin/Syn World, *Journal of Broadcasting and Electronic Media,* December 2009, 636–51; "Waiting for the Web Wonder," *Variety,* December 5, 2010, 1; "Table Scraps," *Broadcasting & Cable,* July 26, 2004, 1; and "Digital Impasse," *Broadcasting & Cable,* August 28, 2006, 8.
11. "Syndies Turning to Cable," *Broadcasting & Cable,* March 19, 2001, 19; "The Waning Days of Syndicated TV," *Hollywood Reporter,* February 18, 2011, 38; and "The New Rules of Syndication," *Broadcasting & Cable,* January 23, 2006, 26–27.
12. "Taking Amateur Video Up a Notch," *Los Angeles Times,* July 16, 2007, C-1; "Pepsi to Put 2 Summer Shows on WB Network," *Los Angeles Times,* April 10, 2003, C-1; and "Coming to America," *Wall Street Journal,* March 11, 2011, D1.
13. "Networks Fear the Net as a Copilot," *Los Angeles Times,* March 27, 2007, E-1; and "Quest for TV Magic," *Los Angeles Times,* November 16, 2003, E-32.
14. "Zucker: 'It's About Less Waste,'" *Hollywood Reporter,* January 30, 2008, 8; "Ready to Air . . . But Where," *Emmy,* December 2001, 36–39; "Play It Again, Shrek," *Los Angeles Times,* January 3, 2005, E-1; and "The Math of a Hit TV Show," *Wall Street Journal,* May 12, 2011, D1.
15. "Radio and TV News Services," *Broadcasting and Cable,* August 14, 2000, 44–45; and "The Changing Face of Broadcast Journalism," *TV Technology*, July 6, 2011, 4.
16. "New Media, New Newsrooms," *Broadcasting & Cable,* January 14, 2008, 22; and "Big Day at the Big News," *Emmy,* Issue No. 3, 2011, 130.
17. Michael C. Keith, *The Radio Station* (Boston: Focal Press, 2004), 84–99.

18. Keith, *The Radio Station,* 106–11.

19. "Day and Dateline," *Hollywood Reporter,* August 2006, 19.

20. "Nervous Time for the TV Set," *Los Angeles Times,* May 8, 2002, 1; "Fox Plans Sizzling Summer," *Broadcasting & Cable,* March 29, 2004, 3; "CBS: Scheduling for Strength," *Broadcasting & Cable,* May 23, 2011, 12; and "Legends of the Fall," *Emmy,* Primetime Special, 2008, 118.

21. "Feathering the Niche," *Emmy,* June 2003, 96–101.

22. "Taming the Wild Web," *Variety,* May 17–23, 2011, 1.

23. Philippe Perebinossoff, Brian Gross, and Lynne Gross, *Programming for TV, Radio & the Internet* (Boston, Focal Press, 2005), 215–38; and "The Death of Viewer Patience," *Hollywood Reporter,* November 25, 2011, 22.

24. "In the Beginning: The Genesis of the Telefilm," *Emmy,* December 1989, 30–35; 1; Saul N. Scher, "Anthology Drama: TV's Inconsistent Art Form," *Television Quarterly,* Winter 1976–77, 29–34; "Roots: 25 Years," *Hollywood Reporter,* January 17, 2002, 14; and "Crying Shame for Fans of Soaps," *Los Angeles Times,* September 23, 2011, D-1.

25. "*24* and More," *Emmy,* June 2003, 114–18; "Why the Sopranos Sing," *Newsweek,* April 2, 2001, 48–55.; "End of an Era," *Hollywood Reporter,* April 2, 2009, 5; and "Truly, Deeply, Madly," *Emmy,* March/April 2008, 28–38.

26. "The Way We Laughed," *Newsweek,* February 19, 2007, 54–55; Erica Scharrer, "From Wise to Foolish: The Portrayal of the Sitcom Father, 1950s–1990s," *Journal of Broadcasting & Electronic Media,* Winter 2001, 23–40; and "When Sitcoms Were King," *Emmy,* September/October 2008, 68–71.

27. "When Reality Got Real," *Emmy,* Issue No. 2, 2011, 10;" "72 Million Join 'Survivor' Tribe," *Hollywood Reporter,* August 25–27, 2000, 1; "Mark Burnett: Reality Survivor," *P3,* July 2008, 20–21; and "Tired Reality Genre Needs Wake-up Call," *Variety,* February 1, 2009, 24.

28. "Got Game," *Emmy,* Primetime Special 2008, 36–38; "Wheel Keeps on Turnin' with Online Fan Club," *Hollywood Reporter,* September 13, 2004, 17; and "Game Show Frenzy Takes Hold," *Broadcasting & Cable,* November 1, 1999, 22–23.

29. "KFI to Let DJ Ladd Get Last Word In," *Hollywood Reporter,* November 3, 2011, 5; Dick Clark Spins Another Record," *Los Angeles Times,* August 26, 1987, B-1; "VH1 Hits a New High Note," *Broadcasting & Cable,* May 5, 2008, 10; "America Loves Talent," *Emmy,* Issue No. 4, 2011, 50; and "Let It Glee," *Emmy,* Issue No. 5, 2010, 102–109.

30. "OMVC Stresses Broadcasting's Importance Following Earthquake," *TV Technology,* September 21, 2011, 6; "Newsrooms Go Multiplatform," *Broadcasting & Cable,* March 26, 2007, 38; and "CNN Rolls Out Election Express," *TV Technology,* October 17, 2007, 6.

31. Tien-Tsung Lee, "The Liberal Media Myth Revisited: An Examination of Factors Influencing Perceptions of Media Bias," *Journal of Broadcasting & Electronic Media,* March 2005, 43–64; "TV Stations Reconsider Live Coverage Policies," *Los Angeles Times,* May 2, 1998, A-19; and "Infoganda: The Real Indecency in Broadcast," *TV Technology,* June 23, 2004, 32.

32. "Stations Game for Sports Growth," *Broadcasting & Cable,* May 30, 2011, 1011; "Money to Burn," *Broadcasting & Electronic Media,* April 25, 2005, 1; "A New Super Bowl Champ," *Los Angeles Times,* February 8, 2011, D-1; and "Losses Predicted on NFL Deals," *Los Angeles Times,* January 15, 1998, D-1.

33. Dale L. Cressman and Lisa Swenson, "The Pigskin and the Picture Tube: The National Football League's First Full Season on the CBS Television Network," *Journal of Broadcasting & Electronic Media,* September 2007, 479–97; "Sports Leagues Impose More Rules on Coverage," *Wall Street Journal,* July 16, 2007, B-1; and "Why TV Needs Sports," *TV Guide,* August 11, 1990, 3–14.

34. "Reconceptualizing Call-in Talk Radio as Listening," *Journal of Radio Studies,* Winter 1998, 36–48; "A Morning TV Wake-up Call," *Newsweek,* March 20, 1995, 68; and "A Bad Joke Ends," *Los Angeles Times,* January 9, 2010, D-1.

35. "'Jenny Jones' Guest Killed after Taping," *Electronic Media,* March 13, 1995, 3; and "Oprah Goes Out on Top," *Broadcasting & Cable,* May 23, 2011, 22.

36. Jill Godnilow, "Kill the Documentary as We Know It," *Journal of Film and Video,* Summer/Fall 2002, 3–10; "Documentary TV: Genre Heats as Demand Grows," *Television Week,* June 6, 2005, 22; "Investigative Journalism Under Fire," *Broadcasting & Cable,* June 23, 2008, 10; "C-SPAN Branches Out," *Broadcasting & Cable,* January 1, 1996, 48; and "'60 Minutes' Keeps Ticking," *Broadcasting & Cable,* September 22, 2008, 14.

37. "Prey TV: Televangelism and Interpellation," *Journal of Film and Video,* Summer/Fall 2002, 23–37; "TV's Religious Revival," *Broadcasting & Cable,* April 25, 2005, 26; "Mourners from Afar Unite Online," *Los Angeles Times,* July 31, 2011, B-1; and "Faith-Based Networks Preach the Multi-Platform Gospel," *Broadcasting & Cable,* October 4, 2010, 14.

38. "Updated Disney.com Offers Networking for Kids," *Wall Street Journal,* January 2, 2007, B-1; George C. Woolery, *Children's Television: The First Thirty-Five Years, 1946–1981* (Metuchen, NJ: Scarecrow Press, 1985); "'Morphing' Karate Teens Provoke Parental Parry of Television Violence," *Christian Science Monitor,* November 16, 1994, 1; "The N Finds Its Niche," *Broadcasting & Cable,* September 19, 2005, 17; "4Kids Makes a Bold Move," *Electronic Media,* March 18, 2002, 11; and "Kids Business Looks for Grown-Up Boost," *Broadcasting & Cable,* March 21, 2011, 8–13.

Chapter 9

SALES AND ADVERTISING

J ust about everyone who works in electronic media is engaged in sales. A talent agent sells a producer on using a particular writer or actor in a production. A producer who pitches a show to a network executive is selling an idea. Recent college graduates need to sell themselves to directors in order to be hired as crew members. But the types of activities that are usually referred to as sales are those that occur when media companies try to sell products or services to consumers, when media companies sell to each other, or when media companies sell to advertisers who then use the media to sell to consumers.

Money is the root of all television

Anonymous

9.1 Media-to-Consumer Sales

Many forms of electronic media sell directly to people who consume or use their product. For example, movie theaters sell tickets, and perhaps even more important, they sell refreshments to the people who eat them while watching the movie (see Exhibit 9.1). Although concessions account for only 25 percent of revenue for most theater chains, they provide a profit margin that averages about 85 percent, with popcorn and soda being particularly profitable. A box of popcorn that sells for $5.00 only costs about 30 cents to make, so the theater makes a profit of

movie theaters

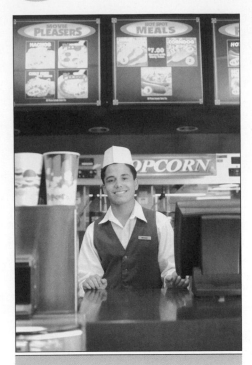

Exhibit 9.1

Refreshments sold to moviegoers provide a great deal of profit to the movie theaters.

Generic Cable TV System Packages	
Product	**Cost per Month**
Digital cable—45 channels	$35.00
Digital cable—150 channels	$45.00
Digital cable—200+ channels	$50.00
Each additional HDTV receiver	$10.00
Digital video recorder	$7.00
Digital video recorder service	$10.00
High-speed internet	$35.00
Phone service	$45.00
Pay-per-view	Depends on event
Video-on-demand	Depends on event

Exhibit 9.2

These are typical offerings of a cable TV system. Usually there are discounts for subscribing to several services.

$4.70. Refreshments are so important to movie theaters that some chains have ushers with pushcarts to sell to people who don't want to wait in line at the concession stand.[1]

radio and TV

Satellite radio, satellite TV, cable TV systems, and phone companies sell services directly to consumers. **Satellite radio** sells packages of audio channels ranging in cost from about $7 to $14 a month, depending on the number of channels you choose. Cable television, satellite TV, and phone services compete with each other, especially in television offerings, but also in terms of **broadband** internet and telephone services (see Exhibit 9.2). In order to remain competitive, they constantly market "deals." They may, for example, offer internet service free for two months if you sign up by next Thursday. Or they may give you three free **pay-per-view** choices if you sign up for caller ID. The marketing departments at the various companies continually eye what the competition is doing and adjust their offerings accordingly.[2]

public broadcasting

Public radio and TV have a particularly difficult sales job in relation to their consumers. They must convince audience members to help pay for public broadcasting even though there are no restrictions on people receiving the programming for free. The stations do this through on-air fundraising campaigns that stress the value of their programming and their need for money. However, the on-air campaigns, although usually successful, often irritate listeners and viewers because they take away from the very programming the stations want the audience members to support. Public broadcasting is constantly looking for new ways to convince people to donate money, from printed mailers to wine tasting parties.[3]

Many media items are sold to consumers in the same manner as other goods—through a wholesale and retail distribution network. Film companies and others distribute **DVD**s for sale or rent through various stores. **Video game** consoles, **smartphones,** and **pads** are often sold the same way. But there is a difference between selling consumer products such as food and furniture and selling many media products because, unlike eggs or a coffee table, media products such as music, video games, and movies can be delivered through the internet. Most sales that are internet-assisted involve a two-step process: The consumer sees a product on the website and then goes to a store to buy it or requests that it be delivered by UPS or a similar service. With some media products, the consumer can view and receive all in one step. This means the website must be a particularly effective sales instrument.[4]

internet selling

9.2 Media-to-Media Sales

Media entities frequently sell to each other. For example, a TV station may rent its studio to an independent production company that wants to use it to record a **corporate video.** A movie studio may sell rights to a video game company so that the company can create a game based on the movie, or a book publisher may sell rights to a studio so it can produce a movie based on the book.[5]

selling examples

Syndicators sell programming to media outlets such as broadcast stations and cable networks. They charge their customers one of three ways. The simplest is **cash.** The station or network writes a check to cover the cost of the programming it wants from the syndicator. Another method is **barter.** The station pays nothing for the program, but the syndicator gets to sell most of the commercials aired within the programming and then keep the money. A few of the commercials are left for the buyer to sell to cover its cost of transmitting the program—electricity, handling, and so on. The third method is **cash plus barter.** The buyer pays the syndicator some money and, in return, sells a larger portion of the commercials than is the case with barter.[6]

syndicators

Major and independent production companies also sell to networks and stations. Sometimes this involves cash or barter, but it can also involve a **license fee** wherein the network helps fund the production in return for the right to air it. This arrangement can get sticky if both the production company and the network are owned by the same parent company (for example, 20th Century Fox and Fox Broadcasting Network). Although it would seem to behoove the network to buy the production company product, the parent company will suffer if the network airs a program from the production company that is subpar.[7]

production companies

Another media-to-media sales process involves cable networks and local cable TV systems. Cable networks such as USA, CNN, and Lifetime depend on local cable systems, such as Comcast and Time Warner, to get their programming seen. If cable systems, especially the big conglomerates, do not include a particular network in their offerings to consumers, the network will not have viewers and, therefore, will not be able to sell advertisements. As a result, cable networks have affiliate representatives who convince cable systems to start carrying or keep carrying the network. Cable networks charge the systems for carrying the networks based on how many subscribers the system has. The price is determined by the degree to which the systems value the network. (ESPN can charge about $4.00 per subscriber while small networks such as Hallmark charge considerably less than one dollar.)[8]

cable networks

broadcast networks

Interestingly, the process involving broadcast TV networks (NBC, CBS, etc.) and their **affiliated** stations is quite different. The networks pay the stations to show the programs. This may seem backward because the stations are the ones obtaining the goods, but the networks retain the rights to sell many of the commercials within their programs and thus make the lion's share of the money. In recent years, as network fortunes have fallen, the networks have tried, occasionally successfully, to reduce their payments to affiliates or even get stations to help pay for the programming.[9]

movie theaters

The movie business has a complicated sales process. Movie theaters obtain the films they show from distributors, which either work independently or are part of the studio structure. The theater owners usually decide what films they want based on hearsay, sales pitches, and **trailers**—not on actually seeing the movies. This is called **blind bidding.** Most exhibitors are large companies with multiplexes in many cities, so they buy for a large group of theaters. Generally, the theater owners keep 30 percent of the money from ticket sales during the first week of a movie's run, and the studios receive 70 percent. As the weeks progress, the studios get less, and the theaters get more, until the percentages reach about 90/10. These percentages are only general; each movie has its own contract between the distributor (studio or independent) and exhibitor (theater), and all the terms are negotiable. For example, a studio might insist on more than 70 percent of the first-week ticket sales for a super blockbuster, arguing that it needs a higher percentage to recover the production costs and, besides, all the people who will flock to the movie will buy popcorn, candy, and soda, adding to the theater's profits. However, movies earn most of their money during the first week and then burn out, so theaters would not be happy with this arrangement.[10]

after theater sales

After movies have been shown in a theater, movie studios or syndicators sell them other places, such as broadcast or cable networks, local stations, DVD distributors, and online websites. They price these movies, which can be sold on a cash or barter basis, based on a percent of the box office take (usually about 10 or 12 percent). A cable network, such as HBO, that obtains the movie shortly after its theatrical release would pay a higher percentage than a local TV station that airs the movie much later. When suppliers sell packages of movies (spooky movies, Clint Eastwood movies, etc.), they average the box office receipts to determine the package price.[11]

international

Syndicators, networks, production companies, and movie studios also sell their products overseas (see Chapter 14). Usually they have foreign sales departments that are separate from the domestic ones. For some movies and TV series, the international market can provide one-third of the revenue.[12]

9.3 Media-to-Advertiser Sales

Most media advertising does not involve direct sales to the consumer. Ads are placed on radio, television, and the internet and are shown at the beginning of DVDs or before a movie starts in hopes that the ads will cause the consumer to buy whatever is advertised. But there is no guarantee that any particular consumer will watch a commercial or that it will affect behavior. A decision to buy something may be the result of hearing an ad on radio, reading a magazine story about the product, searching for it on the internet, glimpsing a commercial while fast-forwarding through a TV program, and hearing about the product from a friend. However, there have been many instances when sales have gone from low to high at the same time a product is heavily advertised. For that reason, advertising is considered to be a very effective way of encouraging people to buy.

People who sell advertising are really selling potential eyes and ears, not a particular product. They convince someone who has a product or service to sell that using their medium is the best way to move the product off the shelf. Advertisers are the customers that media entities deal with, but members of the public are the consumers who will actually buy a product.

indirect sales

Electronic media advertising is in a state of flux. The rash of new media forms that have arisen in recent years has complicated how companies decide on their advertising strategies. In addition consumers have become inured to commercials and have found many ways to ignore them. The base of people that advertisers wish to reach is shifting and so are the methods for reaching them. Traditional ways of advertising aren't working anymore—but newer methods aren't working all that well either.

problems

However, media salespeople still undertake a series of general steps in order to fulfill the needs of their companies and enable advertisers to make the best use of their advertising dollars. They meet with advertisers, convince them to advertise, help them determine the type of ads to use, price the advertising, and help produce and service the ads.

9.4 Contacting Advertisers

Most companies that have products or services to sell to the public need to advertise in order to make people aware that these products or services exist. Some organizations can successfully self-advertise by building a website, writing a **blog**, or sending out tweets. A person who sets up a window washing business may desktop print flyers and personally hang them on doorknobs of local homes. But most companies need more help than that with their advertising. Sometimes someone from the company will contact a radio or TV station and inquire about advertising, but more often it is the other way around.

9.4a Local Salespeople

Selling at the local level is fairly straightforward. Local radio and TV stations and cable systems have sales reps who contact local businesses and try to sell them commercial time (often referred to as **inventory**). At small-town radio stations, the disc jockeys may also be salespeople, spending four hours a day announcing and playing music and four hours calling or going to local restaurants, specialty shops, and used car dealers selling ads. Often the general manager of a small station doubles as a salesperson. In the same manner, the owner of a website aimed at local residents or the operator of a movie theater that shows ads before a movie starts might visit local merchants.

salespeople

process

Larger local electronic media organizations use a distinct sales force. These people are generally paid on a salary-plus-commission basis. Sometimes they specialize according to product line—one person sells to restaurants, another to real estate agents. Generally, the people who sell local ads are expected to service them as well so that advertisers repeat their business. Servicing ads includes making sure the ads are run at the appropriate times, placing information prominently on a website, and facilitating any copy changes that may be needed.

9.4b National Salespeople

sales reps

A local station, cable system, website, or movie theater may also have an on-staff salesperson to handle ads from nationally based companies, but now that many local facilities are owned by conglomerates, most of the dealings related to national ads are handled by headquarters staff for all their media properties. Sometimes local or nationally based media organizations hire outside companies to sell their advertising (see Exhibit 9.3). These companies earn income from commissions on the sales they make for the media organization.

A large portion of advertising dollars goes to national commercial and cable TV networks. These networks maintain significant sales forces that are devoted to selling and servicing major national ads. Network commercial inventory is a fairly limited commodity. Only a certain number of spots are available, and these cannot be expanded as easily as newspapers can add pages when ad demand is heavy. A network has the same amount of time available during the holidays, a heavy season, as it does the rest of the year, so the sales force must be careful to sell in a way that meets the overall needs.

networks

Generally, network management is deeply involved with sales and makes sure that a knowledgeable team presents ideas. For many years, commercial TV

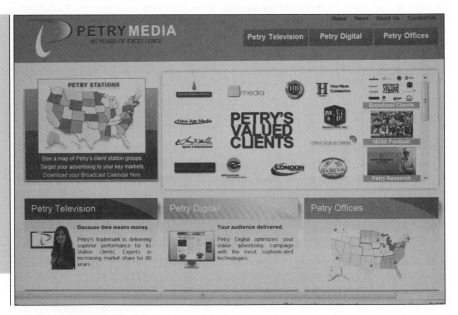

Exhibit 9.3

Petry is one of the oldest of the media sales organizations, which used to be called station representatives. It was founded in 1931 to sell radio advertising but in 1971 sold its radio representation in order to concentrate on TV. Now it is divided into two media areas—television and digital.

network advertising sold out rather easily at high prices. Usually most of it was gone **upfront** (before the fall season actually started). As other forms of media, such as satellite TV and the internet, have eroded the audience, however, network sales have gone soft, and sometimes inventory goes unsold.[13]

9.4c Advertising Agencies

The media people who sell commercial time on a national basis are likely to deal with advertising agencies because they are the organizations that usually make media decisions for large companies that place many ads. Agency employees contact the companies and are the intermediaries between businesses that want to advertise and the media that want the ads.

Most major **advertising agencies** are termed **full-service agencies.** They establish advertising objectives for companies with products or services to sell and try to position their clients so that there is something unique about them that consumers will remember. They place their clients' ads in all forms of media— newspapers, direct mail, radio, TV, internet, portable platforms. They conduct research to test the advertising concept and then attempt to obtain the best buy for the money available. Full-service agencies design the advertisement, oversee its production, and determine when a company should initiate a campaign and how long it should continue. After ads have run, agencies handle post-campaign evaluations to determine the strengths and weaknesses of the campaign. Throughout the process, the ad agency keeps the company executives well informed of the successes and failures of the advertising campaign.

duties

For its efforts, the advertising agency generally receives 15 percent of the billings. In other words, a billing of $1,000 to its client for commercial time on a TV station means that $850 goes to the station and $150 is kept by the ad agency to cover its expenses. Because dollar amounts are fairly constant from agency to agency, the main "product" an ad agency has to sell to its customers is service. Advertisers sometimes change agencies simply because one agency has run out of creative ideas for plugging its product, and a new agency can initiate fresh concepts.

pay

Some of the oldest and largest U.S. ad agencies have undergone mergers and consolidation and some are owned by international holding companies (see "Zoom In" box), in part because advertising has become such an important international business. Most agencies are divided into departments, some of which deal with administrative responsibilities such as accounting, while others deal with creative aspects such as writing and art design, and still others handle media and marketing. A team works on the ad campaign for any one company.[14]

organization

Not all agencies are large, however. Some one-person operations service only a few clients who like the attention they receive from the person directly responsible. Other agencies, sometimes referred to as **boutique agencies,** handle only specific things a company asks for—perhaps the designing of an ad, the post-advertising research, or advice on reaching the Spanish-speaking audience. Usually this type of work is paid for by a negotiated fee rather than a 15 percent commission. Some businesses maintain their own **in-house** services, which amount to an ad agency within the company.[15]

smaller operations

ZOOM IN: **The Saga of the Oldest Advertising Agency**

It is purported that the first person in the United States to use the term "advertising agency" was Volner Palmer, when he formed an agency in Philadelphia in 1841. In 1869, 21-year-old Francis Wayland Ayer opened an agency, also in Philadelphia, that he named N. W. Ayer & Son, after his father. In 1877 Ayer acquired Palmer's firm and self-proclaimed that N. W. Ayer & Son was the oldest advertising agency in the country.

Ayer's agency started with weekly religious newspapers but over the years added many clients and many types of media. It also was instrumental in establishing the 15 percent commission system and in getting employees to work together in creative teams. Among its clients were Camel Cigarettes, AT&T, the U.S. Army, and Morton Salt. For the latter it developed the slogan "When it rains it pours" and the logo of a girl with an umbrella. Morton Salt still uses both of those.

N. W. Ayer & Son, like many other advertising agencies, merged and was acquired. In 1973 it relocated its headquarters to New York, and after mergers involving the MacManus Group and Bcom 3, the N. W. Ayer & Son name was retired. In 2002, the company that had been Ayer was acquired by Publicis Groupe, based in Paris. The Ayer building in Philadelphia was purchased in 2005 and turned into luxury condominiums.

Morton salt.

9.5 Convincing Advertisers

objections

Once someone has gotten a foot in the door of a company, be it a local salesperson, a media sales organization rep, a network executive, or an advertising agency rep, that person needs to convince the people at the company to use their services. Organizations are often hesitant to advertise. They hope that their product is so good that word of mouth will create sales and they will not need to spend money on advertising. Indeed, word of mouth is an outstanding form of advertising, and it has great potential for use within social media. However, there is the risk that the Facebook entry, blog, or review will be negative. When clients advertise, they have control over the content.

particular media

Even if clients do not need to be convinced of the value of advertising, salespeople can find it challenging to convince them to use a particular media. Not only do the electronic media compete with each other, but they also compete against print media, billboards, and mailed coupons (see Exhibit 9.4). A TV station sales representative, for example, needs to discuss the values of TV over radio, the internet newspapers, and other media. Many sales reps, however, are selling **multiple platforms.** In other words, once a salesperson convinces a company to advertise on one property, such as a broadcast network, he or she then tries to get the advertiser to place ads on various other related media properties such as websites, cable networks, and radio stations for "a small extra fee." Part of the job of an advertising agency is to decide on the best media mix for the client.

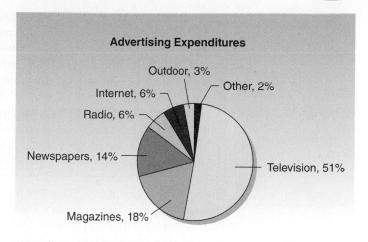

Exhibit 9.4

This is the media breakdown of the $131 billion spent on advertising in 2010.

Beyond the particular media, clients must be convinced to advertise on a specific facility. For example, some radio stations use **ratings** (see Chapter 10) as evidence for the number of people who are listening to the station. Stations that don't have good ratings engage in **concept selling;** they try to sell advertisers on unique elements of their content that will theoretically attract the type of people the advertiser wishes to reach. The characteristics of people listening, watching, or surfing a particular media entity has become an important element of selling advertising. Advertisers want the "right" people to hear or see their message and a salesperson is likely to have the best success if the needs of the client are in line with the demographics of the media entity. Some companies want to advertise to young people because this age group is in the process of forming brand loyalties; some want to target Latinos who are a fast-growing demographic; others prefer the Baby Boomer generation because of their large number.[16]

specific facility

9.6 Determining the Type of Ad

Advertising salespeople must help their clients determine which types of ads best fit their need. The types are almost endless because people in ad agencies and those involved with media are constantly trying to think of new ways to gain the attention of potential consumers. Below is a discussion of some of the different types of ads a company can consider. These are not mutually exclusive—it is possible, for example, to have a local image-oriented ad that is targeted and interactive.

9.6a Geographic Factors

One way to categorize advertising is to divide it into international, national, regional, and local. A business, such as a major shoe company, that distributes throughout the world might prefer to prepare one advertising campaign

international

that operates everywhere. To undertake this **international buy,** the ads can be placed on media outlets in many countries or they can be placed on the internet which, by definition, goes almost anywhere. The company and its ad agency must be careful to take into account cultural differences, however. An ad with a scantily clad American woman may lead to a backlash in a Muslim country.

national

There are several ways to undertake a **national buy** that will cover the entire United States. One is to place an ad on a broadcast or cable network, such as ABC or TBS. That way the ad goes everywhere that the network program goes and plays everywhere in the country at the same time. This type of advertising is used for products with wide appeal such as toothpaste or cereal. Another way is to buy time on individual stations. The advertiser places the ad on many stations, usually enough to cover the whole country, but the ads do not play at the same time on all stations. An advertiser may take this route because its product needs a certain demographic audience. Maybe an automobile manufacturer wants to promote a car that it thinks will particularly appeal to women with small children. It can select stations throughout the country that target that audience.

regional

A **regional buy** covers a particular area of the country and is most often used for products that do not have a national appeal but can be useful in a number of places. A tractor manufacturer, for example, might want to advertise throughout the rural areas of the Midwest. Regional buys can be made by purchasing time on a number of different stations in the region, or they can be made by purchasing time on a regional network. The latter are most common with radio and with cable-TV sports programming.

local

A **local buy** involves placing ads in a limited geographic area. It is used primarily by merchants who service only a local area—used car dealers, computer repair shops. A local advertiser often places the same ad on many different local radio and TV stations, local cable systems, and perhaps even websites that are accessed primarily by local people. In this way, the ad can reach a maximum number of people in a particular area.

A company may decide to undertake international, national, regional, and local advertising and even use the same commercial for all. More often, however, there will be at least slight variations in the advertising to take into account different audience composition.[17]

9.6b Attention Factors

spots

One traditional method of electronic media advertising is **spot buying.** The advertiser (through its ad agency) buys 15, 30, or 60 seconds of airtime for certain times of the day or for insertion within or adjacent to certain programs. Hence, a disc jockey whose show runs from 6:00 A.M. to 9:00 A.M. may present commercials from several dozen advertisers, all falling under the umbrella of spot advertising. In radio, spots can be aired at almost any time because program segments are short—three or four minutes for a musical selection or two or three minutes for news items. In television (both broadcast and cable), spots are aired at more definite times because the programming has natural breaks where ads are inserted.

Another traditional method is **program buying,** in which an advertiser pays the total cost for producing and distributing a program. This is rare today because production costs are high. More frequent is the practice of several noncompeting companies paying for the cost of the program. Then their ads, and usually only their ads, are inserted within the program. These traditional approaches to advertising worked well during the early days of broadcasting when programs had large relatively captive audiences who had little recourse but to sit through commercials. Now people are exposed to approximately 5,000 advertising messages a day; they are so inundated they have developed mental mechanisms to block commercials. In addition, because of channel surfing, mute buttons, and digital video recorders, they have much more control over what they receive.[18]

program

One method that is used to counter the lack of attention created by being inundated with commercials is **product placement.** This practice is actually fairly old, particularly within movies, where companies pay to have their product shown in the film. The Coke can that the actress drinks from is not accidentally a Coke, and the Ford Explorer the actor drives in the movie could be there because Ford paid to have it there. But product placements increased in intensity and number on TV during the 1990s as a way to get viewers to notice products.[19]

product placement

It worked for a while, but viewers learned to ignore the products, so the practice was upped to—**product integration** (often called **branding integration**). In this case, the product is not just shown; it is an integral part of the story—the teenager who has to find a way to earn money so he can buy Reebok shoes to impress his girlfriend, a group of employees who talk Office Depot into sponsoring a talent show. Product integration, which actually was alive and well on old-time radio (see Exhibit 9.5) has brought advertising agencies back into the TV production business to create shows that will highlight their clients.[20]

branding integration

merchandising

A variation on product placement or product integration is **merchandising.** For this, companies create props or characters that can be placed in movies, TV programs, or video games. Then the companies turn these into products they can sell—the cartoon bear that can be sold as a cuddly stuffed animal, the detective's coffee cup that is later included as part of a dish set.[21]

Digital insertion is another way of showing products within programs. The products aren't actually placed in the program but are seen as **virtual ads.** This is common in sports programs where the billboards seen in the background aren't actually on the walls of the stadium but are inserted digitally. Video games have

Exhibit 9.5

The radio program, *Fibber McGee and Molly,* which aired from 1935 to 1959, included a form of product integration. The show's announcer often visited the McGees at their home, and when he did, he talked about the virtues of Johnson's Wax. Shown here are Marian and Jim Jordon, the show's stars.

digital insertion

become an excellent place for placement; players actually seem to enjoy driving past billboards that advertise audio equipment or down a road past a well-known fitness center.[22]

shared screen

Sometimes ads are placed on part of the TV screen that is showing the program—a **shared screen** approach. While the soap opera actors are kissing center screen, a little figure in the corner of the screen is cleaning a messy stove with a well-known detergent.

pod insertion

Another technique is placing an advertisement that looks like part of the program in the middle of a string (pod) of spot commercials—for example, a Vaseline commercial in the middle of commercials running in *Mad Men.* The idea is for this **pod insertion** to get people to stop fast forwarding through the commercials because they think the program has started again.[23]

targeting

Another method designed to get consumers' attention so that they will buy products is **targeting.** Technology allows cable and satellite TV companies to send different commercials to different homes based on the demographics of the occupants. The rich senior citizens living in an affluent neighborhood might see a Cadillac commercial while their poorer nephews will be delivered a Chevy commercial, even though they are watching the same program. Internet ads can be targeted according to what websites a person visits. For example, those who surf boating websites can be shown ads related to water recreation products, while those who access fashion information might see ads for cosmetics and shoes. Sometimes emails and social media postings are analyzed. If you send an email about a concert you attended, you may start seeing music-oriented ads. If you announce on your Facebook page that you are getting married, expect to see ads from wedding planners. Of course, obtaining the information about a person's interests in order to target the ads is fraught with privacy concerns (see Issues section of this chapter).[24]

9.6c Interactive Advertising

Google searches

The interactive capabilities of the internet have brought forth new forms of advertising for companies to consider. The most successful of these has been **keyword search.** Although credit for the original concept is usually given to goto.com, it has been utilized most effectively by Google. Whenever you undertake a search on Google, on the right side of the results page you see a list of sponsored links to products and services related to your search (see Exhibit 9.6). Companies pay Google every time someone clicks on their site link, a process known as **pay-per-click (PPC).** The order in which the sites are listed is determined by a number of factors, including the relevance of the company to the search query and the amount the company bids for each particular concept. Companies (often with the help of ad agencies or consultants) select the search words they want to be identified with and design their sites in such a way that they appear to be obviously relevant to those terms. In addition, companies that want to be at the top of the list are wise to bid high for the terms they really want. The colored sites in the middle of the results page are also positions companies pay for. The white entries are also listed by relevance and other algorithms, but those sites do not pay Google. The keyword search concept is effective because it gives consumers information they

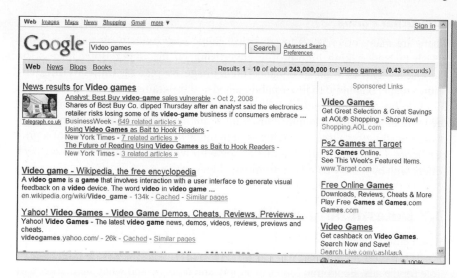

want. Most traditional advertising aims to interest people in something they may never have thought of and may not want until they see the ad. Keyword search gives information, in a low-key manner, for something that they have thought about and may even be looking to buy.[25]

Other types of interactive advertising on the internet have had some degree of success, albeit less than keyword search. For example, many sites sell **banner ads** (see Exhibit 9.7) that they place at the top of their site and other printed ads that they place along the side. Usually the sites charge a set fee for these rather than pay-per-click. There are **pop-up ads** that cover up some of the webpage and disappear only when someone clicks them off. However, there are also pop-up blockers to screen those out because they are generally irritating rather than effective. Companies often place video ads on their own webpages in order to advertise their products; sometimes the video ads are the same ones that appear on TV.

ad placement

Exhibit 9.7
A banner ad.

9.6d Long Forms

Sometimes advertising clients want to develop and position commercials that are longer than the usual 30 seconds. The **infomercial** is in this category. It is an entire program devoted to a particular product or service, such as an exercise machine or a diet plan. Throughout the infomercial people are urged to call to purchase or to obtain more information. Companies pay stations and networks to air their infomercials, so these programs sometimes bring in more money than could be made from commercials, especially in the wee hours of the morning.[26]

infomercials

Another type of long form is **home shopping.** A whole program or entire channel is devoted to selling products, such as jewelry and accessories. Companies supply the products and home shopping networks make their money by keeping a percentage of what viewers pay.

home shopping

9.6e Other Forms

There are many other ways to advertise. Some companies want to make a big splash by undertaking high-profile advertising on the Super Bowl telecast or the Oscars. Others want to enhance their image by placing **underwriting** announcements on public radio or public television programs. Still others engage in **location-based** advertising wherein they place commercials or infomercials near the point of sale—for example, a program about how a particular brand of apples is organically grown that is playing on a monitor in the produce section of a grocery store. Creative minds continue to come up with unique methods to connect sellers with buyers by using electronic media.[27]

9.7 Determining the Cost

Media entities want to charge advertisers as much as they can to air commercials or place ads on the internet. Advertisers, of course, want to pay as little as possible for the ads. Economic forces of supply and demand and what the market will bear affect the interplay of the advertising world, but in both good times and bad there are a number of factors that the media and advertisers keep in mind.

9.7a Cost Factors

CPM

One of these factors is **cost per thousand** or **CPM** (M from the Latin *mille* for thousand). This is the amount of money the media company charges the advertiser to have an advertisement in front of 1,000 people (see Chapter 10). Theoretically, advertisers should want the same CPM for each ad they place, whether it is in an NBC prime-time show or a History Channel morning show. The price for the ad on the History Channel would be much lower because it would probably not have as many thousands of people watching, but the CPM would be the same. But such is not always the case. Advertisers believe the major broadcast networks still have more glitter than cable or syndication, so prime-time broadcasting is able to charge a higher CPM (about $12) than daytime cable (about $2). Also, certain programs can charge a higher CPM than others (see "Zoom In" box).[28]

rate cards

Some media companies, particularly radio and TV stations, local cable channels, and websites, prepare a **rate card,** a listing of the prices they charge for different types of ads (see Exhibit 9.8). Although they usually do not put the CPM in writing, they tie their rate card prices to the number of people who will see or hear the ad. Even if a media company does not have a rate card, company executives go through the process of deciding how much they need to charge for ads in order to cover costs and reap some profit.[29]

frequency

Many variables affect the prices of commercials on radio and TV (and to some extent the ads shown in movie theaters). One is the number of commercials the advertiser wishes to air. Electronic media facilities rarely accept only one ad at a time—it would be too expensive in relation to the time taken by the salesperson to sell the ad. Usually a media company requires that an ad be aired at least 12 times and tries to induce the advertiser to buy even more airtime by offering **frequency discounts**—lower prices per ad as the number of ads increases.

ZOOM IN: **Super Commercials**

The Super Bowl is an outstanding example of selling ads on the basis of what the market will bear—and the market bears a lot. A 30-second Super Bowl ad can cost up to $3 million. Even with 100 million people watching, that is a CPM of $30, about 2.5 times the CPM of prime-time fare. But advertisers love the Super Bowl. It brings a sought-after young male demographic, and it's a time when people actually make a point of watching ads because they have such a great reputation. In fact, the commercials are as likely to be talked about the next day as the game itself. Some of the memorable ones throughout the years are:

- Joe Namath for Noxzema in 1969
- A young boy giving "Mean" Joe Green his Coke in 1980
- Apple's classic 1984 futuristic ad in which a female athlete destroys the Orwellian "Big Brother," symbolically freeing workers from office tedium
- Bugs Bunny and Michael Jordan interacting for Nike in 1992
- Numerous Budweiser commercials including the "Bud-Wise-Er" frogs
- E-Trade's hillbillies and monkey in 2000
- Britney Spears going through various decades with Pepsi in 2002
- Carrier pigeons trying (unsuccessfully) to compete with Federal Express in 2008
- A 2011 Gillette commercial of a man turning his world upside down.

The E-Trade commercial was particularly entertaining and prophetic because it poked fun at all the money dot-com companies were spending on Super Bowl ads. Two hillbillies clapped and a monkey danced while a narrator said, "We just wasted $2 million on a commercial. What are you doing with your money?"

Do you think companies are justified in spending so much for commercials on the Super Bowl? Can you think of any other programming in which commercials might take on the aura that they have with the Super Bowl? What is your favorite Super Bowl commercial?

Britney Spears in Pepsi's Super Bowl commercial.

For example, a company that places an ad 12 times on a radio station might be required to pay $500 per ad, or a total of $6,000. If it places the ad 24 times, it would pay $450 per ad, or a total of $10,800.

Another variable is the length of the ad—usually 15, 30, or 60 seconds. Obviously, a one-minute commercial costs more than a 30-second commercial, but usually not twice as much. Twelve one-minute ads might cost $550 each, and twelve 30-second ads might cost $500 each. Station costs, such as handling, are

length

Exhibit 9.8

An example of the type of rate card that a small radio station chain might use.

Rate Card
Generic Radio Station

Day	Time Slot	Rate
M/F	6:00 A.M. – 10:00 A.M.	$150
M/F	10:00 A.M. – 3:00 P.M.	$120
M/F	3:00 P.M. – 7:00 P.M.	$145
M/F	7:00 P.M. – 12:00 A.M.	$80
Sa/Su	6:00 A.M. – 10:00 A.M.	$115
Sa/Su	10:00 A.M. – 3:00 P.M.	$100
Sa/Su	3:00 P.M. – 7:00 P.M.	$115
Sa/Su	7:00 P.M. – 12:00 A.M.	$75
All days	12:00 A.M. – 6:00 A.M.	$70

30-second spots are 75% of 60-second spots
15-second spots are 45% of 60-second spots

more expensive for two separately produced 30-second commercials than for one 60-second commercial.

daypart

Audiences are of varying sizes at different times of the day (different **dayparts**), so this factor also becomes a variable on rate cards. Radio stations and networks usually have the largest audiences in the morning and early evening, when people are in their cars. The audience is lower during the midmorning and evening, and lower still in the middle of the night. Television is a different story, with most viewers congregating between 7:00 P.M. and 10:00 P.M. The other parts of the day can vary from channel to channel, depending on the programming. Some stations have a different rate for **adjacencies**—commercials that are aired right after or right before a popular program. The advertisers pay extra to be the first or last commercial, rather than one that may get lost in the middle of a pod of commercials.

grid

Some stations create a **grid rate card.** This includes prices for different dayparts but also different prices for the same daypart depending on whether the station has a large number of spots available or has only a few **availabilities (avails).** Obviously, the rates are higher when there are only a few avails.

programs

Television facilities sometimes sell ads based on particular programs rather than for particular times. An ad bought for 9:00 P.M. Tuesday during *The Tuesday Night Movie* might cost more than an ad purchased at 9:00 P.M. Wednesday during *This Week's Report.* Product placements and branded integrations are negotiated on an individual basis, but take into account the popularity of the TV program or the movie actors. Because ads are always available on the internet, the rate structure is different, with the length of time the ad stays up and its physical size being important determinants. In short, there are many variations in the factors that determine the cost of a particular ad.

9.7b Advertising Practices

Media companies create special "deals" to assist and entice advertisers to buy their advertising time. Some of these are:

various practices

trade-out: This is particularly popular in radio and involves trading advertising airtime for some service the station needs. Perhaps the station owns a car that needs occasional service; to receive this service free from Joe's Garage, the station broadcasts 12 ads a week for Joe's Garage with no money changing hands. Similar arrangements are negotiated with stationery suppliers, gas stations, audio equipment stores, and the like.

run-of-schedule (ROS): The salesperson and advertiser decide how many ads should be run and sometimes make up a package that consists of ads in different dayparts. The seller decides on the specific times the ads should run based on the availability of commercial time. For this privilege, the advertiser receives a discount and does not pay the going rate for the times selected.

fixed buy: The advertiser states the exact time each ad should run and pays a premium price. This often involves some negotiating. If two advertisers want 9:00 A.M. Monday, someone must compromise. In this circumstance, some media companies employ the **bump system,** in which the advertiser who offers the most money will get the spot even though some other advertiser was promised it first.

local discount: A local advertiser pays less than a national advertiser for the same airtime. The rationale is that the national advertiser can profit from reaching all the people in a station's coverage area while a local advertiser might not. For example, a national automobile manufacturer has the potential for selling cars to people in an entire city that a station covers, but the people in the southern part of the city are not likely to respond to an ad for a car dealer in the northern part of the city. For this reason, part of the station's coverage area is practically useless to the local car dealer.

orbiting: This practice appeals to advertisers who want many different people to see or hear their ads because ads play at slightly different times each day. For example, all the ads might be aired during morning drive time but on Monday they would be at 6:10, 7:15, and 8:50 while on Tuesday they would play at 6:30, 7:45, and 9:15.

annual flight schedule: Companies that sell leisure products often like to advertise around holiday times, and for them, stations and networks provide an annual flight schedule. The ads run only before major holidays and not at other times of the year.

volume power index (VPI): An advertiser decides who its target audience is and pays only for the number of listeners or viewers who fit that pattern. For example, a cosmetic company may designate women 18 to 34 for a particular product and base the CPM on only those people.

make-goods: Networks promise an advertiser a certain size audience; if the program does not deliver that large an audience, the broadcaster returns money to the advertiser or offers the advertiser free ads to make up for the shortfall.

rate protection: This is usually only available to longtime customers who advertise a great deal. The media organization guarantees that even if the advertising prices increase, these good customers can still buy ads at the old prices.

And on and on. When economic times are bad, media companies tend to offer more enticements to advertisers (and their agencies), trying to find something that will close the deal.[30]

9.8 Producing the Advertisement

Production of commercials is a very important facet of advertising. Companies rarely produce their own commercials because they simply do not have the equipment or know-how to do so. They are in the bread-making, car-selling, or widget-manufacturing business, not the advertising business.

radio

Small businesses that place ads on local radio stations generally have the stations produce the ads. The people who sell the time to the merchant write and produce the commercial at no extra cost. If they are good salespeople, they spend time talking to the merchant to determine what he or she would like to emphasize in the ad, and they check the ad with the merchant before it is aired. Often the commercial is prerecorded with music or sound effects, and occasionally the merchant talks on the commercial. Large companies that advertise on radio usually have much more elaborately produced ads that include jingles, special effects, and top-rated talent. The production costs are generally in addition to the cost of buying time.

TV

Television commercials are even more elaborate. Usually they are slick, costly productions that the advertiser pays for in addition to the cost of commercial airtime. Local stations sometimes produce commercials for local advertisers and charge them production costs—the cost of equipment, supplies, and personnel needed to make the commercial.

agencies

Much of local TV advertising and most network commercial production is handled through advertising agencies. As part of its service to the client, the agency decides the basic content of the commercial, perhaps by coming up with a catchy slogan (see Exhibit 9.9). Usually a **storyboard** (see Exhibit 9.10)—a series of drawings indicating each shot of the commercial—is made. The advertising agency then puts the commercial up for bid. Various independent production companies state the price at which they are willing to produce the commercial and give ideas as to how they plan to undertake production. The ad agency then selects one of these companies and turns the commercial production over to it. Some production companies maintain their own studios and equipment, whereas others rent studio facilities from stations, networks, or other companies.

Slogans from the Past

	Year	Agency	Slogan
1.	1930s	Batten, Barton, Durstine & Osborn	Mmm mm good
2.	1930s	Foote, Cone & Belding	When you care enough to send the very best
3.	1954	Ted Bates & Co.	Melts in your mouth, not in your hand
4.	1957	Foote, Cone & Belding	Does she…or doesn't he?
5.	1959	Ogilvy, Benson & Mather	Good to the last drop
6.	1963	Doyle Dane Bernbach	We try harder
7.	1971	Needham, Hooper & Steers	You deserve a break today
8.	1979	N. W. Ayer	Reach out and touch someone
9.	1984	Dancer-Fitzgerald-Sample	Where's the beef?
10.	1988	Richards Group	We'll leave the light on for you

Answers: 1. Campbell's soup; 2. Hallmark cards; 3. M&Ms candy; 4. Clairol hair color; 5. Maxwell House coffee; 6. Avis car rental; 7. McDonald's restaurants; 8. AT&T phone service; 9; Wendy's restaurants; 10. Motel 6

Exhibit 9.9

Here are 10 advertising slogans that were created a long time ago. See how many you have still heard of today.

Exhibit 9.10

A partial storyboard for a proposed Taco Bell commercial.

Exhibit 9.11

This commercial, featuring Billy Crystal, is being shot on Broadway in New York City.

The time, energy, pain, and money that are invested in producing a commercial often rival what goes into TV programs (see Exhibit 9.11). One commercial often takes weeks to complete, and many use the very latest in visual effects. Once the commercial is "in the can," it may air hundreds of times over hundreds of stations and networks—hence, the obsession with perfection.

internet

Ads for the internet can be the same commercials that are produced for radio or TV, but they are more likely to emphasize graphics. The jury is still out on how fancy these graphics should be. Some people think eye-catching graphics are necessary to grab the attention of web surfers; others think they are negatively distracting and that simple is better.[31]

9.9 Handling Controversies

Media outlets, ad agencies, and companies that advertise have always had to deal with controversies regarding advertising. Hardly anyone likes advertisements—they are too numerous, loud, annoying, insulting, misleading, and uninformative—just to mention a few of the adjectives aimed at them. Over the years there have been public outcries about numerous facets of advertising, one of the most vocal being that of advertising to children.

9.9a Advertising to Children

early programs

Commercials aimed at children generate particularly strong controversies. On early radio and TV, the hosts and stars of children's programs presented many of the ads. For example, in his early programs of the 1950s and 1960s, Captain Kangaroo, after doing a stint about growing vegetables, would walk over to a set featuring boxes of cereal and tell the children how good the cereal was. This practice, called **host selling,** came under fire when research showed that children have difficulty distinguishing between program content and commercial messages. Parents, particularly the group of Boston parents who formed Action for Children's Television (ACT), also complained about the ads (see Chapter 8).

FCC guidelines

As a result of the research and the complaints, the FCC in 1974 issued guidelines stating that programs' hosts should not sell products and that the display of brand names and products should be confined to commercial segments. In 2005, the FCC extended the "host selling" guidelines further to prevent programs from directing children to related commercial websites where they could buy products. The 1974 guidelines also stated that special measures should be taken to provide auditory and/or visual separation between program material and commercials. This led to **islands** at the end of most children's commercials. These were still pictures with no audio followed by a definite fade to black. This was to help children understand that the commercial had ended and the program was about to begin again. Starting about 1983, when the FCC was in a deregulatory mood, these guidelines were no longer enforced, and many of the islands went away.

time for ads

The amount of time devoted to commercials within children's programming has also varied in controversial ways over the years. For several decades, the National Association of Broadcasters had a self-regulatory code that stated the maximum number of minutes per hour that should be devoted to commercials within children's programs. During the 1960s and early 1970s, this number was 16. In 1973, the code was amended (largely at the insistence of ACT) to reduce the number to 12, and soon after, it was further reduced to 9.5 minutes per hour. Although this code was not a law (it was just an advisory standard decided by people within the television industry), most stations abided by it.

The code was outlawed by the Justice Department in 1982, however; and the FCC, in its deregulatory mood, said there should be no limits on the amount of advertising on any programming. This led to increases in the number of ads in children's programs and led to a short-lived phenomenon known as **toy-based programming.** In these programs, a particular toy was the "star" of the show. Often the toy was created before the show with the idea that the program would sell the toy. This did not sit well with ACT and other parents who thought their children were being exposed to commercials that were 30 minutes long.

toys as programs

In 1990, commercials during children's programs were once again restricted, this time by Congress. It passed a bill limiting commercials to 12 minutes per hour on weekdays and 10.5 minutes on weekends. Some stations do not abide by the rule, and the FCC periodically fines them. This 1990 bill essentially outlawed toy-based programs, although they had already fizzled as a programming form because not enough children were watching them.

1990 provisions

In addition, the content of children's commercials has been criticized. For example, all the ads for sugary foods have been related to childhood obesity. The production techniques of children's ads are also questioned, especially those that appear to be deceptive, such as camera lenses that make a toy car look as if it travels faster than it does and sound effects that add to the excitement of a game but are not part of the game. In general, anyone involved in advertising to children needs to take precautions in order to avoid controversy.[32]

content

9.9b Other Controversial Advertising

Not only children's ads are accused of being deceptive; ads aimed at adults are also less than what they seem to be. One classic case occurred when Campbell's put marbles at the bottom of a soup bowl so the vegetables would rise to the top and make for a richer-looking soup. The Federal Trade Commission made Campbell's stop airing the commercial because it was deceptive—no one puts marbles in soup. In a more recent case, the FTC barred Slim Down Solution from making bogus weight-loss claims. Even when demonstrations are valid, they may not be applicable. For example, a watch put through a hot and cold temperature test may operate perfectly at 110 degrees and –20 degrees, but not be satisfactory at normal temperatures.

deceptions

Testimonials have received their share of criticism because the well-known celebrities used for the commercials may not know whether what they are reading from the cue cards is correct or not. Stars actually have to use the product they are advertising (this arose after football star Joe Namath advertised panty hose), but they cannot be expected to know all of its assets and liabilities. Sometimes the implications conveyed by or about the stars are misleading— "John Q. Superstar runs 10 miles a day and eats Crunchies for breakfast." The implication is that the Crunchies enable him to run 10 miles—in all probability, a false premise.

testimonials

Another area of controversy involving commercials concerns the types of products advertised. Congress outlawed cigarette advertising on the airwaves in 1972 after a Surgeon General's report linked cigarettes to cancer (see Exhibit 9.12). Beer, wine, condoms, and personal sanitary products are considered by some groups to be inappropriate TV fare, but advertising them has not

types of products

Blow in her face and she'll follow you anywhere.

Hit her with tangy Tipalet Cherry. Or rich, grape-y Tipalet Burgundy. Or luscious Tipalet Blueberry. It's Wild! Tipalet. It's new. Different. Delicious in taste and in aroma. A puff in her direction and she'll follow you, anywhere. Oh yes....you get smoking satisfaction without inhaling smoke.

Smokers of America, do yourself a favor. Make your next cigarette a **Tipalet.**

New from Muriel.   About 5 for 25¢.

Exhibit 9.12

A type of ad you will never see now. Although this is a print ad, this type of message was prevalent on TV for many years until Congress outlawed cigarette advertising on TV.

been outlawed. The liquor industry, which for many years had a self-imposed ban on advertising hard liquor on radio and TV, lifted its prohibition in 1996, and several stations started accepting liquor ads. Critics claim that advertising medicines over the air and making them available through the internet encourage people to use them excessively.[33]

Political advertising is also criticized for both its content and its presentation. Part of the hostility is directed at politicians who smear each other on minor personal points (or even the quality of each other's commercials) rather than dealing with the issues. Sometimes special interest groups buy ad time and do the smearing, keeping the candidate above the fray. But this, too, is highly controversial, and the Federal Election Commission and others have changed the rules governing such organizations a number of times. Some believe that, given the power of the media, all candidates should be given free time. Politicians favor this idea because it would greatly reduce campaign expenses, eliminating many of the perils inherent in raising large amounts of money to gain office, but broadcasters are opposed to the idea. At present, radio and TV stations are supposed to charge candidates their **lowest unit charge**—that is, the lowest rate they would charge an advertiser wishing to advertise at the same time. Lowest unit charges are hard

political ads

to determine, however, because of the many deals that are made between advertisers and media outlets.[34]

control

Another issue related to advertising is control. Critics point out that "he who pays the piper picks the tune" and think that heads of large companies and advertising agencies control program content because they provide most of the money that supports it. They point to the fact that automobile dealerships pulled advertising from CBS stations after *60 Minutes* aired a segment on financing practices of car dealerships. Not only are there specific instances of advertiser influence, but also overall censorship occurs simply because advertisers refuse to sponsor certain types of programs, such as controversial documentaries. On a more subtle level, advertisers affect program content because they demand certain (young) demographics, and that drives the content of programming that networks, stations, and websites show.[35]

clutter

Then there are the perennial complaints about **clutter.** Recently websites have suffered from these complaints as their owners place more and more ads on each page and utilize pop-ups that block what users are trying to read. But most clutter complaints are aimed at radio and TV, where clutter refers to the amount of nonprogram material (mostly commercials) that occurs within an hour.

As stations and networks see their dollars shrink, they expand the number of minutes devoted to ads. In the early 1980s, the commercial networks were airing no more than 9.5 minutes per hour of ads during prime time, but now some networks program more than 20 minutes. In addition to being annoying to the viewers, this increase in clutter bothers advertisers because their messages get lost. In order to stand out in the clutter, some companies purposely create irritating commercials. Research has demonstrated that ads instilling negative feelings in people often lead to sales of the product because people remember the brand name. Because 15 or 30 seconds is not enough time to explain the assets of a product in an intelligent manner, the intent of irritating commercials is to gain the audience members' attention so they will remember the name without knowing much about the product.[36]

9.10 **Issues** and the Future

All of the controversies addressed in the previous section are likely to remain in the future. Purposeful deception, misleading testimonials, inappropriate products, political influences, advertiser control, and clutter are charges that can be aimed at just about any media. Portable platforms and social media are just starting to deal with these controversies, but as they become more ubiquitous they will encounter more criticism.

One big issue confronting newer media in regard to advertising is privacy (see also Chapter 11). It is valuable to advertisers to target their consumers by placing information about their products in front of people most likely to buy. But determining which people to target involves gathering information. People do not freely give information they know will be used by advertisers, so advertisers gather it in other ways. People do freely share information on social media sites so these are ripe for mining data. Companies that supply DVRs have easy access to information about what TV shows individuals watch, another valuable source of information. **Cookies** (little files placed on surfers' computers) keep track of what websites people have visited. Information-gathering devices can follow smartphones and register how and where they are used. All this information is available for companies to analyze and sell to advertisers. Anyone's chances of keeping such information about themselves hidden are essentially hopeless. While some people worry about loss of privacy in the future, others are conceding that privacy is already lost. The monetary incentives for media companies and advertisers to mine information about specific people and use it for sales purposes is enormous.[37]

privacy

Celebrities may play a part in developing a new form of advertising by monetizing their fans. Those with many followers on Twitter can send out sponsored Twitter messages in exchange for cash from advertisers. Demographic information about people who follow certain musicians or movie stars can definitely help advertisers target potential buyers.[38]

celebrities

media mix

Another issue for the future involves media mix. Currently TV absorbs the lion's share of advertising, but that could change. Network television ratings are continuously dropping, and TV is more difficult than newer media forms to make interactive. DVRs make it easy for people to fast forward through commercials. Both radio and TV ads disappear once they are aired while internet ads stay in front of a person for a longer period of time. And yet, newer media advertising has yet to prove itself in the way that television has for decades.[39]

ad agency programs

Advertising agencies are becoming more aggressive about providing programming to networks that can benefit their advertisers. Some have even designed programs with plots that can accommodate all their client's products in an intense branding integration style. Some programmers are skeptical about accepting programming from agencies, remembering that the quiz show scandals of the 1950s were caused, at least in part, because advertisers were supplying the programs.[40]

effect on society

Some people see advertising as having an overall negative effect on the structure of our society. It encourages a society dominated by style, fashion, and "keeping up with the Joneses," and it retards savings and thrift. It fosters materialistic attitudes that stress inconsequential values and leads to a waste of resources and pollution of the environment. Advertising also fosters monopoly because the big companies that can afford to advertise can convince people that only their brands have merit.[41]

positive elements

Although advertising is severely criticized from many quarters, it has its positive elements. It defrays costs, reducing what the public has to pay directly for media services, it informs people about products available to them, and it drives the world economy. Advertisers need the media, the media need advertisers, and consumers need both. Advertising is not likely to go away.[42]

9.11 Summary

The main forms of selling within electronic media are media to consumer sales, media to media sales, and media to advertiser sales. To summarize advertising, consider a make-believe sales campaign that advertising agency Lynne & Co. put together for a new Telmat Toy Company doll named Carol-o-line that sings Christmas carols.

Lynne & Co., a full-service agency, decided the product required a national ad campaign (as opposed to international, regional, or local) that utilized 30-second TV commercials on children's cable TV channel Dimeon, graphic ads on three well-known internet sites, 30-second audio spots (as opposed to any type of program sponsorship) on several large city radio stations, and free social media advertising utilizing Telmat's president's Twitter followers and other Telmat employees' Facebook pages. Telmat's promotion vice president was skeptical about using radio, but Lynne & Co. convinced her that using certain radio stations with high ratings, as opposed to concept selling, would be a good way to target mothers of young children.

The internet part of the campaign involved bidding for keyword search words "toys," "dolls," and "Christmas music" and making those words more predominant on the Telmat website to better utilize the pay-per-click function. It also involved featuring Carol-o-line on three toy retail websites that do not have clutter. Consideration was given to buying email addresses of mothers with young daughters but ruled out because of privacy concerns.

Also ruled out were product placement, branding integration, merchandizing, infomercials, and home shopping. Carol-o-line will have a very brief selling season that will not merit involvement in any of those processes.

Telmat and Lynne & Co. obtained a CPM of about $2 on the cable channel. They looked at the rate cards of the radio stations and utilized a grid rate card that included favorable dayparts. Because this product is sold primarily during the Christmas season, Lynne & Co. worked particularly hard to negotiate an acceptable annual flight schedule. They also obtained a frequency discount and decided to use ROS. Trade-out, fixed buy, local discount, orbiting, VPI, make good, rate protection, and upfront were not applicable to this advertising campaign.

After Lynne & Co.'s creative department prepared a storyboard for the television commercial, it employed a production company that rented the studio of a local TV station (media to media sales) in order to produce the commercial. The radio commercial was produced at a local radio station. Telmat has an in-house design department and chose to design its own internet graphic ad.

Because Carol-o-line is being marketed primarily for children, Lynne & Co. made sure none of the elements of the TV or radio commercials, the graphic ad, or the social media advertising were deceptive. There was no pod insertion because children have difficulty distinguishing programs from commercials. There also were no testimonials and no pop-up ads.

Lynne & Co. serviced Telmat by doing follow-up studies on the effectiveness of the ad campaign. By using a multiplatform approach, Lynne & Co. hoped to be able counter consumer fatigue and antagonism related to advertising in general.

Suggested Websites

www.adweek.com (Adweek magazine, an industry publication)

www.aaaa.org (American Association of Advertising Agencies, a trade group)

www.omnicomgroup.com (Omnicom, a major advertising agency holding company)

www.rab.com (Radio Advertising Bureau, an organization to help radio organizations advertise effectively)

www.tvb.org (Television Bureau of Advertising, an organization to help television entities advertise effectively)

Notes

1. "Popcorn Is Salt of the Boxoffice," *Hollywood Reporter,* December 10–12, 2004, 14.
2. For examples, see http://www.sirius.com; https://www.directv.com; http://www.comcast.com; and http://www22.verizon.com/.
3. "As Sponsorship Sales Blossom, Public Radio Walks a Fine Line," *Wall Street Journal,* March 17, 2006, 1.
4. "Google Hits Play on Its New Online Music Store," *Los Angeles Times,* November 17, 2011, B-1; and "Store Aims to Plug People into iPhones," *Los Angeles Times,* July 10, 2008, C-1.
5. "TV Turns to Retail," *Broadcasting & Cable,* November 28, 2005, 14.
6. "Syndies Sing Happy Ad Tune," *Hollywood Reporter,* August 25, 2008, 2; and "Cash Could Be King Again," *Broadcasting & Cable,* January 4, 2010, 7.
7. "Table Scraps," *Broadcasting & Cable,* July 26, 2004, 1.
8. "Pot of Gold," *Broadcasting & Cable,* July 7, 2008, 10
9. "Affiliate (Dis)Agreements," *Broadcasting & Cable,* March 21, 2011, 8.
10. "An Ancient Legend Spans the Film Formats," *TV Technology,* November 7, 2007, 18.
11. "The New Rules of Syndication," *Broadcasting & Cable,* January 23, 2006, 26–27.
12. "Biz Without Borders," *Variety,* April 20–26, 2009, 1.
13. "Upfront's Upside," *Broadcasting & Cable,* June 23, 2008, 17; and "Disney Buys Mom Blogs, Plans to Integrate Content, *Wall Street Journal,* November 15, 2011, B1.
14. "Advertising Agencies," *P3,* August 2005, 16; and "Advertising," http://www.designhistory.org/advertising_fall_08.html (accessed November 17, 2011).
15. "Dividing the Advertising Dollars," *Los Angeles Times,* May 17, 2011, B-1.
16. "Marketers Targeting Generation of Millennials," *Broadcasting & Cable,* April 11, 2011, 28; "Nets Put Buy in Bilingual," *Variety,* July 11–17, 2011, 1; and "Television's Senior Moment," *Wall Street Journal,* March 9, 2011, D1.
17. "Local Focus of Spot Runner Has Appeal to Global Investors," *Los Angeles Times,* May 7, 2008, C-1.
18. "DVR, for Divide, Vex, and Rankle," *Los Angeles Times,* May 14, 2007, E-1.
19. "Product Placements Made Easier," *TV Technology,* July 6, 2011, 15.
20. "And Now, A Story from Our Sponsor," *Hollywood Reporter,* March 18, 2008, S-4
21. "The 'Halo' Effect," *Variety,* September 6–12, 2010, 1.
22. "Vid Game Score Will Soar," *Hollywood Reporter,* June 18, 2008, 1.
23. "Hot Pod," *Emmy,* Issue No. 3, 2011, 44.
24. "Targeted TV Ads Set for Takeoff," *Wall Street Journal,* December 20, 2010, B1.
25. "Online Ads Are Google's Strength," *Los Angeles Times,* May 1, 2004, 1; and "Google Sales, Profit Crush Analyst Estimates," *Los Angeles Times,* October 14, 2011, B1.
26. "Infomercials: A Mega-Marketing Tool," *Emmy,* June 1995, 114.
27. "Captive TV Nation: Oh, the Humanity," *Wall Street Journal,* April 16, 2010, W9.
28. "Cheaper by the Thousand," *Broadcasting & Cable,* February 4, 2002, 20–22; and "The Road to Super Bowl XL," *Wall Street Journal,* February 3, 2006.
29. "Loyalty Factor," *Broadcasting & Cable,* May 5, 2004, 42. The rate card is based on one for the Ozark Radio Network eight-station combo found at http://www.ozarkradionetwork.com/rates2.html (accessed July 31, 2008).
30. "Marketing ROI: Every Brand's Opportunity," *ANA/The Advertiser,* October 2001, 30–34; and "Stations Add Incentives and Generate Revenue," *Television Week,* August 15, 2005, 24.
31. Larry Elin and Alan Lapides, *Designing and Producing the Television Commercial* (Boston: Allyn and Bacon, 2003); and "Top 100 Advertising Campaigns," http://adage.com/century/campaigns.html (accessed November 21, 2011).
32. "FTC Commissioner Tackles Ads for Kids," *Wall Street Journal,* August 20, 2008, B7; "Ad Violations Cost Viacom, Disney," *Hollywood Reporter,* October 22–24, 2004, 4; "Senate Unanimously Okays Blurb-Curbing Kidvid Bill," *Daily Variety,* July 20, 1990, 1; and Barbara J. Wilson and Audrey J. Weiss, "Developmental Differences in Children's Reactions to a Toy Advertisement Linked to a Toy-Based Cartoon," *Journal of Broadcasting & Electronic Media,* Fall 1992, 371–94.

33. "Distillers Reverse Ban on Radio, TV Ads," *Broadcasting & Cable,* November 11, 1996, 7; "The Ups and Downs of Ad Rejection," *Broadcasting,* September 16, 1991, 40; and "Radio Executives Open to Condom Spots," *Broadcasting,* November 25, 1991, 46.

34. "FCC Seeking Way Out of 'Lowest Unit Charge' Confusion," *Broadcasting,* June 17, 1991, 21; and "Campaigns Get Personal," *Newsweek,* April 28, 2008, 20.

35. "*60 Minutes* Story Drives Away Ads," http://www.broadcastingcable.com/article/CA411062 (accessed April 19, 2004); and "The Tyranny of Eighteen to Forty-Nine," *Emmy,* Issue No. 6, 2003, 60–63.

36. "Television Networks Fatten Commercial Calf," *Broadcasting,* June 18, 1990, 21; "Ad Clutter Keeps Climbing," *Broadcasting & Cable,* December 22, 2003, 13; "A Word from Our Sponsor," *Newsweek,* August 4, 2008, 58–59.

37. "How Much Should People Worry About the Loss of Online Privacy?" *Wall Street Journal,* November 15, 2011, B7; and "The Web's New Gold Mine: Your Secrets," *Wall Street Journal,* July 31–August 1, 2010, W1.

38. "#Slinging Hash," *Variety,* August 8–14, 2011, 1.

39. "TV Lures Ads as Audiences Scatter," *Wall Street Journal,* September 21, 2011, B1.

40. "The Pitch That You Won't See Coming," *Los Angeles Times,* August 22, 2004, E-1.

41. Arthur Asa Berger, *Manufacturing Desire* (New Brunswick, NJ: Transaction Publishers, 1996).

42. "Survey Says: Ads Support Best," *Hollywood Reporter,* May 5, 2008, 9.

Chapter 10

PROMOTION AND AUDIENCE FEEDBACK

Promotion and audience feedback are, in a manner of speaking, two sides of the same coin. Within the electronic media business, the main purpose of promotion is to attract an audience for a particular product, such as a radio or TV program, a website, a movie, or a video game, in hopes that the feedback from that audience will be positive.

The main reason for desiring positive feedback is financial. For the most part, positive feedback related to video games, DVDs, and movies shown in theaters results in instant financial gratification because consumers pay directly for these products. With much of the internet, television, and radio, the results of the feedback are more indirect.

These media forms sell advertisements and it is the advertisers who provide (or withhold) financial success. It is important for media forms such as radio and TV to have valid proof of their audience feedback so that they can convince potential advertisers to buy commercial time.

> A generation is consuming media differently. More and more they are consuming it socially. For my generation, it was sit back in a chair and watch television. For my children's generation, they are so computer conversant, they are going to consume television with friends all over the world.
>
> **Dick Glover, CEO of video website Funny or Die**

Advertisers know that they are not going to sell products to every person exposed to an ad, but they want to make valid judgments so that they receive maximum return for their advertising dollars. However, they cannot simply depend on the promotion and statistics from members of the electronic media because these practitioners have a vested interest.

For that reason, an independent industry has arisen for the purpose of measuring audience feedback. Promotion (and sales) people use the information from these independent audience research companies to plan their strategies to attract an audience, and thus attract advertisers eager to connect with that audience.

10.1 Promotion

As mentioned in Chapter 7, **promotion** has become very important to media entities because potential viewers and listeners have so many choices. Even getting someone to know about a TV program, let alone sample it, is difficult. A great deal of promotion occurs when something new happens—a network starts airing a new show, a new movie comes out, a radio station starts a new contest, a new video game hits the stores. The purpose of this type of promotion is to build an audience of people who will watch, listen to, or buy a particular media program or product. Promotion is also used for media to advertiser sales and media to media sales.

10.1a Promotion to Build an Audience

One of the easiest and best ways for radio and TV to promote is to place **promotional spots (promos)** on their own stations or networks. People often have loyalty to particular media outlets because they like what they see or hear, so they are a potentially receptive group. In addition, companies that own many media forms often **cross-promote.** A promo for HBO might be cablecast on CNN because Time Warner owns both networks. Promos look like commercials except they are about future programming (see Exhibit 10.1). Promos often contain short scenes (of a teasing nature) from the program, along with information about when it will air. Because promos are like commercials, viewers often skip them in the same way they skip commercials. As a result, stations and networks have started

Exhibit 10.1
A shot from an animated promo for TalkSPORT Radio.

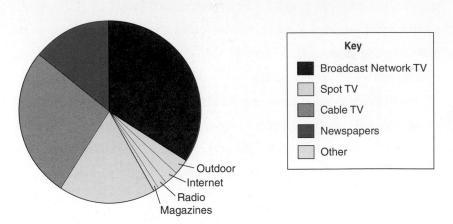

Ad Spending by Major Movie Distributors

using **snipes.** These are pop-ups that appear during a program, usually in a corner of the screen. Viewers cannot fast-forward through them because they are part of the program material the viewer is watching.[1]

promos

Stations and networks are not the only media forms subject to promos. Many DVDs start with promos for other home video products produced by the same company, and **trailers** have been a promotional vehicle for movies for years. An interesting aspect of media promotion is that media forms use each other for promotion. A TV show is advertised on radio; an internet site is advertised on TV; the "sneak" trailer for a movie is placed on YouTube. Exhibit 10.2 shows how the major movie distributors split their advertising dollars.[2]

other promotion

Promotion includes other forms of advertising such as signs on billboards or the sides of buses, listings on internet search sites (see Exhibit 10.3), and ads in newspapers. Most promotion is geared toward the potential audience for the media product, but some promotion is geared toward a particular audience with a particular purpose. For example, at Oscar voting time, the movie studios promote heavily to members of the Academy of Motion Picture Arts and Sciences, whose votes determine the awards.[3]

The best promotion is word of mouth. Friends telling each other about movies, TV programs, or video games they really like have much more impact than anything a media entity can do. Blogs, Facebook, and Twitter have become an important part of promotion; however, the people using social media sometimes express negative opinions that can hurt the promotion process (see "Zoom In" box).[4]

public relations

Promotion is closely tied to public relations and publicity, with the three often being in the same department. **Public relations** builds general goodwill that can enhance sales and audience numbers. Typical public relations activities include giving station tours, answering viewers' emails, and engaging in public-service activities, such as conducting campaigns to stop pollution. Public relations can also include the airing of **public service announcements (PSAs),**

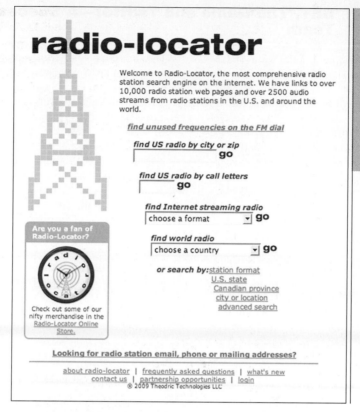

which promote nonprofit organizations or causes. Stations and networks do not charge to air these, so they are often put at undesirable times. But effectively produced PSAs are noticed and often lead to increases in desirable actions, such as people contributing to cancer research.[5]

publicity

Publicity is similar to promotion except that it is free. For example, an advertisement in a local newspaper urging people to tune in to a particular TV newscast would be promotion because a station would pay for the ad. A review of the TV newscast in the same newspaper would be publicity because the station would not pay for it. Publicity is preferred over promotion because it is free, but the problem with publicity is that it may be negative. A positive review of the newscast is helpful, but a negative one is often worse than no review.

cautions

Promotion, public relations, and publicity are all subject to failure. Sometimes networks spend millions of dollars promoting a series only to yank it off the air after two weeks because it hasn't met expectations. Sometimes promotion campaigns go awry because they don't attract their targeted audience. For example, if a cable channel is trying to promote itself to college students, its promotion materials shouldn't feature grade school children. Promotion needs creative minds and energetic bodies that can respond quickly to the changing needs of the media.[6]

ZOOM IN: **BET, *The Game* and Twitter—A Successful Team**

When Black Entertainment Television (BET) premiered *The Game* in 2011, 7.7 million people watched. This set a record for the most watched scripted series premiere on an advertising-supported cable network. And yet there had been very little traditional promotion for the show—mostly a few billboards and some newspaper reviews. The secret to the success was social media.

The Game, a series about pro football players and their significant others, had originally been aired on the CW, but was canceled in 2009. The producers then took the show to BET, which picked it up and decided to have a social media-oriented promotion campaign. However, instead of creating a Facebook site for *The Game*, BET found a fan who had created a page for the show while it was on the CW and paid her to keep the site going.

The network also took advantage of the fact that African Americans, although they are 12 percent of the U.S. population, represent 25 percent of Twitter users. It wasn't hard to get grass roots buzz going about the series. There were very few scripted programs starring AfricanAmericans on TV in 2011, a situation that enabled this show to gain attention and fill a void. The night of the premiere, it was among the top 10 topics on Twitter. During the breaks, fans were tweeting each other with comments and opinions about the story line, thus creating an interactive community in real time.

Social media promotion worked well for BET and *The Game.* Do you think it could work equally well for other shows?

Social media can help promote programs.

10.1b Promotion to Gain a Sale

advertising-related

Although most of the work of a promotion department is geared toward media audience members, some of the work is to aid the sales department. Station and network promotion departments prepare sales packets for the salespeople who deal with advertisers and advertising agencies (see Chapter 9). These packets usually consist of colorful graphics and audio or video samples of station programming that the salesperson can leave with the potential advertiser. Some of the same material can be incorporated into a PowerPoint presentation for the salesperson to present to potential clients. The promo department will cull through statistics from audience measurement companies, obtain pithy quotes from satisfied advertisers, and, in general, compile all the positive material it can that will help the salespeople close a deal.

In the same manner, a promotion department can help a salesperson from a production company or syndicator who is trying to sell a program to a station or network. If a syndicator salesperson wants to target a particular local station, for example, the promotion department can research that local area and also look at the shows the competition is airing. It may suggest the best time for the syndicator's show and may even prepare a promotion campaign that the local station can use to promote the program in its area. Sometimes the promo department comes up with ideas for gifts that the salesperson can leave behind to remind the potential buyers of the show. For example, Warner salespeople gave erase boards to people at stations that were likely to buy *The Big Bang Theory*, a series whose lead characters make frequent use of an erase board.[7]

program related

Like promotion to gain an audience, promotion to make a sale can miss its mark. However, promotion departments have become an integral part of the media business and a primary user of various forms of audience feedback.

10.2 Forms of Audience Feedback

People give feedback to the media in many ways. One of the earliest was fan mail. During the 1920s, research showed that 1 person in 17 who enjoyed a program wrote to make his or her feelings known. During the decades that followed, fan mail was occasionally responsible for keeping a show on the air or resuscitating a canceled show.[8]

fan mail

Today, what was formerly fan mail is more likely to come as text messages or email. In fact, the internet and portable platforms have opened up many more avenues for interaction between fans and their shows. Most shows have websites and encourage the show's stars to engage followers on Twitter. Some producers lean heavily on what happens in the realm of social media. They find out, for example, which subplots and actors their fans like best and emphasize those in upcoming scripts.

texting

The internet, by its structure, can have built-in feedback. Those who operate webpages know how many people use their services because their computers can keep track of the number of **hits.** Even these services, however, would like to know more about the type of users they attract and what new services these people would like.

internet

Sometimes people give feedback unknowingly. For example, radio stations use the number of music downloads and CD purchases as reported in *Billboard* magazine as a basis for deciding what music to play on the air. They also find out what songs people are exchanging, legally and illegally, on the internet and emphasize those on their playlists. People give feedback with their pocketbooks by buying tickets, DVDs, or products from websites.[9]

unwitting feedback

But the type of feedback that is used most often involves formal research with samples of people who supply information about their media habits that is then statistically analyzed and reported. The best-known form of audience research is ratings, which indicate how many people watch or listen to or access

research

media products. However, other research goes beyond tallies to look at what types of people like certain products and why. In addition, companies solicit opinions from people before completing a project so that they can make it better.

10.3 Audience Research Companies

Nielsen

The name most readily associated with audience research is Nielsen, which operates in the United States and many other countries. Nielsen was established in the United States in 1923 by A. C. Nielsen, Sr., and conducted market research primarily for drugstores. Nielsen had a sample of drugstores save their invoices; the company then analyzed these and sold the information to drug manufacturers, so they could predict national sales. In 1942, Nielsen launched a National Radio Index, a report that indicated how many people listened to various programs, and in 1950, it added reports about the television audience. In 1964, because of economic considerations and the changing nature of radio, Nielsen dropped its radio research and concentrated on television.[10]

updating

Nielsen has undertaken many changes over the years. When cable channels proliferated in the 1980s and satellite TV came to the fore soon after, Nielsen was faced with providing information about many more channels than in the days when three networks dominated. One challenge was determining what program was on what channel. Originally this was done through network lineups and phone calls to local stations to determine what they aired, but that became unwieldy as channels multiplied. In 1982, Nielsen introduced the **Automated Measurement of Lineups (AMOL),** in which equipment coded each network and syndicated show in a manner similar to product bar codes. As each program aired, the Nielsen equipment picked up the code and verified whether the program was what was expected. If not, Nielsen employees still made phone calls, but AMOL greatly simplified the verification problem.

Then along came the VCR and Nielsen had to decide what to do about programs that were taped. Should they be ignored? Should they be counted when they were taped? What if no one ever played them back? Nielsen decided, amidst controversy, to count them as being viewed if they were taped. When the DVR came along, it was easier, technologically, to know if someone played the material at a later date, so Nielsen started counting recordings as viewed if they were played back within a week.

Although internet sites can monitor their own hits, the internet is nevertheless a ripe area for validated measurement. Nielsen now publishes reports that include data about which sites are accessed most often. Nielsen measures mobile devices, social media, and other newer forms through analyzing cell phone bills and surveying people by phone, in-person, or with online surveys.

Nielsen has had to adjust its services in other ways. Advertisers want to know how many people watch their ads, not just the programs that surround the ads, and Nielsen has obliged with a special rating for commercials called C3. Because **product placement** and **branding integration** have grown in importance, Nielsen has employees who watch hours and hours of programming, noting each time a product appears on-screen. Program producers want figures on how many total people watch a particular program, even if it is shown on different broadcast, cable, and internet platforms at different times. For this, Nielsen has devised an **unduplicated average audience ratings**.[11]

The other well-known name in audience measurement is Arbitron Inc. Formed in 1948, at one time it measured both local television and radio audiences. In 1994, it dropped the TV ratings because they were unprofitable and concentrated on commercial radio stations and networks. It, too, had to keep up with new technologies, such as satellite radio and internet radio, and it had to accommodate listeners who are constantly on the move. Dealing with the mobile audience led it back into providing information about TV, as well as other platforms. Arbitron developed a **portable people meter (PPM),** a device about the size of a cell phone, which keeps track of its wearer's exposure to any media that has audio, including not only radio and music, but also TV, internet, and even music in elevators. Arbitron also provides information about lifestyle characteristics of people in various communities—information that can be useful to any media or advertiser organizations.[12]

Many companies (for example, AGP, The Pulse, and Percy & Co) have tried to compete with Nielsen and Arbitron in the past and have even received financial support from programmers who would like to see more competition in the audience measurement field. But gathering audience research is expensive, and most of the companies have failed because they simply could not make money. There are still many organizations trying to find a niche in audience measurement, most of them focusing on the user rather than the media. In other words they study how people use cross-platforms as opposed to studying a particular medium, such as radio or TV.[13]

Numerous companies also take ratings data that a station or network obtains from Nielsen or Arbitron and analyze it to find particular strengths that can be pitched to advertisers. They might find, for example, that a station's 4:00 P.M. to 6:00 P.M. slot has the second-highest ratings by combining women and children. Often these companies also offer (for a fee) to make suggestions as to how a particular entity's ratings can be improved. Nielsen and Arbitron also provide these for-fee services.

10.4 Sampling

Companies that undertake research need people they can survey or study in order to compile their data. If a company such as Nielsen wants to know how many people in the entire United States watch TV programs, it tries to reflect in its sample the demographics of the entire United States. This involves using census data to identify a core of counties throughout the country that represent the main U.S. demographics. Nielsen then identifies specific households through **random sampling.** Random sampling involves chance; in essence, the addresses of all the homes that qualify are put in a box and some are drawn out. Of course, a box is not actually used. Most random sampling is now undertaken by computers programmed to select every third (or some other number) household.

Nielsen's base for measuring used to be households; that is, it reported what percentage of households watched a particular program. But as viewing became more individualized, Nielsen changed its base to people. It still selects households for its sample, but it considers what each person over 12 watches when reporting its statistics. A great deal of TV viewing occurs in bars, dorm rooms, hotel rooms,

ZOOM IN: **The Power of College Students**

Advertisers consider college students to be a very important demographic. They are starting to build brand loyalties, and they are fairly easy to convince to try different brands. They are tomorrow's great consumers. But, for many years, Nielsen did not survey college students living away from home. In 2007, after running a three-year test, the company decided to include these students.

The test showed that the addition of college students boosted the ratings for some shows dramatically. For example, ABC's *Grey's Anatomy* increased 53 percent among women 18 to 24 if college students were included. CW's *America's Next Top Model* increased 39 percent among the same group. Knowing that college students are now included in the survey, some programmers have initiated promotions to target them. For example, CW threw campus costume parties to promote the premiere of a reality show, *The Next Pussycat Doll*. ABC arranged college viewing parties for *Jimmy Kimmel Live*. College students now have a greater influence on television programming.

College students who live on campus are now included in Nielsen's surveys.

workplace cafeterias, and the like. For many years, the ratings services ignored this viewing, but Nielsen now includes out-of-home viewers in its sample (see "Zoom In" box).[14]

size

Nielsen has had to increase its sample size as the number of households increased and the number of TV options proliferated. The original sample was 1,000, but now for national ratings, Nielsen samples 23,000 homes (about 60,000 people), which are about .02 percent of the approximate 115 million American households or 312 million people (see Exhibit 10.4). The size of the sample for the local areas that both Nielsen and Arbitron canvas is determined by the population of the particular area.[15]

Number of Households

Exhibit 10.4
This chart, which begins shortly after TV was introduced, shows how households have grown.

focused samples

Not all audience research projects want or need a sample of the entire U.S. population, or even the entire population of a particular city. If a research company wants to know, for example, how many Spanish-speaking people watch the various Spanish-language networks, it will draw a sample only from Spanish-speaking households. A radio station that wants opinions about minor changes in its music would skew its research if it used a broad sample because it's only interested in people who listen to the station and like its music. Much better would be a sample taken from people who call the station to try to win contests. Companies do have to worry about self-selected samples, however. If a sports TV network were to put a poll on its website asking people to rate the importance of sports in overall programming, they would get a biased reply. They could not (or should not) generalize with a claim such as "90 percent of people in the United States think there should be more sports on TV."

replacements

Once a research company selects its sample, representatives try to solicit the cooperation of the households selected. They succeed about 65 percent of the time. When they are not successful, they select alternate homes, which supposedly have similar demographic characteristics. The participants are paid a minimal amount of cash, such as $10, or are given gifts to encourage them to do what is needed to obtain the ratings data. The demographics of the country change fairly rapidly; for example, the divorce rate goes up or average income takes a dip. For this reason, audience measurement companies constantly change their samples. Typically, a household remains in a sample no longer than two years.[16]

10.5 Collecting Data

Once the sample is solidified, the audience measurement company must gather the needed information from the participants. For national or local ratings, this usually involves some sort of equipment—equipment that has evolved over the years (see "Zoom In" box). The equipment that Nielsen currently uses is the **people meter** and its outgrowth, the **local people meter (LPM).** Nielsen

ZOOM IN: **Early Technological Ingenuity**

Nielsen's first machine (a), purchased in 1936 from two MIT professors, was called an audimeter. It was used to launch the 1942 National Radio Index based on 1,000 homes. The machine provided a link between a radio and a moving roll of punched paper tape in such a way that the paper could make a record of what station the radio was tuned to. Specially trained technicians visited the homes at least once a month to take off the old punched tape and put on a new tape—a very involved process.

The sophistication of audimeters increased, and by the 1970s (b) they could be connected directly from TV sets to phone lines that sent the information to a central computer in Florida in the middle of the night. The audimeters could indicate only whether the set was on and what channel it was tuned to, not whether anyone was viewing.

The next step was a different kind of device called a recordimeter that was used in conjunction with a diary (c). This machine was used mainly to make sure the diary entries weren't too different from when the set was actually on. The recordimeter operated somewhat like a mileage counter in that the digits turned over every six minutes that the set was in use. People keeping the diary indicated the "speedometer" reading at the beginning of each day and listed the programs they watched. They also indicated demographic factors about members of the family so that these could be matched with the programs.

a.

b.

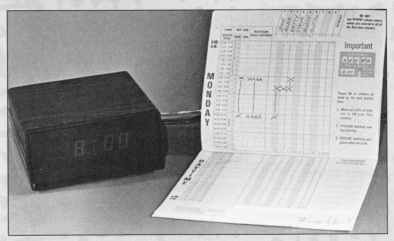

c.

Meters Nielsen has used over the years: (a) a 1936 audimeter utilizing punch tape, (b) an audimeter from the 1970s, (c) a recordimeter and diary.

Exhibit 10.5
A Nielsen people meter.

introduced the people meter in 1987 (see Exhibit 10.5) for its national ratings. The machine includes a handheld keypad that looks something like a remote control. Each member of the family is assigned a particular button on the keypad; extra buttons are provided for visitors. They are to turn on this button when they begin watching TV, push it periodically while they are watching, and turn it off when they are not watching. The people meter gathers information about which channel the set is tuned to and who is watching what programs. This information is sent over phone lines to computers in Nielsen's Florida headquarters.

The local people meter is a device about the size of a cell phone that is similar to Arbitron's portable people meter (PPM). In fact, when Arbitron began work on its meter in the 1990s, it wanted to work jointly with Nielsen, but the two companies eventually went their own ways.[17]

meters

Both Nielsen and Arbitron are still using older methods that involve diaries in some smaller markets. They plan to convert all markets to meters, but the conversion process is expensive, so they are rolling out meters city by city. For the **diary** method, survey participants are mailed packets. Each person in the household over 12 is to fill out a daily diary (see Exhibit 10.6) and then mail the diaries to Nielsen or Arbitron. Getting people to fill out these diaries with any degree of accuracy has become quite difficult and is a major reason both Nielsen and Arbitron are switching to meters.[18]

diaries

Any time a rating company changes its methodology, however, there is a hue and cry from those rated because the ratings change. For example, when Nielsen first introduced the people meter, sports programming increased and children's programming decreased. The speculation was that women, who were the main ones filling out family diaries, knew what their children were watching but were less concerned about reporting what their husbands were watching. With the people meter, men watching a sports event felt compelled to push the button often, fearful they might lose reception of the game. When Arbitron introduced its PPM, radio stations found they had a larger number of people listening than

discrepancies

2	**TUESDAY**							
TIME			**STATION**			**PLACE**		
			Fill in station "call letters" (If you don't know them, fill in program name or dial setting)	Check One (✔)		Check One (✔)		
							Away From Home	
	From	To		AM	FM	At Home	In a Car	Some Other Place
1 ⇨ **Early Morning** (5AM to 10AM)								
2 ⇨ **Midday** (10AM to 3PM)								
3 ⇨ **Late Afternoon** (3PM to 7PM)								
4 ⇨ **Night** (7PM to 5AM)								
IF YOU DID NOT LISTEN TO RADIO TODAY PLEASE CHECK ☑ HERE ➡								

Please review each day's listening to be sure all your entries are complete.

was reported by the diaries but that these people spent less time listening than previously thought. The complaints are loudest when ratings go down and costs go up. Audience measurement companies usually increase their sample size when they switch from diaries to meters and pass the added cost on to the clients who subscribe to the service.[19]

Equipment used for audience research will no doubt continue to evolve. Certainly computers have untapped capabilities for gathering data, and so do set-top boxes, DVRs, and portable devices. As digital technologies grow, the possibilities for tapping into listening and viewing patterns increase, but this raises the issue of privacy rights.

10.6 Analyzing Quantitative Data

Audience research that can be quantified is usually analyzed by computers. These computers are programmed to count how many people watch during various time periods and extrapolate those data into meaningful statistics.

Historically, the main statistics audience research companies reported were **rating** and **share.** A rating is simply the percentage of people (or households) watching a particular TV program or listening to a radio station. Rating percentages are based on the total number of households with TV sets or radios. Assume that the pie in Exhibit 10.7 represents a sample of 1,000 television households drawn from 100,000 households in the market being surveyed. The rating is the percentage of the total sample. Thus, the rating for station WAAA is 160/1000, or 16 percent; the rating for WAAB is 100/1000, or 10 percent; and the rating for WAAC is 140/1000, or 14 percent. Usually when ratings are reported, the percentage sign is eliminated; thus, WAAA has a rating of 16. Ratings may be reported for certain stations or for certain programs. If WAAA aired network evening news at the particular time of this rating pie, then this news

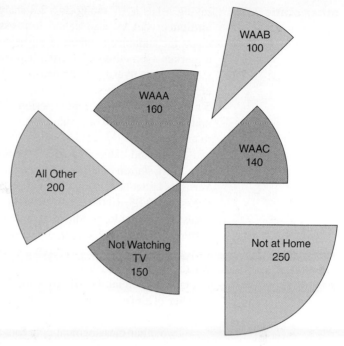

Exhibit 10.7
A ratings pie.

would have a rating of 16 in this particular city. National ratings, or course, are **rating** drawn from a sample of more than just one market.

A share is also a percentage, but it is based on the number of peo- **share** ple (or households) with the TV set (or radio) turned on. In the pie shown in Exhibit 10.7, 600 households had their sets on—160 to WAAA, 100 to WAAB, 140 to WAAC, and 200 to all others. The other 400 households had the TV off, so they did not count in the share of audience total. Therefore, WAAA's share of audience would be 160/600, or 26.7; WAAB's share would be 100/600, or 16.7; and WAAC's share would be 140/600, or 23.3. A share-of-audience calculation is always higher than a rating, unless 100 percent of the people are watching TV—an unlikely phenomenon.

Shares and ratings worked well in the early days of television when there were three networks and a few independent stations to comprise "all other." But times have changed. There are now so many program choices that both ratings and shares for some individual programs or time slots are so small that they are not statistically significant. Also, the original ratings and shares were based on the assumption of one TV set or radio shared by everyone in the household.

As a result, a number of other concepts are now used to convey audience numbers. Frequently the raw numbers, rather than the percentages, are reported. Saying that a program has 3.1 million viewers sounds more impressive than

other statistics

saying it has a 1.7 rating or a 2.8 share. Syndicators like to use **gross average audience (GAA),** also called **impressions.** This measurement takes into account the audience numbers if a particular program is shown more than once in a market—something that often happens with syndicated fare. Another popular statistic is the **average quarter-hour (AQH).** This calculation is based on the average number of persons listening to a particular station (or network) for at least 5 minutes during a 15-minute period. The AQH is particularly popular with radio and some cable networks that have small groups of audience members who tune in and out.

Radio and cable also like the **cume**—the number of different people who tune into a station or network over a period of time. This is valuable for letting advertisers know how many different people hear their message if it airs at different times, say 9:05, 10:05, and 11:05. The cume is important for differentiating services. For example, a radio station with a rating of 1.4 is usually not statistically different from a radio station with a rating of 1.5, but a cume can indicate a wider difference because it draws from a larger time spread. **Reach** and **frequency** are related to cume. Reach is the number of different people that are exposed to a particular commercial, usually over the period of a week. Frequency is the average number of times a person sees or hears a particular commercial over a specific time period.

Two other measurement concepts are **length of tune (LOT)** and **frequency of tune (FOT).** LOT is how long people watch shows on a particular network, and FOT is how often viewers return to a network. The two concepts are particularly valuable to cable TV because they give some idea of viewer loyalty to a particular network. News and sports networks usually rank low in LOT but high in FOT; movie networks register the opposite. Several other useful terms are **people using television (PUT), people using radio (PUR),** and **households using TV (HUT).** These are the percentages of people or households who have the set tuned to anything. In the ratings pie example, the HUT figure is 60; 600 out of 1,000 people had the sets tuned to something.

Two main measurements for the internet are **clicks** and **unique visitors (UV).** Clicks are noted anytime anyone goes to a site, whereas unique visitors are only people who have not visited the site before.[20]

weighing

Even though **quantitative** audience measurement statistics are derived by counting and applying formulas, there is room for controversy and human intervention. Sometimes companies do not get a return of data that represent the sample. For example, Nielsen may give 51 percent of its diaries to women and 49 percent to men, but perhaps 30 percent of the women return the diaries and only 20 percent of the men do. In cases like this, the company weights the sample so that it appears that they are in the proper proportion. In other words, Nielsen would give more weight to each man's returned diary than to each woman's diary.[21]

hyping

During periods when ratings are particularly important, stations and networks often **hype** their programming by sensationalizing their news, having star talent guest on a show, or giving away huge prizes. On occasion, stations have tried to contact members of the sample group either directly or in subtle ways such as airing a promo about ratings. People at the measurement companies have punished such acts by taking the stations out of the ratings report so that they have no ratings at all to tout to advertisers.

On the internet side, some website authors have learned to weave the word "sex" into their sites so they get more clicks, even though the site doesn't deal with sex. Also, there is some disagreement over how to count unique visitors. Should the count be according to computers, so that if two people use the same computer, only one of them will count? Or should it be by individuals, with some sort of safeguard in place to keep people with several computers from counting more than once?[22]

internet count

10.7 Qualitative Research

Ratings, shares, and their kinfolk are considered to be quantitative research because they deal with concrete numbers related to how many people are watching or listening at particular times. Many advertisers and programmers want to know about the quality of the audience. They want to know that they are reaching the right kind of people so that they maximize their **return on investment (ROI).** To take an extreme example, an automobile insurance company may be happy to hear that its commercial reached 15 million people, but if 90 percent of those people are under the age of 16, the company's ROI is not going to be high.

Nielsen and Arbitron break down their data into various **demographics** so that clients at least know the age and sex of their audience, but that is usually still considered quantitative information. What clients often want to know is the **psychographics**—people's lifestyle characteristics and how these relate to media preferences and buying habits. Are people who consider themselves upwardly mobile more likely to shop for organic products than those who are satisfied with their status quo? What brand of smartphone are people who use social networks most likely to buy? What shows are watched by people who are most likely to attend movie theaters? Research on subjects such as these is considered **qualitative** because it deals with factors that are hard to assign number values, even though in the end there may be statistical tests run to attempt to validate a particular concept. People have been divided into many categories—early adopters, brand loyalists, extroverts, imitators, and so on. Advertisers want to learn the psychographics of people who are interested in their products and then place their ads on programs or media forms that also attract those people.

psychographics

Engagement is another qualitative characteristic that has risen to prominence. It looks at the degree to which the creative content of a program or media form results in meaningful communication regarding a brand. In other words, does the content of a program affect the viewer in such a way that he or she wants to buy the product associated with the content? Advertisers are also interested in **brand recall**—whether people remember a brand after they have finished watching a program. One study found, for example, that brand recall for commercials run during the 2008 Olympics was 130 percent greater than for other prime-time shows and 33 percent higher than for spots run during the Academy Awards.[23]

engagement

10.8 Pretesting

Sometimes electronic media organizations want to know what potential audience members think of something before they put it out to the general public, so they engage in **pretesting.** For example, radio stations want to play music that people will listen to so that they do not switch to another station. To help decide which music they should play, stations undertake **music preference research.** Sometimes researchers phone selected people who are likely to enjoy the type of format being tested, play a short section of music for them, and ask their opinion by following a prepared questionnaire. A variation on this approach is to have listeners call a toll-free number where, using a special ID, they can rate songs.

music testing　　Another music preference research method is to invite a group of people to a minitheater and have them listen to music and give reactions, usually on a questionnaire form. Advantages of **minitheater testing** are that the fidelity can be better than it is over the phone and more songs can be played. This form of testing is more expensive than phone testing, however. Another research method involves inviting small groups of people to participate in **focus groups.** Again, the music can be played, but instead of reacting on questionnaires, the people in a group discuss their likes and dislikes. Focus groups can also tackle other issues, such as whether a disc jockey should be removed or whether a format change is in order. Focus groups give more in-depth information, but they are the most expensive method.[24]

video testing　　Minitheater testing and focus groups are often used to pretest movies, TV programs, and commercials (see "Zoom In" box). Producers like to know that a product will be successful before they invest heavily in distributing it. Organizations such as ASI Entertainment gather people in a room and show

 ZOOM IN: **Pretesting in Vegas**

If you are interested in having a say as to what TV programs get on the air, visit Las Vegas. There Viacom and CBS have a 5,000-square-foot facility at the MGM Grand used to pretest programs for CBS, MTV, Nickelodeon, Showtime, and other programming outlets owned by the conglomerate. The theory is that Las Vegas tourists represent the wide demographics that are desired for program testing—Midwesterners, Southerners, rich, poor, male, female, young, old.

The facility includes two small focus group rooms and two large screening rooms, each holding up to 250 viewers. Every seat has a touch screen tied to a central computer so that network executives located in any part of the country can track participant responses. Or, if they prefer to be on-site, they can watch and hear the focus groups through one-way glass.

Would you be interested in pretesting programming in this facility? Why or why not?

The Las Vegas testing facility at the MGM Grand.

them versions of media productions. They elicit reactions by having a focus group discussion, by having them fill out questionnaires, and by using various computer-aided techniques.

The latter includes having people push a button that is attached to a computer when they like something, having them hold devices that measure their perspiration (supposedly the more sweat the higher the person's engagement level), having them wear a belt that measures pulse rate and respiration, or even putting a cap on their heads that transmits brain waves (for example, to see if certain scenes affect the portion of the brain that responds to pleasure). The types of research that utilize body functions are often referred to as **biometrics** or **neuroscience metrics.**[25]

Most TV program pilots are pretested as part of a weeding-out process; those that test poorly don't go into production. But sometimes pretesting points to simple, fixable problems, so the program (or movie or commercial) is returned to the editing room, and the reedited version is pretested again. Or pretesting may result in such things as cast changes, the insertion of more trendy material, or a different marketing plan.

Sometimes website designers have a number of people test their sites before they formally post them. With this help, the authors can find design elements that people don't like and problems with the site navigation. One form of testing used with websites (and sometimes with TV and movie testing, also) is **eye tracking.**

a.

b.

Exhibit 10.8

Eye tracking involves sitting someone down at a computer screen and running a short test to adjust the computer software to his/her particular eyes. Then the person is shown a website (a) and the software indicates, through shading and colors, where the person looks most often (b).

Special software can determine what part of a computer monitor a participant's eyes are drawn to (see Exhibit 10.8). If the idea is to have the person look at the advertisements and that is not happening, the site can be redesigned and retested until the desired outcome is achieved.[26]

web testing

Pretesting has become quite important because the ways that people use media changes so quickly. Companies need to have a crystal ball to know what people will be doing in the future so they can start planning for it at least six months in advance. Pretesting is the best crystal ball they have.

10.9 Other Forms of Research

Q scores

Another form of research delves into the degree to which people are aware of particular shows or talent and how much they like the shows or personalities. Q Scores conducts this type of research. Each month the company mails random people a questionnaire with a list of programs and names. The respondents indicate whether they have heard about each and, if so, the degree to which they like or dislike the performers or shows. The **performer Q** score of each person or **TVQ** score for each program—a number that indicates popularity—is then calculated. Having a low Q can mean unemployment lines for talent and cancellation for shows.[27]

educational

Corporate and educational organizations often undertake effectiveness research. They want to know if the programming they have produced has accomplished its goal in terms of teaching certain information or establishing certain attitudes. Often this research involves giving the people who are going to be watching a particular program a pretest to determine what they know or how they feel. Then, after viewing the program, participants are given the same test again to see if there was a significant change.

pay channels

The pay cable channels, such as HBO and Showtime, are concerned about people disconnecting from the service. Therefore, they sometimes undertake research directed toward finding the right combination of movies and other programs to retain the largest possible number of subscribers.

using tweets

There are metrics that examine **tweets** about a particular program to weigh the positive against the negative. If the number of tweets starts to diminish, the producer needs to swing into action. There are many other forms of audience research, and many companies willing to undertake them—for a fee, of course.[28]

10.10 Reporting Results

Usually after conducting research, the organization that has undertaken the procedures issues reports to the clients who pay for the information. These reports can range from a simple chart to a multipage document. If, for example, the network executives were present when a program was pretested, there may be little need for a detailed report. If the material is distributed widely, as in the case of Nielsen and Arbitron, the reports are more detailed.

changes

The way Nielsen and Arbitron report their results has changed over the years. At first everything was analyzed by hand, and it took months for the reports to be issued after the data were collected. With the advent of computers, this changed. Data sent over phone lines from meters could be analyzed almost instantly. This led to Nielsen's **overnight reports** on the previous night's programming that could be delivered to executives by noon the next day, and later to **fast nationals** that could be delivered by midmorning. The data from both Nielsen and Arbitron diaries took longer to analyze, but it too was aided by the speed of computers and could be used to issue reports within weeks of the time the information was collected. As clients obtained their own computer systems, they could interconnect their computers with those of the measurement companies and obtain the information on screens in their own offices without waiting for hard-copy reports to be delivered.[29]

Cable TV Top 10 Week of November 15				
Rank	Program	Network	Rating	Viewers (000)
1	Wed Night Football	ESPN	7.6	11,289
2	Open Fun	DISC	6.2	10,789
3	Wrestling Night	USA	5.2	9,120
4	Sports Warm-up	TNT	5.0	8,674
5	Angry Women	AMC	5.0	8,526
6	Camp Time	DSNY	4.1	6,276
7	Awards Preview	MTV	4.0	5,876
8	Football Roundup	ESPN	3.8	5,920
9	Roller Rubber	NICK	2.4	3,520
10	The Challenge	BET	2.4	3,515

Exhibit 10.9

A mock-up (using fictional information) of one type of report Nielsen prepares concerning programs on cable TV.

Nielsen

Nielsen offers a large number of national reports that deal with commercial networks, cable TV networks, public broadcasting, syndicated shows, the internet, and cross-platform viewing (see Exhibit 10.9). They give overall numbers related to how many people watch the various programs, and they also break down these data by various subcategories, including age, sex, and part of the country. For reports on local stations, Nielsen divides the country into 210 nonoverlapping **designated market areas (DMAs);** New York City is the largest and Glendive, Montana is the smallest. All areas of the United States are surveyed at least four times a year—February, May, July, and November, periods that are sometimes referred to as **sweeps.** When local people meters are instituted, markets are surveyed on a constant basis.[30]

Arbitron

Arbitron has reports for local radio stations and for radio network programming. For each local market, Arbitron measures two areas, **metro survey area (MSA)** and **total survey area (TSA)** (see Exhibit 10.10). The TSAs are geographically larger than the MSAs and do not receive the low-power stations as clearly as the MSAs. That is why Arbitron has two areas—the low-power stations do not compare favorably with the powerhouses in the TSAs but can hold their own in the MSAs. The station data are analyzed according to **dayparts,** and the reports give overall statistics and a breakdown of various demographics. The network data are referred to as Radio's All Dimension Audience Research (RADAR).[31]

other reports

Nielsen, Arbitron, and other audience measurement companies also prepare special reports that can be purchased by any interested parties. Topics for these reports include a study of airport TVs, an analysis of cinema advertising, a summary report on households using television, a treatise on how people use DVRs, and a study of in-car media habits.

charges

Making improvements that keep up with the evolving media industry and an ever-changing society can be very expensive. This cost is paid by the customers who subscribe to audience measurement services such as networks; advertising agencies; corporations that advertise; radio and TV stations; and cable, satellite, and telco entities. The services raise their prices from time to time, but must be

Exhibit 10.10

Map showing an MSA and a TSA.

Radio Market, USA

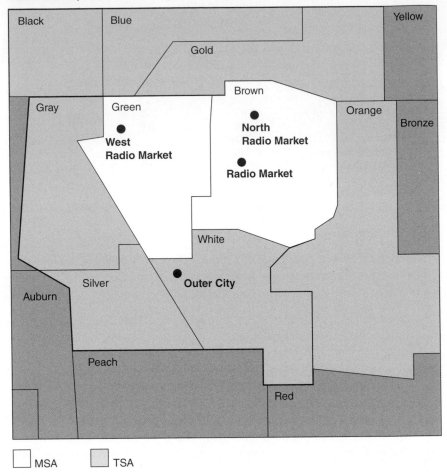

☐ MSA ☐ TSA

sensitive to what the market will bear. They also charge differing amounts to different entities. While TV networks may pay millions of dollars per year for the reports they desire, stations in small markets may only pay thousands per year.

10.11 How Audience Measurement Is Used

selling time

The most important use for audience measurement calculations revolves around selling advertising time (see Chapter 9). The higher the rating (or share, AQH, cume, clicks, etc.) for a particular program, time period, or website, the more the media entity can charge for placing an advertisement within that program, time period, or website. Nielsen estimates that each of its rating points for prime-time broadcast programming is worth about $30,000. That means a program with a rating of 10 can charge about $300,000 for a commercial, whereas a program with a rating of 8 can charge only $240,000. It is no wonder that networks and stations strive for high ratings.

Advertisers use ratings to make sure they are getting a good return on investment. They need the ratings data to determine **cost per thousand,** or CPM (see Chapter 9). This indicates to the advertiser how much it costs to reach 1,000 people (or households). For example, if an advertiser pays $30 for a radio spot and the ratings show that spot is reaching 5,000 people, then the advertiser is paying $6 for each 1,000 people. A related statistic is **cost per point,** or **CPP.** The amount of money the advertiser pays for a week's advertising is divided by the number of ratings points the commercial accrues during a week to determine the cost for each rating point.

CPM and CPP

Audience measurement is also used to determine the overall health of the electronic media industry. When the PUT, PUR, or HUT levels fall, the industry becomes nervous. Ratings and shares also show the relative health of different segments of the electronic media. The three commercial TV networks used to garner about 90 percent of the share of audience. Network programs with ratings of less than 20 usually did not last long. Now, with the broadcast network share sometimes below 20 percent, programs with single-digit ratings are considered acceptable.

industry health

Measurement is also used as a basis of comparison. For example, the share tells a station or network how it is faring in relation to its competition. Although the HUT and ratings may be going down, a station can consider itself successful if its share of the viewing public is increasing. A media organization can also use ratings to compare against its past. If a station's rating (or AQH, cume, etc.) decreases from month to month over the course of a year, the station has reason to worry—the same for a website that is losing unique visitors.

comparison

Audience measurement is also used extensively to make programming decisions. Many programs that flunk pretesting don't get on the air. Programs with high ratings are kept on the air and allowed to build up numerous episodes that can then be sold for syndication. Programs with low ratings are often erased quickly, without having the chance to grow or develop an audience slowly. Similarly, people often disappear from the airwaves as a result of audience measurement. If a radio station's AQH slips during a certain time of day, the disc jockey on at that time can expect a pink slip. Television station news anchors are often removed because they have low Q scores.

program decisions

Sometimes the method of audience research dictates programming policies. For example, when Arbitron switched from diaries to meters, many radio stations stopped their incessant repetition of call letters, a programming philosophy that had been in place so that people with diaries were sure to remember what station they were listening to. Radio stations could also end contests at a time other than the end of a survey week. They had been ending them then because many diary keepers were procrastinators who filled out the diaries at the last minute. A station that made a big splash right before people filled out diaries might see a jump in its ratings.

program policies

Measurement calculations are varied in terms of types and uses because of the needs of different clientele. One advertiser might be more interested in the cumulative number of people hearing an ad than in the number hearing at any particular time; another advertiser might be interested primarily in finding a station that delivers the largest reach.

10.12 Issues and the Future

promotion

Promotion is not as widely criticized as audience measurement, but it does present some issues. Many viewers find snipes to be annoying. Sometimes the promotion department and the sales department are at odds. The sales department wants prime airtime so it can sell commercials for the highest rate, while the promotion department wants that same time for its promos. Promotion's rationale is that ratings will decline if people don't know about the programs, and if ratings go down, sales will decrease.

different results

The customers who subscribe to audience measurement services have many gripes. For starters, the accuracy is frequently questioned because the results do not make common sense. For example, the Nielsen Hispanic TV report, which should be a subset of its overall data, often has radically different numbers from the Spanish population considered in the national reports. Sometimes the report of the number of people watching a program while they record it on a DVR plus the number who watch it within a week is lower than the report that only includes the people watching as they record.

samples

Another factor that affects the validity of ratings is the size and composition of the sample. As media forms proliferate, the number of people watching or listening to any particular program or service shrinks, and the sample size must be increased in order for statistics to be significant. Many contend that a sample that is only .02 percent of the population cannot contain all the different types of people found in society. Although rating companies try to make their samples representative of the entire population, this presents problems. For example, a rating sample might attempt to have the same percentage of households headed by a 30-year-old high-school-educated African American woman with three children living in the city and earning $40,000 per year as in the population of the whole United States. Which of these characteristics are important to audience measurement can be debated. Is a 25-year-old high-school-educated African American woman with no children who earns $35,000 a year a valid substitute?

noncooperation

Even if they can determine the ideal sample, companies are faced with the problem of uncooperative potential samples. About 35 percent of the people contacted refuse to have machines installed on their sets, and about 45 percent do not want to keep diaries. Substitutions must be made for uncooperative people, which may bias the sample in two ways—the substitutes may have characteristics that unbalance the sample, and uncooperative people, as a group, may have particular traits that bias the sample. Particularly troubling is the concept of weighting one demographic group's data more heavily than another because not as many of them responded.

inaccuracies

Problems with ratings methodology do not cease once the size and composition of the sample are decided and the people selected. There is also the problem of receiving accurate information from these people. Any system that uses meters is dealing with a technology that can fail. A certain number of machines develop mechanical malfunctions and a certain number of people use them incorrectly, further reducing the sample size in an unscientific manner. Diaries are also subject to human deceit. People can lie about what they actually watched to appear more intellectual or to help some program they would like to see high in the ratings. The multitude of programming choices taxes people's ability to remember what they saw or heard. Fewer than half the diaries sent out are returned in a form that can be used for analysis.[32]

Because of these flaws and many more, clients want the rating companies to develop better measurement techniques—larger samples, more reliable machines, more minute-by-minute analysis, more qualitative research to predict buying patterns, more analysis of internet and smartphone viewing and listening. Audience research companies can do much of this, but it costs money, and when they do improve methodology or add reports, they find that clients who demanded the improvements are not willing to pay for them. Companies have dropped their subscriptions, sometimes because they are unhappy with the scope and reliability of the ratings and sometimes because the costs are too high. They usually return, however, because the data the researchers provide are valuable for operating their businesses.[33]

cost

Although rating company methodology is often criticized, management interpretation of the data is often faulted to an even greater degree. Rating companies publish results and cannot be held responsible for how they are used. This area of error is the domain of media and advertising executives. The main criticism is that too much emphasis is placed on ratings. Even though rating companies acknowledge that their sampling techniques and methodology yield imperfect results, programs are sometimes removed from the air when they slip one or two rating points. Actors and actresses whose careers are stunted by such action harbor resentment. Television history is full of programs that scored poor ratings initially but were left on the air and went on to gain large, loyal audiences (e.g., *Hill Street Blues, Cheers*). Trade journals sometimes headline the ratings lead of one network over the others when that lead, for all programs totaled, may be only half a rating point. Ratings should be an indication of comparative size and nothing more, but in reality their shadow extends much further.

interpretation

The overdependence on ratings often leads to programming concepts deplored by the critics. In a popularity contest designed to gain the highest numbers, programming tends to become similar, geared toward the audience that will deliver the largest numbers. Programmers emphasize viewer quantity, often to the neglect of creativity, availability to the community, and services to advertisers.

programming concepts

Similar complaints arise against pretesting. Many programs, such as *All in the Family, Batman, The Sopranos,* and *Everybody Loves Raymond* tested poorly but went on to successful runs. Programs that are unique are most likely to test poorly because the testing audience doesn't know what to make of them. But if executives have the courage to try them anyhow, they can sometimes have a hit on their hands.[34]

pretesting

democracy

Looking at it another way, however, ratings' effects on program content are simply the result of the democratic process. Audience members get what they vote for. If programmers were to use another criterion, say creativity, as the basis for advertising rates, the situation would be far more unjust than is the present quantitative rating system. Creativity is an abstract concept that cannot really be defined, let alone counted.

future

Audience measurement technology can stand improvement. One way for it to generate better numbers would be for all radios, TVs, and computers to be equipped so that all viewing and listening are reported to a central location. This could be possible technologically, but it smacks of "Big Brother." However, there would be no need for sampling because everyone would be included. As digital technologies progress further, they are bound to add techniques (and complications) to the audience measurement that already exists.[35]

10.13 Summary

A major function of promotion, publicity, and public relations is to get people to partake of programs or media forms. Another function is to help salespeople. Promotion departments use such elements as promos, PSAs, snipes, cross-promotion, trailers, billboards, and newspaper articles. Audience feedback is one way to tell if promotion has been effective.

Feedback includes fan mail, text messages, website hits, and formalized audience research. A look at Nielsen, Arbitron, and ASI Entertainment shows characteristics of audience research.

Nielsen uses random sampling to undertake TV audience measurement for national networks and for local markets that it divides into DMAs. It has increased its sample size over the years, but some people refuse to be part of the sample. To gather data, it uses people meters and LPMs and still a few diaries. It uses computers to calculate ratings and shares, but with both of these declining for individual networks, other measurements such as number of viewers, GAA, LOT, and FOT have come into vogue. PUTs and HUTs are also important to the industry as a whole. Most of Nielsen's measurements are quantitative, and sometimes those being rated hype their programming to get better ratings. Qualitative research often involves psychographics. Nielsen issues many reports, including the overnights and the fast nationals. Its ratings are used to determine advertising costs, including the CPM and CPP. They are also used, some say too extensively, to make programming decisions. Nielsen has had to keep up with the times by instituting AMOL, figuring out ways to count VCR and DVR recording, adding out-of-home viewing, initiating C3, and rating mobile devices and the internet. Clients resist paying for the added services that they want.

Arbitron measures radio nationally and locally. It uses the PPM and still uses some diaries and encounters resistance when it switches from one data-gathering form to another. Ratings and shares are even less important to radio because the numbers are so low. Popular radio statistics are AQH, cume, reach, frequency, LOT, FOT, and PUR. Arbitron issues a national report (RADAR) and local reports that include MSAs and TSAs. Its ratings are used, like Nielsen's, for advertising and programming decisions.

ASI undertakes pretesting and aims for diverse samples representing the entire country. Some of its sister pretesting services, such as music preference, want people who know and like the particular format being tested. The methods used for pretesting involve personal interaction, usually through minitheaters or focus groups. Pretesting also uses biometrics and neuroscience metrics. The results sometimes involve psychographics as well as demographics. Pretesting is used to make decisions before something is presented to the people it is intended for.

There are many other forms of research, such as Q scores and engagement. New technologies will affect audience feedback of the future.

Suggested Websites

www.arbitron.com (audience research firm Arbitron)

www.asientertainment.com (the pretesting company, ASI Entertainment)

www.marketcastonline.com/Default.asp (a movie and TV pretesting organization)

www.nielsen.com/us/en.html (audience research firm Nielsen)

www.qscores.com (site for the company that supplies performer Q and TVQ scores)

Notes

1. "Pop-Up Promos Drive Industry Crazy," *Broadcasting & Cable,* December 20, 2004, 20.
2. "Slim Pickings," *Hollywood Reporter,* May 30, 2008, 31–32; and "H-wood Calls a Blitz for Super Bowl," *Variety,* January 31–February 6, 2011, 2.
3. "For Your Consideration: A Luxury Tax," *Los Angeles Times,* November 29, 2011, D-1.
4. "*The Game's* Secret Weapon," *Hollywood Reporter,* February 2, 2011, 32–33.
5. "Helping Out, from Coast to Coast," *Broadcasting & Cable,* June 23, 2008, 12.
6. "All or Nothing," *Emmy,* January/February 2007, 44–49; and "Mistakes Marketers Make," *Wall Street Journal,* October 20, 2008, R10.
7. Susan Kantor, Executive Vice President, Warner, at the Warner Media Lab/ Broadcast Education Association Faculty Seminar, July 15, 2011.
8. "Saved! How a Groundbreaking Series Came Back from the Brink," *Emmy,* January/February, 2008, 50–53.
9. "Pirated Music Helps Radio Develop Playlists," *Wall Street Journal,* July 12, 2007, B1; and "New Audience Metrics Aim to Leapfrog Web Buzz," *Broadcasting & Cable,* June 9, 2008, 14.
10. Nielsen's website is www.nielsen.com.
11. "Nielsen on Track of Product Placements," *Media and Technology,* May 31, 2004, 14; "Cable Takes the Measure of C3," *Broadcasting & Cable,* November 12, 2007, 22; and "Measurement Tools Spell Good News," *Television Week,* August 13, 2007, 10.
12. Arbitron's website is www.arbitron.com; "Arbitron to Exit TV Ratings; Cites Sagging Profit," *Los Angeles Times,* October 19, 1993, D-2.

13. "Everyone Hates ComScore," *Fortune,* September 29, 2008, 60; and "How to Count Eyeballs," *Newsweek,* November 27, 2006, 42.

14. "TV Networks Launch Big Campus Push," *Wall Street Journal,* March 5, 2007, B3; and "Nielsen Extends Its Reach," *Broadcasting & Cable,* April 17, 2006, 14.

15. "Nielsen Estimates Number of U. S. Television Homes to be 114.7 Million," http://blog.nielsen.com/nielsenwire/media_entertainment/nielsen-estimates-number-of-u-s-television-homes-to-be-114-7-million/ (accessed December 1, 2011).

16. "Nielsen Adapts Its Methods as TV Evolves," *Wall Street Journal,* September 29, 2003, B-1.

17. "Nielsen: 'Portfolio' over PPM," *Hollywood Reporter,* March 2, 2006, 3.

18. "Dear Diary, Farewell," *Broadcasting & Cable,* July 17, 2006, 26.

19. "Cleveland Rocked by People Meters," *Broadcasting & Cable,* September 8, 2008, 8; and "Programmers, Nielsen Disagree over Claim People meters Underreport Kids," *Broadcasting,* December 21, 1992, 10.

20. "Networks Like When Viewers Watch a LOT," *Broadcasting & Cable,* July 21, 2003, 26; and "TV Households, Viewers Increase in U.S.," *Hollywood Reporter,* August 24–26, 2007, 51.

21. "Nielsen Adds Weight to U.S. Sample," *Broadcasting & Cable,* September 8, 2003, 4.

22 "Duel over Delisting," *Broadcasting & Cable,* December 15, 2003, 16; and "Here's How to Game the System," *Los Angeles Times,* May 7, 2008, E-1.

23. "Measuring Engagement," *Broadcasting & Cable,* April 28, 2008, 12; "It's an Olympic Triumph for Advertisers," *Hollywood Reporter,* August 20, 2008, 6; and Thomas R. Lindlof, "The Qualitative Study of Media Audiences," *Journal of Broadcasting & Electronic Media,* Winter 1991, 23–42.

24. Michael C. Keith, *Radio Programming* (Boston: Focal Press, 2004), 108.

25. "This Test Gets Under Your Skin," *Variety,* October 5–11, 2009, 20; Libby Slate and William J. Adams, "How People Watch Television as Investigated Using Focus Group Techniques," *Journal of Broadcasting & Electronic Media,* Winter 2000, 78–93; and "How CBS Plays in Vegas," *Broadcasting & Cable,* April 23, 2001, 31.

26. "Presentation: Biometrics and Eyetracking," at the Warner Media Lab/ Broadcasting Educations Association Faculty Seminar, July 15, 2011.

27. "Q Scores," http://www.qscores.com/Web/Index.aspx (accessed December 1, 2011); and "Information Please," *Variety,* March 7–13, 2011, 1.

28. "Studios Dance to New Tweet Beat," *Variety,* July 18–24, 2011, 2; and Clark F. Greer and Douglas A. Ferguson, "Using Twitter for Promotion and Branding: A Content Analysis of Local Television Twitter Sites," *Journal of Broadcasting and Electronic Media,* June 2011, 198–214.

29. "Nielsen Adjusts to New Universe," *Hollywood Reporter,* August 24, 2006, 4.

30. "Diary of a Nielsen (Sweeps Week!) Diarist," *Emmy,* Issue No. 2, 2011, 28.

31. "Touch That Dial and Arbitron Will Know Tonight," *Los Angeles Times,* August 24, 2011, D-1; "Arbitron Picks Up RADAR Service in $25 Million Deal," *Hollywood Reporter,* July 3–9, 2001, 43; and Karen S. Buzzard, "James W. Seiler of the American Research Bureau," *Journal of Radio Studies,* December 2003, 186–201.

32. "Nielsen Ratings Come Under Fire," *Wall Street Journal,* November 17, 2003, B-10.

33. "Nielsen Gets Dumped," *Broadcasting & Cable,* June 13, 2005, 16; and "Low-Rated Whine," *Broadcasting & Cable,* July 28, 2008, 4.

34. "When Not to Trust the Feedback," *Los Angeles Times,* July 9, 2002, F-1.

35. "Data Blitz Fits Eye of Beholder," *Variety,* March 7–13, 2011, 10.

Chapter 11

LAWS AND REGULATIONS

Many intermingling governmental entities regulate the electronic media industry. In the U.S. system of government, the legislative branch writes the laws, the executive branch administers them, and the courts adjudicate them. In this way, the branches have checks and balances on one another. This basic process affects media regulation. An electronic media organization that believes it has been wronged by a decision of the Federal Communications Commission can appeal that decision to the courts and also lobby Congress to change the offending law.

Laws and regulations dealing with a wide variety of subjects affect media entities differently. Broadcast stations are highly affected by licensing provisions, whereas the home video industry, which is not licensed, keeps a close eye on copyright legislation. Cable networks that program news must be more concerned about libel than those that deal only with entertainment.

> A function of free speech under our system of government is to invite dispute. It may indeed best serve its highest purpose when it induces a condition of unrest, creates dissatisfaction with conditions as they are, or even stirs people to anger.
>
> **William O. Douglas, former Supreme Court justice**

Different entities regulate to varying degrees. The Federal Aviation Administration is involved only when improperly lit antenna towers may be a hazard to airplanes; the Federal Communications Commission's function encompasses all airwaves. The next few sections deal with the primary regulatory bodies; the rest of the chapter covers the main laws and regulations these bodies create that affect the electronic media industry.

11.1 The Federal Communications Commission

origins

The Federal Communications Commission (FCC) is an independent regulatory body that Congress created because of the mass confusion and interference that arose when early radio stations broadcast on unregulated frequencies. Congress passed the **Radio Act of 1927,** which created the Federal Radio Commission (FRC), and seven years later, it passed the **Communications Act of 1934** (see Chapter 5), which formally established the FCC with powers similar to its predecessor, the FRC. Much later, Congress passed the **Telecommunications Act of 1996** (see Chapters 4 and 5), which did not change the basic structure of the FCC but did change some aspects of what it regulates. Over the years, the FCC's responsibilities have grown. Starting primarily with telephones and radio, its realm now encompasses not only broadcast television but also aspects of other media forms such as cable TV, the internet, and portable platforms.

description

The commission maintains central offices in Washington (see Exhibit 11.1) and field offices throughout the country. It is composed of five commissioners appointed for five-year terms by the president, with the advice and consent of the Senate. The president designates one commissioner to be chairperson, but generally no president has the opportunity to appoint many commissioners because their five-year terms are staggered. No more than three of the commissioners can be from the same political party.

organization

Policy determinations are made by all the commissioners, with the chairperson responsible for the general administration of the commission's affairs. Most of the day-to-day work, such as handling interference complaints, public inquiries, and frequency applications, is undertaken by the staff. The FCC has myriad

Exhibit 11.1
The FCC headquarters in Washington, DC.

functions, many of which are not related to electronic mass media. For example, it has jurisdiction over ship-to-shore radio and police and fire communications.

The FCC establishes rules and regulations that relate to the general operation of the telecommunications industry. FCC policies have addressed issues such as must-carry (see Chapter 3), financial interest–domestic syndication (see Chapter 4), and children's programs (see Chapter 8). Suggestions for these rules can come from media practitioners, the public, Congress, or from within the FCC itself. Once a viable suggestion is received, it is referred to the appropriate FCC department, and the commission then issues a notice asking interested parties to comment. The staff evaluates these comments and reports on them to the commissioners. Sometimes the commissioners hold formal hearings so they can hear from specific individuals or groups and ask pertinent questions. The commissioners then decide whether to issue a new order, amend an old one, ask for more study, or do nothing. If some entity of the electronic media industry does not like the result, it can petition for reconsideration, and the process starts all over.

rules and regs

Many of the FCC functions are technical. It assigns **frequencies** to individual stations, determines the power each can use, and regulates the time of day each may operate. The FCC also controls the general allocation of frequencies, deciding which frequencies go to satellite radio, which to cellular phones, which to wireless internet, and so forth. It also has the jurisdiction to set technical standards, such as those for color television or digital TV (see Chapter 4). The FCC operates two emergency systems. One is the Emergency Alert System (EAS), a national service that ties together all radio and TV stations so that information can be broadcast from the government to the citizenry during a national emergency. The other is the Personal Localized Alert Warning System (PLAN), designed to send emergency warnings to people's mobile devices.[1]

technical

11.2 The Executive Branch

The president influences the media, both formally and informally. Formally, the president can suspend broadcasting operations in time of war and call into action the EAS and PLAN. However, most of the interaction between the president and the media comes informally, with the president seeking positive coverage from radio and TV. Most presidents devise their own ways of handling the media through press secretaries or others who give advice on media relations (see Exhibit 11.2).

president

Various executive departments also interact with the media. For example, the Justice Department oversees antitrust and as such was involved in the breakup of AT&T (see Chapter 3). The Department of State has a bureau that advises on media issues with possible international consequences.

executive departments

Other agencies that are either part of the executive branch or are independent affect broadcasting. The Federal Trade Commission (FTC) deals with fraudulent advertising. If the FTC believes that a company's ads are untruthful, it has the power to order the company to stop broadcasting the ads. The FTC also issues guidelines on potentially controversial subjects such as children's advertising and internet advertising to fend off problems before they occur. In addition, the

agencies

Exhibit 11.2

Reporters are frequently stationed at the White House so that they can report on press conferences and other presidential actions.

scarcity theory

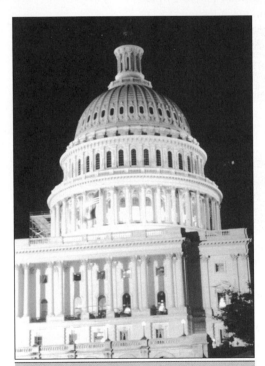

Exhibit 11.3

Many important laws regarding communications are debated and passed by Congress in the Capitol.

Federal Aviation Administration monitors antenna towers so that planes will not crash into them. The Food and Drug Administration occasionally stops the mislabeling of advertised products. The Surgeon General's Office participated in the 1972 ban of cigarette advertising on radio and TV and in reports related to the effects of TV on society (see Chapters 9 and 12).[2]

11.3 The Legislative Branch

Congress generally sets broad policies that are handled on a day-to-day basis by other agencies. These policies are influential in setting direction for the electronic media. The whole basis for the government's intervention in the electronic media business was, and occasionally still is, debated in Congress (see Exhibit 11.3). Ordinarily, the First Amendment would prohibit the government from infringing on the rights of citizens to communicate by whatever means they wish. Congress invaded this area, however, because of the **scarcity theory.** Not everyone who wanted to could broadcast through radio frequencies because this would cause uncontrollable interference. As a result, Congress needed to intervene and determine a mechanism for making decisions regarding who could and could not use the airwaves. Today, with many avenues of distribution available, the scarcity theory doesn't hold much water—hence the controversies.[3]

In addition to overall regulatory decision making that is tied to the 1927, 1934, and 1996 acts, Congress passes other media-related laws, such as copyright laws, cable TV laws, and the law that set up the Corporation for Public Broadcasting (see Chapter 4). Congress monitors the FCC through both the House and Senate subcommittees on communications. These and other committees sometimes conduct investigations into such aspects of communication as the quiz scandals or TV violence.

national laws

State legislative bodies can also affect media. Under the Constitution, federal laws, such as the Communications Act, take precedence over state laws. But occasionally, state laws dealing with privacy, advertising, or state taxes affect elements of the industry. City councils, with local legislative control, have jurisdiction over most cable TV franchising.

state and local laws

11.4 The Judicial Branch

Because FCC decisions can be appealed, the courts of the United States have a significant impact on electronic media. Courts of appeal can confirm or reverse the commission's decisions or send them back to the FCC for further consideration. From these courts, final appeals can be taken to the Supreme Court (see Exhibit 11.4), which can confirm or reject a lower court's decision.

appeals process

Courts also deal with issues other than those arising from FCC decisions. Rulings on such subjects as freedom of speech, obscenity, libel, privacy, copyright, equal time, and even access to the courts determine the direction of electronic media.[4]

court decisions

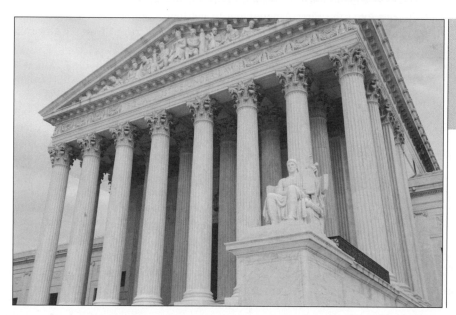

Exhibit 11.4
The United States Supreme Court building, where appeals to cases are heard.

11.5 The First Amendment

freedom of press

The **First Amendment** to the U.S. Constitution is basic to much of what occurs in media. This amendment states that "Congress shall make no law . . . abridging the freedom of speech, or of the press." Issues involving the First Amendment are raised under many banners, one of them being **censorship.** A breach of freedom of the press occurs when the government tries to censor or withhold information. However, the government may contend that giving out the information would be a **clear and present danger** to the country.

clear and present danger

Clear and present danger also extends to individuals. The Supreme Court has ruled that freedom of speech does not give someone the right to falsely yell "Fire" in a crowded theater because this would create a clear and present danger to those in the theater. But governmental agencies are reluctant to label words as dangerous if freedom of speech is involved. During the 1960s, the NAACP wanted the FCC to censor speeches aired on Georgia TV by a candidate for the Senate on the grounds that the speeches contained racially inflammatory remarks that were a danger to the people of Georgia. The FCC refused to issue **prior restraint** in that case, saying the speeches did not literally endanger the nation. Also, plaintiffs wanted to shut down an antiabortion website, saying it contained what they considered dangerous threats, but the courts disagreed.

News reporters often argue that freedom of the press is being violated if they are forced to disclose sources from which they obtained news or to testify in court regarding information they promised would be kept confidential. Reporters were

shield laws

required to testify for years, but during the 1970s, most states passed **shield laws** that gave some protection to news reporters. In most states, they must testify only if the evidence is crucial to the case and cannot be obtained in any other way. Some reporters have gone to jail rather than reveal sources.[5]

WikiLeaks

The First Amendment has been used for many causes. Casino gambling establishments cited the First Amendment to get their commercials broadcast on radio and TV. The courts, citing the First Amendment, struck down a California law that attempted to restrict the sale of violent video games to minors. The issues of the First Amendment became very complicated in 2010 when Julian Assange (see Exhibit 11.5), the editor of WikiLeaks, published American government documents about the Iraq and Afghan wars, some of them classified. These documents were at best embarrassing to U.S. diplomats and at worst a clear and present danger to the country. But Assange is an Australian citizen living in various European countries and operating an international website devoted to publishing news leaks from all over the world with the stated purpose of providing open governments. Other countries do not have anything like the U.S. First Amendment, so there are, at present, no procedures for dealing with Assange and WikiLeaks or similar situations that may arise in the future.[6]

Exhibit 11.5
Julian Assange, the editor-in-chief of WikiLeaks.

11.6 Profanity, Indecency, and Obscenity

Profanity, indecency, and **obscenity** are all major areas where the First Amendment comes into play. They are outlawed by the U.S. Criminal Code, but this code and the First Amendment often clash. It can be difficult to determine when people's freedom of speech should be abridged because what they are saying is profane, indecent, or obscene. Part of the problem is the changing definitions of these words. What was considered indecent in one decade may be perfectly acceptable in the next. In 1937, NBC aired a program in which Mae West (see Chapter 6) performed a sketch about Adam and Eve. Nothing in the script was considered indecent, but her sultry voice sounded suggestive, and the FCC reprimanded NBC. Today this wouldn't cause the slightest stir.

definitions

The three words, even when defined in their most concrete way, often overlap. Profanity is defined as irreverent use of the name of God. The FCC defines indecency as language that, in context, depicts or describes, in terms patently offensive, as measured by contemporary community standards for the broadcast medium, sexual or excretory activities or organs. Obscenity is more extreme than indecency, and its definition was determined in a 1973 court case, *Miller v. California.* To be obscene, a program must contain the depiction of sexual acts in an offensive manner; must appeal to prurient interests of the average person; and must lack serious artistic, literary, political, or scientific value. Obscenity is the most serious of the three; however, the line between indecency and obscenity is fuzzy, and some profanity, combined with sexual references, can be part of indecent or obscene material. In practice, the FCC rarely chastises stations for profanity, but it has handled numerous cases related to indecency.[7]

WBAI

Stern

One of the most famous indecency cases arose in 1973 when a Pacifica Foundation public radio station in New York, WBAI, aired a program on attitudes toward language. It was aired at 2:00 P.M. and included a comical monologue segment performed by George Carlin that spoofed seven dirty words that could not be said on the public airwaves. A father driving in the car with his son heard this monologue and complained to the FCC. The FCC placed a note in WBAI's license renewal file, which led the station to appeal through the courts all the way to the Supreme Court. WBAI claimed the FCC was censoring. The high court determined that censorship was not involved because the FCC did not stop WBAI ahead of time from airing the program. The Supreme Court did say, however, that the program should not have been aired during a time period when children were likely to be in the audience. One of the results of this ruling was that the FCC established a **safe harbor,** a period of time from 10 P.M. to 6 A.M. when indecent material can be aired because children are not expected to be in the audience.

Exhibit 11.6

Howard Stern, an ultimate shock jock, cost Infinity, the company that employed him, $1.7 million in FCC obscenity fines.

In the 1990s, the FCC put more teeth in its indecency actions. It fined Infinity Broadcasting $1.7 million because of numerous sexual and excretory remarks made by its on-air personality Howard Stern (see Exhibit 11.6). At first Infinity fought the fine, but eventually it decided to pay so it could get on with other business.[8]

Then along came Janet Jackson. During the 2004 Super Bowl half-time show, her singing partner, Justin Timberlake, tugged at her black bustier and exposed her right breast. FCC commissioners, politicians, and the public became incensed, especially because the Super Bowl is considered a family event. Janet and Justin apologized and said the idea was theirs and not that of CBS or the National Football League. They claimed there had been a "costume malfunction" and that what was supposed to be exposed was her red bra, not her breast. But the heat that was being generated by indecency on the airwaves in general reached a boil, and a series of actions were taken (see "Zoom In" box).

Jackson

At the time, the maximum fine for indecency was $27,500 per incident, but the FCC fined CBS $550,000, which was $27,500 for each of its 20 owned-and-operated stations. CBS appealed, and while the appeal was in progress, Congress upped the maximum fine to $325,000 per incident. Other indecency complaints surfaced, many of them involving **"fleeting expletives"**—swear words uttered

ZOOM IN: **Janet's Fallout**

A tremendous number of actions took place within a very short time after Janet Jackson's breast-baring incident at the 2004 Super Bowl halftime show produced by MTV. Among them were the following:

- TiVo reports that the incident was by far the most rewatched part of the Super Bowl.
- The FCC receives hundreds of thousands of emails complaining about the incident.
- CBS lengthens the delay time on the Grammy Awards to five minutes to allow video and audio to be stopped before it is aired, but the telecast has no problems.
- *ER* producers decide to blur the breasts of an elderly woman.
- PBS stations review *Antiques Roadshow* programs to make sure no nude etchings are shown.
- House and Senate hold hearings and fire tough questions at network and NFL executives.
- Clear Channel adopts a "zero tolerance" indecency policy, fires shock jock Bubba the Love Sponge, and takes Howard Stern off its owned stations.

Do you think politicians, the media, and the public overreacted, underreacted, or reacted

appropriately to this incident? This all happened during a presidential and congressional election year. Do you think that affected people's actions in any way?

Janet Jackson and Justin Timberlake shortly before the "wardrobe malfunction."

by celebrities or talk-show guests, especially those on awards shows. In 2010 an appeals court ruled that the near zero tolerance for fleeting expletives was a violation of the First Amendment. In 2011, a different appeals court ruled in favor of CBS in the Janet Jackson case, saying that the $550,000 fine was invalid. But this case, and others, can still be appealed to the Supreme Court.[9]

Obscenity is less of a problem for TV broadcasters than indecency. In their attempts to avoid indecent programming, they usually manage to stay away from what might be considered obscene. Radio, however, has potential for obscenity cases because of the lyrics of some modern songs. For example, a Florida court ruled that 2 Live Crew's album *As Nasty As They Wanna Be* was obscene, but the decision was later overturned. Not wanting to tread into the area of obscenity, a number of stations decided not to air Eminem's 2001 release "The Real Slim Shady" (see Exhibit 11.7).[10]

Cable TV is more likely to see legal action regarding obscenity than is commercial broadcasting. Rules are not as strict for cable as for broadcast because, historically, people had to specifically subscribe to cable, whereas broadcast signals were delivered free. A 1984 cable law did not prevent cable from showing indecent material, but it did prohibit obscene material. This gives cable more latitude than broadcasting, so it is more apt to cross the line between indecency and obscenity. The 1996 Telecommunications Act stated that cable operators had to scramble adult programming services, such as Playboy and Spice, or else only offer them between the hours of 10:00 P.M. and 6:00 A.M. But the Supreme Court threw out that provision, so adult channels can be offered 24 hours a day, although most of them are **pay-per-view**.[11]

Exhibit 11.7
Eminem was known for his lyrics that push the envelope. To avoid problems, some stations policed themselves and did not play some of his music.

cable TV

The home video business is also vulnerable to obscenity problems. Video stores have been sued for stocking sexually oriented videos, but store owners have won these cases by using the First Amendment. Video games and movies have codes that help keep them out of trouble. The problem is enforcing the codes—not selling an M video game to a 12-year-old or letting that 12-year-old into an R-rated movie. Both games and movies have been highly criticized for marketing their products to young people by advertising on TV programs that attract children.[12]

other media

The internet is rife with indecency and obscenity problems. In the Telecommunications Act of 1996, Congress tried to make it a crime for online computer services to transmit indecent material, but once again the Supreme Court declared this unconstitutional. In 1998, when members of Congress decided to put the Starr Report detailing the Bill Clinton–Monica Lewinsky affair on the internet, *Newsweek* quipped, "1996: House votes to ban smut on the Web. 1998: House votes to publish smut on the Web.[13]

internet

11.7 Privacy

older media

In the pre-internet days of media, privacy was a concern mostly for movie stars, politicians, and other famous people—primarily those that the **paparazzi** covered aggressively so that they could sell photos to tabloid magazines. States passed **invasion of privacy** laws giving people who were overly pursued the right to sue photographers, reporters, and journalistic organizations. These laws vary from state to state; however, in general, privacy laws allow a person to be left alone. Often the laws deal with giving a person physical solitude. For example, reporters cannot trespass on a person's property and take a photo through the bedroom window. The laws also consider the publication of private facts. In some states, facts are not private if they can be obtained from public records or if they are part of an important news story. For example, the names of rape victims are public record, so they can be broadcast; victims' names are often withheld, however, because broadcasters know the victims do not want their names revealed.[14]

With the coming of the internet, the privacy issue took a new turn—one that involved almost everyone. Technologically, companies operating on the internet can easily gather information (user name, host computer, credit card number, etc.) about anyone who accesses their site and can easily distribute this information to third parties such as advertisers, the government, and people who are developing **apps**.

internet

From the early days of the internet on, companies have had "small print" privacy policies that most users did not read or did not understand. Often these policies required people to **opt out** or else their information could be circulated. In other words, people had to specifically state they did not want their private information distributed. The clamor over this caused by people getting unwanted **spam** led many internet sites to adopt an **opt in** policy, wherein people had to indicate it was all right to share certain information. But this was far from a thorough fix.

social media

The situation worsened with the advent of social media, where the purpose is to share information—albeit with selected people. The innate human desire to connect with others clashed with the concept of privacy. The social networks depended on advertising for income, so the temptation (or even necessity) to give advertisers information about users' interests, hobbies, and such was strong.

children's privacy

A number of laws, regulations, and court cases have dealt with online privacy. For example, the 1998 Children's Online Privacy Protection Act required that written parental consent be given before any information could be collected from children younger than 13. The result of this well-intentioned act was to freeze children out of social networking sites, so children lied about their ages—sometimes encouraged by their parents to do so.[15]

Facebook

In 2009, a watchdog group, the Electronic Privacy Information Center, asked the Federal Trade Commission to investigate acts Facebook had undertaken that the Center felt violated privacy. There were a number of charges, but one of the most flagrant was that Facebook had changed its privacy policy without informing users. With the new policy, certain facts (name, picture, gender, and friends) became public information by default. The result of the FTC's investigation was that, in 2011, Facebook agreed to have an independent privacy audit every two years for the next 20 years. It also agreed to get users' permission before changing privacy settings.

Google and Twitter

In the same year, the FTC investigated Google and found it had told gmail users their information would only be used for email when, in fact, it was also used for the social network service Buzz. Google, like Facebook, agreed to install a privacy review of new products and obtain consent from users for how it used their information. Twitter, too, established privacy audits after hackers broke into its accounts.[16]

smartphones

Smartphones have come under attack for their lack of privacy policies. In 2011 a Senate committee investigated claims that Google and Apple phones contained software that was recording and storing user locations and every keystroke (text messages, photos, etc.) people made using their phones. Such software exists, but the companies said they were not using it to violate privacy but rather to learn ways to improve their phones.[17]

hackers

Hackers also figure into privacy concerns. They can sometimes break into sites and steal information in order to use it for crimes such as **identity theft,** wherein they utilize the information for their own benefit or they sell it to others who use it for illicit purposes, such as fake passports or shopping sprees. If hackers don't get all the information they want from a site, they can engage in **phishing**—they send emails to the addresses they have gathered, pretending to be a legitimate company, such as a bank. They hope to scam recipients into divulging private information, such as passwords and Social Security numbers, that can help them better undertake identity theft. Some hackers engage in a related activity called **spoofing.** They gather an email user's contact list and then send messages to those contacts that look like they are coming from an acquaintance. Sometimes these messages are solicitations for money or sex or other products or services that the apparent sender never sent. Often **viruses** are spread via trusted—yet spoofed— email accounts. All of these activities make people feel uncomfortable and violated, to say the least, and are looked at as invasions of privacy. Most companies try to protect their information from hackers by erecting **firewalls** and installing **filters.** But these cautionary processes are not hacker-proof and there have been many instances of unauthorized people gaining access to the private information of thousands of people.[18]

aiding crime fighters

Ironically, information on the internet and social media sites can help deter hacking and other crimes. People who commit crimes sometimes brag of their exploits on social media and even post videos of themselves committing crimes. Social media sites are open to police, who can browse profiles of suspects, including people who have committed past crimes. Detectives were able to arrest several alleged graffiti artists because they had photos of their work on their profiles; two boys who firebombed an airplane hangar uploaded video of themselves committing the crime; tip-offs regarding stockpiling of guns and ammunition have helped thwart school shootings. Of course, the fact that police can use social media raises issues about privacy. Privacy has become a thorny topic and one that is likely to receive much more attention.[19]

11.8 Libel and Slander

definitions

Most **libel** laws have their roots in the written press. In the early days of radio and television, there was debate as to whether libel applied at all. Libel is defined as **defamation** of character by published word, whereas **slander** is defamation by spoken word. Slander carries less penalty than libel, ostensibly because it is not in a permanent form to be widely disseminated. Some people thought radio and television should be governed by slander laws because words were spoken rather than printed. But because these spoken words are heard by millions, broadcast defamation comes under the libel category.

public figures

Prior to the 1970s, radio and television engaged in little investigative reporting, so libel suits rarely occurred. People who are **public figures** have great difficulty winning a libel suit because the rules and precedents applied to them are stricter than for ordinary citizens. To win a libel suit, a public figure must prove that a journalist acted with **actual malice.** As a result, few public figures bothered to bring libel suits against the broadcast media. By the late 1970s, however, TV was a major source of information and statements about people on TV definitely affected their reputations and livelihoods. As a result, libel cases were on the upswing. During the early 1980s, almost 90 percent of the people who filed libel suits against broadcasters won. This number was soon reduced to 54 percent as broadcasters began fighting these cases more seriously.

Some of the libel cases the courts have heard over the years include: Texas cattlemen who said talk-show host Oprah Winfrey's remarks about beef hurt their business; an eye clinic owner who said ABC falsely reported that the clinic rigged equipment to reveal cataracts that didn't exist; singer Wayne Newton, who claimed that an NBC newscast made it appear that he had strong ties with the Mafia; and General William Westmoreland, who claimed CBS wrongly accused him of purposely deceiving his military superiors about estimates of Vietnam enemy troop strength (see Exhibit 11.8).[20]

Exhibit 11.8

General William Westmoreland's libel case was supposed to be the "libel case of the century" because it involved the credibility of both CBS and the general. However, it settled quietly out of court with neither side declaring victory or defeat.

11.9 Copyright

The issue of **copyright** is one that affects most aspects of electronic media. The copyright principles stem from the U.S. Constitution, which authorizes Congress to promote science and art by giving authors and inventors exclusive rights to their works for a limited time. Congress has passed and amended copyright acts several times, so works created at different times have different rules. But works created starting in 1978 are copyrighted for the life of the author plus 70 years. **Works for hire,** such as movies, are copyrighted for 95 years from the date of first publication.[21]

provisions

After copyrights run out, works are placed in the **public domain** and can be used without obtaining permission. The copyright law also provides for **fair use,** which allows for some use of the work without permission from or payment to the copyright holder. Copyright principles try to balance the need for protection for the creator with the need to make those works available to the public. If artists cannot profit from their works, they are less likely to create them. However, totally protecting works would mean they could not be quoted, even in everyday conversation.[22]

Television stations, cable networks, broadcast and internet radio stations, corporate producers, and others involved with audio or video production must obtain permission and often pay a fee before they can include copyrighted music, photographs, sketches, film clips, or other similar material. Because finding the copyright holders and making arrangements with each individually is a chore, intermediary nonprofit organizations were formed to collect and distribute copyright fees for music. Three such organizations currently exist—the American Society of Composers, Authors, and Publishers (ASCAP); Broadcast Music, Inc. (BMI); and the Society of European Stage Artists and Composers (SESAC).

These music licensing organizations collect money from stations and other programming providers in two ways. One is called **blanket licensing**—for one yearly fee, a station can play whatever music it wants from the license organization without having to negotiate for each piece of music. The other way is called a **per-program fee**—the station pays a set amount for each program that utilizes music from the licensing organization. Radio stations (both over-the-air and internet), because they air so much music, generally opt for the blanket license. Television organizations are more likely to use per-program fees. ASCAP, BMI, and SESAC distribute the money they collect to composers and publishers in accordance with the amount the music is aired. Each organization uses a different method to determine what is aired, but in general they regularly survey media organizations to find out what they are playing. **music licenses**

Organizations that want to use music but do not want to work with one of the music licensing organizations can pay a **needle drop fee** directly to the copyright holder. In other words, they negotiate a set payment for the amount of a particular piece of music they want to use. This is a common method for movies that wish to include current hits. There is no equivalent of ASCAP for video material. Each clip that is used must be cleared individually. The copyright law also provides for **compulsory licenses,** such as those that cable TV systems and satellite programming providers (see Chapter 3) must pay to cover material provided by others, such as movie producers.[23]

It should have come as no surprise that the internet, portable devices, and social media have complicated the concept of copyright. YouTube contains many movie scenes put there by users. People place copyrighted photos, music, clips from their favorite movies, and many other copyrighted "personal" things on their Facebook pages. E-books are awash in copyright complications. At one point Viacom sued Google for placing clips from its copyrighted TV programs on Google-owned YouTube. Other production companies did not join in because they actually liked the publicity that the short YouTube clips provided for their products. The case was more or less settled when Google agreed to remove copyrighted material from YouTube if the copyright owner petitioned to have it taken down.[24] **internet complications**

piracy

Electronic media industry copyright holders are constantly plagued with problems related to violation of copyright, often called **piracy.** It can range from someone making copies of a song for friends to an international ring that distributes illegally dubbed movies to foreign countries even before the movies are released. It has always been a crime to make illegal copies of electronic media material, but now that just about everything is in **digital** form, it is easier to break the law than in **analog** days. The quality of the illegally duplicated material is far better because, unlike analog, digital quality does not degrade as it is copied from one medium to another.[25]

DRM

As a result, companies and the government have devised various methods of **digital rights management (DRM)**—ways to prevent the copyright laws from being violated. DRM includes **scrambling** video signals so they cannot be viewed without equipment that descrambles the signal. For example, someone who has not paid for a pay-cable channel, such as HBO, will see and hear a jumble when they tune to that channel. Of course, people devise illegal **decoder** boxes to unscramble cable and satellite signals, but scrambling methodology has improved, and most decoder boxes do not work for long. Similarly, there are copyright protection technologies that, when incorporated into a DVD, prevent it from being copied. DRM also includes placing digital **fingerprints** on recorded material so that if it is duplicated illegally, it will retain the fingerprint, and the person who duplicated it can be punished. This works well for copyright violations related to uploading and downloading material on the internet. If someone uploads fingerprinted material for which they do not own the rights, the hidden fingerprint will allow the rights owner to prosecute.

laws

Laws are also part of digital rights management, particularly the Digital Millennium Copyright Act of 1998. It made it a crime to circumvent DRM equipment. However, it also set up guidelines so that internet service providers were not responsible for material placed on their sites by users. (This helped Google win the case against Viacom.) Congress also made it a crime to record a movie in a theater. Some people were copying movies by taking a video camcorder into a movie theater and using it to make a grainy (but saleable) copy of the movie as it was projected onto the screen.[26]

FBI

The Federal Bureau of Investigation works to stamp out piracy, both in the United States and elsewhere, but it continues nonetheless. In some foreign countries, particularly in the developing world, people don't understand copyright principles. But most international piracy is not innocent. It is conducted by organizations with large duplicating facilities and elaborate distribution networks.

11.10 Access to the Courts

competing rights

Issues related to cameras in the courtroom arise when there are high profile cases, but the controversy has a long history that involves **competing rights** between the First and the Fifth and Sixth Amendments. Although the First Amendment guarantees freedom of the press, the Fifth Amendment guarantees a fair trial, and the Sixth guarantees a public trial.

In 1937, the American Bar Association adopted a policy, known as **Canon 35,** which barred still cameras and radio from courtrooms. Later, TV cameras were excluded by the same policy. This was not a law, but simply an ABA policy. Most judges abided by this policy, with the rationale being that cameras would cause disruption and lead defendants, lawyers, and jurors to act in ways that they would not act if no cameras were present, thus depriving the defendant of a **fair trial.** In the early days of television, there was potential for actual disruption because of the bulky equipment and lighting needed for TV coverage. During the 1970s, however, when unobtrusive equipment became available and when TV was no longer such a novelty, broadcasters began pressuring for access to courtrooms.

In 1972, the American Bar Association liberalized Canon 35, redesignating it **Canon 3A.** It recommended that individual states and judges be given discretion on whether to allow cameras into their courtrooms. Gradually states began allowing cameras in courtrooms and nothing went awry, so by the mid-1980s all states were allowing cameras. In 1991, the cable channel Court TV was established to cablecast nothing but real courtroom trials. It, and other networks, covered the William Kennedy Smith 1991 rape trial and the 1994 Menendez brothers' trial, where the brothers were accused of murdering their parents—without negative repercussions.[27]

The stage was thus set for cameras in the courtroom for the 1995 trial in which former football star O. J. Simpson was accused of killing his wife, Nicole Brown, and her friend Ron Goldman. One difference between this trial and all previous ones was the extent to which the public watched. The coverage of the trial, not only by Court TV but also by CNN, E! Entertainment Television, and many stations, outdistanced the ratings of all other programming. The verdict was one of the most watched events in TV history (see Exhibit 11.9). Because the trial became a circus, many questions were raised about the efficacy of allowing

Canon 35

Canon 3A

O. J. Simpson

Exhibit 11.9

In front of 150 million TV viewers, O. J. Simpson and his lawyers react to his "not guilty" verdict.

cameras in the courts, especially when a cameraman accidentally showed one of the jurors. Most judges believed the cameras interfered with court proceedings and, as a result, began routinely barring cameras from their courts.[28]

Casey Anthony

However, as time passed and memories faded, the courts began once again opening their doors to television. In 2011, 28-year-old Florida mother, Casey Anthony, was accused of killing her two-year-old daughter. When the trial covered salacious details, the ratings climbed as did the number of cable and broadcast networks covering it. The jury's surprise decision to acquit sparked a media spectacle, not only among some anchors who regaled against the decision but also in the social media.[29]

11.11 Licensing

The FCC is charged with licensing radio and TV stations so that they operate in the **public convenience, interest, and necessity;** without a license, a station cannot operate. The FCC has no direct control over the broadcast networks. It does not license them, but it can control them indirectly through their owned and affiliated stations. For example, when the FCC wanted to punish CBS for the Janet Jackson mishap, it levied fines against the stations CBS owned.[30]

networks

nonlicensed groups

Local cable TV systems, cable networks, satellite providers, and telco TV systems are not licensed, but the FCC has jurisdiction over some aspects of management, such as rate control and must-carry. The FCC has historically had a great deal of regulatory power over the telephone business, not in the form of actual licenses, but by setting rates and overseeing the overall business. Other areas such as home video, movies, the internet, and video games areas are not licensed, but occasionally they are part of antitrust investigations or other ownership considerations. Licensing of TV and radio stations, however, has raised many issues that have permeated the broadcasting industry.

process

When radio and TV station frequencies were first being allocated, companies wishing a license would submit applications to the FCC, and the FCC would decide which one should be given permission to offer the service. This used to be very laborious because FCC staff members sorted through all the applications trying to determine which group or person was most qualified. To alleviate the resulting backup, the FCC changed to allocating stations by **lottery.** The names of all applicants were "put in a hat," and the winner was chosen by chance. That applicant was then carefully checked to make sure it met basic qualifications. Most station frequencies have been given out by now, but when the FCC does allocate frequencies, it often conducts an **auction** and gives the service to the highest bidder, providing that bidder is qualified. Using lotteries and auctions signals a major change in the philosophy of the FCC. Instead of acting as guardian and selecting the best applicant, it now acts more as traffic cop, stopping applicants (who win by chance or money) only if they are undesirable.[31]

After an applicant receives a license, it usually experiences little supervision from the FCC until license renewal time, which currently is every eight years. The renewal process has changed greatly through the years. In the early days, the FRC and FCC renewed licenses almost automatically (see "Zoom In" box).[32]

ZOOM IN: **Two Notable Nonrenewals**

Two cases arose during the late 1920s and early 1930s in which licenses were not automatically renewed. One concerned Dr. J. R. Brinkley, who broadcast medical "advice" over his Milford, Kansas, station. He specialized in goat gland treatments to improve sexual powers and in instant diagnosis over the air for medical problems sent in by listeners. These problems could always be cured by prescriptions obtainable from druggists who belonged to an association Dr. Brinkley operated.

The other culprit was the Reverend Robert Shuler, who used his Los Angeles radio station to berate Catholics, Jews, judges, pimps, and others in his personal gallery of sinners. He professed to have derogatory information regarding unnamed persons who could pay penance by sending him money for his church.

The Federal Radio Commission decided not to renew either of these licenses, and although both defendants cried censorship, the U.S. Supreme Court sided with the FRC on the grounds that with only a limited number of

frequencies available, the commission should consider the quality of service rendered.

In this 1930s photo, Robert Shuler (right) is leaving jail on $500 bail after serving 16 days for alleged radio attacks on judges. He is shaking hands with the Los Angeles County jailer while an assistant jailer looks on.

Blue Book

In 1946, the FCC issued an 80-page document detailing its ideas on license renewal. This document was almost instantly dubbed the **Blue Book,** in part because of its blue cover, but more sarcastically because blue penciling denotes censorship. One of the provisions in it became known as the **promise versus performance** doctrine. It stated that promises made when stations were licensed should be kept and that performance on these promises should be a basis for license renewal. Broadcasters probably would not have objected to that philosophy, but the document went on to detail proper broadcasting behavior. It was particularly adamant about avoiding overcommercialization, broadcasting public-affairs programs, and maintaining well-balanced programming. Broadcasters looked at this document as a violation of the Communications Act that stated the commission was not to have the power of censorship, and on this basis the Blue Book provisions were never implemented.[33]

1960s procedures

In 1960, the FCC issued a much briefer policy statement that listed 14 elements usually necessary to meet public interest. The FCC also changed the license renewal forms so that broadcasters performed **ascertainment,** a process in which they had to interview community leaders to obtain their opinions on the crucial local issues and then design programming to deal with those issues. The results of these interviews and the proposed program ideas were then submitted to the FCC. Along with this material, stations sent copious information concerning station operation for the previous three years, including a **composite week's** list of programming. These seven days from the previous three years were selected at random by the FCC. The FCC's main concern was whether the programs listed adhered to what the station had proposed in its previous application (promise versus performance).[34]

Although the amount of paperwork increased with these 1960 changes, licenses continued to be renewed rather perfunctorily for several more years. This changed during the mid-1960s as community members gradually became involved in license renewal, and the FCC scrutinized license renewal more carefully than in the past.

WLBT-TV

The first major community participation occurred in 1964 when a group from Jackson, Mississippi, led by the United Church of Christ, asked the FCC if it could participate in the license renewal hearing of station WLBT-TV because the group believed the station was presenting racial issues unfairly. The FCC refused this request because, until this time, only people who would suffer technical or economic hardship from the granting of a license were permitted to testify at hearings. The UCC appealed to the courts, stating that ordinary citizens should be heard concerning license renewals. The courts agreed and ordered that a hearing be held that eventually led to WLBT's being given to a nonprofit group. This case established the precedent for citizen participation in license renewal.[35]

WHDH

In 1969, a group of Boston businesspeople successfully challenged the ownership of TV station WHDH, which had been operated by the *Boston Herald Traveler* for 12 years. This was a complicated case and involved rumors of improprieties on the part of all three companies that had originally applied for the station license. The station was awarded to the *Herald Traveler* in 1957, but various allegations kept the ownership in question. In 1962, the *Herald Traveler* was given a four-month temporary license in the hope that the situation would be clarified within that time. Seven *years* later, the commission revoked the *Herald Traveler* license and awarded it to Boston Broadcasters, Inc., an organization that included some of the original unsuccessful applicants for the station license back in the 1950s. This January 1969 decision sent shivers through the entire broadcasting community. Never before had a station license been transferred involuntarily unless the station licensee was found guilty of excessive violations.[36]

RKO

The net result of the WHDH and WLBT cases was the filing of numerous renewal challenges. In some instances, groups requested a **comparative license renewal** hearing because they wanted to operate the stations themselves. In other cases, citizens' groups filed **petitions to deny** license renewal mainly so they could bargain for what they wanted. One license renewal case that dragged on for years involved RKO and its 16 stations. In 1980, the FCC refused to renew the licenses of several RKO stations because RKO's parent corporation, General Tire and Rubber, admitted to the Securities and Exchange Commission that it had bribed foreign officials. The license refusals were appealed and lengthy deliberations began. As the hearings dragged on, RKO gradually (and painfully) sold its stations to other companies. In 1990, the FCC stopped the hearings without deciding whether or not RKO was qualified to be a licensee. The FCC called these "the most burdensome proceedings in the FCC history."[37]

Overall, however, the threat of losing a license abated in the 1980s. The FCC issued statements explaining that the commission would compare the station licensee and any challengers, but if the licensee had provided favorable service in the past, it would be given **renewal expectancy.** In other words, radio and TV stations could now assume that unless they committed serious acts, their licenses would be renewed. The license renewal forms were also changed to decrease the work required of stations. Now stations only need to submit a small amount of information that they send to the FCC over the internet.[38]

renewal expectancy

In addition to renewing licenses, if the FCC finds that a station is not fulfilling its obligations in serving the public convenience, interest, and necessity, it can revoke the license at any time. The FCC has done this for such causes as unauthorized transfer of control, technical violations, fraudulent contests, overcommercialization, and indecent programs. The FCC can also issue lesser punishments such as fines and short-term renewals. The FCC becomes involved when a station is sold and the license is transferred from one party to another. It is the station management's prerogative to set the selling price and select the buyer, but the FCC checks the qualifications of the buyer.[39]

other powers

11.12 Ownership

Various regulatory bodies have a say in who owns media under what conditions. In recent years, the Justice Department has taken on a larger role because of numerous mergers and acquisitions. This department, which oversees the area of antitrust, looks at the mergers to see if monopolies are being created.

monopolies

Historically, the FCC has been very involved with ownership. In general, the trend has been to allow companies to own more and more stations and to own multiple stations in the same market. In the early days of radio and TV, one company could own no more than seven AM, seven FM, and seven TV stations. The numbers were increased over the years and then changed from number of stations to percentage of viewers or listeners reached. For example, in the early 1990s, a station group could only own enough stations to cover a maximum of 35 percent of U.S. TV homes. In 2003, that number was raised to 39 percent.[40]

numbers

A law passed in 1992 required the FCC to set ownership rules for cable, and it decided that no one company should own cable or satellite systems reaching more than 30 percent of television subscribers. Time Warner took this rule to court and succeeded in having it rescinded.[41]

cable

A related area of ownership that the FCC deals with is **cross-ownership.** Many of the early owners of radio and TV stations also owned newspapers. This was considered against the public interest, especially if a town had only one TV station that was owned by the newspaper. The concern was that the public would learn only one version of the news. Similarly, controversies arose over whether one company should be allowed to own radio and also TV stations or TV stations and cable systems in the same market. The FCC has issued several guidelines on cross-ownership, some contradicting each other. Usually it grandfathers cross-ownership that already exists, so many different combinations of newspapers, radio, TV, and cable TV ownership exist.[42]

cross-ownership

11.13 Equal Time

Section 315 of the Communications Act is known as the **equal time** provision. In reality, it deals with **equal opportunity** rather than equal time. It reads as follows: "If any licensee shall permit any person who is a legally qualified candidate for any public office to use a broadcasting station, he shall afford equal opportunities to all other such candidates for that office in the use of such broadcasting station."[43]

provisions

This provision is in effect only during periods of election campaigns and deals only with people who have officially declared for political office. Because Section 315 actually mentions equal opportunity, it guarantees that all candidates for a particular office will be given the same number of minutes of airtime on a particular station. The airtime given must approximate the same time period so that one candidate is not seen during prime time and another in the wee hours of the morning. All candidates must be able to purchase time at the same rate. If one candidate purchases time and other candidates do not have the money to purchase equal time, however, the station does not need to give free time to the poorer candidates. Stations and networks are under pressure from Congress to give free time to all candidates, and some have agreed to do so. However, this is not required.

Through the years, interesting cases have arisen in regard to Section 315 (see "Zoom In" box). Shortly before the 1956 presidential election campaign between Dwight Eisenhower and Adlai Stevenson, Eisenhower, who was the incumbent president, was given free time on all networks to talk to the American people about an urgent crisis in the Middle East. Stevenson's forces immediately demanded equal free time. The FCC, however, decided that Eisenhower's speech was exempt from Section 315 because it did not deal with normal affairs, but with a crisis situation. This precedent has been followed in other election years with other crisis-oriented presidential speeches.

crisis speech

amendment

Exhibit 11.10
Lar Daly campaigning on Chicago TV in his Uncle Sam suit.

In 1959, Lar Daly (see Exhibit 11.10), a candidate for mayor of Chicago, protested that the incumbent mayor, who was running for reelection, was seen on a local news show, and Daly demanded equal time. Had he been an ordinary candidate, he might have been granted time and the issue dropped. He was an eccentric, however, who dressed in an Uncle Sam outfit—complete with a red, white, and blue top hat. Daly ran, unsuccessfully, for some office in every election. Daly was granted his time, but Congress amended Section 315 so that the equal opportunity restrictions would not apply to candidates appearing on newscasts, news interviews, news documentaries, and on-the-spot coverage of news events. Eventually interviews on talk shows such as *Tonight* were lumped in with bona fide news, and candidates have appeared on many of these shows.

In 1960, when Democrat John F. Kennedy and Republican Richard M. Nixon were running for president, the networks wanted the two to debate on television, and the two candidates agreed. But the wording of Section 315 would have necessitated equal debating opportunity for all the splinter candidates on the presidential ballot. Because Congress believed this was a special situation, it suspended Section 315 temporarily for the 1960 presidential and vice presidential offices only (see Exhibit 11.11).

ZOOM IN: **Politics and Entertainment**

The entry of entertainers into politics created a dilemma for broadcasters in terms of Section 315. The issue became prominent when Ronald Reagan ran for president in 1980. Section 315 applied to the movies in which he appeared, so broadcasters did not air the films during the election period. Reagan's opponents made light of the situation, joking that showing the films might actually cause him to lose votes.

In 2003, Arnold Schwarzenegger ran for governor of California, and as with Reagan, the question of his movies arose. This time, however, it was cable TV channels that were considering airing his movies, and it is unclear whether Section 315 applies to cable TV networks. Not wanting to become test cases, networks such as TNT, FX, USA, and HBO, which regularly show Schwarzenegger movies, decided that the prudent thing to do was to cancel their showings until after the election.

In 2007, Fred Thompson, one of the stars of *Law and Order,* decided to run for president. NBC Universal carefully catalogued the shows and was prepared to keep those that included Thompson from airing. But his campaign fizzled, so, for the most part, the shows could air as scheduled.

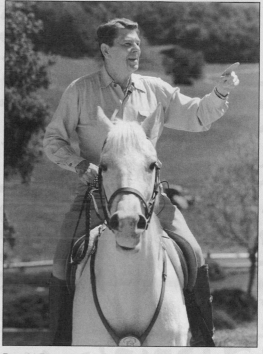

Ronald Reagan, movie star and president.

Exhibit 11.11
Candidate John F. Kennedy speaks while Richard Nixon and moderator Howard K. Smith look on. In the foreground are the newspeople who asked the questions.

debates

Broadcasters hoped that similar suspensions would be forthcoming, but the issue took a different turn. The FCC, under the 1959 Communications Act amendment that allowed on-the-spot coverage of bona fide news events, decided in 1975 that networks and stations could cover candidate debates if these were on-the-spot news events. The broadcasters could not arrange the debates, but if some other group, such as the League of Women Voters, organized the debates, the media could cover the event in much the same way as they cover awards ceremonies or state fairs. In 1976 and 1980, presidential debates were sponsored by the League of Women Voters and telecast as news events. Then in 1983, the FCC ruled that debates could be sponsored by broadcasters, on the grounds that broadcasters should have the same right to hold debates and exclude candidates as civic groups.

The issue of splinter-party candidates came to the fore again in 1992 and 1996. Ross Perot, a strong Reform Party candidate in 1992, was invited to join Democrat Bill Clinton and Republican George H. W. Bush in the debates (see Exhibit 11.12). In 1996, Perot was again a candidate and, of course, wanted to be in the debates. A nonpartisan commission formed to organize the debates decided that Perot did not have a realistic chance of being elected so should not participate. Perot fought the decision and was eventually allowed to participate in one debate.

Because of all the difficulties involved with Section 315, some stations decided they would not offer time to any candidate and thus avoid the question of giving time to opponents. But in 1971, the FCC nixed the idea, stating that stations could have their licenses revoked if they did not allow access to candidates running for federal office. However, for state and local elections, stations were given the option of not dealing with any candidates if they so desired. The FCC has issued thick tomes on political broadcasting, and those, plus relaxation or requirements, have made equal time less of an issue in recent times.[44]

Exhibit 11.12

In the 1992 presidential campaign, Reform Party candidate Ross Perot joined Republican candidate George H. W. Bush and Democratic candidate Bill Clinton for the presidential debates.

11.14 Other Regulations

Many other laws and regulations affect electronic media practitioners. For example, studios sometimes sue actors for **breach of contract** or vice versa. From time to time radio station employees are accused of **payola.** For many years there was a **fairness doctrine** that required stations to present opposing points of view (See "Zoom In" box).[45]

fairness doctrine

The fairness doctrine was never a doctrine but rather a series of rulings dealing with presentation of controversial issues. Various FCC and Congressional statements from the 1940s and 1950s said that licensees must operate on a basis of overall fairness, making facilities available for the expression of contrasting views. For many years, if stations allowed the presentation of information about one point of view, such as reasons for capital punishment, they had to allow time for an opposing presentation (anti-capital punishment).

A hallmark of the fairness doctrine was a court case that became known as the Red Lion case. In 1964, station WGCB in Pennsylvania, operated by the Red Lion Broadcasting Company, broadcast a talk given by the Reverend Billy Hargis that charged author Fred J. Cook with Communist affiliations. Cook demanded that WGCB give him the opportunity to reply. The station said it would if Cook would pay for the time, but Cook took the case to the Supreme Court. The Court ruled that the station should grant Cook the time whether or not he was willing to pay for it, on the grounds that a broadcaster's right of free speech does not include the right to snuff out the free speech of others. The significance of this decision went beyond the dispute between Cook and the Red Lion because it upheld the constitutionality of the fairness concept.

One creative application of the fairness doctrine was a case brought by John F. Banzhaf III. In 1964, the Surgeon General's Office determined there was a link between cigarette smoking and lung cancer, a point that was considered controversial. In 1967, Banzhaf petitioned WCBS-TV in New York, saying that because cigarette commercials showed cigarette smoking in a positive light, free time should be given to antismoking groups to present the other side. WCBS replied that it had presented the negative side of smoking within its news and public-affairs programs and did not think it needed to give equivalent commercial time to the issue. Banzhaf took the matter to the FCC, which sided with him—as did the appeals courts. Therefore, until 1972 when cigarette advertising was banned, any station that aired cigarette commercials had to provide time for anticigarette messages.

The rulings involving the fairness decisions of the 1960s led broadcasters and the public to believe that future decisions by the FCC and the courts would favor those who believed that fairness should be strictly interpreted. However, the pendulum swung, and the decisions of the 1970s began to turn around. When an ecology group tried to emulate Banzhaf's case by requesting that ads for gasoline be countered by antipollution announcements, the attempt was not successful. The FCC stated that the cigarette ruling was not to be used as a precedent because that case was unique.

During the 1980s, the number of complaints brought under the fairness doctrine waned, and the doctrine itself became the focus of attention. A court decision stated that the doctrine was not law but merely an FCC regulation that the FCC could abolish. In 1987, Congress passed a bill that would have codified the fairness doctrine and made it a law rather than an FCC policy, but President Reagan vetoed it. Soon after, the FCC said it was going to stop enforcing fairness

This meant that stations could air programming about controversial issues without having to worry about complaints or contrasting points of view. One thing this enabled was the rise of talk radio, where issues discussed on programs are often one-sided. From time to time members of Congress tried to pass bills to reinstate the fairness doctrine. When this happened, talk-show hosts railed against the bills, with conservative talk show host Rush Limbaugh calling them "crush Rush" bills.

In 2011, the FCC took the doctrine totally off the books.

John F. Banzhaf III used the fairness doctrine to enable antismoking messages to be aired.

lotteries

The U.S. Criminal Code outlaws **lotteries** sponsored by radio or TV. Stations are allowed to have contests, though, and sometimes cases arise as to whether a station is conducting a contest or a lottery. Generally, something is considered a lottery if a person pays to enter, if chance is involved, and if a prize is offered. Stations usually avoid lotteries by making sure people do not have to pay to enter contests.[46]

hoaxes

The FCC also has rules against **hoaxes.** In 1990, after two Los Angeles disc jockeys faked a murder confession on the air that led to a nationwide police search for a nonexistent killer, the FCC established a mechanism for fining stations up to $250,000 for such hoaxes.[47]

Many of the issues discussed in other chapters of this book, such as **network neutrality** (see Chapters 2 and 3) and the proposals to use broadcast station frequencies for wireless broadband internet (see Chapter 4), will be affected by legal processes. Any elements of electronic media business procedures that become controversial are likely to be dealt with through the FCC, Congress, or the courts.[48]

11.15 Issues and the Future

At varying times in history, different laws and regulations take on increased importance. For many years equal time and licensing were major issues. Today privacy and copyright merit more press, mainly because the internet has brought forth a host of issues. It is a democratic tool that people can access and alter and it can distribute anything quickly and thoroughly. The same

privacy and copyright

people who want their information kept private want private information about others so that they can market their widgets. Software providers want their material copyright protected but, at the same time, seek provisions that allow them to violate other companies' copyrights. TV and movie production companies in Hollywood fight for copyright protection while internet companies in the Silicon Valley want people to be able to post or sell anything, regardless of its origin. People who have their identity stolen because hackers break into a company and steal information fret because the companies take a hands-off approach to helping them straighten out the problems caused by identity theft.[49]

balance

The amount and type of regulation is likely to change as newer media take a bigger bite from the audience apple. Broadcasters resent the many licensing restrictions that have tied their hands over the years while cablecasters, video stores, satellite systems, the internet, and others operate with much less regulation. The main reason for this is timing. Broadcasters were in business during the 1960s when heavy regulation was in vogue. Most of the other media systems arose during the 1980s and 1990s when deregulation was the watchword. Broadcasters are unleashing themselves from some of the regulations, but it is a hard pull.

Auctions and lotteries reduce the amount of time the FCC staff spends deciding who should get what frequencies, but they do not ensure that the best people receive access to the media. Particularly with auctions, money rather than morality decides who earns the right to program to the American people.

auctions

There are occasional murmurs that Section 315 should be abolished. This is not likely to happen because it affects the members of Congress who would have to vote to abolish it. Politicians want to make sure they have access to radio and TV. Although they would like to amend Section 315 so that they would have free time instead of having to pay for it, they are unlikely to destroy the equal time concept.

Section 315

Some have questioned whether the Emergency Alert System is still needed. Tests to check its technical reliability have not gone well. It was not put into effect during the terrorist attacks of September 11, 2001. The news media effectively undertook the role of keeping the populace informed. Maybe the system is an idea whose time has passed.[50]

EAS

Regulation suffers from people problems. Senators and representatives depend on the support of media to be elected and, hence, are often heavily influenced by broadcasting lobbies. FCC commissioners, because they know their decisions can be appealed to the courts, sometimes make conservative decisions that are unlikely to be overturned. Some have suggested that the FCC be abolished because the commissioners and staff institute so much red tape that they stifle ingenuity and progress of electronic media businesses.[51]

people problems

Regulation policies are in a constant state of flux—a situation having both advantages and disadvantages. The state of flux allows for changes to keep up with the times, but it also creates internal inconsistencies among the various regulatory bodies. It inhibits rigidity on the part of elected and appointed officials, but it also causes confusion and uncertainty for those who must comply with regulations.

11.16 Summary

The electronic media industry interrelates with all three branches of government—legislative, executive, and judicial—and with independent regulatory bodies. The main independent regulatory board is the FCC. Some of its chores are technical and have not changed much. Others, such as licensing, are more philosophical and are subject to changes as society's outlook alters. Licensing has caused broadcasters varying degrees of consternation through the years. Decisions regarding WLBT, WHDH, and RKO affected the regulatory direction of the industry. Ownership and cross-ownership are also important topics. The FCC has issued fines against obscenity, as in the Howard Stern case, and decided when equal time provisions were violated, as in cases regarding presidential crisis speeches. On occasion, the FCC has issued guidelines or rulings such as the Blue Book. Another regulatory body, the FTC, has dealt with advertising and privacy complaints against Facebook and others.

The executive branch is most likely to claim clear and present danger if the president believes reporters are acting irresponsibly. The president can veto communication legislation, as in the case of the fairness bill. In addition, the president nominates commissioners and can activate the Emergency Alert System. The Justice Department handles matters related to monopoly.

The legislative branch passes and amends many laws that affect telecommunications. The amendment to Section 315 that removed equal time restrictions from bona fide newscasts affected election campaigns. Congress wrestles with copyright laws and all their ramifications. Other criminal and civil laws passed by Congress, such as those dealing with lotteries and hoaxes, affect broadcasting, as do state laws dealing with shielding reporters and invasion of privacy. Congressional committees hold hearings on communications-related issues, and the Senate approves the appointment of FCC commissioners.

The courts are the place of appeal for those who think they are treated unjustly by other branches of the government or by elements of society. Media and the courts have a double-edged relationship. On one hand, a battle was waged regarding the right of radio and TV to have access to the courts for news coverage—a battle that received a setback because of the O. J. Simpson case. On the other hand, the courts make many decisions that directly affect broadcasters, such as those involving the First Amendment. Indecency and obscenity rulings on subjects such as WBAI's "seven dirty words," radio lyrics, and the CBS fine for the Janet Jackson "wardrobe malfunction" are taken to the courts. Likewise, libel cases such as Westmoreland's, as well as privacy invasions, are fought in the courts. Although the various branches of government disagree with one another from time to time, equilibrium is maintained by the checks and balances system.

Suggested Websites

www.ascap.org (American Society of Composers, Authors and Publishers, a music licensing organization)

www.fcc.gov (the Federal Communications Commission)

www.ftc.gov (the Federal Trade Commission)

www.supremecourt.gov (the Supreme Court)

www.whitehouse.gov (news about the president and others in the executive branch)

Notes

1. The Federal Communications Commission website is www.fcc.gov. "First National EAS Test Date Set." *TV Technology,* July 6, 2011, 6; and "FCC Launches Alert System for Mobile," *TV Technology,* June 22, 2011, 1.
2. "Presidential Privilege," *Emmy,* January/February 2008, 32; and "Ma Bell's Big Breakup," *Newsweek,* January 18, 1982, 58–59.
3. Steven Phipps, "'Out of Chaos': A Reexamination of the Historical Basis for the Scarcity of Channels Concept," *Journal of Broadcasting & Electronic Media,* Winter 2001, 57–74.

4. "Second to None," *Broadcasting & Cable,* July 19, 2010, 34.

5. "Press Shield Law Upheld," *Broadcasting & Cable,* November 8, 1999, 37; and "Jailing of Reporter Sends Jolt," *Hollywood Reporter,* July 7, 2005, 1.

6. "State's Law on Video Games Voided," *Los Angeles Times,* June 28, 2011, 1; and "U.S. May Try to Extradite Founder of WikiLeaks," *Los Angeles Times,* December 8, 2010, A-9.

7. "Contradictions in U.S. Law on Obscenity and Indecency in Broadcasting: A Bleeping Critique," *Feedback,* August 2002, 28–34.

8. "Stern's Blue Streak Costs Infinity a Cool $1.7 Mil," *Daily Variety,* September 10, 1995, 6.

9. "Super Bowl Halftime Stunt Angers NFL, CBS, FCC," *Wall Street Journal,* February 3, 2004, B-1; "Super Bowl Episode Prompts CBS to Heighten Safeguards for Grammys," *Los Angeles Times,* February 4, 2004, C-1; "Firing of 'Love Sponge' Signals Cleanup of Shock Radio," *Wall Street Journal,* February 25, 2004, B-1; "Bared Breast Nets $550K Penalty," *Hollywood Reporter,* September 26–October 4, 2004, 71; "Court Tosses FCC Ban on Foul Speech," *Los Angeles Times,* July 14, 2010, 1; and "CBS Wins Ruling on Indecency," *Los Angeles Times,* November 3, 2011, B-3.

10. "Crew Acquitted in Obscenity Case," *Daily Variety,* October 27, 1990, 1; and "Don't Mess Around with Slim," *Broadcasting & Cable,* June 11, 2001, 14.

11. "Court Clears Way for More Playboy," *Electronic Media,* May 29, 2000, 21.

12. "Push to Allow DVDs to Be 'Sanitized' Alarms Studios," *Los Angeles Times,* June 23, 2004, C-1; and "Games under the Gun," *Hollywood Reporter,* September 19–25, 2000, 14–15.

13. "High Court Strikes Down Internet Indecency Rules," *Electronic Media,* June 30, 1997, 37; "Special Too Much Information Edition," *Newsweek,* September 21, 1998, 8; and Ven-hwei Lo and Ran Wei, "Third-Person Effect, Gender, and Pornography on the Internet," *Journal of Broadcasting & Electronic Media,* March 2002, 13–33.

14. "Providing Coverage, Protecting Victims: Rape Trials on Trial," *Broadcasting,* April 30, 1984, 134.

15. "No One under 13 Admitted, but Who Told Them to Lie?" *Los Angeles Times,* February 22, 2001, T-1.

16. "Facebook 'Unfair' on Privacy," *Wall Street Journal,* November 30, 2011, B1; and "Facebook Privacy Deal Sends Message," *Los Angeles Times,* November 12, 2011, B-1.

17. "Apple, Google Officials Testify," *Los Angeles Times,* May 11, 2011, B-1.

18. "Security Center," http://www.buysafe.com/security_center/security_glossary.html (accessed December 12, 2011); and "Think Before You Click," *Broadcasting & Cable,* May 23, 2011, 30.

19. "How to Avoid the Prying Eyes," *Wall Street Journal,* July 31–August 1, 2010, W3; and Miriam J. Metzger and Sharon Doctor, "Public Opinion and Policy Initiatives for Online Privacy Protection," *Journal of Broadcasting & Electronic Media,* September 2003, 350–74.

20. "Newton's NBC Libel Damage Award Nixed," *Daily Variety,* August 31, 1990, 1; "The General's Retreat," *Newsweek,* March 4, 1985, 59–60; and "ABC Takes Double Hit in Court," *Broadcasting & Cable,* December 30, 1996, 10.

21. *The United States Constitution,* Section 8; and "Justices OK Copyright Extension," *Los Angeles Times,* January 16, 2003, 1.

22. Matt Jackson, "Commerce Versus Art: The Transformation of Fair Use," *Journal of Broadcasting & Electronic Media,* Spring 1995, 190–99.

23. "ASCAP Singing with Radio Deal," *Hollywood Reporter,* October 19–25, 2004, 1; and "Copyright Office Proposes—Cable Opposes—Higher Fees," *Broadcasting & Cable,* August 11, 1997, 18.

24. "Google Wins Key Copyright Decision," *Wall Street Journal,* June 24, 2010, B1; and "Build the Library Without Google?" *Los Angeles Times,* March 27, 2011, B-1.

25. "Pirate Party Fires Volley," *Variety,* June 14–20, 2010, A-4" and "Latest Plot Twist for 'Star Wars': Attack of the Cloners," *Los Angeles Times,* May 10, 2002, 1.

26. "Safer Digital Information," *Broadcasting & Cable,* July 14, 2008, 16; "Policing Web Video with 'Fingerprints,'" *Wall Street Journal,* April 23, 2007, B-1; and Public Law No. 105-304, Digital Millennium Copyright Act, October 28, 1998.

27. Susanna Barber, *News Cameras in the Courtroom: A Free Press-Fair Trial Debate* (Norwood, NJ: Ablex, 1987); and "Courtroom Doors Begin to Open for TV, Radio," *Broadcasting,* September 3, 1990, 25.

28. "Court TV's O. J. Duties Put on Trial," *Electronic Media,* January 30, 1995, 1.

29. "A Trial Too Juicy to Resist," *Los Angeles Times,* July 6, 2011, D-1.

30. Section 307 of the Communications Act of 1934 states: "The Commission, if public convenience, interest, or necessity will be served thereby, subject to the limitation of this Act, shall grant to any applicant therefore a station license provided for by this Act." This section has become the keystone of regulation that the FCC has often used to justify regulations, especially those aimed at programming.

31. "Auction Worries Multiply," *Broadcasting & Cable,* July 9, 2001, 8.

32. "From Fighting Bob to the Fairness Doctrine," *Broadcasting,* January 5, 1976, 46.

33. Michael J. Socolow, "Questioning Advertising's Influence over American Radio: The Blue Book Controversy of 1945–1947," *Journal of Radio Studies,* December 2002, 282–302.

34. Erik Barnouw, *The Golden Web* (New York: Oxford University Press, 1968), 227–36.

35. "Looking Back to WLBT(TV)," *Broadcasting,* April 16, 1984, 43.

36. "The Checkered History of License Renewal," *Broadcasting,* October 16, 1978, 30.

37. "FCC Gives RKO Green Light to Sell Stations," *Broadcasting,* July 25, 1988, 33; and "The Trials of RKO," *Channels,* January 1990, 70–73.

38. "The Next Best Thing to Renewal Legislation," *Broadcasting,* January 10, 1977, 20.

39. Charles E. Clift III, "Station License Revocations and Denials of Renewal, 1970–1978," *Journal of Broadcasting,* Fall 1980, 411–21.

40. Jennifer M. Proffitt, "Juggling Justifications: Modifications to National Television Station Ownership Rules," *Journal of Broadcasting & Electronic Media*, December 2007, 575–95.

41. "FCC Fears Cable Deal Firestorm," http:/www.thedeal.com (accessed May 25, 2004).

42. "It's Almost as If There's No Rule," *Broadcasting & Cable,* March 20, 2000, 8; and "No Hard, or Fast, Rules," *Broadcasting & Cable,* May 24, 2010, 28.

43. Public Law No. 416, Section 315.

44. "Appeals Court Agrees with FCC: Broadcasters May Sponsor Debates," *Broadcasting,* May 12, 1984, 69; "FCC Wearing 2-Party Hat, Claims Critic," *Daily Variety,* August 2, 1991, 1; "Debate Continues over Debates," *Broadcasting & Cable,* September 23, 1996, 14; and "NBCU Ready for Thompson White House Run," *Broadcasting & Cable,* July 16, 2007, 6.

45. Timothy J. Brennan, "The Fairness Doctrine as Public Policy," *Journal of Broadcasting & Electronic Media,* Fall 1989, 419–40; "Who's Afraid of the Fairness Doctrine?" *Broadcasting & Cable,* July 28, 2008, 6; "Fairness Doctrine, R.I.P., *Wall Street Journal,* August 25, 2011, A14; and "Case of the Year," *Hollywood Reporter,* July 22, 2011, 49.

46. *Lotteries and Contests: A Broadcasters Handbook* (Washington, DC: National Association of Broadcasters, 1985).

47. "FCC Adopts $25,000 Fine for Hoaxes," *Broadcasting,* May 18, 1992, 5.

48. "Defending Your (Spectrum) Life," *Broadcasting & Cable,* May 23, 2011, 23; and "FCC OKs Rules on Net Access," *Los Angeles Times,* December 22, 2010, B-1.

49. "The Piracy Showdown," *Hollywood Reporter,* December 16, 2011, 30; and "The Great Privacy Debate," *Wall Street Journal,* August 7–8, 2010, W1.

50. "Mixed Results for National EAS Test," *TV Technology,* December 7, 2011, 1.

51. "Time to Shut Down the FCC," *Wall Street Journal,* December 3, 2010, A21.

Chapter 12

ETHICS AND EFFECTS

One by-product of deregulation is an increased emphasis on ethics. When electronic media operations are heavily controlled through laws and regulations, individuals encounter legal constraints that tell them what they can and cannot do. When there are few laws, individuals and "the corporate conscience" are in a position to make many fundamental decisions. Often, they must rely on a sense of ethics, and ethics can be influenced by knowing the effects of media on the public.

Media, through their persuasive powers, can affect individuals—their behavior, their beliefs, and their purchases. Children are particularly prone to media influences that can be both confusing and enlightening. Media also affect society as a whole and the various institutions that operate within society. Some of these institutions (such as networks and websites) are part of the media, while others (such as the FCC and citizens' groups) act as influences on the ethics and regulation of the media, and still others (such as churches and schools) are affected in a more indirect but nevertheless important manner.

> The speed of communication is wonderful to behold. It is also true that speed can multiply the distribution of information that we know to be untrue. The most sophisticated satellite has no conscience—and in the end the communicator will be confronted with the age-old problem of what to say and how to say it.
>
> **Edward R. Murrow, former CBS newscaster**

12.1 Interrelationships of Laws and Ethics

thin line

Often there is a thin line between laws and ethics. Something that is illegal can also be unethical. For example, a **payola** law prohibits a disc jockey from accepting money from a record company in exchange for playing that company's music on the airwaves without reporting it (see Chapter 5). If a disc jockey gets caught engaging in payola, he or she can be fined or even imprisoned. But what if the disc jockey feels 99 percent sure of not getting caught? In that case, accepting the money is both a legal and an ethical issue.

stakes

Sometimes ethics and the law collide because of what is at stake. Although it is illegal for talk-show talent to say something obscene over the air, doing so can increase ratings. The extra money from advertisers based on the increased ratings can offset the fine from the FCC. Should the talk-show talent be obscene? Should management encourage this **obscenity**? Again, ethics and legality are intertwined.

degree

The degree of regulation also affects ethics. For example, when cable rates are regulated (see Chapter 3), cable companies know how much they can or cannot raise rates. When no government agency is policing how much they charge subscribers, managers must use their conscience and their sense of economic fairness when designing their costs.

justification

Many aspects of hacking are illegal and yet **hackers**, too, have ethical dilemmas. Some have said they hacked into a company's computers to prove to the company that it had a security problem and that they had no intent of using the material they obtained in a malicious way. Is this acceptable ethically? Others have condoned hacking into smartphones in order to get facts for a news story that, when released, would benefit the greater society. Does that justify the hacking? On a less grandiose level, computer buffs who figure out how to download a video game for free rationalize that the rich company selling the product won't suffer from selling one less game.

In short, even though there are laws or regulations that are meant to prevent or allow certain actions, these laws do not rule out the need for consideration of ethics. Education regarding ethics is needed when dealing with the implementation of laws, the justifications for laws, and the ease of treading between legal and illegal, ethical and unethical.[1]

12.2 Ethical Guidelines

To help managers and employees make proper ethical decisions, some electronic media organizations draw up guidelines of **self-regulation** dos and don'ts. For example, a professional association for news people, the Radio Television Digital News Association (RTDNA), has codes and guidelines for a large number of situations such as airing 911 calls, amber alerts, blogging, avoiding conflict of interest, and covering bomb threats. Exhibit 12.1 gives some of the points listed in its Code of Ethics and Professional Conduct. The original code was created in 1946 and is frequently rewritten to keep it up-to-date. This code has no legal force, and

RTDNA code

Sample RTDNA Code Provisions

Professional electronic journalists should:

- Fight to ensure that the public's business is conducted in public.
- Clearly disclose the origin of information and label all material provided by outsiders.
- Not present images or sounds that are reenacted without informing the public.
- Treat all subjects of news coverage with respect and dignity, showing particular compassion to victims of crime or tragedy.
- Disseminate the private transmissions of other news organizations only with permission.
- Not accept gifts, favors, or compensation from those who might seek to influence coverage.
- Gather and report news without fear or favor, and vigorously resist undue influence from any outside forces, including advertisers, sources, story subjects, powerful individuals, and special interest groups.
- Seek support for and provide opportunities to train employees in ethical decision-making.

Exhibit 12.1

A few provisions of the RTDNA code.

there are no penalties for violating it, but it is something the organization hopes that journalists follow.[2]

In the early part of the 21st century, many of the practices related to judging the Oscars went a little over the top. Companies and individuals were blatantly promoting their movies to the industry people who vote and, in some cases, even starting smear campaigns against competing films. As a result, the Academy of Motion Picture Arts and Sciences adopted a code of behavior for the awards season. Among other things, it advised industry members not to write letters to the editor or be quoted in ads. Campaigners were to avoid advertising that bad-mouthed other films and were not to throw special parties for voters.[3]

Oscar code

Much of ethical self-regulation comes from individual stations or networks, which have their own written or unwritten codes. At the commercial broadcast networks, the business of making sure all programs and commercials adhere to good taste falls to the Department of Standards and Practices (often called **broadcast standards**), a group operating independently of programming or sales and reporting directly to top network management. This department often reviews program and commercial ideas when they are in outline or **storyboard** form and then screens them several times again as they progress through scripting and production. If any of the proposed ideas run counter to what are determined to be the prevailing standards, broadcast standards personnel request changes before the idea can proceed to the next step (see Exhibit 12.2).

broadcast standards

Naturally there is conflict between broadcast standards and program or commercial producers. But there is also often cooperation so that problems can be averted. For example, NBC decided to air Steven Spielberg's movie *Schindler's*

To: Executive producer of the series
From: Broadcast Standards & Practices editor for the show
Subject: Broadcast Standards & Practices report
CC: Programming executive responsible for the show, the head of the programming department, the head of the Standards Department, and the in-house legal counsel

Page 2: Please ensure that there is plenty of coverage for the fight scene in the bar. Delete having Mark break a beer bottle on Sam's face.

Page 4: Delete "Christ" in Molly's dialogue, "Christ, what did I do to deserve this!"

Page 6: In the bedroom scene, do not have Molly "moving sensuously" on top of Mark. There can be no grinding action in this sequence, nor can there be any nudity. Molly must remain appropriately covered as she gets out of bed. Again, we suggest that you provide adequate coverage to avoid problems at the rough cut stage.

Page 22: Overly graphic images of the crime scene need to be avoided.

Page 24: Please make sure you have the proper clearances for the use of the song, "Stop in the Name of Love."

Page 38: The medical information about Alzheimer's disease must be correct. Please have your medical consultant provide documentation that confirms the scripted information.

Page 42: Substitute for scripted dialogue about illegal immigrants being the cause of the nation's ills. We do not want to include advocacy positions in this entertainment program.

Page 43: Do not have the teenagers smoking cigarettes, as scripted.

Page 47: Avoid a "how to" when Molly commits suicide. Do not include every step of the process she uses as we do not want viewers to be able to imitate her actions. Extreme care must be exercised to avoid making suicide appear to be a viable solution to her problems.

Page 55: At the airport, revise having the security guard portrayed as a buffoon ("You look like a nice guy who wouldn't want to harm all these nice people who are flying home for the holidays") who allows passengers to board without having their baggage inspected, as we do not want to ridicule necessary homeland security procedures.

List uncut, even though it had gruesome scenes and some nudity. Spielberg and a network executive spoke at the start of the movie, stating that the story was too important to edit, warning the audience about the graphic nature of the scenes, and suggesting that children not be allowed to watch. Having framed the broadcast this way, the network did not receive complaints but rather letters of congratulations.

At local radio and TV stations, the broadcast standards functions may not be as formal. The general manager frequently performs the function on an as-needed basis, and sometimes the function is delegated to whichever group or person handles the station's legal matters or public relations. In any organization, the person who is the "boss" plays an enormous role in setting the tone for ethical behavior.

local stations

Within the cable TV and satellite broadcast industries, individual networks have their own standards. Arts & Entertainment, for example, has a policy against frontal nudity—a policy that it knowingly violates when it shows certain Woody Allen movies because Allen insists that none of his movies be edited.

cable TV

Network, station, and internet self-regulation occurs constantly and informally at all levels through the actions of individuals who work in the electronic media. Writers, producers, directors, actors, editors, and website designers are constantly basing decisions on their own ideas of propriety and appropriateness, even when management provides no direction (see "Zoom In" box).[4]

individuals

In his book *Real-World Media Ethics,* Philippe Perebinossoff proposes an ethics rubric for media practitioners to use as an approach to a wide range of ethical dilemmas (see Exhibit 12.3). His Evaluate, Truth, Harm, Investigation, Codes of Ethics, and Situational Ethics rubric provides media practitioners (and

rubric

An Ethics Rubric

E *Evaluate*
The ethical situation needs to be examined in a number of different ways, not just from a single perspective. Though it is important to consider a creator's intention and goals, do not simply buy into one person's point of view. Take the time to analyze.

T *Truth*
Make sure you have a clear definition of the facts as well as a definition that can be agreed upon by others. The truth is not always black and white. In a world where exaggeration seems to be the norm, it is often difficult to get to the essential truth.

H *Harm*
Consider what harm is likely to ensue from a given action. Real-world situations are involved, and media rumors can ruin lives. Stop to evaluate negative outcomes that can ensue, even from seemingly ethical decisions. Of course, intentional harm should similarly be evaluated.

I *Investigation*
Investigation involves going beyond a cursory review and digging deep to gather the necessary information. Do not fall into the trap of getting there first and getting it wrong. This holds especially true for news, but it is applicable elsewhere.

C *Codes of Ethics*
Codes provide valuable guidelines that can facilitate ethical decision making. Before you make a final determination about a course of action, it's wise to pause to check if there's a code of ethics that addresses the case in question.

S *Situational Ethics*
Approach issues on a case-by-case basis that allows you to adjust ethical beliefs to meet a particular situation. Doing so creates a sensitivity to a set of particular circumstances and avoids the tendency to rush to judgment based on other, possibly very different cases.

Exhibit 12.3
An easy-to-remember method for dealing with ethical situations.

ZOOM IN: **Ethical Decisions Gone Awry**

Most ethical decisions never come to the fore. The people making them come to the right decision and life goes on. When the decisions go awry, however, they receive publicity and scrutiny. Here are four such decisions.

The people at NBC news were faced with a tough ethical decision in the spring of 2007 when the network received a package of video, photographs, and writings from Cho Seung-Hui, the gunman who killed people on the campus of Virginia Tech. Staffers disagreed about what to do with the material; the debate was about weighing the value of the material as vital information versus the perception of glorifying a madman. In the end, the network aired an edited video of Cho's rantings and some stills of him looking threatening. For the most part, the network received negative feedback from the public for its decision to air any of the material.

Don Imus made a personal decision in 2007 when he called the Rutgers women's basketball team "nappy-headed hos." Known for a series of sexist and racist comments, Imus said he was just trying to make a sarcastic point. But the description lost him his jobs on CBS radio and MSNBC. About a year later, however, he returned to work with a new show on WABC-AM.

Shock DJs Andy and Opie also lost their jobs at WNEW-FM in New York when, in 2002, they broadcast a live account of a couple allegedly having sex in St. Patrick's Cathedral. This stunt was part of a regular feature on the show in which couples could win a trip by having sex in risky places, but the public and station management thought a place of worship was ethically tasteless.

In 2011 some staffers at NBC decided to edit the Pledge of Allegiance in a piece about the U.S. Open Golf Tournament. In a montage of students reciting the pledge, which was intercut with patriotic images, the staffers cut out the words "under God," "one nation," and "indivisible." The complaints, especially those in the form of tweets, came immediately. NBC quickly apologized and said that the decision to edit the pledge, made by a small group of people, was a bad decision.

St. Patrick's Cathedral.

students) with a comprehensive way to analyze what is at stake ethically so that they can make reasoned decisions.[5]

12.3 Ethical Considerations

Making ethical decisions within the fast-paced communications industry is not easy. It involves heavy thinking regarding such subjects as fairness, taste, conflict of interest, trust, and accuracy. Individuals within all facets of life have a responsibility to act in an ethical manner, but the burden is often greater within the electronic media because they are so visible.

Most of the ethical decisions those engaged in electronic media must make involve their responsibilities to their audience. For example, audiences believe that the news they are receiving is actually news, but if they hear that a network has given an airplane ride to an important person in the news and then received an exclusive interview with that person, they can question the efficacy of the news.[6]

toward audience

In addition to ethical actions toward the audience, media practitioners must also consider ethical practices toward each other. Many "deals" are made in the entertainment business, and if the agreements arrived at are not honored, individual and corporate credibility suffers. People want to do business with other people who keep their word, but sometimes in the rush to make the deal, ethics becomes a low priority. Once people know each other and trust that they will act ethically, they don't need to check details as carefully as they would with new people. This makes it harder for new people to break into the business because people like to work with those they already trust, and it makes it extremely important that someone act ethically when hired for the first time. An easy way to destroy career potential is to gossip about a show's star or divulge a show's plot lines in a blog.

toward others

The temptation for unethical practices is great within the field. Hollywood has always had a reputation for living outside the bounds of morality. The entertainment business is one in which a few people can get rich very fast, legitimately. Many other people who want to get rich fast are walking the thin line between right and wrong. This does not justify unethical behavior, but it makes it seem more acceptable because "everyone is doing it." An aspiring actor who knows that a competitor received a part in a movie because his uncle is a friend of the producer may feel justified in telling people he once played Hamlet, even though it was just a short scene in his high school English class. Movie studios sometimes "overestimate" their box office take to appear to beat the competition. One studio created a fake critic and several fake fans to hype its movies.[7]

temptations

Ethical decisions are not clear-cut. Deciding to do something may harm one segment of society while deciding not to may harm another. For example, condom advertisements on TV are opposed by people who say the ads promote promiscuity and favored by people who say stations' refusal to air the ads hinders progress in the control of teenage pregnancies and AIDS.

murkiness

Many media-related ethical decisions, especially those concerning broadcast journalism, must be made quickly and without complete information. When a person holding hostages calls the news director of a station and threatens to kill the hostages unless allowed to broadcast demands immediately, the news director does not have time to read the ethics manual or hold a meeting with the station's top management. The news director does not know what the demands will be. Perhaps they will involve the threat to kill more people, thus making the situation worse. Providing airtime may lead others who are unbalanced to demand airtime; however, if the airtime is not given, the hostages may be killed. This is a no-win ethical situation.

speed and pressure

Exhibit 12.4

News Corp. CEO Rupert Murdoch, who built a worldwide media empire from an Australian newspaper he inherited from his father, finds himself involved in a major phone tapping scandal that has destroyed parts of his company and the lives of some of his most trusted employees.

Sometimes important decisions must be made in situations where there is a great deal of pressure. A network pulled an episode of *Law & Order* after Procter & Gamble canceled its advertising on the show because it didn't like content that dealt with the accidental shooting of a child. Responsible programming or caving into pressure?[8]

Sometimes the pressure comes internally—for example, if a news department wants a scoop. Rupert Murdoch's massive multimedia company, News Corp., is involved in a major scandal involving phone hacking (see Exhibit 12.4). Reporters are accused of making illegal taps into phones of celebrities, politicians, members of the British royal family, and victims of crime in order to gain information about their private lives that could then be printed in the British tabloid, *News of the World*. They also stand accused of bribing the police for information and obtaining it in other unsavory ways. The company has admitted to many of the crimes, apologized, and shut down *News of the World*. Top managers, who have been investigated for knowing about the wire tapping and even encouraging it, have lost their jobs and been arrested. Rupert Murdoch and his son James have been asked tough questions by members of the British Parliament, and Murdoch withdrew his bid to obtain a satellite company because of the scandal. Reporters often started with minor ethical breaches, such as befriending a celebrity and talking him/her into having a picture taken in a bar. The unethical actions escalated to illegalities that went undiscovered for years but eventually caused a major downfall for individuals and the company.[9]

scoops

thin line

Sometimes there can be a thin line between an ethical slip and a joke or a promotion campaign. For example, in 2004, when filmmaker M. Night Shyamalan had a new film, *The Village,* coming out, he and the Sci Fi Channel tried to develop a marketing stunt by creating a documentary that supposedly contained information about Shyamalan's life that he did not want revealed. They issued press releases about a rift between the filmmaker and the documentarians when, in reality, there was no rift or revealing information. It was all a hoax.[10]

time and place

Ethical decisions can also vary depending on time and geography. The ethics involved in deciding whether to air a program on child pornography at 3:00 in the afternoon could be quite different from the factors that go into deciding whether to air that program at 11:00 at night. A news story about a man in St. Louis who has unusual ways of extracting sexual favors from women might be exploitatively titillating when aired in Denver. It might even cause copycat crimes. If aired in St. Louis, however, the story can help protect women by letting them know the man's procedures.

technology

Technological advances make for ever-changing ethical dilemmas because they make possible things no one had thought of previously. For example, computer technology now allows for parts of a picture to be removed and something else inserted, a procedure that couldn't be done in times past. When CBS was covering the millennium celebrations, it placed a CBS "virtual" billboard into Times Square—replacing a real NBC sign. Was this an ethical breach, a prank, or a creative use of technology? Technologies that have been around for a long time, such as simple editing, also have ethical ramifications. Showing a cutaway of someone chewing nervously on a pencil can give a news story a different slant than showing the same person smiling.[11]

Something may appear unethical to a certain group of people that genuinely appears ethical to the person engaged in it. For example, a salesperson may sell a package of station ads to a particular diet company. This diet is attacked by a group of health food store owners as being useless or even harmful. Both the person selling the ad and the station have a great deal to lose monetarily if the diet commercial is removed. In addition, the salesperson may have used the diet and believes it works well. The health food store owners may be against the diet because it takes business away from them. Continuing to air the ads, although this may appear unethical to many, may at worst be confusing. **mixed opinions**

Entertainment companies are businesses and have an obligation to shareholders to maximize profits. Given that violence sells, movie producers sometimes highlight a violent scene in a movie trailer even though that may be the only violence in the movie. Is this a deception or just clever marketing that will sell tickets and thus enhance profits? Reality TV is a money-maker, to some extent because it exploits people who are weak or mentally ill or who have an obsessive need for fame. When the husband of a woman who was appearing on *The Real Housewives of Beverly Hills* committed suicide, the producers and the industry as a whole took stock of how reality TV might be affecting people—but the show went on.[12] **profits**

Sometimes conflicting loyalties affect ethical decisions. A reporter who learns of infidelity on the part of a political candidate can find that the decision about whether or not to report the information cuts across loyalties to him/herself, the employer, the audience, a political party, the nation, and an ideological stand. If the reporter releases the information, his or her stature as an investigative journalist will increase, the station or network involved can boast of a scoop, and the audience will be informed about a character trait of the candidate. The reporter, however, may be a member of the same political party as the candidate and may believe the nation will suffer if this candidate is not elected. The reporter may also think that private sex life has nothing to do with the ability to govern. **conflicting loyalties**

Ethical decisions are rarely easy, but being unable to resolve an ethical issue doesn't mean you shouldn't grapple with it. See how you and your classmates would handle the ethical dilemmas posed in Exhibit 12.5. Sometimes hindsight makes ethical decisions look easy. But because of lack of facts, peer pressure, the desire to succeed financially, and genuine differences of opinion, deciding what is right in a particular circumstance can be difficult. Ethics is basically doing the right thing from a moral point of view when decision making is required. In fact, sometimes good ethics is nothing more than good manners.

Exhibit 12.5

Here are a few examples of situations that involve ethical decision making. Read them, decide what you would do, and discuss them with others. The situations cover a variety of aspects of the communications business because no facet of the business is exempt from ethical problems.

Ethical Problems

1   You are the producer for a potential new TV series call *The New Hit*. You have talked to the network about this show and indicated several leading ladies that you think you could obtain. The network executives responded most favorably to Betty Bigname, so you make a concerted effort to hire her. But her agent tells you there is no way; she is overcommitted. You pursue your second choice, Mary Mediumname. She is available and eager for the part. The network gives you the go-ahead to make a pilot with Mary Mediumname, but you can tell the executives are not as excited about the series as they were when they thought Betty Bigname would star. But you sign Mary to a contract and begin planning the production. One day Betty Bigname's agent calls and says the major movie Betty was to star in fell through, so she is now available for your series. You know that legally you can buy out Mary—pay her what she would have earned but don't use her. Since she really wants the part, she will probably drive a hard bargain. You would then be paying for two leading ladies. In addition, Mary's public relations firm issued a great deal of publicity saying she will be starring in this pilot. What do you do?

2   You are the salesperson for radio station KICK. Last month you sold a large package of ads to the Goody Food Restaurant. This earned you your biggest commission ever. You want Goody Food to buy an even more lucrative package of ads, but the manager is stalling because she doesn't think the ads she bought did much good. You hit on an idea. You could call some of your friends and have them make reservations at Goody Food, making sure to mention that they heard an ad on KICK. You could then call the manager and ask again if she wants the ads. Of course, your friends could later cancel their reservations, but not until you had the ad deal signed. Should you do this?

3   You are the assistant to the president of an internet company. At a company party the president, to whom you are somewhat attracted, becomes a little drunk and asks you to go out with him/her. What should you say? A little later in the evening, after he/she has had a few more drinks, he/she asks you for a ride home. What should you do?

4   As a news reporter, you are covering the death of a famous rock star who died under mysterious circumstances. The other members of the rock group, who probably know how the rock star actually died, will not talk to reporters. The anchor at your station suggests you pose as someone from the coroner's office and see if you can get the rock group members to talk to you. How would you react to this suggestion?

5   You are producing a commercial for a vitamin company. One suggestion for the production is to juxtapose a shot of the vitamin bottle next to a bodybuilding champion. You have no proof that taking the vitamins will make anyone look like this champion, so you will not say anything on the audio track to imply or disclaim a relationship between the two. Is it all right to produce the commercial this way?

6   You and a friend made a video in which you are horsing around, cracking off-color jokes, and pretending you are co-hosts of a late-night talk show. When you watch your video, it is actually funny, so you put it on YouTube. It is starting to gain a following, and you have even had an inquiry from the booking agent of a stand-up comedy club where you have been wanting to appear. But the next day your friend pleads with you to take the video off YouTube. She has applied for a job as an elementary school teacher and fears the principal who interviewed her will search the internet, find the video, and decide not to hire her. Should you take down the video, try to convince her that the principal probably won't find it and that it won't hurt her if it is found, tell her your career is more important than hers, or find some other solution?

12.4 Effects of Media

The influence that media exert on our society is extensive. The mere ability to **influence** communicate instantaneously affects the process of communication. Beyond this, the permeation of opinions, emotions, and even fads can often be attributed to various elements of the media.

Sometimes communications practitioners try to downplay the effect they have on society, especially when they are under attack for their violent programming. They say that no one takes what they report in the news, dramatize in movies, or show in video games seriously enough for it to affect anyone's actions. However, they weaken their own argument when, in the next breath, they tell advertisers how effective commercials are at getting people to buy products.

A number of people have blamed media for deaths. The families of victims **accusations** of the Columbine High School shootings filed a lawsuit against several companies that create video games and sex-oriented websites. They cited a home videotape of the teenage shooters with one holding a shotgun he called "Arlene," after a character in the *Doom* video game. In several court cases, indicted murderers used "television intoxication" as a contributing factor in their defense. They claimed (unsuccessfully) that they committed brutal acts because of things they saw on television.[13]

Not all media effects are considered bad, however. Radio and television pro- **positive effects** grams cause people to evaluate social problems. Whether the evaluations lead to the proper conclusions depends on one's point of view, but electronic media expose the issues. Portions of documentaries and dramas have been played before Congress to obtain funding for such causes as AIDS and the homeless. Showing footage of starving children in Africa helped develop a climate for approving humanitarian aid.

One problem with determining the effects electronic media have on individ- **ubiquity** uals is that it is essentially impossible to isolate media from other aspects of society. Gone are the days when researchers could find a group of people who never watched TV to compare with a group that did. Many other aspects of society—family, church, school, friends—reinforce, influence, or reflect effects that can also be attributed to media. Despite this, many people and organizations investigate the effects of electronic media and have deep-seated opinions about these effects.

12.5 Organizations That Consider Effects

As already indicated, the communications industry considers the effects of its programming through self-imposed codes and standards. Government agencies also consider effects—Congress through its hearings on such subjects as violence and news, the FCC through its regulations such as those dealing with obscenity. Critics who write reviews of TV programs, movies, and video games for newspapers and magazines sometimes address both positive and negative effects that they think the materials will create. Two other entities that are involved with effects are citizen groups and academic institutions.

Exhibit 12.6

Michael Moore's film *Fahrenheit 9/11* galvanized political sides.

TV-focused

other focuses

12.5a Citizen Groups

Many national citizens' organizations are critical of the role of media in society. Some of these are organized specifically to affect television programming. For example, Action for Children's Television (ACT), founded by a group of Boston parents, had as its mission the improvement of children's programming. Media Research Center's main objective is to neutralize the impact of what it sees as broadcasting's liberal bias on the American political scene.

Other organizations have their own larger agendas but see the media as having a major role in helping them reach their goals. For example, the National Organization for Women (NOW) is vocal about the portrayal of women on TV, the sexist lyrics of songs heard on the radio, and the large number of sex sites on the internet. The National Association for the Advancement of Colored People (NAACP) speaks out about the portrayals of minorities on TV. The Parent-Teacher Association (PTA) and the American Medical Association (AMA) both have objected to violent programming. The left-leaning organization MoveOn.org applauded Michael Moore's film *Fahrenheit 9/11* (see Exhibit 12.6) and its stated purpose of helping to get President Bush out of the White House, while right-leaning organizations condemned it.[14]

12.5b Academic Institutions

purpose

Much of the research on the effects of electronic media comes from professors at colleges and universities (see Exhibit 12.7). These studies are scientific and supposedly unbiased and are usually undertaken with the intent of adding to the overall basic knowledge of the effects of media on society. Citizens' groups, broadcasters, and government agencies often use the studies to support their points of view or guide their actions.

techniques

Academicians use a wide variety of techniques when they undertake research. Some studies are conducted in a **laboratory** setting (people might be brought to a university classroom where they are given a pretest about their feelings toward Native Americans, shown a movie about Native Americans, and then given a posttest on their feelings); others involve **field research** (researchers might interview family members and observe them watching TV in their own homes to determine whether fathers, mothers, or children are most likely to decide what TV programs are watched). Sometimes they involve **surveys** (radio station programmers might be sent questionnaires about their tweets that are then analyzed to determine, among other things, whether music stations or news stations have the most Twitter followers). Research can also involve **content analysis** (researchers might view video games and count the number of male versus female characters).

As with audience measurement (see Chapter 10), academic research can be divided into **quantitative** and **qualitative.** In a quantitative research study, a researcher might count the number of times each family member pushes the remote control button to change the channel. The number of button pushings could then be studied statistically to compare it with other factors, such as family income. The researcher's **hypothesis** that children are more likely to control what is seen on TV in high-income families than in low-income families could then be mathematically substantiated or rejected. Qualitative research would take place, however, if the researcher interviewed the families and obtained anecdotal information that led to the conclusion that children are more likely to decide what the family watches on TV when they are tired and grumpy than when they are in good spirits.

Research is often biographical, historical, or aesthetic in nature. A biographical study of Senator Joseph McCarthy's relationship with media before he started his **blacklisting** inquiries might give insight into actions that could prevent this type of activity from recurring. A historical study of detergent commercials through the years can reveal a great deal about changing social mores. A study of the films of John Ford can uncover particular characteristics of his directing techniques. Some studies try to determine **cause and effect:** Does listening to antipolice lyrics cause people to lower their opinions of the police? Others look at **uses and gratifications:** What are the primary reasons people use smartphones—convenience, mobility, relaxation?[15]

Academicians also develop models to explain media functions and effects. Exhibit 12.8 shows one such model. It illustrates communication as an ongoing process that includes a source, a message, a channel, a receiver, barriers, and feedback. The **source** includes the people who decide what is sent out to others. In the case of the internet, anyone in the world with access to a computer can act as a source. For many media forms, such as movies, the source is a group of people—actors, directors, writers, cinematographers, producers. Some people are more important than others in terms of their influence on what is communicated. For example, the people who decide which news will be seen on CNN have more influence than the camera operator for a corporate video on fixing a carburetor. People, such as news directors, who decide what a large number of other people will see or hear are often referred to as **gatekeepers** (see Chapters 1 and 8).

The people who act as the source are concerned with sending a **message** that has a purpose. Some messages are intended to inform, some are designed to entertain, and some are planned to persuade. Messages are transmitted through **channels.** For electronic media, some of the most common channels are radio, broadcast and cable TV, the phone, and the internet. Various devices and processes can influence the effectiveness of a channel. For example, instant replay, which is possible on the TV medium, enables sportscasting to communicate to the fans in ways that other channels, such as radio, cannot.

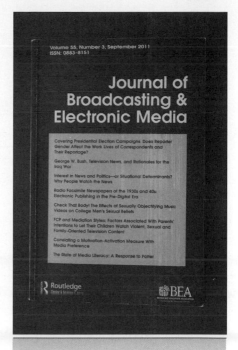

Exhibit 12.7

Journal of Broadcasting & Electronic Media is one of the main academic journals that publish the research of college professors in this field.

types of research

source

message

channel

Exhibit 12.8
Communication
model.

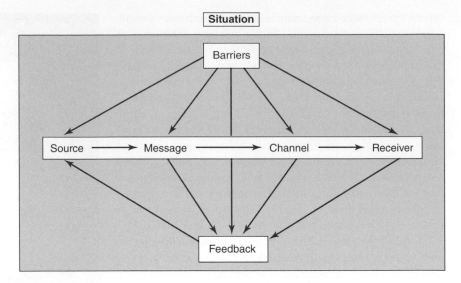

receiver

The **receiver** of the message is the audience. For some forms of telecommunications, primarily broadcast TV, the audience is a composite of individuals that is generally large, heterogeneous, and fairly anonymous. Cable systems that **narrowcast** are seeking a more homogeneous audience. For corporate video, the receiver might be even narrower—for example, the people who sell a new line of women's clothes. For email or tweets, the receiver is often only one person.

barriers

Many **barriers,** sometimes referred to as **noise,** can obstruct the communication process or reduce its effectiveness. The source can have built-in physical or psychological barriers. For example, if all the people making a movie live and work in California, they may not have a proper frame of reference to design a product that will communicate to people in Vermont. Messages also have barriers. A poorly written joke may not entertain. An informational piece delivered in Spanish will not communicate to someone who does not understand that language. A campaign speech intended to persuade might only inform. A message can be distorted simply because information presented on radio or TV takes on added importance.

The receiver, too, is affected by many barriers. Some of these are in the receiver's background or environment. For example, a person who has lived in France might perceive a program about French politics in an entirely different way from a person who has never even visited France. A person playing a video game in a hot room might react differently from someone playing in a cold room. Interruptions or distractions, such as a child crying or a cell phone call that cuts off, can also be barriers for the receiver.

feedback

The message, channel, and receiver all serve as foundations of **feedback** to the source. For example, if no one laughs at a joke during rehearsal, this can be a signal to the creator that it is not funny. Managers of affiliated radio and TV stations often express their opinions to the people who provide the network programs.

Email and text messaging involve frequent feedback, with the source and the receiver switching roles as each exchange occurs. Through ratings and social media interactions, receivers can alter the decisions made by the source, as is evidenced by the cancellation of shows with poor ratings. There are also barriers to feedback. People can laugh out of politeness, not bother to complain, or fill out a rating form incorrectly.[16]

12.6 High-Profile Effects

Individuals, organizations, and academicians consider many topics related to the effects of communications—how and why people use the internet to acquire political information, the puritanical impulses of David Lynch's films, the role of women in radio during World War II, the structure of China's national television market, partisan balance in local TV election coverage, public radio's culture coverage, the relationship of cell phones to brain tumors, how sports fans differ from fans of other forms of programming.[17]

topics

Some of the subjects related to possible effects of communications are discussed and studied more than others. Primary among these are violence, children and media, women and minorities, sex, and news.

12.6a Violence

Violence in media is highly criticized, especially when the violence seems gratuitous. Movie previews on DVDs are deemed too violent. The internet comes under attack for websites that teach how to build bombs. The violence depicted in music videos is decried, especially since their target audience is the age group that instigates much of the violent behavior in society. The same goes for violent lyrics played on radio and violent video games. There is debate as to how much violence news programs need to show. Sports programming is accused of inciting fired-up men to beat up on their significant others; battered women's crisis centers report that for victims of domestic violence, Super Bowl day is one of the worst days of the year.[18]

examples

Congress has investigated violence many times. As far back as 1950, Senator Estes Kefauver suggested in the U.S. Senate that there was too much violence on TV. A major outcry arose in 1963 after the assassination of President Kennedy with claims being made that violence on TV led to the possibility of assassination. In 1972, the Surgeon General issued a report stating that the causal relationship between violent TV and antisocial behavior was sufficient to merit immediate attention. Hardly anyone paid immediate attention, but a growing protest against violence reached a crescendo in 1977, leading to network program changes that led to diminished protest. During the 1980s, the subject of violence was resurrected by Reverend Jerry Falwell, head of the Moral Majority, and Reverend Donald Wildmon, who organized the Coalition for Better Television. They took credit for the fact that several advertisers canceled sponsorship of violent programs. In 1992, the Senate and the networks reached an agreement under which the networks would receive a three-year exemption from antitrust laws in return for curbing violence on the tube. The networks did very little, so in 1993

history

Capitol Hill was once again summoning TV network leaders asking them to void their programs of violence. The networks (both broadcast and cable) responded by agreeing to put violence warnings on the air before showing programs that they deemed to be heavily violent. But very few shows were so deemed. In 1996, Congress passed legislation that mandated V-chips in new television sets so that parents could block out violence. Very few people used these chips, but violence complaints continued. In 2007, the FCC issued a report suggesting powers that Congress could give the FCC, so it could curb violence, but Congress has done little to implement the recommendations.[19]

measurement problems

Innumerable studies have been conducted concerning violence, but they have built-in problems. Measuring violence is not like measuring cups of sugar. Is pushing someone in front of a runaway cactus the same violent act as pushing someone in front of a car? Is it violent for one cartoon character to push another off a cliff when the one pushed soars through the air and arrives at the bottom with nothing injured but pride? Should a heated argument be treated the same as a murder? Is it worse to sock a weak old woman than a young virile man? Should a gunfight be considered one act of violence, or should each shot of the gun be counted?

indexes

Despite all these measurement pitfalls, indexes abound in an attempt to tell whether media violence is increasing or decreasing. One of the oldest violence-measuring systems was developed by Professor George Gerbner of the University of Pennsylvania. He trained observers watching one week of TV fare a year to count acts of violence according to his complicated formula. The networks took offense at some of the acts he called violent, such as comedic violence, and commissioned a study through UCLA. That university did not give the networks much credit for curbing violence either. The National Citizens' Committee for Broadcasting, somewhat with tongue in cheek, developed a "violence index" that calculated how many years each broadcast network would spend in jail if convicted of all the crimes it portrayed in one week—the range was from 1,063 to 1,485 years.[20]

theories

Measurement is not the only pitfall connected with violence. The effect of violence on society is also debated and hard to determine. Some people who subscribe to the **catharsis theory** say it can be good for people to watch violence. Watching it can provide a vicarious thrill that gives people the excitement they need in their lives and stifles their urges to actually act in a violent manner. Other people hold to the **observational theory**—violent programming incites people to commit crimes and shows them how to do it. They point to numerous copycat crimes in which someone has committed a crime very much like one shown in a movie or on TV. Some researchers have investigated the **mean world syndrome**—the fear that people have about undertaking their daily tasks because they think, from watching TV, movies, and the internet, that the world is a much more violent place than it actually is. Still others look at the **desensitizing effect**—watching violence makes people think that actual violence isn't such a bad thing (see "Zoom In" box).[21]

points of view

The bottom line is that violent programming sells. People watch it and advertisers buy time on it. Networks say they are just giving the people what they

ZOOM IN: **Violence Results and Counter-Results**

Many research projects and surveys about violence have been conducted, the findings of which are generally severely (perhaps even violently) challenged by both friends and foes of TV fare. Some of the results are enlightening.

1. People who watch violence on a large screen show greater tendencies toward aggressive behavior than do those who watch on a small screen.
2. The inclusion of humor in a program dampens the tendency toward aggressive behavior on the part of the viewer.
3. Cartoons have more acts of violence in them than do dramas.
4. Men are more likely than women to seek out violent programming and more likely to enjoy it.
5. The more frequently children watch TV at age 8, the more serious are the crimes they are convicted of by age 30.
6. There is little difference between news programs that contain only nonviolent news and ones that contain both violent and nonviolent

items in terms of increased inclination toward aggression on the part of viewers.

7. The more children identify with violent characters in a program, the greater is their inclination toward aggression.
8. There is little correlation between what children consider to be violent acts and what mothers consider to be violent acts.
9. Four out of 10 people believe that watching violence is harmful to the general public and to children in particular.
10. Hardly anyone believes that watching violence hurts him or her personally.

want and that stifling violent programming is against the First Amendment. Many government agencies, individuals, and organizations believe that media program suppliers should invoke their collective ethical conscience and keep violent material off the channels.

12.6b Children and Media

Much of the discussion and research related to children and media involves violence. The people and organizations that speak out against violence in general usually are especially vocal about the negative effects violence has on children. As already indicated, the scientific research yields conflicting results. The preponderance of research, however, indicates that media violence is bad for children, especially those already predisposed toward aggressive behavior.

In one study, sixth graders were divided into three groups. One group acted as a control and was not shown any television. The other two groups were shown a *Woody Woodpecker* cartoon in which Woody knocks a man unconscious. One group was simply shown the cartoon; the other was told to think about the feelings of the man while they were watching. The children who were told to think

violence

ZOOM IN: **Kids and Media**

Here are some other results of research involving children and media.

1. Children do learn reading and vocabulary from TV, but the children who watch TV the most and children who play video games the most are the ones who perform the worst in school.
2. Children three and younger understand very little of what they watch on TV, yet they sometimes sit mesmerized before the set.
3. White (but not black) adolescents who have a TV in the bedroom are at greater odds of initiating health risk behaviors, such as cigarette smoking and sexual intercourse, than are white adolescents who do not have a TV in the bedroom.
4. Of children ages 8 to 18, 92 percent play video games and 8.5 percent of them can be classified as addicted in that their play interferes with other aspects of their lives.
5. When asked to name their favorite TV character, almost all boys select a male, but only half the girls select a female.
6. It is difficult for children to understand time leaps in television programming, but children who watch the most TV understand them the best.
7. More TV ads are aimed at boys than at girls.
8. Children develop attitudes about alcohol based on what they see on TV, but these attitudes are also formed by what their parents do.

about feelings liked the man better and thought the violence was less funny than either of the other groups.[22]

other subjects   A great deal besides violence is studied in relation to children and media, given that an estimated 4,000+ studies have dealt with the subject (see "Zoom In" box). For example, one study examined Nickelodeon's *Dora, the Explorer* to assess the extent to which the show empowered preschoolers, girls, and Latinas. Studies that have been conducted on childhood obesity have found that it correlates with video game playing.[23]

parents   Another area that is frequently discussed concerning children and media is the role of parents. Network executives hold that parents are the ones who should control and influence their children's use of media, but parents point out that they are not always with their children when they are using media and that radio, TV networks, and internet sites should take responsibility for including material that is healthy for children's minds and emotions. The government gets in and out of the middle of this debate in fairly regular cycles, regulating and deregulating aspects of children's programming and commercials. Research studies that attempt to assess the extent to which parents control what their children listen to and look at show that such involvement is not universal. However, they also reveal that if parents talk to their children about media, they can improve their children's ability to learn and shape their attitudes toward how they use media.[24]

Electronic media are very much a part of the home. As such, they touch the lives of children at least as much as those of adults. The effects of media on children have been subjected to a great deal of research and dialogue, but thought and discussion regarding these effects are bound to continue because of the importance of the values and behavior of future generations.

12.6c Women and Minorities

Also receiving extensive consideration regarding the effects of media is the area of women and minorities. Some scholars study the ways that women and minorities use media. One study, for example, found that when women are in a bad mood, they prefer media (specifically, music) that are not involving or absorbing so that they can think about their stress, whereas men tend to distract themselves with high-absorbing messages.[25]

uses and portrayals

Most of the research, and the controversy, about women and minorities involves how these groups are portrayed on television and in films (see Exhibit 12.9). Highly criticized is the portrayal of minority groups that conveys negative **stereotypes**—the doddering old man, the lazy Mexican American, the servile African American, the brawny lesbian, the subservient wife. Largely as a result of criticism and research, radio, TV, and movies have corrected many of their blatant stereotypes. For example, studies of the 1970s found that very few African Americans were portrayed as professionals or managers; studies of the 1990s found that African Americans and European Americans were equally likely to be portrayed in those categories.[26]

Another issue related to women and minorities is that they are underrepresented. This criticism often emanates from Chicano, Asian American, Native American, African American, and physically disabled actors who have trouble finding work. Criticism of underrepresentation, however, also affects the self-esteem and inclusion feelings of viewers. Children, for example, who do not see people who look like them on TV feel left out and are not able to build positive TV role models.[27]

12.6d Sex

An issue closely related to women is the portrayal of sex on various media platforms. This subject, like violence, is a perennial thorn. Sexual permissiveness,

Exhibit 12.9

During the 1950s, most women on TV, such as June Cleaver of *Leave It To Beaver,* were portrayed as loving, calm, protective, nurturing, happily married, stay-at-home mothers. By the 1970s, women were resentful of these portrayals and wanted to be shown in more aggressive out-of-home roles. It took a while, however, for the concept of working women to be incorporated into TV scripts.

both in society and on the screen, has increased over the years. The V-neck dresses that raised eyebrows during the 1950s are considered modest by today's standards. Television drama has broached sexually sensitive subjects, such as homosexuality and incest, usually to the instant outcry of critics. But the hue and cry dies down, and the networks go on to challenge another taboo.

type and amount   Both the type and amount of sex depicted draw fire. The barrage of sexual innuendos on sitcoms, the bedroom scenes in movies, the titillating "news stories" about prostitutes, the sexual setups of reality shows, the abundance of sex sites on the internet, the use of sexy women as targets in video games—all are decried. Radio talk shows, which periodically rediscover sex, receive a great deal of criticism and some government regulatory restrictions. After quieting down, the subject once again emerges. The lyrics of rock music aired on radio and the semiclad, sensuous women seen in music videos are criticized by public-interest groups. When sex is combined with violence against women, it receives some of its strongest criticism because of the fear of copycat crimes and a belief that such material desensitizes men in general to act against women.[28]

promiscuity   One of the main criticism of sex centers on the idea that people, seeing so much sex, become promiscuous. Research has born this out. For example, one study showed that exposure to sexually explicit music videos was associated with more permissive attitudes toward premarital sex and stronger endorsement of the sexual double standard, regardless of gender, overall TV viewing, or previous sexual experience.[29]

In addition, researchers theorize that the sex shown on TV and in movies is idealized and makes people feel cheated or inadequate in relation to their own sex lives. The media enhance sexual expectations that reality does not meet. Showing (or even talking about) sex can be negatively instructive, teaching young children **safe sex**   things they shouldn't know. Studies also deal with the depiction of safe sex. For example, in one research study, one group of college students was shown a program with sexual intercourse that depicted the use of condoms, another group was shown a program with sexual intercourse but no condoms, and the third group was shown a program with no sexual content. The women who saw the show with the condoms then had a more positive attitude toward condom use than the women in either of the other groups, but there was no significant difference among men in the three groups. Despite the outcries against sex in the media, it, like violence, continues because sex sells.[30]

12.6e News

sensationalism   Much of the research and discussion concerning news is tied to the types of stories shown on the news. People decry sensationalism, such as the showing of dead bodies and flaming automobiles. Other forms of sensationalism also come under attack, such as barging in on grieving relatives or reporting details of rapes. Individual news organizations have policies regarding the depiction of violent and sensational events, but many show a great deal of this material, often at the expense of weightier public-interest subjects such as international relations.[31]

Exhibit 12.10
One study found that news items read by female anchors were perceived to be more credible than those read by males but that male newscasters were considered to be more credible people.

Bias is another concern. Conservatives believe that news is a product of the eastern liberal establishment, and liberals decry the conservative commentators, especially those on radio and Fox TV. Studies show that the nature of radio and TV news presentations can bias audience members, but the studies of evidence of bias are murkier, with many of them concluding that newscasts, as a whole, are not biased toward any particular point of view. As with violence, research techniques used for bias studies have their shortcomings. What one researcher considers a biased story, another might give a clean bill of health.[32]   **bias**

A fair amount of news research is in the uses-and-gratifications category, attempting to learn how and why certain groups of people (senior citizens, working women) use various media forms (cable TV, radio, the internet) to obtain news. This type of research can also explore the impact of different types of stories (serious versus light, long versus short).[33]   **uses and gratification**

Somewhat related is research that explores the effects of various forms of news presentation. Do people remember more about a story if it contains graphics than if it is just read by an anchor? Does the gender or age of a newscaster affect perceived credibility (see Exhibit 12.10)? Do people pay more attention to stories that are preceded by a teaser than stories that are not? What types of sites are most likely to be linked to from news websites?[34]   **presentation**

12.7 Issues and the Future

Most issues related to ethics and effects will be around for a long time. Naysayers predict that ethics are on the way out—or that they have already disappeared. Those among us who have faith in human nature and in future generations believe that people will always be faced with ethical dilemmas but

regulation

that most people will make the right decisions for the right reason most of the time.

Given the nation's two-party checks and balances system, the relationship between regulation and ethics is bound to fluctuate periodically. Sometimes the government leaders are in the mood to regulate actions that at other periods are considered individual ethical issues. The amount of regulation is often tied to the ethical beliefs of those in power.

sex and violence

The issue of violence generates a great deal of heat and no doubt will continue to do so. As in the past, violence will figure in debates about how to program for children, whether to cut down on news sensationalism, and how to depict women in movies and video games. Sexual content, in terms of both talking about sex and showing sexual activity, will also continue to be a thorny issue.

citizens groups

The influence of citizen groups on the media has been a roller-coaster phenomenon. During the 1960s, the groups had a great deal of power, but their influence waned in the 1980s, in part because they lost regulatory battles and in part because people seemed to tire of their watchdog role. However, some current grassroots groups are concerned enough about media effects to try to force reform.

The government, citizen groups, and academicians are turning increased attention to the ethics and effects of the newer platforms. The number of pornographic sites on the internet has caused watchdogs to become alarmed, as has the fact that people using the internet sometimes lure children into sexual encounters. Academic researchers are always looking for new areas to explore, and the newer media lend themselves to unexplored topics. Digital video re-

future studies

corders, smartphones, social media, internet sites, and iPads are all worthwhile topics for future research. Researchers have barely begun to examine how constantly being connected affects the social and intellectual development of young people. Other pertinent future topics could be cyber bullying, online hate speech, and news coverage of health-related issues. In addition, researchers will continue to study further aspects of the array of subjects that they presently study, including violence, children, women and minorities, sex, and news.

12.8 Summary

Ethics and effects are intertwined. Someone who programs a TV network and knows that violence appears to affect children negatively must consider that fact when making programming decisions. The people who develop self-regulation codes, such as the RTDNA one, make provisions for avoiding news bias and negative stereotypes mainly because their sense of ethics leads them in that direction. People who enforce broadcast standards watch for gratuitous sex and unsavory stereotyping in part because it is their job and in part because they want to further ethical standards. Government officials who make laws to try to enforce ethical behavior often do so because of some undesirable effect on society such as hacking or cable TV prices that are too high. The ethics rubric contains principles that can be used to examine how actions might affect audience members and individuals.

Unfortunately, ethical decisions are not always easy. They are hampered by temptations, murkiness, speed, pressures, variations over time and space, technological changes, need for profit, and conflicting loyalties. Citizen groups often have one opinion of right and wrong while industry groups have another.

Academic research, both quantitative and qualitative, helps delineate negative and positive effects and can help with ethical decisions. It can involve a laboratory, field research, surveys, content analysis, cause and effect, and uses and gratifications. Despite measurement shortfalls, a great deal of research is conducted on the issue of violence, with the catharsis, observational, mean world, and desensitizing theories receiving study. Research on children and TV also encompasses the effects of violence, while other studies and comments focus on the responsibility of parents. Research on minorities and women has led to changes in media programming. Research on sex shows negative effects and varying points of view. News research centers on sensationalism, bias, and presentation techniques, but it, too, has violent elements.

Models, most of them formed by academicians, also aid in pinpointing effects. They can, for example, show the role of gatekeepers, barriers, and feedback. Although many resources are available to help people understand effects and make appropriate ethical decisions, in the end it is the innate character of each individual that really counts.

Suggested Websites

www.kff.org/entmedia (the Kaiser Family Foundation, which sponsors research related to media)

www.mediaresearch.org (Media Research Center, a conservative watchdog organization)

www.moveon.org (MoveOn, a liberal watchdog organization)

www.now.org (National Organization for Women, abbreviated NOW)

www.rtdna.org (Radio-Television Digital News Association, abbreviated RTDNA)

Notes

1. "FCC Launches Payola Probes of 4 Radio Giants," *Los Angeles Times,* April 20, 2006, 1; "Stern's Blue Streak Costs Infinity a Cool $1.7 Mil," *Daily Variety,* September 10, 1995, 6; "Cable Price Hike," *Broadcasting & Cable,* October 23, 2000, 29; "Where Have All the "Good" Hackers Gone?" *Mix,* August 2011, 6; and "The Really Smart Phone," *Wall Street Journal,* April 23–24, 2011, C1
2. Radio Television Digital News Association, "Ethics," http://www.rtdna.org/pages/best-practices/ethics.php (accessed December 22, 2011).
3. "Acad Voters Catch a Code," *Daily Variety,* September 4, 2003, 1.
4. "NBC Bashed for Unleashing a Killer's Rants on Its Airwaves," *Los Angeles Times,* April 20, 2007, 1; "Finding a Replacement for Imus Won't Be Easy," *Wall Street Journal,* April 16, 2007,

B1; "FCC Investigates Church Coupling; WNEW Axes DJs," *Hollywood Reporter,* August 23–25, 2002, 1; and "NBC Says Cutting Pledge During U.S. Open Was Bad Decision," http://www.broadcastingcable.com/article/470026.php (accessed December 23, 2011).

5. Philippe Perebinossoff, *Real-World Media Ethics* (Burlington, MA: Focal Press, 2008), 19–21.

6. "It's Time to Drag Checkbook News Into the Open," *Variety,* August 1–2, 2011, 10.

7. "Untruths and Consequences," *Los Angeles Times Calendar,* June 24, 2001, 5.

8. "Wells Scolds CBS for Pulling 'Law' Episode," *Hollywood Reporter,* August 20, 2001, 2

9. "Scandal Reaches to Top at News Corp." *Variety,* July 11, 2011, 2; and "Confessions of a *News of the World* Reporter," *Hollywood Reporter,* July 22, 2011, 10.

10. "Shyamalan Documentary a Hoax, Sci Fi Admits," *Los Angeles Times,* July 19, 2004, E-1.

11. "CBS' Virtual Logos a Real Pain," *Broadcasting & Cable,* January 17, 2000, 20; and "Do New Technologies Create New Ethical Issues?" *Beyond Computing,* June 2000, 10.

12. "A 'Real' Shame," *Los Angeles Times,* September 6, 2011, D-9; and Sarah M. Coyne et al., "Does Reality Backbite? Physical, Verbal, and Relational Aggression in Reality Television Programs," *Journal of Broadcasting and Electronic Media,* June 2010, 282–98.

13. "Columbine Families Sue Game Makers, Web Sites," *Hollywood Reporter,* April 24–30, 2001, 101; and "*Sopranos* Scenario in Slaying?" *Los Angeles Times,* January 28, 2003, B-1.

14. "Kidvid: A National Disgrace," *Newsweek,* October 17, 1983, 81–83; "Media Research Center," http://www.mrc.org/public/default.aspx (accessed December 23, 2011); and "Michael Moore," http://front.moveon.org/?s=Michael+Moore (accessed December 23, 2011).

15. Material dealing with research methodology includes Joy Keiko Asamen and Gordon L. Berry, *Research Paradigms, Television and Social Behavior* (Thousand Oaks, CA: Sage, 1998); and Arthur Asa Berger, *Media and Communication Research Methods* (Thousand Oaks, CA: Sage, 2001).

16. This model is based on Bert E. Bradley, *Fundamentals of Speech Communication* (Dubuque, IA: William C. Brown, 1991), 5.

17. Barbara K. Kaye and Thomas J. Johnson, "Online and in the Know: Uses and Gratifications of the Web for Political Information," *Journal of Broadcasting & Electronic Media,* March 2002, 54–71; Jeff Johnson: Pervert in the Pulpit: The Puritanical Impulse of the Films of David Lynch," *Journal of Film and Video,* Winter 2003, 3–14; Jim Grubbs, "Women Broadcasters of World War II," *Journal of Radio Studies,* June 2004, 40–54; Elaine J. Yuan and Thomas B. Ksiazek, "The Duality of Structure in China's National Television Market: A Network Analysis of Audience Behavior," *Journal of Broadcasting & Electronic Media,* June 2011, 180–97; Sue Carter, Frederick Fico, and Jocelyn S. McCabe, "Partisan and Structural Balance in Local Television Election Coverage," *Journalism and Mass Communication Quarterly,* Winter 2002, 41–53; "Sara Magee, "All Things Cultured: An Analysis of Popular Culture Coverage on National Public Radio's *All Things Considered,*" *Journal of Radio and Audio Media,* May 2011, 47–64; Vini G. Khurana et. al., "Cell Phones and Brain Tumors: A Review Including the Long-term Epidemiologic Data," *Surgical Neurology,* September 2009, 205–14; and Walter Gantz et al., "Sports Versus All Comers: Comparing TV Sports Fans with Fans of Other Programming Genres," *Journal of Broadcasting & Electronic Media,* March 2006, 95–118.

18. Mary Beth Oliver and Sriram Kalyanaraman, "Appropriate for All Viewing Audiences: An Examination of Violent and Sexual Portrayals in Movie Previews Featured on Video Rentals," *Journal of Broadcasting & Electronic Media,* June 2002, 283–99; R. E. Caplan, "Violent Program Content in Music Videos," *Journalism Quarterly,* Spring 1995, 144–47; "Super Violence Comes Home," *Mother Jones,* January 1987, 15; and "Plugged In, but Tuned Out," *Wall Street Journal,* October 6, 2005, D-1.

19. "Simon Introduces TV Violence Bill, *Broadcasting,* March 30, 1987, 148; "The TV Violence Proposal: Let's Get Cynical," *Los Angeles Times,* July 1, 1993, F-1; "TV Violence No Longer a Front-Burner Issue in Washington," *Broadcasting & Cable,* January 23, 1995, 9; "TV Violence in the Cross-Hairs," *Hollywood Reporter,* April 28, 1999, 4; "Lawmakers, Parent Groups Laud Media Violence Findings," *Los Angeles Times,* January 18, 2001, C-1; "Remember the V-chip? TV Guide Cuts Icons," *Daily Variety,* September 16, 2003, 5; and "Violence: The New Indecency?" *Broadcasting & Cable,* January 22, 2007, 18–19.

20. "More Violence Than Ever Says Gerbner's Latest," *Broadcasting,* February 28, 1977, 20; George Gerbner, "Reclaiming Our Cultural Mythology," *The Ecology of Justice,* Spring 1994, 40; and Jack Glascock, "Direct and Indirect Aggression on Prime-Time Network Television," *Journal of Broadcasting & Electronic Media,* June 2008, 268 81.

21. Andrew J. Weaver, "A Meta-Analytical Review of Selective Exposure to and the Enjoyment of Media Violence," *Journal of Broadcasting & Electronic Media,* June 2011, 232–50; W. James Potter and Stacy Smith, "The Context of Graphic Portrayals of Television Violence," *Journal of Broadcasting & Electronic Media,* Spring 2000, 301–23; Nancy Signorielli, "Prime-Time Violence 1993–2001: Has the Picture Really Changed?" *Journal of Broadcasting & Electronic Media,* March 2003, 36–57; and "A New View on TV," *Wall Street Journal,* September 6–7, 2008, 1.

22. Amy I. Nathanson and Joanne Cantor, "Reducing the Aggression-Promoting Effect of Violent Cartoons by Increasing Children's Fictional Involvement with the Victim: A Study of Active Mediation," *Journal of Broadcasting & Electronic Media,* Winter 2000, 125–42.

23. Erin L. Ryan, "*Dora the Explorer*: Empowering Preschoolers, Girls, and Latinas," *Journal of Broadcasting & Electronic Media,* March 2010, 54–68; "Generation Wired," *Parade,* October 9. 2011, 14; Erica Weintraub and Heidi Kay Meili, "Effects of Interpretations of Televised Alcohol Portrayals on Children's Alcohol Beliefs," *Journal of Broadcasting & Electronic Media,* Fall 1994, 417–35; Robert Abelman, "You Can't Get There from Here: Children's Understanding of Time-Leaps on Television," *Journal of Broadcasting & Electronic Media,* Fall 1990, 469–76; Cynthia Hoffer, "Children's Wishful Identification and Para-Social Interaction with Favorite Television Characters," *Journal of Broadcasting & Electronic Media,* Summer 1996, 389–402; Christine Jackson, Hane D. Brown, and Carol J. Pardun, "The TV in the Bedroom: Implications for Viewing Habits and Risk Behaviors during Early Adolescence," *Journal of Broadcasting & Electronic Media,* September 2008, 349–67; and "Facing Off Over Video Games," *Los Angeles Times,* May 3, 2010, E-1.

24. Stacey J. T. Hust, W. Joann Wong, and Yi-Chun Chen, "FCP and Mediation Styles: Factors Associated with Parents' Intentions to Let Their Children Watch Violent, Sexual and Family-Oriented Television Content," *Journal of Broadcasting & Electronic Media,* September 2011, 380–99; Lynne Schafer Gross, Susan Plumb Salas, and Cindy Miller-Perin, "Active Guidance: A Study of the Degree to Which Parents Will Engage in Activities in Order to Enhance Their Involvement in Their Children's TV Viewing," *Journal of Research,* Fall 2003, 20–29; Moniek Buijzen et al., "Parent Versus Child Reports of Parental Advertising Mediation: Exploring the Meaning of Agreement," *Journal of Broadcasting & Electronic Media,* December 2008, 509–25; and Sonia Livingstone and Ellen J. Helsper, "Parental Mediation of Children's Internet Use," *Journal of Broadcasting & Electronic Media,* December 2008, 581–99.

25. Silvia Knobloch-Westerwick, "Gender Differences in Selective Media Use for Mood Management and Mood Adjustment, *Journal of Broadcasting & Electronic Media,* March 2007, 73–92.

26. Martha M. Lauzen, David M. Dozier, and Nora Horan, "Constructing Gender Stereotypes through Social Roles in Prime-Time Television," *Journal of Broadcasting & Electronic Media,* June 2008, 200–214; Tom Robinson and Caitlin Anderson, "Older Characters in Children's Animated Television Programs: A Content Analysis of Their Portrayal," *Journal of Broadcasting & Electronic Media,* June 2006, 287–304; Joan McGettigan, "Interpreting a Man's World: Female Voices in *Badlands* and *Days of Heaven,*" *Journal of Film and Video,* Winter 2001, 33–43; Leigh M. Moscowitz, "Gay Marriage in Television News: Voice and Visual Representation in the Same-Sex Marriage Debate," *Journal of Broadcasting & Electronic Media,* March 2010, 24–39; and Rick Busselle and Heather Crandall, "Television Viewing and Perceptions about Race Differences in Socioeconomic Success," *Journal of Broadcasting & Electronic Media,* June 2002, 265–82.

27. W. H. Anderson, Jr., and B. M. Williams, "TV and the Black Child: What Black Children Say about the Shows They Watch," *Journal of Black Psychology,* Spring 1983, 27–42; "Fewer Women at TV Series Helm," *Hollywood Reporter,* July 19, 2004, 5; and Christina Pieraccini and Douglas Alligood, *Color Television: Fifty Years of African American and Latino Images on Prime-Time Television.* (Dubuque, IA: Kendall/Hunt, 2005).

28. Wanjiri G. Mbure, "Check That Body! The Effects of Sexually Objectifying Music Videos on College Men's Sexual Beliefs, *Journal of Broadcasting & Electronic Media,* September 2011, 360–79; LeeAnn Kahlor and Matthew S. Eastin, "Television's Role in the Culture of Violence Toward Women: A Study of Television Viewing and the Cultivation of Rape Myth Acceptance in the United States," *Journal of Broadcasting & Electronic Media,* June 2011, 215–31; and Mary Beth Oliver et al., "Sexual and Violent Imagery in Movie Previews: Effects on Viewers' Perceptions and Anticipated Enjoyment," *Journal of Broadcasting & Electronic Media,* December 2007, 596–614.

29. Yuanyuan Zhang, Laura E. Miller, and Kristen Harrison, "The Relationship between Exposure to Sexual Music Videos and Young Adults' Sexual Attitudes," *Journal of Broadcasting & Electronic Media,* September 2008, 368–86.

30. Kirstie M. Farrar, "Sexual Intercourse on Television: Do Safe Sex Messages Matter?" *Journal of Broadcasting & Electronic Media,* December 2006, 635–50.

31. Travis L. Dixon, Cristina L. Azocar, and Michael Casas, "The Portrayal of Race and Crime on Television Network News," *Journal of Broadcasting & Electronic Media,* December 2003, 498–523.

32. Renita Coleman, "The Intellectual Antecedent of Public Journalism," *Journal of Communication Inquiry,* Spring 1997, 60–76; and "Cuts at TV-News Divisions Augur Leaner Approach," *Wall Street Journal,* February 26, 2010, B5.

33. Anke Wonneberger, Klaus Schoenbach, and Les van Meurs, "Interest in News and Politics— or Situational Determinants? Why People Watch the News," *Journal of Broadcasting & Electronic Media,* September 2011, 325–43; Carolyn Johnson and Lynne Gross, "Mass-Media Use by Women in Decision-Making Positions," *Journalism Quarterly,* August/September 1985, 850–53; Henry Grunwald, "Opening Up 'Valleys of the Uninformed,'" *Media Studies Journal,* Fall 1993, 29–32; and David Tewksbury, "The Seeds of Audience Fragmentation: Specialization in the Use of Online News Sites," *Journal of Broadcasting & Electronic Media,* September 2005, 332–48.

34. Maria Elizabeth Grabe, et. al., "Covering Presidential Election Campaigns: Does Reporter Gender Affect the Work Lives of Correspondents and Their Reportage?" *Journal of Broadcasting & Electronic Media,* September 2011, 285–306; Itai Himelboim, "The International Network Structure of News Media: An Analysis of Hyperlinks Usage in News Web Sites," *Journal of Broadcasting & Electronic Media,* September 2010, 373–90; " Hao-chieh Chang, "The Effect of News Teasers in Processing TV News," *Journal of Broadcasting & Electronic Media,* Summer 1998, 327–39; and David Weibel, Bartholomaus Wissmath, and Tudolf Groner, "How Gender and Age Affect Newscasters' Credibility," *Journal of Broadcasting & Electronic Media,* September 2008, 466–84.

Chapter 13

TECHNICAL UNDERPINNINGS

The quote about the three-year-old is just one bit of evidence of how much technology changes during the life of just about everyone. We used to communicate in chatrooms; now we communicate with social media. We used to blog; now we tweet. The electronic media are grounded in technology, and although the average person does not need to know exactly how the electrons operate for each media form, everyone needs to understand some basics in order to exist in our technological world. Those who work in media industries need a more thorough knowledge of technical underpinnings so that they can take advantage of innovation and converse with those responsible for it. Engineers, of course, need to be thoroughly versed in electronics. They are the ones who invent and improve the equipment and processes that make telecommunication possible.

One way to look at technical underpinnings is to divide them into production, distribution, and exhibition. Regardless of the form of electronic media used, its messages must be produced utilizing some sort of equipment—microphones,

> A three-year-old goes to the family TV set and swipes. Nothing happens. She turns to her dad and says, "Daddy, the TV is broken."
>
> **Anonymous**

cameras, computers. The production must then be distributed by wired or wireless means—cable TV, satellite TV, the internet, a smartphone. However, the program material is of little use if it simply remains in the distribution pipe; it must be seen and heard through an exhibition device—a radio, a TV set, a computer monitor, a motion picture screen. This chapter is not intended to make anyone an expert in technology, but it should serve as an introduction to the equipment and processes needed to deliver electronic media content.

13.1 Production Overview

digital and analog

technological changes

Today most electronic media programming is produced through **digital** means. But prior to the 1990s, the underlying process used by electronic media was **analog** (see "Zoom In" box). Some media forms, such as radio and movies, are still in the process of converting from analog to digital; others, such as television, have converted recently; and others, such as the internet and DVRs, came to the fore during the digital era and have been digital since their inception.[1]

Changes in technology change production techniques. Some production methods used to be mechanical rather than electronic. For example, audio tape was edited by cutting out unwanted material with a razor blade and then connecting the desired material together with a special adhesive tape. Film was edited in much the same way. Mechanical editing has given way to electronic editing, which allows for more flexibility and effects. **High-definition television** (see Chapter 4) included a different **aspect ratio.** The screen changed from a fairly square one to a wide screen. This brought about changes in how much could be seen on the screen and how items could be placed.

Production equipment used to be bulky, expensive, and temperamental. Only skilled technicians could operate it. Now most people carry a camera with them in their phone—one that sports a much higher quality picture than the professional cameras of the early days of TV. Today there are many different forms of production. Almost anyone can operate a camera well enough to produce acceptable video and sound (see Exhibit 13.1). However, the production process for movies and TV programs is often complicated, sometimes involving hundreds of people who pay careful attention to sets, costumes, sound quality, lighting, and other production elements. In some cases productions that used to be

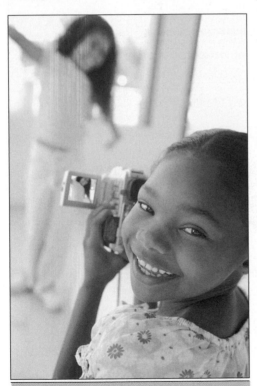

Exhibit 13.1

Even small children can operate video cameras—a big change from years past.

ZOOM IN: **What's the Difference between Analog and Digital?**

The technical difference between digital and analog is that digital utilizes discrete on and off impulses, whereas analog involves a continuous method of signal recognition. Analog is similar to creating a line graph for a statistical analysis. All measurements are on a continuum and the line curves up and down. Digital sound is similar to a person looking at individual numbers and writing them down in a set order. It is, in essence, many samples of the analog signal.

When the analog method is used to take an electronic signal from one place to another (e.g., one recording device to another), the signal changes shape and degrades slightly in quality. This is similar to someone trying to trace a curve on a graph. The reproduction will not be exactly like the original. When the digital method is used to transport the signal, it does not waver. As it travels from one source to another, separate bits of information transmit with little loss of quality. This would compare to someone copying the numbers of the statistical study. The numbers would be copied accurately, so the results would not be distorted.

This gives digital an advantage over analog because material can be dubbed or duplicated with little or no loss of quality. With analog dubbing, colors run together, the picture becomes washed out, and the audio develops hisses and pops. In general, both audio and video signals are sharper and crisper with digital than with analog, even in first generation.

Analog is a continuous wave, whereas digital is a series of discrete samples from the wave that are turned into off-on (0-1) binary numbers.

Cardioid   Omnidirectional

Exhibit 13.2
Two of the most common microphone pickup patterns.

complicated have been simplified. A news reporter used to have a crew of several people. Now that reporter can act as a one-man band—setting up the camera, positioning him/herself in front of it for an interview, handling the microphone, shooting the footage, editing the material on a laptop, and sending the story back to the station over the internet.[2]

Exhibit 13.3
A boom microphone. For movies, a microphone of this type is held by a crew member who moves it above the various actors as each is speaking.

microphones

recorders

13.2 Audio Production

Some of the main equipment used to produce stand-alone audio material (such as radio programs or music concerts) or audio that accompanies video includes microphones, audio players/recorders, and audio boards. **Microphones** convert sound into electronic impulses that can be transmitted through the rest of the equipment. Microphones come in many forms designed for different purposes. For example, some microphones, called **omnidirectional,** pick up sound from all directions, while others, referred to as **cardioid,** pick up mainly from one direction (see Exhibit 13.2). The omnidirectional microphone would be good to use for crowd noises, while the cardioid would be more suited to situations in which one person is talking. Some microphones are designed to pick up the wide range of sounds of musical instruments, whereas others optimize the sound of the human voice. Some are very small—just part of a **chip** in an iPod—whereas others, such as a boom microphone (see Exhibit 13.3), are quite large so that they can pick up dialogue of various people on a movie set.

Audio players and recorders include **compact disc (CD)** players, **memory sticks,** and computer **hard drives.** Sometimes sound goes directly from the microphone to a recorder. The microphone can be built into the recorder, the signal can be sent through wireless means, or the sound is sent through a cable that is connected to the microphone on one end and the recorder on the other. Recorders/players are also used to play back recorded material, such as music and sound effects, so that it can be incorporated into a production.

Audio boards (see Exhibit 13.4) are used to mix various sounds together. For example, an audio production may consist of two people talking (each into a separate microphone) and music coming from a hard drive. All three signals would be sent into an audio board, and an operator could then raise and lower the volume on each so that the music did not overpower the voices and the voices meshed well together. Sound from an audio board can be sent to a recorder, where it can be stored and played back whenever it is needed. Audio boards also have other functions. They can be used to change the quality of a sound (e.g., give a voice an echo so it sounds like it is coming from a cave) or determine which sounds go to the right and left channels of a **stereo** recording.

boards

Exhibit 13.4
An audio board.

For modern digital audio work, the functions of the audio board and the audio recorder are often combined in a computer program. The technician gathers the sounds needed by plugging a microphone directly into a computer, by transferring sound from a memory stick into the computer program, or by downloading sound from an internet site. Then, using the computer program, the technician mixes and edits the sounds into a finished product. The computer programs have innumerable effects, often referred to as **signal processing,** which can be used to enhance and alter the various sounds. Sounds can be stored on individual computers until they are distributed. They can also be stored on large computers called **servers,** some of which may be at a distant location from the production facility, referred to as a **cloud** (see Chapter 6).[3]

computerized production

13.3 Video Production

Video production utilizes all the audio equipment but also requires additional equipment such as cameras, video recorders, switchers, monitors, lights, editors, and visual effects equipment. **Cameras** are at the heart of any video system because they capture the image through a **lens** and send it on to other equipment—in much the same way that a microphone captures sound.

Sometimes picture information is shot with film cameras, which operate in an analog chemical manner. They have a shutter behind the lens that opens and closes to allow the image to reach photosensitive frames of film stock that can later be developed into individual pictures at a laboratory (see Exhibit 13.5). When video cameras were analog, film cameras provided a far superior picture to video. But video cameras that are high-definition digital rival or exceed the quality of film, and many movies and TV shows are now being shot with video (see Exhibit 13.6). Some movies, whether shot with a film camera or a video camera, are produced as **three-dimensional (3-D)** movies. The production process for 3-D usually involves using two cameras that can approximate the vision of two eyes.[4]

cameras

Video cameras often come in a package, known as a **camcorder,** which also includes a recorder. Originally video recorders used tape as the recording

Exhibit 13.6

This video camera, called The Red One, is frequently used to shoot movies.

Exhibit 13.5

A film camera on a pedestal.

medium, but today they are more likely to use discs or hard drives. Cameras can also be separate from their recorders, a configuration that is common in studio situations where several cameras that are wheeled around on **pedestals** capture different angles of the same scene and all the images are sent to a switcher.

switchers

A **switcher** for video is similar to an audio board for sound in that it mixes various pictures together (for example, credits that roll over the end of a drama, a fade from black to the beginning of a show, or a scene from a fire that appears in a box behind a news anchor) and also creates effects, such as a picture that swirls on or off the screen. Some switchers also incorporate the ability to create graphics, such as words that appear in titles or as identification. In other instances the **graphics generator** is a separate computer with more capabilities—graph construction, overlaid drawings on football plays. The output of a switcher usually goes to a recording device—a videotape recorder or a computer server—where the picture and its sound are stored.

monitors

Monitors are similar to TV sets, except they don't show regular TV channels. Instead, they show the pictures that are being created and manipulated in the production facility. There are usually a large number of them in a studio setting because all the inputs (each camera, graphics, satellite feeds, etc.) are shown on separate monitors so that a director can select the image that he or she wants to go through the switcher to be recorded.

lights

Although it is possible for cameras to capture an image using only the light that is available, professionals usually augment a scene with additional light either to

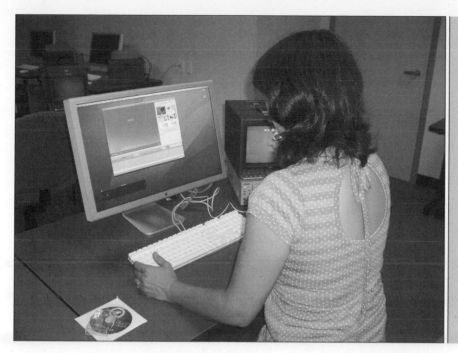

Exhibit 13.7
This editor is booting up editing software for use with a computer.

boost the available light or to create a particular mood. The trend in lighting is to use bulbs, such as **LEDs,** that are cool, small, and energy efficient. In a studio situation, lights hang from a ceiling **grid;** in other locations, they mount on light stands.

Once the video images and their sound are captured, they often need to be edited. For the most part, this is undertaken on computers with **nonlinear editing** software (see Exhibit 13.7). This type of editing allows picture and sound to be manipulated easily. Any shot can be placed anywhere on the final product and then moved about easily—for example, the third and fifth shots could be interchanged with little or no difficulty. If the director decides to lengthen a shot by two seconds, the computer automatically moves all the following shots ahead by two seconds.

editing

Computers are also used to create the elaborate **visual effects,** such as fiery crashes, flying people, exotic backgrounds, and lumbering dinosaurs. Generally, the computers for movie projects are configured to handle large volumes of complicated footage, and the software programs for visual effects are sophisticated. However, simpler effects operate within nonlinear editing programs and can be utilized by people producing wedding videos, corporate productions, and material to distribute over the internet.[5]

effects

13.4 Computer Production

Computers are not only used in conjunction with video but are also used to create complete products. Many animated movies and video games are made entirely in computers. The line blurs when **motion capture** is used. The process involves

types of products

scanning the movements of a real person and using those basic movements for a computerized "person." The actors wear bodysuits that have reflective markings at each joint. They are surrounded by cameras that record their performance data on computers. An artist then uses this data as a basis of movements for the computerized character. Is this video or computer animation?

web pages

Another type of computer production involves the construction of websites or social networking pages. Although these often contain audio and video that can be created with equipment similar to that used for movies and TV shows, they also require text, photos, and graphics. A fundamental purpose of web-based material is that it be interactive, so ease of navigation and attractive design are important elements. Many software programs (Intuit Website Creator, Adobe Contribute) are available to help professionals and members of the public build websites, and the social networking sites provide templates and instructions that can enable anyone to create personalized information. Needless to say, much of this material is saved on servers.[6]

13.5 Distribution Overview

wholesale-retail

Once production has been completed, it is ready to be distributed to an audience. Most of the electronic media use either **wired** or **wireless** means to distribute their content. Wired technologies are obviously ones that carry information over wires. Wireless technologies are those that send signals through the airwaves. Electronic media are unlike industries that produce concrete physical products, such as furniture, bread, or shoes. Those industries distribute primarily through wholesalers and retailers. Some facets of the electronic media also use the wholesale-retail pattern—for example, video stores that sell or rent **DVD**s. The program material is duplicated onto many discs, which are then shipped to wholesale houses that distribute them to video stores so that consumers who go to the stores can purchase them. But this model is breaking down as more movies and TV programs are being distributed through the internet.

wired and wireless

Some of the electronic media forms that use wires are cable TV, telco TV, and landline phones. Some of the major forms of wireless distribution include radio broadcasting, TV station broadcasting, satellites, cell phones, and wi-fi. Signals sometimes utilize both wireless and wired methods to get from starting point to destination. For example, a phone call from a wireless cell phone might arrive at a landline phone by way of a satellite. Someone can use a laptop computer to access the internet by wire when in an office and by wireless technology when in a coffee shop. However, the two technologies have different characteristics, different uses, and different advantages.

13.6 Wire Transmission

short and long distance

Wires can be used for sending electronic signals short and long distances. Short-distance use includes running a wire from a consumer DVD player to a TV set, from a microphone to an audio board, from a studio camera to a switcher, or from a projector to speakers in a movie theater. Much longer hauls are made when wires are used to transmit phone calls and email messages around the world or to deliver cable TV channels throughout a community.

Not all wires are alike. Voice and data can use simpler wires than video. For many years, the copper **twisted-pair** was the standard for telephone operations. Television signals required a new type of wire called **coaxial cable,** which was the type that cable TV systems used when they first built their systems. Both twisted-pairs and coax are still used, but most applications that use wire have switched to **fiber optics** (see Exhibit 13.8).

types of wire

With this technology, audio, video, or other data can be sent through an optic strand that is less than a hundredth of an inch in diameter. Because this strand is made of glass, it is relatively inexpensive, lightweight, strong, and flexible. A fiber optic cable that is less than an inch in diameter can carry 400,000 phone calls simultaneously—10 times the amount that could be carried on older copper wire. Fiber optics carry digital information through the glass fiber on light produced by laser diodes. Using light makes transmission less susceptible to electrical interference than with coaxial cable or twisted-pair lines.[7]

cable TV

Wires are the workhorses of cable TV systems, which consist of a **headend** where all the inputs, such as local TV stations, pay cable networks, and internet phone services are received. At this headend, all the services are placed on a wire that is either buried underground or hung on telephone poles. This wire branches and goes to various subscribers' homes, where it is connected to TV sets or home communications systems. Because the wire is physically in the home, signals can be sent back up the wire to the headend, enabling cable to be interactive. Although wires must be shielded in some way, they are not as subject to interference as signals traveling through the airwaves. Therefore, it is possible to put a large number of signals in a fairly small wire. Most cable systems have converted from coaxial cable to fiber optics except for the wires at the end of the line that go into consumer homes.[8]

Exhibit 13.8
A fiber optic.

Wires are also the primary carriers of the internet, although, as already mentioned, it can also be distributed in a wireless manner. One of the problems of internet transmission, wired or wireless, is the possibility of **gridlock.** When material streams over the internet, each computer is delivered a different stream. Unlike over-the-air broadcasts or satellites where one signal can go to many receivers, each person accessing the internet receives a separate stream of information, even though everyone accessing the internet may be seeing or hearing the same content. If too many people try to access one website at the same time, most of them cannot get through because there are not enough streams available, and that is how gridlock sets in. Organizations that host websites often charge by the number of streams a particular website owner wants to have available.

internet

Speed is also important for the internet. The more quickly the information can move from one point to another, the more complicated that information can be. Originally, internet data were sent over dial-up phone lines at what, by today's standards, were very slow speeds—1,200 bits per second (bps). This meant that only words, not pictures, sound, or video, could get through, and even then it took a long time for information to download. Speeds increased to more than 28.8 kilobits per second (28,800 bps) using phone wires, but it wasn't until both phone companies and cable companies developed technologies (primarily **cable modems** and **DSL** phone lines) that speed increased to 6 megabits per second (6,000,000 bps) and then upwards of 100 Mbps. These faster technologies, which usually use fiber optics, are referred to as **broadband** and have facilitated the transmission of audio and video.[9]

Wires and wireless often compete for the same business. Wireless is more flexible in that it has the potential to be picked up anywhere, and it can be changed relatively easily. Once wires are installed, it is difficult and expensive to replace them with a newer technology. But wires are more secure. It is harder to pirate a signal that is riding securely in a wire than one that is floating through the air.

13.7 Wireless Transmission

frequencies

Wireless technologies use the **electromagnetic spectrum,** a continuing series of energies at different **frequencies.** The frequencies can be compared to the different frequencies involved with sound. The human ear is capable of hearing sounds between about 16 cycles per second (low bass) and upward of 16,000 cycles per second (high treble). This means that a very low bass sound makes a vibration that cycles at a rate of 16 times per second.

hertz

These rates are usually measured in **hertz** in honor of the early radio pioneer Heinrich Hertz. One hertz (Hz) is one cycle per second. A low bass note would be at the frequency of 16 Hz, a higher note would be at 400 Hz, and a very high note would be at 16,000 Hz. As the numbers become larger, prefixes are added to the term *hertz* so the zeros do not become unmanageable. One thousand hertz is referred to as one kilohertz (kHz), one million hertz is one megahertz (MHz), and a billion hertz is one gigahertz (GHz). Therefore, the 16,000-hertz high note could also be said to have a frequency of 16 kHz.

Radio waves, which are part of the electromagnetic spectrum, also have frequencies and are measured in hertz. Their frequencies are higher, however, ranging from about 30 kHz to 300 GHz. They are capable of carrying sound and pictures, and it is through these radio waves that wireless electronic media distribution occurs.

Above radio waves on the electromagnetic spectrum are infrared rays and then light waves, with each color occupying a different frequency range. After visible light come ultraviolet rays, X rays, gamma rays, and cosmic rays (see Exhibit 13.9).

Although all radio frequencies in the electromagnetic spectrum are capable of carrying sound and pictures, they are not all the same. Frequencies toward

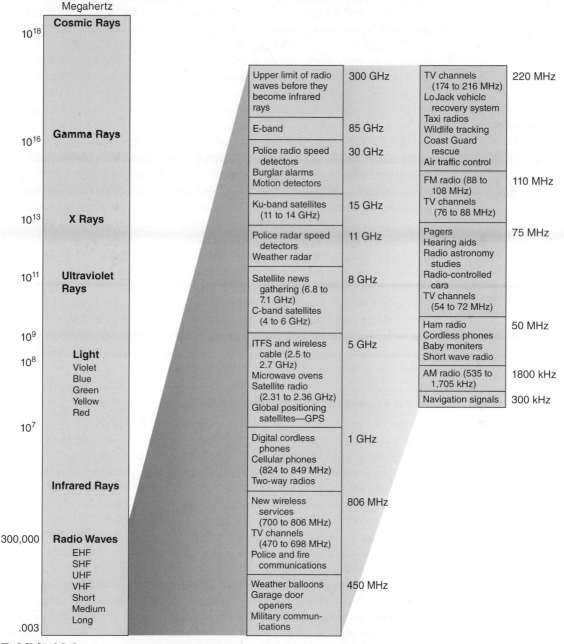

Exhibit 13.9

The electromagnetic spectrum and the main services of the radio wave portion.

the lower end of the spectrum behave more like sound than do frequencies at the higher end, which behave more like light. For example, the lower frequencies can go around corners better than the higher frequencies, in the same way that you can hear people talking around a corner but cannot see them.

radio waves

Radio waves also have many uses other than the distribution of entertainment and information material usually associated with the electronic media industry. These uses range from the opening of garage doors to secret reconnaissance functions. Some of the most common media and nonmedia uses are shown in Exhibit 13.9.

The spot on the radio portion of the spectrum at which a particular service is placed depends somewhat on the needs of the service. The lower frequencies have longer ranges in the earth's atmosphere. For example, **shortwave** radio, which travels long distances, uses very low frequencies; motion detectors that need to detect movement only in one or two rooms operate on high frequencies.

placement of services

Many placements, however, are an accident of history. The lower frequencies were understood and developed earlier than the higher frequencies. Not long ago, people were not even aware the higher frequencies existed. AM radio was developed earlier than FM (see Chapter 5), so the former was placed on the part of the spectrum that people then knew and understood. Ultra-high frequencies were discovered during World War II and led to the FCC's reallocating television frequencies after the war into two categories, **very high frequency (VHF)** and **ultra-high frequency (UHF)** (see Chapter 4).

These VHF and UHF frequencies were used for analog TV, but when it came time to convert to digital, some of the frequencies were not suitable for digital, so the FCC gave stations new frequencies. This allocation also enabled the stations to continue broadcasting analog signals while they were working to establish their digital transmissions. Once the nation converted to **digital TV,** the stations had to return their old frequencies to the FCC. The FCC auctioned off the old television frequencies, most of which were secured by companies that want to expand or develop new high-speed wireless services.[10]

13.7a Terrestrial Radio Broadcasting

definitions

Terrestrial radio broadcasting uses the electromagnetic spectrum to distribute signals close to the earth. These signals travel only a short distance in the earth's atmosphere, as opposed to satellite broadcasting that goes into outer space. AM and FM radio are terrestrial broadcasting forms, as is the new form of digital radio called **HD radio,** sometimes referred to as **in-band on-channel** or IBOC radio (see Chapter 5). The parts of the electromagnetic spectrum that are most important to these services are 88 to 108 MHz, where FM resides, and 535 to 1705 kHz, the home of AM. IBOC can be squeezed into those same frequencies; that's how it gets its name—it is in the same frequency band and on the same channel as its AM or FM counterpart. The position in the spectrum, however, has nothing to do with **AM (amplitude modulation), FM (frequency modulation),** or **PCM (pulse code modulation),** the type of modulation that is used for HD radio.

modulation

Sound, when it leaves the radio station studio in the form of radio energy, travels to the station's **transmitter** and then to the **antenna.** At the transmitter it is **modulated,** which means the electrical energy is superimposed onto the

Consider this to be an electrical wave representing the original sound.

Exhibit 13.10
Diagram of an AM wave.

Consider this to be the carrier wave of a particular radio station. Notice it is of much higher frequency than the electrical wave.

This would be the modulated carrier wave taking the sound signal. Note that the sound signal makes an image of itself and that the amplitude, or height, of the carrier wave is changed—hence, amplitude modulation.

carrier wave that represents that particular radio station's frequency (e.g., 710 AM, 97.1 FM). The transmitter generates this carrier wave and places the sound wave on it, using the process of modulation. Amplitude, frequency, or pulse code modulation can occur regardless of where the carrier wave is located on the spectrum. In amplitude modulation, the amplitude (or height) of the carrier wave is varied to fit the characteristics of the sound wave (see Exhibit 13.10). In frequency modulation, the frequency of the carrier wave is changed instead (see Exhibit 13.11). Pulse code modulation, because it is a digital form, encodes information as 0s and 1s (see Exhibit 13.12).

Consider this to be the electrical wave representing the original sound wave.

Exhibit 13.11
Diagram of an FM wave.

Consider this to be the carrier wave.

This would be the modulated carrier wave. The frequency is increased where the sound wave is highest (positive), and the frequency is decreased where the sound wave is lowest (negative). The amplitude does not change.

Perhaps this can be better seen by superimposing the sound wave over the carrier wave.

0101110101010   Pulse code modulation is a digital form that consists
1111000011010   of a series of on (1) and off (0) pulses.
1110001010

**modulation
differences**

AM, FM, and PCM have different characteristics caused by the modulation methods. For example, AM is much more subject to static because static appears at the top and bottom of the wave cycle. Because FM depends on varying the frequency of the wave and PCM is just a code, the top and bottom can be eliminated without distorting the signal. AM, however, depends on height, so the static regions must remain with the wave.

**spectrum
differences**

AM and FM also have differences because of their placement on the spectrum, differences that will also affect PCM depending on whether it is in the frequency band of AM or FM. AM signals can travel great distances around the earth, while FM signals sometimes cannot be heard if an obstruction, such as a large building, comes between the transmitter and the radio that is attempting to receive the station. FM is higher on the spectrum and closer to light than is AM, and just as light waves do not travel through buildings or hills, FM signals are similarly affected, making them **line of sight.** AM, at the lower end of the spectrum, is not so affected, but these lower frequencies are affected by a nighttime condition of the ionosphere that, when hit by radio waves, bounces the wave back to earth. AM waves can be bounced great distances around the earth's surface—from New York to London, for example. Because of this phenomenon, some AM stations are authorized to broadcast only during daylight hours so they will not interfere with other radio station signals that are traveling long distances because they are bouncing. FM is not affected by this because of its position in the spectrum, not because of its manner of modulation. Theoretically, if FM waves were transmitted on the lower frequencies, such as 535 kHz, they could bounce in a manner similar to AM.

bandwidth

Another difference between AM and FM is that the **bandwidth** is greater for FM stations. Although each station is given a specific frequency, such as 550 kHz or 88.5 MHz, the spectrum actually used covers a wider area. For an AM radio station, this width (bandwidth) is 10 kHz; for FM, the bandwidth per station is 200 kHz. An AM station at 550 kHz actually operates at from 545 to 555 so that it can have room to modulate the necessary signals and prevent interference from adjacent channels. Because FM stations have a broader bandwidth, they can produce higher fidelity than AM stations. This makes FM more adaptable to stereo broadcasting because there is room for two channels of sound. AM stereo does exist, but not all stations use it because it is not as effective as FM stereo.

IBOC

FM's broader bandwidth also makes it easier to add PCM digital radio so that it comes from the same frequency area as the FM station. Engineers involved with IBOC had to work much harder to superimpose digital radio in the AM band. One plan, however, is for both AM and FM stations to broadcast the same programming in both analog and digital and, eventually, after listeners have bought radios that can receive the PCM signals, to abandon analog and only broadcast in digital.

The FCC, however, is not mandating that radio switch to digital; it is purely voluntary on the part of the stations.

In addition, the broader bandwidth of FM enables independent signals other than those needed for digital and stereo sound to be **multiplexed** on an FM radio station signal. This information is carried on part of the FM signal, but it can be received only by those with special receivers. Some of the services include piped music to doctors' offices and reading for the blind.

multiplexing

After the sound waves are modulated (AM, FM, or PCM) onto the proper frequency carrier wave at the transmitter, the carrier wave is radiated into the air. It is sent into the airwaves at the assigned frequency and power from the radio station antenna. Because FM frequencies travel line of sight, FM antennas are usually positioned on high places overlooking a large area. AM antennas can operate effectively at relatively low heights.

antennas

The FCC has established a complicated chart of frequency and power allocations to allow a maximum number of stations around the country to broadcast without interference. There is room for 117 stations of 10 kHz each between 535 and 1,705 kHz, but there are more than 14,000 AM stations nationwide. This is possible because many stations throughout the country broadcast on the same frequency, but in a controlled way that considers geographic location and power.[11]

stations

13.7b Terrestrial Television Broadcasting

As with radio, the terrestrial television transmitter is the device for superimposing or modulating information onto a carrier wave. With the analog television signal that was used from the early days of television until 2009, audio and video were sent to the transmitter separately. The video signal was amplitude modulated, and the audio signal was frequency modulated in either monaural or stereo. The two were then joined and broadcast from the station antenna. In the early days, this signal went from the station antenna through the local airwaves to receiving antennas on people's rooftops and from there to a TV set with "rabbit ears" (see Exhibit 13.13). Most households do not receive their TV stations this way anymore. They are more likely to get them through cable TV, satellite TV, or telco TV. But stations still send out their terrestrial signal, and often cable, satellite, and telco systems pick up that signal and transpose it into their own systems.

modulation

Digital TV is modulated in a manner similar to digital radio because it consists of a series of on and off pulses. The digital TV situation is much more complicated than digital radio, however. For one thing, unlike radio, the FCC mandated that all TV stations switch from analog to digital whether they wanted to or not. For another, the digital stations are not all on the same frequency that their analog stations were. For example, a station that used to be channel 4 may now be channel 38. Also, there is the confusion between digital TV and high-definition TV (see Chapter 4). Digital is a

digital TV

Exhibit 13.13
This dipole antenna for UHF and VHF TV shows why such antennas were referred to as "rabbit ears."

transmission form based on pulses rather than analog waves; HDTV incorporates digital but also provides more lines of resolution so that the picture looks sharper than the old analog picture, which only had 525 lines.

scanning

To further complicate things, several different formats of HDTV have different numbers of lines and different methods of **scanning** (the process for creating the picture). A video picture is never an entire frame. It is a series of very rapidly illuminated dots (**pixels**) that look like full-frame pictures to us because our eyes retain the image produced by the pixels. Analog TV employed **interlace scanning,** in which all the odd lines of information created by the dots were laid down first, followed by the even lines in order to form a frame. This interlace process is used by some forms of high-definition television, but others use **progressive scanning** that lays information on the screen one line at a time from top to bottom (see Exhibit 13.14). When TV was developed in the 1930s and 1940s, progressive scanning was not a viable technical option, but by the time HDTV was in development, it was possible for HDTV to utilize either form of scanning. Many combinations of scanning and number of lines have been developed, but the ones that are used the most are 720p, 1080i, and 1080p. The numbers stand for the number of lines while "p" stands for progressive scan and "i" stands for interlace. Fortunately, TV sets switch seamlessly, so consumers aren't saddled with dealing with the different formats.

**portable
platforms**

Terrestrial TV stations have an added challenge of getting their signal to people on the go. They want to participate in the portable platform revolution, so an engineering group developed a standard for all stations to use to broadcast to mobile devices. However, it is not as simple as it sounds. Servicing all the devices involves a great deal of **transcoding** (changing electronic characteristics from one form to another). Not only do iPad, Kindle, iPhone, Blackberry, Android, etc, have different operating systems, but they have different screen sizes, aspect ratios, audio requirements, and copyright protection. Making terrestrial broadcasting work with all the new gadgets is no easy chore.[12]

13.7c Satellites

transponders

Terrestrial signals travel only a short distance, usually staying within the confines of one city. Satellites can be used to distribute to a wider area. Signals are sent from satellite dishes on earth and are received on satellites in outer space that have **transponders**—

essentially reception channels that can hold video, audio, and data information. The information goes from the satellite back down to earth where it can be received by any equipped facility. Being equipped to receive the signal means owning a satellite dish positioned in such a way that it lines up with the signal being sent from the satellite.

The satellites used for telecommunications transmit in two main frequency bands, **C-band** and **Ku-band.** Those in C-band operate between 4 and 6 GHz, and those in Ku-band operate between 11 and 14 GHz. The C-band satellites were put up first and carry much of the cable TV network programming. Additional cable programming is carried on Ku-band satellites, and satellite TV services such as DirecTV and Dish Network transmit from this frequency range. **Satellite radio** operates from slightly lower frequencies, in the 2.3 GHz range. Satellites are used for many other purposes such as international news feeds and network program distribution.

bands

Most of the satellites are positioned 22,300 miles above the equator and are powered, at least in part, by energy they gather from the sun. These **synchronous satellites** travel in an orbit that is synchronized with the speed of the earth's rotation, thus appearing to hang motionless in space. This way they can continually receive and send signals to the same points on earth. It is not difficult for signals to travel 22,300 miles because once they leave the earth's atmosphere, they do not encounter the interference and inhospitable weather conditions that waves traveling through the earth's atmosphere encounter.

orbit

The satellites that transmit to the United States are positioned along the equator between 55 and 140 degrees west longitude. From there they can cast a signal, called a **footprint** (see Exhibit 13.15), over the entire United States. Satellites

position

Exhibit 13.15
A satellite and its footprint.

positioned at other longitudes have footprints over other sections of the world. Most of the earth's surface can be covered by three strategically placed satellites. In this way, instant worldwide communication is possible through a satellite network, and pictures can be beamed from anywhere in the world to the United States.

low-orbit

Some satellites are not synchronous because they are closer to the earth than the synchronous satellites. These **low-orbit satellites** hand off signals to each other so that they can continue to cover specific areas. They are often used by telephone companies to distribute phone calls and by corporations for data distribution, such as credit card transactions. One reason for using them is that they do not have as much latency as synchronous satellites have. When having back-and-forth telephone conversations, it is annoying to have the degree of delay that occurs when signals travel 22,300 miles.[13]

13.7d Cell Phone Technology

early

Wireless phones existed as far back as the 1920s, but they were cumbersome and expensive and did not catch on with the general public. AT&T's Bell Labs developed the basic concept for cellular phones in the 1940s, but the FCC did not authorize the technology until 1981.

technology

Cellular technology divides geographic areas into small, discrete parts called **cells,** with the average cell covering an area of several miles. Each cell is served by low-power transmitters and receivers. They are so low power that several phones can share the same frequency in the same cell without causing interference. As a person travels from one cell to another, the system hands off signals (see Exhibit 13.16).

digital functions

Cell phones of the 1980s and early 1990 used analog technology and only had voice capability, but they caught on quickly with the public. In the mid-1990s, digital cell phone systems were developed. Because the 0s and 1s of digital technology take up less space than analog, there was opportunity for the phones to serve more functions than solely phone calls. Cameras, games, internet access, and the like were added and by the 2000s cell phones were being called **smartphones** (see Chapter 2).

Twitter

In 2006, Twitter added the ability to send short text messages called **tweets** to the repertoire of smartphones. These messages, which can be up to 240 characters long, use very little bandwidth so can hitchhike on a smartphone with ease. Twitter is designed in a **distributed network** pattern so that, if the text message cannot get through one way, it can be rerouted another way. For this reason, text messaging often keeps working during a disaster when other forms of communication are destroyed.[14]

13.7e Wi-Fi Technology

frequencies

Wi-fi (wireless fidelity) enables laptops, smartphones, tablets, game consoles, and other equipment to connect to the internet if they are within range of a wi-fi signal. The technology is the outgrowth on a 1985 decision by the FCC to open several bands of frequency and allow them to be used without a government license. These were not considered to be good frequencies and, in fact, were

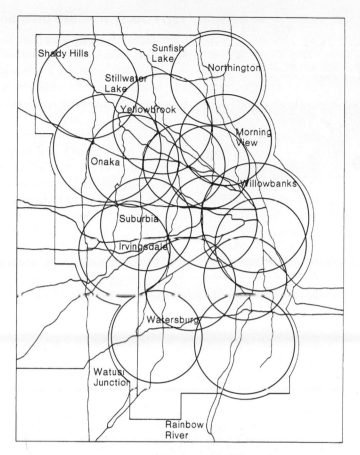

Exhibit 13.16
This drawing shows how the wireless cells of a cellular telephone system overlap so that signals can be handed from one wireless cell phone tower to another.

called "garbage bands" at the time. The frequencies were already allocated to equipment, such as microwave ovens, and anyone using the frequencies was not allowed to cause interference to the equipment. The solution to this problem was called **spread spectrum**—a method to spread a signal out over a wide range of frequencies so that it could fill in little spaces that were not being used.

Several of the companies interested in using these frequencies decided there needed to be a standard so that applications developed by one company could be used by another. This standard was ratified in January 2000 and named wi-fi. **standard** The first significant use of it was by Apple, which put a slot for wi-fi in one of its laptop computers so that owners could access the internet wirelessly. This proved the value of wi-fi and soon other computer manufacturers followed suit.

Wi-fi has a very small range, about 120 feet indoors and 300 feet outdoors, **range** although there are constant technological advances aimed at improving its range. It is used within homes and offices to allow several computers to share a broadband link to the internet. Businesses, such as coffee shops, have set up wi-fi areas called **hotspots**, with the idea that people will frequent their establishments to use the internet and then purchase whatever they are selling.[15]

Exhibit 13.17

The top of this truck holds microwave apparatus for sending news from its location back to the TV station.

13.7f Other Wireless Distribution

The electromagnetic spectrum is used for many forms of telecommunications other than radio, broadcast TV, satellite distribution, cell phones, and wi-fi. One of the oldest uses is **microwave** transmission. Located between 1 and 30 GHz, microwaves are higher in the electromagnetic spectrum than radio and TV stations, but they are terrestrial in that they do not go into outer space. They are line of sight and travel only about 30 miles. Microwave transmitters were once used to send network signals across the country. Towers were built about every 30 miles, each one picking up a signal from a previous tower and sending it on to the next. When satellites were developed, it was much easier to send signals to a satellite so they could

microwave

be received anywhere in the country. Microwaves are still sometimes used to transmit signals from TV studios to transmitters and from news trucks to stations (see Exhibit 13.17).

media uses

Radio and TV stations use electromagnetic spectrum frequencies for **translators.** These are towers that pick up a signal and send it to a particular area, such as a spot within a station's coverage area that has poor reception. Cordless phones, video game controls, TV set remote controls, and other wireless equipment also take advantage of low-power signals. Wireless mics that enable performers to move around unrestricted by wires are basically tiny radio stations that send sound from the mic to a receiver using the electromagnetic spectrum. Similarly, cameras used in the field can have antennas on them to send their signals through the airwaves to a switcher or recorder.

other uses

In short, media companies use the electromagnetic spectrum in many ways. However, they are not its only occupants (refer back to Exhibit 13.9). It is also important for health and safety; police and fire departments use it for communications, as do air traffic controllers and the Coast Guard. A fair amount of the spectrum is used to track weather conditions and wildlife. It is also the home of many of life's conveniences, such as baby monitors, LoJacks, and global positioning systems.[16]

13.8 Exhibition Overview

gadgets

A broadcast antenna, a satellite, a wire, or a hotspot does not succeed in distributing program material unless someone actually watches or listens. The number of gadgets that are available for exhibiting electronic media content has grown rapidly in recent years. The motion picture screen, the radio, and the TV set were the main exhibition devices for many years, but they have been joined by the likes of computer monitors, pads, pods, game consoles, and smartphones.

Exhibition has been slower than production and distribution to adopt digital. Part of the reason is that in its final form exhibition must be analog because our eyes cannot see digital technologies' 0s and 1s and our ears cannot hear them. But exhibition has also been slower because it involves many consumers. While executives at a TV network can decide to spend the money to convert to digital production and transmission, it is the millions of TV set owners who must pay for the new sets or converters to see and hear the digital signals. Making this sort of transition with any speed is very difficult.

digital

On the other hand, many people are enamored with new ways to view and listen to their favorite programs and websites. They accept, and even demand, increasingly more convenient, user-friendly products that put the world at their fingertips regardless of where they are.

13.9 Motion Picture Exhibition

For many years movies were exhibited by placing film prints (delivered in a can by mail or a similar service) on a projector where frames were pulled down in front of a light that showed through a lens. The picture was projected onto a beaded screen responsive to picking up the light images. The sound for the film usually rode beside the picture frames and was sent to multiple speakers to give audience members the feeling of being surrounded by the sound.

film projection

However, many motion picture theaters have now converted to digital projection. Referred to as **digital cinema** (see Chapter 6), this methodology involves showing movies using digital media such as hard drives and servers rather than film. The drives can be hand delivered or the movies can be sent over satellite and stored on the server. Obviously, the projector needed is different from that used for film. One basic design for a digital cinema projector involves more than a million tiny mirrors, each mounted on a hinge that can tilt thousands of times per second. Some of these mirrors respond to digital data representing reds, some to blues, and some to greens. The 0s and 1s to which the image has been reduced instruct each mirror to pivot so that it either reflects or deflects the colored light needed for that image. The light from the mirrors is magnified and focused on the cinema screen to reproduce the image.

digital cinema

In 2005 seven movie studios established standards for digital cinema that covered many technological aspects. They included specifications for such things as the distribution master, protection of content from piracy, and parameters for two digital projection formats—2K (2,048 horizontal pixels by 1,080 vertical pixels) and 4K (4,096 horizontal pixels by 2,160 vertical pixels). It is generally conceded that 4K is about the quality of 35mm film.

It has also been found that 4K projection lends itself well to 3-D movies. This has brought about a revival of 3-D production (see "Zoom In" box). Some theaters, in order to attract moviegoers, have installed equipment that makes the seats shake and tilt in tandem with the action on the screen, and some serve gourmet food delivered to VIP seats set aside in a special section of the theater.[17]

other attractions

ZOOM IN: **Why Do We Need Those 3-D Glasses?**

Basically, we need 3-D glasses to fool our brains. People's eyes are spaced several inches apart so each eye has a slightly different view. Our brains put these two images together to form an image that appears to have depth (three dimensions), providing what we are looking at has three dimensions. A movie screen is flat, so even though each eye views it slightly differently, it still looks flat.

In order to give a three-dimensional feel, two images must be projected onto the screen and in some way affect each eye slightly differently. In production, the images are created by having the same scene recorded through two different lenses, each approximating the position of one eye. During exhibition these two images are projected onto the screen. If you look at projected 3-D without glasses, you will see the fuzziness of the two images.

What the glasses do is filter out one image for each eye so that each eye is only looking at one of the images on the screen. One way to do this is to project each image in a different color—usually red and green. The glasses for viewing this have one red lens (filter) and one green lens (filter). The colored filters separate the two images so that each image only enters one eye. Then the brain puts the two images together—and the monsters look like they are coming right at you.

Another method uses **polarization,** a process that deals with the angle and vibration of light. The movie is originally shot with lenses that are polarized differently. This still requires projecting two images on the screen, but they have different polarization as opposed to different colors. The glasses are also polarized so that only one image enters one eye and the brain, once again, is fooled into making the image 3-D.

Engineers are working on ways to create 3-D that is **autostereoscopic** (no, it's not a disease; it means 3-D without glasses). But don't count on ditching those glasses anytime soon.

People wearing 3-D glasses.

13.10 Radio and Audio Reception

radios

For radio broadcasts, radio receivers pick up and amplify radio waves that have been sent out from the antenna, separate the information from the carrier wave, and reproduce this information as analog sounds that can be heard through a

speaker or **headphones.** Some radios also have digital displays that list facts about songs and other information. The major change in radios over the years is that they have shrunk; some are now small enough to fit in the ear (thanks to transistors and silicon chips). A radio has been developed that can handle both digital and analog AM and FM, but at present, a different receiver is needed to hear satellite radio.

The speakers and headphones that allow people to hear sound from a radio or from some other device that produces sound (a computer, a CD player, a TV set, a video game console) come in many different forms. Speakers are stand-alone boxes that allow anyone within their range to hear the audio. They usually have several components—a **woofer** for low frequencies, a **tweeter** for high frequencies, and a **crossover** to divide the audio signal and send the proper frequencies to the woofer and tweeter. Headphones fit in or on ears and allow one person to hear the sound. **Closed-cushion headphones** have a ring-shaped muff that surrounds the ear but rests on the head. **Open-air headphones** have muffs that rest directly on the ear. **Earbuds** are tiny and fit into the ear.[18]

speakers

13.11 Video Exhibition

An array of devices is currently available for viewing video, but historically, the main one was the family TV set. For many years, these sets were **cathode-ray tube** based. An **electron gun** located at the back of the picture tube sends a stream of electrons to a **phosphor screen** at the front of the tube. When the electrons hit the phosphor screen, they cause it to glow, creating the television picture. Tube-based sets are deep because there needs to be room between the gun and the screen. Most TVs manufactured now are thin sets, often referred to as **flat-screen TV.** The two main forms are **liquid crystal display (LCD)** and **plasma.** LCD screens are made up of two transparent pads with crystal molecules between them. These molecules light up according to the voltage applied to them, and the voltage relates to the characteristics of the electrons making up the picture. Plasma screens are made up of two glass panels with gas between them. The gas activates colored dots according to the pattern of voltages applied.[19]

TV sets

Television sets have improved in many ways. For example, TV sets used to contain tiny three-inch speakers that delivered low-quality monaural sound. When stereo TV was authorized in the 1980s, this changed rapidly. Now TV sets have excellent speakers that produce high-quality sound. Some people build themselves "home theaters" (see Exhibit 13.18) that include speakers placed around the room to give a surround-sound feeling. Another big improvement of the 1980s was the remote control that allowed viewers to change channels from the comfort of their armchairs. Through the years, the remote control has added many features, such as muting, freeze-frame, and the ability to view several TV programs at once.[20]

Computers have screens that look very much like TV sets and are constructed similarly, with tube-based, LCD, or plasma technology. For the most part, however, they cannot receive over-the-air, cable, or satellite TV signals. They are used primarily for displaying the internet, video games, movies, and documents

computer screens

Exhibit 13.18
A home theater.

created with computer programs such as Word and Excel. There are sets that can display both traditional television and the internet, and they may be the wave of the future.

projected TV

portable screens

Video material, whether from a TV set or a computer, can also be sent from a projector onto a screen. The oldest technology for **projection TV** consisted of a unit that took the signals from a conventional TV tube, magnified them, and projected them onto a large screen. This form of projector was heavy, however, and when LCD technologies were developed, they were integrated into smaller projectors that could be placed on a table or hung from a ceiling (see Exhibit 13.19).

Small, portable screens can also be used to display TV signals and computer-based material. Screens that previously were used only for video games have been altered so they can also show other forms of video. Pads and smartphone screens also serve as a display areas for many forms of video. In some cases the process of exhibiting video or audio on newer devices is complicated; other times it is just a matter of using a simple **app.**[21]

Exhibit 13.19
An LCD video projector.

13.12 **Issues** and the Future

New types of screens will no doubt be developed in the future. The trend is definitely toward devices that can exhibit the product of many media entities—TV networks, movie studios, internet websites, Twitter feeds. People seem comfortable switching from one screen to another, but they do want their entertainment and information at their fingertips. There may be a dip in TV set

screens

sales as people use pads and smartphones rather than second or third TV sets. Desktop computers are losing favor to laptops and other more portable equipment, so the sale of large computer monitors may dip also. The conversion to digital cinema seems to be a given, but people may not even realize they are viewing video rather than film on the movie theater large screen.

Issues surrounding the electronic spectrum are likely to continue. The radio waves portion of the spectrum is finite. It does not go above 300 GHz because at that point it turns into infrared light. Many media entities want to use radio waves, and although the potential demands have not yet exceeded the supply, various organizations are arguing for more space on the spectrum. The Department of Homeland Security established after 9/11 definitely feels the need for spectrum space, as do other safety and security agencies, and they believe their needs should take precedence over providing entertainment. Add to this the government's desire to make money by auctioning off the frequencies to the highest bidder, and the future management of the electromagnetic spectrum could be in for some rocky controversies.

spectrum

On the other hand, engineers are constantly devising ways to squeeze more information into existing spectrum. Wi-fi, in particular, can be developed to a much greater degree. For example, if all homes had public wi-fi systems that could be used by anyone walking or driving down the street, whole cities could become hotspots. The privacy and security issues related to that are likely to be thorny in that these public sites would have to be kept totally separate from private sites, but it would make internet use easy and universal. Engineers are also finding ways to move information more quickly and efficiently through both wired and wireless transmission.

wi-fi

New technologies may change business models. If it is possible to receive broadcast TV programming everywhere, the networks may no longer need the affiliated stations. They can simply send their programming by satellite or internet directly to people's screens. Even if TV stations still show network programming, they may do so through a pull method rather than the current push method. In other words, instead of the networks sending (pushing) programming to the stations, the stations may decide which shows they want and pull them from the network servers by using internet feeds. PBS is experimenting with this approach.

business models

Production changes constantly as technology evolves. Each movie seems to sport new, more complicated visual effects, and sophisticated 3-D has become a reality. As production equipment becomes smaller and easier to handle, stations, networks, and the internet rely more on material from the general public. Pieces of production equipment take on more functions. Because most of them are computer based, they can be used for switching, graphics, audio, lighting, and other functions all at once. This reduces the need for some members of the crew.

evolution

Many other technical marvels are bound to punctuate the future. Smartphones may shrink further so that they are the size of a wrist watch. The disabled may profit from better interfaces with the computer. For example, there are computers that understand speech and can talk back. Engineers are working

other innovations

on ways to project three dimensions on TV sets without the need for glasses, so autostereoscopic 3-D TV may be available in the future. There are bound to be problems with each new technology. However, these types of problems are not new to the electronic media world. Color TV, satellite TV, and high-definition TV went through similar throes. The technologies for production, distribution, and exhibition will no doubt continue to change at a rapid rate.

13.13 Summary

Various media have different production, distribution, and exhibition processes, and these processes are constantly evolving. Most of them are now digital, although some remain analog and others are in the process of converting.

Radio and audio are produced with microphones, recorders, audio boards, and computers. Radio signals are sent to transmitters, where they are modulated as AM, FM, or PCM and distributed in a wireless fashion by antennas. The various forms of radio have different characteristics caused by their positions on the electromagnetic spectrum (designated by hertz), their bandwidth, and accidents of history. Some radio is sent from satellite. Radio receivers demodulate and amplify signals and play them through devices that have greatly shrunk in size over the years. Radio and other forms of audio are played back using speakers and various forms of headphones.

Broadcast, cable, satellite and telco TV programming is produced digitally with both audio and video equipment. Cameras capture the image with aspect ratio being a consideration; recorders and clouds store the image; switchers mesh pictures together; and monitors display them. Lights are trending toward cooler, more energy-efficient bulbs; editors are nonlinear; and visual effects are computer-based. Broadcast signals utilize the electromagnetic spectrum; their digital transmissions encompass HDTV with either interlace or progressive scanning. Cable TV systems depend on wires for distribution from the headend, using both coaxial cable and fiber optic cable. Telco systems also use fiber optics. Satellite TV broadcasts use synchronous satellites with transponders and footprints and frequencies that are higher up on the electronic spectrum than broadcast—either C-band or Ku-band. All are displayed on TV sets that have changed from tube based to LCD or plasma based. Sound accompanying TV has improved greatly, and some people make home theaters.

Movies are shot either with video equipment or film, which is an analog chemical medium. In either case, they are edited electronically. They can be distributed by mail or satellite. The exhibition process varies depending on whether film or digital material is used. Film projectors pull individual frames in front of a lens and light. Digital cinema projectors consist of many mirrors responding to 0s and 1s. Some films are produced, distributed, and exhibited in 3-D for which people wear glasses.

Computers, which have always been digital, are used to produce visual effects, video games, and sometimes entire movies or TV shows. They are also used to produce websites and social network sites. They are tied to the internet, which uses both wired and wireless methods of distribution. Gridlock and broadband play a role in the distribution. The internet (and sometimes TV signals) can be viewed on plasma or LED computer monitors, laptops, and smaller screens, such as pads and smartphones. Smartphones are part of cell phone technology that uses cells and sometimes needs transcoding. Phones and other digital devices can be tied to wi-fi, which utilizes hotspots and spread spectrum. These newer media present many opportunities and issues for the future.

Suggested Websites

www.apple.com (the main site for Apple computers, phones, pads, and other products)

www.audio-technica.com (Audio-Technica, an audio company specializing in microphones and headsets)

www.panasonic.com (Panasonic, a manufacturer of video and audio equipment such as cameras and TV sets)

www.smpte.org (Society of Motion Picture and Television Engineers, a trade organization that, among other things, sets technical standards)

www.sony.com (Sony, a company known for audio and video equipment, particularly cameras and TV sets)

Notes

1. "Digital Compression," *CTI,* October 2000, 46–51.
2. "A Thrilling 40-Year Ride from Portapak to iPhone," *TV Technology,* January 20, 2010; and "A New Tune for One-Man Bands," *Broadcasting & Cable,* May 3, 2010, 22.
3. "Directional Mic Behavior and Usage Examined," *TV Technology,* June 13, 2007, 34; "Shotgun Microphones," *Mix,* April 2009, 34; "Audio Consoles Get Heard," *TV Technology,* May 26, 2003, 60–62; "The Source of Sound Effects," *American Lifestyle,* July/August 2010; and "Broadcasters Take on the Cloud," *TV Technology,* July 6, 2011, 1.
4. "Fresh Kodak Concerns Surface," *Wall Street Journal,* July 29, 2010, B5; and "Bowing to the Shift to Digital," *Los Angeles Times,* October 26, 2011, B-3.
5. "The Red Revolution," *Los Angeles Times Magazine,* September 2011, 24; "3D Dominates Tech Retreat," *TV Technology,* April 1, 2010, 22; "Have Lenses Passed Cameras in Quality?" *TV Technology,* February 16, 2011, 46; "Energy, Variety Drive Lighting Technology," *TV Technology,* July 20, 2011, 14; "Switchers Evolve to Meet Increasing Production Demands," *TV Technology,* December 21, 2011, 8; "21st Century News Graphics," *TV Technology,* January 20, 2010, 14; "Monitors Get Smaller, Lighter," *TV Technology,* October 6, 2010, 27; and "Mixing Formats in the Edit," *TV Technology,* December 23, 2009, 16.
6. "The Art of Gold," *The Envelope,* December 8, 2011, S24; "Animated Performance," *Millimeter,* November/December 2007, 24–27; and "With Heads in the Clouds," *Los Angeles Times,* December 18, 2011, D-4.
7. "Coaxial Cable: The Name of the Game," *Computer Technology,* October 2000, 74; and "Connecting Fiber Optics," *TV Technology,* October 18, 2006, 22.

8. "Time Warner's Phone Service Shows Cable's Growing Clout," *Wall Street Journal,* February 23, 2005, B1.

9. "Broadband Raises the Bar," *Broadcasting & Cable,* June 23, 2008, 19; "DSL's Big Push," *Los Angeles Times,* December 21, 2000, T-1; and "SMPTE of Standardize HD Over IP," *TV Technology,* October 6. 2010, 20.

10. "Spectrum Squeeze," *Fortune,* July 25, 2011, 15; and "The Battle for Bandwidth," *Mix,* October 2008, 56–59.

11. "Radio Tunes in Warily to Its Digital Future," *Los Angeles Times,* April 7, 2003, C-1; and "System Sends High-Speed Data with FM Subcarriers," *Microwaves,* February 1995, 6–7.

12. "The Digital Pace," *Broadcasting & Cable,* September 29, 2008, 24; "FCC Awards New DTV Channels," *TV Technology,* May 8, 1997, 20; and "Transcoding for Mobile," *TV Technology,* October 19, 2011, 12.

13. "Space Odyssey," *Aviation Week & Space Technology,* March 19/26, 2007, 86–88; and "Satellite Soaring," *Mix,* April 2006, 34–35.

14. "Cellphone Gridlock," *Fortune,* March 22, 2010, 38; "New Spec Published for TV Everywhere," *TV Technology,* December 22, 2010, 18; and "Why Twitter Survives Disasters," *TV Technology,* April 6, 2011, 12.

15. "Wi-Fi and the Mobile Meltdown," *Wall Street Journal,* October 19, 2011, A13; and "FCC Names White Space Database Managers," *TV Technology,* February 16, 2011, 18.

16. "Microwave Community Faces Major Facilities Relocation," *Enterprise Communications,* March 1995, 62; "ENG Cameras Cut the Cord," *TV Technology,* June 23, 2004, 12; and "Wireless Mics Search for RF Haven," *TV Technology,* November 23, 2005, 16

17. "Digital Switch Halfway Home," *Hollywood Reporter,* April 1, 2011, 55; "Sony Tries to Build Buzz on 4K Projector," *Hollywood Reporter,* June 26, 2008, 6; "When Can We Ditch the 3D Glasses?" *TV Technology,* July 6, 2011, 1; and "Exhibs Shake Out Extra Coin," *Variety,* March 28–April 3, 2011, 14.

18. "New Chip for HD Radio," *Broadcasting & Cable,* September 8, 2003, 17; and David E. Reese, Lynne S. Gross, and Brian Gross, *Audio Production Worktext* (Burlington, MA: Focal Press, 2009), 125–26.

19. "LCDs Versus Plasmas," *Sound and Video Contractor,* June 2003, 26–30; and "Plasma Please?" *Emmy,* Issue No. 4, 2009, 16.

20. "Revolution by Remote," *Los Angeles Times,* April 13, 2003, E-29; and "Dolby's Transition to Greatness?" *Hollywood Reporter,* February 19, 2008, 9.

21. "Connected TVs: What to Watch For," *Broadcasting & Cable,* May 23, 2011, 27; "Google Expands Video Offerings," *Los Angeles Times,* October 29, 2011, B-1; and "'Four Screens' System Integration," *TV Technology,* June 22, 2011, 10.

Chapter 14

THE INTERNATIONAL SCENE

Electronic media are very important to the world. The ability to communicate almost anything to the most remote part of the earth instantly has changed the way people and governments act. Conversely, the entire world is very important to electronic media. Technologies such as satellites and the internet have created a worldwide market for advertised products.

Media systems in most countries have developed very differently from those in the United States. Knowledge of the history and customs of various systems around the world is crucial to anyone who intends to deal with global media. Organizations vary as boundary lines are crossed, yet common elements glue the world's media systems into a unified whole.

The orbiting satellites herald a new day in world communications. For telephone, message, data, and television, new pathways in the sky are being developed. They are sky trails to progress in commerce, business, trade, and in relationships and understanding among peoples. Understanding among peoples is a precondition for a better and more peaceful world. The objectives of the United States are to provide orbital messengers, not only of words, speech, and pictures, but of thought and hope.

President Lyndon B. Johnson

14.1 Early Film

France

Producing theatrical movies is expensive, so many countries engaged in little or no early film production. In the early 1900s, Hollywood came to dominate the production and distribution of popular movies, but other countries historically have contributed to film's repertoire. As mentioned previously (see Chapter 6), the Lumière brothers of France were instrumental in creating turn-of-the-century short movies and developing a film projection system.

During the 1920s, France was the gathering place for artistic experimentation. Directors such as Salvador Dali, Jean Renoir, and René Clair produced movies with such techniques as dream effects, slow motion, distortion, multiple exposures, and visual symbolism. Films reflected the artistic sensibilities of these directors who were considered the **auteurs** (authors) of the films. In René Clair's 1923 *The Crazy Ray,* a scientist with a magical ray freezes activity in Paris so that only a few people can move about. Clair uses the frozen motion for social commentary by showing such scenes as an unfaithful wife frozen in the arms of her lover and a pickpocket with the wallet of a frozen victim (see Exhibit 14.1).[1]

Germany

Germans also developed film techniques during the 1920s, many of them starting in the 1919 film *The Cabinet of Doctor Caligari.* Almost all German shooting of this period was confined to studios, where the filmmakers could carefully control lighting, sets, and other elements. The main studio, Ufa (Universum Film AG), had repertory players, not movie stars, and directors who favored expressionistic lighting that emphasized highlights and shadows. Many of the directors and technicians who worked in Germany came to the United States in the 1930s and were instrumental in developing Hollywood films.[2]

Russia

Exhibit 14.1

In René Clair's *The Crazy Ray,* a man is frozen on the side of a building.

Russia was another country whose practitioners made major contributions to early film techniques. The Russians, particularly Sergei Eisenstein, are best known for developing editing techniques. One of Eisenstein's best-known films, *Potemkin* (1925), was about a 1905 rebellion on the battleship *Potemkin* and the reprisals by the czarist government. One scene involves a sailor smashing a dish, an action that takes but a few seconds, but Eisenstein uses an edited sequence of 11 shots to emphasize the sailor's rage. In another scene, in which innocent people are killed as they run down steps, Eisenstein uses a rhythmic variety of shots—long shots from the bottom and top of the steps, close-ups of faces expressing horror, moving shots that reinforce the chaotic movement of the people (see Exhibit 14.2).[3]

14.2 Early Radio

Most countries of the world experimented with radio broadcasting during the 1920s. In some countries, private radio clubs were the initial broadcasters; in other countries, the government took the lead. Radio was slow to develop in the Middle East because the conservative Muslim leaders, who could not understand how wireless worked, suspected radio to be the work of the devil. Ibn Saud, Saudi Arabia's leader, who wanted radio, devised an experiment to satisfy the religious leaders. He asked a group of them to travel to Mecca, where they were to await a wireless transmission that he would send from Riyadh. At the appointed time, he read passages of the Koran to them. Because the devil cannot pronounce the word of the Koran, he convinced them that radio must be the work of human beings, not the devil.[4]

Saudi Arabian experiment

Exhibit 14.2

One of the close-ups of a human face from the slaughter on the steps in Eisenstein's *Potemkin*.

Three basic structures for broadcasting eventually developed throughout the world—private, public, and authoritarian. **Private** radio stations were owned by private businesses. This U.S. model was also the predominant model in Latin America. In Mexico and South America, the radio stations were owned by media barons who handed their broadcasting empires down from one generation to another. The main electronic media company in Mexico was founded by Emilio Azcárraga and was passed on to his son and grandson, also named Emilio. The elder Azcárraga started the company with a chain of radio stations. In the 1930s, he introduced trumpets into Mexican mariachi bands so the music would sound livelier on radio, and today all mariachi bands have horns. In Brazil, the major early radio network was Diários e Emissoras, led by Assis Chateaubriand, but Rádio Globo also held a dominant role. The latter was headed by Roberto Marinho, who would later lead his company to overwhelming dominance in television. Most of these moguls came from the newspaper business, so radio and print journalism were linked. Radio was supported by commercials and featured live news, variety programs, comedies, and **rádionovelas** (serials or soap operas).[5]

private systems

The **public** broadcasting structure was closely aligned to the government and was supported by **license fees** collected from members of the public who owned radios. Britain developed this model in 1922 and it was then adopted by most of Europe and by British colonies throughout the world. The British Broadcasting Corporation (BBC) was under a royal **charter** that gave the BBC a monopoly on all radio broadcasting and created a board of governors appointed for five-year terms. This board was the policy-making group, while a director-general and

public systems

staff performed the day-to-day operations of the BBC. The charter stated that there could be no advertisements on the BBC; the license fees that supported it were collected by the post office. Programming on the early BBC was very paternalistic. Designed to upgrade tastes, it was often referred to as programming from "Auntie BBC." The original organization consisted of three national program services, each designed to lead the listener to the next for a higher cultural experience. At the lowest level was the Light Programme, which consisted of quiz shows, light music, children's adventure, and serials. Level two was the Home Service, which included dramas, school broadcasts, and news. The highest level, called the Third Programme, was classical music, literature, talk, and drama. All these services were national, although the BBC later introduced local stations.[6]

authoritarian systems

The **authoritarian** broadcasting structure was closely supervised by the government. It predominated in countries with dictatorships. Russia provides the main model because, from the beginning, broadcasting in Russia was a state monopoly. When the Communists came to power in 1917, one of Vladimir Lenin's first acts was to centralize radio, which was then just developing. In 1924, the Communists founded an organization called Radio for All Society that started radio stations in major cities. Several years later, the Communists formed a state bureaucracy that eventually oversaw all Soviet radio and TV. Radio programming consisted primarily of news and information that the government wanted the people to hear. Educational and cultural programs were evident, but entertainment programs were scarce. The whole system was supported from general tax dollars and did not broadcast commercials.[7]

14.3 The Colonial Era

During the formative days of radio, many European countries had colonies in Africa, the Middle East, and Asia. The British, who had widespread holdings, exported their public, noncommercial, charter-oriented model of broadcasting, with its license fees and paternalistic programming, throughout the world. They also established the British Empire Service, a **shortwave** service that sent news and other programming from England to its colonies and dominions in such far-flung places as Australia, Canada, India, and Nigeria.

British style

The British style was to encourage British subjects to use radio to preserve and enhance the local culture. As a result, Britain started the radio organizations with British citizens but focused on training natives to run the stations and networks. After several years, the number of local people working in broadcasting far surpassed the number of British. By the 1940s, some of the colonies even offered services in the vernacular language along with their English services.

This was different from other colonial powers, which exerted stronger governing influence. The French, for example, had a policy known as "assimilation" that used radio broadcasting to tie the colonies firmly to the motherland. Not only were most of the employees French, but many of the programs were produced in France.

When the colonial era ended in the 1950s and 1960s, people in the British colonies continued broadcasting operations because they knew how, while people in the French colonies started over from scratch. The Algerians, for example, forced the French to leave very quickly in 1962, but this left hardly anyone capable of maintaining or operating the broadcasting structure. Almost all the technicians had been French, and when they left, the entire broadcasting system came to a temporary standstill.[8]

French style

14.4 World War II and Its Aftermath

As tensions grew in Europe in the late 1930s, countries used radio for propaganda purposes. In 1937, Benito Mussolini's Fascist Italian army invaded Ethiopia and set up a shortwave station to broadcast anti-British propaganda in Arabic to the Arab world. The British concluded that they could no longer concentrate just on their Empire Service. They needed to counter propaganda transmissions. To do this, they set up an **external service,** the BBC World Service, to broadcast worldwide over short-wave in many different languages. During and after the war, people in many countries listened to this BBC service.[9]

BBC World Service

In 1940, the United States started an external service, which later became known as Voice of America (VOA). Originally, it was aimed at Central and South America because these areas were friendly to Germany, which by then had achieved military victories in Europe. Eventually, VOA broadcast to other areas and became as well known as the BBC. During the cold war period that followed World War II, the United States established Radio Free Europe and Radio Liberty, both of which were designed mainly to get America's message into the Soviet Union and its affiliated countries.[10]

VOA

Russia also strengthened its external service, Radio Moscow, during the war. The service was formed in 1925 when a live report of a military parade in Red Square was broadcast to foreign listeners in English, German, and French. During the cold war, Radio Moscow was a widespread Soviet propaganda service that reached many countries.[11]

Radio Moscow

Another American service that developed during the war was the Armed Forces Radio Service (AFRS). Enterprising servicemen in Alaska set up a transmitter and wrote to Hollywood stars asking for radio programs. The stars could not send the programs because of security regulations, so the servicemen contacted the War Department in Washington, which set up AFRS to provide servicemen with American programming they could hear in the field. Some of the broadcasting was accomplished by shortwave, and some was undertaken by troop-operated stations. Several stations actually moved along with the advancing armies, but most were stationary. Studios were set up in Los Angeles so that popular stars could perform on programs, such as *Mail Call,* that were sent to AFRS facilities (see Exhibit 14.3). AFRS was later changed to AFRTS (American Forces Radio and Television Service) and still programs for military personnel and others.[12]

AFRS

Exhibit 14.3

Walter Brennan (left) and Gary Cooper perform for AFRS's *Mail Call* about 1943. They read letters to entertain and boost morale of people fighting in World War II.

Before the war, Germany had a decentralized radio system. The government wanted to cover all of Germany with just one central radio station, but this plan failed because in the 1920s it was technically impractical to transmit one signal to all the little towns and valleys. As a consequence, Germany was divided into broadcast regions, each operating at least semi-independently. When Adolf Hitler rose to power in the early 1930s, he quickly realized the power of radio. In 1933, the government, which by then was controlled by his Nazi Party, established a Ministry for Public Information and Propaganda and put all radio stations under its power. People who had been top radio administrators were sent to concentration camps, and most employees lost their jobs. All information programming was subject to directives from the Nazis, and entertainment programming was not allowed to be "destructive." This meant that compositions by Jewish composers were forbidden, and jazz disappeared from the airwaves.

Germany

After the war, the Allied powers that occupied West Germany reestablished a decentralized form of radio, this time not for technical reasons but for political ones—they did not want radio to aid the resurgence of a strong central government. They set up the ARD, an umbrella organization for stations in nine regions, but it did not broadcast anything nationally. ARD was the only broadcast organization service in West Germany for a number of years. East Germany went its own way with an authoritarian system along the lines of that of its occupying power, the Soviet Union.[13]

Japan

Japan, before the war, had a government-regulated, nonprofit, private broadcasting system. Private companies (primarily newspapers) owned the stations and collected the license fees, but they were heavily overseen by the government. In 1926, the government formed NHK, a national public-service network that provided much of the programming for the stations. During the war, radio was under state control. After the war, the Allied powers reorganized broadcasting to include both NHK, as a government public-service network, and new private commercial stations that were not allowed to form networks. They were intended to be local stations serving local needs. However, large newspaper companies bought commercial stations in several areas of Japan and played similar programming on all of them, thus creating a semi-network.[14]

China

As Mao Tse-tung was rising to power in China in the 1940s, he and his revolutionaries set up guerrilla radio stations built with Russian transmitters and scavenged parts. These stations operated out of caves and partially destroyed buildings but were the basis for what eventually became China's centralized radio system, CPBS.[15]

Film, too, was used during World War II for propaganda purposes, especially by Mussolini in Italy. After the war, filmmaking in Europe gradually returned, largely as an artistic experience with the director firmly in charge of style and content. One well-known Italian director was Federico Fellini, whose main star was his wife, Giulietta Masina. With her, he made such films as *La Strada* (1954) and *Night of Cabiria* (1956). Fellini's main theme was sensuality versus spirituality (see Exhibit 14.4). Ingmar Bergman of Sweden was another influential director who probed human emotions and was concerned with spiritual conflict and the fragility of the psyche.[16]

Some of the French directors who had made movies before the war picked up again, making the same type of artistic films. A group of film critics, including André Bazin, François Truffaut, and Jean-Luc Goddard, harshly criticized French films, but eventually some of them joined the production process and became directors. England's films

Exhibit 14.4
Giulietta Masina (right) in a scene from *La Strada*.

of the 1940s and 1950s tended to be somewhat stuffy adaptations of classic literature. The British also shot "quota quickies"—**B pictures** that met the quota of British films that theater owners had to show. These were screened as part of double features to go with American movies that people were more interested in seeing.[17]

postwar film

14.5 Early Television

Television developed later internationally than it did in the United States. One reason was that much of the world was physically recovering from World War II and had other priorities. Also, television was much more expensive than radio, so poorer countries could not easily afford it. TV also was not adopted for social reasons. In South Africa, TV was not introduced until 1976 because the apartheid rulers did not want to disturb the "South African way of life." They feared programming from outside the country because they thought it would create dissatisfaction among the nonwhites who might see how people of their races lived in other countries.[18]

South Africa

In Muslim countries, religion inhibited the introduction of television even more than it had the introduction of radio because the Muslim religion prohibits the creation of graven images—which television was considered to do. In Saudi Arabia, the introduction of TV proved to be fatal to the king. When test TV transmissions started in 1965, Saudi religious conservatives marched on the station. One of the conservatives, Khalid, was killed by a policeman during a struggle with a government official. Khalid's family appealed to King Faisal to punish the person who shot him, but Faisal said the policeman had acted properly. Ten years later, Khalid's younger brother shot and killed King Faisal and was reported to have said, "Now my brother is avenged."[19]

Saudi Arabia

Britain

Television eventually developed almost everywhere, and once again the British model was the most common. The British still had many of their colonies during the early days of TV, but even the countries that were no longer tightly allied with Britain included television in their already established radio structures. Britain had televised the coronation of George VI in 1937—quite a feat for that time. World War II interrupted development, and it was not until 1953, with the televised coronation of Queen Elizabeth II, that the British people became aware of TV and purchased sets.

Latin America

The Latin American countries, which, like the United States, did not experience the ravages of World War II within their borders, started TV relatively early. Part of the reason for this early start was that media companies in the United States, seeking profits, invested in Latin American media. NBC assisted Argentina; ABC was active in Venezuela; CBS invested in Uruguay; and Time-Life gave money and advice to Brazil's TV Globo. In general, the same newspaper moguls who dominated radio also dominated television.[20]

14.6 Broadcasting's Development

pirate stations

Between the 1950s and the 1980s, the private, public, and authoritarian systems of broadcasting continued, but they underwent changes and amalgamations. In Britain, the programming's paternalistic nature was criticized. In 1963, **pirate stations** located on ships anchored off the coast of England began broadcasting rock music, which BBC radio disdained. This programming became so popular that when the government planned to suppress it, a huge public outcry prompted the BBC instead to revamp its radio programming from three to four services, one of which played rock music.

ITA

A heated 1954 debate in Parliament about the quality and role of television led to the establishment of the Independent Television Authority (ITA), a new television service that was structured very differently from the BBC. The ITA was a regionally based national network that did not produce programs. All programming came from 15 independent companies, called ITVs, selected and franchised by the ITA. Each of these companies served a different area of the country and programmed local material, as well as contributing to the national fare (see Exhibit 14.5). After 1954, a number of new TV services (both BBC- and ITA-operated) were added in Britain, and public broadcasters expanded their offerings in other parts of Europe. Advertising was a controversial subject, with broadcasters trying to maintain services with few or no commercials. But television was too expensive to be supported totally by license fees, and slowly but surely, television commercials were accepted by Europe's public systems.[21]

Canada

The public systems adapted in other ways to meet their local needs. Canada provides a good example. Because of its ties to Britain, it has a government-run broadcasting system, the Canadian Broadcasting Corporation (CBC). It also has a private broadcasting system, CTV, similar in structure to that of the United States. Most Canadians live near the U.S. border, and the private stations cannot make money servicing the remote areas, so the CBC's mission includes serving these outlying regions. Canada started cable TV in 1950, two years before it had

Exhibit 14.5

A production scene from *Coronation Street*, one of independent British TV's most popular early programs. Its cast of characters often interacted in the pub, Rovers Return Inn.

a broadcast TV network. There were 140,000 TV receivers in Canada before it officially started television broadcasting because cable TV systems were bringing in U.S. stations for subscribers to watch. The presence of American programming in Canada is a thorn in the side of the Canadian government. Politicians are constantly trying to stem the tide of U.S. cultural invasion by setting up rules and **quotas** that are enacted, changed, and opposed, all in an attempt to enable Canada to express its cultural identity.[22]

The authoritarian model of broadcasting continued in full force in the Soviet Union (see Exhibit 14.6) and spread to other Communist countries, most of which were in Eastern Europe. The pattern of central control, however, was not as heavy-handed in these countries as in the USSR. For example, Hungary had local cable TV. Unlike the United States, where cable TV became popular because of the national pay and basic channels, Hungarian cable started because the people saw it as a way of showing locally produced programming that was more liberal in content than the national product.[23]

The Latin American private systems continued to grow. In the 1960s, they cast off the American companies and assumed all responsibilities, financial and operational. Television, which during its early years was viewed

Eastern Europe

Exhibit 14.6

In the 1950s, the Russians built this television tower on the outskirts of Moscow next to a monument to conquerors of space.

Latin America

primarily by the economic elite, spread to the masses. The video version of the rádionovela, the **telenovela,** became extremely popular, and Latin American countries (particularly Mexico and Brazil) built worldwide markets for these productions.[24]

14.7 The Concerns of Developing Nations

Ethiopia

The poorer nations of the world had trouble developing television and filmmaking because of the cost. National pride, however, led them to develop TV systems as best they could. For example, in 1963, Haile Selassie of Ethiopia persuaded the newly formed Organization of African Unity to hold its first meeting in his capital city. A European manufacturer supplied closed-circuit TV for the event. Haile Selassie was so impressed that he ordered a broadcast television station to be installed in time for the imperial birthday—always a big event. A British firm built the station in six months—just in time for the celebration. Thus it was that Ethiopia, a country with one of the world's lowest per capita incomes, had a national television service in 1964 but hardly any sets on which to view its programs.

Middle East

When oil was discovered in the Middle East, this desert area became important to the world economy. In the 1970s, oil prices skyrocketed and these countries became rich. They used some of their money to build fancy broadcasting systems, but the population of the area was so small that the countries did not have adequate personnel to operate the systems and produce programs.[25]

India

Some of the developing countries that did engage in moviemaking—Brazil, Argentina, Egypt—tended to produce movies of a somewhat pedantic nature. An exception was India (see Exhibit 14.7), which developed a thriving film production community that produced more movies per year than Hollywood. The films were mainly formula musicals intended to entertain. The people of India

Exhibit 14.7

An Indian film shoot in Delhi, near Qutub Minar, the world's tallest minaret.

loved their homegrown movies; movie stars became celebrities, and the music of the films became very popular. Eventually the term "Bollywood" was coined—short for "Bombay Hollywood"—to refer to the movie industry of India, much of which is in Bombay (now called Mumbai).[26]

Whether poor in financial or human resources, these developing countries were happy to accept money and technical expertise from other countries. But they did not want the philosophical and social strings that came with foreign programming. Most of the developing countries had just emerged from colonialism and did not want to be subjected to "electronic colonialism." However, these countries could not afford to produce much of their own TV programming, particularly expensive dramas. They were even less likely to produce movies, which cost even more. As a result, they imported TV programs and movies, particularly the readily available American material. Although the residents of developing nations usually liked the American fare, their governments were uneasy about it. They feared that the lifestyles shown on such programs as *Dallas* would make their people discontent or materialistic. They did not want their youth corrupted by American fashion or mores. Also, the amount of sex and violence in American movies did not sit well with government officials.

electronic colonialism

Some of the major conflict between developed and developing countries manifested itself in the area of news. Most of the democratic developed nations were in favor of the **free flow** of information. They believed that any country or media organization should be able to send information to any other country. The developing nations favored **national identity,** believing that each country should decide what information should be allowed to cross its borders.

The United Nations set up a commission to address the free flow–national identity issue and create a New World Information Order (NWIO). The commission tackled the complexities, changing realities, and possible solutions concerning the world's communication structure. Its 1980 report, called the MacBride Report after the commission's chairman, supported the free flow of information but strongly suggested that developing countries be provided with the means to contribute as well as receive. It recommended setting up training programs and giving countries more access to technology. Although the report was hailed when it first came out, eventually it was criticized by both sides, and the issues are still not resolved. Satellite broadcasting further exacerbated the problem because signals from satellites reach much farther than broadcast signals.[27]

MacBride Report

14.8 The Coming of Satellites

The first American communication satellite, Telstar I, was launched in 1962, and soon after, the U.S. Congress set up Comsat, an agency to handle American satellite issues. At Comsat's urging, Intelsat was formed in 1964 to handle satellite needs for many countries. At first Comsat managed Intelsat, but in 1973 Intelsat became an independent organization owned by a consortium of countries, each of which paid a yearly fee based on its use of services (see Exhibit 14.8). When a nation wanted to use a satellite for an event, such as telecasting the Olympics or a world soccer championship, it could rent satellite time from Intelsat. In that

Intelsat

Exhibit 14.8
The lobby of the
former Intelsat
building in
Washington, DC,
displaying some of
its early satellites.

Exhibit 14.8
The lobby of the former Intelsat building in Washington, DC, displaying some of its early satellites.

way, any nation, no matter how small, could have access to satellite technology by paying a modest fee.[28]

CNN

Satellites were used for many purposes including beaming farm information to rural India (see "Zoom In" box), broadcasting directly to homes in Europe and Brazil, and the distribution of CNN throughout the world. Although Ted Turner started CNN in 1980 as a cable TV network for American viewers, he had internationalization in mind from the beginning. When the service went worldwide in the mid-1980s, entities in various countries slowly subscribed to (or bootlegged) the satellite feeds, until today most countries air CNN.[29]

STAR

Another use of satellites was for the Satellite Television Asia Region (STAR) system. Started in Hong Kong in 1991 by property developer Li Ka-shing, it broadcast unscrambled signals of music videos, movies, sports, and other fare to countries from Egypt to Japan. It created a huge appetite for its programming. For example, in India, where the only television programming was from the sleepy, paternalistic public system Doordarshan, enterprising entrepreneurs hooked up rudimentary cable systems to serve large apartment buildings. For a fee, each apartment was wired to a VCR for movies and to a satellite dish for CNN and STAR. The hookup rate was phenomenal. The fate of the characters on *The Bold and the Beautiful* became a main topic of Indian conversation. In 1993, Rupert Murdoch purchased a controlling interest in STAR for $525 million. Li Ka-shing had originally invested $250 million in the service, and after Murdoch's purchase, he still owned one-third of the company.[30]

objections

Satellite programming did not receive instant acclaim from governments that disliked their citizens receiving information and entertainment with views and attitudes different from those espoused by the government. The people, however, liked the diversity, and, in the end, the governments gave in. At one time the Greek government said it would shoot down any satellites that flew over its airspace, but by 1988 the Greek government broadcasting system was airing foreign programs brought in by satellite. China, while trying to position itself as a major manufacturer of satellite dishes, forbade its citizens from owning them. This didn't work and the Chinese gained access to satellite programming.[31]

ZOOM IN: **A Satellite Experiment**

One of the first forays into large-scale use of satellites for communication occurred in India. In 1975, the Indian Space Research Organization, in conjunction with the Indian public television organization, Doordarshan, launched the Satellite Instructional Television Experiment (SITE), one of the most ambitious experiments in television history. With the help of the United States, it used a NASA satellite to beam farm, health, hygiene, and family-planning programs four hours each day to 2,400 villages in rural India.

SITE was also used to telecast entertainment programs, such as *I Love Lucy*. Because few people in rural areas had their own TV sets, they watched SITE programs in communal areas.

SITE's goal of educating people about how they could implement solutions to the country's problems was not met. Tests showed that farmers who watched the SITE programs were not any more innovative than farmers who didn't.

NASA had lent India the satellite for only one year, and when NASA disconnected the satellite in 1976, the SITE experiment ended. It brought the wonders of TV to audiences who otherwise would not have seen them, however, and set the stage for later satellite development. It also resulted in many Indian baby girls being named Lucy, after Lucille Ball.

Would you call this experiment a success or a failure? Why?

Viewers watching a SITE program at a communal location in the Indian village of Gujarat.

14.9 Privatization

Privatization was rampant in the 1980s, particularly in Western Europe where the staid public broadcasting systems seemed to be out of step with the times. Privately owned advertising-supported stations and networks, organized along the lines of those in the United States and offering similar programming, multiplied during the

illegal radio stations

decade. As might be expected, established government broadcasters fought the introduction of these new services. In many countries, the original private stations were illegal local radio stations that operated without a license. They became so popular that eventually they were legalized. In France, the government suppressed most of them until 1981, when Socialist candidate François Mitterand came out in favor of them. He won the election and passed a law legalizing private radio. In most countries, once private radio was authorized, private TV was not far behind.[32]

Germany

The advent of satellite services and cable TV aided privatization. By the late 1970s, West Germany had two government TV systems, ARD, the loosely connected state-based system, and ZDF, a more centralized network started in 1963. In 1978, German politicians decided to launch four cable TV pilot projects to improve reception. They also decided to use this pilot to experiment with programming ideas, primarily by allowing private program suppliers to provide material for the cable projects. The cable pilots failed, mainly because of marketing inexperience. For example, one company tried to force all subscribers to sign a 12-year contract. In an attempt to solve the cable problem, the states amended their broadcasting laws so the private programming suppliers could operate in other ways. The most common way was by forming private advertising-supported TV stations. Eventually, they also supplied programming to German satellite services and to revived cable systems.[33]

France

Privatization affected the public systems, which over the years had become bloated with people and aging equipment. The new entrepreneurs—with slim staffs, new technologies, popular programming, and advertising dollars—stole the audience. Many of the public systems lightened their programming, amid anguished cries about the effects of lowering cultural standards. Others went out of business; the French government in 1987, in a very controversial move, privatized its original government service.[34]

Britain

Even the venerable BBC was attacked for overspending and for forgetting its public-service function. When its charter came up for renewal in the 1990s, Parliament scrutinized it carefully; as a result, the BBC streamlined itself and stayed in business, but not as the same old "Auntie." Independent television in Britain underwent its share of turmoil also. All the regional ITV franchises came up for renewal, and some broadcasters who had been in business for years lost their franchises to newcomers.[35]

Privatization changed the nature of broadcasting, not only in Europe but also in Asia, Africa, and other parts of the world that had not previously had a private structure. As a result, many people who 15 years earlier had had one or two program choices now had more than 30.

14.10 The VCR

Adding to the choices were the movies and other programs available on videocassette. **Videocassette recorders (VCRs)** became popular in almost every country. In the early 1980s, much of their use was illegal. Cassettes and VCRs were small enough to be easily smuggled into a country. The programming material on the cassettes was easy to duplicate, so pirated copies of tapes were abundant.

Many of the countries where early **piracy** abounded were poor countries that did not have **copyright** laws. Even people in the governments did not understand royalties and saw nothing wrong with dubbing copies of programs. Over the years, the United States and other developed countries have persuaded many of them to support the provisions of copyright laws, so the situation is not as bad as it used to be.

piracy

Videocassettes were attractive in some countries because they contained material that was not available otherwise. In Saudi Arabia, for example, companies at first duplicated the tapes legally and brought them into the country despite very strict Muslim censors. The censors did not know what they were dealing with— they couldn't see anything on the physical tapes. When they discovered the forbidden cultural and sexual content of many of the tapes, they outlawed the videos. The result was a thriving underground industry that smuggled, duplicated, and sold tapes any way it could.

censorship

Legal tapes, as well as illegal ones, became very popular. The African country of Cameroon, which had delayed the establishment of television, finally started a television broadcast system in 1986, in part to lure viewers away from videocassettes. In India, video clubs and parlors sprang up, and it became the fashion to ride around in buses that showed videos. Eastern European black markets were a hotbed of pirated tapes during the 1980s. Some people in this part of the world got their first view of Western life from videocassettes. The tapes were instrumental in raising discontent with the Communist lifestyle.[36]

popularity

14.11 The Collapse of Communism

When Polish leader Lech Walesa was asked what caused the collapse of Communism, he pointed to a TV set and said, "It all came from there."[37]

Communist governments tried hard to keep their citizens from obtaining information from outside countries. They jammed signals of external services and even employed wired radio that carried only government stations. But as technology progressed, information on broadcast radio and TV, satellite, and videocassettes did seep in. Most citizens within Communist countries knew they were not getting complete information from their government systems. The desire for more communication with the outside world was part of what led to the uprisings that undermined Communism.

The media also acted as a messenger to show the outside world what was really happening in these countries. Individuals, armed with audiotape recorders and camcorders, taped injustices within their countries and got the material to CNN, VOA, or the BBC. In one 1988 incident, a Czechoslovakian radio hobbyist sent information to Radio Free Europe in Munich describing intervention by Communist troops against people who were praying on Good Friday. Several months later, Czechoslovakian television staffers disobeyed their bosses and aired student protests against Communism. This led to the downfall of Communism in Czechoslovakia.[38]

outside communication

After Communism fell, Eastern European countries struggled to build a new electronic media system. Political instability racked these countries, and laws

new systems

could not be drafted fast enough to handle all the societal changes, let alone the changes in broadcasting. But things eventually settled down, and this part of the world also adopted privatization, cable TV, satellite TV, Western-style programming, and advertising.[39]

China

Even in countries where Communism still survived, such as China, the effects of media could be felt. In 1989, Mikhail Gorbachev, then head of the Soviet Union, visited China, and to demonstrate its new openness, the Chinese government allowed media from throughout the world into the country. The government planned a grand ceremonial event, but China's own citizens had learned about using the media and turned this event into an opportunity to publicly embarrass the leadership by demonstrating in Tiananmen Square (see Exhibit 14.9) for additional freedoms. The media, of course, covered this uprising, and CNN was able to get live pictures out to the world even after the government started restricting media access. Since that time, the Chinese government has periodically become more open. It allowed foreign correspondents to see the devastation of the Sichuan Province 8.3 earthquake in May 2008, and when it hosted the 2008 summer Olympics, it did exhibit more openness than in the past.[40]

Russia

Russian media have taken a slightly different tack. After the fall of Communism, the government-run media services struggled with programming philosophy because their programming had been so highly pedantic. New private companies (primarily joint ventures between Russian companies and Western companies) sprang up—radio stations that played rock music and TV stations that showed American movies and TV series. Eventually a new TV service, NTV, built from scratch by a private Russian company, became very popular. It aired Western material, much of which had not been seen in Russia before, but also began producing slick, gritty, realistic dramas and miniseries as well as some

Exhibit 14.9

A young man facing down tanks was one of the most memorable shots of the Tiananmen Square incident, which was shown throughout the world.

comedies. This helped revive the Russian film industry, which had essentially disappeared when American movies were introduced. However, NTV also aired news that dared to criticize the government. When Vladimir Putin became president, he did not take kindly to this approach, and the government started to thwart NTV and other private media operations. In 2001, the government gas monopoly, Gazpron, took over NTV and brought it back to the more staid philosophy of the old authoritarian model. Today both TV and film products are geared mainly to supporting the ideals of the government.[41]

Another result of the fall of Communism was a change in the Voice of America and similar external services. As previously mentioned, the main mission of these services during the cold war was to send information to the Soviet Union and its satellites. When this was no longer needed, VOA, BBC World Service, and other similar services lost some of their importance.[42]

VOA

14.12 Indigenous Programming

Most countries have always had the desire to produce radio, television, and film material themselves, but economics and logistics impeded them. Poorer countries found they could purchase imported (mostly American) entertainment much more cheaply than they could produce it themselves. Richer nations, when they first incorporated privatization, had such a great need for programming to fill all the new channels that they, too, relied largely on American fare. As these markets developed, American production studios became dependent on exportation. Most TV shows and movies produced in the United States did not make a profit through their national sales; the black ink came only after the products were sold overseas.[43]

American shows

But the media world is changing and more countries are producing for themselves. Generally, the indigenous radio and TV fare is preferred over imported programming if it is of an entertaining (as opposed to pedantic or propagandistic) nature. Soap operas, talk shows, game shows, dramas, news (see "Zoom In" box)—all have more appeal if they feature people speaking the native language without subtitles or dubbed dialogue and engaging in actions that are familiar to the listeners and viewers.[44]

appeal

Sometimes the indigenous programming features local talent and crew but is based on a concept that is **franchised** from another country. One of the most successful early franchised shows was *Wheel of Fortune*. King World, the show's distributor, sent a booklet describing the show and a consultant to every country that wanted to air the program. It required that the format be essentially the same as that shown in the United States, but the "Vanna Whites" and "Pat Sajaks" were local, as were all the contestants. King World charged the stations or networks for using the idea, but the cost was less than buying a U.S. version and the series was more successful because it looked local.[45]

franchises

More countries are also producing movies. China has become a major producer of movies that are well accepted in other countries, bringing profits as well as recognition to China. New Zealand developed an active national campaign to produce its own quality movies. Eastern European countries, which had a history

movies

ZOOM IN: **Al Jazeera: A Loud Voice from a Tiny Nation**

Al Jazeera is an indigenous satellite news service established in the Middle East that has taken on an important role in world politics. It was launched in 1996 with $150 million in start-up money from Hamad bin Khalifa alThani, the emir of the tiny peninsula country of Qatar (Al Jazeera means "peninsula" in Arabic).

He had overthrown his father in a bloodless coup and decided to make Qatar into a modern democracy, in part by abolishing the country's Information Ministry, which had been responsible for censorship. Although it was pro-Arab, Al Jazeera was unlike other news programs in the Middle East, which were filled with footage of government officials greeting other government officials; its reporters were encouraged to report on such forbidden subjects as women's rights, polygamy, and the legitimacy of some Arab regimes.

With footage such as that showing the destruction of two ancient Buddha statues in Afghanistan and the burning of an Egyptian flag by Palestinians who felt Egypt was going soft on Israel, it angered neighboring governments that tried to shield their inhabitants from such news. Several Mideast countries briefly recalled their ambassadors from Qatar over stories they didn't like, and many other countries tried, futilely, to keep their citizens from viewing Al Jazeera.

After the terrorist attack on the World Trade Center and Pentagon on September 11, 2001, Al Jazeera became well known worldwide. Initially, it was the only network allowed inside the Taliban-controlled areas of Afghanistan, and it was the network Osama bin Laden sent tapes to when he decided to talk about his views of America.

Al Jazeera has expanded over the years to include more channels, such as ones devoted to sports, documentaries, and children's programming. It also broadcasts in several languages, including English, and can be accessed on the internet and through some American cable TV systems.

It covered the uprisings in Egypt in 2011 that led to the ouster of Egyptian President Hosni Mubarak in a more open manner than the government-owned media, which were characterizing the demonstrations as organized by a small minority of foreign-influenced hooligans. The Egyptian government shut down Al Jazeera's Cairo bureau and revoked its license to broadcast from Egypt, but its journalists continued to report anyhow. The viewership of its English-language service greatly increased during the uprising underscoring that it has rightly gained an important place in the world media structure.

Qatar and its Middle Eastern neighbors.

of making quality films, revived the industry after coming out from under Communism. Albania, Armenia, Croatia, Tanzania, Thailand, and Uruguay have been among the countries recently submitting films to the Academy of Motion Picture Arts and Sciences for Oscar consideration in the foreign-language category.[46]

Worldwide, the cost of production equipment has fallen and production techniques have improved. Poorer countries are able to incorporate the same flashy effects as wealthier countries and well-trained cast and crew members can be found in many parts of the world.

Despite the recent increase in indigenous programming, American programming is still the most common import. It is popular enough that countries institute quotas to protect their local production from this "media imperialism." For example, the European Union requires that 50 percent of programming in its member countries must be from Europe. Some countries are even stricter. French law says that 60 percent must be European, and of that amount, 40 percent must be French.[47]

quotas

14.13 Globalization

In the 1960s, Canadian professor Marshall McLuhan predicted that television would create a "global village" in which all parts of the world could communicate with each other. Today we are close to reaching that global village and it has greatly changed the electronic media production and distribution structure.

Originally, American radio and TV companies produced mainly for American audiences. If their works attracted audiences overseas, that was simply icing on the cake. But as the international market grew, Hollywood realized media products could earn more money overseas than domestically. That led to more aggressive selling to other countries.

Gradually, countries such as Australia, Mexico, Brazil, and Britain, which had always exported some material, increased their share of the world market, somewhat at the expense of the United States. In addition, new countries, such as Poland and the Czech Republic, entered the TV program distribution field. All these countries found that distributing their TV programs and movies became harder as countries started relying on their own indigenous material. As a result, countries that wished to export programming began undertaking new strategies.[48]

early distribution

For one, companies began forming alliances and **joint ventures** to increase multinational involvement. The theory, which proved correct, was that a company that had participation in a movie or TV show would be more likely to buy the product to show in its country. This would, naturally, increase the revenue for the product.

Some of the initial international cooperation simply involved shooting all or part of a project in another country. An American company, for example, might shoot in New Zealand because of particular scenery needs or in Italy so it could have access to world-renowned costume designers. Or it might shoot in Germany because of that country's generous film subsidies or in Australia, which houses some excellent production and postproduction facilities. Countries such as Japan and India, which have a history of filmmaking, could be counted on to have knowledgeable crews.[49]

shooting in other countries

**financial
arrangements**

The cooperation moved beyond one company in a particular country utilizing strengths of another country. What developed were financial and creative liaisons. A number of countries would put money into a movie or TV series, thus spreading the risk. The fact that all countries would show this **co-production** helped assure its financial success. Companies that had money invested also wanted creative control, which might lead to Mexican and Italian actors, a British producer, a French director, and a Japanese cinematographer. Expectations were initially low for these films. They were considered to be a financial marriage of convenience. And, indeed, some of the cultural clashes that occurred among executives, cast, and crew inhibited effective production. Particularly difficult were co-productions that involved Russia. People found it very annoying to work through the Russian red tape in order to find out whom they needed to go to or what they needed to do to get government money.[50]

**co-production
successes**

Eventually, the co-production process settled down and some excellent films have raised the creative bar. In 2003 New Zealand came onto the film scene in a big way by winning 11 Oscars, including best picture, for *Lord of the Rings: The Return of the King*. It was the final film of a trilogy that had been funded by two American companies as well as director Peter Jackson's New Zealand-based company (see

Exhibit 14.10). It was a risky, highly creative undertaking, in part because of its special effects and in part because the footage for all three movies was shot all at once before any of the movies were released. In 2009 the Oscar for best picture went to *Slumdog Millionaire*, a production that involved Britain and India. The director was British but most of the cast and crew were from India, where the movie was shot. One of the British companies involved owned the rights to the British TV series *Who Wants to Be a Millionaire?* so was able to give the rights to use that concept for the movie.[51]

There have been many other co-productions and will be many more. The TV series, *The Tutors*, is a co-production between Canada and Ireland. Warner, Disney, and Fox have co-production deals with an Indian company and Universal has one with a Mexican production company. When South Africa hosted the 2010 World Cup, visiting media personnel found that the country had the equipment, crew, and support services needed for production. This led to a number of productions including the movie *The First Grader* about an 84-year-old Kenyan who learns to read. The story was written by a South African and included participation by Britain, Kenya, and the U.S. National Geographic[52]

Exhibit 14.10

New Zealand director Peter Jackson holds the Oscar for best picture for *The Lord of the Rings: The Return of the King*.

Another form of international electronic media sharing involves franchises. As countries developed their indigenous TV programming, they began franchising their series to each other. The United States,

franchises

too, now franchises more from other countries than the other way around. Two of the first popular series were *Survivor*, started in Sweden in 1997 and first aired in the United States in 2000, and *Who Wants to Be a Millionaire?* on air in Britain in 1998 and started in the United States and many other countries in 1999. Interestingly, many of the most popular franchise show ideas (*Big Brother, Deal or No Deal, Fear Factor, The Voice*) have come from the Netherlands. Dick de Rijk, one of the creators of these shows, attributes the success to the fact that, because Holland is such a small country, programs produced there have to be able to cross borders in order to gain enough audience to be successful. That approach gives Dutch producers a different mindset than that found in program creators from larger countries.[53]

remakes

A variation on franchising is **remakes,** something that is common within the film industry. One country will remake another country's popular movie, using cast and crew members from its own country and producing the movie in its native language. Sweden's 2009 award-winning crime movie *Men Who Hate Women* was remade by several countries including the United States, where it was named *The Girl with the Dragon Tattoo*. Spain's movie *Three Meters above the Sky* was remade by Italian moviemakers and France's *Love Crime* became a British remake. Remakes are popular because they are somewhat of a sure thing. A concept that was popular in one country is likely to be popular in another.[54]

local productions

Once countries found they could produce material popular in a number of other countries, some production companies came up with the idea of producing programming that would appeal primarily to another country. Disney produced *High School Musical* in Chinese for the Chinese audience. Sony produced a movie about a 1970s British soccer manager, well-known in the UK but unknown in other countries, and marketed it to the British audience.[55]

bypassing studios

Some international production companies are bypassing deals with Hollywood studios and working directly with stars. George Clooney, Brad Pitt, and Julia Roberts have signed independently with an Indian company (see Exhibit 14.11). A Korean-based company has a deal with American director Chris Columbus.[56]

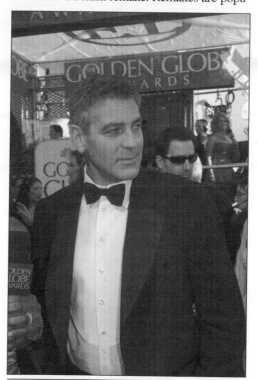

Exhibit 14.11
George Clooney is one of the American actors who has signed with an international company independently, as opposed to being part of an American project.

**other
arrangements**

Many other types of international electronic media procedures are developing. StudioCanal, a French company, is producing audience-friendly English-language movies and also has a large library that includes English-language films. Sometimes companies don't bother with temporary alliances; they buy each other. Sony (Japanese) bought Columbia (American) and renamed it Sony Pictures. A Canadian company owns a New Zealand TV network.[57]

**American
imports**

One of the main outcomes of globalization is that the United States, which for many years was somewhat insular and cocky about its movie and TV program dominance, is now very much aware of the rest of the world. Many broadcast and cable networks buy foreign products—children's programs from Australia, dramas from Britain, films from France. In addition, minority audiences in the United States are eager to see programming in their native languages. Whole cable channels or independent stations that are devoted to programming in Spanish, Vietnamese, Korean, and other languages buy programming from those countries.[58]

American still leads the world in film and TV production, but other countries have carved out spots for themselves. What seems to be working well is spreading risk by securing funding and distribution in a cooperative manner with companies and governments throughout the world. Marshall McLuhan would concur.

14.14 The Digital Age

**obtaining
and providing
information**

Digital telecommunication has come to all parts of the globe. The internet and portable devices have already brought enormous changes to communication. For the first time, theoretically everyone in the entire world has access to the same base of information (or jewelry advertisements or titillating photos). For the most part, this information is uncensored and free of the **gatekeepers** who decide what people will or will not hear or see with most other media. Perhaps even more important, anyone can be a provider of information or entertainment—again without outside control.

**Mideast and
China**

Tweets and **emails** between individuals from different countries and **chatrooms** that are not bound by geography greatly enhance interpersonal communications. During the 2011 Arab Spring uprisings in the Middle East, insurgents organized their plans primarily through Facebook and Twitter. Some of the same countries that tried to keep satellite out have also tried to protect their citizens from the internet. China, for example, went to great lengths to police the internet, but hookups became common. The response from the government was akin to "if you can't lick them, join them." Chinese authorities trained and paid bloggers to try to steer online discussions in ways favorable to the government, and government officials sent text messages with inspirational Maoist quotes.[59]

phone systems

Until fairly recently, large areas of the world had antiquated, unreliable rotary-dial telephone systems. They have been able to skip several generations of telephone improvements and go straight to cellular, internet, or satellite-based phones. These new phone technologies greatly enhance the ability of people and organizations to communicate internationally.

Many parts of the world are in the process of converting to digital radio and television. Some had hopes that all countries would use the same standard to facilitate ease of program exchange, but that is not happening. Brazil and Japan developed standards to compete with the American one and are working to talk other countries into adopting those standards.[60]

Other aspects of digital technologies are popular throughout the world. Pods, pads, and video games (see Exhibit 14.12) have been as much a success in other countries as they have in the United States. European movie producers started shooting movies entirely with digital video well before this practice was common in the United States. Digital technologies are increasing the speed, depth, and breadth of communication.

popularity

Exhibit 14.12
One never knows where video game consoles are going to show up—in this case, in a Scottish hospital where Prince Charles was visiting children.

14.15 Issues and the Future

The proliferation of new electronic media forms has affected the rest of the world as much as it has the United States. Although digital-based companies such as Twitter and Facebook allow people to communicate more thoroughly and quickly than old-fashioned letters, landline phone calls, or even broadcast signals or satellite feeds, they present problems. As recently as the 1960s, President John F. Kennedy had six days to ponder what to do before going public about the Cuban missile crisis. In 1991, during the Persian Gulf conflict, President George H. W. Bush was lucky to have six hours before making a major decision—and then it was with the whole world watching. In 2011 the uprisings in the Middle East could be photographed, reported, analyzed, and sometimes blown out of proportion within minutes. Although this ability to communicate rapidly keeps people informed, it can also aggravate situations that would cool down on their own.

time change

problems

The rapidity with which new forms of communication have swept the world also caused problems and societal changes. The Middle East did not have enough people to operate its hastily constructed broadcasting structure. The people of Eastern Europe needed to change their philosophical and legal mind-set to cope with media after the fall of Communism. Public broadcasting systems around the world had to react to the financial impact of privatization. The future effects of digital media on government structure, transportation, and commerce are still unknown. For example, multiplatform advertising may help strengthen weak economies or it may turn people into avid materialists who are frustrated because they cannot buy what they see.

cost

The cost of adopting every new technological wonder that comes along is daunting, not only for individuals but also for countries. Poor nations and poor people are particularly affected in that the gap between the "haves" and "have-nots" becomes wider. Because much of media consumption relates to obtaining information, the economically poor also become the information poor. Despite the United Nations' attempt to create a New World Information Order, the developed countries still do most of the sending, and developing countries are left to receive information that they do not necessarily want.

effect on America

Throughout much of the 1900s, the most popular entertainment was American. However, many countries are now producing a larger share of their own programming and are successfully exporting it. These programs compete with Hollywood, which by now depends on international sales to make ends meet. American content producers and producers throughout the world are making cooperative adjustments in order to create an equitable media stage. Working internationally presents both exciting opportunities and major challenges for those who will work in the electronic media industry in the future.

14.16 Summary

There have been many changes in the international electronic media scene over the years. The early distinct private, public, and authoritarian broadcasting systems have given way to a mixture of systems that emphasize privatization. Pirate radio stations, satellites, and cable TV were instrumental in leading to the changes. The Colonial era, when powerful nations developed and operated the broadcasting systems of less powerful nations, is long gone. However, the free flow/national identity conflict still exists with wealthy nations dominating.

External services, such as VOA, BBC World Service, and Radio Moscow no longer serve the propaganda purposes they did during World War II and the Cold War. Likewise, the German and Japanese broadcasting systems the Allies formulated after World War II have been altered by media proliferation.

The VCR, satellites, and world programming services such as CNN led to a downfall of Communism and a restructuring of the formerly Communistic media systems. China, although still Communistic, was also forced to develop more open communication even though it attempted to counteract effects of satellites and the internet. Mideastern countries that once opposed radio and TV on religious grounds now find they are confronted with the realities of texting, social networking, and Al Jazeera.

The early movies in countries such as France, Germany, and Russia were largely artistic expressions. Filming was too expensive for most of the world. Today many countries have entered the mainstream movie business. Even poor countries can produce movies or join in co-productions so that they have a say in film production and distribution. Companies also recreate movie concepts from other countries, produce indigenous material that they franchise or sell to each other, and bypass Hollywood studios to work directly with stars.

World communication has developed at a rapid pace, which has created some problems. The tying together of countries through media, however, is bound to continue.

Suggested Websites

http://afrts.dodmedia.osd.mil (the American Forces Radio and Television Service)

www.bbc.co.uk (the British Broadcasting Corporation)

www.cbc.ca (the Canadian Broadcasting Corporation)

www.intelsat.com (satellite provider Intelsat)

www.voa.gov (the external service Voice of America)

Notes

1. Gerald Mast, *A Short History of the Movies* (New York: Macmillan, 1986), 207.
2. "A Modern Take on *Dr. Caligari*," *American Cinematographer,* April 2006, 30–33.
3. Jack C. Ellis, *A History of Film* (Englewood Cliffs, NJ: Prentice Hall, 1990), 92–94.
4. Douglas A. Boyd, *Broadcasting in the Arab World* (Ames: Iowa State University Press, 1993), 138–39.
5. "El Tigre," *Los Angeles Times,* November 10, 1991, 26; and "Battle Intensified over Control of Mexican TV," *Los Angeles Times,* January 17, 2005, C-1.
6. R. W. Burns, *British Television: The Formative Years* (London: Peter Peregrinos, 1986); and "Britain's BBC-TV," *Broadcasting,* November 3, 1986, 43–53.
7. Bernard Redmont, "Soviet TV: Ballet and Brezhnev, Serials and Symphony," *Television Quarterly,* Spring 1981, 27–35.
8. Boyd, *Broadcasting in the Arab World,* 205–8.
9. "BBC World Service.com," www.bbc.co.uk/worldservice/index.shtml (accessed August 2, 2011).
10. "Voice of America," http://www.voanews.com/english/programs/ (accessed August 2, 2011).
11. Sergei V. Erofeev, "Russia," in Gross, *The International World of Electronic Media,* 190.
12. "The GI Joe Network," *Emmy,* August 1990, 70–74.
13. *Radio and Television in the Federal Republic of Germany* (Frankfurt, Germany: Hessicher Rundfunk, 1980), 5–45.
14. Nobuo Otsuka, "Japan," in Gross, *The International World of Electronic Media,* 301–3.
15. Joseph S. Johnson, "China," in Gross, *The International World of Electronic Media,* 278.
16. Ellis, *A History of Film,* 314–17.
17. Mast, *A Short History of the Movies,* 339–49, 380–87.

18. Alan Brender, "After a 25-Year Wait . . ." *TV Guide,* August 14, 1976, 24–26.

19. Boyd, *Broadcasting in the Arab World,* 147–49.

20. Joseph Straubhaar, "Brazil," in Gross, *The International World of Electronic Media,* 63–67.

21. *This Is Independent Broadcasting* (London: Independent Broadcasting Authority, n.d.), 3–14.

22. "Canada Wants to Raise CBC's Native Program Levels to 90 Percent," *Broadcasting,* March 9, 1987, 43; "Good Fences," *Hollywood Reporter,* July 7–13, 1998, 12; and "CRTC Mulls Changing the Channel on TV Rules," *National Post,* April 7, 2008, FP-1.

23. "Hungary: A Goulash of Media Activity," *Broadcasting,* July 23, 1990, 81–83.

24. Everett M. Rogers and Livia Antola, "Telenovelas: A Latin American Success Story," *Journal of Communication,* Autumn 1985, 4–12; and "Mexico's Televisa Searches for Global Stardom," *Wall Street Journal,* May 30, 1995, A10.

25. From Drought to Deluge," *Cable Satellite Europe,* December 1993, 20–21.

26. "To Make a Big Movie in Less Than a Day, Forget the Script," *Wall Street Journal,* May 6, 1999, 1.

27. Kusum Singh and Bertram Gross, "'MacBride': The Report and the Response," *Journal of Communication,* Autumn 1981, 104–17.

28. "The Expanding International Horizon of Satellites," *Broadcasting,* July 25, 1988, 36.

29. "From Ahnadabad to Makapura," *TV Guide,* June 19, 1976, 10–12; and "CNN: The Channel to the World," *Los Angeles Times,* January 29, 1991, 1.

30. "TV Is Exploding All Over Asia," *Fortune,* January 24, 1994, 98–101; and "Murdoch Star Deal Transforms Asia," *Broadcasting & Cable,* August 2, 1993, 34.

31. "Chinese Wiring the Countryside for Satellite TV," *Los Angeles Times,* September 23, 1999, C-1.

32. "Europe Braces for Free-Market TV," *Fortune,* February 20, 1984, 74–82; and "France: A Revolution in the Making," *Channels,* September/October 1985, 60–61.

33. "Pay TV Comes to Germany," *Broadcasting,* March 25, 1991, 90; and Wolfram Peiser, "The Television Generation's Relation to the Mass Media in Germany: Accounting for the Impact of Private Television," *Journal of Broadcasting & Electronic Media,* Summer 1999, 364–85.

34. "Whole Lotta Shakin' Going On in French TV," *Daily Variety,* February 3, 1988, 63.

35. "TV: Revolution Brewing in Thatcher's Britain," *Wall Street Journal,* January 3, 1989, A-9; and "Auction Action Shakes Up U.K. TV," *Daily Variety,* October 17, 1991, 1.

36. Lalit Acharya and Surekha Acharya, "India," in Gross, *The International World of Electronic Media,* 267.

37. "Tuning in the Global Village," *Los Angeles Times,* October 20, 1992, H-1.

38. Ivan Stadtrucker, "The Slovak Republic and the Czech Republic," in Gross, *The International World of Electronic Media,* 162; and "Cable in Poland," *International Cable,* June 1997, 24–26.

39. Colin Sparks, *Communism, Capitalism, and the Mass Media* (Thousand Oaks, CA: Sage, 1998); and "Maverickski," *Hollywood Reporter,* August 8–14, 2000, 18–19.

40. "Chinese See TV Face-Off as New Page in History," *Los Angeles Times,* June 28, 1998, 1; "Politics at Play, Again," *Denver Post,* August 7, 2008, C-1; and "China's Agony of Defeat," *Newsweek,* August 4, 2008, 39–41.

41. Anna Yudin and Michael C. Keith, "Russian Radio and the Age of Glasnost and Perestroika," *Journal of Radio Studies,* December 2003, 246–54; "Russia Alters Direct Hold on Government Channels," *Hollywood Reporter,* December 23–25, 2005, 8; and "Un-Hollywood: In Russia, Films Promote the State," *Wall Street Journal,* January 9, 2008, 1.

42. "Pentagon Channel: Not Just for the Military," *TV Technology,* May 31, 2006, 12.

43. "Worldwide Opening," *Hollywood Reporter,* July 28, 2005, S1-S7.

44. "Vive le Funding for Arte TV in Europe," *Wall Street Journal,* December 28, 2010, 47; and "Uprising Draws New Viewers to Al Jazeera," *Wall Street Journal,* February 1, 2011, B8.

45. "Format Fever: The Risks and Rewards," *Broadcasting & Cable,* January 23, 1995, 94.

46. "How Mr. Kong Helped Turn China into a Film Power," *Wall Street Journal,* September 14, 2005, A1; "The Jackson Effect," *Hollywood Reporter,* November 25, 2011, 59; and "Bumper Crop for Academy," *Hollywood Reporter,* December 3, 2001, 84.

47. "The World Turns to U.S. TV," *Broadcasting & Cable,* January 8, 2007, 23; and "B. O.'s House of BRIC," *Variety,* January 17–23, 2011, 1.

48. "Brits Jack Up Share of Int'l TV," *Hollywood Reporter,* October 7, 1998, 9; and "Eastern Europe Puts Programs into Mix," *Electronic Media,* January 7, 2002, 18.

49. "Studios & Facilities Update," *Variety,* May 9–15, 2011, S1–S8.
50. "Russia May Give H'wood a Break," *Variety,* July 25–31, 2011, 4.
51. "The Fate of Middle Earth," *American Cinematographer,* January 2004, 54–61; and "Indian Stunner," *Hollywood Reporter,* May 2010, 39.
52. "Made in South Africa," May 13, 2011, 91–92; and "Global Focus," *Hollywood Reporter,* November 21, 2008, 1–2.
53. "How to Use a 'Lifeline,'" *Newsweek,* February 28, 2000, 46–47; and "Why the Dutch Are Dominating TV," *Hollywood Reporter,* May 20, 2011, 10.
54. "Remake Mania Strikes Europe," *Variety,* February 21–27, 2011, 6; "Original 'Girl' Buoys Swedes," *Variety,* July 18–24, 2011, 4.
55. "Biz Without Borders," *Variety,* April 20–26, 2009, 1.
56. "H'Wood Sign of Change," *Variety,* November 30–December 6, 2009, 1.
57. "New Global Recipe," February 8–14, 2010, 1.
58. "LATV's Strategic Shift," *Broadcasting & Cable,* May 4, 2009, 14.
59. "China Goes One-on-One with the Net," *Los Angeles Times,* January 27, 2001, 1; and "Rise of the Online Autocrats," *Wall Street Journal,* October 2, 2010, C3.
60. "Latin America Goes Its Own Way on DTV," *TV Technology,* July 22, 2009, 12; and "DAB UK," *Diffusion EBU,* 2005/2, 16–19.

GLOSSARY

A

above-the-line Refers to expenses related to administrative and conceptual aspects of a production, mainly those related to producing, directing, writing, and acting. (7.12a)

actor A person portraying someone other than himself or herself. (7.12a)

actual malice In libel suits, taking something that was known to be harmful and saying or printing it anyway, with reckless disregard. (11.8)

adjacencies Commercials that are the first to be aired after programming ends or right before programming starts. (9.7a)

advertising agency An organization that decides on and implements an advertising strategy for a customer. (4.6, 5.9, 9.4c)

affiliate A station or system that receives programming from a broadcast or cable network. (1.2f, 4.2, 8.1b, 9.2)

agent A person who seeks work for other people, such as actors or directors, and, in return, gets a percent of what the people earn. (7.10)

à la carte Offering cable subscribers the opportunity to buy only the channels they want rather than packages of channels the cable system puts together. (3.14)

alternator A device for converting mechanical energy into electrical energy in the form of alternating current (AC). (5.3)

amplitude modulation (AM) Changing the height of a transmitting radio wave according to the sound being broadcast; stations that broadcast in the 535 to 1,705 kHz range. (5.8, 13.7a)

analog A device or circuit in which the output varies as a continuous function of the input. (1.2i, 4.18, 6.12, 11.9, 13.1)

anamorphic A lens that squeezes a wide picture into a frame of film in a camera and then unsqueezes it in the projector. (6.9)

anchor person A person who reads the news on radio or television. (7.12b)

annual flight schedule A plan for running commercials that are aired only near holidays. (9.7b)

antenna A wire or set of wires or rods used both to send and to receive radio waves. (13.7a)

anthology drama A television play, most commonly associated with the 1950s, that probed character and emphasized life's complexities. (8.6)

application (app) Usually a small specialized computer program, often developed by a third party, that can be downloaded onto a mobile platform such as a smartphone, pod, or pad. (2.13, 5.18, 11.7, 13.11)

ARPANET The original name for what became the internet, developed by the Defense Department's Advanced Research Projects Agency. (1.2e, 2.1)

ascertainment A process stations used to undertake to keep their licenses that involved interviewing community leaders to learn what they believed were the major problems in the community. (11.11)

aspect ratio The relationship of the height of a TV picture to its width. (13.1)

assignment editor A person in a news room who keeps track of the stories that need to be covered and decides which reporters should be sent out to cover each story. (7.12b, 8.3a)

auction To sell something, such as frequency spectrum, to the highest bidder. (4.18, 11.11)

audience flow The ability to hold an audience from one program to the next program shown on the same channel. (8.5b)

audio board A mixer used to combine various sound inputs, adjust their volume, and then send them to other pieces of equipment. (13.2)

audiocassette recorder A machine that records and plays sound from tape on encased reels. (5.18)

audion tube A three-electrode vacuum tube invented by Lee De Forest that was instrumental in amplifying voice so it could be sent over wireless and used for movies. (5.1, 6.6)

audiotape recorder A machine that records and plays sound from a magnetic tape that is usually either 1/4-inch or 1/8-inch wide. (5.12) auteur   The French word for "author," hence the primary creator of a movie; usually used to refer to the director. (6.10, 14.1)

authoritarian   A media system owned and closely overseen by the government and supported by general government funds. (14.2)

Automated Measurement of Lineups (AMOL)   A method that picks up special codes from programs so that Nielsen can determine what programs are on what channels in each market. (10.3)

autostereoscopic   An experimental process wherein 3-D images can be seen as three-dimensional without the use of glasses. (13.9)

availabilities (avails)   Times in a station or network schedule when it can air commercials. (9.7a)

average quarter-hour (AQH)   A ratings calculation based on the average number of persons listening to a particular station for at least 5 minutes during a 15-minute period. (10.6)

B

backyard satellite   A process through which individual households received satellite signals by putting a receiving dish on their property. (3.5)

bandwidth   The number of frequencies within given limits that are occupied by a particular transmission, such as one radio station; the amount of space (hence, speed) given to particular internet material. (13.7a)

banner ad   An advertisement that appears at the top of a webpage. (5.20, 9.6c)

barrier   In a communication model, anything that reduces the effectiveness of the communication process. (12.5b)

barter   To receive a program for free because much of the advertising time is sold by the seller. (9.2)

basic cable   Channels, often supported by advertising, for which the cable subscriber does not pay a large extra fee. (3.6)

below-the-line   Refers to expenses for a production that are in the craft or technical areas, such as salaries for camera operators and editors. (7.12a)

Betamax   The first consumer videotape format. (6.12)

bicycle network   A system in which stations shared program material but did not air it at the same time because the programs were physically transported from one station to another. (4.5, 5.14)

Biltmore Agreement   A settlement between newspapers and radio, worked out at the Biltmore Hotel in the 1930s, that stipulated what radio stations could and could not air in the way of news. (5.10)

biometrics   Any audience research method that uses biological data such as perspiration, fingerprints, heart rate, or DNA. (10.8)

blacklisting   A phenomenon of the 1950s when many people in the entertainment business were accused of leaning toward Communism and, as a result, could not find work. (4.5, 6.9, 12.5b)

blackout   Not allowing a particular program, usually sports, to be shown in a particular area because the event is not sold out. (8.12)

blanket licensing   Obtaining the right to use a large catalog of musical selections by paying one set fee. (11.9)

blind bidding   When a theater owner selects a movie to show in theaters without actually seeing it, depending only on publicity and trailers. (9.2)

block booking   A movie distribution technique in which an exhibitor was forced to rent a group of films (some good, some bad) to get any of them. (6.5)

block programming   Airing one type of programming, such as comedies, for an entire evening. (8.5b)

blog   Short for web log, a chronicle placed on the internet with information written by one or just a few individuals, although users may post comments. (2.7, 8.3a, 9.4)

blogger   A person who places chronicles or other diary-like information on the internet. (7.12b)

Blue Book   The nickname given to a 1946 FCC document that set forth principles regarding license renewal. (11.11)

Bluetooth   A wireless technology that connects portable devices such as cell phones to the internet and to each other by using low-power radio transmission. (2.12)

Blu-ray   Sony's format for high-definition videodiscs that has been accepted as the standard format. (6.13)

boutique agency   An advertising agency that handles only a limited number of tasks for a client. (9.4c)

B picture   A movie that was inexpensive to produce and was usually the lesser film of a double feature. (6.7, 14.4) brand recall   The ability of people to remember the name of a product advertised at some point after they have seen an ad for it. (10.7)

branding integration   Incorporating a particular product within a TV show in exchange for money from the company that produces the product; also called product integration. (9.6b, 10.3)

breach of contract   Failure to do something that is in a written or oral agreement without a legitimate excuse. (11.14)

broadband   High-speed data transmission using relatively wide bandwidths. (2.9, 9.1, 13.6)

broadcasting   The sending of radio and television programs through the airwaves. (1.2a)

broadcast standards   The department (often called the Department of Standards and Practices) at a network or station that oversees the general standards of acceptability of program and commercial content. (12.2)

browser   Computer software that aids in searching the world wide web. (2.6)

buffer   An area, usually related to a computer, where streamed material stops temporarily so that all of it can be gathered and played as though it were being played in real time. (2.8)

bulletin board   A service that allows people to post electronic messages using the internet. (2.7)

bump system   When a station or network removes an advertiser from a particular time spot because another advertiser has offered to pay more. (9.7b)

C

cable modem   An electronic device provided by a cable TV company that provides a high-speed connection to the internet. (13.6)

camcorder   A single unit that consists of both a camera and a videocassette recorder. (8.3a, 13.3)

camera   A device that transduces light waves into electrical waveforms. (13.3)

Canon 35   An American Bar Association policy that banned cameras in courtrooms. (11.10)

Canon 3A   An American Bar Association policy that let individual states and judges decide whether or not cameras should be allowed in their courtrooms. (11.10)

capacitance disc   A videodisc system that used a stylus that moved over grooves in a manner similar to a record player. (6.12)

cardioid   A microphone that picks up sound primarily from one direction in a heart-shaped pattern. (13.2)

carrier wave   A high-frequency wave that can be sent through the air and is modulated by a lower-frequency wave containing information. (13.7a)

cash   Paying a set amount for a program and then being able to sell all the commercial time. (9.2)

cash plus barter   Paying a reduced amount for a program but letting the seller fill some of the advertising time. (9.2)

catharsis theory   A postulate related to violence research that states it is good for people to watch violence because it gives them vicarious excitement that keeps them from inciting real violence. (12.6a)

cathode-ray tube   A special type of TV set vacuum tube consisting of an electron gun that shoots electrons at a phosphor screen in order to create an image. (13.11)

cause and effect   A method of research that tries to determine the relationship between two or more modes of behavior. (12.5b)

C-band   A satellite frequency band between 4 and 6 GHz. (13.7c)

cell   An area several miles in diameter that constitutes the reception area for one transmitter of a cellular phone system. (13.7d)

cellular phone (cell phone)   A mobile phone that operates by relaying signals from one small area to another through the use of low-powered transmitters. (1.3, 2.12)

censorship   Not allowing certain information to be disseminated. (11.5)

channel   In a communication model, the element through which messages are transmitted. (12.5b)

charter   A right to operate that is given to a broadcasting corporation (such as the BBC) by the government. (14.2)

chatroom   A computer service that allows many people to write messages that others in the group can see as long as they are online. (2.7, 14.14)

chief executive officer (CEO)   The highest-ranking person within an organization who actively makes decisions for the organization. (7.12f)

chief financial officer (CFO)   A high-ranking person within a company who is in charge of monetary matters. (7.12f)

chip A tiny piece of silicon with electronic circuits that can store and manipulate data. (13.2)

CinemaScope A 1950s film experiment that used an anamorphic lens to squeeze a picture so it could be unsqueezed and shown on a large, curved screen. (6.9)

Cinerama A 1950s film experiment in which three interlocking projectors showed movies on a wraparound screen. (6.9)

clear and present danger A threatening of the security of the nation if certain information is made public. (11.5)

click A visit to a website that is counted even if the person or computer has visited the site before. (10.6)

clock A circle that shows all the segments that appear in an hour's worth of radio station programming. (8.5)

closed-cushion headphone A ring-shaped muff that rests on the head and covers the ear through which a person hears sound. (13.10)

cloud A large server onto which users place their documents, music, movies, and such that is at a location that is remote from the user. (6.15, 13.2)

clutter Having a large number of commercials at one time. (9.9b)

coaxial cable A transmission line in which one conductor surrounds the other, making a cable that is not susceptible to external interference from other sources. (13.6)

commentator Someone who gives his or her own opinions about news events. (5.10)

common carrier A communication distribution system available for use by those that do not own it. (3.3)

Communications Act of 1934 The congressional law that established the FCC and set the guidelines for the regulation of telecommunications. (3.12, 5.8, 11.1)

community antenna television (CATV) An early name for cable television. (1.2d)

compact disc (CD) An audio disc on which sound is recorded digitally with optical technology. (1.3, 5.18, 13.2)

comparative license renewal A procedure by which a group could challenge the license of incumbent station owners. (11.11)

competing rights Different provisions of the Constitution that allow for conflicting actions. (11.10)

composite week Seven days over a three-year period that were randomly selected by the FCC so that a station's programming record could be judged for license renewal purposes. (11.11)

compression A process by which redundant information is removed from a digital file, making it smaller so that it can be transmitted more quickly and stored more efficiently. (2.8)

compulsory license A copyright fee that must be paid and that is usually a set fee, such as a percentage of income. (3.2, 11.9)

concept selling When a station or network uses something unique about itself to sell commercial time to an advertiser, usually because its ratings are so low they are unreliable. (9.5)

content analysis A research method that involves studying something (such as the number of violent acts) within a group of programs to test a hypothesis. (12.5b)

controller A person who oversees profit and loss and expenditures for a company or other organization. (7.12f)

control room An area where the director, technical director, and other crew members select and mix the video and audio coming from a studio. (7.12a)

convergence The coming together of various media forms and facilities, such as television and computers, so that they merge and share characteristics. (1.7)

cookies Small files placed in a computer whenever someone visits a site that indicate what pages a person looked at on the site. (9.10)

co-production A TV program or movie that has financial and/or creative input from two or more companies or government agencies, sometimes in different countries. (14.13)

copyright The exclusive right to publication, production, or sale of a literary, dramatic, musical, or artistic work. (3.2, 11.9, 14.10)

corporate video The use of video by corporations and similar organizations for training, orientation, and similar purposes. (7.12a, 9.2)

cost per point (CCP) The cost an advertiser pays per ratings point, calculated by dividing what the advertiser paid by the rating points a commercial accumulates during a week. (10.11)

cost per thousand (CPM)   The price that an advertiser pays for each thousand households or people a commercial reaches (M is from the Latin *mille,* for thousand). (9.7a, 10.11)

cover letter   A letter sent with a résumé that highlights aspects of the résumé that are applicable to a particular job. (7.6)

cross-ownership   A situation in which one company owns different media in one market, such as a newspaper owning a TV station. (11.12)

crossover   An electronic component within a speaker that sends low frequencies to the woofer and high frequencies to the tweeter. (13.10)

cross-promote   When one network or station promotes something on another network or station, usually because they have common ownership. (10.1a)

cume   The number of households or people that tune in to a particular station at different times. (10.6)

customer service   A department within a company that handles complaints and also sometimes sells services such as cable TV subscriptions. (7.12e)

D

datagram   Encoded delivery information attached to a digital packet when it launches onto the internet, including the senders' and receivers' names and computer addresses. (2.2)

dayparts   Segments of the day that reflect the size and composition of the available audience. (8.5, 9.7a, 10.10)

decoder   A device that can descramble scrambled television signals. (11.8)

decompression   The process of taking file material that has been compressed and getting it back into its original form so that it can be heard and seen through a monitor or TV set. (2.8)

deep focus   Shots that have both the foreground and a faraway background in sharp focus. (6.7)

defamation   An attack on someone's reputation. (11.8)

demographics   Information pertaining to vital statistics of a population, such as age, sex, marital status, and geographic location. (8.2, 10.7)

demo reel   A compilation of audio and video material that a person has been involved with that is usually given to a potential employer. (7.6)

deregulation   The removal of laws and rules that spell out government policies. (3.8, 4.15, 5.17)

desensitizing effect   A theory that watching violence makes people think that seeing someone commit an act of violence is common and not worth dealing with. (12.6a)

designated market area (DMA)   Nielsen's term for the various individual markets it surveys. (10.10)

development   The process that a TV program goes through to get from idea to exhibition. (8.2)

diary   A booklet used for audience measurement in which people write down the programs they listen to or watch. (10.5)

digital   A device or circuit in which the output varies in discrete on-off steps. (1.2, 6.12, 11.9, 13.1)

digital cinema   A method of projecting movies in a theater that uses digital technology rather than film projectors. (6.16, 13.9)

digital insertion   Advertising material that is placed in a video but it not actually there because it is a virtual image. (9.6b)

digital rights management (DRM)   Technology that uses encryption for file security or in other ways prevents illegal copying. (2.14, 11.9)

digital subscriber line (DSL)   A high-speed telephone-based connection from a computer to the internet that is always on and that can allow for both data and voice communication simultaneously. (13.6)

digital television (DTV)   A technical form of TV that allows for high-definition broadcast pictures and/or additional program channels. (1.3, 4.18, 13.7)

digital versatile disc (DVD)   A round disc that can be used to store and retrieve audio, video, and data. (6.13, 13.5)

digital videodisc   The original name for the digital versatile disc, or DVD, because its first use was to store video. (6.13, 9.1)

digital video recorder (DVR)   A hard-disk drive that can record and compress video from off-air, cable TV, or satellite TV and can pause recording and pick up where it left off; often referred to by the name of the popular brand TiVo. (1.3, 6.14, 8.5a)

direct broadcast satellite (DBS)   A process of transmission and reception in which signals sent to a satellite can be received directly by TV sets in homes that have small satellite receiving dishes mounted on them; now often called satellite TV. (3.5)

director   The person in charge of the creative aspects of a TV program or movie. (7.12a)

distance learning   Instructional programs, usually offered by a college, that are intended to bring education to people who live far from an educational institution or who prefer not to travel to the college. (2.7)

distant signal importation   The bringing in of stations from other parts of the country by a cable system. (1.2e, 3.1)

distributed network   A way of interconnecting computer signals in a "fishnet" pattern so that data can flow along many paths, rather than to and from a central computer. (2.2, 13.7d)

diversity   A set of conscious practices that involve an understanding and appreciation of various cultures and a respect for differing experiences. (7.9)

docudrama   A fictionalized production that is based on fact. (8.6)

Dolby   A noise reduction technique that raises the volume of the movie sound track elements most likely to be affected by inherent noise during production and then lowers them again during projection so that the noise seems lower in relation to the wanted elements of the sound track. (6.11)

download   To take something from the internet and put it on a computer so that it can be accessed at a future

time as opposed to being viewed at the moment. (2.8, 3.10, 4.19)

DVD player   A machine that plays back video material from a round disc. (1.3)

E

earbud   A tiny headphone that fits within the ear. (13.10)

earphones   Small devices placed over the ears to hear audio signals. (5.9)

e-book   A computerized version of a printed book that can be read on a computer or a device such as a Kindle that is specifically designed for the purpose. (2.14)

e-commerce   Short for "electronic commerce"; buying and selling goods and services on the internet, often referred to as online shopping. (2.7)

electromagnetic spectrum   A continuing series of energies that encompasses frequencies that can carry audio and video signals. (4.19, 13.7)

electron gun   The part of a TV tube that shoots a steady stream of electrons that scan from top to bottom. (13.11)

electronic mail (email)   Messages sent over the internet from one person to another person or group, which recipients can read at their convenience. (2.3, 14.14)

electronic scanning   A method that analyzes the density of areas to be copied and translates this into a moving arrangement of electrons that can later reproduce the densities in the form of a picture. (4.1)

embedded   Mixed in with another group, as reporters were mixed in

with troops during the war in Iraq. (8.3a)

encoding   Using computer software to translate sound or picture from analog to digital. (2.8)

engagement   The degree to which the creative content of a media product, such as a TV show, results in a strong connection with an audience member, preferably so that person will have a positive response to the commercials within the program. (10.7)

episodic dramas   Televised plays that have set characters and problems that are dealt with in each program. (8.6)

equal opportunity   Giving the same treatment to political candidates. *See* equal time. (11.13)

equal time   A rule stemming from Section 315 of the Communications Act stating that TV and radio stations should give the same treatment and opportunity to all political candidates for a specific office. (11.13)

event video   The use of video to record important milestones such as birthdays and weddings. (7.12a)

external service   Radio and TV programs that one country produces to influence other countries. (14.4)

eye tracking   A media research method wherein special computer software indicates the parts of a monitor screen that a person looks at the most. (10.8)

F

fairness doctrine   A policy that evolved from FCC decisions, court cases, and congressional actions stating that radio and TV stations had to present all sides of controversial issues they discussed. (11.14)

fair trial Making sure someone accused of a crime is treated equitably by the courts. (11.10)

fair use Allowing part of a copyrighted work to be used without copyright clearance or payment. (11.9)

family hour A policy stating that all programs aired between 7:30 P.M. and 9:00 P.M. should be suitable for children as well as adults. (4.13)

fast national A rating report on national viewing that Nielsen gets to subscribers the morning after the programs air. (10.10)

feedback In a communication model, anything that gives information back to the source. (12.5b)

fiber optic A glass strand through which large amounts of information can be sent. (3.13, 13.6)

field research Studies that are conducted in environments where people naturally are, rather than in special controlled environments. (12.5b)

file sharing An online activity in which computer users engage in digital swapping of content, such as music and video files. (2.8)

filter Software that attempts to identify and block spam, viruses, and other undesirable matter sent over the internet. (11.7)

financial interest—domestic syndication (fin-syn) A policy that used to preclude networks from receiving any monetary remuneration from programs aired on the network or any rights to distribute those programs within the country after they had aired on the network. (4.13, 8.1c)

fingerprints Invisible markings on copyrighted goods that travel with them if they are copied illegally, in order to try to prevent piracy. (11.9)

fireside chats Radio talks given by President Franklin Roosevelt. (5.9)

firewall A software barrier designed to keep unwanted information from coming into or going out of a computer network. (11.7)

First Amendment The part of the U.S. Constitution that guarantees freedom of speech and freedom of the press. (11.5)

first-person shooter A type of video game in which the screen represents the player's eyes and players see their hands and usually a gun. (2.16)

first-run syndication Programs produced for distribution to stations and cable TV rather than for the commercial networks. (8.1d)

fixed buy When the advertiser states a specific time that a commercial should air and the station or network abides by that time. (9.7b)

flat-screen TV A thin television or computer screen that usually incorporates plasma or LCD technology. (13.10)

fleeting expletives Swear words that someone says in an extemporaneous manner on a live telecast. (11.6)

focus group An in-depth discussion session to determine what people do and do not like about various aspects of the media. (10.8)

footprint The section of the earth that a satellite's signal covers. (13.7c)

format The type of programming a radio station selects, usually

described in terms of the music it plays, such as contemporary, jazz, rock, and so on. (1.2b, 8.4)

franchise A special right granted by a government or corporation to operate a facility, such as a cable TV system; the right to produce a TV program that has the format of another TV program. (3.6, 14.12)

free flow A philosophy that any country or media organization should be able to send information to any other country. (14.7)

freelance To work on a per-project basis rather than as a full-time employee. (7.7)

freeze Immobilization or cessation of an activity, such as a stop in the assigning of radio or TV station frequencies. (1.2c, 4.3)

frequencies The number of recurrences of a periodic phenomenon, such as a carrier wave, during a set time period, such as a second. (11.1, 13.7)

frequency The average number of times a person is exposed to a particular commercial over a period of time, such as a week. (10.6)

frequency discount A lessening of cost to an advertiser that airs numerous commercials often on a station or network. (9.7a)

frequency modulation (FM) Placing a sound wave on a carrier wave in such a way that the number of recurrences is varied; stations that broadcast between 88 and 108 MHz. (5.14, 13.7a)

frequency of tune (FOT) An audience measurement that indicates how many times viewers return to a particular network. (10.6) full-motion video   Refers to video games that utilize TV or movie quality video as opposed to lower quality graphics. (2.16)

full-service agency   An advertising agency that handles all the advertising needs for a particular client. (9.4c)

G

gatekeeper   A person who makes important decisions regarding what will or will not be communicated through the media. (1.6, 8.11, 12.5b, 14.14)

genre   A categorization of programs, such as drama or documentary. (4.16, 8.6)

graphics generator   A stand-alone computer system or part of a nonlinear editing system that can be used to create words and pictures for TV programs. (13.3)

grid   Metal bars that are suspended from a ceiling and are used to hang lights. (13.3)

gridlock   When so many people are trying to access a particular internet site that it cannot handle them all. (13.6)

grid rate card   A list of prices a station or network charges for ads, which vary according to when there is a lot of availability and when the commercial schedule is fairly full. (9.7a)

gross average audience (GAA) The average number of people watching a program over several showings in a market. (10.6)

guild   A unionlike organization for above-the-line people such as actors and directors. (7.10)

H

hacker   A person who uses a computer to get unauthorized access to data. (11.7, 12.1)

hammocking   Programming a new or weak program between two successful programs. (8.5b)

hard drive   The part of a computer system that holds most of the information. (13.2)

HD DVD   A high-definition videodisc format that lost out to Blu-ray. (6.13)

HD radio   Digital radio transmission that is broadcast in the same frequency band as conventional AM and FM stations; also called in-band on-channel. (5.19, 13.7a)

headend   The part of a cable TV system where all the network and other programming that is going to be on the system is received. (13.6)

headphones   Small speakers encased in something that can be placed in or near the ear. (13.10)

hertz   A frequency unit of one cycle per second; abbreviated as Hz. (13.7)

high-definition television (HDTV) Television that scans at approximately 1,000 lines a frame and has a wide aspect ratio. (4.18, 13.1)

hit   Each time a user accesses a website. (10.2)

hoax   A deceptive trick, often done in mischief, that, if done on radio or TV, is punishable by fines. (11.14)

Hollywood 10   Ten creative people from the movie industry who refused to answer questions of the House Un-American Activities Subcommittee and were sent to jail during the blacklisting era. (6.9)

home shopping   Programs showing products that viewers can buy

instantly by calling a particular phone number. (1.5c, 9.6d)

host selling   A practice that has been outlawed on children's TV of having the host or star of a show also sell products during the show. (9.9a)

hotspot   The area served by a wi-fi transmitter in which users can receive a wireless signal to connect to the internet. (2.11, 13.7e)

households using TV (HUT)   The percentage of homes that have a TV set tuned to any channel. (10.6)

human resources   A department within a company that deals with personnel issues, such as benefits, union negotiations, and hiring and firing procedures. (7.12f)

hype   To make something extraordinary in an attempt to increase ratings; for example, having a big giveaway during sweeps period. (10.6)

hyperlink   A word or image in a document that can be clicked to take the internet user to another document or file automatically. (2.4)

hypothesis   In research, a supposition that is proposed to draw a conclusion or test a point. (12.5b)

I

iconoscope   The earliest form of TV camera tube, in which a beam of electrons scanned a photoemissive mosaic screen. (4.1)

identity theft   An act by which a hacker steals personal information, such as credit card numbers and passwords, from consumers via computers, telephones, or other telemedia. (11.7)

impressions The average number of people watching a program over several showings in a market. (10.6)

in-band on-channel (IBOC) A radio technology that allows digital signals to be broadcast in the same frequency band as conventional AM and FM stations; often called HD radio. (13.7a)

indecency Language that, in context, depicts or describes sexual or excretory activities or organs in terms patently offensive, as measured by contemporary community standards for the broadcast medium. (11.6)

independents TV or radio stations that are not affiliated with one of the major networks; small film and television production companies. (1.2f, 4.11, 6.10, 8.1c)

infomercial A program of about 30 minutes that extols the virtues of a particular product. (1.5e, 9.6d)

information superhighway A metaphor for the internet in which a road system represents the connections among networks and computers, which can be accessed by users through on-ramps. (2.5)

in-house Performing some service within a company rather than hiring outside help. (9.4c)

instant messaging (IM) A service that allows users to correspond simultaneously by typing messages into various devices, including computers and cell phones. (2.7)

interactive cable Two-way capability that allows interaction between the subscriber and sources provided by the cable TV system. (3.7)

Interface Message Processor (IMP) A small computer that used

to be connected to a main computer to translate data from the main computer into a standard protocol for sharing files with other networked computers. (2.1)

interlace scanning A technical method of building a TV picture in which odd lines are laid down and then even lines are laid down in order to build a frame. (13.7b)

international buy To purchase advertising time in such a way that the product to be advertised will be seen throughout the world. (9.6a)

internet service provider (ISP) A company that facilitates the use of information on the internet by providing easy ways for customers to access the information. (2.6)

internship The chance to work and learn within a company without actually being hired. (7.4)

invasion of privacy Not leaving someone alone who wishes to be left alone, or divulging facts about a person that he or she does not wish divulged. (11.7)

inventory The amount of commercial time that a station or network has to sell. (9.4a)

island A still picture at the end of commercials aimed at children to help them differentiate between the commercial and the program. (9.9a)

J

joint venture A business agreement, usually between companies in several different countries, designed to share the risk associated with producing an electronic media product such as a movie or TV series because each party agrees to contribute equity for a specified period of time. (14.13)

K

keyword search A type of internet advertising in which links to appropriate sites come up when a person types a request into a search engine. (9.6c)

kinescope An early form of poor-quality TV program reproduction that basically involved making a film of what was shown on a TV screen. (4.6)

Kinetoscope An early film viewer that had a peephole for the person to look through in order to see a short movie. (6.1)

Ku-band A satellite frequency band between 11 and 14 GHz. (13.7c)

L

laboratory research A form of research conducted in a controlled environment that is not a person's usual environment. (12.5b)

landline A hard-wired telephone line, usually in a home or business. (1.3)

laser disc A videodisc system that uses a laser to read the information on the disc. (6.12)

leased access A basic cable channel on which time can be purchased by a business or other organization willing to pay to cablecast a message. (3.7)

length of tune (LOT) An audience measurement that indicates how long viewers watch a particular network. (10.6)

lens The front part of a camera that gathers light and focuses it to create the image. (13.3)

libel To broadcast or print something unfavorable and false about a person. (11.8)

license fee   The amount a network pays a producing company or sports franchise to air the program the company produces or the game the sports franchise owns; the amount individuals in some countries pay the government to own a radio or TV set. (9.2, 14.2)

light-emitting diode (LED)   A type of light bulb that consists of tiny electron tubes that put out light. (13.3)

line of sight   Transmission in which the transmitting agent needs to be lined up with the receiving agent in such a way that there could be visual communication between them. (13.7a)

liquid crystal display (LCD)   Devices that use chemical elements that show black or a particular color when power is applied. (13.10)

local buy   To purchase advertising time on stations in a limited geographic area. (9.6a)

local discount   A reduction in cost given to an advertiser who can't profit from the whole coverage area because its place of business is located too far from some of the areas the station reaches. (9.7b)

local-into-local   The process in which satellite TV transmits local broadcast TV stations into the local areas as part of its service. (3.9)

local origination   Programs produced for the local community, particularly as it applies to programming created by cable TV systems. (3.3, 8.1a)

local people meter (LPM)   Nielsen's portable audience measurement device that people carry with them to track their video exposure. (10.5)

location-based   Television programs or commercials that are shown in places such as doctors' offices or grocery stores, where people have not chosen to watch the video but are somewhat captive to it. (1.7, 9.6e)

log   A listing of program and commercial material that is aired on a radio or TV station. (7.12e)

lottery   A game or contest that involves chance, prizes, and consideration (money); a random selection method the FCC uses for assigning licenses. (11.11, 11.14)

loudspeaker   A device that amplifies sound so that a large group of people can hear it. (5.9)

low angle   A camera shot that is taken from below, which makes the person in the shot look powerful and dominant. (6.7)

lowest unit charge   The amount that may be charged for a politician's commercial, equal to the lowest rate a regular advertiser would have to pay. (9.9b)

low-orbit satellite   A satellite that circles the earth at a height of about 485 miles and is not synchronous with the rotation of the earth. (13.7c)

M

made-for   A movie that is specially produced for TV. (4.11)

magazine concept   Placing ads of various companies within a program rather than having the entire program sponsored by one company. (4.6)

magazine show   A program divided into short segments. (4.13)

majors   Large film and television production companies. (8.1c)

make-good   An electronic media outlet's need to pay back an advertiser some of its money if a promised audience size is not obtained. (9.7b)

mean world syndrome   A theory that watching violence makes people afraid to go out because they think the world is a more dangerous place than it actually is. (12.6a)

mechanical scanning   An early form of scanning in which a rotating device, such as a disc, broke up a scene into a rapid succession of narrow lines for conversion into electrical impulses. (4.1)

memory stick   A USB-based digital data storage device developed by Sony that is palm-sized and can be used for various computer applications. (13.2)

merchandising   Selling the rights to characters or concepts of a TV show or movie that have been purposely included so they can be developed into saleable products, such as toys or clothing. (9.6b)

message   In a communication model, that which is communicated. (12.5b)

metro survey area (MSA)   Arbitron's division for radio ratings of areas that receive radio stations clearly. (10.10)

microphone   A device that transduces spoken words or other sounds into electrical waveforms. (13.2)

microwave   Radio waves, 1,000 MHz and up, that can travel fairly long distances. (3.4, 13.7f)

minidoc   A short documentary, often within a newscast. (8.14)

miniseries A dramatic production of several hours shown on TV across a number of different nights. (8.6)

minitheater testing A pretesting procedure that involves bringing participants into a medium-sized room and showing them a movie, program, or commercial in order to get their reactions. (10.8)

mobisode A TV production specifically made to play on a mobile portable platform such as a smartphone. (2.13, 8.1c)

mockumentary A program made in the form of a documentary but which makes fun of something. (8.1a)

modem Short for "modulation-demodulation," a device that allows computer-generated data to be sent over phone lines or cable TV systems. (2.8)

modulate To place information from one wave onto another so that the wave that is carrying it represents the signal of the original wave. (13.7a)

monitor A TV set that does not receive signals sent over the air but can receive signals from a camera or recorder. (13.3)

motion capture Scanning the movements of humans into a computer and then using the scan as a pattern for a computer-generated movie character. (13.4)

MP3 A compression system for audio that is part of the video MPEG compression system and is also used for stand-alone audio applications. (1.3, 2.8, 5.18)

multi-platforms Related areas that media companies can present to advertisers, such as a TV station and its website, in hopes that the advertiser will buy ads in all the areas. (9.5)

multiple-system operator (MSO) A company that owns and operates several cable systems in different locations. (3.2)

multiplex To place more than one service on an allocated band of frequencies. (13.7a)

music preference research Determining what music people would be likely to stay tuned to by playing them samples over the phone or in a theater and soliciting their reactions. (10.8)

must-carry A ruling that cable or satellite TV systems must put certain broadcast stations on their channels. (3.2, 4.15)

N

narrowcasting Playing program material that appeals to a small segment of the population, rather than a broad segment. (1.2g, 3.7, 8.5a, 12.5b)

national buy To buy advertising time on individual stations throughout the whole country. (9.6a)

national identity A philosophy that each country should decide for itself what information should be allowed to enter its borders. (14.7)

near-video-on-demand (NVOD) A cable TV, satellite, or telco service in which the same movie starts on different channels at frequent intervals, such as every 15 minutes, so that subscribers can tune in at a time that is convenient for them. (3.10)

needle drop fee A fee for using music one time that includes as a factor the length of the cut used. (11.9)

network neutrality A proposed legal requirement that all internet sites be treated equally when they are delivered by ISPs; ISPs oppose it because they want to manage traffic on their networks. (2.19, 3.12, 11.14)

neuroscience metrics Research method calculations that use the brain or nervous system for the data collection. (10.8)

news agency An organization that provides news to various media entities. (7.12b, 8.3a)

news director The head of a news department. (8.3b)

news producer A person who decides which stories will be presented on a particular newscast. (7.12b, 8.3b)

news release Information put out by a company or other organization that it wishes to have included in the news. (8.3a)

news reporter A person who gathers news and information outside the studio environment. (7.12b)

nickelodeon An early movie theater that charged customers a nickel to see a movie. (6.3)

node A computer in a distributed network that relays packets of information from the previous relay point to the next. (2.2)

noise Something physical or psychological that reduces the effectiveness of the communication process. (12.5b)

nonlinear editing A method of editing in which material can be accessed in any order and easily rearranged. (13.3)

O

obscenity   Something that depicts sexual acts in an offensive manner, appeals to prurient interests of the average person, and lacks serious artistic, literary, political, or scientific value. (11.6, 12.1)

observational theory   In discussions about violence, the idea that people will learn how to be violent by watching it on TV. (12.6a)

off-net   Syndicated shows that at one time played on a network. (8.1d)

omnidirectional   A microphone that picks up sound from all directions. (13.2)

on-demand   Material, usually video or audio, that subscribers can request and store on discs or a computer so they can access it when they want it. (2.8, 5.20)

open-air headphone   A muff that rests on the air through which a person hears sound (13.10)

opt in   The ability to select what you will allow an internet company to do with information about you, such as opting in to allow it to give your email address to a third party. (11.7)

opt out   The ability to prohibit an internet company from doing things with information about you, such as opting out of allowing it to give your email address to a third party. (11.7)

orbiting   Placing ads at a slightly different time each day so that more people have a chance to hear or see them. (9.7b)

overnight reports   Ratings reports that are delivered to customers by noon of the day after the programs air. (10.10)

P

packet switching   The method of operation of the internet, in which information is broken down and sent to its destination in small pieces that are then reassembled. (2.2)

pad   A portable screen about the length and width of a piece of paper that can access the internet and many other electronic applications. (2.14, 9.1)

paradigm shift   A complete change in thinking or a belief system that allows for the creating of something that was previously thought to be impossible. (1.6)

parallel editing   Cutting between two actions or story lines, usually until the two merge. (6.4)

pay cable   A method by which people pay a monthly fee to receive cable programming that is usually free of commercials. (3.7)

payola   The practice of paying a disc jockey under the table so that he or she will air music that might not otherwise be aired. (5.13, 11.14, 12.1)

pay-per-click (PPC)   A process through which one internet site pays another if someone clicks on a link posted on one site in order to access the other. (9.6c)

pay-per-view (PPV)   Charging the customer for a particular program watched. (3.10, 8.1c, 9.1, 11.6)

pedestal   A mechanism that holds a camera and allows it to be raised

or lowered, usually by hydraulic or pneumatic means. (13.3)

PEG   Cable TV channels that are set aside for public, educational, and government access. (3.6)

people meter   A machine used for audience measurement that includes a keypad to be pushed by each person to indicate when he or she is watching TV. (10.5)

people using radio (PUR)   The percentage of people who have a radio tuned to any station. (10.6)

people using television (PUT)   The percentage of people who have a TV set tuned to any channel. (10.6)

performer Q   A measurement that indicates the degree to which people are aware of and like a particular radio, TV, or movie personality. (10.9)

per-program fee   A right to use music that is obtained by paying a fee for each program that utilizes the music. (11.9)

persistence of vision   A phenomenon in which the eye retains images for a short period of time, enabling fast-moving still pictures to look like constant movement. (6.1)

personal digital assistant (PDA)   A handheld minicomputer that provided convenient functions and could be connected to a computer for full functionality. (2.13)

petition to deny   A process by which citizen groups expressed the desire that a license be taken away from a station. (11.11)

phishing   A kind of spam in which a cybercriminal pretends to be a legitimate company in order to get people to divulge personal information that can be used for identity theft. (11.7)

phonograph A device for playing records that includes a turntable on which the record spins and a tone arm with a needle at the end that picks up the sound by vibrating in the grooves of the record. (5.12)

phosphor screen A layer of material on the inner face of the TV tube that fluoresces when bombarded by electrons. (13.11)

pilot A recording of a single program of a proposed series that is produced to obtain acceptance and commercial support. (8.2)

pipes The physical elements that make up the internet grid, including copper wires, coaxial cables, fiber optics, satellites, and the like. (2.9)

piracy Obtaining electronic signals or programs by illegal means and gaining financially from them. (6.17, 11.9, 14.10)

pirate stations Illegal radio stations located on boats off the coast of Great Britain that broadcast rock music during the 1960s. (14.6)

pitch To try to sell a program idea. (8.2)

pixel Short for "picture element," one of the small dots that illuminate to make a picture on a television set or computer screen. (13.7d)

plasma A TV set technology that consists of two glass panels with gas between them that is activated by voltage and, in turn, activates colored dots to create a picture. (13.10)

pod A portable device to which material can be sent through the internet or by other means so that it can be heard or seen using a small screen. (2.14)

podcast To transmit material so it can be viewed or heard on a

portable device such as an iPod. (2.14, 5.18)

pod insertion Placing a commercial that looks like program material in the middle of a series of spot commercials. (9.6b)

polarization A process in which rays of light exhibit different properties in different directions, especially the state in which all the vibration takes place in one plane causing light to vibrate in a particular direction or path. (13.9)

pop-up ad An ad that shows up on an internet site that can be removed by clicking it off. (9.6c)

portable people meter (PPM) A pager-size audience measurement device that people take with them so that their radio listening is determined for ratings purposes wherever they are. (10.3)

portfolio A compilation of a person's materials, usually of an artistic nature, that the person puts together in order to show a potential employer his or her skills. (7.6)

postdivestiture The time after AT&T was broken up in 1980 during which there were many innovations in the phone business. (3.11)

potted palm music Soft music played on early radio that derived its name because this type of music was usually played at teatime in restaurants by orchestras flanked by potted palm trees. (5.5)

prequel A movie that is produced after another movie but which tells the story of what happened before the time depicted in the previous movie. (6.11)

press-radio war A dispute in the 1930s between radio and newspapers

over news that could be broadcast on radio. (5.10)

pretesting Determining ahead of time what programs or commercials people are likely to respond to in a positive manner by having a group of people give written or oral opinions. (10.8)

primary channel The main digital channel of a broadcast station, the one that is high definition. (4.18)

prime-time access rule (PTAR) A former FCC ruling declaring that stations should program their own material or syndicated material rather than network fare during one hour of prime time. (4.13)

prior restraint When some entity (such as the government) tries to censor material before it is disseminated. (11.5)

private A media system in which businesses own the media and finance them primarily by advertising, and the government has only minimal oversight. (14.2)

privatization A movement of the 1980s in which countries that had public or authoritarian media systems added or changed to privately owned electronic media. (14.9)

producer The person who is in overall charge of a production, especially the schedule and money. (7.12a)

product integration Incorporating a particular product within the plot of a TV show in exchange for money from the company that produces the product. (9.6b)

product placement Charging a company to have something that it sells included in a movie, television program, or video game, usually as a prop or set dressing. (1.5c, 9.6b, 10.3)

profanity Irreverent use of the name of God. (11.6)

program buying When one company pays the costs of an entire program and has its ads inserted within that program. (9.6b)

progressive scanning A technical method of building a TV picture in which information is laid down one line at a time from top to bottom to create a frame. (13.7b)

projection TV A television screen that is very large, with the signal coming from the rear or front. (13.11)

proliferation The distribution of media content over an increasing number of venues and platforms. (1.7)

promise versus performance A procedure in which broadcasters promised what they would do during a license period and then were judged on the fulfillment of their promises when their license came up for renewal. (11.11)

promotion Publicizing a program, station, organization, or the like to enhance an image, build goodwill, and ultimately get more customers. (7.12e, 10.1)

promotional spot (promo) An advertisement for a station's or network's own programs that is shown on its own channel. (10.1a)

psychographics Information pertaining to lifestyle characteristics of a group of people, such as their desire to be involved with new technologies. (10.7)

public A media system that is closely aligned with the government and is usually supported, at least in part, by license fees. (14.2)

public access Programming conceived and produced by members of the public for cable TV channels. (1.6, 3.3)

public broadcasting A noncommercial form of broadcasting that gets money from audience members, corporations, and, to some extent, the government. (4.12)

public convenience, interest, or necessity A phrase in the Communications Act of 1934 that the FCC uses as a basis for much of its regulatory power. (11.11)

public domain Works that are not copyrighted, such as very old material or government publications. (11.9)

public figure A well-known person who would have to prove actual malice in order to win a libel suit. (11.8)

publicity Free articles or other forms of enhancement that will garner public attention. (10.1a)

public relations The attempt to build goodwill for a particular organization. (10.1a)

public service announcements (PSAs) Advertisements for non-profit organizations. (10.1a)

pulse code modulation (PCM) An audio recording and transmitting pattern that records sound digitally. (13.7a)

Q

qualitative Research that is not statistical in nature but is based on other forms of analysis, such as anecdotal, historical, or biographical. (10.7, 12.5b)

quantitative Research that can be analyzed through numerical and statistical methodology. (10.6, 12.5b)

quiz scandals The discovery during the 1950s that some of the contestants on quiz shows were given the answers to questions ahead of time. (4.9, 8.9)

quota A limit set on something, such as the amount of foreign programming a country allows on its broadcasting systems. (14.6)

R

Radio Act of 1927 The congressional law that established the Federal Radio Commission. (5.8, 11.1)

rádionovelas A form of radio soap opera, developed in Latin America, in which stories are serialized for a period of time. (14.2)

radio waves The electrical impulses of the radio frequency band of the electromagnetic spectrum. (5.1, 13.7)

random sampling A method of selection whereby each unit has the same chance of being selected as any other unit. (10.4)

rate card A chart-like listing of what a station, cable system, internet site, or network charges for different types of ads or other services. (9.7a)

rating The percentage of households or people watching or listening to a particular program. (7.12e, 9.5, 10.6)

rate protection Guaranteeing a customer a certain advertising fee, even if the rate card increases. (9.7b)

raw website return A type of internet search in which a user enters keywords into a box and the search engine returns a list of websites with those keywords. (2.6)

reach   The number of different people or households exposed to a particular commercial over a time period, usually a week. (10.6)

reality TV   A genre of programming in which people are actually trying to accomplish real acts, such as getting to a finish line first or winning a singing contest. (4.16)

receiver   In a communication model, the person or group that hears or sees a message. (12.5b)

record   An analog-based disc that holds sound impulses in its grooves and is played on a phonograph. (5.12)

regional Bell operating company (RBOC)   A local telephone company created as a result of the breakup of AT&T. (3.11)

regional buy   To buy advertising time on stations in a particular part of the country. (9.6a)

remake   A movie that one country makes that is based on a movie that another country has produced at an earlier time. (14.13)

renewal expectancy   An FCC statement that if a station provided favorable service, its license was not likely to be in jeopardy. (11.11)

reregulation   Imposing new rules on some group after rules have been eliminated, usually by the government. (3.8)

resilience   The ability of various forms of electronic media to adapt and continue to exist, even under adverse conditions. (1.7)

résumé   A written document that lists a person's career accomplishments; it is usually used to try to obtain a job. (7.6)

retransmission consent   The ability of TV stations to ask cable systems

to pay for the right to carry the TV station. (3.8, 4.15)

return on investment (ROI)   The value a company or individual gets for the amount of money it spends. (10.7)

rights fee   Money paid to broadcast something, such as a sports contest. (8.12)

robotic cameras   Studio cameras that do not have individual operators behind them but are run by a person sitting in a remote location. (7.1)

run-of-schedule (ROS)   When a station, rather than the advertiser, decides on the time that a particular commercial will air. (9.7b)

S

safe harbor   A period of time when indecent material can be aired because children are not likely to be in the audience. (11.6)

satellite radio   Transmission and reception of audio signals from a satellite that can be received directly by radios designed to receive the signals. (1.3, 5.19, 9.1, 13.7c)

scanners   Radio devices that can be used to listen in on police and fire communications. (8.3a)

scanning   The process of producing a video image by illuminating individual pixels one at a time, row by row. (13.7b)

scarcity theory   Reasoning that broadcasters should be regulated because there are not enough station frequencies for everyone to have one. (11.3)

scrambling   Changing transmitted electronic signals so they cannot be received properly without some sort of decoding system. (3.9, 11.9)

search engine   A type of index to the internet. (2.6)

secondary channels   Digital signals sent out by broadcast stations that are not their main HDTV channel. (4.18)

Section 315   The portion of the Communications Act that states that political candidates running for the same office must be given equal treatment. (11.13)

segment producer   A person who oversees a particular part of a newscast, such as entertainment news. (8.3b)

self-regulation   Rules that people within the electronic media industry set for themselves. (12.2)

sequel   A second movie that picks up where an earlier, usually successful, movie left off. (6.16, 8.2)

server   A large-capacity computer used to store and place information on the internet, a TV station, or some other entity. (2.5, 3.10, 6.15, 13.2)

share   The percentage of households or people watching a particular program in relation to all programs available at that time. (10.6)

shared screen   When an advertisement is placed, usually in a lower corner, on the same screen and at the same time as a TV program. (9.6b)

shield law   A state law that has the effect of allowing reporters to keep sources of information secret. (11.5)

shortwaves   Radio waves that can travel long distances. (13.7, 14.3)

signal processing   Changing elements of sound, such as loudness or pitch, so that the resulting sound is different from the original sound. (13.2)

slander   To say something false that is harmful to a person's character or reputation. (11.8)

smartphone   A cell phone that performs more functions than just phone calls, such as accessing the internet and interacting with GPS. (1.3, 2.13, 5.18, 9.1, 13.7d)

snipe   A pop-up in the lower portion of a TV screen that promotes an upcoming program. (10.1a)

social networking   Using internet sites to set up pages where you give information about yourself that others can access and respond to. (2.10)

sound bite   A short audio statement about something in the news. (8.3a)

source   In a communication model, the total number of people needed to communicate a message. (12.5b)

spam   Largely unwanted and unsolicited email messages, usually sent to large numbers of people. (11.7)

speaker   A sound box that converts electrical energy back into sound. (13.10)

spin-off   A series that is created out of characters or ideas that have appeared on other series. (4.13, 8.2)

spoofing   A crime in which a hacker gains access to a person's email account and sends messages from that account that the person does not authorize. (11.7)

spot buying   When a company purchases advertising time within or between programs in such a way that the company is not specifically identified with the program. (9.6b)

spread spectrum   Disseminating a signal over a wide range of frequencies so it can occupy whatever spaces of the electromagnetic spectrum are available. (13.7e)

standard definition (SD)   Television signals with a 3:4 aspect ratio and 525 lines of resolution. (4.18)

stereo   Sound reproduction using two channels through left and right speakers to give a feeling of reality. (13.2, 5.14)

stereotype   A fixed notion about a group of people that is often not true, especially for individuals within the group. (1.5d, 12.6c)

storyboard   A chart that contains step-by-step pictorialization of a commercial, TV program, or movie. (9.8, 12.2)

streaming audio   Sound that comes over the internet to a computer in real time without being stored on the computer. (2.8, 5.20)

streaming video   Moving pictures that come over the internet to a computer in real time without being stored on the computer. (2.9, 4.19)

stringer   A person who is paid for the stories or footage he or she gathers if that material is used by some news-gathering organization. (8.3a)

stripping   To air programs, often old network shows, at the same time every day of the week. (8.5b)

stroboscopic   An instrument that makes still images look like they are moving and can also be used to observe moving objects by making them appear stationary, usually using pulsed illumination. (6.1)

studio   A space that contains cameras, sets, lights, and microphones

where acting and performing takes place. (7.12a)

studio years   The period during the 1930s and 1940s when Hollywood movie studios dominated the movie business by having stars under contract and engaging in all phases of production, distribution, and exhibition. (6.7)

super 8   A type of movie film with a small 8 millimeter frame that was used mainly for home movies and has been replaced by video equipment. (6.12)

superstation   A broadcast station that is put on satellite and shown by cable systems. (3.4)

surround sound   Sound that comes from at least six different speakers, giving the effect of sound all around the person who is listening to or watching TV or a movie. (4.18)

surveys   Research study that involves questionnaires that are administered, tabulated, and analyzed. (12.5b)

sweeps   The period of time when ratings data are collected for local areas. (10.10)

switcher   A piece of equipment used to select the video input that will be taped or shown live. (13.3)

synchronous satellite   A satellite whose orbit is synchronized with the earth's rotation, so that it appears to hang motionless in space. (13.7c)

syndicated exclusivity   A cable TV rule stating that if a local station was carrying a particular program, the cable system could not show that same program on a service imported from a distant location. (3.2)

syndicator   A company that produces or acquires programming and sells it to stations, cable networks, and other electronic media. (1.2f, 4.11, 8.1d, 9.2)

T

targeting   Delivering an advertisement to the people who are most likely to be interested in the product being advertised. (9.6b)

Telecommunications Act of 1996   A congressional law that allows many electronic media companies into each other's businesses, deregulates media, and has provisions related to violence and pornography. (3.12, 4.15, 5.17, 11.1)

telenovela   A form of soap opera, developed in Latin America, in which stories are serialized for several months. (4.17, 8.6, 14.6)

teleprompter   A mechanical device that, through the use of mirrors, projects a script in front of a camera lens. (7.12b)

tentpoling   Programming a successful program between two weak or new programs. (8.5b)

10-watter   A public radio station that once broadcast with low power and was used mainly to train students, although now most 10-watters have increased their power to at least 100 watts. (5.16)

testimonials   Positive statements about a commercial product usually given by a well-known person. (9.9b)

text messaging   A system that allows short messages to be sent from one smartphone user to another without necessarily having access to the internet. (2.10)

third-person perspective   Refers to video games dependent on how the

player moves characters through the game as opposed to a set procedure each time the game is played. (2.16)

three-dimensional (3-D)   Material that is produced in such a way that it approximates the way the eyes see two images and can then be projected back so that it appears to have multidimensions. (1.2d, 6.9, 13.3)

toll station   A name for the type of radio programming WEAF initiated in 1922 that allowed anyone to broadcast a public message by paying a fee, similar to the way that one pays a toll to communicate a private message by a pay telephone. (5.6)

total survey area (TSA)   Arbitron's division for radio ratings of geographically large areas that may not receive all stations equally clearly. (10.10)

toy-based programming   Children's programming that was designed around toys as the main characters. (9.9a)

trade-out   To give goods or services (such as advertising time) in exchange for other goods or services. (9.7b)

trades   Journals and magazines that deal with the media industry. (7.3)

traffic   A department that keeps track of programs and commercials that are aired by maintaining a daily log. (7.12e)

trailer   An advertisement for, or preview of, a movie that includes scenes from the movie. (2.9, 9.2, 10.1a)

transcoding   Converting one digital format into another so that the material can be viewed or heard on various playback devices. (13.7b)

translator   An antenna tower that boosts a station's signal and sends it

to an area that the signal could not reach on its own. (13.7d)

Transmission Control Protocol/ Internet Protocol (TCP/IP)   The standard computer network language that allows different computer networks to connect to each other. (2.2)

transmitter   A piece of equipment that generates and amplifies a carrier wave and modulates it with information that can be radiated into space. (13.7a)

transponder   The part of a satellite that carries a particular signal. (13.7c)

treasurer   A person who handles cash for a company or other organization. (7.12f)

TVQ   A measurement that indicates the degree to which people are aware of and like a particular program. (10.9)

TV receive-only (TVRO)   A satellite dish that can receive but not send signals. (3.5)

twisted-pair   Copper wires used primarily to carry phone conversations. (13.6)

tweet   A written posting, often from a smartphone, of up to 140 characters that can be sent in a wireless or wired fashion from a person to another person or group of people. (2.10, 10.9, 13.7d, 14.14)

tweeter   The part of an audio speaker that produces high frequencies. (13.10)

U

ultra-high frequency (UHF)   The area in the spectrum between 300 and 3,000 MHz that was used by analog broadcast TV stations above channel 13. (4.3, 13.7)

umbrella deal An agreement between an independent producer and a studio or network in which the studio provides money, office space, and other amenities to the independent in exchange for the right to distribute its programming. (8.1c)

underwriting Helping pay for public broadcasting in return for a brief mention of the contribution. (9.6e)

unduplicated average audience ratings A total of the percent of people who watch a particular program, even though they watch on different platforms, such as a local station, a cable network, and over the internet. (10.3)

uniform resource locator (URL) A specific address for a page on the world wide web. (2.4)

union An organization that establishes pay rates and working conditions for people in a particular part of the industry that production units then need to abide by. (7.10)

unique visitor (UV) A person who visits a website who has not gone there before. (10.6)

upfront Ads for programs that are sold before the fall season begins. (9.4b)

user-generated content Information or entertainment material put into the media systems by ordinary people who are not usually employed by a media organization. (1.6)

uses and gratifications A field of research that tries to determine the perceived value people feel by becoming involved with certain actions. (12.5b)

V

vacuum tube An electron tube evacuated of air to the extent that its electrical characteristics are unaffected by the remaining air. (2.1, 5.1)

vast wasteland A term coined by FCC chairman Newton Minow in 1961 to refer to the lack of quality TV programming. (4.11)

V-chip Circuitry in TV sets that allows people to block out programs with violent or sexual content. (4.15)

vertical integration A situation in which one company produces, distributes, and exhibits its products without decision making from any other sources. (6.5)

very high frequency (VHF) The area in the spectrum between 30 and 300 MHz that was used by analog TV stations that broadcast on channels 2 to 13. (4.1, 13.7)

videocassette recorder (VCR) A taping and playback machine that uses magnetic videotape enclosed in a container that is automatically threaded when the machine is engaged. (1.3, 6.12, 14.10)

videodisc A round, flat device that contains video and audio information and can display this information on a TV or computer screen. (6.12)

video game A form of play that involves interaction between the person or people playing and a TV or other screen. (1.3, 8.9, 9.1)

video home system (VHS) The consumer-grade half-inch videocassette format developed by Matsushita. (6.12)

video news release (VNR) Recorded material given to the media that has information a

company, politician, or other person or group wants to have publicized. (8.3a)

video-on-demand (VOD) The ability for subscribers to request a program or other material and then store it so they can access it when they want it. (3.10)

video store A physical building where movies and other video material can be rented or purchased. (6.12)

virtual ad An advertisement, usually in the form of a billboard, that isn't part of the real scene but is inserted electronically. (9.6b)

virus An intentionally destructive program that can attack computers, erasing files and in other ways damaging them. (11.7)

visual effects Complicated movie scenes or portions of them that are created in a computer. (13.3)

Voice over Internet Protocol (VoIP) A telephone technique that uses packet switching to route phone calls via the internet. (2.8)

voice tracking Making a radio program sound local even though the person doing the talking is in another city. (5.17, 8.1b)

volume power index (VPI) A measure that is used when an advertiser pays only for the consumers watching or listening who fit into the advertiser's target audience. (9.7b)

W

webcasting Sending audio or video material over the internet. (2.9)

webisode A TV production specifically made to be shown over the internet. (2.9, 8.1c)

wi-fi Short for "wireless fidelity," technology that provides broadband connectivity without cables by connecting a low-power radio transmitter to the internet to modulate the data onto radio waves. (2.11, 13.7e)

window The period between the time a movie is shown in a theater and the time it is released for showing on other media, such as pay cable or network TV. (6.17, 8.1c)

wired Equipment or distribution methods that use cable, fiber optics, or other wires that hold the signal within them. (13.5)

wireless Any equipment or distribution method that uses the electromagnetic spectrum. (5.1, 13.5)

wire recording A form of audio recording that predated tape and used wire that had to be cut and tied in order to edit. (5.12)

wire services Organizations that supply news to various media. (5.10, 8.3a)

woofer The part of an audio speaker that produces low frequencies. (13.10)

works for hire Collaborative artistic creations, such as movies or TV programs, for which a company rather than an individual usually owns the copyright. (11.9)

world wide web (www) Computerized information that is made available from organizations and people to other organizations and people. (2.4)

writer The person who creates a script for a fictional or news program. (7.12a)

PHOTO CREDITS

Chapter 1

Exhibit 1.1: © HFPA, 63rd Golden Globe Awards; p. 4: Courtesy of KDKA Pittsburgh; p. 5: © NBC/Globe Photos/Zuma (top), © CBS/Globe Photos/Zuma (middle), © Photo/Viacom, Hlwd (bottom); p. 6: © Broadcasting Magazine (top), © Photo/Viacom, Hlwd (middle), Courtesy of USA Network (bottom); p. 7: Courtesy of Hughes Communications, Inc. (top), Photos and screenshots courtesy of Google Inc. Used with permission. (middle), © Matt Buchanan/Wikimedia Creative Commons (bottom); 1.4: © Academy of Television Arts & Sciences Foundation; 1.5: © Image Source/Corbis RF; 1.6: © Marty Bahamonde/FEMA; 1.7: © Flying Colours Ltd/Getty RF; 1.8: © Ingram Publishing/SuperStock RF; 1.9: © McGraw-Hill Companies, Inc. photographer David Planchet; 1.10: © Ingram Publishing RF; 1.11: Courtesy of Author; p. 21: © AP/Wide World Photos; 1.12: © Corbis RF.

Chapter 2

Exhibit 2.1: ©AP Photo/Lindlar; 2.2: © BBN Technologies; 2.3: © AP Photo/Damian Dovarganes; 2.5: © AP Photo/Paul Sakuma; 2.7: © Dan Murphy/BBN Technologies; p. 33: © BBN Technologies; 2.8: © Nemereofsky/IPOL/Globe Photos/Zuma; 2.9: © Globe Photos/Zuma; 2.10: Photos and screenshots courtesy of Google Inc. Used with permission; 2.11: © Amazon; 2.12: © Joi/Wikimedia GNU Free Documentation License; 2.13: Photos and screenshots courtesy of Google Inc. Used with permission; 2.14: © Steve Rogers/Wikimedia Creative Commons Attribution ShareAlike; 2.15: © Matt Buchanan/Wikimedia Creative Commons; p. 48: © Max Photography for GDC Online/Wikimedia Creative Commons; 2.16–2.17: Courtesy of the Author.

Chapter 3

Page 58: © Brian Gross; 3.2: © TeleCable of Overland Park, Kansas; 3.3: © HBO; 3.5: © Showtime; 3.6: © Bravo Networks; 3.7: © USA Network; 3.8: © Hughes Communication; p. 72: © Alan Light/Wikimedia Creative Commons; 3.10: © AP Photo/Mark Elias; 3.11: © AP Photo/Comedy Central; 3.12: © AP Photo; 3.13: © Academy of Television Arts & Sciences Foundation.

Chapter 4

Exhibit 4.1: Courtesy of AT&T Co. Phone Center; 4.2: © Smithsonian Institution; 4.3–4.4: © RCA; 4.5: © NBC/Globe Photos/Zuma; 4.6: © Photos/Viacom, Hlwd; p. 89: © Culver Pictures; 4.7: © Everett Collection; 4.8: © NBC/Globe Photos/Zuma; 4.9: © Great Plains National Instructional Television Library; 4.10: © Globe Photos/Zuma; 4.11: © United Press International/Corbis; 4.12–4.13: © NBC/Globe Photos/Zuma; 4.14: © Broadcasting Magazine; 4.15: © Broadcasting & Cable 1987–1994/Cahners Publishing Company; p. 96: © Walter Bennett/Getty Images; 4.16: © Bruce Bilson; 4.17: © Family Communications; 4.18: © Photo/Viacom, Hlwd; 4.19: © Fitzroy Barrett/Globe Photos/Zuma; 4.21: © CBS Photo Archive; 4.22: © ABC Photo Archive; 4.23: © HFPA 63rd Golden Globe Awards.

Chapter 5

Exhibits 5.1–5.2: © Smithsonian Institution; 5.3: © RCA; 5.4–5.5: © KDKA, Pittsburgh; p. 120: © KFI, Los Angeles; 5.6: © KFI, Los Angeles; 5.7: © UPI/Bettman News Photos/Corbis; 5.8: © RCA; 5.9–5.11: ©KFI, Los Angeles; p. 126: © NBC/Globe Photos/Zuma (left & bottom), © KFI, Los Angeles (right); 5.12–5.13: © NBC/Globe Photos/Zuma; 5.14: © KFI, Los Angeles; 5.15: © NBC/Globe Photos/Zuma; 5.16: © CBS/Globe Photos/Zuma; 5.17: © Bettmann/Corbis; 5.18: © Donald M. McLaren; p. 133: © AP Photo; 5.19a-b: Courtesy of Author; 5.20: © NPR; 5.21: Courtesy John Carroll University, Ohio; 5.22: © LoudCity.

Chapter 6

Exhibit 6.1: © Corbis; 6.2: © Steve Gainee, ASC American Society of Cinematographers; 6.3: Courtesy of Thomas Edison National Historical Park collection,

NPS; 6.4: Courtesy of Library of Congress, Thomas Edison National Historical Park collection, NPS; 6.5: Courtesy of Argonne National Laboratory, University of Chicago; p. 150: © VPPA/IPOL/Globe Photos/Zuma; 6.6: © Bettmann/Corbis; 6.7: Hulton Archive/Getty; 6.8: © Globe Photos/Zuma; 6.9: © Photofest; 6.10: © Globe Photos/Zuma; 6.12: © ADH/ Globe Photos/Zuma; 6.14: © Globe Photos/Zuma; p. 161: Courtesy of Author; 6.15: © Dynamic Graphics/ JupiterImages RF; 6.16–6.17: © Globe Photos/Zuma; 6.18: © JVC Industries; 6.19: © RCA; 6.20: © 2002 TiVo, Inc; 6.21: © Nick White/Getty Rf; p. 169: © The McGraw-Hill Companies, Inc. Erica Simone Leeds, Photographer (left), © The McGraw-Hill Companies, Inc. Jill Braaten, Photographer (top), Courtesy of Author (bottom right).

Chapter 7

Exhibit 7.1: © Digital Vision Ltd./Superstock RF; 7.2: © Image Source/Getty RF; 7.3: Courtesy of the Author; 7.6: © Academy of Television Arts and Sciences Foundation; 7.12: © Pete Souza/Wikimedia Creative Commons; 7.15: © Zion Lutheran Church, Anaheim, California; 7.16: Courtesy of the Author; p. 198; © Emily Ibarra; p. 203: © Sony Corporation of America.

Chapter 8

Exhibit 8.1: © Kathryn Indiek/Globe Photos/Zuma; p. 210: © TheBuiBrothers.com, http://TheBuiBrothers.com; 8.2: © Academy of Television Arts & Sciences Foundation; 8.4: © Patchett Kaufman Entertainment; 8.5: © Rhodes/USMC/Globe Photos/Zuma; 8.6: © KFWB, Los Angeles; 8.9–8.10: © HFPA, 63rd Golden Globes Awards; 8.11: © Academy of Television Arts & Sciences Foundation; 8.12: © NBC/Globe Photos/Zuma; 8.13: © Keith McDuffee, http://flic.kr/p/6Qy1oG; 8.14: © The McGraw-Hill Companies, Inc. Jill Braaten, photographer; 8.16: © The McGraw-Hill Companies, Inc. Jill Braaten, photographer; p. 231: © John J. Kruzel/American Forces Press Service; 8.17: © A film by Carlos Sandoval and Catherine Tambini, photo courtesy of P.O.V. and Camino Bluff Productions; 8.18: © Crystal Cathedral Ministries; 8.19: © Henry McGee/Globe Photos/Zuma.

Chapter 9

Exhibit 9.1: © Randy Faris/Corbis RF; 9.3: Courtesy of the Author; p. 248: Courtesy of the Author; 9.5: © NBC/Globe Photos/Zuma; 9.6: Photos and screenshots courtesy of Google Inc. Used with permission; 9.7: Courtesy Powells.com; p. 255: © Getty Images; 9.10: © N8VanDyke/Wikimedia Creative Commons; 9.11: © Rick Mackler/Globe Photos/Zuma.

Chapter 10

Exhibit 10.1: © Alpha/Globe Photos/Zuma; p. 272 & 276: Courtesy of the Author; p. 278 a-c: © A. C. Nielsen Company; 10.5: © A. C. Nielsen Company; p. 284: © Donny Sianturi; 10.8a-b: Courtesy of the Author.

Chapter 11

Exhibit 11.2: © Bettmann/Corbis; 11.4: © The McGraw-Hill Companies, Inc./Jill Braaten, photographer; 11.5: © Marina Haris/Julian Assange; 11.6: © Rick Mackler/Globe Photos/Zuma; p. 302: © Alec Michael/ Globe Photos/Zuma; 11.7: © Colin Broley/Reuters/ TimePix/Getty; 11.8: © UPI/Bettmann/Corbis; 11.9: © SYGMA/Corbis; p. 311: © Bettmann/Corbis; 11.10: © BROADCASTING & CABLE, 1987 © 1994 BY Cahners Publishing Company; p. 315: Courtesy Ronald Reagan Presidential Library, National Archives and Records Administration; 11.11: © UPI/Bettmann/ Corbis; 11.12: © Wally McNamee/Corbis; p. 317: © John F. Banzhaf III.

Chapter 12

Exhibit 12.4: © Monika Flueckiger; 12.6: © The McGraw-Hill Companies, Inc./Jill Braaten, photographer; 12.7: Courtesy of the Author; p. 339: Courtesy Library and Archives Canada/PA-202189; p. 340: © Ingram Publishing RF; 12.9: © Library of Congress, Prints and Photographs Division, NYWT&S; 12.10: © Blend Images/Getty RF.

Chapter 13

Exhibit 13.1: © BananaStock/PunchStock RF; 13.3: © Ingram Publishing/Fototsearch RF; 13.4: © Sony Enterprises; 13.5: © Burke/Triolo/Brand X Pictures/ Jupiterimages RF; 13.6: © Red Digital Cinema; 13.7:

Courtesy of the Author; 13.8: © Corning Glass Works; 13.15: © Hughes Aircraft Company; 13.17: Courtesy of the Author; p. 370: © Charlie Edwards/Getty RF; 13.18: © William Casey/Alamy RF; 13.19: © Sharp Electronics Corporation.

Chapter 14

Exhibit 14.1: © Photofest; 14.2: © Kobal Collection; 14.3: © True Boardman; 14.4: © Photofest; 14.5: © Granada Television; 14.6: © AP Photo/Alexander Zemlianichenko; 14.7: © The McGraw-Hill Companies, Inc. Erica Simone Leeds, photographer; 14.8: Courtesy of the Author; p. 389: © Indian Space Research Organization; 14.9: © AP Photos/Jeff Widener; 14.10: © Superstar Images/Globe Photos/Zuma; 14.11: © HFPA, 63rd Golden Globe Awards; 14.12: © Globe Photos/Zuma.

INDEX